PHILIP'S

# ESSENTIAL WORLD ATLAS

PHILIP'S

# ESSENTIAL WORLD ATLAS

## SECOND EDITION

IN ASSOCIATION WITH

THE ROYAL GEOGRAPHICAL SOCIETY

WITH THE INSTITUTE OF BRITISH GEOGRAPHERS

# Contents

**Cartography by Philip's**

**Text**
Keith Lye

**Picture Acknowledgements**
**Robert Harding Picture Library** /Photri 1
**Image Bank** /Lionel Brown 10
**Rex Features** /Sipa 6, 24
**Still Pictures** 26, /Anne Piantanida 8, /Chris Caldicott 16, /Mark Edwards 18, 20, /Hartmut Schwarzbach 14, 22, /Luke White 4
**Tony Stone Images** /Kevin Kelley 2, /Art Wolfe 12

First published in Great Britain in 1996 under the title *Philip's Desk Reference Atlas*

This edition first published in 1998 by George Philip Limited, a division of Octopus Publishing Group Limited, 2–4 Heron Quays, London E14 4JP

Second edition 1999

Revised reprint 2000

A CIP catalogue record for this book is available from the British Library.

ISBN 0-540-07757-7

Printed in China

Details of other Philip's titles and services can be found on our website at: www.philips-maps.co.uk

## World Statistics

*vi–ix* *Countries*
*x–xi* *Cities*
*xii–xv* *Physical*
*xvi* *Climate*

## The Earth in Focus

*2–3* *The Universe and Solar System*
*4–5* *The Changing Earth*
*6–7* *Earthquakes and Volcanoes*
*8–9* *Water and Ice*
*10–11* *Weather and Climate*
*12–13* *Landforms and Vegetation*
*14–15* *Population*
*16–17* *Languages and Religions*
*18–19* *Agriculture and Industry*
*20–21* *Trade and Commerce*
*22–23* *Transport and Travel*
*24–27* *International Organizations*
*28–29* *Regions in the News*
*30–32* *World Flags*

## World Maps

1 General Reference
2–3 Northern Hemisphere
4–5 Southern Hemisphere
6–7 Europe
8–9 Scandinavia
10–11 British Isles
12–13 France
14–15 Germany and Benelux
16–17 Central Europe
18–19 Spain and Portugal
20–21 Italy and the Adriatic
22–23 Greece and the Balkans
24–25 Eastern Europe
26–27 Asia
28–29 Western Russia and Central Asia
30–31 Eastern Siberia
32–33 Japan
34–35 China
36–37 South-east Asia
38–39 Philippines and Eastern Indonesia
40–41 Eastern India, Bangladesh and Burma
42–43 Western India and Pakistan
44–45 Iran, the Gulf and Afghanistan
46–47 The Middle East and Turkey
48–49 Arabia and the Horn of Africa
50–51 Africa
52–53 North-east Africa
54–55 North-west Africa
56–57 Central Africa
58–59 Southern Africa
60–61 Australia
62–63 South-east Australia
64–65 New Zealand, Central and South-west Pacific
66–67 North America
68–69 Eastern Canada
70–71 Western Canada
72–73 North-east USA
74–75 South-east USA
76–77 North-central USA
78–79 Southern USA
80–81 North-west USA
82–83 South-west USA
84–85 Mexico
86–87 Caribbean and Central America
88–89 South America
90–91 South America – North-west
92–93 South America – North-east
94–95 South America – South
96 Antarctica

97–160 **Index to World Maps**

# World Statistics – Countries

Listed below are all the countries of the world; the more important territories are also included. If a territory is not completely independent, then the country it is associated with is named. The area figures give the total area of land, inland water and ice. Annual income is the GNP per capita. The figures are the latest available: usually 1997.

| *Country / Territory* | *Area (1,000 sq km)* | *Area (1,000 sq mls)* | *Population (1,000s)* | *Capital City* | *Annual Income US$* |
|---|---|---|---|---|---|
| **Afghanistan** | 652 | 252 | 24,792 | Kabul | 600 |
| **Albania** | 28.8 | 11.1 | 3,331 | Tirana | 750 |
| **Algeria** | 2,382 | 920 | 30,481 | Algiers | 1,490 |
| **Andorra** | 0.45 | 0.17 | 75 | Andorra La Vella | 16,200 |
| **Angola** | 1,247 | 481 | 11,200 | Luanda | 340 |
| **Argentina** | 2,767 | 1,068 | 36,265 | Buenos Aires | 8,750 |
| **Armenia** | 29.8 | 11.5 | 3,422 | Yerevan | 530 |
| **Australia** | 7,687 | 2,968 | 18,613 | Canberra | 20,540 |
| **Austria** | 83.9 | 32.4 | 8,134 | Vienna | 27,980 |
| **Azerbaijan** | 86.6 | 33.4 | 7,856 | Baku | 510 |
| **Azores (Portugal)** | 2.2 | 0.87 | 238 | Ponta Delgada | – |
| **Bahamas** | 13.9 | 5.4 | 280 | Nassau | 11,940 |
| **Bahrain** | 0.68 | 0.26 | 616 | Manama | 7,840 |
| **Bangladesh** | 144 | 56 | 125,000 | Dhaka | 270 |
| **Barbados** | 0.43 | 0.17 | 259 | Bridgetown | 6,560 |
| **Belarus** | 207.6 | 80.1 | 10,409 | Minsk | 2,150 |
| **Belgium** | 30.5 | 11.8 | 10,175 | Brussels | 26,420 |
| **Belize** | 23 | 8.9 | 230 | Belmopan | 2,700 |
| **Benin** | 113 | 43 | 6,101 | Porto-Novo | 380 |
| **Bhutan** | 47 | 18.1 | 1,908 | Thimphu | 390 |
| **Bolivia** | 1,099 | 424 | 7,826 | La Paz/Sucre | 950 |
| **Bosnia-Herzegovina** | 51 | 20 | 3,366 | Sarajevo | 300 |
| **Botswana** | 582 | 225 | 1,448 | Gaborone | 4,381 |
| **Brazil** | 8,512 | 3,286 | 170,000 | Brasília | 4,720 |
| **Brunei** | 5.8 | 2.2 | 315 | Bandar Seri Begawan | 15,800 |
| **Bulgaria** | 111 | 43 | 8,240 | Sofia | 1,140 |
| **Burkina Faso** | 274 | 106 | 11,266 | Ouagadougou | 240 |
| **Burma (= Myanmar)** | 677 | 261 | 47,305 | Rangoon | 1,790 |
| **Burundi** | 27.8 | 10.7 | 5,531 | Bujumbura | 180 |
| **Cambodia** | 181 | 70 | 11,340 | Phnom Penh | 300 |
| **Cameroon** | 475 | 184 | 15,029 | Yaoundé | 650 |
| **Canada** | 9,976 | 3,852 | 30,675 | Ottawa | 19,290 |
| **Canary Is. (Spain)** | 7.3 | 2.8 | 1,494 | Las Palmas/Santa Cruz | – |
| **Cape Verde Is.** | 4 | 1.6 | 399 | Praia | 1,010 |
| **Central African Republic** | 623 | 241 | 3,376 | Bangui | 320 |
| **Chad** | 1,284 | 496 | 7,360 | Ndjaména | 240 |
| **Chile** | 757 | 292 | 14,788 | Santiago | 5,020 |
| **China** | 9,597 | 3,705 | 1,236,915 | Beijing | 860 |
| **Colombia** | 1,139 | 440 | 38,581 | Bogotá | 2,280 |
| **Comoros** | 2.2 | 0.86 | 545 | Moroni | 450 |
| **Congo** | 342 | 132 | 2,658 | Brazzaville | 660 |
| **Congo (= Zaïre)** | 2,345 | 905 | 49,001 | Kinshasa | 110 |
| **Costa Rica** | 51.1 | 19.7 | 3,605 | San José | 2,640 |
| **Croatia** | 56.5 | 21.8 | 4,672 | Zagreb | 4,610 |
| **Cuba** | 111 | 43 | 11,051 | Havana | 1,300 |

| Country/Territory | Area (1,000 sq km) | Area (1,000 sq mls) | Population (1,000s) | Capital City | Annual Income US$ |
|---|---|---|---|---|---|
| **Cyprus** | 9.3 | 3.6 | 749 | Nicosia | 13,420 |
| **Czech Republic** | 78.9 | 30.4 | 10,286 | Prague | 5,200 |
| **Denmark** | 43.1 | 16.6 | 5,334 | Copenhagen | 32,500 |
| **Djibouti** | 23.2 | 9 | 650 | Djibouti | 850 |
| **Dominica** | 0.75 | 0.29 | 78 | Roseau | 3,090 |
| **Dominican Republic** | 48.7 | 18.8 | 7,999 | Santo Domingo | 1,670 |
| **Ecuador** | 284 | 109 | 12,337 | Quito | 1,590 |
| **Egypt** | 1,001 | 387 | 66,050 | Cairo | 1,180 |
| **El Salvador** | 21 | 8.1 | 5,752 | San Salvador | 1,810 |
| **Equatorial Guinea** | 28.1 | 10.8 | 454 | Malabo | 530 |
| **Eritrea** | 94 | 36 | 3,842 | Asmara | 570 |
| **Estonia** | 44.7 | 17.3 | 1,421 | Tallinn | 3,330 |
| **Ethiopia** | 1,128 | 436 | 58,390 | Addis Ababa | 110 |
| **Fiji** | 18.3 | 7.1 | 802 | Suva | 2,470 |
| **Finland** | 338 | 131 | 5,149 | Helsinki | 24,080 |
| **France** | 552 | 213 | 58,805 | Paris | 26,050 |
| **French Guiana (France)** | 90 | 34.7 | 162 | Cayenne | 10,580 |
| **French Polynesia (France)** | 4 | 1.5 | 237 | Papeete | 7,500 |
| **Gabon** | 268 | 103 | 1,208 | Libreville | 4,230 |
| **Gambia, The** | 11.3 | 4.4 | 1,292 | Banjul | 320 |
| **Georgia** | 69.7 | 26.9 | 5,109 | Tbilisi | 840 |
| **Germany** | 357 | 138 | 82,079 | Berlin/Bonn | 28,260 |
| **Ghana** | 239 | 92 | 18,497 | Accra | 370 |
| **Greece** | 132 | 51 | 10,662 | Athens | 12,010 |
| **Grenada** | 0.34 | 0.13 | 96 | St George's | 2,880 |
| **Guadeloupe (France)** | 1.7 | 0.66 | 416 | Basse-Terre | 9,200 |
| **Guatemala** | 109 | 42 | 12,008 | Guatemala City | 1,500 |
| **Guinea** | 246 | 95 | 7,477 | Conakry | 570 |
| **Guinea-Bissau** | 36.1 | 13.9 | 1,206 | Bissau | 240 |
| **Guyana** | 215 | 83 | 820 | Georgetown | 690 |
| **Haiti** | 27.8 | 10.7 | 6,781 | Port-au-Prince | 330 |
| **Honduras** | 112 | 43 | 5,862 | Tegucigalpa | 700 |
| **Hong Kong (China)** | 1.1 | 0.40 | 6,707 | – | 22,990 |
| **Hungary** | 93 | 35.9 | 10,208 | Budapest | 4,430 |
| **Iceland** | 103 | 40 | 271 | Reykjavik | 26,580 |
| **India** | 3,288 | 1,269 | 984,000 | New Delhi | 390 |
| **Indonesia** | 1,905 | 735 | 212,942 | Jakarta | 1,110 |
| **Iran** | 1,648 | 636 | 64,411 | Tehran | 4,700 |
| **Iraq** | 438 | 169 | 21,722 | Baghdad | 2,000 |
| **Ireland** | 70.3 | 27.1 | 3,619 | Dublin | 18,280 |
| **Israel** | 27 | 10.3 | 5,644 | Jerusalem | 15,810 |
| **Italy** | 301 | 116 | 56,783 | Rome | 20,120 |
| **Ivory Coast (Côte d'Ivoire)** | 322 | 125 | 15,446 | Yamoussoukro | 690 |
| **Jamaica** | 11 | 4.2 | 2,635 | Kingston | 1,560 |
| **Japan** | 378 | 146 | 125,932 | Tokyo | 37,850 |
| **Jordan** | 89.2 | 34.4 | 4,435 | Amman | 1,570 |
| **Kazakstan** | 2,717 | 1,049 | 16,847 | Astana | 1,340 |
| **Kenya** | 580 | 224 | 28,337 | Nairobi | 330 |
| **Korea, North** | 121 | 47 | 21,234 | Pyŏngyang | 1,000 |
| **Korea, South** | 99 | 38.2 | 46,417 | Seoul | 10,550 |

| Country / Territory | Area (1,000 sq km) | Area (1,000 sq mls) | Population (1,000s) | Capital City | Annual Income US$ |
|---|---|---|---|---|---|
| **Kuwait** | 17.8 | 6.9 | 1,913 | Kuwait City | 17,390 |
| **Kyrgyzstan** | 198.5 | 76.6 | 4,522 | Bishkek | 440 |
| **Laos** | 237 | 91 | 5,261 | Vientiane | 400 |
| **Latvia** | 65 | 25 | 2,385 | Riga | 2,430 |
| **Lebanon** | 10.4 | 4 | 3,506 | Beirut | 3,350 |
| **Lesotho** | 30.4 | 11.7 | 2,090 | Maseru | 670 |
| **Liberia** | 111 | 43 | 2,772 | Monrovia | 770 |
| **Libya** | 1,760 | 679 | 4,875 | Tripoli | 6,510 |
| **Lithuania** | 65.2 | 25.2 | 3,600 | Vilnius | 2,230 |
| **Luxembourg** | 2.6 | 1 | 425 | Luxembourg | 45,360 |
| **Macau (China)** | 0.02 | 0.006 | 429 | Macau | 7,500 |
| **Macedonia** | 25.7 | 9.9 | 2,009 | Skopje | 1,090 |
| **Madagascar** | 587 | 227 | 14,463 | Antananarivo | 250 |
| **Madeira (Portugal)** | 0.81 | 0.31 | 253 | Funchal | – |
| **Malawi** | 118 | 46 | 9,840 | Lilongwe | 220 |
| **Malaysia** | 330 | 127 | 20,993 | Kuala Lumpur | 4,680 |
| **Maldives** | 0.30 | 0.12 | 290 | Malé | 1,080 |
| **Mali** | 1,240 | 479 | 10,109 | Bamako | 260 |
| **Malta** | 0.32 | 0.12 | 379 | Valletta | 12,000 |
| **Martinique (France)** | 1.1 | 0.42 | 407 | Fort-de-France | 10,000 |
| **Mauritania** | 1,030 | 412 | 2,511 | Nouakchott | 450 |
| **Mauritius** | 2.0 | 0.72 | 1,168 | Port Louis | 3,800 |
| **Mexico** | 1,958 | 756 | 98,553 | Mexico City | 3,680 |
| **Micronesia, Fed. States of** | 0.70 | 0.27 | 127 | Palikir | 2,070 |
| **Moldova** | 33.7 | 13 | 4,458 | Chişinău | 540 |
| **Mongolia** | 1,567 | 605 | 2,579 | Ulan Bator | 390 |
| **Morocco** | 447 | 172 | 29,114 | Rabat | 1,250 |
| **Mozambique** | 802 | 309 | 18,641 | Maputo | 90 |
| **Namibia** | 825 | 318 | 1,622 | Windhoek | 2,220 |
| **Nepal** | 141 | 54 | 23,698 | Katmandu | 210 |
| **Netherlands** | 41.5 | 16 | 15,731 | Amsterdam/The Hague | 25,820 |
| **Netherlands Antilles (Neths)** | 0.99 | 0.38 | 210 | Willemstad | 10,400 |
| **New Caledonia (France)** | 18.6 | 7.2 | 192 | Nouméa | 8,000 |
| **New Zealand** | 269 | 104 | 3,625 | Wellington | 16,480 |
| **Nicaragua** | 130 | 50 | 4,583 | Managua | 410 |
| **Niger** | 1,267 | 489 | 9,672 | Niamey | 200 |
| **Nigeria** | 924 | 357 | 110,532 | Abuja | 260 |
| **Norway** | 324 | 125 | 4,420 | Oslo | 36,090 |
| **Oman** | 212 | 82 | 2,364 | Muscat | 4,950 |
| **Pakistan** | 796 | 307 | 135,135 | Islamabad | 490 |
| **Panama** | 77.1 | 29.8 | 2,736 | Panama City | 3,080 |
| **Papua New Guinea** | 463 | 179 | 4,600 | Port Moresby | 940 |
| **Paraguay** | 407 | 157 | 5,291 | Asunción | 2,010 |
| **Peru** | 1,285 | 496 | 26,111 | Lima | 2,460 |
| **Philippines** | 300 | 116 | 77,736 | Manila | 1,220 |
| **Poland** | 313 | 121 | 38,607 | Warsaw | 3,590 |
| **Portugal** | 92.4 | 35.7 | 9,928 | Lisbon | 10,450 |
| **Puerto Rico (US)** | 9 | 3.5 | 3,860 | San Juan | 7,800 |
| **Qatar** | 11 | 4.2 | 697 | Doha | 11,600 |
| **Réunion (France)** | 2.5 | 0.97 | 705 | Saint-Denis | 4,500 |

| *Country/Territory* | *Area (1,000 sq km)* | *Area (1,000 sq mls)* | *Population (1,000s)* | *Capital City* | *Annual Income US$* |
|---|---|---|---|---|---|
| **Romania** | 238 | 92 | 22,396 | Bucharest | 1,420 |
| **Russia** | 17,075 | 6,592 | 146,861 | Moscow | 2,740 |
| **Rwanda** | 26.3 | 10.2 | 7,956 | Kigali | 210 |
| **St Lucia** | 0.62 | 0.24 | 150 | Castries | 3,500 |
| **St Vincent & Grenadines** | 0.39 | 0.15 | 120 | Kingstown | 2,370 |
| **São Tomé & Príncipe** | 0.96 | 0.37 | 150 | São Tomé | 330 |
| **Saudi Arabia** | 2,150 | 830 | 20,786 | Riyadh | 6,790 |
| **Senegal** | 197 | 76 | 9,723 | Dakar | 550 |
| **Sierra Leone** | 71.7 | 27.7 | 5,080 | Freetown | 200 |
| **Singapore** | 0.62 | 0.24 | 3,490 | Singapore | 32,940 |
| **Slovak Republic** | 49 | 18.9 | 5,393 | Bratislava | 3,700 |
| **Slovenia** | 20.3 | 7.8 | 1,972 | Ljubljana | 9,680 |
| **Solomon Is.** | 28.9 | 11.2 | 441 | Honiara | 900 |
| **Somalia** | 638 | 246 | 6,842 | Mogadishu | 500 |
| **South Africa** | 1,220 | 471 | 42,835 | C. Town/Pretoria/ Bloemfontein | 3,400 |
| **Spain** | 505 | 195 | 39,134 | Madrid | 14,510 |
| **Sri Lanka** | 65.6 | 25.3 | 18,934 | Colombo | 800 |
| **Sudan** | 2,506 | 967 | 33,551 | Khartoum | 800 |
| **Surinam** | 163 | 63 | 427 | Paramaribo | 1,000 |
| **Swaziland** | 17.4 | 6.7 | 966 | Mbabane | 1,210 |
| **Sweden** | 450 | 174 | 8,887 | Stockholm | 26,220 |
| **Switzerland** | 41.3 | 15.9 | 7,260 | Bern | 44,220 |
| **Syria** | 185 | 71 | 16,673 | Damascus | 1,150 |
| **Taiwan** | 36 | 13.9 | 21,908 | Taipei | 12,400 |
| **Tajikistan** | 143.1 | 55.2 | 6,020 | Dushanbe | 330 |
| **Tanzania** | 945 | 365 | 30,609 | Dodoma | 210 |
| **Thailand** | 513 | 198 | 60,037 | Bangkok | 2,800 |
| **Togo** | 56.8 | 21.9 | 4,906 | Lomé | 330 |
| **Trinidad & Tobago** | 5.1 | 2 | 1,117 | Port of Spain | 4,230 |
| **Tunisia** | 164 | 63 | 9,380 | Tunis | 2,090 |
| **Turkey** | 779 | 301 | 64,568 | Ankara | 3,130 |
| **Turkmenistan** | 488.1 | 188.5 | 4,298 | Ashkhabad | 630 |
| **Uganda** | 236 | 91 | 22,167 | Kampala | 320 |
| **Ukraine** | 603.7 | 233.1 | 50,125 | Kiev | 1,040 |
| **United Arab Emirates** | 83.6 | 32.3 | 2,303 | Abu Dhabi | 17,360 |
| **United Kingdom** | 243.3 | 94 | 58,970 | London | 20,710 |
| **United States of America** | 9,373 | 3,619 | 270,290 | Washington, DC | 28,740 |
| **Uruguay** | 177 | 68 | 3,285 | Montevideo | 6,020 |
| **Uzbekistan** | 447.4 | 172.7 | 23,784 | Tashkent | 1,010 |
| **Vanuatu** | 12.2 | 4.7 | 185 | Port-Vila | 1,290 |
| **Venezuela** | 912 | 352 | 22,803 | Caracas | 3,450 |
| **Vietnam** | 332 | 127 | 76,236 | Hanoi | 320 |
| **Virgin Is. (US)** | 0.34 | 0.13 | 118 | Charlotte Amalie | 12,000 |
| **Western Sahara** | 266 | 103 | 200 | El Aaiún | 300 |
| **Western Samoa** | 2.8 | 1.1 | 224 | Apia | 1,170 |
| **Yemen** | 528 | 204 | 16,388 | Sana | 270 |
| **Yugoslavia** | 102.3 | 39.5 | 10,500 | Belgrade | 2,000 |
| **Zambia** | 753 | 291 | 9,461 | Lusaka | 380 |
| **Zimbabwe** | 391 | 151 | 11,044 | Harare | 750 |

# World Statistics – Cities

Listed below are all the cities with more than 600,000 inhabitants (only cities with more than 1 million inhabitants are included for Brazil, China and India). The figures are taken from the most recent censuses and surveys, and are in thousands. As far as possible the figures are for the metropolitan area, e.g. greater New York or Mexico City.

| | *Population (1,000s)* |
|---|---|
| **Afghanistan** | |
| Kabul | 1,565 |
| **Algeria** | |
| Algiers | 2,168 |
| Oran | 916 |
| **Angola** | |
| Luanda | 2,418 |
| **Argentina** | |
| Buenos Aires | 11,256 |
| Córdoba | 1,208 |
| Rosario | 1,118 |
| Mendoza | 773 |
| La Plata | 642 |
| San Miguel de Tucumán | 622 |
| **Armenia** | |
| Yerevan | 1,248 |
| **Australia** | |
| Sydney | 3,770 |
| Melbourne | 3,217 |
| Brisbane | 1,489 |
| Perth | 1,262 |
| Adelaide | 1,080 |
| **Austria** | |
| Vienna | 1,595 |
| **Azerbaijan** | |
| Baku | 1,720 |
| **Bangladesh** | |
| Dhaka | 6,105 |
| Chittagong | 2,041 |
| Khulna | 877 |
| **Belarus** | |
| Minsk | 1,700 |
| **Belgium** | |
| Brussels | 948 |
| **Bolivia** | |
| La Paz | 1,126 |
| Santa Cruz | 767 |
| **Brazil** | |
| São Paulo | 16,417 |
| Rio de Janeiro | 9,888 |
| Salvador | 2,211 |
| Belo Horizonte | 2,091 |
| Fortaleza | 1,965 |
| Brasília | 1,821 |
| Curitiba | 1,476 |
| Recife | 1,346 |
| Pôrto Alegre | 1,288 |
| Manaus | 1,157 |
| Belém | 1,144 |
| Goiânia | 1,004 |
| **Bulgaria** | |
| Sofia | 1,116 |
| **Burkina Faso** | |
| Ouagadougou | 690 |
| **Burma (Myanmar)** | |
| Rangoon | 2,513 |
| **Cambodia** | |
| Phnom Penh | 920 |
| **Cameroon** | |
| Douala | 1,200 |
| Yaoundé | 800 |
| **Canada** | |
| Toronto | 4,344 |
| Montréal | 3,337 |
| Vancouver | 1,831 |
| Ottawa–Hull | 1,022 |
| Edmonton | 885 |
| Calgary | 831 |
| Québec | 693 |
| Winnipeg | 677 |
| Hamilton | 643 |
| **Chile** | |
| Santiago | 5,067 |
| **China** | |
| Shanghai | 15,082 |
| Beijing | 12,362 |
| Tianjin | 10,687 |
| Hong Kong (SAR)* | 6,502 |
| Chongqing | 3,870 |
| Shenyang | 3,860 |
| Wuhan | 3,520 |
| Guangzhou | 3,114 |
| Harbin | 2,505 |
| Nanjing | 2,211 |
| Xi'an | 2,115 |
| Chengdu | 1,933 |
| Dalian | 1,855 |
| Changchun | 1,810 |
| Jinan | 1,660 |
| Taiyuan | 1,642 |
| Qingdao | 1,584 |
| Fuzhou, Fujian | 1,380 |
| Zibo | 1,346 |
| Zhengzhou | 1,324 |
| Lanzhou | 1,296 |
| Anshan | 1,252 |
| Fushun | 1,246 |
| Kunming | 1,242 |
| Changsha | 1,198 |
| Hangzhou | 1,185 |
| Nanchang | 1,169 |
| Shijiazhuang | 1,159 |
| Guiyang | 1,131 |
| Ürümqi | 1,130 |
| Jilin | 1,118 |
| Tangshan | 1,110 |
| Qiqihar | 1,104 |
| Baotou | 1,033 |
| Hefei | 1,000 |
| **Colombia** | |
| Bogotá | 6,004 |
| Cali | 1,985 |
| Medellín | 1,970 |
| Barranquilla | 1,157 |
| Cartagena | 812 |
| **Congo** | |
| Brazzaville | 937 |
| **Congo (Zaïre)** | |
| Kinshasa | 1,655 |
| Lubumbashi | 851 |
| Mbuji-Mayi | 806 |
| **Costa Rica** | |
| San José | 1,220 |
| **Croatia** | |
| Zagreb | 931 |
| **Cuba** | |
| Havana | 2,241 |
| **Czech Republic** | |
| Prague | 1,209 |
| **Denmark** | |
| Copenhagen | 1,362 |
| **Dominican Republic** | |
| Santo Domingo | 2,135 |
| Santiago | 691 |
| **Ecuador** | |
| Guayaquil | 1,973 |
| Quito | 1,487 |
| **Egypt** | |
| Cairo | 9,900 |
| Alexandria | 3,431 |
| El Gîza | 2,144 |
| Shubra el Kheima | 834 |
| **El Salvador** | |
| San Salvador | 1,522 |
| **Ethiopia** | |
| Addis Ababa | 2,112 |
| **France** | |
| Paris | 9,319 |
| Lyon | 1,262 |
| Marseille | 1,087 |
| Lille | 959 |
| Bordeaux | 696 |
| Toulouse | 650 |
| **Georgia** | |
| Tbilisi | 1,300 |
| **Germany** | |
| Berlin | 3,470 |
| Hamburg | 1,706 |
| Munich | 1,240 |
| Cologne | 964 |
| Frankfurt | 651 |
| Essen | 616 |
| Dortmund | 600 |
| **Ghana** | |
| Accra | 949 |
| **Greece** | |
| Athens | 3,097 |
| **Guatemala** | |
| Guatemala | 1,167 |
| **Guinea** | |
| Conakry | 1,508 |
| **Haiti** | |
| Port-au-Prince | 1,255 |
| **Honduras** | |
| Tegucigalpa | 813 |
| **Hungary** | |
| Budapest | 1,885 |
| **India** | |
| Bombay (Mumbai) | 12,572 |
| Calcutta | 10,916 |
| Delhi | 7,207 |
| Madras (Chennai) | 5,361 |
| Hyderabad | 4,280 |
| Bangalore | 4,087 |
| Ahmadabad | 3,298 |
| Pune | 2,485 |
| Kanpur | 2,111 |
| Nagpur | 1,661 |
| Lucknow | 1,642 |
| Surat | 1,517 |
| Jaipur | 1,514 |
| Coimbatore | 1,136 |
| Vadodara | 1,115 |
| Indore | 1,104 |
| Patna | 1,099 |
| Madurai | 1,094 |
| Bhopal | 1,064 |
| Vishakhapatnam | 1,052 |
| Varanasi | 1,026 |
| Ludhiana | 1,012 |
| **Indonesia** | |
| Jakarta | 11,500 |
| Surabaya | 2,701 |
| Bandung | 2,368 |
| Medan | 1,910 |
| Semarang | 1,366 |
| Palembang | 1,352 |
| Tangerang | 1,198 |
| Ujung Pandang | 1,092 |
| Bandar Lampung | 832 |
| Malang | 763 |
| Padang | 721 |
| **Iran** | |
| Tehran | 6,750 |
| Mashhad | 1,964 |
| Esfahan | 1,221 |
| Tabriz | 1,166 |
| Shiraz | 1,043 |
| Ahvaz | 828 |
| Qom | 780 |
| Bakhtaran | 666 |
| **Iraq** | |
| Baghdad | 3,841 |
| Diyala | 961 |
| As Sulaymaniyah | 952 |
| Arbil | 770 |
| Al Mawsil | 664 |
| **Ireland** | |
| Dublin | 952 |
| **Israel** | |
| Tel Aviv-Yafo | 1,502 |
| **Italy** | |
| Rome | 2,775 |
| Milan | 1,369 |
| Naples | 1,067 |
| Turin | 962 |
| Palermo | 698 |
| Genoa | 678 |
| **Ivory Coast (Côte d'Ivoire)** | |
| Abidjan | 2,500 |
| **Jamaica** | |
| Kingston | 644 |
| **Japan** | |
| Tokyo–Yokohama | 26,836 |
| Osaka | 10,601 |
| Nagoya | 2,152 |
| Sapporo | 1,757 |
| Kyoto | 1,464 |
| Kobe | 1,424 |
| Fukuoka | 1,285 |
| Kawasaki | 1,203 |
| Hiroshima | 1,109 |
| Kitakyushu | 1,020 |
| Sendai | 971 |
| Chiba | 857 |
| Sakai | 803 |
| Kumamoto | 650 |
| Okayama | 616 |
| **Jordan** | |
| Amman | 1,300 |
| Az-Zarqā | 609 |

| | Population (1,000s) |
|---|---|
| **Kazakstan** | |
| Almaty | 1,150 |
| **Kenya** | |
| Nairobi | 2,000 |
| Mombasa | 600 |
| **Korea, North** | |
| Pyŏngyang | 2,639 |
| Hamhung | 775 |
| Chŏngjin | 754 |
| Chinnampo | 691 |
| **Korea, South** | |
| Seoul | 11,641 |
| Pusan | 3,814 |
| Taegu | 2,449 |
| Inchon | 2,308 |
| Taejŏn | 1,272 |
| Kwangju | 1,258 |
| Ulsan | 967 |
| Sŏngnam | 869 |
| Puch'on | 779 |
| Suwŏn | 756 |
| **Latvia** | |
| Riga | 846 |
| **Lebanon** | |
| Beirut | 1,900 |
| **Libya** | |
| Tripoli | 1,083 |
| **Madagascar** | |
| Antananarivo | 1,053 |
| **Malaysia** | |
| Kuala Lumpur | 1,145 |
| **Mali** | |
| Bamako | 800 |
| **Mauritania** | |
| Nouakchott | 735 |
| **Mexico** | |
| Mexico City | 15,048 |
| Guadalajara | 2,847 |
| Monterrey | 2,522 |
| Puebla | 1,055 |
| León | 872 |
| Ciudad Juárez | 798 |
| Tijuana | 743 |
| Culiacán Rosales | 602 |
| Mexicali | 602 |
| **Moldova** | |
| Chişinău | 700 |
| **Mongolia** | |
| Ulan Bator | 627 |
| **Morocco** | |
| Casablanca | 3,079 |
| Rabat-Salé | 1,344 |
| Fès | 735 |
| Marrakesh | 621 |
| **Mozambique** | |
| Maputo | 2,000 |
| **Netherlands** | |
| Amsterdam | 1,101 |
| Rotterdam | 1,076 |
| The Hague | 694 |
| **New Zealand** | |
| Auckland | 997 |
| **Nicaragua** | |
| Managua | 864 |
| **Nigeria** | |
| Lagos | 10,287 |
| Ibadan | 1,365 |
| Ogbomosho | 712 |
| Kano | 657 |
| **Norway** | |
| Oslo | 714 |
| **Pakistan** | |
| Karachi | 9,863 |
| Lahore | 5,085 |
| Faisalabad | 1,875 |
| Peshawar | 1,676 |
| Gujranwala | 1,663 |
| Rawalpindi | 1,290 |
| Multan | 1,257 |
| Hyderabad | 1,107 |
| **Paraguay** | |
| Asunción | 945 |
| **Peru** | |
| Lima–Callao | 6,601 |
| Callao | 638 |
| Arequipa | 620 |
| **Philippines** | |
| Manila | 9,280 |
| Quezon City | 1,989 |
| Davao | 1,191 |
| Caloocan | 1,023 |
| Cebu | 662 |
| **Poland** | |
| Warsaw | 1,638 |
| Lódz | 825 |
| Kraków | 745 |
| Wroclaw | 642 |
| **Portugal** | |
| Lisbon | 2,561 |
| Oporto | 1,174 |
| **Romania** | |
| Bucharest | 2,060 |
| **Russia** | |
| Moscow | 9,233 |
| St Petersburg | 4,883 |
| Nizhniy Novgorod | 1,425 |
| Novosibirsk | 1,400 |
| Yekaterinburg | 1,300 |
| Samara | 1,200 |
| Omsk | 1,200 |
| Chelyabinsk | 1,100 |
| Kazan | 1,100 |
| Ufa | 1,100 |
| Volgograd | 1,003 |
| Perm | 1,000 |
| Rostov | 1,000 |
| Voronezh | 908 |
| Saratov | 895 |
| Krasnoyarsk | 869 |
| Togliatti | 689 |
| Simbirsk | 678 |
| Izhevsk | 654 |
| Krasnodar | 645 |
| Vladivostok | 632 |
| Yaroslavl | 629 |
| Khabarovsk | 618 |
| **Saudi Arabia** | |
| Riyadh | 1,800 |
| Jedda | 1,500 |
| Mecca | 630 |
| **Senegal** | |
| Dakar | 1,571 |
| **Singapore** | |
| Singapore | 3,104 |
| **Somalia** | |
| Mogadishu | 1,000 |
| **South Africa** | |
| Cape Town | 2,350 |
| East Rand | 1,379 |
| Johannesburg | 1,196 |
| Durban | 1,137 |
| Pretoria | 1,080 |
| West Rand | 870 |
| Port Elizabeth | 853 |
| Vanderbijlpark–Vereeniging | 774 |
| **Spain** | |
| Madrid | 3,029 |
| Barcelona | 1,614 |
| Valencia | 763 |
| Sevilla | 719 |
| Zaragoza | 607 |
| **Sri Lanka** | |
| Colombo | 1,863 |
| **Sudan** | |
| Nyala | 1,267 |
| Khartoum | 925 |
| Sharg el Nil | 879 |
| **Sweden** | |
| Stockholm | 1,744 |
| Göteburg | 775 |
| **Switzerland** | |
| Zürich | 1,175 |
| Bern | 942 |
| **Syria** | |
| Aleppo | 1,591 |
| Damascus | 1,549 |
| Homs | 644 |
| **Taiwan** | |
| Taipei | 2,653 |
| Kaohsiung | 1,405 |
| Taichung | 817 |
| Tainan | 700 |
| **Tanzania** | |
| Dar-es-Salaam | 1,361 |
| **Thailand** | |
| Bangkok | 5,572 |
| **Togo** | |
| Lomé | 590 |
| **Tunisia** | |
| Tunis | 1,827 |
| **Turkey** | |
| Istanbul | 7,490 |
| Ankara | 3,028 |
| Izmir | 2,333 |
| Adana | 1,472 |
| Bursa | 1,317 |
| Konya | 1,040 |
| Gaziantep | 930 |
| Icel | 908 |
| Antalya | 734 |
| Diyarbakir | 677 |
| Kocaeli | 661 |
| Urfa | 649 |
| Kayseri | 648 |
| Manisa | 641 |
| **Uganda** | |
| Kampala | 773 |
| **Ukraine** | |
| Kiev | 2,630 |
| Kharkiv | 1,555 |
| Dnipropetrovsk | 1,147 |
| Donetsk | 1,088 |
| Odesa | 1,046 |
| Zaporizhzhya | 887 |
| Lviv | 802 |
| Kryvyy Rih | 720 |
| **United Kingdom** | |
| London | 8,089 |
| Birmingham | 2,373 |
| Manchester | 2,353 |
| Liverpool | 852 |
| Glasgow | 832 |
| Sheffield | 661 |
| Nottingham | 649 |
| Newcastle | 617 |
| **United States** | |
| New York | 16,329 |
| Los Angeles | 12,410 |
| Chicago | 7,668 |
| Philadelphia | 4,949 |
| Washington, DC | 4,466 |
| Detroit | 4,307 |
| Houston | 3,653 |
| Atlanta | 3,331 |
| Boston | 3,240 |
| Dallas | 2,898 |
| Minneapolis–St Paul | 2,688 |
| San Diego | 2,632 |
| St Louis | 2,536 |
| Phoenix | 2,473 |
| Baltimore | 2,458 |
| Pittsburgh | 2,402 |
| Cleveland | 2,222 |
| San Francisco | 2,182 |
| Seattle | 2,180 |
| Tampa | 2,157 |
| Miami | 2,025 |
| Newark | 1,934 |
| Denver | 1,796 |
| Portland (Or.) | 1,676 |
| Kansas City (Mo.) | 1,647 |
| Cincinnati | 1,581 |
| San Jose | 1,557 |
| Norfolk | 1,529 |
| Indianapolis | 1,462 |
| Milwaukee | 1,456 |
| Sacramento | 1,441 |
| San Antonio | 1,437 |
| Columbus (Oh.) | 1,423 |
| New Orleans | 1,309 |
| Charlotte | 1,260 |
| Buffalo | 1,189 |
| Salt Lake City | 1,178 |
| Hartford | 1,151 |
| Oklahoma | 1,007 |
| Jacksonville (Fl.) | 665 |
| Omaha | 663 |
| Memphis | 614 |
| **Uruguay** | |
| Montevideo | 1,378 |
| **Uzbekistan** | |
| Tashkent | 2,107 |
| **Venezuela** | |
| Caracas | 2,784 |
| Maracaibo | 1,364 |
| Valencia | 1,032 |
| Maracay | 800 |
| Barquisimeto | 745 |
| **Vietnam** | |
| Ho Chi Minh City | 4,322 |
| Hanoi | 3,056 |
| Haiphong | 783 |
| **Yemen** | |
| Sana | 972 |
| **Yugoslavia** | |
| Belgrade | 1,137 |
| **Zambia** | |
| Lusaka | 982 |
| **Zimbabwe** | |
| Harare | 1,189 |
| Bulawayo | 622 |

* SAR = Special Administrative Region of China

# World Statistics – Physical

Under each subject heading, the statistics are listed by continent. The figures are in size order beginning with the largest, longest or deepest, and are rounded as appropriate. Both metric and imperial measurements are given. The lists are complete down to the > mark; below this mark they are selective.

## Land and Water

| | km$^2$ | miles$^2$ | % |
|---|---|---|---|
| The World | 509,450,000 | 196,672,000 | – |
| Land | 149,450,000 | 57,688,000 | 29.3 |
| Water | 360,000,000 | 138,984,000 | 70.7 |
| | | | |
| Asia | 44,500,000 | 17,177,000 | 29.8 |
| Africa | 30,302,000 | 11,697,000 | 20.3 |
| North America | 24,241,000 | 9,357,000 | 16.2 |
| South America | 17,793,000 | 6,868,000 | 11.9 |
| Antarctica | 14,100,000 | 5,443,000 | 9.4 |
| Europe | 9,957,000 | 3,843,000 | 6.7 |
| Australia & Oceania | 8,557,000 | 3,303,000 | 5.7 |
| | | | |
| Pacific Ocean | 179,679,000 | 69,356,000 | 49.9 |
| Atlantic Ocean | 92,373,000 | 35,657,000 | 25.7 |
| Indian Ocean | 73,917,000 | 28,532,000 | 20.5 |
| Arctic Ocean | 14,090,000 | 5,439,000 | 3.9 |

## Seas

| Pacific Ocean | km$^2$ | miles$^2$ |
|---|---|---|
| South China Sea | 2,974,600 | 1,148,500 |
| Bering Sea | 2,268,000 | 875,000 |
| Sea of Okhotsk | 1,528,000 | 590,000 |
| East China & Yellow | 1,249,000 | 482,000 |
| Sea of Japan | 1,008,000 | 389,000 |
| Gulf of California | 162,000 | 62,500 |
| Bass Strait | 75,000 | 29,000 |

| Atlantic Ocean | km$^2$ | miles$^2$ |
|---|---|---|
| Caribbean Sea | 2,766,000 | 1,068,000 |
| Mediterranean Sea | 2,516,000 | 971,000 |
| Gulf of Mexico | 1,543,000 | 596,000 |
| Hudson Bay | 1,232,000 | 476,000 |
| North Sea | 575,000 | 223,000 |
| Black Sea | 462,000 | 178,000 |
| Baltic Sea | 422,170 | 163,000 |
| Gulf of St Lawrence | 238,000 | 92,000 |

| Indian Ocean | km$^2$ | miles$^2$ |
|---|---|---|
| Red Sea | 438,000 | 169,000 |
| The Gulf | 239,000 | 92,000 |

## Mountains

| Europe | | m | ft |
|---|---|---|---|
| Elbrus | Russia | 5,642 | 18,510 |
| Mont Blanc | France/Italy | 4,807 | 15,771 |
| Monte Rosa | Italy/Switzerland | 4,634 | 15,203 |
| Dom | Switzerland | 4,545 | 14,911 |
| Liskamm | Switzerland | 4,527 | 14,852 |
| Weisshorn | Switzerland | 4,505 | 14,780 |
| Taschorn | Switzerland | 4,490 | 14,730 |
| Matterhorn/Cervino | Italy/Switzerland | 4,478 | 14,691 |
| Mont Maudit | France/Italy | 4,465 | 14,649 |
| Dent Blanche | Switzerland | 4,356 | 14,291 |
| > Nadelhorn | Switzerland | 4,327 | 14,196 |
| Grandes Jorasses | France/Italy | 4,208 | 13,806 |
| Jungfrau | Switzerland | 4,158 | 13,642 |
| Barre des Ecrins | France | 4,103 | 13,461 |
| Gran Paradiso | Italy | 4,061 | 13,323 |
| Piz Bernina | Italy/Switzerland | 4,049 | 13,284 |

| Europe (cont.) | | m | ft |
|---|---|---|---|
| Eiger | Switzerland | 3,970 | 13,025 |
| Monte Viso | Italy | 3,841 | 12,602 |
| Grossglockner | Austria | 3,797 | 12,457 |
| Wildspitze | Austria | 3,772 | 12,382 |
| Monte Disgrazia | Italy | 3,678 | 12,066 |
| Mulhacén | Spain | 3,478 | 11,411 |
| Pico de Aneto | Spain | 3,404 | 11,168 |
| Marmolada | Italy | 3,342 | 10,964 |
| Etna | Italy | 3,340 | 10,958 |
| Zugspitze | Germany | 2,962 | 9,718 |
| Musala | Bulgaria | 2,925 | 9,596 |
| Olympus | Greece | 2,917 | 9,570 |
| Triglav | Slovenia | 2,863 | 9,393 |
| Monte Cinto | France (Corsica) | 2,710 | 8,891 |
| Gerlachovka | Slovak Republic | 2,655 | 8,711 |
| Torre de Cerrado | Spain | 2,648 | 8,688 |
| Galdhöpiggen | Norway | 2,468 | 8,100 |
| Hvannadalshnúkur | Iceland | 2,119 | 6,952 |
| Kebnekaise | Sweden | 2,117 | 6,946 |
| Ben Nevis | UK | 1,343 | 4,406 |

| Asia | | m | ft |
|---|---|---|---|
| Everest | China/Nepal | 8,848 | 29,029 |
| K2 (Godwin Austen) | China/Kashmir | 8,611 | 28,251 |
| Kanchenjunga | India/Nepal | 8,598 | 28,208 |
| Lhotse | China/Nepal | 8,516 | 27,939 |
| Makalu | China/Nepal | 8,481 | 27,824 |
| Cho Oyu | China/Nepal | 8,201 | 26,906 |
| Dhaulagiri | Nepal | 8,172 | 26,811 |
| Manaslu | Nepal | 8,156 | 26,758 |
| Nanga Parbat | Kashmir | 8,126 | 26,660 |
| Annapurna | Nepal | 8,078 | 26,502 |
| Gasherbrum | China/Kashmir | 8,068 | 26,469 |
| Broad Peak | China/Kashmir | 8,051 | 26,414 |
| Xixabangma | China | 8,012 | 26,286 |
| Kangbachen | India/Nepal | 7,902 | 25,925 |
| Jannu | India/Nepal | 7,902 | 25,925 |
| Gayachung Kang | Nepal | 7,897 | 25,909 |
| Himalchuli | Nepal | 7,893 | 25,896 |
| Disteghil Sar | Kashmir | 7,885 | 25,869 |
| Nuptse | Nepal | 7,879 | 25,849 |
| Khunyang Chhish | Kashmir | 7,852 | 25,761 |
| Masherbrum | Kashmir | 7,821 | 25,659 |
| Nanda Devi | India | 7,817 | 25,646 |
| Rakaposhi | Kashmir | 7,788 | 25,551 |
| Batura | Kashmir | 7,785 | 25,541 |
| Namche Barwa | China | 7,756 | 25,446 |
| Kamet | India | 7,756 | 25,446 |
| Soltoro Kangri | Kashmir | 7,742 | 25,400 |
| Gurla Mandhata | China | 7,728 | 25,354 |
| Trivor | Pakistan | 7,720 | 25,328 |
| > Kongur Shan | China | 7,719 | 25,324 |
| Tirich Mir | Pakistan | 7,690 | 25,229 |
| K'ula Shan | Bhutan/China | 7,543 | 24,747 |
| Pik Kommunizma | Tajikistan | 7,495 | 24,590 |
| Demavend | Iran | 5,604 | 18,386 |
| Ararat | Turkey | 5,165 | 16,945 |
| Gunong Kinabalu | Malaysia (Borneo) | 4,101 | 13,455 |
| Yu Shan | Taiwan | 3,997 | 13,113 |
| Fuji-San | Japan | 3,776 | 12,388 |

| Africa | | m | ft |
|---|---|---|---|
| Kilimanjaro | Tanzania | 5,895 | 19,340 |
| Mt Kenya | Kenya | 5,199 | 17,057 |
| Ruwenzori | Uganda/Congo (Zaïre) | 5,109 | 16,762 |
| Ras Dashan | Ethiopia | 4,620 | 15,157 |

| Africa (cont.) | | m | ft |
|---|---|---|---|
| Meru | Tanzania | 4,565 | 14,977 |
| Karisimbi | Rwanda/Congo (Zaïre) | 4,507 | 14,787 |
| Mt Elgon | Kenya/Uganda | 4,321 | 14,176 |
| Batu | Ethiopia | 4,307 | 14,130 |
| Guna | Ethiopia | 4,231 | 13,882 |
| Toubkal | Morocco | 4,165 | 13,665 |
| Irhil Mgoun | Morocco | 4,071 | 13,356 |
| Mt Cameroon | Cameroon | 4,070 | 13,353 |
| Amba Ferit | Ethiopia | 3,875 | 13,042 |
| Pico del Teide | Spain (Tenerife) | 3,718 | 12,198 |
| Thabana Ntlenyana | Lesotho | 3,482 | 11,424 |
| Emi Koussi | Chad | 3,415 | 11,204 |
| Mt aux Sources | Lesotho/South Africa | 3,282 | 10,768 |
| Mt Piton | Réunion | 3,069 | 10,069 |

| Oceania | | m | ft |
|---|---|---|---|
| Puncak Jaya | Indonesia | 5,029 | 16,499 |
| Puncak Trikora | Indonesia | 4,750 | 15,584 |
| Puncak Mandala | Indonesia | 4,702 | 15,427 |
| Mt Wilhelm | Papua New Guinea | 4,508 | 14,790 |
| Mauna Kea | USA (Hawaii) | 4,205 | 13,796 |
| Mauna Loa | USA (Hawaii) | 4,170 | 13,681 |
| Mt Cook (Aoraki) | New Zealand | 3,753 | 12,313 |
| Mt Balbi | Solomon Is. | 2,439 | 8,002 |
| Orohena | Tahiti | 2,241 | 7,352 |
| Mt Kosciuszko | Australia | 2,237 | 7,339 |

| North America | | m | ft |
|---|---|---|---|
| Mt McKinley (Denali) | USA (Alaska) | 6,194 | 20,321 |
| Mt Logan | Canada | 5,959 | 19,551 |
| Citlaltepetl | Mexico | 5,700 | 18,701 |
| Mt St Elias | USA/Canada | 5,489 | 18,008 |
| Popocatepetl | Mexico | 5,452 | 17,887 |
| Mt Foraker | USA (Alaska) | 5,304 | 17,401 |
| Ixtaccihuatl | Mexico | 5,286 | 17,342 |
| Lucania | Canada | 5,227 | 17,149 |
| Mt Steele | Canada | 5,073 | 16,644 |
| Mt Bona | USA (Alaska) | 5,005 | 16,420 |
| Mt Blackburn | USA (Alaska) | 4,996 | 16,391 |
| Mt Sanford | USA (Alaska) | 4,940 | 16,207 |
| Mt Wood | Canada | 4,848 | 15,905 |
| Nevado de Toluca | Mexico | 4,670 | 15,321 |
| Mt Fairweather | USA (Alaska) | 4,663 | 15,298 |
| Mt Hunter | USA (Alaska) | 4,442 | 14,573 |
| Mt Whitney | USA | 4,418 | 14,495 |
| Mt Elbert | USA | 4,399 | 14,432 |
| Mt Harvard | USA | 4,395 | 14,419 |
| Mt Rainier | USA | 4,392 | 14,409 |
| Blanca Peak | USA | 4,372 | 14,344 |
| Longs Peak | USA | 4,345 | 14,255 |
| Tajumulco | Guatemala | 4,220 | 13,845 |
| Grand Teton | USA | 4,197 | 13,770 |
| Mt Waddington | Canada | 3,994 | 13,104 |
| Mt Robson | Canada | 3,954 | 12,972 |
| Chirripó Grande | Costa Rica | 3,837 | 12,589 |
| Mt Assiniboine | Canada | 3,619 | 11,873 |
| Pico Duarte | Dominican Rep. | 3,175 | 10,417 |

| South America | | m | ft |
|---|---|---|---|
| Aconcagua | Argentina | 6,960 | 22,834 |
| Bonete | Argentina | 6,872 | 22,546 |
| Ojos del Salado | Argentina/Chile | 6,863 | 22,516 |
| Pissis | Argentina | 6,779 | 22,241 |
| Mercedario | Argentina/Chile | 6,770 | 22,211 |
| Huascaran | Peru | 6,768 | 22,204 |
| Llullaillaco | Argentina/Chile | 6,723 | 22,057 |
| Nudo de Cachi | Argentina | 6,720 | 22,047 |
| Yerupaja | Peru | 6,632 | 21,758 |
| N. de Tres Cruces | Argentina/Chile | 6,620 | 21,719 |
| Incahuasi | Argentina/Chile | 6,601 | 21,654 |
| Cerro Galan | Argentina | 6,600 | 21,654 |
| Tupungato | Argentina/Chile | 6,570 | 21,555 |

| South America (cont.) | | m | ft |
|---|---|---|---|
| Sajama | Bolivia | 6,542 | 21,463 |
| Illimani | Bolivia | 6,485 | 21,276 |
| Coropuna | Peru | 6,425 | 21,079 |
| Ausangate | Peru | 6,384 | 20,945 |
| Cerro del Toro | Argentina | 6,380 | 20,932 |
| Siula Grande | Peru | 6,356 | 20,853 |
| Chimborazo | Ecuador | 6,267 | 20,561 |
| Cotapaxi | Ecuador | 5,896 | 19,344 |
| Pico Colon | Colombia | 5,800 | 19,029 |
| Pico Bolivar | Venezuela | 5,007 | 16,427 |

| Antarctica | m | ft |
|---|---|---|
| Vinson Massif | 4,897 | 16,066 |
| Mt Kirkpatrick | 4,528 | 14,855 |
| Mt Markham | 4,349 | 14,268 |

## Ocean Depths

| Atlantic Ocean | m | ft |
|---|---|---|
| Puerto Rico (Milwaukee) Deep | 9,220 | 30,249 |
| Cayman Trench | 7,680 | 25,197 |
| Gulf of Mexico | 5,203 | 17,070 |
| Mediterranean Sea | 5,121 | 16,801 |
| Black Sea | 2,211 | 7,254 |
| North Sea | 660 | 2,165 |
| Baltic Sea | 463 | 1,519 |

| Indian Ocean | m | ft |
|---|---|---|
| Java Trench | 7,450 | 24,442 |
| Red Sea | 2,635 | 8,454 |
| Persian Gulf | 73 | 239 |

| Pacific Ocean | m | ft |
|---|---|---|
| Mariana Trench | 11,022 | 36,161 |
| Tonga Trench | 10,882 | 35,702 |
| Japan Trench | 10,554 | 34,626 |
| Kuril Trench | 10,542 | 34,587 |
| Mindanao Trench | 10,497 | 34,439 |
| Kermadec Trench | 10,047 | 32,962 |
| New Guinea Trench | 9,140 | 29,987 |
| Peru–Chile Trench | 8,050 | 26,410 |

| Antarctica | m | ft |
|---|---|---|
| Molloy Deep | 5,608 | 18,399 |

## Land Lows

| | | m | ft |
|---|---|---|---|
| Dead Sea | Asia | –403 | –1,322 |
| Lake Assal | Africa | –156 | –512 |
| Death Valley | North America | –86 | –282 |
| Valdés Peninsula | South America | –40 | –131 |
| Caspian Sea | Europe | –28 | –92 |
| Lake Eyre North | Oceania | –16 | –52 |

## Rivers

| Europe | | km | miles |
|---|---|---|---|
| Volga | Caspian Sea | 3,700 | 2,300 |
| Danube | Black Sea | 2,850 | 1,770 |
| Ural | Caspian Sea | 2,535 | 1,575 |
| Dnepr (Dnipro) | Black Sea | 2,285 | 1,420 |
| Kama | Volga | 2,030 | 1,260 |
| Don | Black Sea | 1,990 | 1,240 |
| Petchora | Arctic Ocean | 1,790 | 1,110 |
| Oka | Volga | 1,480 | 920 |
| Belaya | Kama | 1,420 | 880 |

| Europe (cont.) | | km | miles |
|---|---|---|---|
| Dnister (Dniester) | Black Sea | 1,400 | 870 |
| Vyatka | Kama | 1,370 | 850 |
| Rhine | North Sea | 1,320 | 820 |
| North Dvina | Arctic Ocean | 1,290 | 800 |
| Desna | Dnepr (Dnipro) | 1,190 | 740 |
| Elbe | North Sea | 1,145 | 710 |
| Wisla | Baltic Sea | 1,090 | 675 |
| Loire | Atlantic Ocean | 1,020 | 635 |
| West Dvina | Baltic Sea | 1,019 | 633 |

| Asia | | km | miles |
|---|---|---|---|
| Yangtze | Pacific Ocean | 6,380 | 3,960 |
| Yenisey–Angara | Arctic Ocean | 5,550 | 3,445 |
| Huang He | Pacific Ocean | 5,464 | 3,395 |
| Ob–Irtysh | Arctic Ocean | 5,410 | 3,360 |
| Mekong | Pacific Ocean | 4,500 | 2,795 |
| Amur | Pacific Ocean | 4,400 | 2,730 |
| Lena | Arctic Ocean | 4,400 | 2,730 |
| Irtysh | Ob | 4,250 | 2,640 |
| Yenisey | Arctic Ocean | 4,090 | 2,540 |
| Ob | Arctic Ocean | 3,680 | 2,285 |
| Indus | Indian Ocean | 3,100 | 1,925 |
| Brahmaputra | Indian Ocean | 2,900 | 1,800 |
| Syrdarya | Aral Sea | 2,860 | 1,775 |
| Salween | Indian Ocean | 2,800 | 1,740 |
| Euphrates | Indian Ocean | 2,700 | 1,675 |
| Vilyuy | Lena | 2,650 | 1,645 |
| Kolyma | Arctic Ocean | 2,600 | 1,615 |
| Amudarya | Aral Sea | 2,540 | 1,575 |
| Ural | Caspian Sea | 2,535 | 1,575 |
| Ganges | Indian Ocean | 2,510 | 1,560 |
| Si Kiang | Pacific Ocean | 2,100 | 1,305 |
| Irrawaddy | Indian Ocean | 2,010 | 1,250 |
| Tarim–Yarkand | Lop Nor | 2,000 | 1,240 |
| Tigris | Indian Ocean | 1,900 | 1,180 |
| Angara | Yenisey | 1,830 | 1,135 |
| Godavari | Indian Ocean | 1,470 | 915 |
| Sutlej | Indian Ocean | 1,450 | 900 |
| Yamuna | Indian Ocean | 1,400 | 870 |

| Africa | | km | miles |
|---|---|---|---|
| Nile | Mediterranean | 6,670 | 4,140 |
| Congo | Atlantic Ocean | 4,670 | 2,900 |
| Niger | Atlantic Ocean | 4,180 | 2,595 |
| Zambezi | Indian Ocean | 3,540 | 2,200 |
| Oubangi/Uele | Congo (Zaïre) | 2,250 | 1,400 |
| Kasai | Congo (Zaïre) | 1,950 | 1,210 |
| Shaballe | Indian Ocean | 1,930 | 1,200 |
| Orange | Atlantic Ocean | 1,860 | 1,155 |
| Cubango | Okavango Swamps | 1,800 | 1,120 |
| Limpopo | Indian Ocean | 1,600 | 995 |
| Senegal | Atlantic Ocean | 1,600 | 995 |
| Volta | Atlantic Ocean | 1,500 | 930 |
| Benue | Niger | 1,350 | 840 |

| Australia | | km | miles |
|---|---|---|---|
| Murray–Darling | Indian Ocean | 3,750 | 2,330 |
| Darling | Murray | 3,070 | 1,905 |
| Murray | Indian Ocean | 2,575 | 1,600 |
| Murrumbidgee | Murray | 1,690 | 1,050 |

| North America | | km | miles |
|---|---|---|---|
| Mississippi–Missouri | Gulf of Mexico | 6,020 | 3,740 |
| Mackenzie | Arctic Ocean | 4,240 | 2,630 |
| Mississippi | Gulf of Mexico | 3,780 | 2,350 |
| Missouri | Mississippi | 3,780 | 2,350 |
| Yukon | Pacific Ocean | 3,185 | 1,980 |
| Rio Grande | Gulf of Mexico | 3,030 | 1,880 |
| Arkansas | Mississippi | 2,340 | 1,450 |
| Colorado | Pacific Ocean | 2,330 | 1,445 |
| Red | Mississippi | 2,040 | 1,270 |

| North America (cont.) | | km | miles |
|---|---|---|---|
| Saskatchewan | Lake Winnipeg | 1,940 | 1,205 |
| Snake | Columbia | 1,670 | 1,040 |
| Churchill | Hudson Bay | 1,600 | 990 |
| Ohio | Mississippi | 1,580 | 980 |
| Brazos | Gulf of Mexico | 1,400 | 870 |
| St Lawrence | Atlantic Ocean | 1,170 | 730 |

| South America | | km | miles |
|---|---|---|---|
| Amazon | Atlantic Ocean | 6,450 | 4,010 |
| Paraná–Plate | Atlantic Ocean | 4,500 | 2,800 |
| Purus | Amazon | 3,350 | 2,080 |
| Madeira | Amazon | 3,200 | 1,990 |
| São Francisco | Atlantic Ocean | 2,900 | 1,800 |
| Paraná | Plate | 2,800 | 1,740 |
| Tocantins | Atlantic Ocean | 2,750 | 1,710 |
| Paraguay | Paraná | 2,550 | 1,580 |
| Orinoco | Atlantic Ocean | 2,500 | 1,550 |
| Pilcomayo | Paraná | 2,500 | 1,550 |
| Araguaia | Tocantins | 2,250 | 1,400 |
| Juruá | Amazon | 2,000 | 1,240 |
| Xingu | Amazon | 1,980 | 1,230 |
| Ucayali | Amazon | 1,900 | 1,180 |
| Maranón | Amazon | 1,600 | 990 |
| Uruguay | Plate | 1,600 | 990 |
| Magdalena | Caribbean Sea | 1,540 | 960 |

## Lakes

| Europe | | km$^2$ | miles$^2$ |
|---|---|---|---|
| Lake Ladoga | Russia | 17,700 | 6,800 |
| Lake Onega | Russia | 9,700 | 3,700 |
| Saimaa system | Finland | 8,000 | 3,100 |
| Vänern | Sweden | 5,500 | 2,100 |
| Rybinskoye Reservoir | Russia | 4,700 | 1,800 |

| Asia | | km$^2$ | miles$^2$ |
|---|---|---|---|
| Caspian Sea | Asia | 371,800 | 143,550 |
| Lake Baykal | Russia | 30,500 | 11,780 |
| Aral Sea | Kazak./Uzbek. | 28,687 | 11,086 |
| Tonlé Sap | Cambodia | 20,000 | 7,700 |
| Lake Balqash | Kazakstan | 18,500 | 7,100 |
| Lake Dongting | China | 12,000 | 4,600 |
| Lake Ysyk | Kyrgyzstan | 6,200 | 2,400 |
| Lake Orumiyeh | Iran | 5,900 | 2,300 |
| Lake Koko | China | 5,700 | 2,200 |
| Lake Poyang | China | 5,000 | 1,900 |
| Lake Khanka | China/Russia | 4,400 | 1,700 |
| Lake Van | Turkey | 3,500 | 1,400 |
| Lake Ubsa | China | 3,400 | 1,300 |

| Africa | | km$^2$ | miles$^2$ |
|---|---|---|---|
| Lake Victoria | East Africa | 68,000 | 26,000 |
| Lake Tanganyika | Central Africa | 33,000 | 13,000 |
| Lake Malawi/Nyasa | East Africa | 29,600 | 11,430 |
| Lake Chad | Central Africa | 25,000 | 9,700 |
| Lake Turkana | Ethiopia/Kenya | 8,500 | 3,300 |
| Lake Volta | Ghana | 8,500 | 3,300 |
| Lake Bangweulu | Zambia | 8,000 | 3,100 |
| Lake Rukwa | Tanzania | 7,000 | 2,700 |
| Lake Mai-Ndombe | Congo (Zaïre) | 6,500 | 2,500 |
| Lake Kariba | Zambia/Zimbabwe | 5,300 | 2,000 |
| Lake Mobutu | Uganda/Congo (Zaïre) | 5,300 | 2,000 |
| Lake Nasser | Egypt/Sudan | 5,200 | 2,000 |
| Lake Mweru | Zambia/Congo (Zaïre) | 4,900 | 1,900 |
| Lake Cabora Bassa | Mozambique | 4,500 | 1,700 |
| Lake Kyoga | Uganda | 4,400 | 1,700 |
| Lake Tana | Ethiopia | 3,630 | 1,400 |
| Lake Kivu | Rwanda/Congo (Zaïre) | 2,650 | 1,000 |
| Lake Edward | Uganda/Congo (Zaïre) | 2,200 | 850 |

| Australia | | $km^2$ | $miles^2$ |
|---|---|---|---|
| Lake Eyre | Australia | 8,900 | 3,400 |
| Lake Torrens | Australia | 5,800 | 2,200 |
| Lake Gairdner | Australia | 4,800 | 1,900 |

| North America | | $km^2$ | $miles^2$ |
|---|---|---|---|
| Lake Superior | Canada/USA | 82,350 | 31,800 |
| Lake Huron | Canada/USA | 59,600 | 23,010 |
| Lake Michigan | USA | 58,000 | 22,400 |
| Great Bear Lake | Canada | 31,800 | 12,280 |
| Great Slave Lake | Canada | 28,500 | 11,000 |
| Lake Erie | Canada/USA | 25,700 | 9,900 |
| Lake Winnipeg | Canada | 24,400 | 9,400 |
| Lake Ontario | Canada/USA | 19,500 | 7,500 |
| Lake Nicaragua | Nicaragua | 8,200 | 3,200 |
| Lake Athabasca | Canada | 8,100 | 3,100 |
| Smallwood Reservoir | Canada | 6,530 | 2,520 |
| Reindeer Lake | Canada | 6,400 | 2,500 |
| Nettilling Lake | Canada | 5,500 | 2,100 |
| Lake Winnipegosis | Canada | 5,400 | 2,100 |
| Lake Nipigon | Canada | 4,850 | 1,900 |
| Lake Manitoba | Canada | 4,700 | 1,800 |

| South America | | $km^2$ | $miles^2$ |
|---|---|---|---|
| Lake Titicaca | Bolivia/Peru | 8,300 | 3,200 |
| Lake Poopo | Peru | 2,800 | 1,100 |

## Islands

| Europe | | $km^2$ | $miles^2$ |
|---|---|---|---|
| Great Britain | UK | 229,880 | 88,700 |
| Iceland | Atlantic Ocean | 103,000 | 39,800 |
| Ireland | Ireland/UK | 84,400 | 32,600 |
| Novaya Zemlya (North) | Russia | 48,200 | 18,600 |
| West Spitzbergen | Norway | 39,000 | 15,100 |
| Novaya Zemlya (South) | Russia | 33,200 | 12,800 |
| Sicily | Italy | 25,500 | 9,800 |
| Sardinia | Italy | 24,000 | 9,300 |
| North-east Spitzbergen | Norway | 15,000 | 5,600 |
| Corsica | France | 8,700 | 3,400 |
| Crete | Greece | 8,350 | 3,200 |
| Zealand | Denmark | 6,850 | 2,600 |

| Asia | | $km^2$ | $miles^2$ |
|---|---|---|---|
| Borneo | South-east Asia | 744,360 | 287,400 |
| Sumatra | Indonesia | 473,600 | 182,860 |
| Honshu | Japan | 230,500 | 88,980 |
| Sulawesi (Celebes) | Indonesia | 189,000 | 73,000 |
| Java | Indonesia | 126,700 | 48,900 |
| Luzon | Philippines | 104,700 | 40,400 |
| Mindanao | Philippines | 101,500 | 39,200 |
| Hokkaido | Japan | 78,400 | 30,300 |
| Sakhalin | Russia | 74,060 | 28,600 |
| Sri Lanka | Indian Ocean | 65,600 | 25,300 |
| Taiwan | Pacific Ocean | 36,000 | 13,900 |
| Kyushu | Japan | 35,700 | 13,800 |
| Hainan | China | 34,000 | 13,100 |
| Timor | Indonesia | 33,600 | 13,000 |
| Shikoku | Japan | 18,800 | 7,300 |
| Halmahera | Indonesia | 18,000 | 6,900 |
| Ceram | Indonesia | 17,150 | 6,600 |
| Sumbawa | Indonesia | 15,450 | 6,000 |
| Flores | Indonesia | 15,200 | 5,900 |
| Samar | Philippines | 13,100 | 5,100 |
| Negros | Philippines | 12,700 | 4,900 |
| Bangka | Indonesia | 12,000 | 4,600 |
| Palawan | Philippines | 12,000 | 4,600 |
| Panay | Philippines | 11,500 | 4,400 |
| Sumba | Indonesia | 11,100 | 4,300 |
| Mindoro | Philippines | 9,750 | 3,800 |

| Asia (cont.) | | $km^2$ | $miles^2$ |
|---|---|---|---|
| Buru | Indonesia | 9,500 | 3,700 |
| Bali | Indonesia | 5,600 | 2,200 |
| Cyprus | Mediterranean | 3,570 | 1,400 |

| Africa | | $km^2$ | $miles^2$ |
|---|---|---|---|
| Madagascar | Indian Ocean | 587,040 | 226,660 |
| Socotra | Indian Ocean | 3,600 | 1,400 |
| Réunion | Indian Ocean | 2,500 | 965 |
| Tenerife | Atlantic Ocean | 2,350 | 900 |
| Mauritius | Indian Ocean | 1,865 | 720 |

| Oceania | | $km^2$ | $miles^2$ |
|---|---|---|---|
| New Guinea | Indon./Papua NG | 821,030 | 317,000 |
| New Zealand (South) | New Zealand | 150,500 | 58,100 |
| New Zealand (North) | New Zealand | 114,700 | 44,300 |
| Tasmania | Australia | 67,800 | 26,200 |
| New Britain | Papua NG | 37,800 | 14,600 |
| New Caledonia | Pacific Ocean | 19,100 | 7,400 |
| Viti Levu | Fiji | 10,500 | 4,100 |
| Hawaii | Pacific Ocean | 10,450 | 4,000 |
| Bougainville | Papua NG | 9,600 | 3,700 |
| Guadalcanal | Solomon Is. | 6,500 | 2,500 |
| Vanua Levu | Fiji | 5,550 | 2,100 |
| New Ireland | Papua NG | 3,200 | 1,200 |

| North America | | $km^2$ | $miles^2$ |
|---|---|---|---|
| Greenland | Greenland | 2,175,600 | 839,800 |
| Baffin Is. | Canada | 508,000 | 196,100 |
| Victoria Is. | Canada | 212,200 | 81,900 |
| Ellesmere Is. | Canada | 212,000 | 81,800 |
| Cuba | Cuba | 110,860 | 42,800 |
| Newfoundland | Canada | 110,680 | 42,700 |
| Hispaniola | Atlantic Ocean | 76,200 | 29,400 |
| Banks Is. | Canada | 67,000 | 25,900 |
| Devon Is. | Canada | 54,500 | 21,000 |
| Melville Is. | Canada | 42,400 | 16,400 |
| Vancouver Is. | Canada | 32,150 | 12,400 |
| Somerset Is. | Canada | 24,300 | 9,400 |
| Jamaica | Caribbean Sea | 11,400 | 4,400 |
| Puerto Rico | Atlantic Ocean | 8,900 | 3,400 |
| Cape Breton Is. | Canada | 4,000 | 1,500 |

| South America | | $km^2$ | $miles^2$ |
|---|---|---|---|
| Tierra del Fuego | Argentina/Chile | 47,000 | 18,100 |
| Falkland Is. (East) | Atlantic Ocean | 6,800 | 2,600 |
| South Georgia | Atlantic Ocean | 4,200 | 1,600 |
| Galapagos (Isabela) | Pacific Ocean | 2,250 | 870 |

# World Statistics – Climate

For each city, the top row of figures shows total rainfall in millimetres; the bottom row shows the average temperature in ° Celsius or centigrade. The total annual rainfall and average annual temperature are given at the end of the rows.

| | *Jan.* | *Feb.* | *Mar.* | *Apr.* | *May* | *June* | *July* | *Aug.* | *Sept.* | *Oct.* | *Nov.* | *Dec.* | *Total* |
|---|---|---|---|---|---|---|---|---|---|---|---|---|---|
| **Europe** | | | | | | | | | | | | | |
| Berlin, Germany | 46 | 40 | 33 | 42 | 49 | 65 | 73 | 69 | 68 | 49 | 46 | 43 | 603 |
| Altitude 55 metres | 1 | 0 | 4 | 9 | 14 | 17 | 19 | 18 | 15 | 9 | 5 | 1 | 9 |
| London, UK | 54 | 40 | 37 | 37 | 46 | 45 | 57 | 59 | 49 | 57 | 64 | 48 | 593 |
| 5 m | 4 | 5 | 7 | 9 | 12 | 16 | 18 | 17 | 15 | 11 | 8 | 5 | 11 |
| Málaga, Spain | 61 | 51 | 62 | 46 | 26 | 5 | 1 | 3 | 29 | 64 | 64 | 62 | 474 |
| 33 m | 12 | 13 | 16 | 17 | 19 | 29 | 25 | 26 | 23 | 20 | 16 | 13 | 18 |
| Moscow, Russia | 39 | 38 | 36 | 37 | 53 | 58 | 88 | 71 | 58 | 45 | 47 | 54 | 624 |
| 156 m | −13 | −10 | −4 | 6 | 13 | 16 | 18 | 17 | 12 | 6 | −1 | −7 | 4 |
| Paris, France | 56 | 46 | 35 | 42 | 57 | 54 | 59 | 64 | 55 | 50 | 51 | 50 | 619 |
| 75 m | 3 | 4 | 8 | 11 | 15 | 18 | 20 | 19 | 17 | 12 | 7 | 4 | 12 |
| Rome, Italy | 71 | 62 | 57 | 51 | 46 | 37 | 15 | 21 | 63 | 99 | 129 | 93 | 744 |
| 17 m | 8 | 9 | 11 | 14 | 18 | 22 | 25 | 25 | 22 | 17 | 13 | 10 | 16 |
| **Asia** | | | | | | | | | | | | | |
| Bangkok, Thailand | 8 | 20 | 36 | 58 | 198 | 160 | 160 | 175 | 305 | 206 | 66 | 5 | 1,397 |
| 2 m | 26 | 28 | 29 | 30 | 29 | 29 | 28 | 28 | 28 | 28 | 26 | 25 | 28 |
| Bombay (Mumbai), India | 3 | 3 | 3 | <3 | 18 | 485 | 617 | 340 | 264 | 64 | 13 | 3 | 1,809 |
| 11 m | 24 | 24 | 26 | 28 | 30 | 29 | 27 | 27 | 27 | 28 | 27 | 26 | 27 |
| Ho Chi Minh, Vietnam | 15 | 3 | 13 | 43 | 221 | 330 | 315 | 269 | 335 | 269 | 114 | 56 | 1,984 |
| 9 m | 26 | 27 | 29 | 30 | 29 | 28 | 28 | 28 | 27 | 27 | 27 | 26 | 28 |
| Hong Kong, China | 33 | 46 | 74 | 137 | 292 | 394 | 381 | 361 | 257 | 114 | 43 | 31 | 2,162 |
| 33 m | 16 | 15 | 18 | 22 | 26 | 28 | 28 | 28 | 27 | 25 | 21 | 18 | 23 |
| Tokyo, Japan | 48 | 74 | 107 | 135 | 147 | 165 | 142 | 152 | 234 | 208 | 97 | 56 | 1,565 |
| 6 m | 3 | 4 | 7 | 13 | 17 | 21 | 25 | 26 | 23 | 17 | 11 | 6 | 14 |
| **Africa** | | | | | | | | | | | | | |
| Cairo, Egypt | 5 | 5 | 5 | 3 | 3 | <3 | 0 | 0 | <3 | <3 | 3 | 5 | 28 |
| 116 m | 13 | 15 | 18 | 21 | 25 | 28 | 28 | 28 | 26 | 24 | 20 | 15 | 22 |
| Cape Town, South Africa | 15 | 8 | 18 | 48 | 79 | 84 | 89 | 66 | 43 | 31 | 18 | 10 | 508 |
| 17 m | 21 | 21 | 20 | 17 | 14 | 13 | 12 | 13 | 14 | 16 | 18 | 19 | 17 |
| Lagos, Nigeria | 28 | 46 | 102 | 150 | 269 | 460 | 279 | 64 | 140 | 206 | 69 | 25 | 1,836 |
| 3 m | 27 | 28 | 29 | 28 | 28 | 26 | 26 | 25 | 26 | 26 | 28 | 28 | 27 |
| Nairobi, Kenya | 38 | 64 | 125 | 211 | 158 | 46 | 15 | 23 | 31 | 53 | 109 | 86 | 958 |
| 1,820 m | 19 | 19 | 19 | 19 | 18 | 16 | 16 | 16 | 18 | 19 | 18 | 18 | 18 |
| **Australia, New Zealand & Antarctica** | | | | | | | | | | | | | |
| Christchurch, New Zealand | 56 | 43 | 48 | 48 | 66 | 66 | 69 | 48 | 46 | 43 | 48 | 56 | 638 |
| 10 m | 16 | 16 | 14 | 12 | 9 | 6 | 6 | 7 | 9 | 12 | 14 | 16 | 11 |
| Darwin, Australia | 386 | 312 | 254 | 97 | 15 | 3 | <3 | 3 | 13 | 51 | 119 | 239 | 1,491 |
| 30 m | 29 | 29 | 29 | 29 | 28 | 26 | 25 | 26 | 28 | 29 | 30 | 29 | 28 |
| Mawson, Antarctica | 11 | 30 | 20 | 10 | 44 | 180 | 4 | 40 | 3 | 20 | 0 | 0 | 362 |
| 14 m | 0 | −5 | −10 | −14 | −15 | −16 | −18 | −18 | −19 | −13 | −5 | −1 | −11 |
| Sydney, Australia | 89 | 102 | 127 | 135 | 127 | 117 | 117 | 76 | 73 | 71 | 73 | 73 | 1,181 |
| 42 m | 22 | 22 | 21 | 18 | 15 | 13 | 12 | 13 | 15 | 18 | 19 | 21 | 17 |
| **North America** | | | | | | | | | | | | | |
| Anchorage, Alaska, USA | 20 | 18 | 15 | 10 | 13 | 18 | 41 | 66 | 66 | 56 | 25 | 23 | 371 |
| 40 m | −11 | −8 | −5 | 2 | 7 | 12 | 14 | 13 | 9 | 2 | −5 | −11 | 2 |
| Kingston, Jamaica | 23 | 15 | 23 | 31 | 102 | 89 | 38 | 91 | 99 | 180 | 74 | 36 | 800 |
| 34 m | 25 | 25 | 25 | 26 | 26 | 28 | 28 | 28 | 27 | 27 | 26 | 26 | 26 |
| Los Angeles, USA | 79 | 76 | 71 | 25 | 10 | 3 | <3 | <3 | 5 | 15 | 31 | 66 | 381 |
| 95 m | 13 | 14 | 14 | 16 | 17 | 19 | 21 | 22 | 21 | 18 | 16 | 14 | 17 |
| Mexico City, Mexico | 13 | 5 | 10 | 20 | 53 | 119 | 170 | 152 | 130 | 51 | 18 | 8 | 747 |
| 2,309 m | 12 | 13 | 16 | 18 | 19 | 19 | 17 | 18 | 18 | 16 | 14 | 13 | 16 |
| New York, USA | 94 | 97 | 91 | 81 | 81 | 84 | 107 | 109 | 86 | 89 | 76 | 91 | 1,092 |
| 96 m | −1 | −1 | 3 | 10 | 16 | 20 | 23 | 23 | 21 | 15 | 7 | 2 | 11 |
| Vancouver, Canada | 154 | 115 | 101 | 60 | 52 | 45 | 32 | 41 | 67 | 114 | 150 | 182 | 1,113 |
| 14 m | 3 | 5 | 6 | 9 | 12 | 15 | 17 | 17 | 14 | 10 | 6 | 4 | 10 |
| **South America** | | | | | | | | | | | | | |
| Antofagasta, Chile | 0 | 0 | 0 | <3 | <3 | 3 | 5 | 3 | <3 | 3 | <3 | 0 | 13 |
| 94 m | 21 | 21 | 20 | 18 | 16 | 15 | 14 | 14 | 15 | 16 | 18 | 19 | 17 |
| Buenos Aires, Argentina | 79 | 71 | 109 | 89 | 76 | 61 | 56 | 61 | 79 | 86 | 84 | 99 | 950 |
| 27 m | 23 | 23 | 21 | 17 | 13 | 9 | 10 | 11 | 13 | 15 | 19 | 22 | 16 |
| Lima, Peru | 3 | <3 | <3 | <3 | 5 | 5 | 8 | 8 | 8 | 3 | 3 | <3 | 41 |
| 120 m | 23 | 24 | 24 | 22 | 19 | 17 | 17 | 16 | 17 | 18 | 19 | 21 | 20 |
| Rio de Janeiro, Brazil | 125 | 122 | 130 | 107 | 79 | 53 | 41 | 43 | 66 | 79 | 104 | 137 | 1,082 |
| 61 m | 26 | 26 | 25 | 24 | 22 | 21 | 21 | 21 | 21 | 22 | 23 | 25 | 23 |

# The Earth in Focus

> Landsat image of the San Francisco Bay area. The narrow entrance to the bay (crossed by the Golden Gate Bridge) provides an excellent natural harbour. The San Andreas Fault runs parallel to the coastline.

# The Universe & Solar System

BETWEEN 10 AND 20 billion (or 10,000 to 20,000 million) years ago, the Universe was created in a huge explosion known as the 'Big Bang'. In the first $10^{-24}$ of a second the Universe expanded rapidly and the basic forces of nature, radiation and subatomic particles, came into being. The Universe has been expanding ever since. Traces of the original 'fireball' of radiation can still be detected, and most scientists accept the Big Bang theory of the origin of the Universe.

**The Nearest Stars ▾**

The 20 nearest stars, excluding the Sun, with their distance from Earth in light-years.*

|  |  |
|---|---|
| Proxima Centauri | 4.25 |
| Alpha Centauri A | 4.3 |
| Alpha Centauri B | 4.3 |
| Barnard's Star | 6.0 |
| Wolf 359 | 7.8 |
| Lalande 21185 | 8.3 |
| Sirius A | 8.7 |
| Sirius B | 8.7 |
| UV Ceti A | 8.7 |
| UV Ceti B | 8.7 |
| Ross 154 | 9.4 |
| Ross 248 | 10.3 |
| Epsilon Eridani | 10.7 |
| Ross 128 | 10.9 |
| 61 Cygni A | 11.1 |
| 61 Cygni B | 11.1 |
| Epsilon Indi | 11.2 |
| Groombridge 34 A | 11.2 |
| Groombridge 34 B | 11.2 |
| L789-6 | 11.2 |

** A light-year equals approximately 9,500 billion km [5,900 billion miles].*

*> The Lagoon Nebula is a huge cloud of dust and gas. Hot stars inside the nebula make the gas glow red.*

## GALAXIES

Almost a million years passed before the Universe cooled sufficiently for atoms to form. When a billion years had passed, the atoms had begun to form protogalaxies, which are masses of gas separated by empty space. Stars began to form within the protogalaxies, as particles were drawn together, producing the high temperatures necessary to bring about nuclear fusion. The formation of the first stars brought about the evolution of the protogalaxies into galaxies proper, each containing billions of stars.

Our Sun is a medium-sized star. It is

Mercury Venus Earth Mars Jupiter

**PLANETARY DATA**

| | Mean distance from Sun *(million km)* | Mass *(Earth = 1)* | Period of orbit *(Earth years)* | Period of rotation *(Earth days)* | Equatorial diameter *(km)* | Escape velocity *(km/sec)* | Number of known satellites |
|---|---|---|---|---|---|---|---|
| **Sun** | – | 332,946 | – | 25.38 | 1,392,000 | 617.5 | – |
| **Mercury** | 58.3 | 0.06 | 0.241 | 58.67 | 4,878 | 4.27 | 0 |
| **Venus** | 107.7 | 0.8 | 0.615 | 243.0 | 12,104 | 10.36 | 0 |
| **Earth** | 149.6 | 1.0 | 1.00 | 0.99 | 12,756 | 11.18 | 1 |
| **Mars** | 227.3 | 0.1 | 1.88 | 1.02 | 6,787 | 5.03 | 2 |
| **Jupiter** | 777.9 | 317.8 | 11.86 | 0.41 | 142,800 | 59.60 | 16 |
| **Saturn** | 1,427.1 | 95.2 | 29.46 | 0.42 | 120,000 | 35.50 | 20 |
| **Uranus** | 2,872.3 | 14.5 | 84.01 | 0.45 | 51,118 | 21.30 | 15 |
| **Neptune** | 4,502.7 | 17.2 | 164.79 | 0.67 | 49,528 | 23.3 | 8 |
| **Pluto** | 5,894.2 | 0.002 | 248.54 | 6.30 | 2,300 | 1.1 | 1 |

one of the billions of stars that make up the Milky Way galaxy, which is one of the millions of galaxies in the Universe.

## THE SOLAR SYSTEM

The Solar System lies towards the edge of the Milky Way galaxy. It consists of the Sun and other bodies, including planets (together with their moons), asteroids, meteoroids, comets, dust and gas, which revolve around it.

The Earth moves through space in three distinct ways. First, with the rest of the Solar System, it moves around the centre of the Milky Way galaxy in an orbit that takes 200 million years.

As the Earth revolves around the Sun once every year, its axis is tilted by about 23.5 degrees. As a result, first the northern and then the southern hemisphere lean towards the Sun at different times of the year, causing the seasons experienced in the mid-latitudes.

The Earth also rotates on its axis every 24 hours, causing day and night. The movements of the Earth in the Solar System determine the calendar. The length of a year – one complete orbit of the Earth around the Sun – is 365 days, 5 hours, 48 minutes and 46 seconds. Leap years prevent the calendar from becoming out of step with the solar year.

*> The diagram below shows the planets around the Sun. The sizes of the planets are relative but the distances are not to scale. Closest to the Sun are dense rocky bodies, known as the terrestrial planets. They are Mercury, Venus, Earth and Mars. Jupiter, Saturn, Uranus and Neptune are huge balls of gas. Pluto is a small, icy body.*

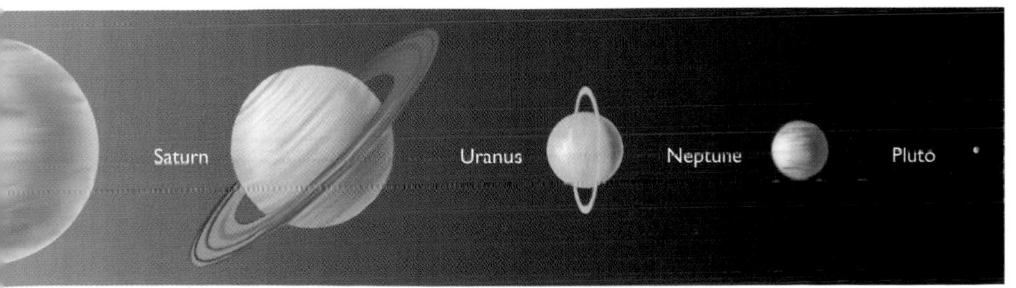

# The Changing Earth

THE SOLAR SYSTEM was formed around 4.7 billion years ago, when the Sun, a glowing ball of gases, was created from a rotating disk of dust and gas. The planets were then formed from material left over after the creation of the Sun.

After the Earth formed, around 4.6 billion years ago, lighter elements rose to the hot surface, where they finally cooled to form a hard shell, or crust. Denser elements sank, forming the partly liquid mantle, the liquid outer core, and the solid inner core.

> Fold mountains, such as the Himalayan ranges which are shown above, were formed when two plates collided and the rock layers between them were squeezed upwards into loops or folds.

## EARTH HISTORY

The oldest known rocks on Earth are around 4 billion years old. Natural processes have destroyed older rocks. Simple life forms first appeared on Earth around 3.5 billion years ago, though rocks formed in the first 4 billion years of Earth history contain little evidence of life. But rocks formed since the start of the Cambrian period (the first period in the Paleozoic era), about 590 million years ago, are rich in fossils. The study of fossils has enabled scientists to gradually piece together the long and complex story of life on Earth.

### THE PLANET EARTH

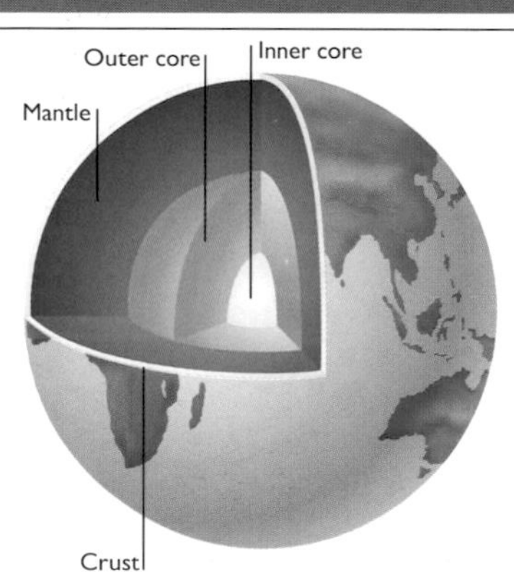


**CRUST** The continental crust has an average thickness of 35–40 km [22–25 miles]; the oceanic crust averages 6 km [4 miles].

**MANTLE** 2,900 km [1,800 miles] thick. The top layer is solid, resting on a partly molten layer called the asthenosphere.

**OUTER CORE** 2,100 km [1,300 miles] thick. It consists mainly of molten iron and nickel.

**INNER CORE (DIAMETER)** 1,350 km [840 miles]. It is mainly solid iron and nickel.

### ELEMENTS

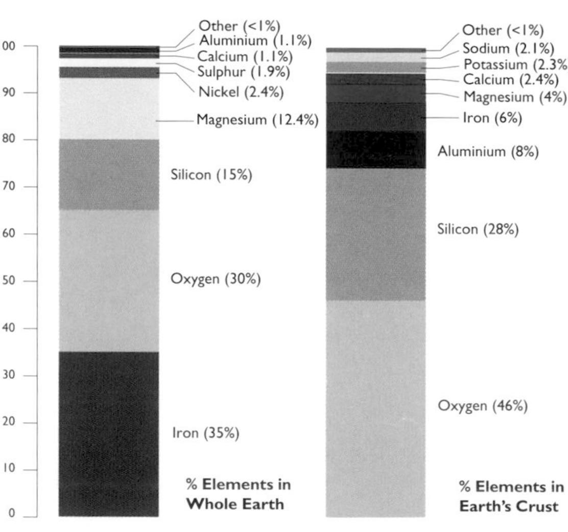


> The Earth contains about 100 elements, but eight of them account for 99% of the planet's mass. Iron makes up 35% of the Earth's mass, but most of it is in the core. The most common elements in the crust – oxygen and silicon – are often combined with one or more of the other common crustal elements, to form a group of minerals called silicates. The mineral quartz, which consists only of silicon and oxygen, occurs widely in such rocks as granites and sandstones.

## PLATE BOUNDARIES

> The Earth's lithosphere is divided into six huge plates and several small ones. Ocean ridges, where plates are moving apart, are called constructive plate margins. Ocean trenches, where plates collide, are subduction zones. These are destructive plate margins. The map shows the main plates and the directions in which they are moving.

Plate boundaries

Direction of plate movements

PACIFIC Major plates

## THE DYNAMIC EARTH

The Earth's surface is always changing because of a process called plate tectonics. Plates are blocks of the solid lithosphere (the crust and outer mantle), which are moved around by currents in the partly liquid mantle. Around 250 million years ago, the Earth contained one super-continent called Pangaea. Around 180 million years ago, Pangaea split into a northern part, Laurasia, and a southern part, Gondwanaland. Later, these huge continents, in turn, also split apart and the continents drifted to their present positions. Ancient seas disappeared and mountain ranges, such as the Himalayas and Alps, were pushed upwards.

## PLATE TECTONICS

In the early 1900s, two scientists suggested that the Americas were once joined to Europe and Africa. Together they proposed the theory of continental drift to explain the similarities between rock structures on both sides of the Atlantic. But no one could offer an explanation as to how the continents moved.

Evidence from the ocean floor in the 1950s and 1960s led to the theory of plate tectonics, which suggested that the lithosphere is divided into large blocks, or plates. The plates are solid, but they rest on the partly molten asthenosphere, within the mantle. Long ridges on the ocean floor were found to be the edges of plates which were moving apart, carried by currents in the asthenosphere. As the plates moved, molten material welled up from the mantle to fill the gaps. But at the ocean trenches, one plate is descending beneath another along what is called a subduction zone. The descending plate is melted and destroyed. This crustal destruction at subduction zones balances the creation of new crust along the ridges. Transform faults, where two plates are moving alongside each other, form another kind of plate edge.

## GEOLOGICAL TIME SCALE

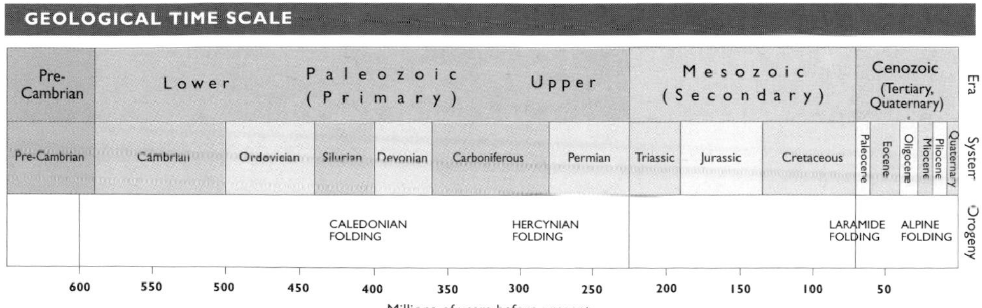

# Earthquakes & Volcanoes

PLATE TECTONICS HELP us to understand such phenomena as earthquakes, volcanic eruptions, and mountain building.

## EARTHQUAKES

Earthquakes can occur anywhere, but they are most common near the edges of plates. They occur when intense pressure breaks the rocks along plate edges, making the plates lurch forward.

**Major Earthquakes since 1900** ▾

| Year | Location | Mag. | Deaths |
|---|---|---|---|
| 1906 | San Francisco, *USA* | 8.3 | 503 |
| 1906 | Valparaiso, *Chile* | 8.6 | 22,000 |
| 1908 | Messina, *Italy* | 7.5 | 83,000 |
| 1915 | Avezzano, *Italy* | 7.5 | 30,000 |
| 1920 | Gansu, *China* | 8.6 | 180,000 |
| 1923 | Yokohama, *Japan* | 8.3 | 143,000 |
| 1927 | Nan Shan, *China* | 8.3 | 200,000 |
| 1932 | Gansu, *China* | 7.6 | 70,000 |
| 1934 | Bihar, *India/Nepal* | 8.4 | 10,700 |
| 1935 | Quetta, *Pakistan* | 7.5 | 60,000 |
| 1939 | Chillan, *Chile* | 8.3 | 28,000 |
| 1939 | Erzincan, *Turkey* | 7.9 | 30,000 |
| 1960 | Agadir, *Morocco* | 5.8 | 12,000 |
| 1964 | Anchorage, *Alaska* | 8.4 | 131 |
| 1968 | North-east Iran | 7.4 | 12,000 |
| 1970 | North Peru | 7.7 | 66,794 |
| 1976 | Guatemala | 7.5 | 22,778 |
| 1976 | Tangshan, *China* | 8.2 | 255,000 |
| 1978 | Tabas, *Iran* | 7.7 | 25,000 |
| 1980 | El Asnam, *Algeria* | 7.3 | 20,000 |
| 1980 | South Italy | 7.2 | 4,800 |
| 1985 | Mexico City, *Mexico* | 8.1 | 4,200 |
| 1988 | North-west Armenia | 6.8 | 55,000 |
| 1990 | North Iran | 7.7 | 36,000 |
| 1993 | Maharashtra, *India* | 6.4 | 30,000 |
| 1994 | Los Angeles, *USA* | 6.6 | 51 |
| 1995 | Kobe, *Japan* | 7.2 | 5,000 |
| 1997 | North-east Iran | 7.1 | 2,400 |
| 1998 | Takhar, *Afghanistan* | 6.1 | 4,200 |
| 1998 | Rostaq, *Afghanistan* | 7.0 | 5,000 |

> The earthquake that struck Kobe in January 1995 was the worst one experienced in Japan since 1923. Japan lies alongside subduction zones.

Earthquakes are common along the mid-ocean ridges, but they are a long way from land and cause little damage. Other earthquakes occur near land in subduction zones, such as those that encircle much of the Pacific Ocean. These earthquakes often trigger off powerful sea waves, called tsunamis. Other earthquakes occur along transform faults, such as the San Andreas fault in California, a boundary between the North American and Pacific plates. Movements along this fault cause periodic disasters, such as the earthquakes in San Francisco (1906) and Los Angeles (1994).

> The section between the Pacific and Indian oceans shows a subduction zone under the American plate, with spreading ocean ridges in the Atlantic and Indian oceans. East Africa may one day split away from the rest of Africa as plate movements pull the Rift Valley apart.

## VOLCANOES & MOUNTAINS

Volcanoes are fuelled by magma (molten rock) from the mantle. Some volcanoes, such as in Hawaii, lie above 'hot spots' (sources of heat in the mantle). But most volcanoes occur either along the ocean ridges or above subduction zones, where

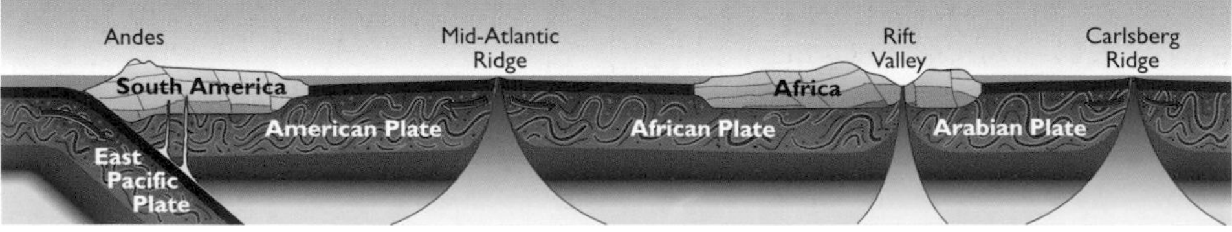

## EARTHQUAKES

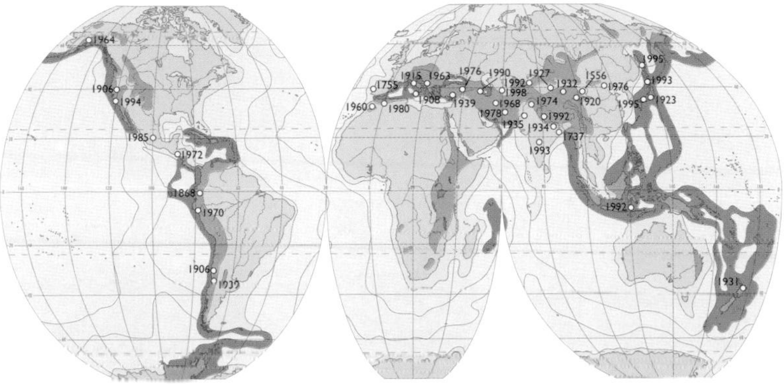

1976 ○ Selected major earthquakes & dates

Mobile land areas

Submarine zones of mobile land areas

Stable land platforms

Submarine extensions of land platforms

Mid-oceanic volcanic ridges

Oceanic platforms

## VOLCANOES

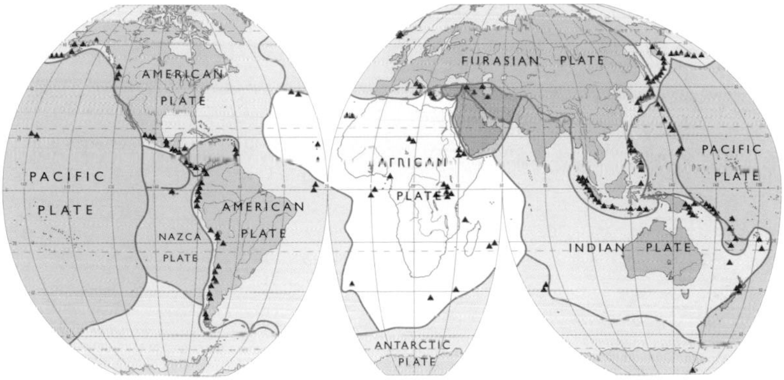

▲ Land volcanoes active since 1700

Boundaries of tectonic plates

The maps show that the main earthquake zones follow plate edges. Most volcanoes are also in these zones, whereas some lie over 'hot spots', far from plate edges.

magma is produced when the descending plate is melted.

Volcanic mountains are built up gradually by runny lava flows or by exploded volcanic ash. Fold mountains occur when two plates bearing land areas collide and the plate edges are buckled upwards into fold mountain ranges. Plate movements also fracture rocks and block mountains are formed when areas of land are pushed upwards along faults or between parallel faults. Blocks of land sometimes sink down between faults, creating deep, steep-sided rift valleys.

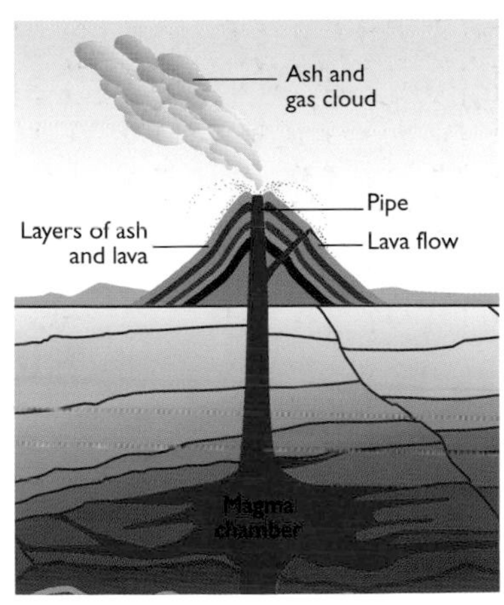


*> Volcanoes occur when molten magma reaches the surface under pressure through long vents. 'Quiet' volcanoes emit runny lava (called pahoehoe). Explosive eruptions occur when the magma is sticky. Explosive gases shatter the magma into ash, which is hurled upwards into the air.*

# Water & Ice

A VISITOR FROM outer space might be forgiven for naming our planet 'Water' rather than 'Earth', because water covers more than 70% of its surface. Without water, our planet would be as lifeless as the Moon. Through the water cycle, fresh water is regularly supplied from the sea to the land. Most geographers divide the world's water into four main oceans: the Pacific, the Atlantic, the Indian and the Arctic. Together the oceans contain 97.2% of the world's water.

The water in the oceans is constantly on the move, even, albeit extremely slowly, in the deepest ocean trenches. The greatest movements of ocean water occur in the form of ocean currents. These are marked, mainly wind-blown

> Ice breaks away from the ice sheet of Antarctica, forming flat-topped icebergs. Researchers fear that warmer weather is melting Antarctica's ice sheets at a dangerous rate, after large chunks of the Larsen ice shelf and the Ronne ice shelf broke away in 1997 and 1998, respectively.

## EXPLANATION OF TERMS

**GLACIER** A body of ice that flows down valleys in mountain areas. It is usually narrow and hence smaller than ice caps or ice sheets.

**ICE AGE** A period of Earth history when ice sheets spread over large areas. The most recent Ice Age began about 1.8 million years ago and ended 10,000 years ago.

**ICEBERG** A floating body of ice in the sea. About eight-ninths of the ice is hidden beneath the surface of the water.

**ICE SHEET** A large body of ice. During the last Ice Age, ice sheets covered large parts of the northern hemisphere.

**OCEAN** The four main oceans are the Pacific, the Atlantic, the Indian and the Arctic. Some people classify a fifth southern ocean, but others regard these waters as extensions of the Pacific, Atlantic and Indian oceans.

**OCEAN CURRENTS** Distinct currents of water in the oceans. Winds are the main causes of surface currents.

**SEA** An expanse of water, but smaller than an ocean.

## JANUARY TEMPERATURE AND OCEAN CURRENTS

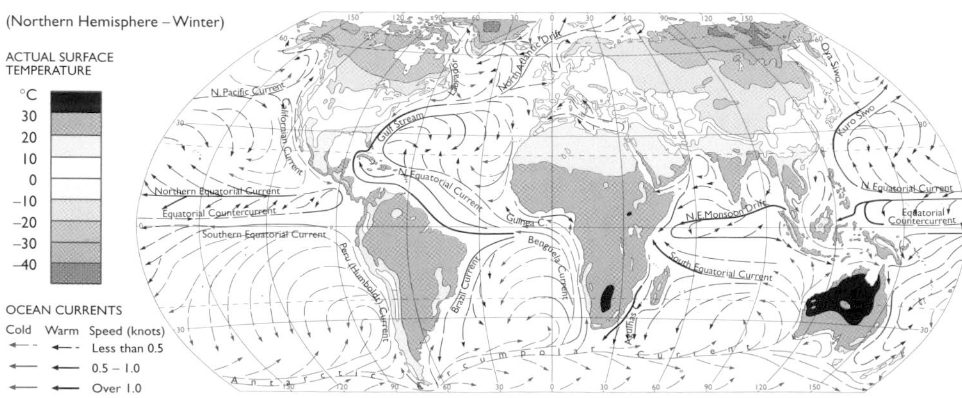

## CROSS-SECTION OF ANTARCTICA

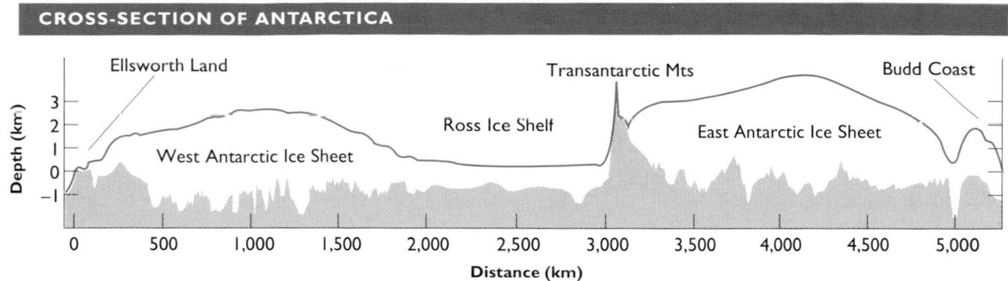


> *This section across Antarctica shows the concealed land areas in brown, with the top of the ice in blue. The section is divided into the West and East Antarctic Ice Sheets. The vertical scale has been exaggerated*

movements of water on or near the surface. Other dense, cold currents creep slowly across the ocean floor. Warm and cold ocean currents help to regulate the world's climate by transferring heat between the tropics and the poles.

### ICE

About 2.15% of the world's water is locked in two large ice sheets, several smaller ice caps and glaciers. The world's largest ice sheet covers most of Antarctica. The ice is up to 4,800 m [15,750 ft] thick and it represents 70% of the world's fresh water. The volume of ice is about nine times greater than that contained in the world's other ice sheet in Greenland. Besides these two ice sheets, there are some smaller ice caps in northern Canada, Iceland, Norway and Spitzbergen, and many valley glaciers in high mountain regions throughout the world.

If global warming was to melt the world's ice, the sea level could rise by as much as 100 m [330 ft], flooding low-lying coastal regions. Many of the world's largest cities and most fertile plains would vanish beneath the waves.

### Composition of Seawater ▾

The principal components of seawater, by percentage, excluding the elements of water itself:

|  |  |  |  |
|---|---|---|---|
| Chloride (Cl) | 55.04% | Potassium (K) | 1.10% |
| Sodium (Na) | 30.61% | Bicarbonate ($HCO_3$) | 0.41% |
| Sulphate ($SO_4$) | 7.69% | Bromide (Br) | 0.19% |
| Magnesium (Mg) | 3.69% | Strontium (Sr) | 0.04% |
| Calcium (Ca) | 1.16% | Fluorine (F) | 0.003% |

*The oceans contain virtually every other element, the more important ones being lithium, rubidium, phosphorus, iodine and barium.*

## JULY TEMPERATURE AND OCEAN CURRENTS

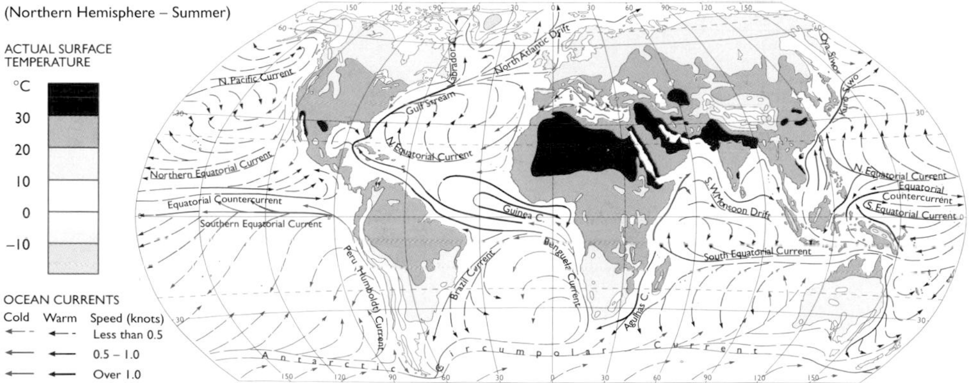

# Weather & Climate

WEATHER IS A description of the day-to-day state of the atmosphere. Climate, on the other hand, is weather in the long term: the seasonal pattern of temperature and precipitation averaged over time.

In some areas, the weather is so stable and predictable that a description of the weather is much the same as a statement of the climate. But in parts of the mid-latitudes, the weather changes from hour to hour. Changeable weather is caused mainly by low air pressure systems, called cyclones or depressions, which form along the polar front where warm subtropical air meets cold polar air.

The main elements of weather and climate are temperature and rainfall. Temperatures vary because the Sun heats the Earth unequally, with the most intense heating around the Equator. Unequal heating is responsible for the general circulation of the atmosphere and the main wind belts.

Rainfall occurs when warm air containing invisible water vapour rises. As the rising air cools, the capacity of the air to hold water vapour decreases and so the water vapour condenses into droplets of water or ice crystals, which collect together to form raindrops or snowflakes.

*> Lightning occurs in clouds and also between the base of clouds and the ground. Lightning that strikes the ground can kill people or start forest fires.*

## LIGHTNING

Lightning is a flash of light in the sky caused by a discharge of electricity in the atmosphere. Lightning occurs within cumulonimbus clouds during thunderstorms. Positive charges build up at the top of the cloud, while negative charges build up at the base. The charges are finally discharged as an electrical spark. Sheet lightning occurs inside clouds, while cloud to ground lightning is usually forked. Thunder occurs when molecules along the lightning channel expand and collide with cool molecules.

*> The rainfall map shows areas affected by tropical storms, which are variously called hurricanes, tropical cyclones, willy willies and typhoons. Strong polar winds bring blizzards in winter.*

## ANNUAL RAINFALL

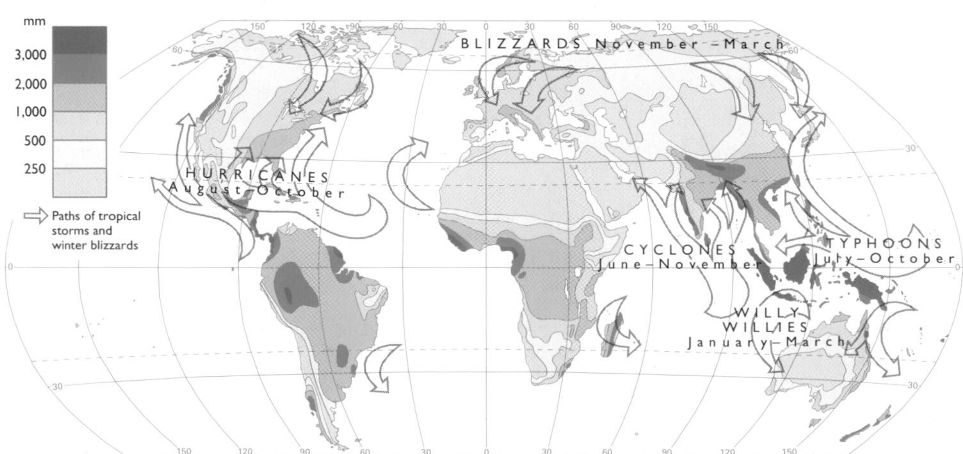

## GLOBAL WARMING

The Earth's climates have changed many times during its history. Around 11,000 years ago, much of the northern hemisphere was buried by ice. Some scientists believe that the last Ice Age may not be over and that ice sheets may one day return. Other scientists are concerned that air

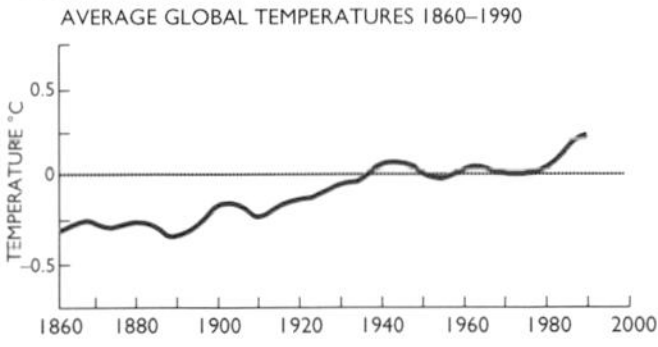


pollution may be producing an opposite effect – a warming of the atmosphere. Since 1900, average world temperatures have risen by about 0.5°C [0.9°F] and increases are likely to continue. Global warming is the result of an increase in the amount of carbon dioxide in the atmosphere, caused by the burning of coal, oil and natural gas, together with deforestation. Short-wave radiation from the Sun passes easily through the atmosphere. But, as the carbon dioxide content rises, more of the long-wave radiation that returns from the Earth's surface is absorbed and trapped by the carbon dioxide. This creates a 'greenhouse effect', which will change the world's climates with, perhaps, disastrous environmental consequences.

## CLIMATE

The world contains six main climatic types: hot and wet tropical climates; dry climates; warm temperate climates; cold temperate climates; polar climates; and mountain climates. These regions are further divided according to the character and amount of precipitation and special features of the temperature, notably seasonal variations. Regions with temperate climates include Mediterranean areas with hot, dry summers and mild, moist winters. The British Isles have a different type of temperate climate, with warm, rather than hot, summers and rain throughout the year.

## CLIMATIC REGIONS

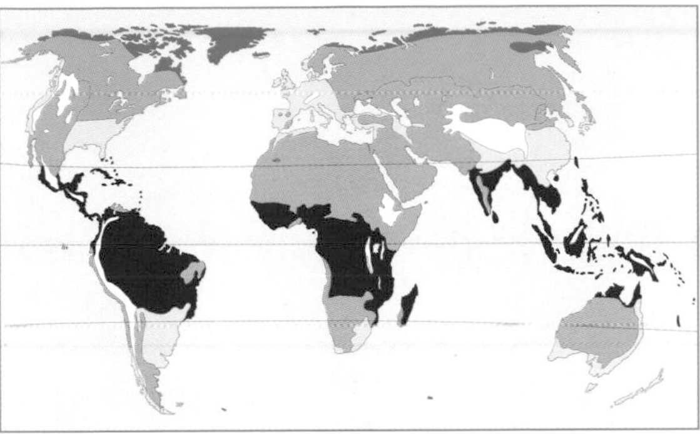

- Tropical Climate (hot & wet)
- Dry Climate (desert & steppe)
- Temperate Climate (warm & wet)
- Continental Climate (cold & wet)
- Polar Climate (very cold & wet)
- Mountainous Areas (where altitude affects climate types)

## WORLD CLIMATIC RECORDS

**Highest Recorded Temperature**
Al Aziziyah, Libya: 58°C [136.4°F] on 13 September 1922

**Highest Mean Annual Temperature**
Dallol, Ethiopia: 34.4°C [94°F] from 1960–66

**Lowest Mean Annual Temperature**
Polus, Nedostupnosti, Pole of Cold, Antarctica: –57.8°C [–72°F]

**Lowest Recorded Temperature (outside poles)**
Verkhoyansk, Siberia, Russia: –68°C [–90°F] on 6 February 1933

**Windiest Place**
Commonwealth Bay, Antarctica: gales often exceed 320 km/h [200 mph]

**Longest Heatwave**
Marble Bar, Western Australia: 162 days over 38°C [94°F], 23 October 1923 to 7 April 1924

**Driest Place**
Calama, northern Chile: no recorded rainfall in 400 years to 1971

**Wettest Place (average)**
Tututendo, Colombia: mean annual rainfall 11,770 mm [463 in]

**Wettest Place (24 hours)**
Cilaos, Réunion, Indian Ocean: 1,870 mm [73.6 in] from 15–16 March 1952

**Wettest Place (12 months)**
Cherrapunji, Meghalaya, north-east India: 26,470 mm [1,040 in], August 1860 to 1861. Cherrapunji also holds the record for rainfall in one month: 2,930 mm [115 in] in July 1861

**Heaviest Hailstones**
Gopalganj, central Bangladesh: up to 1.02 kg [2.25 lbs] in April 1986, which killed 92 people

**Heaviest Snowfall (continuous)**
Bessans, Savoie, France: 1,730 mm [68 in] in 19 hours over the period 5–6 April 1969

**Heaviest Snowfall (season/year)**
Paradise Ranger Station, Mt Rainier, Washington, USA: 31,102 mm [1,224 in] fell from 19 February 1971 to 18 February 1972

# Landforms & Vegetation

THE CLIMATE LARGELY determines the nature of soils and vegetation types throughout the world. The studies of climate and plant and animal communities are closely linked. For example, tropical climates are divided into tropical forest and tropical grassland climates. The tropical forest climate, which is hot and rainy throughout the year, is ideal for the growth of forests that contain more than half of the world's known plant and animal species. But tropical grassland, or savanna, climates have a marked dry season. As a result, the forest gives way to grassland, with scattered trees.

> The tropical broadleaf forests are rich in plant and animal species. The extinction of many species because of deforestation is one of the great natural disasters of our time.

## CLIMATE & SCENERY

The climate also helps to shape the land. Frost action in cold areas splits boulders apart, while rapid temperature changes in hot deserts make rock surfaces peel away like the layers of an onion. These are examples of mechanical weathering.

Chemical weathering usually results from the action of water on rocks. For example, rainwater containing dissolved carbon dioxide is a weak acid, which reacts with limestone. This chemical process is responsible for the erosion of the world's most spectacular caves.

Running water and glaciers play a major part in creating scenery, while in

**NATURAL VEGETATION**

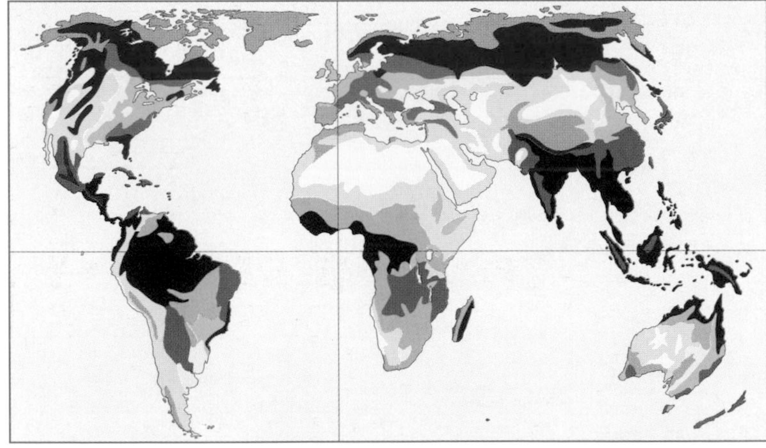

- Tundra & mountain vegetation
- Needleleaf evergreen forest
- Broadleaf deciduous forest
- Mixed needleleaf evergreen & broadleaf deciduous trees
- Mid-latitude grassland
- Semi-desert scrub land
- Evergreen broadleaf & deciduous trees & scrub
- Desert
- Tropical grassland (savanna)
- Tropical broadleaf & monsoon rainforest
- Subtropical broadleaf & needleleaf forest

> Human activities, especially agriculture, have greatly modified plant and animal communities throughout the world. As a result, world vegetation maps show the natural 'climax vegetation' of regions – that is, the kind of vegetation that would grow in a particular climatic area, had that area not been affected by human activities. For example, the climax vegetation of western Europe is broadleaf, deciduous forest, but most of the original forest, together with the animals which lived in it, was destroyed long ago.

## DESERTIFICATION AND DEFORESTATION

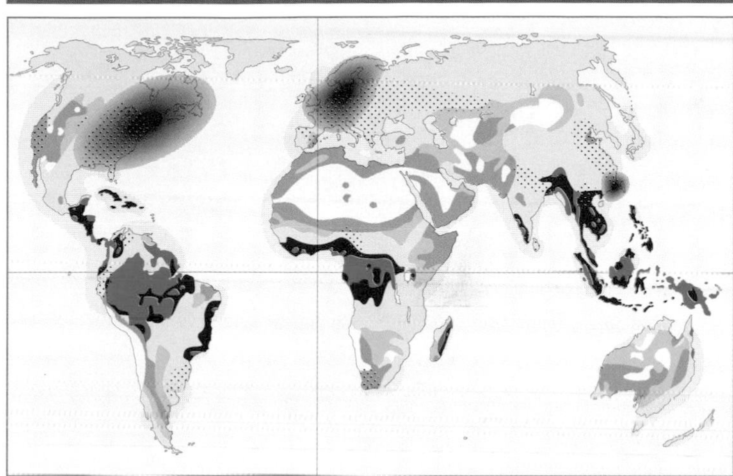

Pollution

Polluted seas

Main areas of sulphur & nitrogen emissions

Areas of acid rain

Desertification

Existing deserts

Areas with a high risk of desertification

Areas with a moderate risk of desertification

Deforestation

Former areas of rainforest

Existing rainforest

dry areas, wind-blown sand is a powerful agent of erosion. Most landforms seem to alter little in one person's lifetime. But geologists estimate that natural forces remove an average of 3.5 cm [1.4 in] from land areas every 1,000 years. Over millions of years, these forces reduce mountains to flat plains.

### HUMAN INTERFERENCE

Climate also affects people, though air conditioning and central heating now make it possible for us live in comfort almost anywhere in the world.

However, human activities are damaging our planet. Pollution is poisoning rivers and seas, while acid rain, caused by air pollution, is killing trees and acidifying lakes. The land is also harmed by such things as nuclear accidents and the dumping of toxic wastes.

Some regions have been overgrazed or so intensively farmed that once fertile areas have been turned into barren deserts. The clearance of tropical forests means that some plant and animal species are disappearing before scientists have had a chance to study them.

## MOULDING THE LAND

Powerful forces inside the Earth buckle rock layers to form fold mountain ranges. But even as they rise, the forces of erosion wear them away. On mountain slopes, water freezes in cracks in rocks. Because ice occupies more space than the equivalent amount of water, this 'frost action' shatters rocks, and the fragments tumble downhill. Some end up on or inside moving glaciers. Other rocks are carried away by running water. The glaciers and streams not only transport rock fragments, but they also wear out valleys and so add to their load. The eroded material breaks down into fragments of sand, silt and mud, much of which reaches the sea, where it piles up on the sea floor in layers. These layers eventually become compacted into sedimentary rocks, such as sandstones and shales. These rocks may eventually be squeezed up again by a plate collision to form new fold mountains, so completing a natural cycle of mountain building and destruction.

## MAJOR FACTORS AFFECTING WEATHERING

| | WEATHERING RATE | | |
|---|---|---|---|
| | SLOW ← | | → FAST |
| **Mineral solubility** | low<br>*(e.g. quartz)* | moderate<br>*(e.g. feldspar)* | high<br>*(e.g. calcite)* |
| **Rainfall** | low | moderate | heavy |
| **Temperature** | cold | temperate | hot |
| **Vegetation** | sparse | moderate | lush |
| **Soil cover** | bare rock | thin to moderate soil | thick soil |

*Weathering is the breakdown and decay of rocks in situ. It may be mechanical (physical), chemical or biological.*

# Population

THE ADVENT OF agriculture around 10,000 years ago had a great impact on human society. People abandoned their nomadic way of life and settled in farming villages. With plenty of food, some people were able to pursue jobs unconnected with farming. These developments eventually led to rapid social changes, including the growth of early cities and the emergence of civilization.

## THE POPULATION EXPLOSION

The social changes had a major effect on the world's population, which rose from around 8 million in 8000 BC, to about 300 million by AD 1000. The rate of population increase then began to accelerate further, passing the 1 billion mark in the 19th century, the 2 billion mark in the 1920s, and the 4 billion mark in the 1970s.

Today the world has a population of more than 6 billion and experts forecast that it will reach around 11 billion by 2200. However, they then predict that it will stabilize at this level or even begin to decline. Most of the expected increase will occur in developing countries in Africa, Asia and Latin America.

*> Many cities in India, such as Bombay (also known as Mumbai), have grown so quickly that they lack sufficient jobs and homes for their populations. As a result, slums now cover large areas.*

### POPULATION PYRAMIDS

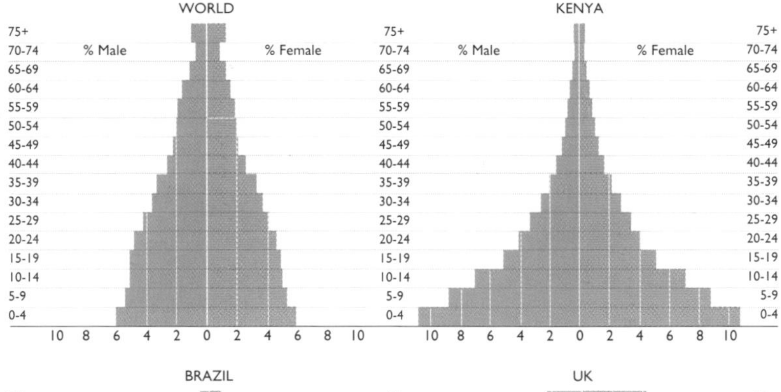


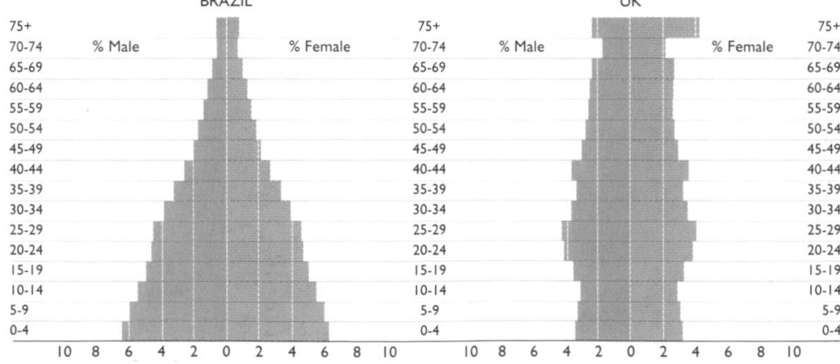


*> The population pyramids compare the average age structures for the world with those of three countries at varying stages of development. Kenya, a developing country, had, until recently, one of the world's highest annual rates of population increase. As a result, a high proportion of Kenyans are aged under 15. Brazil has a much more balanced economy than Kenya's, and a lower rate of population increase. This is reflected in a higher proportion of people aged over 40. The UK is a developed country with a low rate of population growth, 0.3% per year between 1985–95, much lower than the world average of 1.6%. The UK has a far higher proportion of people over 60 years old.*

## The World's Largest Cities ▾

Early in the 21st century, for the first time ever, the majority of the world's population live in cities. Below is a list of the 20 largest cities (in thousands) based on 1997 figures.

| | | |
|---|---|---|
| 1 | Tokyo, *Japan* | 26,836 |
| 2 | São Paulo, *Brazil* | 16,417 |
| 3 | New York, *USA* | 16,329 |
| 4 | Shanghai, *China* | 15,082 |
| 5 | Mexico City, *Mexico* | 15,048 |
| 6 | Bombay (Mumbai), *India* | 12,572 |
| 7 | Los Angeles, *USA* | 12,410 |
| 8 | Beijing, *China* | 12,362 |
| 9 | Seoul, *South Korea* | 11,641 |
| 10 | Jakarta, *Indonesia* | 11,500 |
| 11 | Buenos Aires, *Argentina* | 11,256 |
| 12 | Calcutta, *India* | 10,916 |
| 13 | Tianjin, *China* | 10,687 |
| 14 | Osaka, *Japan* | 10,601 |
| 15 | Lagos, *Nigeria* | 10,287 |
| 16 | Cairo, *Egypt* | 9,900 |
| 17 | Rio de Janeiro, *Brazil* | 9,888 |
| 18 | Karachi, *Pakistan* | 9,863 |
| 19 | Paris, *France* | 9,319 |
| 20 | Manila, *Philippines* | 9,280 |

This population explosion has been caused partly by better medical care, which has reduced child mortality and increased the average life expectancy at birth throughout the world. But it has also created problems. In some developing countries, nearly half of the people are children. They make no contribution to the economy, but they require costly education and health services. In richer countries, the high proportion of retired people is also a strain on the economy.

In the 21st century, for the first time in 10,000 years, the majority of people are no longer forced to rely on farming for their livelihood. Instead, nearly half of them live in cities where many of them enjoy a high standard of living. But rapid urbanization also creates problems, especially in the developing world, with the growth of slums and an increase in homelessness and crime.

## POPULATION BY CONTINENT

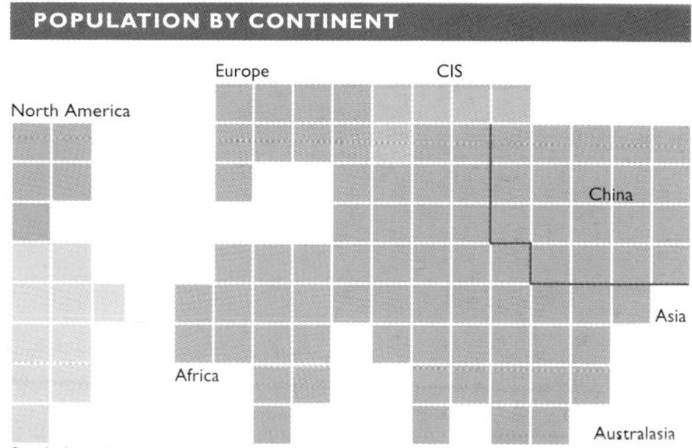


> *The cartogram shows the populations of the continents in a diagrammatic way, with each square representing 1% of the world's population. For example, North America is represented by five squares, which means that it contains about 5% of the world's population, while Asia, the most populous continent even excluding the Asian part of the former USSR, is represented by 56 squares (China accounting for 19 of these). By contrast, Australasia is represented by less than half of a square because it contains only 0.15% of the world's population.*

## WORLD DEMOGRAPHIC EXTREMES

**Fastest growing population; average annual % growth (1992–2000)**

| | | |
|---|---|---|
| 1 | Nigeria | 5.09 |
| 2 | Afghanistan | 4.21 |
| 3 | Ivory Coast | 3.54 |
| 4 | Oman | 3.52 |
| 5 | Syria | 3.51 |

**Slowest growing population; average annual % growth (1992–2000)**

| | | |
|---|---|---|
| 1 | Kuwait | -1.39 |
| 2 | Ireland | -0.24 |
| 3 | St Kitts & Nevis | -0.22 |
| 4 | Bulgaria | -0.13 |
| 5 | Latvia | -0.10 |

**Youngest populations; % aged under 15 years (1996)**

| | | |
|---|---|---|
| 1 | West Bank/Gaza | 51.7 |
| 2 | Uganda | 48.6 |
| 3 | Benin | 48.4 |
| = | Niger | 48.4 |
| 5 | Zambia | 48.2 |

**Oldest populations; % aged over 65 years (1996)**

| | | |
|---|---|---|
| 1 | Sweden | 17.3 |
| 2 | Italy | 16.1 |
| 3 | Greece | 15.9 |
| = | Norway | 15.9 |
| 5 | Belgium | 15.8 |

**Highest urban populations; % of population in urban areas (1996)**

| | | |
|---|---|---|
| 1 | Singapore | 100.0 |
| = | Bermuda | 100.0 |
| 3 | Macau | 99.0 |
| 4 | Kuwait | 97.0 |
| 5 | Hong Kong | 95.0 |

**Lowest urban populations; % of population in urban areas (1996)**

| | | |
|---|---|---|
| 1 | Bhutan | 6.0 |
| = | Rwanda | 6.0 |
| 3 | Burundi | 8.0 |
| 4 | Ethiopia | 13.0 |
| = | Uganda | 13.0 |

**Most male populations; number of men per 100 women (1997)**

| | | |
|---|---|---|
| 1 | Qatar | 193.3 |
| 2 | United Arab Emirates | 176.4 |
| 3 | Bahrain | 133.7 |
| 4 | Saudi Arabia | 125.1 |
| 5 | Oman | 113.4 |

**Fewest male populations; number of men per 100 women (1997)**

| | | |
|---|---|---|
| 1 | Latvia | 84.3 |
| 2 | Ukraine | 86.8 |
| 3 | Russia | 88.0 |
| 5 | Estonia | 88.7 |
| 4 | Belarus | 88.8 |

# Languages & Religions

ALL PEOPLE BELONG to one species, *Homo sapiens*, but within that species is a great diversity of cultures. Two of the main factors that give people an identity and sense of kinship with their neighbours are language and religion.

Definitions of languages vary and as a result estimates of the total number of languages in existence range from about 3,000 to 6,000. Many languages are spoken only by a small number of people. Papua New Guinea, for example, has only 4.2 million people but 869 languages.

The world's languages are grouped into families, of which the Indo-European is the largest. Indo-European languages are spoken in a zone stretching from

> Religion is a major force in South-east Asia. About 94% of the people in Thailand are Buddhists, and more than 40% of men over the age of 20 spend some time, if only a few weeks, serving as Buddhist monks. Confucianism, Islam, Hinduism, and Christianity are also practised in Thailand.

## THE WORLD'S LANGUAGES

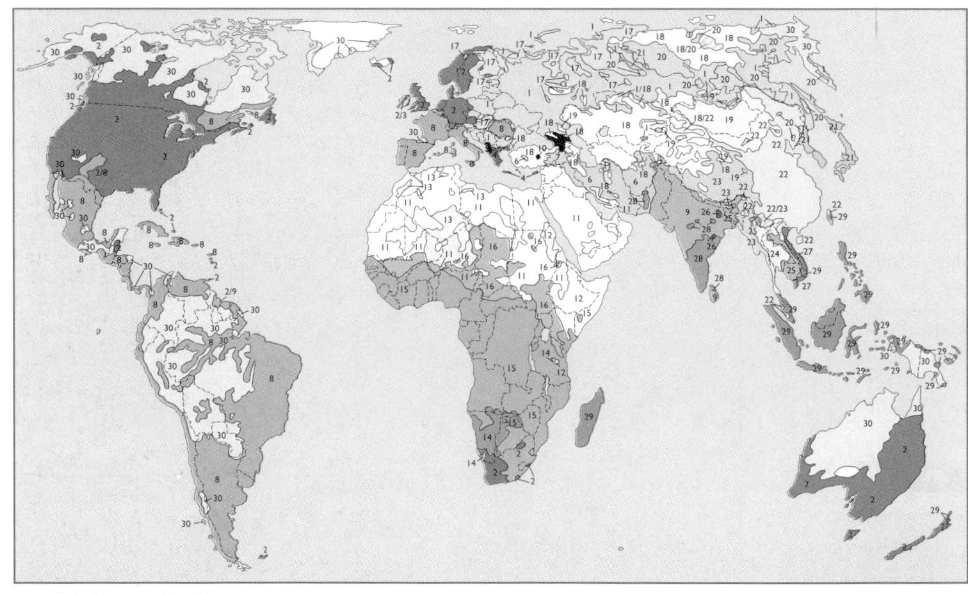

**Indo-European Family**
- 1 Balto-Slavic group (inc. Russian, Ukrainian)
- 2 Germanic group (inc. English, German)
- 3 Celtic group
- 4 Greek
- 5 Albanian
- 6 Iranian group
- 7 Armenian
- 8 Romance group (inc. Spanish, Portuguese, French, Italian)
- 9 Indo-Aryan group (inc. Hindi, Bengali, Urdu, Punjabi, Marathi)
- 10 **Caucasian Family**

**Afro-Asiatic Family**
- 11 Semitic group (inc. Arabic)
- 12 Kushitic group
- 13 Berber group

- 14 **Khoisan Family**
- 15 **Niger-Congo Family**
- 16 **Nilo-Saharan Family**
- 17 **Uralic Family**

**Altaic Family**
- 18 Turkic group
- 19 Mongolian group
- 20 Tungus-Manchu group
- 21 Japanese & Korean

**Sino-Tibetan Family**
- 22 Sinitic (Chinese) languages
- 23 Tibetic-Burmic languages

- 24 **Tai Family**

**Austro-Asiatic Family**
- 25 Mon-Khmer group
- 26 Munda group
- 27 Vietnamese

- 28 **Dravidian Family** (inc. Telugu, Tamil)
- 29 **Austronesian Family** (inc. Malay-Indonesian)
- 30 **Other Languages**

## NATIVE SPEAKERS

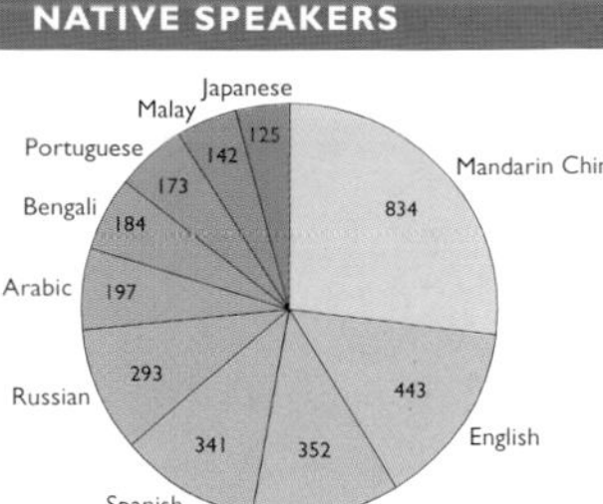


> The chart shows the native speakers of major languages in millions. Mandarin Chinese is the language of 834 million, as compared with English, which has 443 million speakers. However, many other people speak English as a second language.

Europe, through south-western Asia into the Indian subcontinent. In addition, during the period of European colonization, they spread throughout North and South America and also to Australia and New Zealand. Today about two-fifths of the world's people speak an Indo-European language, as compared with one-fifth who speak a language belonging to the Sino-Tibetan language.

The Sino-Tibetan language family includes Chinese, which is spoken as a first language by more people than any other. English is the second most important first language, but it is more important than Chinese in international affairs and business, because so many people speak it as a second language.

> Most languages have alphabetic systems of writing. The Greek alphabet uses some letters from the Roman alphabet, such as the A and B. Russians use the Cyrillic alphabet, which is based partly on Roman and partly on Greek letters. The Cyrillic alphabet is also used for Bulgarian and some central Asian languages. Serbs use either the Cyrillic or the Roman alphabet to write Serbo-Croat.

### RELIGIONS

Christianity is the religion of about a third of the world's population. Other major religions include Buddhism, Islam, Hinduism, Judaism, Chinese folk religions and traditional tribal religions.

Religion is a powerful force in human society, establishing the ethics by which people live. It has inspired great music, painting, architecture and literature, yet at the same time religion and language have contributed to conflict between people throughout history. Even today, the cause of many of the conflicts around the world are partly the result of linguistic and religious differences.

**Religious Adherents ▾**

The world's major religions, with the number of adherents in millions (latest available year)

| Religion | Millions |
|---|---|
| **Christian** | 1,669 |
| Roman Catholic | 952 |
| Protestant | 337 |
| Orthodox | 162 |
| Anglican | 70 |
| Other Christian | 148 |
| **Muslim** | 945 |
| Sunni | 841 |
| Shia | 104 |
| **Hindu** | 663 |
| **Buddhist** | 312 |
| **Chinese folk** | 172 |
| **Ethnic/local** | 92 |
| **Jewish** | 18 |
| **Sikh** | 17 |

## ALPHABETS

**The Greek Alphabet**

| Α | Β | Γ | Δ | Ε | Ζ | Η | Θ | Ι | Κ | Λ | Μ | Ν | Ξ | Ο | Π | Ρ | Σ | Τ | Υ | Φ | Χ | Ψ | Ω |
|---|---|---|---|---|---|---|---|---|---|---|---|---|---|---|---|---|---|---|---|---|---|---|---|
| A | V/B | G | D | E | Z | E | TH | I | K | L | M | N | X | O | P | R | S | T | Y | F | CH | PS | O |

**The Cyrillic Alphabet**

| А | Б | В | Г | Д | Е | Ё | Ж | З | И | Й | К | Л | М | Н | О | П | Р | С | Т | У | Ф | Х | Ц | Ч | Ш | Щ | Ю | Я |
|---|---|---|---|---|---|---|---|---|---|---|---|---|---|---|---|---|---|---|---|---|---|---|---|---|---|---|---|---|
| A | B | V | G | D | E | YO | ZH | Z | I | Y | K | L | M | N | O | P | R | S | T | U | F | KH | TS | CH | SH | SHCH | YU | YA |

# Agriculture & Industry

> The cultivation of rice, one of the world's most important foods, is still carried out by hand in many areas. But the introduction of new strains of rice has greatly increased yields.

Because it supplies so many basic human needs, agriculture is the world's leading economic activity. But its relative importance varies from place to place. In most developing countries, agriculture employs more people than any other activity. For example, the diagram at the bottom of this page shows that more than 90% of the people of Nepal are employed in farming.

Many farmers in developing countries live at subsistence level, producing barely enough to supply the basic needs of their families. Alongside the subsistence sector, some developing countries produce one or two cash crops that they export. Dependence on cash crops is precarious: when world commodity prices fall, the country is plunged into financial crisis.

In developed countries, by contrast, the proportion of people engaged in agriculture has declined over the last 200 years. Yet, by using farm machinery and scientific methods, notably the selective breeding of crops and animals, the production of food has soared. For example, although agriculture employs only 3% of its workers, the United States is one of the world's top food producers.

## EMPLOYMENT

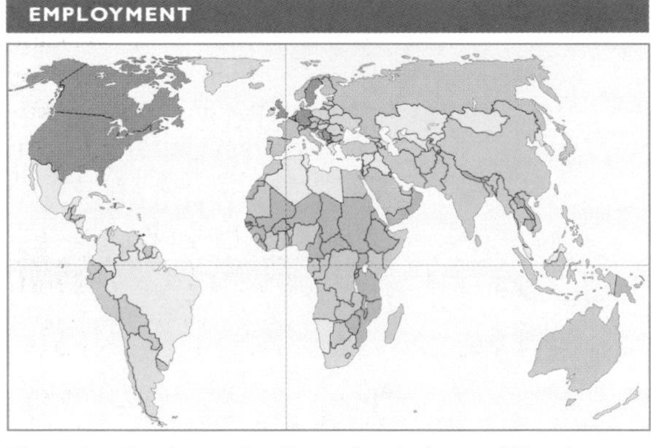

The number of workers employed in manufacturing for every 100 workers engaged in agriculture (latest available year)

- Under 10
- 10 – 50
- 50 – 100
- 100 – 200
- 200 – 500
- Over 500

## INDUSTRIALIZATION

The Industrial Revolution began in Britain in the late 18th century and soon spread to mainland Europe and other parts of the world. Industries first arose in areas with supplies of coal, iron ore and cheap water power. But later, after oil and gas came into use as industrial fuels, factories could be set up almost anywhere.

The growth of manufacturing led to an increase in the number of industrial cities. The flight from the land was accompanied by an increase in efficiency in agriculture. As a result, manufacturing replaced agriculture as the chief source of

## DIVISION OF EMPLOYMENT

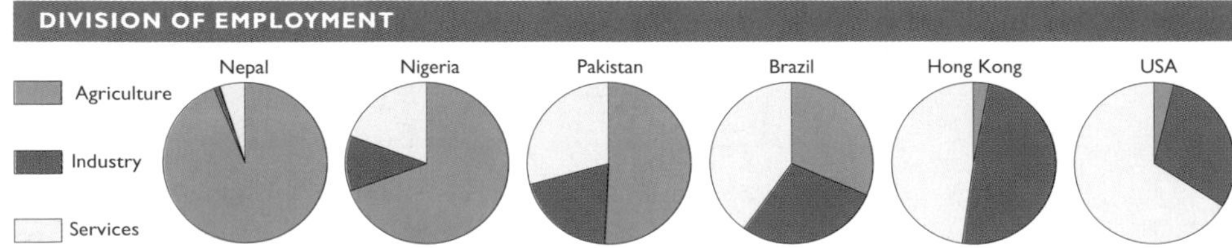

## PATTERNS OF PRODUCTION

*> The table shows how the economy breaks down (in terms of the Gross Domestic Product for 1997) in a selection of industrialized countries. Agriculture remains important in some countries, though its percentage share has steadily declined since the start of the Industrial Revolution. Industry, especially manufacturing, accounts for a higher proportion, but service industries account for the greatest percentage of the GDP in most developed nations. The figures for Manufacturing are shown separately from Industry because of their importance in the economy.*

| Country | Agriculture | Industry (excl. manufacturing) | Manufacturing | Services |
|---|---|---|---|---|
| Australia | 3% | 24% | 12% | 61% |
| Austria | 1% | 24% | 14% | 61% |
| Brazil | 10% | 28% | 18% | 44% |
| Denmark | 4% | 7% | 20% | 69% |
| Finland | 5% | 3% | 28% | 64% |
| France | 2% | 20% | 13% | 65% |
| Germany | 1% | 8% | 24% | 67% |
| Greece | 17% | 13% | 23% | 47% |
| Hungary | 4% | 24% | 14% | 58% |
| Ireland | 8% | 7% | 3% | 82% |
| Italy | 3% | 8% | 21% | 68% |
| Japan | 1% | 28% | 19% | 52% |
| Kuwait | 0% | 46% | 9% | 45% |
| Mexico | 4% | 18% | 17% | 61% |
| Netherlands | 3% | 21% | 12% | 64% |
| Norway | 2% | 24% | 10% | 64% |
| Singapore | 0% | 29% | 17% | 54% |
| Sweden | 3% | 8% | 28% | 61% |
| UK | 2% | 8% | 23% | 67% |
| USA | 3% | 10% | 20% | 67% |

income and employment in industrialized countries, and rapidly widened the wealth gap between them and the poorer non-industrialized countries whose economies continued to rely on agriculture.

### SERVICE INDUSTRIES

Eventually, the manufacturing sector became so efficient that it could supply most of the things that people wanted to buy. Trade between industrialized countries also increased, so widening the choice for consumers in the developed world. These factors led to a further change in the economies of developed countries, namely a reduction in the relative importance of manufacturing and the growth of the service sector.

Service industries include such activities as government, transport, insurance, finance, and even the writing of computer software. In the United States, service industries now account for about two-thirds of the Gross National Product (GNP), while in Japan they account for just over half. But the wealth of both countries still rests on their massive industrial production.

## AGRICULTURE

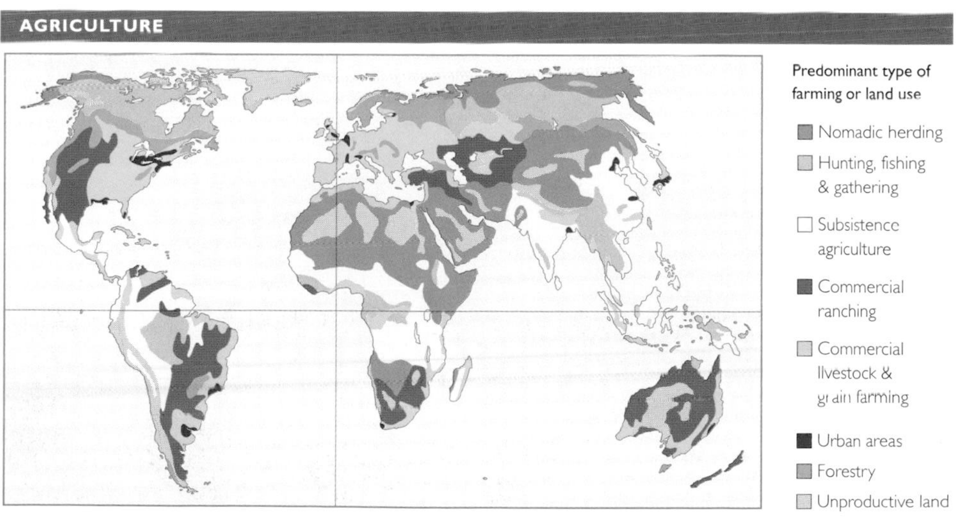

Predominant type of farming or land use

- Nomadic herding
- Hunting, fishing & gathering
- Subsistence agriculture
- Commercial ranching
- Commercial livestock & grain farming
- Urban areas
- Forestry
- Unproductive land

# Trade & Commerce

TRADE HAS ALWAYS been an important human activity. It has widened the choice of goods available in any country, lowered prices and generally raised living standards. People regard any growth of world trade as a sign that the world economy is healthy, whereas a decline indicates a world recession.

Exports and imports are of two main kinds. Visible imports and exports include primary products, such as food and manufactures. Invisible imports and exports include services, such as banking, insurance, interest on loans, and money spent by tourists.

World trade, both visible and invisible, is dominated by the 29 members of the OECD (Organization for Economic Development), which includes the world's top trading nations, namely the United States, Japan, Germany, France, Italy and the United Kingdom, as well as Australia, New Zealand, Canada and Mexico. Hungary, Poland and South Korea joined in 1996.

> The new port of the historic Italian city of Ravenna is linked to the Adriatic Sea by a canal. The port has large oil refining and petrochemical industries.

## DEBT AND AID

International debtors and the development aid they receive (1996)

The provision of aid by rich countries to developing countries is part of international politics. But the grants made to developing countries are often dwarfed by the burden of debt which the countries are expected to repay. In 1990, the debts of Mozambique, one of the world's poorest countries, were estimated to be 75 times its entire earnings from exports.

Debt, US$ per capita

Aid, US$ per capita

$5,014

2,750
2,500
2,250
2,000
1,750
1,500
1,250
1,000
750
500
250
0

50
100
200
$391

India
Tanzania
Sierra Leone
Nigeria
Madagascar
Mozambique
Laos
Guinea Bissau
Egypt
Honduras
Zambia
Papua New Guinea
Mauritania
Ecuador
Ivory Coast
Jordan
Nicaragua
Israel
Jamaica
Congo
Panama

## CHANGING EXPORTS

From the late 19th century to the 1950s, primary products, including farm products, minerals, natural fibres, timber and, in the latter part of this period, oil

### The World's Largest Businesses ▼

The world's largest businesses in 1997 by sales, in billions of US$.

| | | |
|---|---|---|
| 1 | General Motors, *USA* | 168.4 |
| 2 | Ford Motor, *USA* | 147.0 |
| 3 | Mitsui, *Japan* | 144.9 |
| 4 | Mitsubishi, *Japan* | 140.2 |
| 5 | Itochu, *Japan* | 135.5 |
| 6 | Royal Dutch/Shell Group, *UK/Neths* | 128.2 |
| 7 | Marubeni, *Japan* | 124.0 |
| 8 | Exxon, *USA* | 119.4 |
| 9 | Summitomo, *Japan* | 119.3 |
| 10 | Toyota Motor, *Japan* | 108.7 |
| 11 | Wal-Mart Stores, *USA* | 106.1 |
| 12 | General Electric, *USA* | 79.2 |
| 13 | Nissho Iwai, *Japan* | 78.9 |
| 14 | Nippon Telegraph/Telephone, *Japan* | 78.3 |
| 15 | Intl. business Machines, *USA* | 75.9 |
| 16 | Hitachi, *Japan* | 75.7 |
| 17 | AT&T, *USA* | 74.5 |
| 18 | Nippon Life Insurance, *Japan* | 72.6 |
| 19 | Mobil, *USA* | 72.3 |
| 20 | Daimler-Benz, *Germany* | 71.6 |

## TRADED PRODUCTS

The character of world trade has greatly changed in the last 50 years. While primary products were once the leading commodities, world trade is now dominated by manufactured products. Cars are the single most valuable traded product, followed by vehicle parts and engines. The next most valuable goods are high-tech products such as data processing (computer) equipment, telecommunications equipment, and transistors. Other items include aircraft, paper and board, trucks, measuring and control instruments, and electrical machinery. Trade in most manufactured products is dominated by the OECD countries. For example, the leading vehicle exporter is Japan, which became the world's leading car manufacturer in the 1990s. The United States, Germany, the United Kingdom, France and Japan lead in the production of data processing equipment.

and natural gas, dominated world trade.

Many developing countries still remain dependent on exporting mineral ores, fossil fuels, or farm products such as cocoa or coffee whose prices fluctuate according to demand. But today, manufactured goods are the most important commodities in world trade. The OECD nations lead the world in exporting manufactured goods, though they are being challenged by a group of 'tiger economies' in eastern Asia, notably Singapore, Hong Kong and Taiwan. Other rapidly industrializing countries in Asia include Thailand, Malaysia and the Philippines. The generally cheap labour costs of these countries have enabled them to produce manufactured goods for export at prices lower than those charged for goods made in Western countries.

Private companies carry on most of the world's trade. The small proportion handled by governments decreased recently with the collapse of Communist regimes in eastern Europe and the former Soviet Union.

## SHARE OF WORLD TRADE

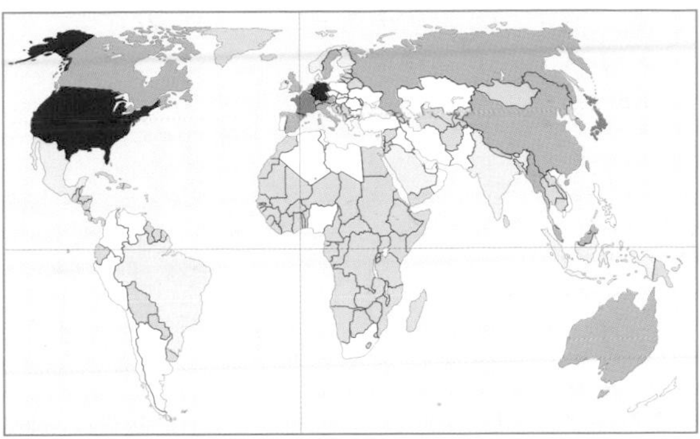

Percentage share of total world exports by value (1996)

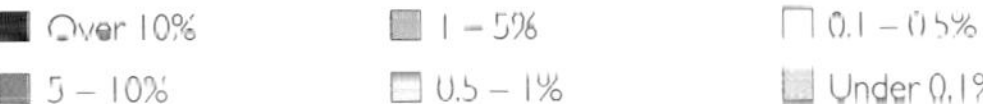


## DEPENDENCE ON TRADE

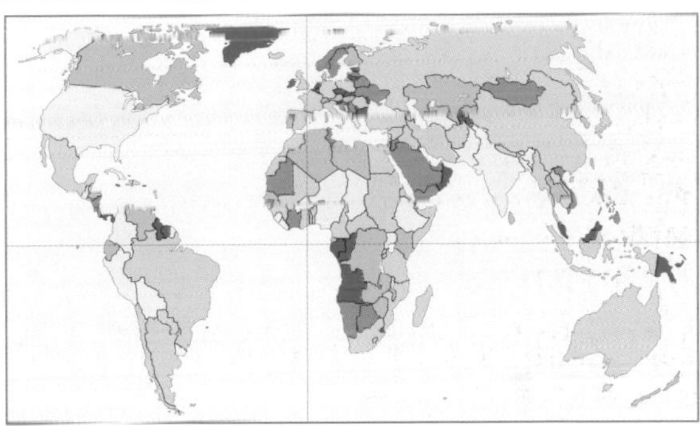

Value of exports as a percentage of Gross Domestic Product (1997)

Over 50% GDP
30 – 40% GDP
10 – 20% GDP
40 – 50% GDP
20 – 30% GDP
Under 10% GDP

### Trade in Oil ▾

Major world trade in oil in millions of tonnes (1997)

|  |  |
|---|---|
| Middle East to Asia (not Japan) | 294.4 |
| Middle East to Japan | 218.1 |
| Middle East to W. Europe | 187.9 |
| S. and C. America to USA | 132.1 |
| N. Africa to W. Europe | 97.9 |
| CIS to Western Europe | 90.8 |
| Middle East to USA | 86.9 |
| Canada to USA | 72.7 |
| West Africa to USA | 68.3 |
| Mexico to USA | 68.0 |
| W. Africa to W. Europe | 40.1 |
| Western Europe to USA | 32.9 |
| Middle East to Africa | 32.0 |
| Middle East to South and Central America | 27.8 |
| CIS to Central Europe | 31.8 |
| Middle East to Central Europe | 19.3 |
| *Total world trade* | 1,978.9 |

# Transport & Travel

About 200 years ago, most people never travelled far from their birthplace. But adventurous travellers can now reach almost any part of the world.

Transport is concerned with moving goods and people around by land, water and air. Land transport was once laborious, and was dependent on pack animals or animal-drawn vehicles. But during the Industrial Revolution, railways played a vital role in moving bulky materials and equipment required by factories. They were also important in the opening up and development of remote areas around the world in North and South America, Africa, Asia and Australia.

Today, however, motor vehicles have taken over many of the functions once served by railways. Unlike railways, motor vehicles provide a door-to-door service and, through the invention of heavy trucks, they can also carry large loads. In the mid-1990s, about 90% of inland freight in Britain was carried by road, while car and van travel accounted for 86% of passenger travel, as compared with 6% by buses and coaches, 5% by rail and less than 1% by air.

*> Traffic jams and vehicle pollution have affected cities throughout the world. Many of Bangkok's beautiful old canals have been filled in to provide extra roads to cope with the enormous volume of traffic in the city.*

## TRAVEL & TOURISM

Sea transport, which now employs huge bulk grain carriers, oil tankers and container ships, still carries most of the world's trade. But since the late 1950s, fewer passengers have travelled overseas by sea, because air travel is so much faster, though many former ocean liners now operate successfully as cruise ships.

Air travel has played a major part in the rapid growth of the tourist industry,

### AIR TRAVEL

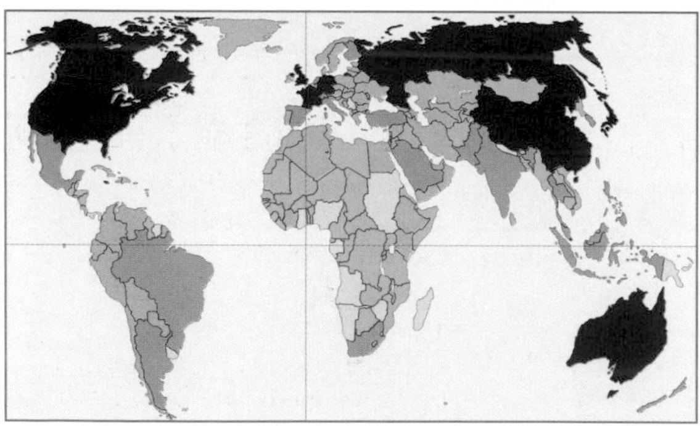

Number of passenger kilometres flown, in millions (1996). Passenger kilometres are the number of passengers (both international and domestic) multiplied by the distance flown by each passenger from airport of origin.

- Over 100,000
- 50,000 – 100,000
- 10,000 – 50,000
- 1,000 – 10,000
- 500 – 1,000
- Under 500

### The World's Busiest Airports ▾

Total number of passengers, in thousands (1997)

| |  |  |
|---|---|---|
| 1 | O'Hare Intl., *Chicago* | 70,295 |
| 2 | Hartsfield Atlanta Int., *Atlanta* | 68,206 |
| 3 | Dallas/Fort Worth Int., *Dallas* | 60,489 |
| 4 | Los Angeles Intl., *Los Angeles* | 60,143 |
| 5 | Heathrow, *London* | 57,975 |
| 6 | Haneda, *Tokyo* | 49,302 |
| 7 | San Francisco Intl., *San Francisco* | 40,500 |
| 8 | Frankfurt/Main, *Frankfurt* | 40,263 |
| 9 | Kimpo Intl., *Seoul* | 36,757 |
| 10 | Charles de Gaulle, *Paris* | 35,294 |
| 11 | Denver Intl., *Denver* | 34,973 |
| 12 | Miami Intl., *Miami* | 34,533 |
| 13 | Schiphol, *Amsterdam* | 31,570 |
| 14 | Metro Wayne County, *Detroit* | 31,521 |
| 15 | John F. Kennedy Intl., *New York* | 31,229 |

## The Longest Rail Networks ▼

Extent of rail network, in thousands of kilometres (1996)

| | | |
|---|---|---|
| 1 | USA | 243.3 |
| 2 | Russia | 87.1 |
| 3 | India | 62.9 |
| 4 | China | 56.7 |
| 5 | Germany | 40.8 |
| 6 | Argentina | 34.2 |
| 7 | France | 31.9 |
| 8 | Mexico | 26.5 |
| 9 | South Africa | 25.9 |
| 10 | Poland | 23.4 |

which accounted for 7.5% of world trade by the mid-1990s. Travel and tourism have greatly increased people's understanding and knowledge of the world, especially in the OECD countries, which account for about 8% of world tourism.

Some developing countries have large tourist industries which have provided employment and led to improvements in roads and other facilities. In some cases, tourism plays a vital role in the economy. For example, in Kenya, tourism provides more income than any other activity apart from the production and sale of coffee. However, too many tourists can damage fragile environments, such as the wildlife and scenery in national parks. Tourism can also harm local cultures.

## THE IMPORTANCE OF TOURISM

Nations receiving the most from tourism, millions of US$ (1996)

| | | |
|---|---|---|
| 1 | USA | 64,400 |
| 2 | Spain | 28,400 |
| 3 | France | 28,200 |
| 4 | Italy | 27,300 |
| 5 | UK | 20,400 |
| 6 | Austria | 15,100 |
| 7 | Germany | 13,200 |
| 8 | Hong Kong | 11,200 |
| 9 | China | 10,500 |
| 10 | Switzerland | 9,900 |

Number of tourist arrivals, millions (1996)

| | | |
|---|---|---|
| 1 | France | 66,800 |
| 2 | USA | 49,038 |
| 3 | Spain | 43,403 |
| 4 | Italy | 34,087 |
| 5 | UK | 25,960 |
| 6 | China | 23,770 |
| 7 | Poland | 19,514 |
| 8 | Mexico | 18,667 |
| 9 | Canada | 17,610 |
| 10 | Czech Republic | 17,400 |

Fastest growing tourist destinations, % change in receipts (1994–95)

| | | |
|---|---|---|
| 1 | South Korea | 49% |
| 2 | Czech Republic | 27% |
| 3 | India | 21% |
| 4 | Russia | 19% |
| 5 | Philippines | 18% |
| 6 | Turkey | 17% |
| 7 | Thailand | 15% |
| 8 | Poland | 13% |
| 9 | China | 12% |
| 10 | Israel | 12% |

Overseas travellers to the USA, thousands (1997)

| | | |
|---|---|---|
| 1 | Canada | 13,900 |
| 2 | Mexico | 12,370 |
| 3 | Japan | 4,640 |
| 4 | UK | 3,350 |
| 5 | Germany | 1,990 |
| 6 | France | 1,030 |
| 7 | Taiwan | 885 |
| 8 | Venezuela | 860 |
| 9 | South Korea | 800 |
| 10 | Brazil | 785 |

## THE WORLD'S VEHICLES

Proportion of the world's vehicles by region (1994)

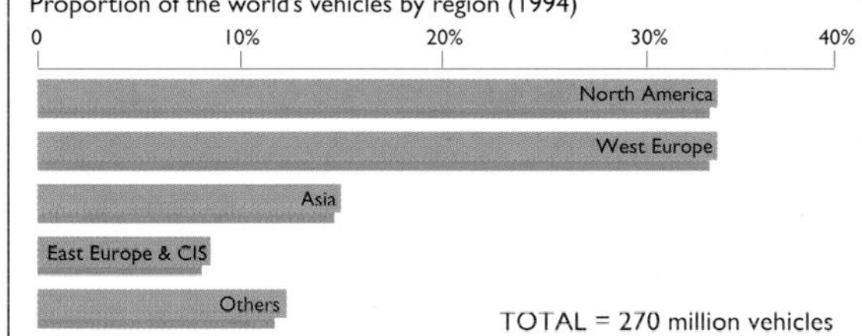


## CAR OWNERSHIP

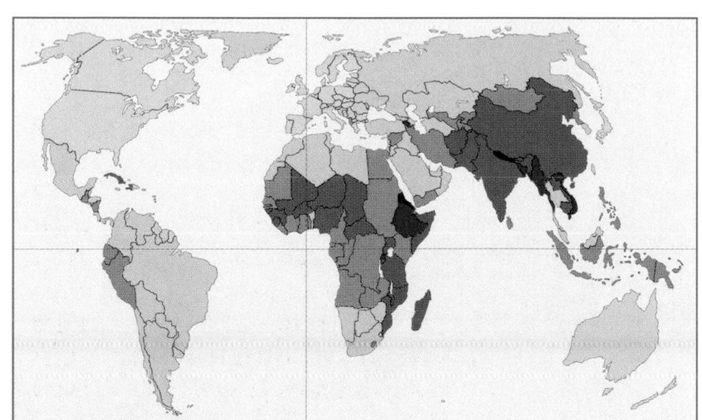

Number of people per car (1996)

- Over 1,000
- 500 – 1,000
- 100 – 500
- 25 – 100
- 5 – 25
- Under 5

Two-thirds of the world's vehicles are found in the developed countries of Europe and North America. Car ownership is also high in Australia and New Zealand, as well as in Japan, the world's leading car exporter. Car transport is the most convenient form of passenger travel, but air pollution caused by exhaust fumes is a serious problem in many large cities.

# International Organizations

In the late 1980s, people rejoiced at the collapse of Communist regimes in eastern Europe and the former Soviet Union, because this brought to an end the Cold War, a long period of hostility between East and West. But hope of a new era of peace was shattered when ethnic and religious rivalries led to civil war in Yugoslavia and in parts of the former Soviet Union.

In order to help maintain peace, many governments have formed international organizations to increase co-operation. Some, such as NATO (North Atlantic Treaty Organization), are defence alliances, while others aim to encourage economic and social co-operation. Some organizations such as the Red Cross are non-governmental organizations, or NGOs.

*> In the early 1990s, the United Nations peacekeeping mission worked to end the civil war in Bosnia-Herzegovina and also to bring aid to civilians affected by the fighting.*

**UN Contributions ▾**

In 1996–97, the top ten contributing countries to the UN budget, which was US$2.6 billion, were as follows:

| |  |  |
|---|---|---|
| 1 | USA | 25.0% |
| 2 | Japan | 15.4% |
| 3 | Germany | 9.0% |
| 4 | France | 6.4% |
| 5 | UK | 5.3% |
| 6 | Italy | 5.2% |
| 7 | Russia | 4.5% |
| 8 | Canada | 3.1% |
| 9 | Spain | 2.4% |
| 10 | Brazil | 1.6% |

## UNITED NATIONS

The United Nations, the chief international organization, was formed in October 1945 and now has 185 member countries. The only independent nations that are not members are Kiribati, Nauru, Switzerland, Taiwan, Tonga, Tuvalu and the Vatican City.

### THE UNITED NATIONS

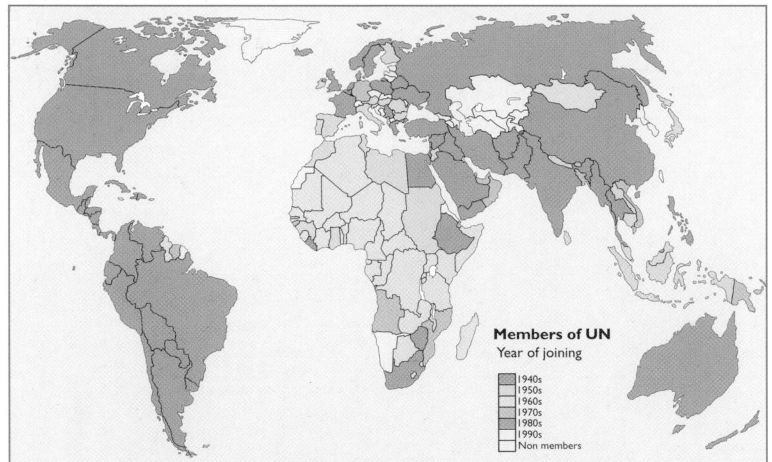


*> The membership of the UN had risen from 51 in 1945 to 185 by the end of 1998. The first big period of expansion came in the 1960s when many former colonies achieved their independence. The membership again expanded rapidly in the 1990s when new countries were formed from the former Soviet Union and Yugoslavia. The most recent addition, Palau, is a former US trust territory in the Pacific Ocean and joined in 1994.*

The United Nations was formed at the end of World War II to promote peace, international co-operation and security, and to help solve economic, social, cultural and humanitarian problems. It promotes human rights and freedom and is a forum for negotiations between nations.

The main organs of the UN are the General Assembly, the Security Council, the Economic and Social Council, the Trusteeship Council, the International Court of Justice and the Secretariat.

The UN also operates 14 specialized agencies concerned with particular issues, such as agriculture, education, working conditions, communications and health. For example, UNICEF (the United Nations International Children's Fund), established in 1946 to deliver post-war relief to children, now aims to provide basic health care to children and mothers worldwide. The ILO (International Labour Organization) seeks to improve working conditions, while the FAO (Food and Agricultural Organization) aims at improving the production and distribution of food. The WTO (World Trade Organization) was set up as recently as January 1995 to succeed GATT (General Agreements on Tariffs and Trade).

## THE UNITED NATIONS

**THE GENERAL ASSEMBLY** is the meeting of all member nations every September under a newly-elected president to discuss issues affecting development, peace and security.

**THE SECURITY COUNCIL** has 15 members, of which five are permanent. It is responsible for maintaining international peace.

**THE SECRETARIAT** consists of the staff and employees of the UN, including the Secretary-General (appointed for a five-year term), who is the UN's chief administrator.

**THE ECONOMIC & SOCIAL COUNCIL** works with the specialized agencies to implement UN policies on improving living standards, health, cultural and educational co-operation.

**THE TRUSTEESHIP COUNCIL** was designed to bring several dependencies to independence. This work is now complete.

**THE INTERNATIONAL COURT OF JUSTICE**, or World Court, deals with legal problems and helps to settle disputes. Its headquarters are at The Hague, in the Netherlands.

## UN DEPARTMENTS

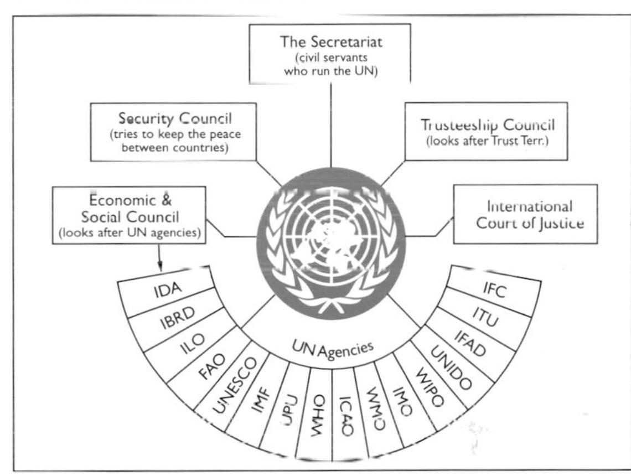


## UN PEACEKEEPING MISSIONS

The United Nations tries to resolve international disputes in several ways. It sends unarmed observer missions to monitor cease-fires or supervise troop withdrawals, and the Security Council members also send peacekeeping forces.

The first of these forces was sent in 1948 to supervise the cease-fire between Arabs and Jews in disputed parts of Palestine and, since then, it has undertaken more than 30 other missions. The 'Blue Berets', as the 25,650 UN troops are called, must be impartial in any dispute and they can fire only in self-defence. Hence, they can operate only with the support of both sides, which leaves them open to criticism when they are unable to prevent violence by intervening.

By the mid-1990s, the UN was involved in 15 world conflicts, was policing the boundary in partitioned Cyprus, and was seeking to enforce a peace agreement in Angola after 20 years of civil war. Other UN missions were in Tajikistan, Georgia, the Israeli-occupied Golan Heights, Haiti, Kuwait, southern Lebanon, the India–Pakistan border, Liberia, Mozambique, Western Sahara and the former Yugoslavia. A force known as UNPROFOR (UN Protection Force) had been operating in Bosnia-Herzegovina and, by 1995, it accounted for 60% of the total UN peacekeeping budget. In February 1996, the Secretary-General of the UN approved the setting up of a new force, the United Nations Mission in Bosnia-Herzegovina (UNMIBH). Its main objective was to help create the right climate for the elections held in September 1996.

> The European Parliament, one of the branches of the EU, consists of 626 members. The number of members for each country is based mainly on population.

## ECONOMIC ORGANIZATIONS

Over the last 40 years, many countries have joined common markets aimed at eliminating trade barriers and encouraging the free movement of workers and capital.

The best known of these is the European Union. Other organizations include ASEAN (the Association of South-east Asian Nations), which aims at reducing trade barriers between its nine members: Brunei, Burma, Indonesia, Laos, Malaysia, the Philippines, Singapore, Thailand and Vietnam.

APEC (the Asia-Pacific Co-operation Group) was founded in 1989 and includes the countries of East and South-east Asia, as well as North America, plus Australia, New Zealand and Chile. APEC aims to create a free trade zone by 2020.

Together the United States, Canada and Mexico form NAFTA (North American Free Trade Agreement), which aims at eliminating trade barriers within 15 years of its foundation on 1 January 1994. Other economic groupings link the countries of Latin America.

Another economic group with more limited aims is OPEC (Organization of Petroleum Exporting Countries). It works to unify policies concerned with the sale of petroleum on world markets.

The central aim of the Colombo Plan is to provide economic development assistance for South and South-east Asia.

## OTHER ORGANIZATIONS

Some organizations exist for consultation on matters of common interest. The Commonwealth of Nations grew out of the links created by the British Empire, while the OAS (Organization of American States) works to increase understanding throughout the Western hemisphere. The OAU (Organization of

### THE EUROPEAN UNION

At the end of World War II (1939–45), many Europeans wanted to end the ancient emnities that had caused such destruction and rebuild the shattered continent. It was in this mood that Belgium, France, West Germany, Italy, Luxembourg and the Netherlands signed the Treaty of Paris in 1951. This set up the European Coal and Steel Community (ECSC), the forerunner of the European Union.

In 1957, through the Treaty of Rome, the same six countries created the European Economic Community (EEC) and the European Atomic Community (EURATOM). In 1967, the ECSC, the EEC and EURATOM merged to form the single European Community (EC).

Another economic group, the European Free Trade Association (EFTA), was set up in 1960 by seven countries: Austria, Denmark, Norway, Portugal, Sweden, Switzerland, and the United Kingdom. However, Denmark, Ireland and the UK left to become members of the EC in 1973, followed by Greece in 1981, Spain and Portugal in 1986, and Austria, Finland and Sweden in 1995. The expansion of the EC to 15 members left EFTA with just four members: Iceland, Liechtenstein, Norway and Switzerland.

In 1993, following the signing of the Maastricht Treaty, the EC was reconstituted as the European Union (EU). The aims of the EU include economic and monetary union, a single currency for all 15 countries, and closer co-operation on foreign and security policies and also on home affairs. This step has led to a debate. Some people would like the EU to develop into a federal Europe, but others fear that this would lead to a loss of national identity. Another matter of importance is the future enlargement of the EU. By 1995, formal applications for membership had been received from Turkey, Malta, Cyprus, Poland, Hungary, Slovakia and Romania. Other possible members include the Czech Republic, Estonia, Latvia and Lithuania.

## AUSTRALIA'S NEW ROLE

Most of the people who settled in Australia between 1788 and the mid-20th century came from the British Isles. However, the strong ties between Australia and Britain were weakened after Britain joined the European Community in 1973. Since 1973, many Australians have argued that their world position has changed and that they are part of a Pacific community of nations, rather than an extension of Europe. Some want closer integration with ASEAN, the increasingly powerful economic group formed by seven South-east Asian nations. But in 1995, the prime minister of Malaysia, Dr Mahathir Mohamad, argued that Australia could not be regarded as Asian until at least 70% of its people were of ethnic Asian origin.

African Unity) has a similar role in Africa, while the Arab League is made up of Arabic-speaking North African and Middle Eastern states. The recently formed CIS (Commonwealth of Independent States) aims to maintain links between 12 of the 15 republics which made up the Soviet Union.

## NORTH–SOUTH DIVIDE

The deepest division in the world today is the divide between rich and poor nations. In international terms, this is called the North–South divide, because the North contains most of the world's developed countries, while the developing countries lie mainly in the South. The European Union recognizes this division and gives special trading terms to more than 60 former European dependencies, which form the ACP (African, Caribbean and Pacific) states. One organization containing a majority of developing countries is the Non-Aligned Movement. This Movement was created in 1961 during the Cold War as a political bloc allied neither to the East nor to the West. However, the aims of the 113 members who attended the movement's 11th gathering in 1995 were concerned mainly with economic matters. The 113 countries between them produce only about 7% of the world's gross output and they can speak for the poorer South.

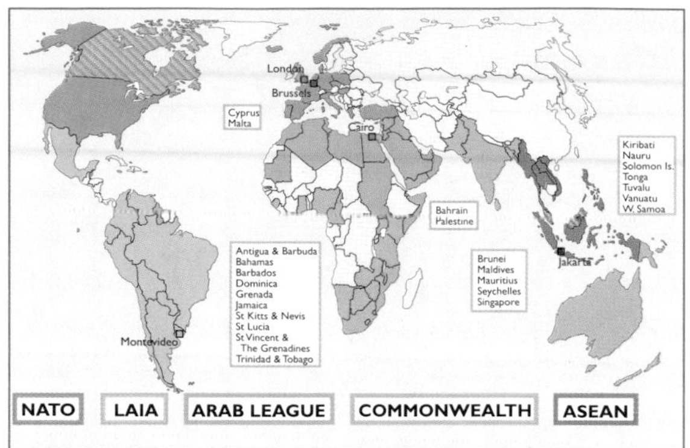


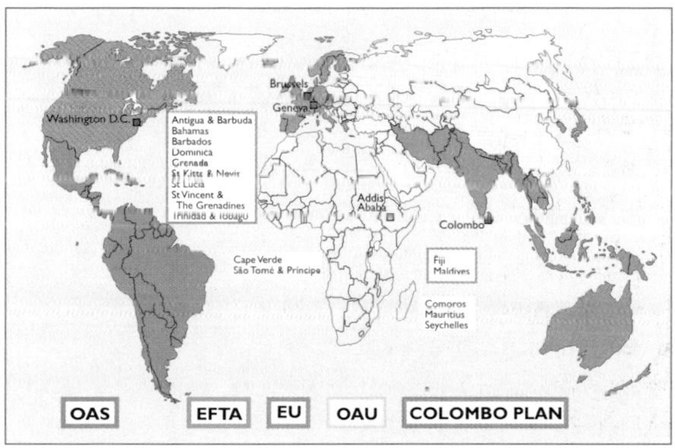


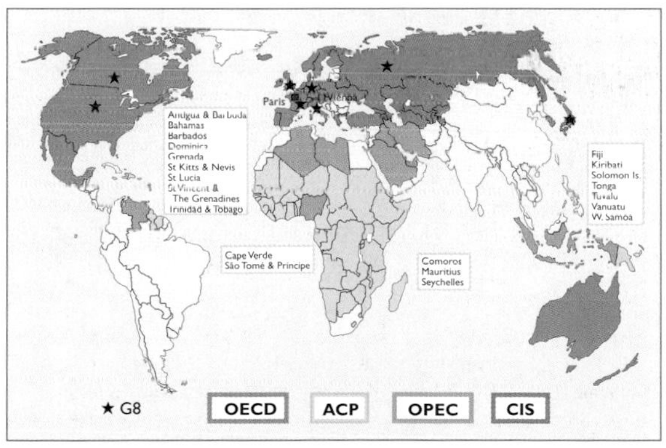


*> The maps above show the membership of major international organizations. One important grouping shown on the bottom map is the Group of Eight (often called 'G8'). This group of eight leading industrial nations (comprising Canada, France, Germany, Italy, Japan, Russia, the United Kingdom and the United States) holds periodic meetings to discuss major problems, such as world recessions.*

# Regions in the News

## THE BREAK-UP OF YUGOSLAVIA

> The former Yugoslavia, a federation of six republics, split apart in 1991–92. Fearing Serb domination, Croatia, Slovenia, Macedonia and Bosnia-Herzegovina declared themselves independent. This left two states, Serbia and Montenegro, to continue as Yugoslavia. The presence in Croatia and Bosnia-Herzegovina of Orthodox Christian Serbs, Roman Catholic Croats and Muslims led to civil war and 'ethnic cleansing'. In 1995, the war ended when the Dayton Peace Accord affirmed Bosnia-Herzegovina as a single state partitioned into a Muslim-Croat Federation and a Serbian Republic. But the status of Kosovo, a former autonomous Yugoslav region, remained unresolved. Kosovo's autonomy had been abolished in 1989 and the Albanian-speaking, Muslim Kosovars were forced to accept direct Serbian rule. After 1995, support grew for the rebel Kosovo Liberation Army. The Serbs hit back and thousands of Kosovars were forced to flee their homes. In March 1999, NATO launched an aerial offensive in an attempt to halt the 'ethnic cleansing'. A Serb military withdrawal from Kosovo was finally agreed in June 1999.

### Population Breakdown ▾

Population totals and the proportion of ethnic groups (1995)

| | |
|---|---|
| **Yugoslavia** | **10,881,000** |
| Serb 63%, Albanian 17%, Montenegrin 5%, Hungarian 3%, Muslim 3% | |
| Serbia | 6,017,200 |
| *Kosovo* | *2,045,600* |
| *Vojvodina* | *2,121,800* |
| Montenegro | 696,400 |
| **Bosnia-Herzegovina** | **4,400,000** |
| Muslim 49%, Serb 31%, Croat 17% | |
| **Croatia** | **4,900,000** |
| Croat 78%, Serb 12% | |
| **Slovenia** | **2,000,000** |
| Slovene 88%, Croat 3%, Serb 2% | |
| **Macedonia (F.Y.R.O.M.)** | **2,173,000** |
| Macedonian 64%, Albanian 22%, Turkish 5%, Romanian 3%, Serb 2% | |

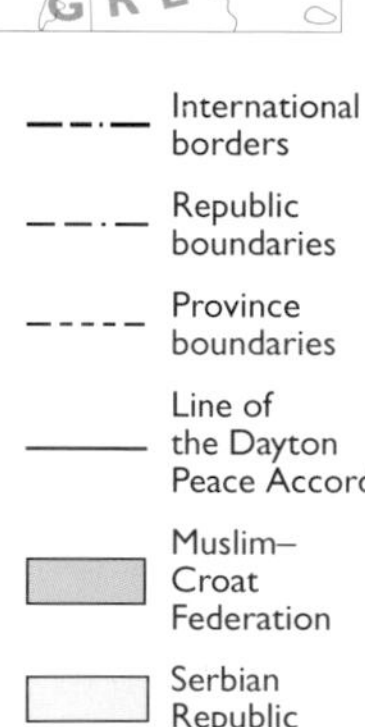

> Since its establishment in 1948, the State of Israel has seldom been out of the news. During wars with its Arab neighbours in 1948–49, 1956, 1967 and 1973, it occupied several areas. The largest of the occupied territories, the Sinai peninsula, was returned to Egypt in 1979 following the signing of an Egyptian–Israeli peace treaty. This left three Israeli-occupied territories: the Gaza Strip, the West Bank bordering Jordan, and the Golan Heights, a militarily strategic area overlooking south-western Syria.

Despite the peace agreement with Egypt, conflict continued in Israel with the PLO (Palestine Liberation Organization), which claimed to represent Arabs in Israel and Palestinians living in exile. Finally, on 13 September 1993 Israel officially recognized the PLO, and Yasser Arafat, leader of the PLO, renounced terrorism and recognized the State of Israel. This led to an agreement signed by both sides in Washington, DC. In May 1994, limited Palestinian self-rule was established in the Gaza Strip and in parts of the occupied West Bank. A Palestinian National Authority (PNA) was created and took over from the Israeli military administration when Israeli troops withdrew from the Gaza Strip and the city of Jericho. On 1 July 1994 the Palestinian leader, Yasser Arafat, stepped on to Palestinian land for the first time in 25 years.

Many people hoped that these developments would eventually lead to the creation of a Palestinian state, which would co-exist in peace with its neighbour Israel. But groups on both sides sought to undermine the peace process. In November 1995, a right-wing Jewish student assassinated the Israeli prime minister, Yitzhak Rabin, who was succeeded by Símon Peres.

In 1996, a right-wing coalition led by Binyamin Netanyahu was returned to power in a general election. The peace talks with the PLO were temporarily halted, but an agreement was reached in early 1997 over the withdrawal of Israeli troops from the town of Al Khalil (Hebron), on the West Bank. One-fifth of this town remained in the hands of about 400 Israeli settlers. Negotiations with Syria, however, over the Golan Heights were halted in 1996.

## THE NEAR EAST

—·—·— 1949 Armistice Line

- - - - - 1974 Cease-fire Lines (Golan Heights)

Efrata ● Main Jewish settlements in the West Bank and Gaza Strip

Halhul □ Main Palestinian Arab towns in the West Bank and Gaza Strip – under Palestinian control since May 1994 (Gaza and Jericho) and 28 September 1995 (West Bank)

### Population Breakdown ▾

Population totals and the proportion of ethnic groups (1995)

| | |
|---|---|
| **Israel** | **5,696,000** |
| Jewish 82%, Arab Muslim 14%, Arab Christian 3%, Druse 2% | |
| *West Bank* | *973,500* |
| Palestinian Arab 97% (Arab Muslim 85%, Christian 8%, Jewish 7%) | |
| *Gaza Strip* | *658,200* |
| Arab Muslim 98% | |
| **Jordan** | **5,547,000** |
| Arab 99% (Palestinian Arab 50%) | |
| **Syria** | **14,614,000** |
| Arab 89%, Kurdish 6% | |

# World Flags

Afghanistan

Albania

Algeria

Angola

Argentina

Armenia

Australia

Austria

Azerbaijan

Bahamas

Bahrain

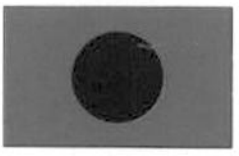
Bangladesh

Belarus

Belgium

Benin

Bhutan

Bolivia

Bosnia-Herzegovina

Botswana

Brazil

Bulgaria

Burkina Faso

Burma (Myanmar)

Burundi

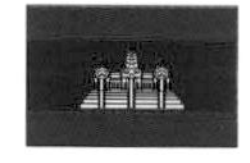
Cambodia

Cameroon

Canada

Central African Rep.

Chad

Chile

China

Colombia

Congo

Congo (Zaïre)

Costa Rica

Croatia

Cuba

Cyprus

Czech Republic

Denmark

Djibouti

Dominican Republic

Ecuador

Egypt

El Salvador

Equatorial Guinea

Eritrea

Estonia

Ethiopia

Finland

France

Gabon

Georgia

Germany

Ghana

Greece Guatemala Guinea Guinea–Bissau Guyana

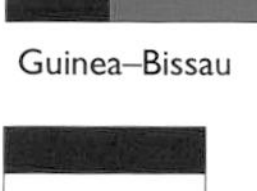

Haiti Honduras Hong Kong Hungary Iceland

India Indonesia Iran Iraq Ireland

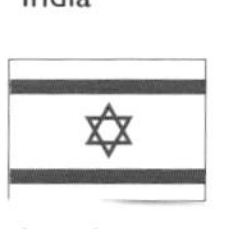
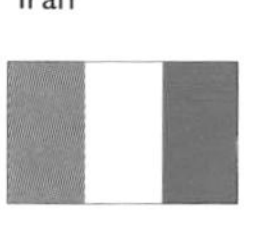

Israel Italy Ivory Coast Jamaica Japan

Jordan Kazakstan Kenya Korea, North Korea, South

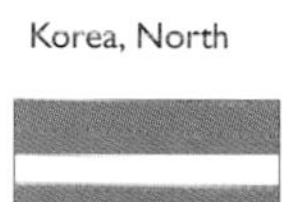

Kuwait Kyrgyzstan Laos Latvia Lebanon

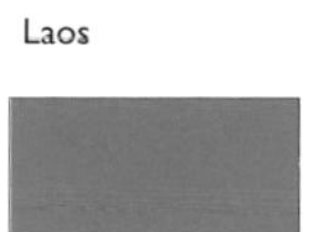

Lesotho Liberia Libya Liechtenstein Lithuania

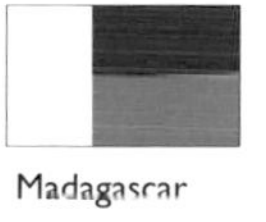

Luxembourg Macedonia Madagascar Malawi Malaysia

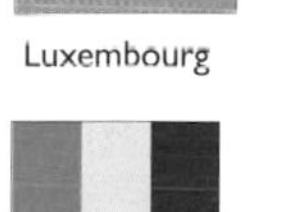

Mali Malta Mauritania Mexico Moldova

Mongolia Morocco Mozambique Namibia Nepal

Netherlands New Zealand Nicaragua Niger Nigeria

Norway

Oman

Pakistan

Panama

Papua New Guinea

Paraguay

Peru

Philippines

Poland

Portugal

Puerto Rico

Qatar

Romania

Russia

Rwanda

São Tomé & Príncipe

Saudi Arabia

Senegal

Sierra Leone

Singapore

Slovak Republic

Slovenia

Somalia

South Africa

Spain

Sri Lanka

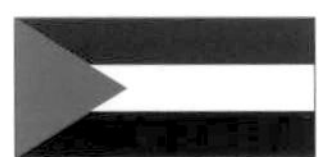
Sudan

Surinam

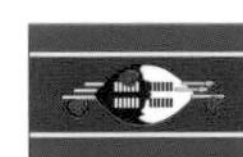
Swaziland

Sweden

Switzerland

Syria

Taiwan

Tajikistan

Tanzania

Thailand

Togo

Trinidad & Tobago

Tunisia

Turkey

Turkmenistan

Uganda

Ukraine

UAE

United Kingdom

USA

Uruguay

Uzbekistan

Vatican City

Venezuela

Vietnam

Yemen

Yugoslavia

Zambia

Zimbabwe

# World Maps — GENERAL REFERENCE

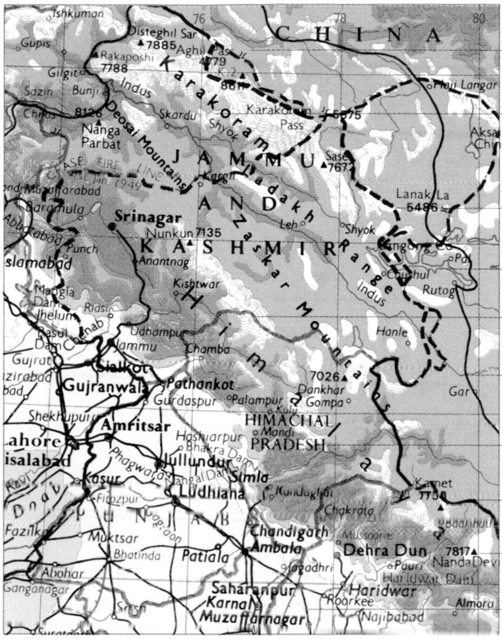

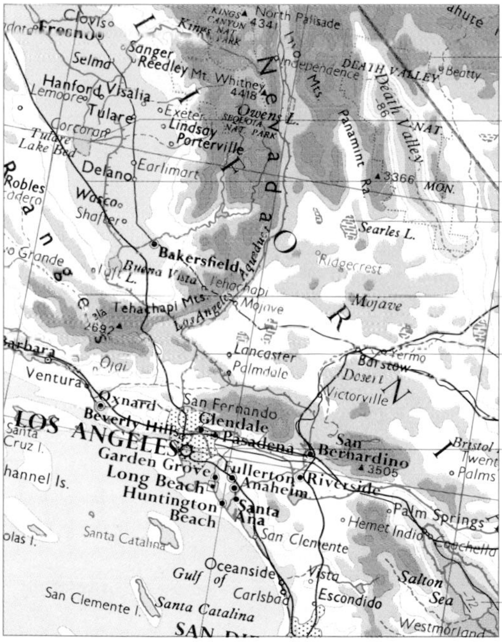

Pass

Permanent Ice and Glaciers

International Boundary (undefined or disputed)

Perennial Lake

Internal Boundary

Perennial Stream

Administrative Area Name

International Boundary

Elevation (m)

Railway

National Park Boundary

Seasonal or Dry Lake

Road

Salt Lake

Intermittent Stream

Principal Canal

Airport or Airfield

Height of Lake Surface (m)

Settlements

Settlement symbols and type styles vary according to the scale of each map and indicate the importance of towns rather than specific population figures.

2 NORTHERN HEMISPHERE

1:100 000 000

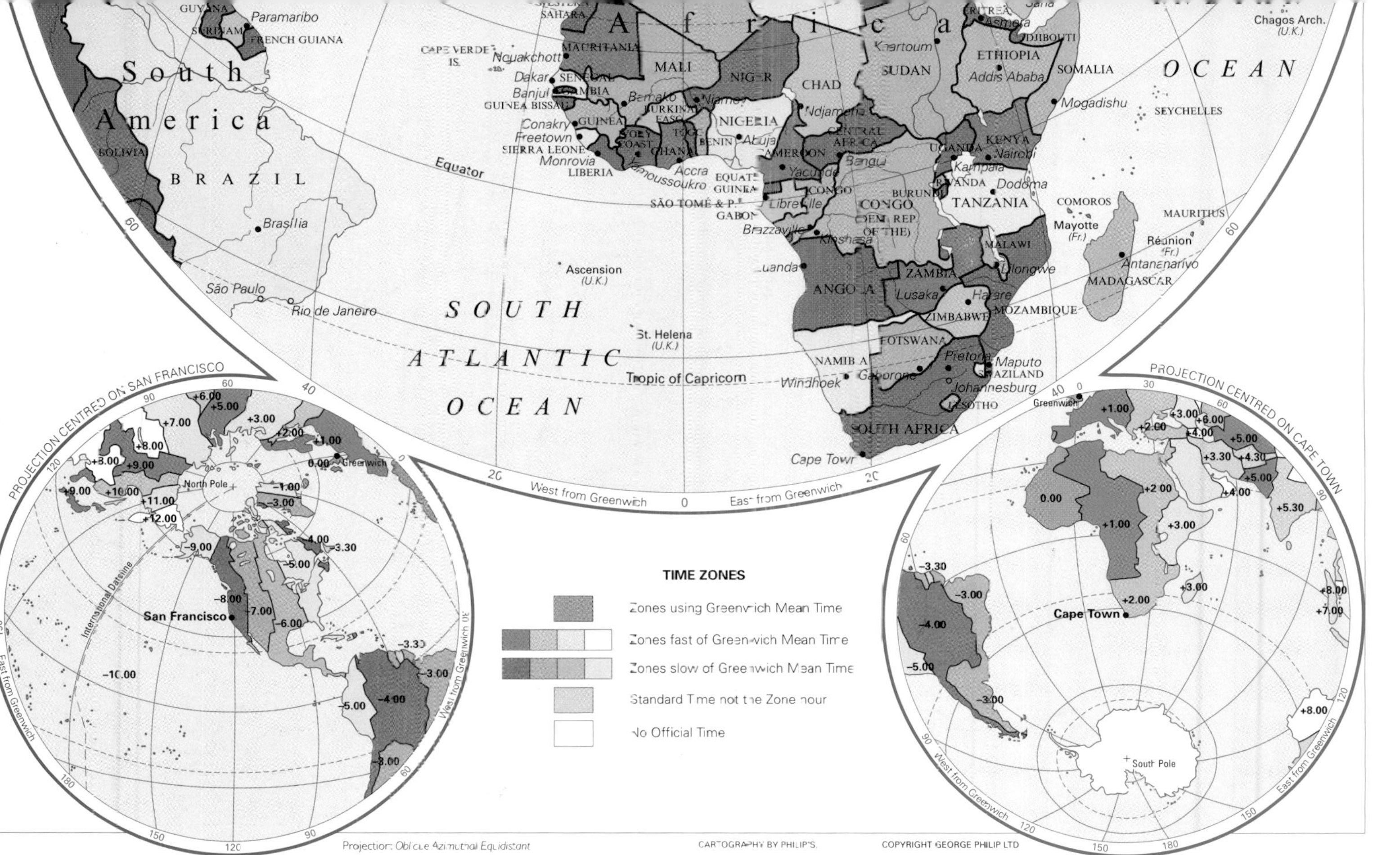


Projection: Oblique Azimuthal Equidistant

CARTOGRAPHY BY PHILIP'S

# SOUTHERN HEMISPHERE

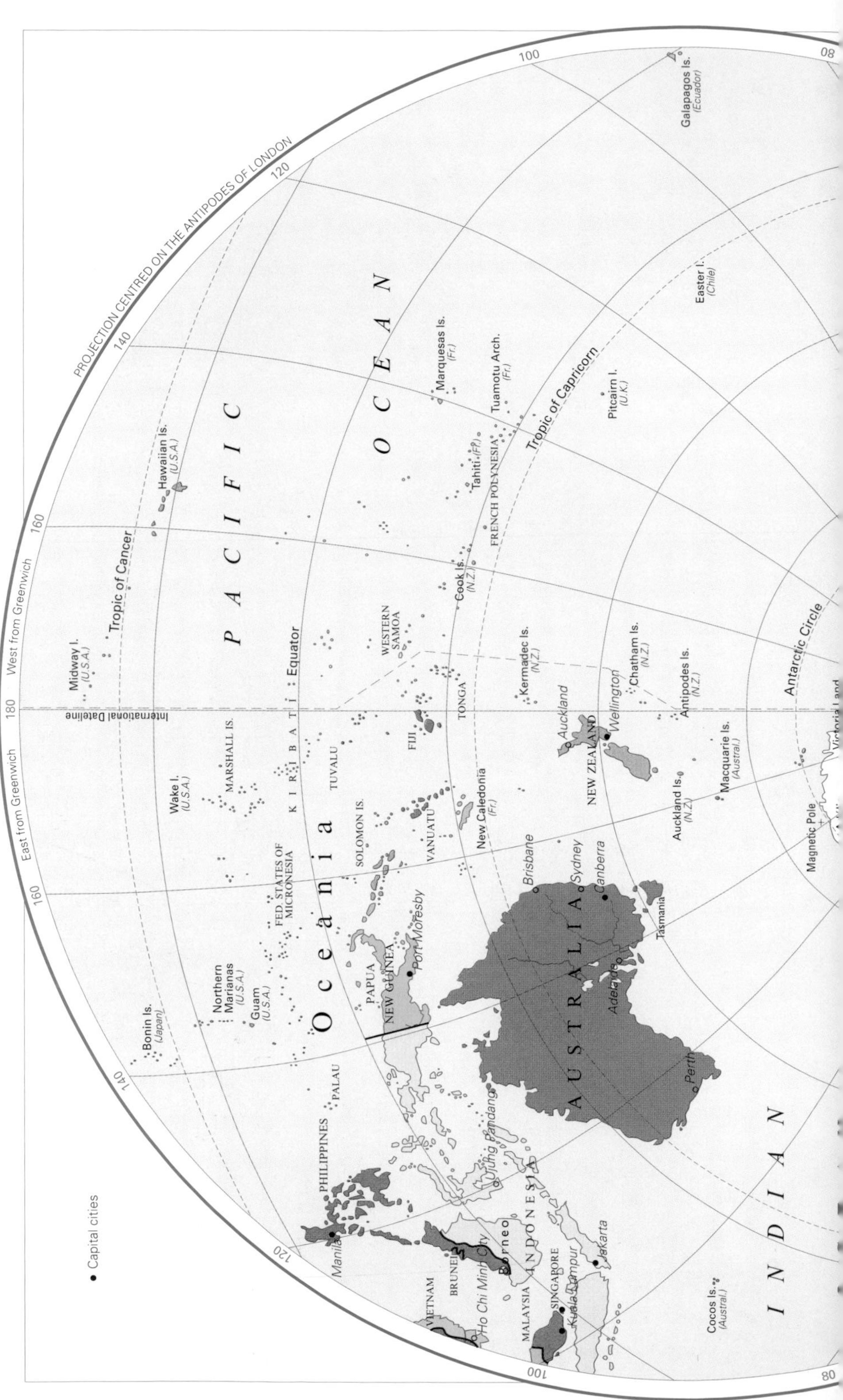

Antarctica
Wilkes Land
Byrd Land
Ellsworth Land
South Pole
Enderby Land
Queen Maud Land
Kerguelen
(Fr.)
Heard I.
(Austral.)
Crozet I.
(Fr.)
Pr. Edward I.
(S. Africa)
Bouvet I.
(Norw.)
South Sandwich Is.
(U.K.)
South Georgia
(U.K.)
Falkland Is.
(U.K.)
South America
PERU
BOLIVIA
CHILE
Santiago
ARGENTINA
PARAGUAY
Buenos Aires
URUGUAY
Montevideo
BRAZIL
SOUTH
ATLANTIC
OCEAN
PROJECTION CENTRED ON CAIRO
PROJECTION CENTRED ON SHANGHAI
North Pole
Greenwich
Cairo
Shanghai
International Dateline
Equator
West from Greenwich
East from Greenwich
TIME ZONES
Zones using Greenwich Mean Time
Zones fast of Greenwich Mean Time
Zones slow of Greenwich Mean Time
Standard Time not the Zone hour
Projection: Oblique Azimuthal Equidistant
CARTOGRAPHY BY PHILIP'S.

ICELAND
Reykjavík
Arctic Circle
Norwegian Sea
Faroe Is. (Den.)
Shetland Is.
Orkney Is.
ATLANTIC OCEAN
UNITED KINGDOM
Hebrides
SCOTLAND
Aberdeen
Glasgow
Dundee
Edinburgh
N. IRELAND
Belfast
IRELAND
Dublin
Cork
Newcastle-upon-Tyne
Manchester
Leeds
Liverpool
Sheffield
Birmingham
WALES
Cardiff
ENGLAND
Bristol
LONDON
Plymouth
Southampton
English Channel
Channel Is. (U.K.)
North Sea
NORWAY
Bergen
Stavanger
Oslo
Trondheim
SWEDEN
Gävle
Uppsala
Örebro
Vänern
Vättern
Jönköping
Gothenburg
Skagerrak
Kattegat
Ålborg
DENMARK
Århus
Copenhagen
Malmö
Baltic
Kiel
Hamburg
Bremen
Elbe
Amsterdam
The Hague
Rotterdam
NETHERLANDS
Antwerp
BELGIUM
Brussels
Lille
Essen
Dortmund
Cologne
Bonn
Wiesbaden
Frankfurt am Main
GERMANY
Hannover
Magdeburg
Berlin
Halle
Leipzig
Chemnitz
Dresden
Szczecin
Gdańsk
Bydgoszcz
POLAND
Oder
Poznań
Łódź
Wrocław
Katowice
Prague
CZECH REP.
Ostrava
LUX.
Luxembourg
Meuse
Le Havre
Rouen
Brest
Seine
PARIS
FRANCE
Strasbourg
Rhine
Stuttgart
Nuremberg
Munich
Vienna
Bratislava
Linz
Salzburg
AUSTRIA
Graz
HUNGARY
Bay of Biscay
Nantes
Loire
Dijon
Limoges
Lyons
Bordeaux
St.-Étienne
Zürich
Bern
LIECH.
Vaduz
Innsbruck
SWITZERLAND
Geneva
Grenoble
Milan
SLOVENIA
Ljubljana
Zagreb
Trieste
CROATIA
Venice
Turin
Genoa
Bologna
Garonne
Toulouse
Rhône
La Coruña
Vigo
Porto
Douro
Bilbao
Valladolid
Ebro
ANDORRA
Andorra la-Vella
Zaragoza
Marseilles
Toulon
Nice
MONACO
Florence
SAN MARINO
Tiber
Adriatic Sea
Split
BOSNIA-HERZ.
Sarajevo
PORTUGAL
Lisbon
Tagus
SPAIN
Madrid
Guadiana
Barcelona
Valencia
Corsica
Ajaccio
ITALY
Rome
Balearic Is.
Minorca
Palma
Majorca
Ibiza
Sardinia
Seville
Córdoba
Guadalquivir
Murcia
Alicante
Granada
Naples
Bari
Taranto
Tyrrhenian Sea
Cádiz
Str. of Gibraltar
Málaga
Gibraltar (U.K.)
Tangier
Ceuta (Sp.)
Cagliari
Mediterranean Sea
Algiers
Melilla (Sp.)
Annaba
Palermo
Messina
Sicily
Catánia
Ionian Sea
MOROCCO
Africa
ALGERIA
Constantine
TUNISIA
Tunis
Pantelleria (Italy)
MALTA
Valletta
Projection: Bonne
West from Greenwich
East from Greenwich
■ LONDON Capital Cities

1: 20 000 000
100 0 100 200 300 400 500 miles
100 0 200 400 600 800 km
White Sea
Murmansk
Arkhangelsk
N. Dvina
Kotlas
Ob
Perm
Nizhniy Tagil
Yekaterinburg
Chelyabinsk
Kirov
FINLAND
Vaasa
Luleå
Turku
Helsinki
Vyborg
L. Ladoga
L. Onega
ST. PETERBURG
Vologda
Rybinsk Res.
Kostroma
Yaroslavl
Ivanovo
Nizhniy Novgorod
Kazan
Ufa
Magnitogorsk
Orenburg
R U S S I A
ESTONIA
Tallinn
L. Chudskoye
LATVIA
Riga
MOSCOW
Simbirsk
Samara
W. Dvina
LITHUANIA
Kaunas
Vilnius
Kaliningrad (Russia)
Vitebsk
Smolensk
Tula
Penza
Volga
Uralsk
Ural
Mogilev
Minsk
BELARUS
Pripet
Brest
Białystok
Warsaw
Vistula
Lublin
Kraków
Orel
Tambov
Saratov
Kursk
Voronezh
Gomel
Chernigov
KAZAKSTAN
Atyraū
Kiev
Dnieper
Zhitomir
Kharkov
Volgograd
Don
Astrakhan
Caspian Sea
UKRAINE
Lvov
Dniester
Donetsk
Dnepropetrovsk
Zaporozhye
Taganrog
Rostov
Krivoy Rog
Bug
Kherson
Nikolayev
Odessa
MOLDOVA
Kishinev
Stavropol
Krasnodar
Makhachkala
Crimea
ROMANIA
Cluj-Napoca
Debrecen
Timişoara
Braşov
Galaţi
Ploieşti
Bucharest
Constanţa
Sevastopol
Black Sea
GEORGIA
Tbilisi
AZERBAIJAN
Baku
ARMENIA
Yerevan
Araks
Danube
Belgrade
SERBIA
Niš
Sofia
BULGARIA
Varna
Samsun
Erzurum
Tabriz
Bosporus
ISTANBUL
Skopje
MACEDONIA
Plovdiv
Thessaloniki
Bursa
Ankara
TURKEY
Kayseri
Diyarbakır
IRAN
GREECE
Ægean Sea
İzmir
Konya
Adana
Asia
Aleppo
Euphrates
IRAQ
Tigris
Patrai
Athens
Antalya
SYRIA
Baghdad
Rhodes
CYPRUS
Nicosia
Crete
CARTOGRAPHY BY PHILIPS.
C
D
E
F
G
H
J

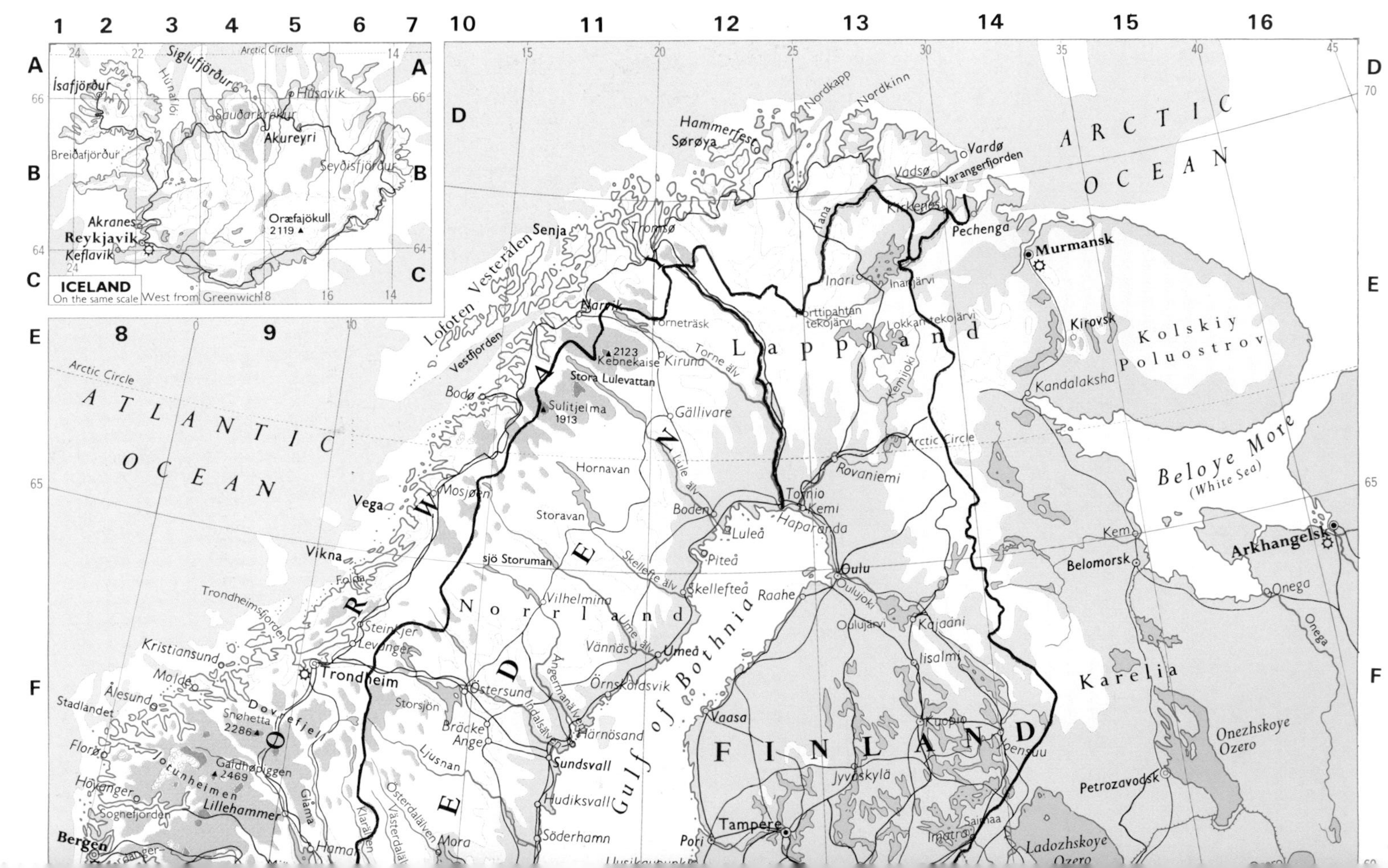

ARCTIC OCEAN
ATLANTIC OCEAN
Lappland
FINLAND
NORWAY
SWEDEN
Norrland
Karelia
Kolskiy Poluostrov
Beloye More
(White Sea)
Gulf of Bothnia
Arctic Circle
Nordkapp
Nordkinn
Hammerfest
Sørøya
Vardø
Vadsø
Varangerfjorden
Kirkenes
Pechenga
Murmansk
Kirovsk
Kandalaksha
Kem
Belomorsk
Arkhangelsk
Onega
Onezhskoye Ozero
Petrozavodsk
Ladozhskoye Ozero
Inari
Inarijärvi
Rovaniemi
Kemijoki
Tornio
Kemi
Haparanda
Oulu
Oulujoki
Oulujärvi
Kajaani
Iisalmi
Kuopio
Jyväskylä
Raahe
Vaasa
Tampere
Pori
Luleå
Piteå
Skellefteå
Umeå
Örnsköldsvik
Härnösand
Sundsvall
Hudiksvall
Söderhamn
Boden
Gällivare
Kiruna
Torne älv
Lule älv
Skellefte älv
Ume älv
Ångermanälven
Indalsälven
Kebnekaise
2123
Stora Lulevattan
Sulitjelma
1913
Hornavan
Storavan
sjö Storuman
Vilhelmina
Vännäs
Östersund
Storsjön
Bräcke
Ånge
Ljusnan
Mora
Österdalälven
Klarälven
Tromsø
Senja
Narvik
Vesterålen
Lofoten
Vestfjorden
Bodø
Mosjøen
Vega
Vikna
Folda
Steinkjer
Levanger
Trondheim
Trondheimsfjorden
Kristiansund
Molde
Ålesund
Dovrefjell
Snøhetta
2286
Glåma
Hamar
Lillehammer
Galdhøpiggen
2469
Jotunheimen
Sognefjorden
Florø
Stadlandet
Bergen
ICELAND
On the same scale
West from Greenwich
Ísafjörður
Breiðafjörður
Húnaflói
Siglufjörður
Sauðárkrókur
Akureyri
Húsavík
Seyðisfjörður
Öræfajökull
2119
Akranes
Reykjavík
Keflavík

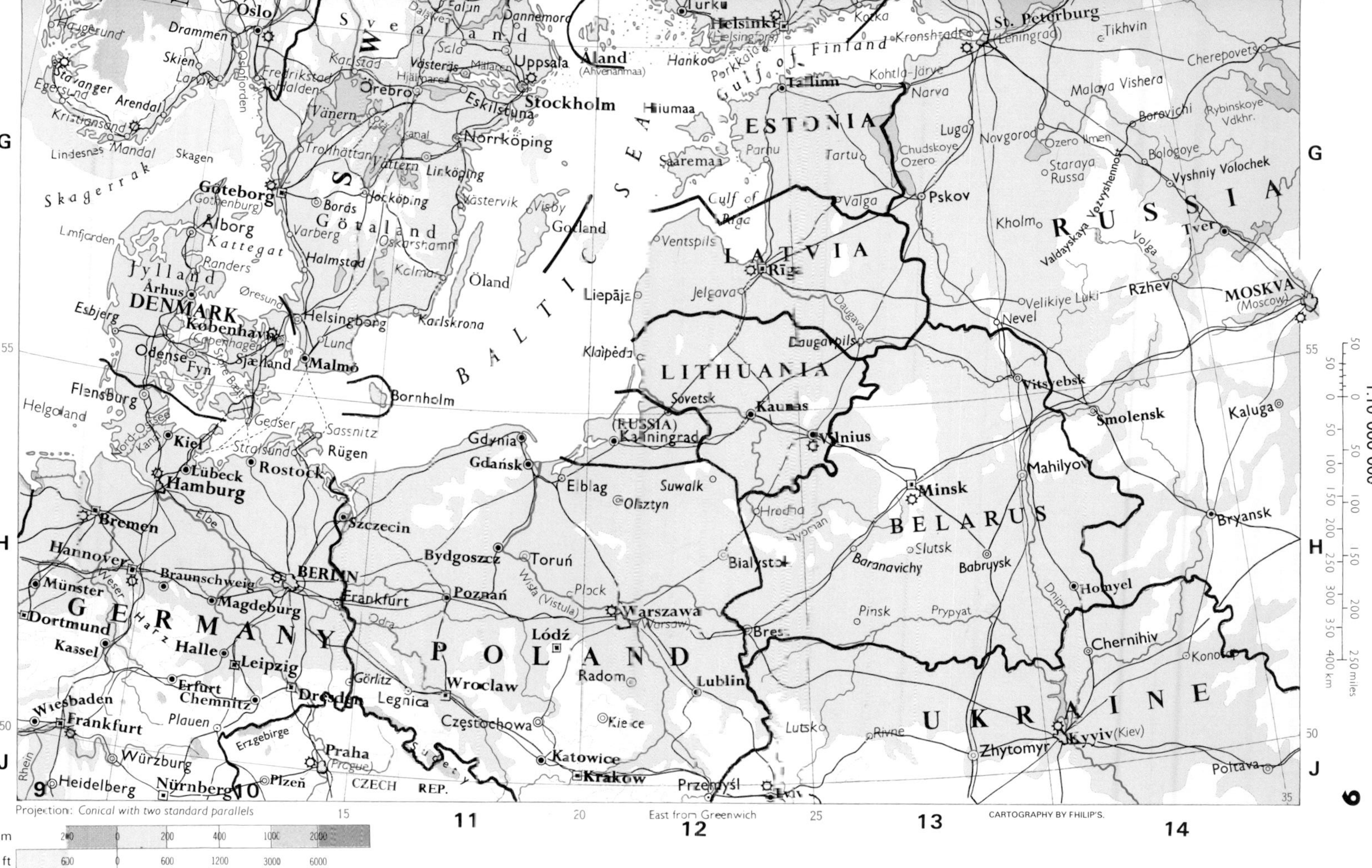

1:10 000 000
50 0 50 100 150 200 250 miles
50 0 50 100 150 200 250 300 350 400 km
Projection: Conical with two standard parallels
East from Greenwich
CARTOGRAPHY BY PHILIP'S.
BALTIC SEA
RUSSIA
ESTONIA
LATVIA
LITHUANIA
BELARUS
UKRAINE
POLAND
GERMANY
DENMARK
CZECH REP.
(RUSSIA)
Oslo
Stockholm
Helsinki (Helsingfors)
St. Petersburg (Leningrad)
Tallinn
Rīga
Vilnius
Minsk
MOSKVA (Moscow)
Kyyiv (Kiev)
Warszawa (Warsaw)
BERLIN
København (Copenhagen)
Praha (Prague)
Göteborg (Gothenburg)
Malmö
Hamburg
Bremen
Hannover
Gdańsk
Gdynia
Kaliningrad
Kaunas
Smolensk
Gulf of Finland
Gulf of Riga
Skagerrak
Kattegat
Götaland
Jylland
Gotland
Öland
Bornholm
Rügen
Lódź
Kraków
Katowice
Wrocław
Poznań
Szczecin
Lublin
Leipzig
Dresden
Frankfurt
Nürnberg
Heidelberg
Chernihiv
Zhytomyr
Poltava
Bryansk
Kaluga
Tver
Pskov
Novgorod
Vitsyebsk
Mahilyow
Homyel
Babruysk
Pinsk
Brest
Lutsk
Rivne
Przemyśl

m 2000 1000 500 200 100 50 0 200 500 1000
ft 6000 3000 1500 600 300 150 0 600 1500 3000
ATLANTIC OCEAN
NORTH SEA
NORWAY
SCOTLAND
Shetland Is.
Yell
Unst
Fetlar
Mainland
Lerwick
Foula
Fair Isle
Orkney Is.
Westray
Sanday
Stronsay
Mainland
Kirkwall
Hoy
South Ronaldsay
Pentland Firth
Thurso
Wick
Helmsdale
C. Wrath
Lairg
Golspie
Moray Firth
Tain
Invergordon
Dingwall
Buckie
Banff
Fraserburgh
Peterhead
Nairn
Elgin
Huntly
Inverness
Spey
Don
Inverurie
Aberdeen
Aviemore
Dee
Ballater
Stonehaven
Grampian Mts.
North West Highlands
North Minch
Ullapool
L. Ness
Ben Nevis
1342
1182
1311
Fort William
Mallaig
Portree
Skye
Rhum
Eigg
Coll
Tiree
Tobermory
Mull
Oban
Colonsay
Jura
Islay
Outer Hebrides
Inner Hebrides
Lewis
Stornoway
789
Harris
St. Kilda
North Uist
Benbecula
South Uist
Barra
Montrose
Arbroath
Forfar
Dundee
Tay
Perth
St. Andrews
1214
L. Lomond
973
Stirling
Dunfermline
Glenrothes
Kirkcaldy
Dunbar
Greenock
Clyde
Glasgow
Edinburgh
Paisley
East Kilbride
Hamilton
Irvine
Kilmarnock
Ayr
Arran
Campbeltown
Malin Hd.
Southern Uplands
Galashiels
Jedburgh
840
816
Hawick
Berwick-upon-Tweed
Alnwick
Cheviot Hills
Askøy
Bergen
Osøyri
Stord
Bømlo
Leirvik
Haugesund
Kopervik
Åkrahamn
Boknafjorden
Stavanger
Sandnes
Bryne
Nærbø
1224
316
238

1: 5 000 000
UNITED KINGDOM
IRELAND
NORTHERN IRELAND
ENGLAND
WALES
NETHERLANDS
BELGIUM
FRANCE
IRISH SEA
CELTIC SEA
English Channel
St. George's Channel
Bristol Channel
Cardigan Bay
Str. of Dover
Dublin
Belfast
LONDON
BIRMINGHAM
Manchester
Liverpool
Leeds
Sheffield
Kingston upon Hull
Cork
Limerick
Galway
Waterford
Londonderry
Cardiff
Bristol
Southampton
Portsmouth
Plymouth
Brighton
Norwich
Cambridge
Oxford
Nottingham
Leicester
Coventry
Stoke on Trent
Derby
York
Middlesbrough
Sunderland
South Shields
Newcastle-upon-Tyne
Scarborough
Swansea
Newport
Reading
Milton Keynes
Southend-on-Sea
Ipswich
Great Yarmouth
Lowestoft
ROTTERDAM
's-Gravenhage (Den Haag)
Haarlem
BRUSSEL (Bruxelles)
Antwerpen
Lille
Dunkerque
Calais
Le Havre
Rouen
Caen
Cherbourg
Channel Is. (U.K.)
Guernsey
Jersey
Isle of Wight
Land's End
Isles of Scilly
Pennines
Cambrian Mts.
Cumbrian Mts.
Projection Conical with two standard parallels
West from Greenwich
East from Greenwich
CARTOGRAPHY BY PHILIP'S.

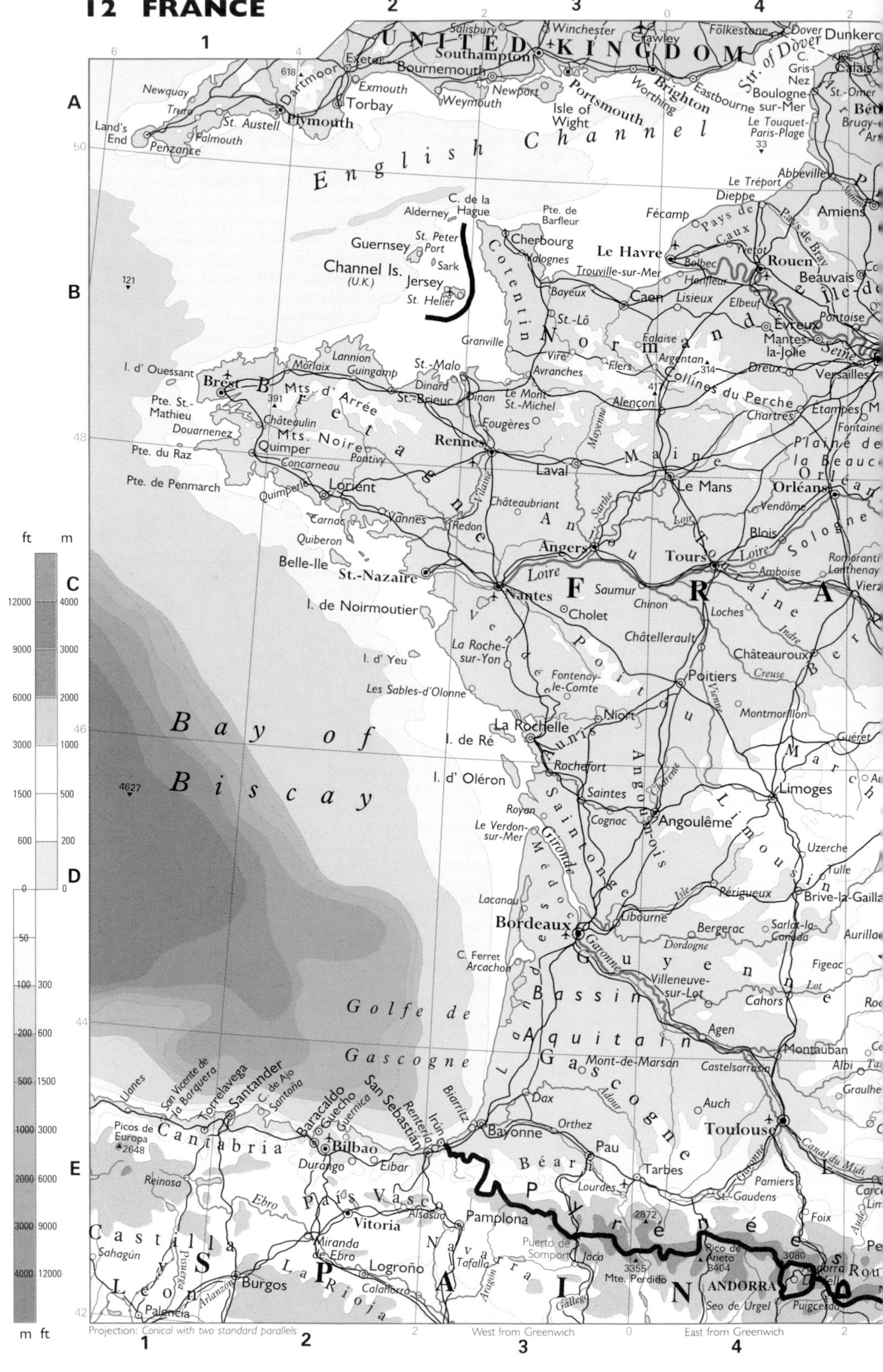
English Channel
Bay of Biscay
Golfe de Gascogne
FRANCE
SPAIN
UNITED KINGDOM
Projection: Conical with two standard parallels
West from Greenwich
East from Greenwich

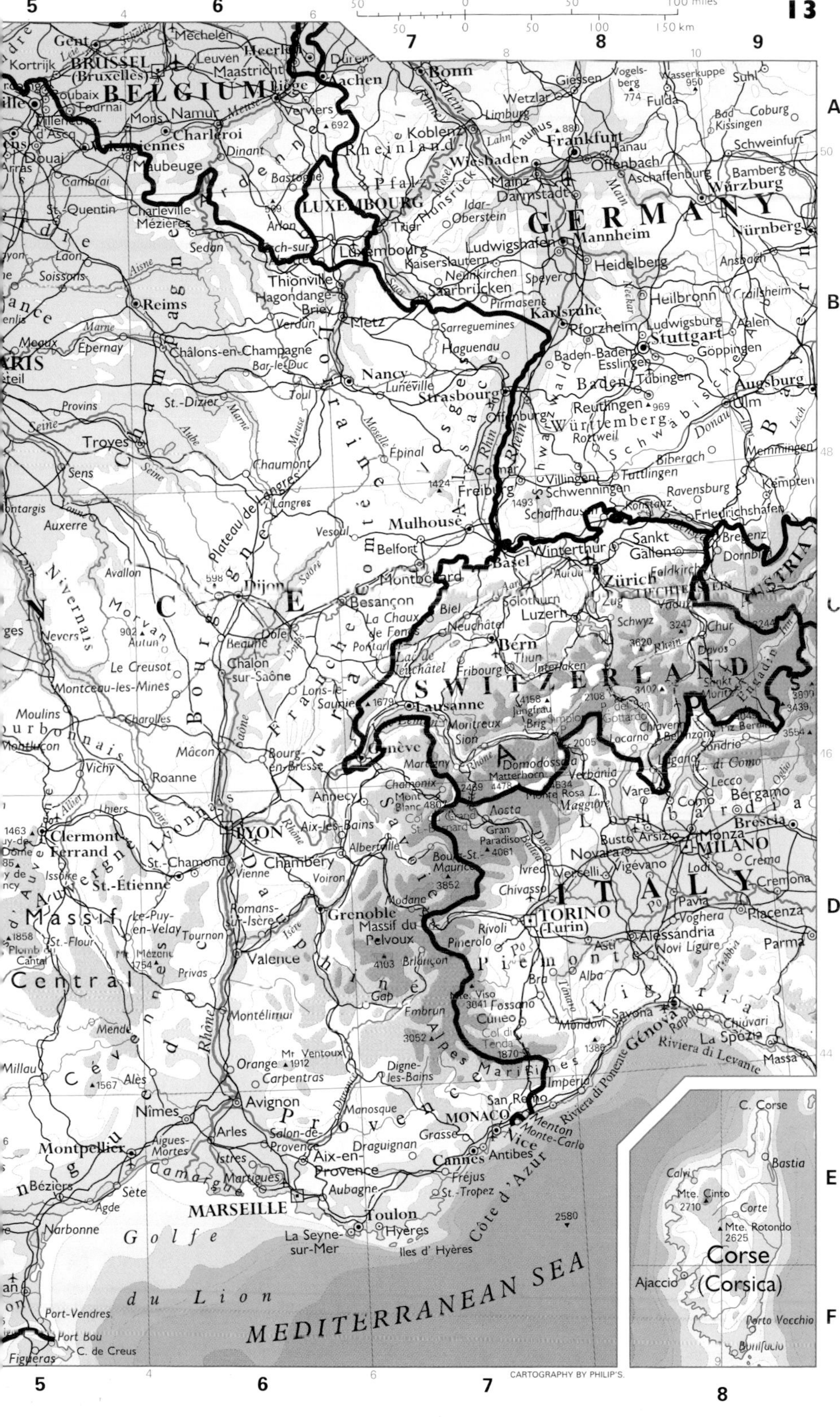
1: 5 000 000
50 0 50 100 miles
50 0 50 100 150 km
BELGIUM
LUXEMBOURG
GERMANY
SWITZERLAND
ITALY
AUSTRIA
BRUSSEL (Bruxelles)
Gent
Kortrijk
Mechelen
Leuven
Heerlen
Maastricht
Liège
Aachen
Düren
Bonn
Namur
Mons
Charleroi
Tournai
Roubaix
Douai
Valenciennes
Maubeuge
Cambrai
St.-Quentin
Verviers
Dinant
Bastogne
Arlon
Charleville-Mézières
Sedan
Laon
Soissons
Reims
Thionville
Hagondange-Briey
Verdun
Metz
Luxembourg
Trier
Koblenz
Rheinland-Pfalz
Wiesbaden
Mainz
Darmstadt
Frankfurt
Hanau
Offenbach
Aschaffenburg
Würzburg
Bamberg
Schweinfurt
Coburg
Bad Kissingen
Suhl
Fulda
Wasserkuppe 950
Vogelsberg 774
Giessen
Wetzlar
Limburg
Taunus
Hunsrück
Idar-Oberstein
Kaiserslautern
Neunkirchen
Saarbrücken
Pirmasens
Ludwigshafen
Mannheim
Heidelberg
Speyer
Karlsruhe
Pforzheim
Heilbronn
Nürnberg
Ansbach
Crailsheim
Ludwigsburg
Stuttgart
Aalen
Göppingen
Esslingen
Baden-Baden
Tübingen
Reutlingen 969
Baden-Württemberg
Schwäbische Alb
Augsburg
Ulm
Rottweil
Biberach
Memmingen
Kempten
Tuttlingen
Villingen-Schwenningen
Ravensburg
Friedrichshafen
Konstanz
Schaffhausen
Bregenz
Dornbirn
Feldkirch
Vaduz
Sarreguemines
Haguenau
Strasbourg
Nancy
Lunéville
Toul
Épinal
Colmar
Offenburg
Freiburg
Mulhouse
Belfort
Basel
Winterthur
Zürich
Sankt Gallen
Montbéliard
Besançon
Biel
Solothurn
Luzern
Zug
Schwyz
Chur
Davos
Neuchâtel
Bern
Thun
Interlaken
Fribourg
La Chaux de Fonds
Pontarlier
Lac de Neuchâtel
Lausanne
Montreux
Sion
Genève
Martigny
Jungfrau 4158
Brig
Simplon
Domodossola
Matterhorn 4478
Locarno
Bellinzona
Lugano
Sondrio
Sankt Moritz
Engadin
Chamonix
Mont Blanc 4807
Aosta
Gran Paradiso 4061
Verbania
Lago Maggiore
Varese
Como
Lecco
Bergamo
Brescia
Monza
MILANO
Busto Arsizio
Novara
Vigévano
Vercelli
Lodi
Crema
Cremona
Pavia
Voghera
Piacenza
Parma
Ivrea
Chivasso
TORINO (Turin)
Rivoli
Pinerolo
Asti
Alessándria
Novi Ligure
Alba
Bra
Piemonte
Mte. Viso 3841
Fossano
Cuneo
Mondovi
Col di Tenda 1870
Savona
Génova
Liguria
Rapallo
Chiavari
La Spézia
Riviera di Levante
Riviera di Ponente
Massa
Imperia
San Remo
Menton
Monte-Carlo
MONACO
Nice
Antibes
Cannes
Grasse
Fréjus
St.-Tropez
Draguignan
Côte d'Azur
Toulon
Hyères
Îles d'Hyères
La Seyne-sur-Mer
Aubagne
MARSEILLE
Aix-en-Provence
Martigues
Istres
Salon-de-Provence
Arles
Camargue
Aigues-Mortes
Avignon
Nîmes
Montpellier
Sète
Agde
Béziers
Narbonne
Port-Vendres
Port Bou
C. de Creus
Figueras
Golfe du Lion
MEDITERRANEAN SEA
Manosque
Digne-les-Bains
Provence
Alpes Maritimes
Mt. Ventoux 1912
Orange
Carpentras
Montélimar
Valence
Privas
Tournon
Romans-sur-Isère
Grenoble
Massif du Pelvoux
Briançon
Gap
Embrun
Modane
Bourg-St.-Maurice
Albertville
Chambéry
Voiron
Aix-les-Bains
Annecy
Vienne
LYON
St.-Chamond
St.-Étienne
Le-Puy-en-Velay
Roanne
Thiers
Vichy
Clermont-Ferrand
Issoire
Auvergne
Massif Central
Mt. Mézenc 1754
St.-Flour
Plomb du Cantal 1858
Cévennes
Mende
Alès
Millau
Mâcon
Bourg-en-Bresse
Lons-le-Saunier
Jura
Franche-Comté
Chalon-sur-Saône
Le Creusot
Montceau-les-Mines
Charolles
Moulins
Bourbonnais
Montluçon
Nevers
Nivernais
Morvan
Autun
Beaune
Dole
Dijon
Bourgogne
Avallon
Auxerre
Sens
Troyes
Provins
Seine
Chaumont
Langres
Plateau de Langres
Vesoul
St.-Dizier
Bar-le-Duc
Châlons-en-Champagne
Champagne
Épernay
Meaux
Marne
Lorraine
Vosges
Alsace
Rhein
Schwarzwald
Corse (Corsica)
C. Corse
Bastia
Calvi
Mte. Cinto 2710
Corte
Mte. Rotondo 2625
Ajaccio
Porto Vecchio
Bonifacio
CARTOGRAPHY BY PHILIP'S.

# GERMANY AND BENELUX

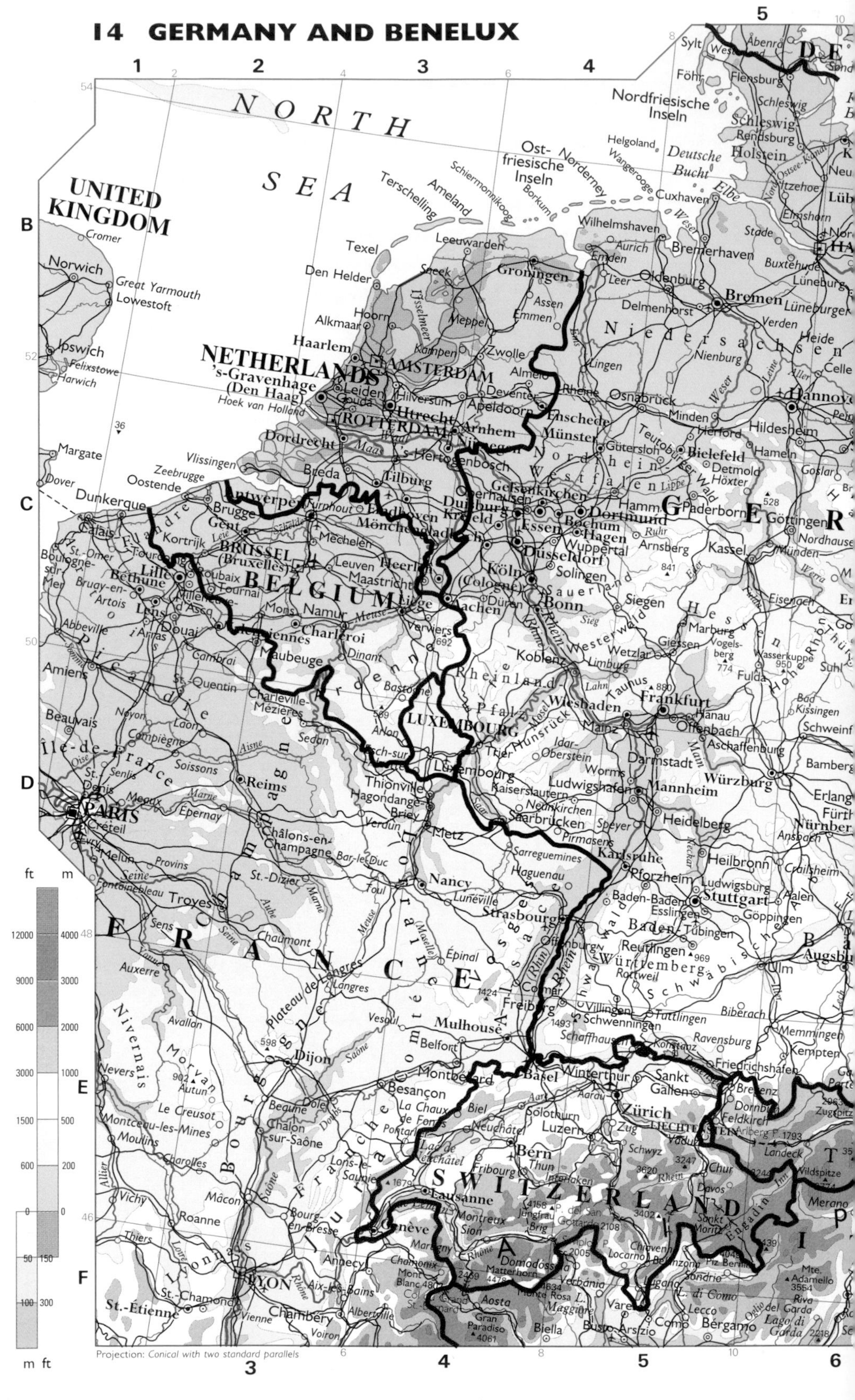


Projection: *Conical with two standard parallels*

1: 5 000 000

50 0 50 100 miles

50 0 50 100 150 km

6 7 8 9 10

A B C D E

7 8 9 10

# 16 CENTRAL EUROPE

1: 5 000 000
50 0 50 100 miles
50 0 50 100 150 km
BELARUS
UKRAINE
MOLDOVA
ROMANIA
MINSK
Marijampolė
Alytus
Suwałki
Druskininkai
Augustów
Lida
Hrodna
Navahrudak
Dzyarzhynsk
Hrodzyanka
Bykhaw
Slawharad
Sokółka
Białystok
Masty
Dzyatlava
Stowbtsy
Nyasvizh
Asipovichy
Babruysk
Rogachow
Zhlobin
Vawkavysk
Slonim
Baranavichy
Slutsk
Klyetsk
Glusk
Aktsyabrski
Homyel
Svislach
Lyakhavichy
Hantsavichy
Salihorsk
Svyetlahorsk
Rechytsa
Hajnówka
Ivatsevichy
Tsyelyakhany
Vasilevichi
Bielsk Podlaski
Pruzhany
Bereza
Pyetrikaw
Kalinkavichy
Luninyets
Loyew
Kobryn
Dragichyn
Yaselda
Mazyr
Khoyniki
Zhabinka
Ivanava
Pinsk
Davyd Haradok
Biała Podlaska
Brest
Stolin
Yelsk
Malaryta
Międzyrzec Podlaski
Pripet Marsh
Chornobyl
Kamin-Kashyrskyy
Dubrovytsya
Ovruch
Włodawa
Oster
Olevsk
Kyyivske Vdskh.
Belokorovichi
Lyuboml
Kovel
Staryy Chartoriysk
Korosten
Dymer
Chełm
Kostopil
Malyn
Irpin
Rozhyshche
Kivertsi
Novohrad-Volynskyy
Radomyshl
KYYIV (Kiev)
Novovolynsk
Volodymyr-Volynskyy
Lutsk
Rivne
Zdolbuniv
Zhytomyr
Korostyshev
Vasylkiv
Zamość
Horokhiv
Dubno
Slavuta
Pershotravensk
Fastiv
Chervonohrad
Ostroh
Radekhiv
Berestechko
Kremenets
Shepetivka
Polonne
Berdychiv
Bila Tserkva
Rava-Ruska
Izyaslav
Nesterov
Kamyanka-Buzka
Brody
Skvyra
Tarashcha
Kozyatyn
Yavoriv
Starokonstyantyniv
Khmelnik
Mostyska
Lviv (Lvov)
Zolochiv
Zbarazh
Tetiyev
Przemyśl
Horodok
Ternopil
Khmelnytskyy
Lipovets
Zhashkiv
Sanok
Skalat
Vinnytsya
Sambir
Khodoriv
Berezhany
Hrymayliv
Drohobych
Rogatyn
Terebovlya
Kopychyntsi
Bar
Zhmerynka
Haysyn
Boryslav
Truskavets
Stryy
Uman
Skole
Kalush
Buchach
Chortkiv
Skala-Podilska
Tulchyn
Dniester
Kamyanets-Podilskyy
Hayvoron
Bolekhiv
Vapnyarka
Ivano-Frankivsk
Horodenka
Zalishchyky
Mohyliv-Podilskyy
Bershad
Nadvirna
Kolomyya
Khotyn
Uzhhorod
Volovets
Pechenizhyn
Ocnița
Balta
Yaremcha
Snyatyn
Novoselytsya
Lipcani
Yampil
Mukacheve
Chernivtsi
Drochia
Soroca
Ananyiv
Berehove
Yasinya
Storozhynets
Hlyboka
Edineț
Florești
Khust
Rakhiv
Dorohol
Bălți
Rîbnița
Kotovsk
Tyachiv
Dubăsari Vdkhr.
Sighetu Marmației
Rădăuți
Fălești
Satu Mare
Suceava
Botoșani
Dubăsari
Baia Mare
Borșa
Fălticeni
Orhei
Carei
Pietrosul
Pașcani
Ungheni
Chișinău
Tiraspol
Vatra-Dornei
Iași
Tighina
Bistrița
Roman
Huși
Cimișlia
Zalău
Dej
Piatra Neamț
Vaslui
Leova
Basarabeasca
Bilhorod-Dnistrovskyy
Oradea
Reghin
Cluj-Napoca
Tîrgu Mureș
Bacău
Comrat
Turda
Odorheiu Secuiesc
Miercurea Ciuc
Bîrlad
Artsyz
Munții Bihor
Onești
Ceadîr-Lunga
Abrud
Tîrnăveni
Sighișoara
Cahul
Tatarbunary
Mediaș
Sfîntu Gheorghe
Tecuci
Ozero Sasyk
Brad
Alba-Iulia
Vulcănești
Bolhrad
Kiliya
Focșani
Izmayil
Vylkove
Deva
Făgăraș
Brașov
Reni
Sibiu
Galați
Sulina
Simeria
Săcele
Rîmnicu Sărat
Lugoj
Hunedoara
Carpații Meridionali
Brăila
Tulcea
Petroșani
Moldoveana
Caransebeș
Vf. Peleaga
Cîmpulung
Vf. Omul
Cîmpina
Buzău
Babadag
Vulcan
Paringul Mare
Curtea de Argeș
Dunărea (Danube)
Prut
Siret
Mureș
Olt
Someș
Bistrița
Nyoman
Pripyats
Sluch
Uzh
Teterev
Prypyat
Sozh
Drut
Byarezina
Ptsich
Ubort
Styr
Horyn
Nistru
Buzău
Bîrlad
East from Greenwich
CARTOGRAPHY BY PHILIP'S.

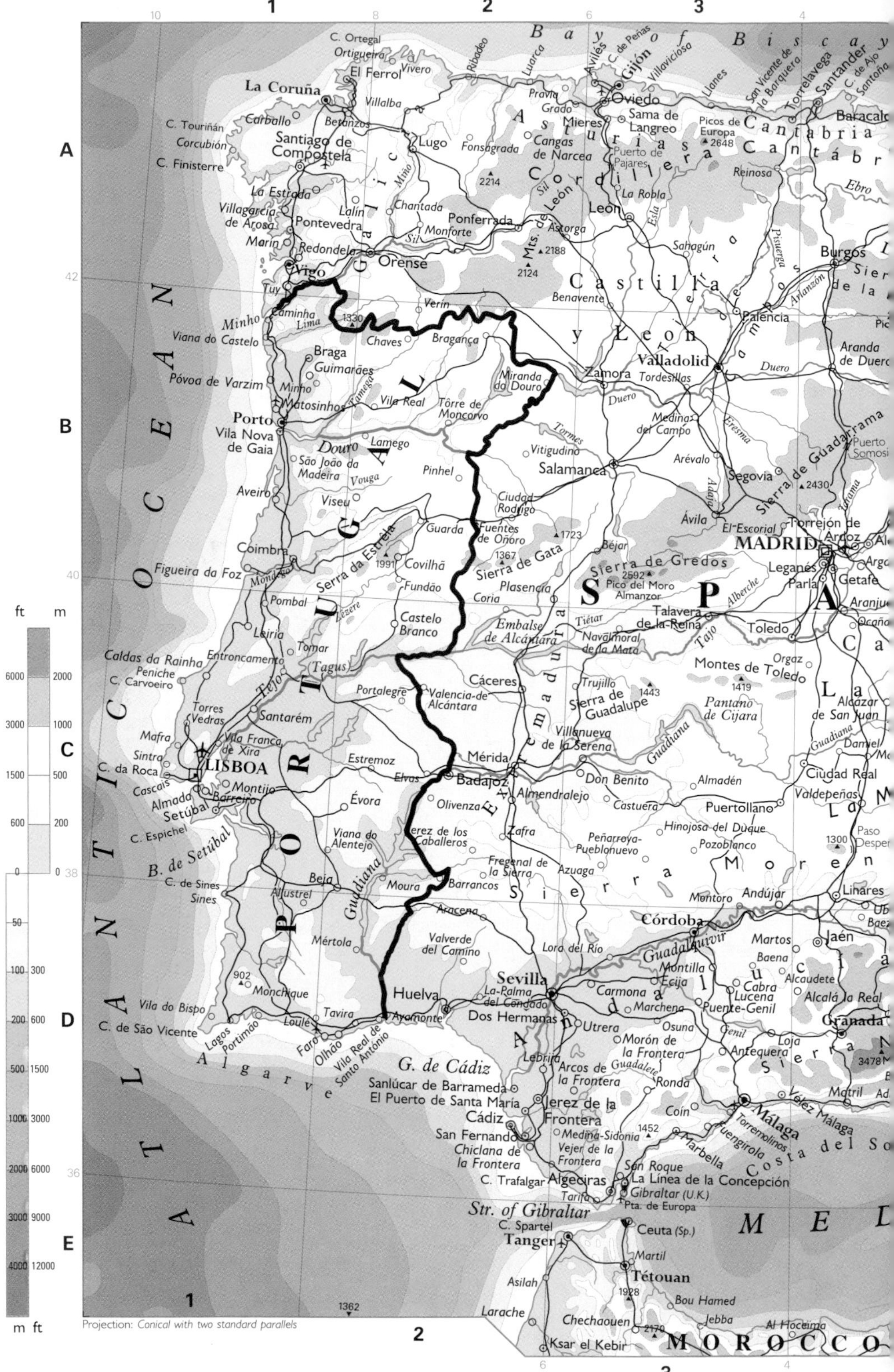
1
2
3
A
B
C
D
E
Bay of Biscay
ATLANTIC OCEAN
PORTUGAL
SPAIN
MOROCCO
C. Ortegal
Ortigueira
El Ferrol
Vivero
La Coruña
Carballo
Betanzos
Villalba
C. Touriñán
Corcubión
C. Finisterre
Santiago de Compostela
Lugo
Fonsagrada
Ribadeo
Luarca
Avilés
C. de Peñas
Gijón
Villaviciosa
Pravia
Grado
Oviedo
Mieres
Sama de Langreo
Cangas de Narcea
Llanes
San Vicente de la Barquera
Torrelavega
Santander
C. de Ajo
Santoña
Baracaldo
Picos de Europa
2648
Puerto de Pajares
Reinosa
Ebro
La Robla
León
Asturias
Cordillera Cantábrica
La Estrada
Villagarcía de Arosa
Marín
Lalín
Pontevedra
Chantada
Monforte
Sil
Miño
Ponferrada
Astorga
Mts. de León
2214
2188
2124
Redondela
Vigo
Orense
Tuy
Caminha
Lima
Minho
Viana do Castelo
Verín
1330
Chaves
Bragança
Braga
Guimarães
Póvoa de Varzim
Minho
Matosinhos
Tâmega
Vila Real
Tôrre de Moncorvo
Miranda do Douro
Porto
Vila Nova de Gaia
Douro
Lamego
São João da Madeira
Vouga
Pinhel
Aveiro
Viseu
Guarda
Coimbra
Mondego
Serra da Estrela
1991
Covilhã
Fundão
Figueira da Foz
Pombal
Zêzere
Castelo Branco
Leiria
Tomar
Caldas da Rainha
Peniche
C. Carvoeiro
Entroncamento
Tagus
Tejo
Torres Vedras
Santarém
Portalegre
Mafra
Sintra
C. da Roca
Cascais
LISBOA
Vila Franca de Xira
Montijo
Barreiro
Almada
Setúbal
C. Espichel
B. de Setúbal
Estremoz
Elvas
Évora
Viana do Alentejo
Beja
Aljustrel
C. de Sines
Sines
Guadiana
Moura
Mértola
902
Monchique
Vila do Bispo
C. de São Vicente
Lagos
Portimão
Loulé
Faro
Olhão
Tavira
Vila Real de Santo António
Algarve
Sahagún
Pisuerga
Burgos
Arlanzón
Castilla y León
Benavente
Palencia
Valladolid
Zamora
Tordesillas
Duero
Aranda de Duero
Medina del Campo
Eresma
Tormes
Vitigudino
Salamanca
Arévalo
Segovia
Sierra de Guadarrama
Puerto de Somosierra
2430
Ciudad Rodrigo
Fuentes de Oñoro
1723
Ávila
Adaja
El Escorial
Torrejón de Ardoz
MADRID
1367
Sierra de Gata
Béjar
Sierra de Gredos
2592
Pico del Moro Almanzor
Leganés
Parla
Getafe
Aranjuez
Plasencia
Coria
Alberche
Talavera de la Reina
Tiétar
Embalse de Alcántara
Navalmoral de la Mata
Tajo
Toledo
Ocaña
Orgaz
Montes de Toledo
1419
Cáceres
Valencia de Alcántara
Trujillo
Sierra de Guadalupe
1443
Pantano de Cijara
Alcázar de San Juan
Extremadura
Villanueva de la Serena
Guadiana
Daimiel
Mérida
Badajoz
Don Benito
Almadén
Ciudad Real
Almendralejo
Olivenza
Castuera
Puertollano
Valdepeñas
Zafra
Peñarroya-Pueblonuevo
Hinojosa del Duque
Pozoblanco
Jerez de los Caballeros
Fregenal de la Sierra
Azuaga
1300
Paso Despeñaperros
Barrancos
Sierra Morena
Montoro
Andújar
Linares
Aracena
Córdoba
Valverde del Camino
Lora del Río
Guadalquivir
Martos
Jaén
Baena
Montilla
Écija
Cabra
Alcaudete
Lucena
Alcalá la Real
Huelva
Ayamonte
La Palma del Condado
Sevilla
Carmona
Marchena
Puente-Genil
Dos Hermanas
Utrera
Osuna
Genil
Loja
Granada
Andalucía
Morón de la Frontera
Antequera
Lebrija
Arcos de la Frontera
Guadalete
Ronda
3478
G. de Cádiz
Sanlúcar de Barrameda
El Puerto de Santa María
Jerez de la Frontera
Cádiz
San Fernando
Chiclana de la Frontera
Medina-Sidonia
1452
Vejer de la Frontera
Coín
Málaga
Vélez Málaga
Motril
Torremolinos
Fuengirola
Marbella
Costa del Sol
C. Trafalgar
Algeciras
San Roque
La Línea de la Concepción
Gibraltar (U.K.)
Pta. de Europa
Tarifa
Str. of Gibraltar
C. Spartel
Tanger
Ceuta (Sp.)
Martil
Tétouan
Asilah
1928
Bou Hamed
Larache
Chechaouen
Jebba
2170
Al Hoceima
Ksar el Kebir
1362
10
8
6
4
42
40
38
36
ft
m
6000
2000
3000
1000
1500
500
600
200
0
0
50
100
300
200
600
500
1500
1000
3000
2000
6000
3000
9000
4000
12000
m
ft
Projection: Conical with two standard parallels

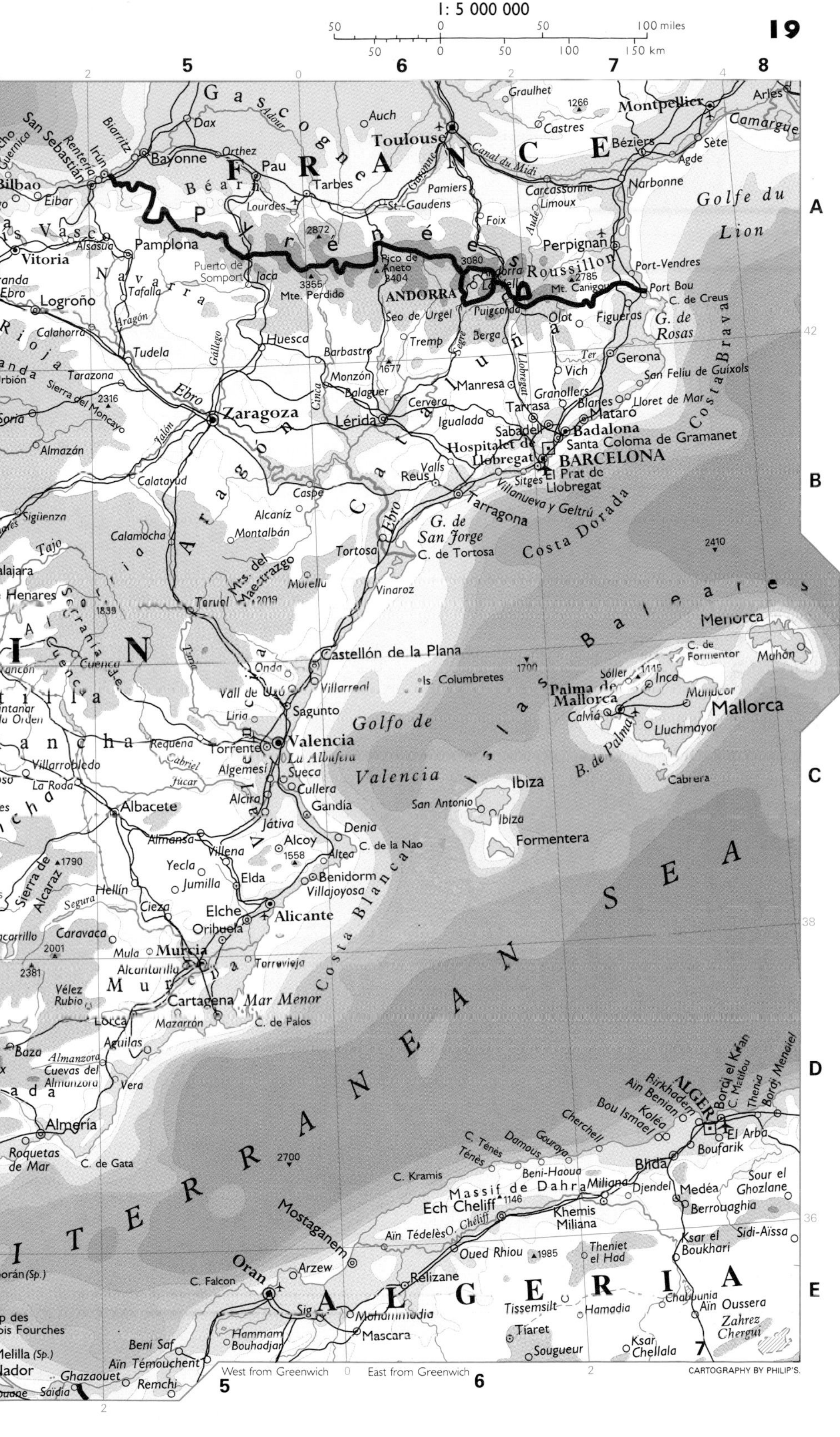
1: 5 000 000
50
0
50
100 miles
50
0
50
100
150 km
5
6
7
8
A
B
C
D
E
Gascogne
FRANCE
Toulouse
Auch
Graulhet
Castres
Montpellier
Arles
Camargue
Béziers
Sète
Agde
Narbonne
Golfe du Lion
Canal du Midi
Carcassonne
Limoux
Garonne
Adour
Dax
Biarritz
Bayonne
Orthez
Pau
Béarn
Tarbes
Lourdes
Pamiers
St.-Gaudens
Foix
Aude
Perpignan
Port-Vendres
Port Bou
Roussillon
Mt. Canigou
2785
Pyrénées
2872
3080
Pico de Aneto
3404
3355
Mte. Perdido
ANDORRA
Puerto de Somport
Jaca
Seo de Urgel
Puigcerdá
Olot
Figueras
C. de Creus
G. de Rosas
Costa Brava
San Sebastián
Rentería
Irún
Guernica
Bilbao
Eibar
Vitoria
Alsasua
Pamplona
Navarra
Tafalla
Logroño
Ebro
Rioja
Calahorra
Tudela
Aragón
Gállego
Huesca
Barbastro
Tremp
Berga
Cataluña
Ter
Gerona
Vich
1677
Segre
Llobregat
San Felíu de Guíxols
Lloret de Mar
Blanes
Granollers
Tarazona
Sierra del Moncayo
2316
Soria
Zaragoza
Cinca
Monzón
Balaguer
Lérida
Cervera
Manresa
Igualada
Tarrasa
Mataró
Sabadell
Badalona
Santa Coloma de Gramanet
Hospitalet de Llobregat
BARCELONA
El Prat de Llobregat
Almazán
Jalón
Calatayud
Caspe
Valls
Reus
Sitges
Villanueva y Geltrú
Tarragona
Costa Dorada
Sigüenza
Alcañiz
Montalbán
Calamocha
Tajo
G. de San Jorge
C. de Tortosa
Tortosa
Mts. del Maestrazgo
Morella
2019
Vinaroz
Teruel
Henares
Serranía de Cuenca
1839
2410
Baleares
Menorca
Mahón
C. de Formentor
Cuenca
Castellón de la Plana
Onda
Villarreal
Is. Columbretes
1700
Sóller
1445
Inca
Manacor
Palma de Mallorca
Mallorca
Calviá
Lluchmayor
B. de Palma
Cabrera
Vall de Uxó
Sagunto
Liria
Golfo de Valencia
Islas
Mancha
Requena
Valencia
Cabriel
Torrente
La Albufera
Algemesí
Sueca
Cullera
Júcar
Villarrobledo
La Roda
Albacete
Alcira
Gandía
Ibiza
San Antonio
Formentera
Játiva
Alcoy
Denia
C. de la Nao
1558
Altea
Almansa
Villena
Yecla
Elda
Benidorm
Villajoyosa
Jumilla
Sierra de Alcaraz
1790
Hellín
Segura
Cieza
Elche
Alicante
Orihuela
Costa Blanca
Caravaca
2001
Mula
Murcia
Torrevieja
2381
Alcantarilla
Vélez Rubio
Cartagena
Mar Menor
Lorca
Mazarrón
C. de Palos
Baza
Águilas
Almanzora
Cuevas del Almanzora
Vera
Almería
Roquetas de Mar
C. de Gata
MEDITERRANEAN SEA
2700
ALGER
Bordj el Kiffan
C. Matifou
Thenia
Bordj Menaiel
Birkhadem
Aïn Benian
Koléa
Bou Ismaël
Cherchell
Gouraya
Damous
C. Ténès
Ténès
El Arba
Boufarik
Blida
Beni-Haoua
C. Kramis
Massif de Dahra
Miliana
Djendel
Médéa
Sour el Ghozlane
Ech Cheliff
1146
Khemis Miliana
Berrouaghia
Mostaganem
Aïn Tédelès
Chéliff
Ksar el Boukhari
Sidi-Aïssa
Oued Rhiou
1985
Theniet el Had
Oran
Arzew
Relizane
C. Falcon
ALGERIA
Tissemsilt
Hamadia
Chabounia
Aïn Oussera
Sig
Mohammadia
Zahrez Chergui
Mascara
Tiaret
Hammam Bouhadjar
Beni Saf
Aïn Témouchent
Sougueur
Ksar Chellala
Melilla (Sp.)
Ghazaouet
Remchi
Saïdia
West from Greenwich
East from Greenwich
CARTOGRAPHY BY PHILIP'S.

SWITZERLAND
AUSTRIA
HUNGARY
SLOVENIA
CROATIA
BOSNIA-HERZEGOVINA
FRANCE
MONACO
SAN MARINO
VATICAN CITY
ITALIA
ADRIATIC SEA
LIGURIAN SEA
Golfo di Génova
Golfo di Venézia
Corse
TORINO (Turin)
MILANO
ROMA
Venézia (Venice)
Firenze (Florence)
Génova
Bologna
Verona
Pádova
Trieste
Ljubljana
Zagreb
Sarajevo
Split
Rijeka
Zadar
Ancona
Pescara
Rímini
Ravenna
Pisa
Livorno
Perúgia
Elba
Piemonte
Lombardia
Liguria
Toscana
Lazio
Dolomiti
Alpes Maritimes
Karnische Alpen
Velebit Planina
Dinara Planina
Dalmacija
Istra
Drava
Sava
Po
Adige
1
2
3
4
5
6
7
A
B
C
D

1: 5 000 000

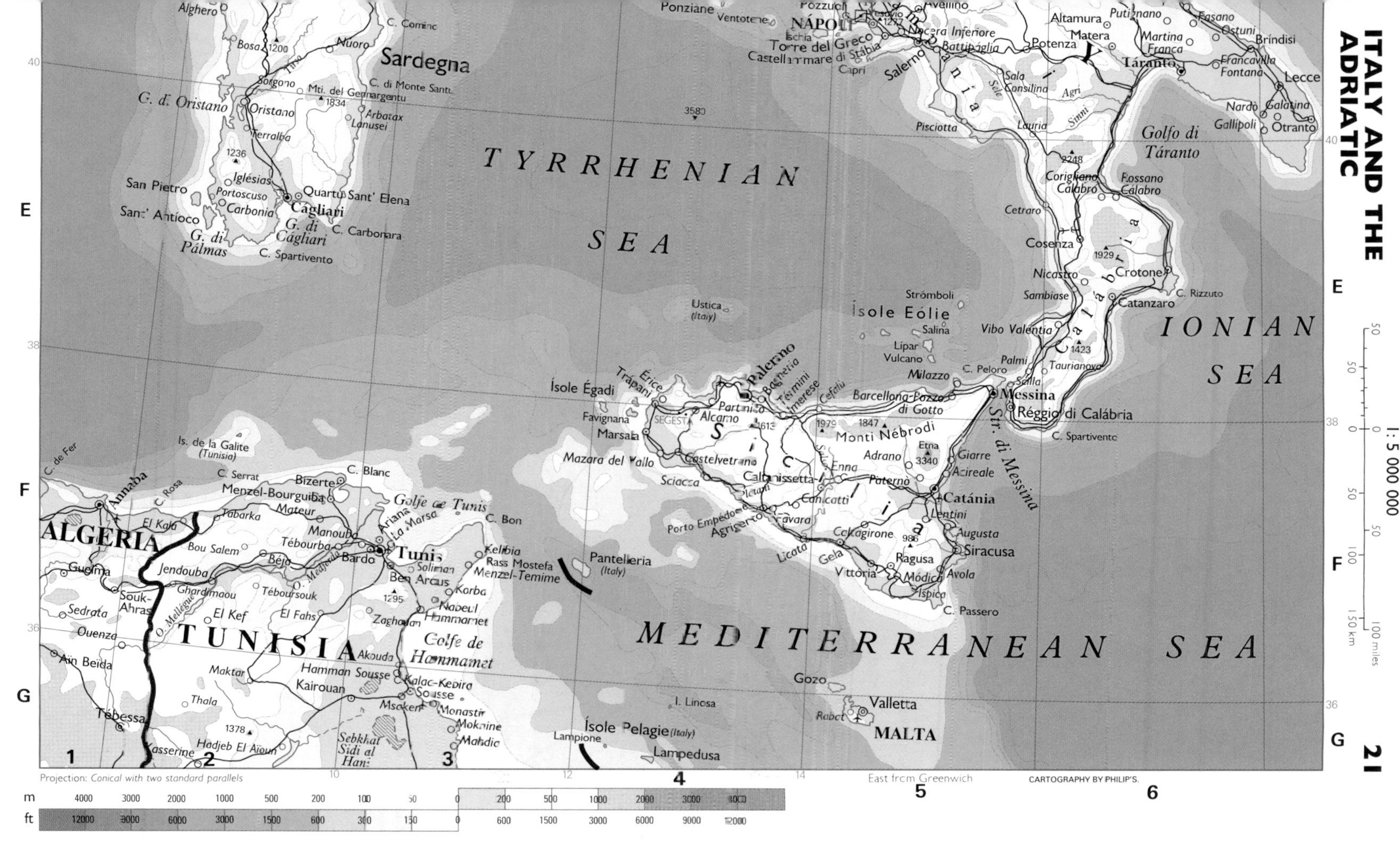
TYRRHENIAN SEA
IONIAN SEA
MEDITERRANEAN SEA
Sardegna
Sicilia
Calábria
TUNISIA
ALGERIA
MALTA
Valletta
Gozo
NÁPOLI
Palermo
Messina
Réggio di Calábria
Catánia
Siracusa
Táranto
Brindisi
Lecce
Otranto
Potenza
Cosenza
Catanzaro
Crotone
Salerno
Cágliari
Oristano
Nuoro
Alghero
Tunis
Bizerte
Sousse
Kairouan
Annaba
Ísole Eólie
Ísole Égadi
Ísole Pelagie (Italy)
Lampedusa
Pantelleria (Italy)
Ustica (Italy)
Str. di Messina
Golfo di Táranto
Golfe de Tunis
Golfe de Hammamet
Etna 3340
Trápani
Marsala
Agrigento
Caltanissetta
Ragusa
Gela
Enna
Projection: Conical with two standard parallels
East from Greenwich
CARTOGRAPHY BY PHILIP'S
m
ft

# 22 GREECE AND THE BALKANS

1: 5 000 000
50 0 50 100 miles
50 0 50 100 150 km
D E F G
1 2 3 4 5 6
ITALY
TURKEY
IONIAN SEA
MEDITERRANEAN SEA
Str. of Otranto
Thessaloníki
ATHÍNAI (Athens)
IZMIR (Smyrna)
Bursa
Balikesir
Manisa
Lárisa
Vólos
Lamía
Pátrai
Pelopónnisos
Kríti
Iráklion
Khaniá
Ródhos (Rhodes)
Kárpathos
Kásos
Kos
Sámos
Ikaría
Khíos
Lésvos
Límnos
Évvoia
Náxos
Páros
Thíra
Mílos
Kíthira
Zákinthos
Kefallinía
Levkás
Kérkira (Corfu)
Lecce
Brindisi
C. Santa Maria di Leuca
Vlóra
Korça
Kikládhes
Dhodhekánisos
Voríai Sporádhes
Projection: Conical with two standard parallels
East from Greenwich
CARTOGRAPHY BY PHILIP'S.

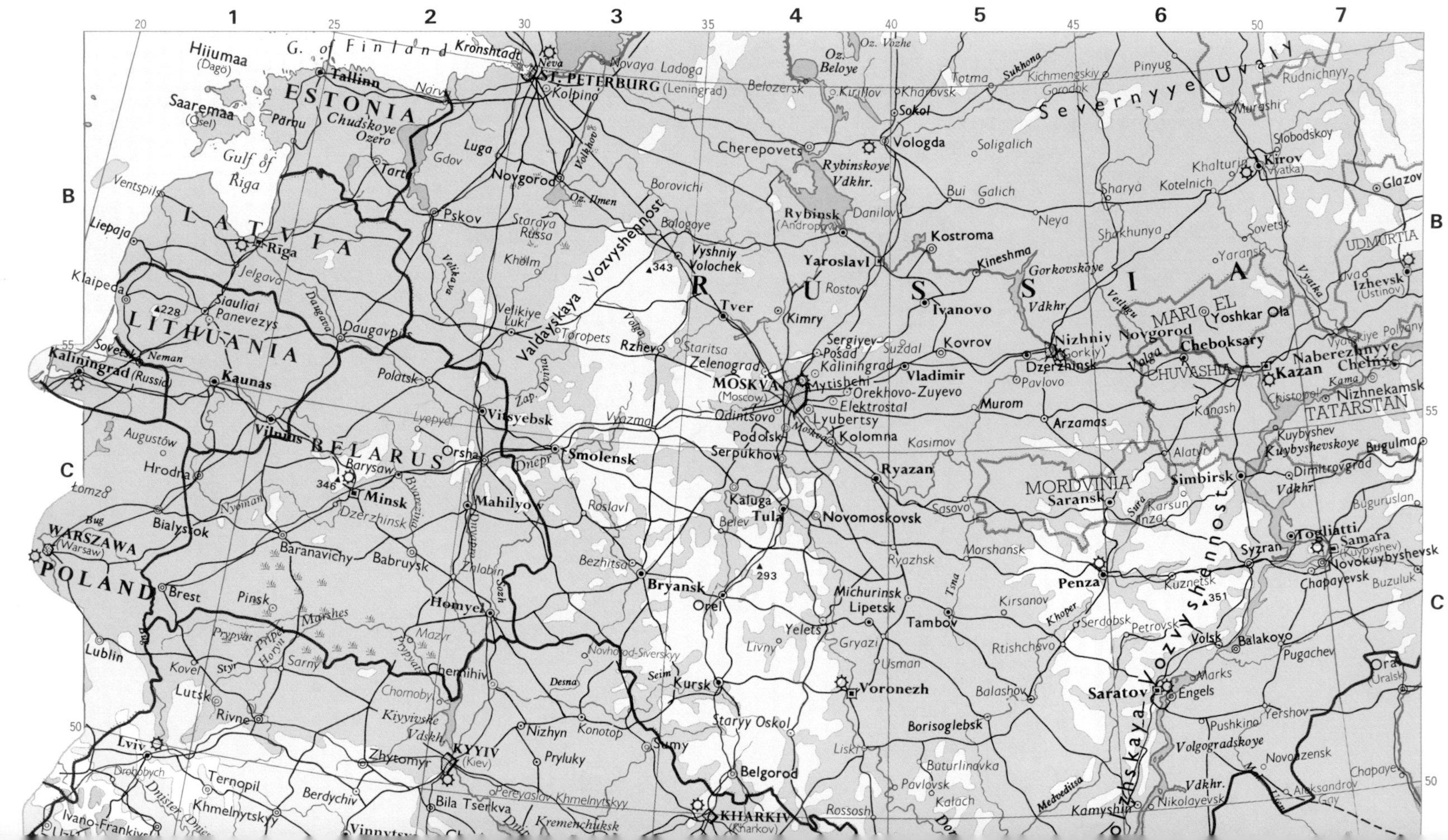

ESTONIA
LATVIA
LITHUANIA
BELARUS
POLAND
RUSSIA
UDMURTIA
MARI EL
CHUVASHIA
TATARSTAN
MORDVINIA
Severnyye Uvaly
Valdayskaya Vozvyshennost
Privolzhskaya Vozvyshennost
G. of Finland
Gulf of Riga
Hiiumaa (Dagö)
Saaremaa (Ösel)
Tallinn
Pärnu
Tartu
Chudskoye Ozero
Narva
Kronshtadt
ST. PETERBURG (Leningrad)
Kolpino
Novaya Ladoga
Oz. Ilmen
Novgorod
Luga
Gdov
Pskov
Velikaya
Riga
Jelgava
Liepaja
Ventspils
Daugavpils
Daugava
Siauliai
Panevezys
Kaunas
Klaipeda
Sovetsk
Neman
Kaliningrad (Russia)
Vilnius
Hrodna
Augustów
Łomża
Bialystok
Brest
WARSZAWA (Warsaw)
Lublin
Bug
Minsk
Barysaw
Baranavichy
Babruysk
Pinsk
Polatsk
Vitsyebsk
Orsha
Mahilyow
Homyel
Dnyapro
Sozh
Smolensk
Roslavl
Vyazma
Rzhev
Velikiye Luki
Staraya Russa
Borovichi
Bologoye
Vyshniy Volochek
Tver
Volga
Zelenograd
MOSKVA (Moscow)
Odintsovo
Podolsk
Serpukhov
Kaluga
Tula
Bryansk
Orel
Kursk
Belgorod
KHARKIV (Kharkov)
Sumy
Konotop
Chernihiv
KYYIV (Kiev)
Bila Tserkva
Zhytomyr
Rivne
Lutsk
Kovel
Ternopil
Lviv
Dnister
Khmelnytskyy
Berdychiv
Nizhyn
Pryluky
Desna
Kremenchuksk
Voronezh
Lipetsk
Yelets
Staryy Oskol
Rossosh
Borisoglebsk
Tambov
Michurinsk
Ryazan
Novomoskovsk
Kolomna
Orekhovo-Zuyevo
Elektrostal
Lyubertsy
Mytishchi
Sergiyev Posad
Vladimir
Kovrov
Ivanovo
Kostroma
Kineshma
Yaroslavl
Rybinsk (Andropov)
Rybinskoye Vdkhr.
Cherepovets
Vologda
Sokol
Oz. Beloye
Belozersk
Kirov
Kotelnich
Sharya
Nizhniy Novgorod (Gorkiy)
Dzerzhinsk
Arzamas
Murom
Saransk
Penza
Kuznetsk
Saratov
Engels
Volgogradskoye Vdkhr.
Balakovo
Volsk
Syzran
Simbirsk
Togliatti
Samara (Kuybyshev)
Novokuybyshevsk
Kazan
Cheboksary
Yoshkar Ola
Naberezhnyye Chelny
Nizhnekamsk
Izhevsk (Ustinov)
Glazov
Bugulma
Buzuluk
Uralsk
Kamyshin
Balashov
Rtishchevo
Kirsanov
Morshansk

1: 10 000 000
100 50 0 50 100 150 200 miles
100 0 100 200 300 km
1. Karachey-Cherkessia
2. Kabardino-Balkaria
3. North Ossetia
4. Ingushetia
Projection: Conical with two standard parallels
35 East from Greenwich
CARTOGRAPHY BY PHILIP'S.
m 4000 2000 1000 200 0 200 400 1000 2000 4000
ft 12 000 6000 3000 600 0 600 1200 3000 6000 12 000
UKRAINE
MOLDOVA
ROMANIA
BULGARIA
TURKEY
GEORGIA
ARMENIA
AZERBAIJAN
KAZAKSTAN
IRAN
KALMYKIA
DAGESTAN
CHECHENIA
ABKHAZIA
ADYGEA
AJARIA
CRIMEA
NAXCIVAN
BLACK SEA
Sea of Azov
CASPIAN SEA
Caucasus Mountains
Caspian Depression
Anadolu Dağları
Kuzey
Volgograd (Stalingrad)
Astrakhan
Donetsk
Rostov
Krasnodar
Sochi
Tbilisi
Yerevan
BAKI (Baku)
ISTANBUL
Ankara
BUCUREŞTI (Bucharest)
Chişinău (Kishinev)
Odesa
Sevastopol
Simferopol
Novorossiysk
Samsun
Trabzon
Erzurum
Grozny
Makhachkala
Vladikavkaz
Nalchik
Stavropol
Varna
Burgas
Constanţa
Zonguldak
Kayseri
Sivas

C
B
A
D
E
F
G
H
J
K
L
ATLANTIC OCEAN
ARCTIC
GREENLAND
ICELAND
Arctic Circle
Svalbard
Barents Sea
Novaya Zemlya
Kara Sea
UNITED KINGDOM
North Sea
NORWAY
SWEDEN
FINLAND
Murmansk
White Sea
Arkhangelsk
Vorkuta
Salekhard
Ob
Yenisei
LONDON
PARIS
FRANCE
GERMANY
Berlin
Europe
Prague
Vienna
Warsaw
ST. PETERSBURG
Nizhniy Novgorod
MOSCOW
Kazan
Perm
Yekaterinburg
Irtysh
RU
ITALY
Rome
UKRAINE
Belgrade
Odessa
Danube
Volga
Ufa
Chelyabinsk
Samara
Omsk
Don
Rostov
Volgograd
Astrakhan
Astana
Pavlodar
Karaganda
KAZAKSTAN
Mediterranean Sea
Athens
Black Sea
ISTANBUL
Bursa
Izmir
TURKEY
Ankara
Konya
Adana
GEORGIA
Tbilisi
Yerevan
ARMENIA
AZERBAIJAN
Baku
Caspian Sea
Aral Sea
Syrdarya
L. Balkhash
UZBEKISTAN
Tashkent
Alma Ata
Bishkek
KYRGYZSTAN
Nicosia
CYPRUS
Beirut
LEBANON
Aleppo
SYRIA
Euphrates
Mosul
Tabriz
TURKMENISTAN
Ashkhabad
Samarkand
TAJIKISTAN
Dushanbe
Kashi
Alexandria
ISRAEL
Damascus
'Ammān
Jerusalem
JORDAN
LIBYA
CAIRO
Suez
EGYPT
Nile
IRAQ
Baghdād
Tigris
Basra
Mashhad
TEHRĀN
IRAN
Eşfahān
Herāt
Kābul
AFGHANISTAN
Qandahār
Islamabad
JAMMU & KASHMIR
Hotan
Aswân
KUWAIT
Kuwait
Shīrāz
Zāhedān
Faisalabad
Lahore
SAUDI ARABIA
Red Sea
Medina
Riyadh
BAHRAIN
The Gulf
Al Manāmah
QATAR
Doha
UNITED ARAB EMIRATES
Abu Dhabi
G. of Oman
Muscat
PAKISTAN
Indus
KARACHI
DELHI
New Delhi
Jaipur
Lucknow
Kanpur
Varanasi
INDIA
Jedda
Mecca
Port Sudan
SUDAN
Khartoum
ERITREA
Sana'
YEMEN
Aden
G. of Aden
OMAN
Ahmadabad
Vadodara
Bhopal
Indore
Surat
Nagpur
MUMBAI (Bombay)
Pune
Hyderabad
DJIBOUTI
Arabian Sea
Socotra (Yemen)
Addis Ababa
ETHIOPIA
SOMALI REP.
Africa
Bangalore
CHENNAI (Madras)
UGANDA
L. Victoria
KENYA
Lakshadweep Is. (India)
Madurai
SRI
Colombo
CONGO (DEM. REP. OF THE)
Mogadishu
Nairobi
Equator
INDIAN OCEAN
MALDIVES
Male
TANZANIA
Mombasa
Dar es Salaam
SEYCHELLES
Victoria
ZAMBIA
MALAWI
Aldabra Is. (Seychelles)
Amirante Is. (Seychelles)
Chagos Arch. (U.K.)
Projection: Bonne
East from Greenwich
Hanoi ● Capital Cities
6
7
8
9
10
11

1: 67 000 000

OCEAN
Laptev Sea
New Siberian Is.
Wrangel I.
ALASKA (U.S.A.)
Bering Sea
Aleutian Is. (U.S.A.)
Khatanga
Verkhoyansk
Gizhiga
Magadan
Okhotsk
Petropavlovsk-Kamchatskiy
Sea of Okhotsk
Yakutsk
Lena
S I A
Sakhalin
Kuril Is.
Komsomolsk
Yuzhno-Sakhalinsk
Khabarovsk
Angara
Krasnoyarsk
Bratsk
L. Baikal
Chita
Novokuznetsk
Irkutsk
Ulan Ude
Amur
Blagoveshchensk
Hailar
Qiqihar
Harbin
Changchun
Jilin
Vladivostok
Hokkaido
Sapporo
Honshū
OCEAN
MONGOLIA
Ulan Bator
Sea of Japan
NORTH KOREA
P'yongyang
SEOUL
SOUTH KOREA
Pusan
TŌKYŌ
Yokohama
JAPAN
Kyōto
Nagoya
Ōsaka
Hiroshima
Kyūshū
Bonin Is. (Japan)
SHENYANG
Anshan
Jinzhou
Dalian
BEIJING
TIANJIN
Taiyuan
Jinan
Baotou
Ürümqi
Hami
Yumen
Lanzhou
Hwang-ho
Xi'an
Yellow Sea
SHANGHAI
Nanjing
East China Sea
Ryukyu Is.
Volcano Is. (Japan)
Tropic of Cancer
PACIFIC
CHINA
Wuhan
HANGZHOU
Nanchang
Fuzhou
Taipei
TAIWAN
Chengdu
CHONGQING
Yangtze
Changsha
Lhasa
Thimphu
BHUTAN
Brahmaputra
Kunming
GUANGZHOU
Si Kiang
HONG KONG
Macau
GUAM (U.S.A.)
Ganges
BANGLADESH
DACCA
Patna
Chittagong
BURMA (MYANMAR)
Hanoi
Haiphong
Hainan
Luzon
PHILIPPINES
FED. STATES OF MICRONESIA
PALAU
MANILA
LAOS
Vientiane
Mekong
VIETNAM
Irrawaddy
Salween
Bay of Bengal
Rangoon
THAILAND
BANGKOK
CAMBODIA
Phnom Penh
Ho Chi Minh City
South China Sea
Cebu
Mindanao
Davao
Palawan
Sulu Sea
Zamboanga
Andaman Is. (India)
G. of Thailand
BRUNEI
SABAH
Bandar Seri Begawan
Celebes Sea
Manado
Halmahera
IRIAN JAYA
Nicobar Is. (India)
PEN. MALAYSIA
Str. of Malacca
Kuala Lumpur
MALAYSIA
SARAWAK
Ceram
Ambon
Medan
SINGAPORE
Borneo
Celebes
Banda Sea
Sumatra
Banjarmasin
Ujung Pandang
Arafura Sea
INDONESIA
Palembang
Java Sea
Semarang
Surabaya
Flores
Timor
JAKARTA
Bandung
Java
Sumba
Timor Sea
AUSTRALIA
CARTOGRAPHY BY PHILIP'S.

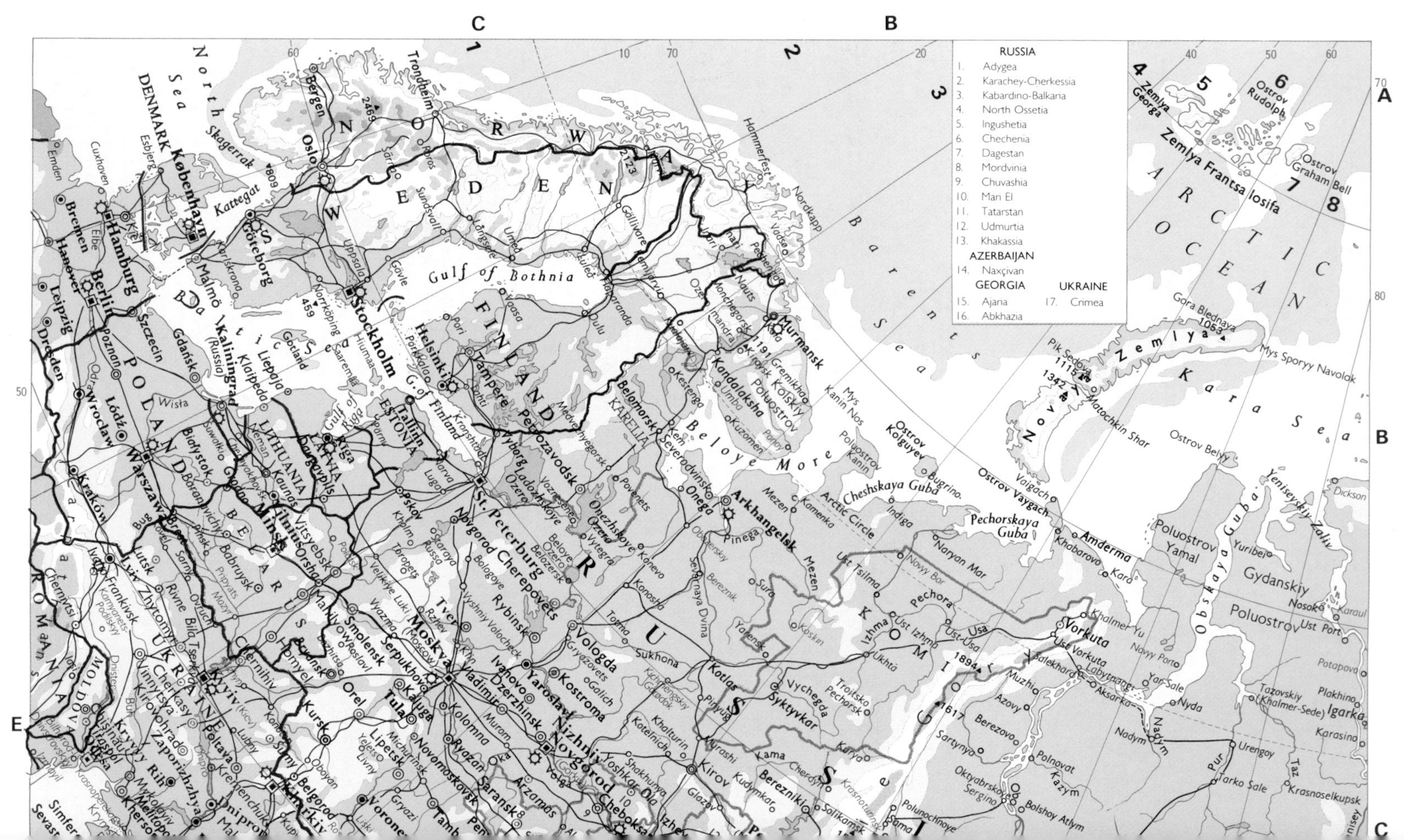
RUSSIA
1. Adygea
2. Karachey-Cherkessia
3. Kabardino-Balkaria
4. North Ossetia
5. Ingushetia
6. Chechenia
7. Dagestan
8. Mordvinia
9. Chuvashia
10. Mari El
11. Tatarstan
12. Udmurtia
13. Khakassia
AZERBAIJAN
14. Naxçivan
GEORGIA
15. Ajaria
16. Abkhazia
UKRAINE
17. Crimea
ARCTIC OCEAN
Barents Sea
Kara Sea
Zemlya Frantsa Iosifa
Novaya Zemlya
Beloye More
Gulf of Bothnia
G. of Finland
Gulf of Riga
Baltic Sea
North Sea
Skagerrak
Kattegat
NORWAY
SWEDEN
FINLAND
KARELIA
ESTONIA
LATVIA
LITHUANIA
BELARUS
POLAND
UKRAINE
MOLDOVA
ROMANIA
DENMARK
RUSSIA
KOMI
Arctic Circle
Murmansk
Arkhangelsk
St. Peterburg
Moskva (Moscow)
Helsinki
Stockholm
Oslo
København
Berlin
Hamburg
Warszawa
Kyyiv (Kiev)
Minsk
Riga
Tallinn
Vilnius
Kaliningrad (Russia)
Nizhniy Novgorod
Vorkuta
Kirov
Syktyvkar
Kotlas
Vologda
Yaroslavl
Kostroma
Tver
Smolensk
Kursk
Orel
Tula
Kaluga
Ryazan
Saransk
Lipetsk
Belgorod
Kharkiv
Poltava
Zaporizhzhya
Amderma
Naryan Mar
Nadym
Urengoy
Igarka

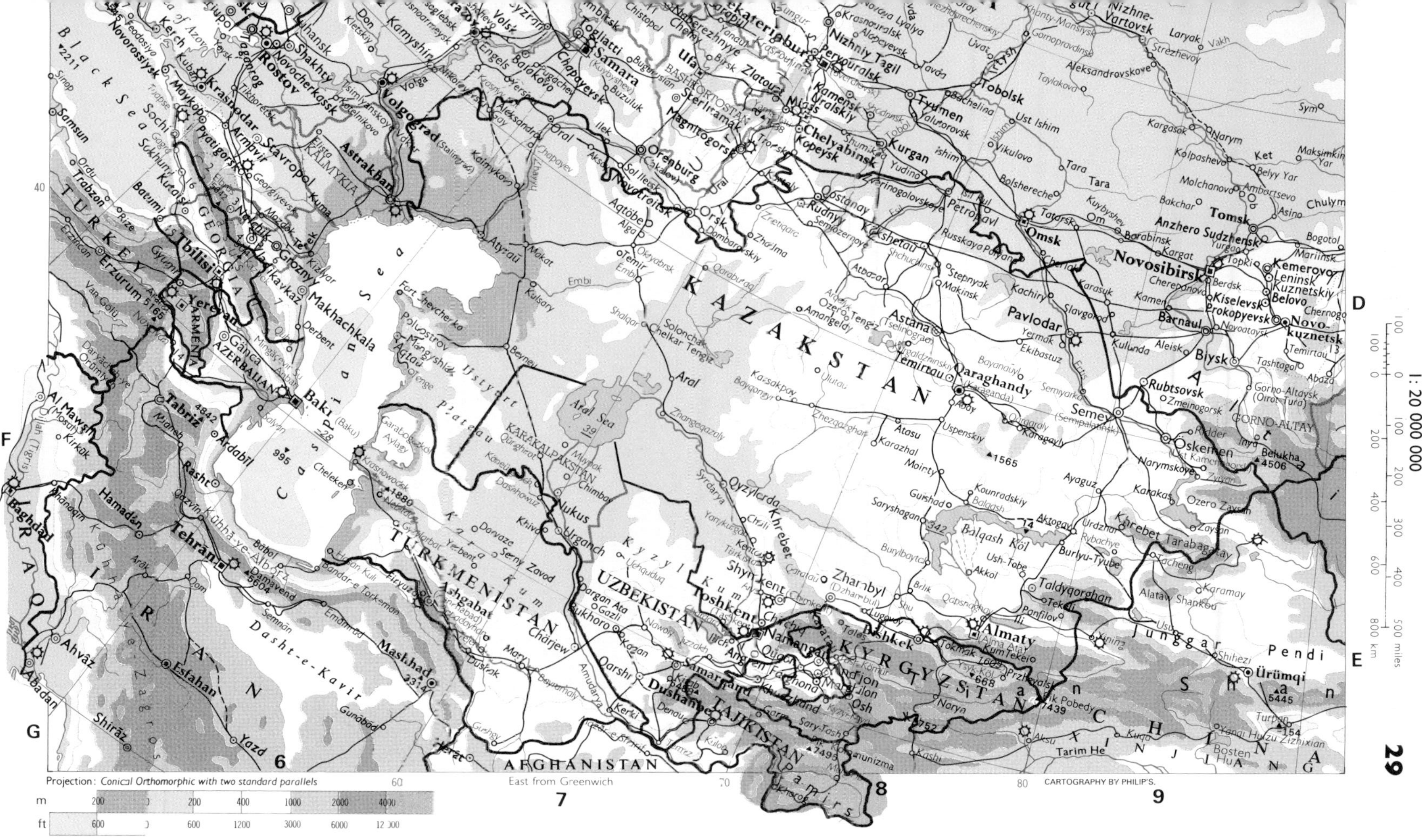


1: 20 000 000

100 0 100 200 300 400 500 miles

100 0 200 400 600 800 km

# 30 EASTERN SIBERIA

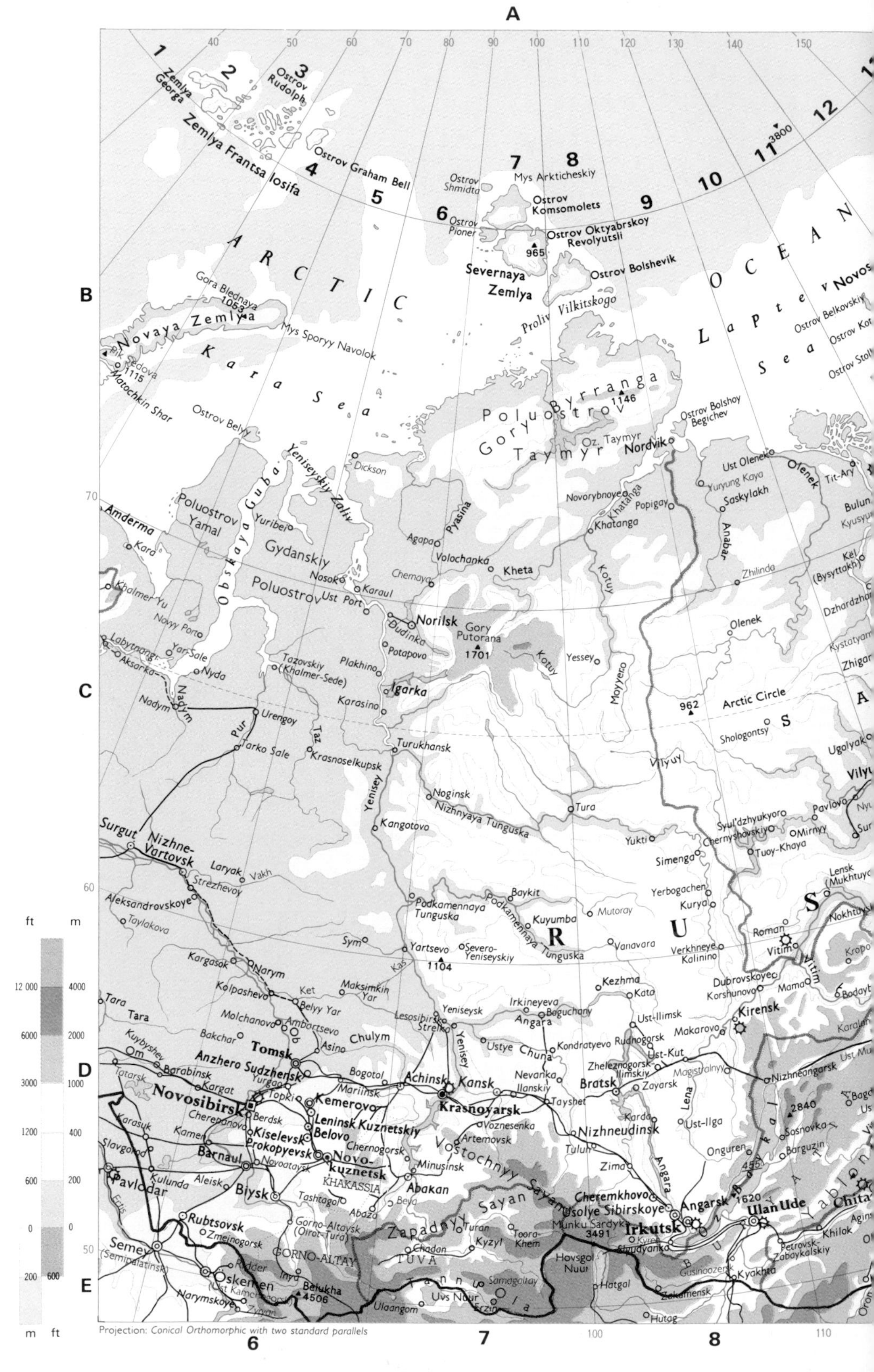

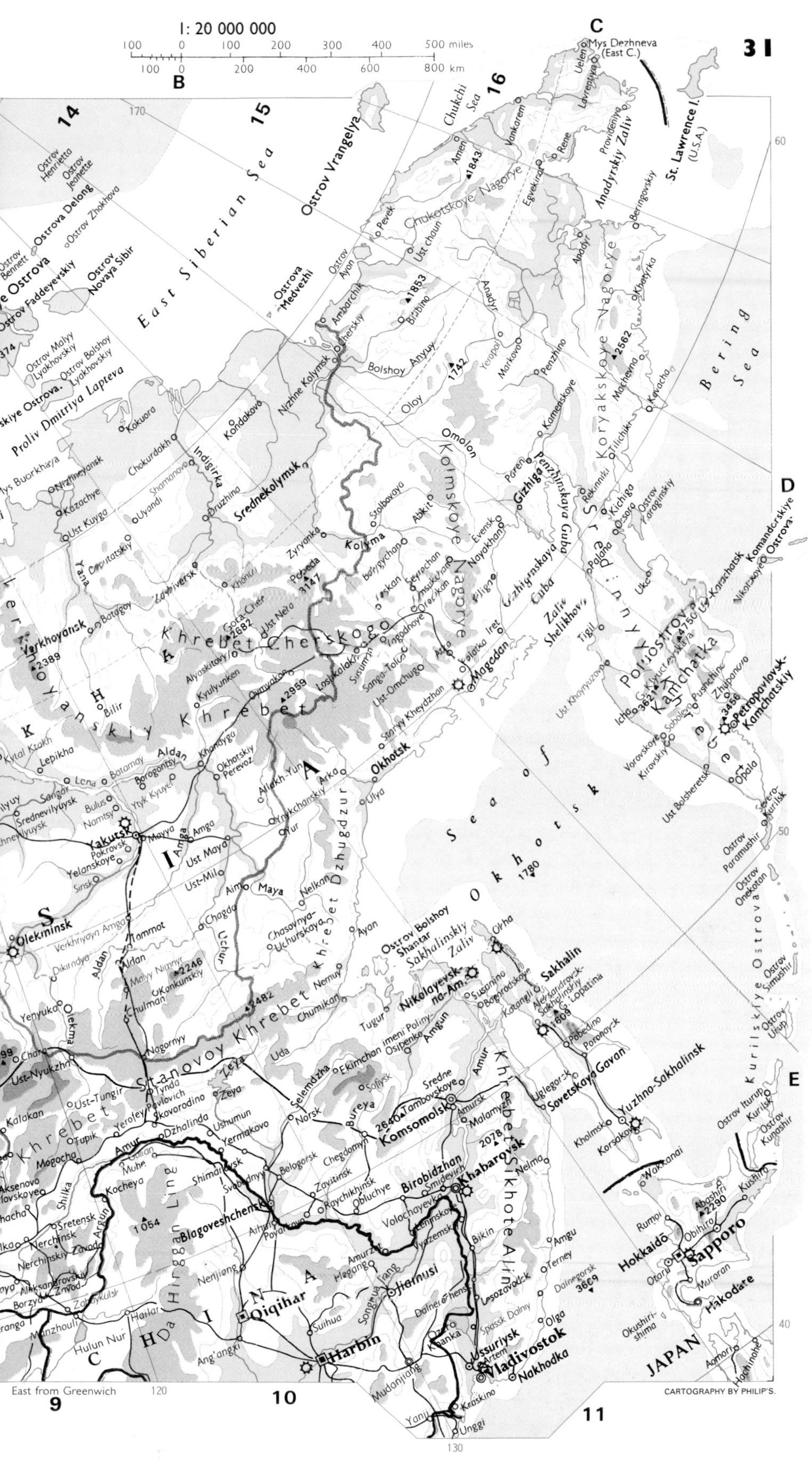


CARTOGRAPHY BY PHILIP'S.

## SOUTHERN HONSHU, KYUSHU AND SHIKOKU

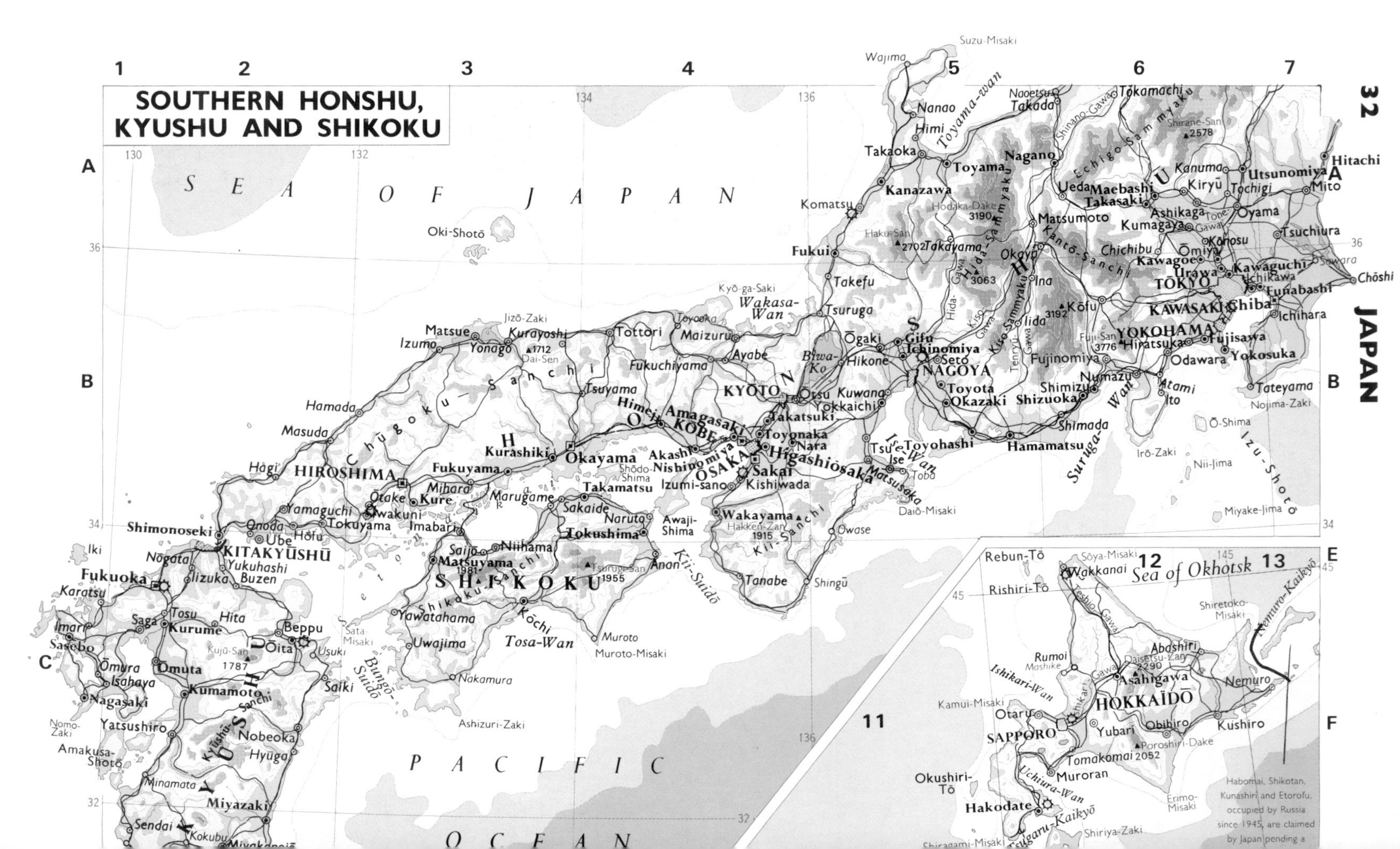

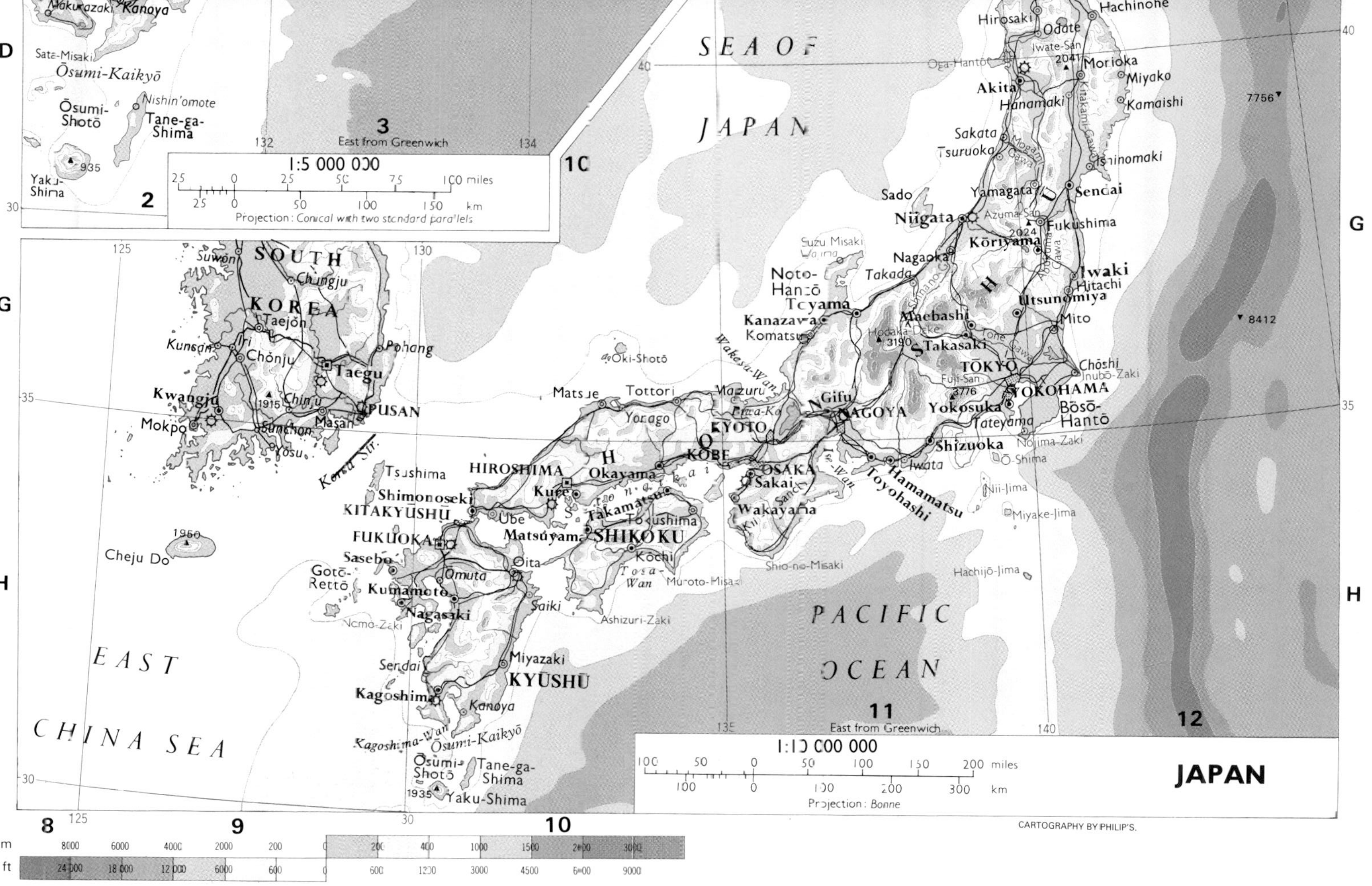
JAPAN
SEA OF JAPAN
PACIFIC OCEAN
EAST CHINA SEA
SOUTH KOREA
HONSHU
SHIKOKU
KYŪSHŪ
TŌKYŌ
YOKOHAMA
NAGOYA
KYOTO
OSAKA
KOBE
HIROSHIMA
KITAKYŪSHŪ
FUKUOKA
PUSAN
Hachinohe
Hirosaki
Odate
Morioka
Miyako
Kamaishi
Akita
Hanamaki
Sakata
Tsuruoka
Ishinomaki
Sendai
Yamagata
Fukushima
Niigata
Sado
Kōriyama
Nagaoka
Takada
Iwaki
Hitachi
Utsunomiya
Mito
Noto-Hantō
Toyama
Kanazawa
Komatsu
Maebashi
Takasaki
Chōshi
Inubō-Zaki
Yokosuka
Bōsō-Hantō
Tateyama
Nojima-Zaki
Shizuoka
Ō-Shima
Nii-Jima
Miyake-Jima
Hachijō-Jima
Iwata
Hamamatsu
Toyohashi
Gifu
Ise-Wan
Sakai
Wakayama
Shio-no-Misaki
Wakasa-Wan
Maizuru
Tottori
Yonago
Matsue
Oki-Shotō
Okayama
Kure
Takamatsu
Tokushima
Matsuyama
Kōchi
Tosa-Wan
Muroto-Misaki
Ashizuri-Zaki
Ube
Shimonoseki
Tsushima
Korea Str.
Ōita
Saiki
Sasebo
Gotō-Rettō
Kumamoto
Omuta
Nagasaki
Nomo-Zaki
Miyazaki
Sendai
Kagoshima
Kanoya
Kagoshima-Wan
Ōsumi-Kaikyō
Ōsumi-Shotō
Tane-ga-Shima
Yaku-Shima
Suwon
Chŏngju
Taejŏn
Kunsan
Iri
Chŏnju
Taegu
Pohang
Kwangju
Chinju
Masan
Mokpo
Sunchon
Yŏsu
Cheju Do
Makurazaki
Sata-Misaki
Nishin'omote
1:5 000 000
Projection: Conical with two standard parallels
1:10 000 000
East from Greenwich
Projection: Bonne
miles
km
m
ft
CARTOGRAPHY BY PHILIP'S

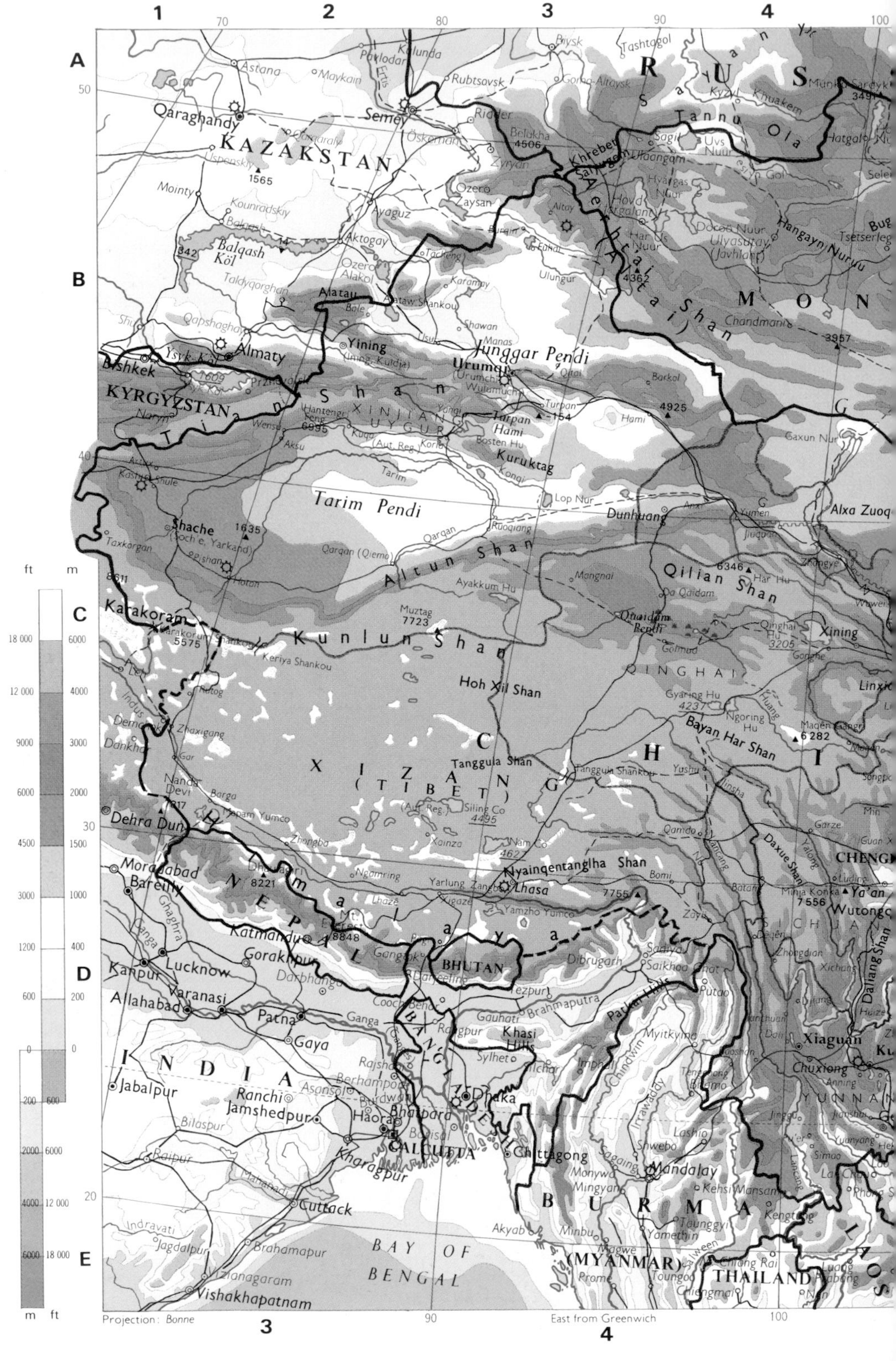

KAZAKSTAN
Astana
Qaraghandy
Pavlodar
Kulunda
Maykain
Semey
Rubtsovsk
Biysk
Tashtagol
Gorno-Altaysk
Ridder
Öskemen
Qarqaraly
Uspenskiy
1565
Mointy
Kounradskiy
Balqash
Balqash Köl
342
Ayaguz
Aktogay
Ozero Alakol
Zyryan
Ozero Zaysan
Taldyqorghan
Alatau
Qapshaghay
Almaty
Bishkek
Ysyk-Köl
1609
Przhevalsk
KYRGYZSTAN
Naryn
Tian Shan
Yining
Bole
Alataw Shankou
Karamay
Tacheng
Shawan
Manas
Urumqi
Junggar Pendi
Qitai
Turpan
Tarpan Hami
-154
Hantengri Feng
6995
XINJIANG UYGUR (Aut. Reg.)
Kuqa
Korla
Aksu
Bosten Hu
Kuruktag
Kongi
Tarim
Tarim Pendi
Lop Nur
Kashi
Shule
Artux
Shache (Soch'e, Yarkand)
1635
Taxkorgan
Pishan
Hotan
Qarqan
Qarqan (Qiemo)
Ruoqiang
Altun Shan
Ayakkum Hu
Muztag
7723
8611
Karakoram
Karakorum Shankou
5575
Kunlun Shan
Keriya Shankou
Hoh Xil Shan
Leh
Rutog
Indus
Demchok
Zhaxigang
Gar
Nanda Devi
7817
Barga
Mapam Yumco
Dehra Dun
XIZANG (TIBET) (Aut. Reg.)
CHINA
Tanggula Shan
Tanggula Shankou
Siling Co
4495
Nam Co
4627
Xainza
Zhongba
Ngamring
Nyainqentanglha Shan
Lhasa
Yarlung Zangbo
Xigaze
Yamzho Yumco
Lhazê
Dhaulagiri
8221
Mt. Everest
8848
Himalaya
NEPAL
Katmandu
Gangtok
Darjeeling
BHUTAN
7755
Moradabad
Bareilly
Ghaghra
Ganga
Lucknow
Kanpur
Gorakhpur
Darbhanga
Allahabad
Varanasi
Patna
Gaya
Cooch Behar
Rangpur
BANGLADESH
Rajshahi
Berhampore
Asansol
Ranchi
Jamshedpur
Burdwan
Haora
Bhatpara
CALCUTTA
Barisal
Dhaka
Kharagpur
Jabalpur
INDIA
Bilaspur
Raipur
Mahanadi
Cuttack
Indravati
Jagdalpur
Brahamapur
Vizianagaram
Vishakhapatnam
BAY OF BENGAL
Gauhati
Brahmaputra
Tezpur
Dibrugarh
Sadiya
Saikhoa Ghat
Khasi Hills
Sylhet
Silchar
Imphal
Patkai Hills
Putao
Myitkyina
Chindwin
Irrawaddy
Chittagong
Akyab
Bhamo
Lashio
Shwebo
Monywa
Sagaing
Mandalay
Mingyan
Minbu
Magwe
Yamethin
Taunggyi
Kehsi Mansam
BURMA (MYANMAR)
Prome
Toungoo
Chiengmai
Chiang Rai
THAILAND
Kengtung
Luang Prabang
LAOS
RUSSIA
Sayan
Kyzyl
Tannu Ola
Khuakem
Mönh Sarıdag
3491
Hatgal
Selenge
Belukha
4506
Khrebet Saylyugem
Sagil
Uvs Nuur
Ulaangom
Hyargas Nuur
Hovd
Jargalant
Har Us Nuur
Altay
Altai Shan
Burqin
Fuhai
Ulungur
4362
Dzavhan Gol
Ulyasutay (Javhlant)
Hangayn Nuruu
Tsetserleg
MONGOLIA
Chandmani
3957
Barkol
4925
Hami
Gaxun Nur
Dunhuang
Yumen
Jiuquan
Alxa Zuoqi
Anxi
Mangnai
6346
Qilian Shan
Zhangye
Da Qaidam
Qaidam Pendi
Wuwei
Qinghai Hu
3205
Xining
Golmud
QINGHAI
Gonghe
Linxia
Gyaring Hu
4237
Ngoring Hu
Huang
Bayan Har Shan
Maqên Gangri
6282
Yushu
Jinsha
Songpan
Qamdo
Garze
Min
Lancang
Daxue Shan
Yalong
CHENGDU
Bomi
Batang
Minya Konka
7556
Ya'an
Wutongqiao
Luding
SICHUAN
Zayü
Dêqên
Zhongdian
Xichang
Dalliang Shan
Huize
Dali
Xiaguan
Chuxiong
Kunming
Anning
Tengchong
YUNNAN
Jinggu
Jianshui
Yuanyang
Simao
Lai Chau
Phong Saly
Lancang
70
80
90
100
50
40
30
20
1
2
3
4
A
B
C
D
E
ft
m
18 000
12 000
9000
6000
4500
3000
1200
600
0
6000
4000
3000
2000
1500
1000
400
200
0
200
600
2000
6000
4000
12 000
6000
18 000
Projection: Bonne
East from Greenwich

1: 20 000 000
100 0 100 200 300 400 500 miles
100 0 200 400 600 800 km
5
6
7
8
110
120
130
A
B
C
D
E
Cheremkhovo
Angarsk
Ozero Baykal
Bukachacha
Sretensk
Ulan Ude
Chita
Shilka
Nerchinsk
Khilok
Yablonovyy Khrebet
Babushkin
Kyakhta
Olovyannaya
Borzya
Argun
Yilehuli Shan
Heilong
Amur
Shimanovsk
Svobodnyy
Bureya
Chegdomyn
2640
Blagoveshchensk
Obluchye
Birobidzhan
Khabarovsk
Leninskoye
Xiao Hinggan Ling
Manzhouli
Hailar
Hulun Nur
Buir Nur
Nenjiang
Bei'an
Butha Qi
HEILONGJIANG
Qiqihar
Hailun
Yichun
Hegang
Jiamusi
Shuangyashan
Dalnerechensk
Altanbulag
Hentiyn Nuruu
Bulgan
Ulaanbaatar
(Ulan Bator)
Kerulen
Choybalsan
Ondorhaan
Matad
Dzuunmod
Arxan
Solon
Horqin Youyi Qianqi
Suihua
HARBIN
Mudanjiang
O L I A
Huld
Saynshand
Dzamin Üüd
Erenhot
Dalandzadgad
1949
Da Hinggan Ling
Tao'an
Da'an
Changchun
Jilin
Ussuriysk
Vladivostok
Artem
Tongliao
Siping
Liaoyuan
Yanji
Hailong
Najin
Chongjin
2744
Fuxin
Fushun
SHENYANG
Benxi
Tonghua
Liaoyang
Anshan
Dandong
NORTH
Jinzhou
Chengde
Yingkou
Qinhuangdao
Hamhung
Hungnam
Sonid Youqi
Bayan Obo
NEI MONGOL
Hohhot
Jining
Zhangjiakou
Xuanhua
BAOTOU
Datong
BEIJING
(Peking)
Tong Xian
Tangshan
Liaodong Wan
Korea Bay
Sinuiju
Anju
KOREA
P'yongyang
Wonsan
Mu Us Shamo
3015
2834
Shijiazhuang
Baoding
TIANJIN
(Tientsin)
Hangu
DALIAN
Bo Hai
Yantai
SOUL
SOUTH KOREA
Inch'on
Taejon
Andong
Kunsan
Kwangju
Mokpo
Taegu
Pusan
Masan
Tsushima
TAIYUAN
Yangquan
Yuci
Xingtai
Handan
Anyang
Bozhen
Zibo
Jinan
Weifang
QINGDAO
SHANDONG
Boshan
Linyi
YELLOW SEA
Wuzhong
Linyi
Tongchuan
Pingliang
Tianshui
Baoji
Dali
XI'AN
4107
Xinxiang
Jiaozuo
Jining
Yanzhou
Kaifeng
Zhengzhou
Shangqiu
Xuzhou
Lianyungang
Huai'an
JIANGSU
Luoyang
Xuchang
HENAN
Shangshui
Nanyang
Huainan
Bengbu
Cheju
Cheju Do
1950
Fukuoka
Sasebo
Nagasaki
Korea Str.
JAPAN
Hanzhong
Ankang
Zhumadian
NANJING
Zhenjiang
Changzhou
Daba Shan
Xiangfan
Xinyang
Hefei
Ma'anshan
Wuxi
Suzhou
SHANGHAI
Chang
Nanchong
Fengjie
Yichang
HUBEI
WUHAN
ANHUI
Anqing
Wuhu
Jiaxing
Hangzhou
Shaoxing
Ningbo
Wanxian
Shashi
Huangshi
Jiujiang
Tunxi
Jingdezhen
ZHEJIANG
EAST CHINA SEA
Beibei
CHONGQING
Zigong
Luzhou
Dongting Hu
Nanchang
Poyang Hu
Qu Xian
Changde
Yiyang
Changsha
Shangrao
Wenzhou
Xiangtan
Zhuzhou
Fuzhou
2120
Ryukyu-Retto
Okinawa
750
Zunyi
HUNAN
Shaoyang
Hengyang
JIANGXI
Ji'an
Nanping
Fuzhou
GUIZHOU
Guiyang
Zhenyuan
Wuyi Shan
FUJIAN
Anshun
Duyun
Ganzhou
Quanzhou
Taibei
(Taipei)
Jilong
Xinzhu
Yilan
Miaoli
Taizhong
Guilin
Shaoguan
Zhangzhou
Xiamen
Zhanghua
Jiayi
TAIWAN
Sakishima-Gunto
Tropic of Cancer
Liuzhou
Mei Xian
GUANGDONG
Chao'an
Shantou
Yu Shan
3950
GUANGXI
ZHUANGZU
Wuzhou
Sanshui
GUANGZHOU
(Canton)
Tainan
Taidong
Nanning
Foshan
Jiangmen
Gaoxiong
Pingdong
Pingxiang
Lang Son
(Aut.Reg.)
Qinzhou
Beihai
Macau
Kowloon
Hong Kong
Bashi Channel
Batan Is.
HANOI
G. of Tonkin
Haiphong
Zhanjiang
SOUTH CHINA SEA
Nam Dinh
Ninh Binh
Thanh Hoa
Vinh
VIETNAM
Leizhou Bandao
Haikou
Hainan Dao
Wuzhi Shan
1867
HAINAN
Huangliu
PHILIPPINES
Luzon
Laoag
40
30
20
5
6
7
CARTOGRAPHY BY PHILIP'S.

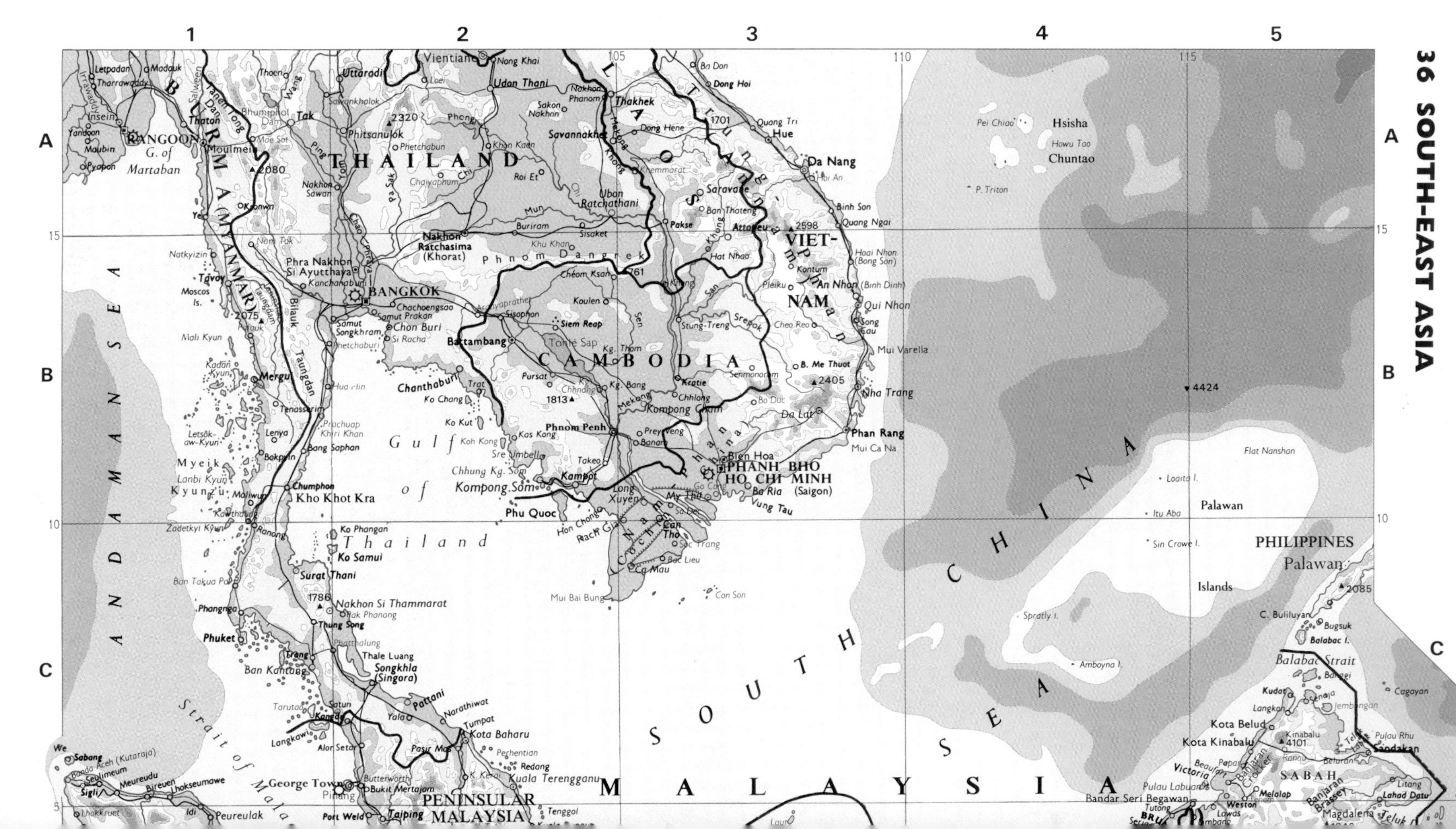

1
2
3
4
5
A
B
C
THAILAND
LAOS
CAMBODIA
VIET-NAM
BURMA (MYANMAR)
PHILIPPINES
SABAH
PENINSULAR MALAYSIA
MALAYSIA
SOUTH CHINA SEA
ANDAMAN SEA
Gulf of Thailand
G. of Martaban
Strait of Mala
Palawan
Palawan
Islands
Hsisha
Howu Tao
Chuntao
Pei Chiao
P. Triton
Flat Nanshan
Loaita I.
Itu Aba
Sin Crowe I.
Spratly I.
Amboyna I.
BANGKOK
RANGOON
Moulmein
Phnom Penh
PHANH BHO HO CHI MINH (Saigon)
Vientiane
Nong Khai
Udon Thani
Da Nang
Hue
Quang Tri
Dong Hoi
Ba Don
Binh Son
Quang Ngai
Qui Nhon
Nha Trang
Phan Rang
Mui Ca Na
Mui Varella
Da Lat
Bien Hoa
Vung Tau
Ba Ria
Phu Quoc
Kompong Som
Kampot
Battambang
Siem Reap
Tonle Sap
Kompong Cham
Kratie
Stung-Treng
Pakse
Saravane
Attopeu
Savannakhet
Thakhek
Nakhon Phanom
Sakon Nakhon
Khon Kaen
Roi Et
Ubon Ratchathani
Nakhon Ratchasima (Khorat)
Buriram
Sisaket
Phnom Dangrek
Phitsanulok
Uttaradit
Tak
Nakhon Sawan
Phra Nakhon Si Ayutthaya
Kanchanaburi
Chon Buri
Si Racha
Chanthaburi
Trat
Ko Chang
Ko Kut
Tavoy
Mergui
Ye
Thaton
Chumphon
Kho Khot Kra
Ranong
Surat Thani
Ko Samui
Ko Phangan
Nakhon Si Thammarat
Songkhla (Singora)
Phuket
Phangnga
Trang
Pattani
Narathiwat
Kota Baharu
Kuala Terengganu
George Town
Butterworth
Taiping
Port Weld
Kota Kinabalu
Kota Belud
Sandakan
Bandar Seri Begawan
Balabac Strait
Balabac I.
C. Buliluyan
Victoria
Mui Bai Bung
Con Son
Can Tho
Ca Mau
Long Xuyen
My Tho
Sabang
Banda Aceh (Kutaraja)
Sigli
Lhokseumawe
Langkawi
Lanbi Kyun
Myeik Kyunzu
Zadetkyi Kyun
Moscos Is.
Mali Kyun
Natkyizin

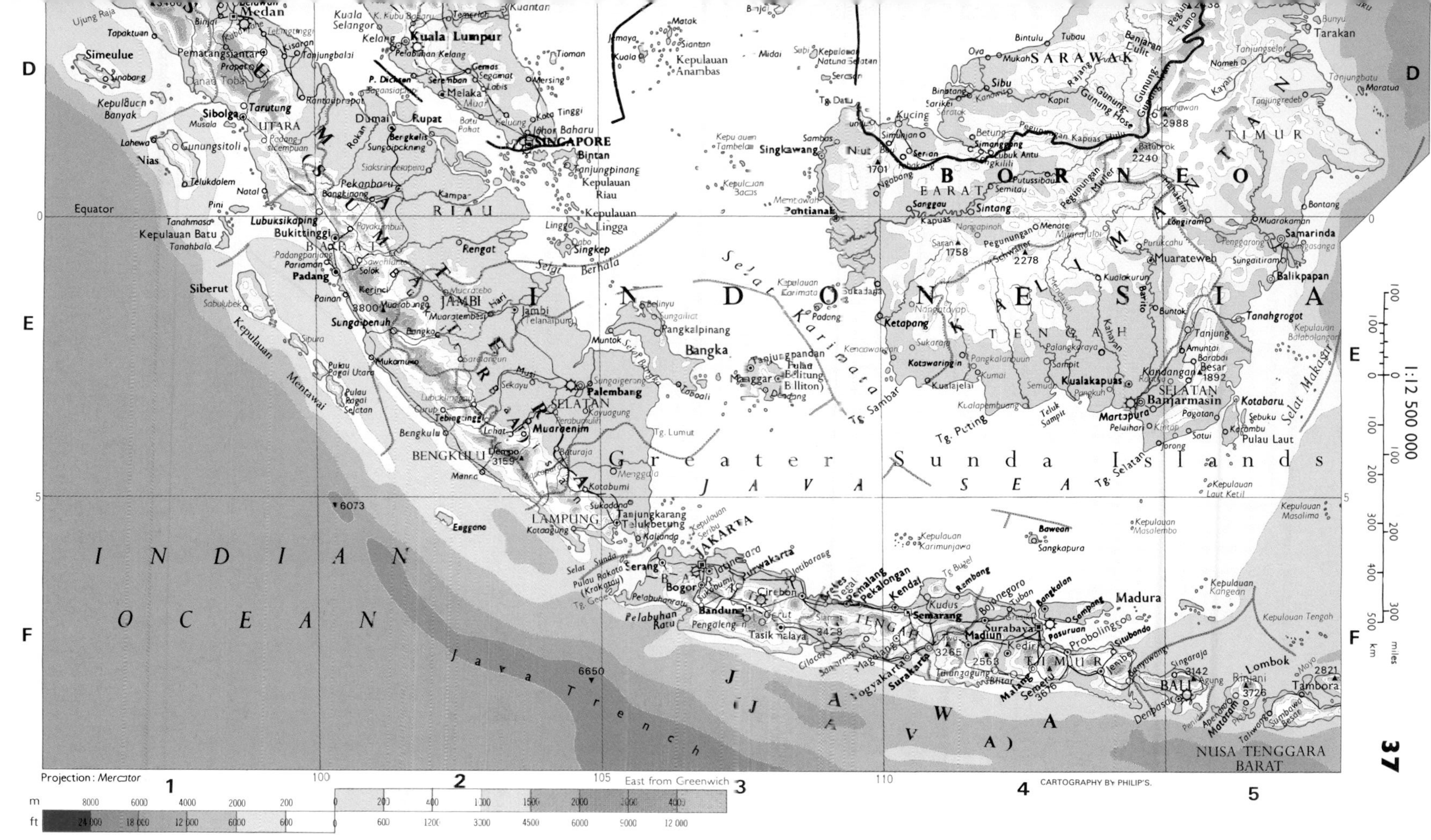
1:12 500 000
INDIAN OCEAN
Java Trench
Greater Sunda Islands
JAVA SEA
INDONESIA
SUMATERA
BORNEO
KALIMANTAN
SARAWAK
JAWA
Selat Karimata
Selat Makasar
Equator
Medan
Kuala Lumpur
SINGAPORE
Padang
Palembang
Pontianak
Banjarmasin
Balikpapan
Samarinda
JAKARTA
Bandung
Semarang
Surabaya
Yogyakarta
Surakarta
Malang
Bali
Lombok
Madura
Bangka
Belitung
Siberut
Nias
Simeulue
Kepulauan Riau
Kepulauan Anambas
NUSA TENGGARA BARAT
East from Greenwich
Projection: Mercator
CARTOGRAPHY BY PHILIP'S.

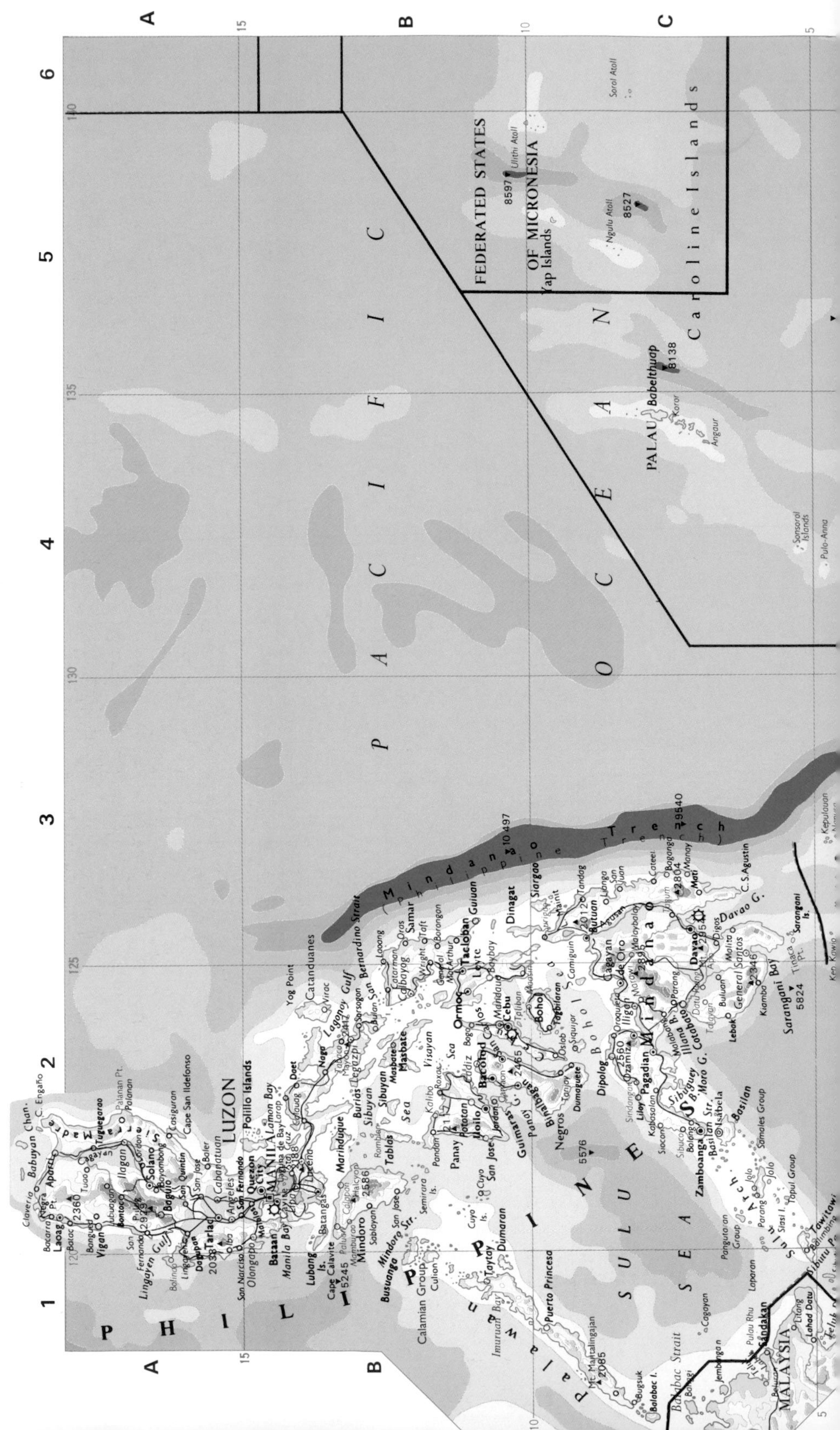

A
B
C
1
2
3
4
5
6
P A C I F I C
O C E A N
P H I L I P P I N E S
LUZON
MANILA
Quezon City
Polillo Islands
Lamon Bay
Manila Bay
Bataan
Olongapo
San Fernando
Angeles
Cabanatuan
Tarlac
Dagupan
Lingayen Gulf
Baguio
Bontoc
Ilagan
Tuguegarao
Aparri
Laoag
Vigan
Babuyan Chan.
C. Engaño
Palanan Pt.
Cape San Ildefonso
Casiguran
Baler
Solano
Lucena
Batangas
Lubang Is.
Cape Calavite
Mindoro
Mindoro Str.
Marinduque
Tablas
Sibuyan
Sibuyan Sea
Burias
Naga
Lagonoy Gulf
Legazpi
Sorsogon
Catanduanes
Virac
Yog Point
San Bernardino Strait
Samar
Catarman
Calbayog
Borongan
Tacloban
Guiuan
Leyte
Ormoc
Masbate
Visayan Sea
Panay
Iloilo
Roxas
Kalibo
San Jose
Guimaras
Negros
Bacolod
Cebu
Bohol
Tagbilaran
Bohol Sea
Dumaguete
Dinagat
Siargao
Surigao
Butuan
Cagayan de Oro
Iligan
Dipolog
Mindanao
Pagadian
Cotabato
Moro G.
Illana B.
Sibuguey B.
Zamboanga
Basilan
Basilan Str.
Isabela
Davao
Davao G.
Mati
General Santos
Sarangani Bay
Sarangani Is.
C. S. Agustin
Tandag
Mindanao Trench
Samales Group
Jolo
Tapul Group
Sulu Arch.
Tawitawi
SULU SEA
Cuyo Is.
Semirara Is.
Calamian Group
Culion
Busuanga
Taytay
Dumaran
Palawan
Puerto Princesa
Imuruan Bay
Mt. Mantalingajan
2085
Balabac Strait
Balabac I.
Bugsuk
Cagayan
Sandakan
Lahad Datu
MALAYSIA
PALAU
Babelthuap
Koror
Angaur
8138
Sonsorol Islands
Pulo Anna
FEDERATED STATES OF MICRONESIA
Yap Islands
Ulithi Atoll
Ngulu Atoll
Sorol Atoll
8597
8527
Caroline Islands
10 497
9540
5245
5576
5824
2360
2930
2465
2804
2954
Mayon 2462
120
125
130
135
140
15
10
5

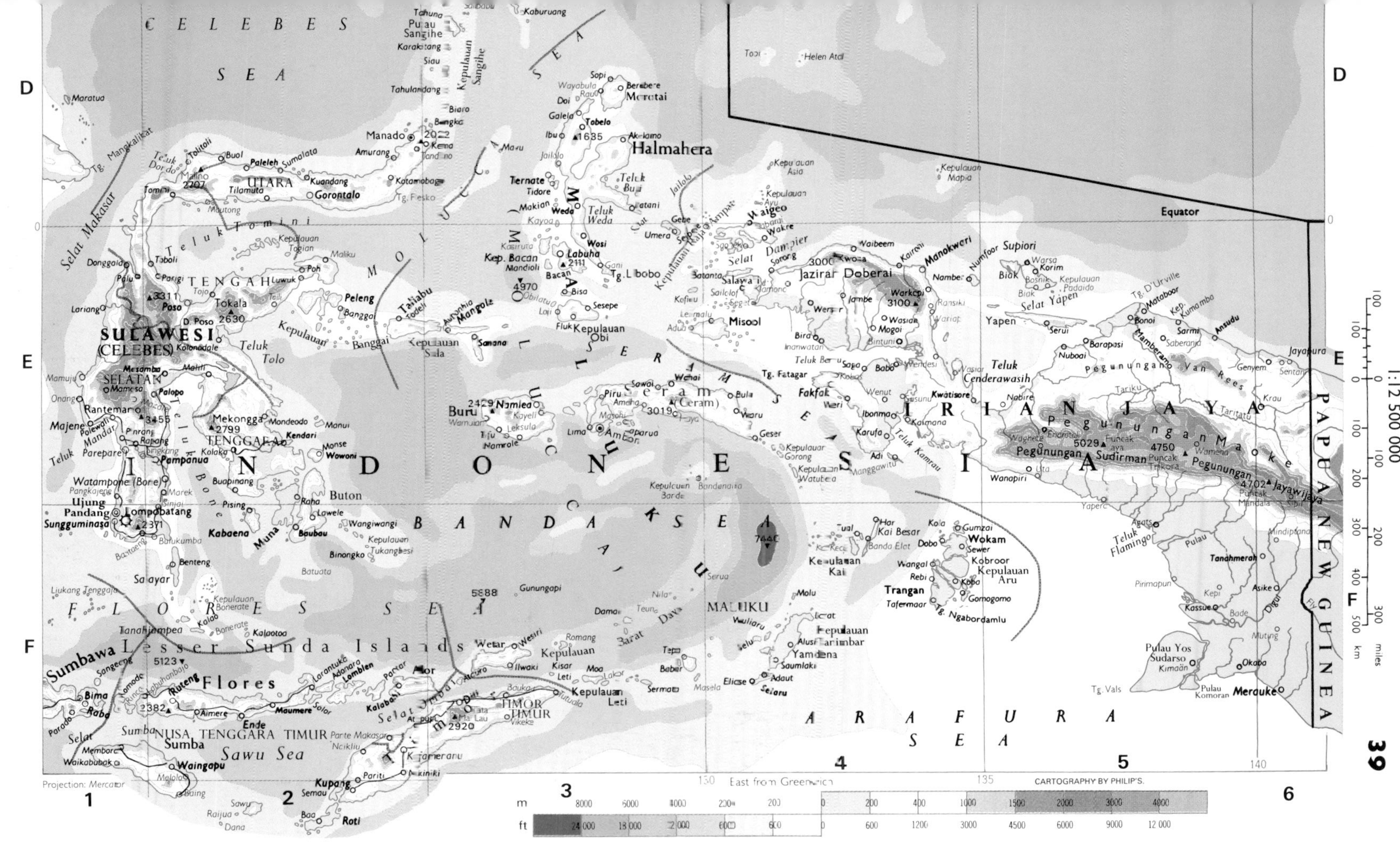
1:12 500 000
miles
km
PAPUA NEW GUINEA
CELEBES SEA
MOLUCCA SEA
Equator
Halmahera
SULAWESI (CELEBES)
INDONESIA
IRIAN JAYA
BANDA SEA
FLORES SEA
ARAFURA SEA
MALUKU
Lesser Sunda Islands
NUSA TENGGARA TIMUR
Flores
Sumba
Sawu Sea
TIMOR
Buru
Seram (Ceram)
Teluk Cenderawasih
Jazirah Doberai
Yapen
Biak
Kepulauan Aru
Kepulauan Kai
Kepulauan Tanimbar
Manado
Ujung Pandang
Ambon
Kupang
Jayapura
Merauke
Sorong
Manokwari
Pegunungan Jayawijaya
Pegunungan Sudirman
Projection: Mercator
East from Greenwich
CARTOGRAPHY BY PHILIP'S.

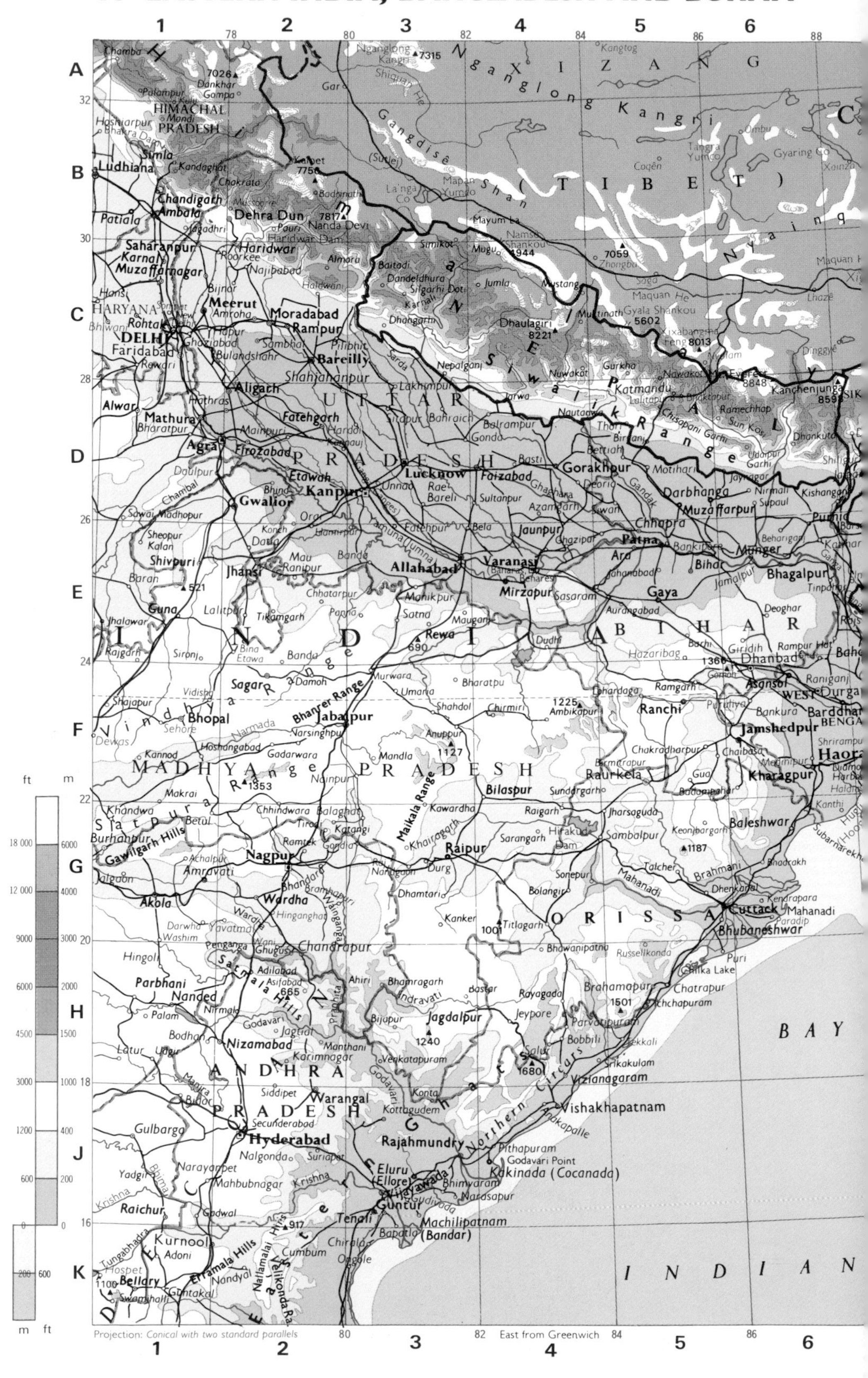
HIMACHAL PRADESH
Ludhiana
Chandigarh
Dehra Dun
Saharanpur
Meerut
Moradabad
DELHI
Bareilly
Aligarh
Agra
Gwalior
Kanpur
Lucknow
Allahabad
Varanasi
Patna
Gaya
Gorakhpur
Muzaffarpur
Darbhanga
Bhagalpur
Ranchi
Jamshedpur
Kharagpur
Cuttack
Bhubaneshwar
Jabalpur
Bhopal
Nagpur
Raipur
Bilaspur
Hyderabad
Warangal
Vishakhapatnam
Rajahmundry
Kakinada (Cocanada)
Guntur
Vijayawada
Machilipatnam (Bandar)
Kurnool
Bellary
UTTAR PRADESH
MADHYA PRADESH
ANDHRA PRADESH
ORISSA
BIHAR
HARYANA
XIZANG (TIBET)
Nganglong Kangri
Gangdisê Shan
Kanchenjunga
Everest 8848
Katmandu
Dhaulagiri 8221
Siwalik Range
Vindhya Range
Satpura Range
Maikala Range
Gawilgarh Hills
Northern Circars
Eastern Ghats
BAY
INDIAN
ft
m
Projection: Conical with two standard parallels
East from Greenwich

1: 10 000 000
50 0 50 100 150 200 250 miles
50 0 50 100 150 200 250 300 350 400 km
CHINA
SICHUAN
YUNNAN
Lhasa
BHUTAN
ARUNACHAL PRADESH
ASSAM
NAGALAND
MANIPUR
MIZORAM
TRIPURA
MEGHALAYA
KACHIN
CHIN
SHAN
KAYAH
BURMA (MYANMAR)
THAILAND
Shillong
Dhaka
CALCUTTA
Chittagong
Mandalay
Rangoon
Maulamyaing (Moulmein)
Akyab
Ramree I.
Cheduba I.
Arakan Coast
Arakan Yoma
Pegu Yoma
Gulf of Martaban
BAY OF BENGAL
INDIAN OCEAN
Preparis North Channel
Preparis South Channel
Tropic of Cancer
Tak (Raheeng)
Tavoy
CARTOGRAPHY BY PHILIP'S.

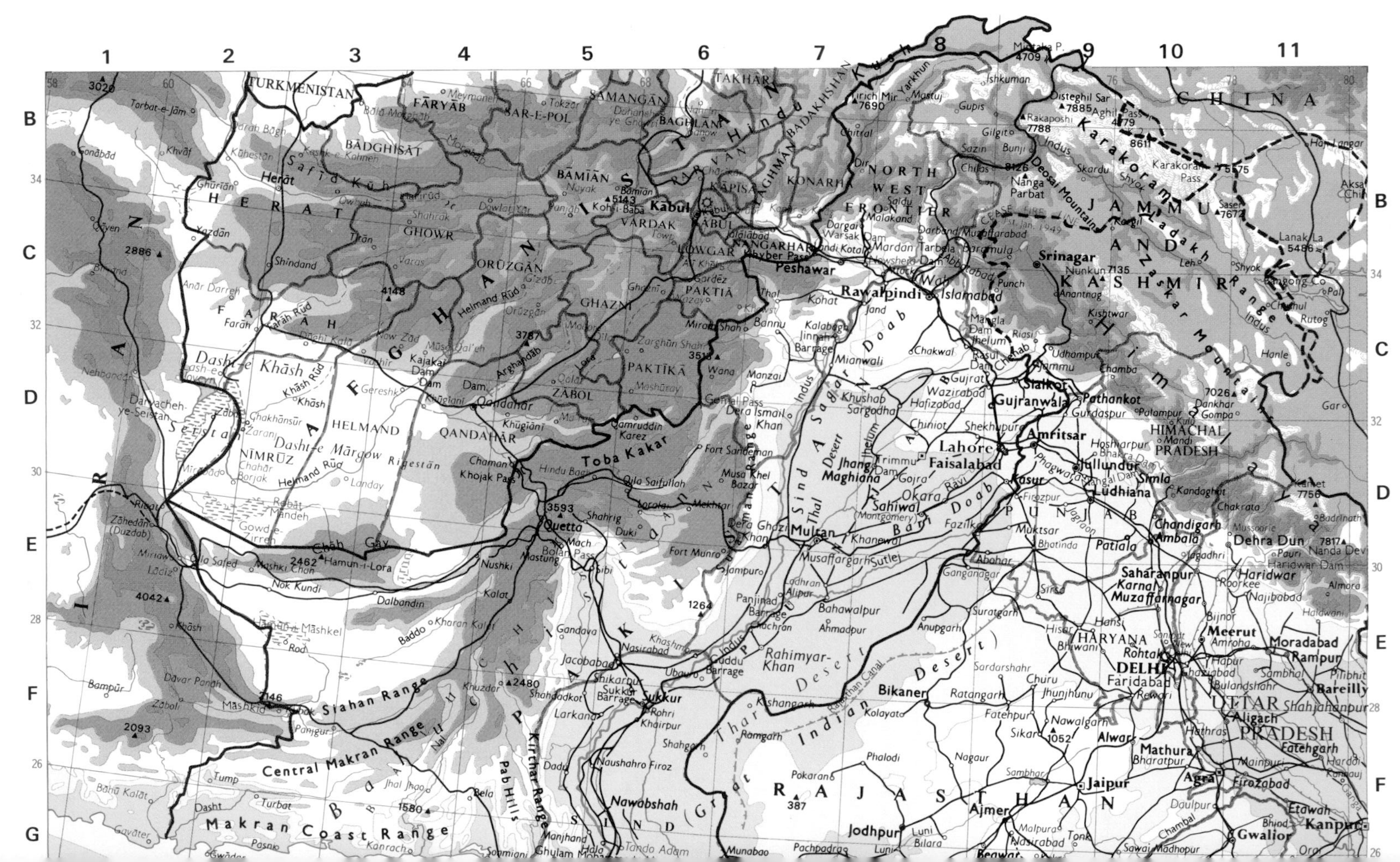
CHINA
TURKMENISTAN
AFGHANISTAN
IRAN
PAKISTAN
Karakoram
Hindu Kush
JAMMU AND KASHMIR
NORTH WEST FRONTIER
HIMACHAL PRADESH
PUNJAB
HARYANA
UTTAR PRADESH
RAJASTHAN
SIND
BALUCHISTAN
Thar or Great Indian Desert
Central Makran Range
Makran Coast Range
Siahan Range
Kirthar Range
Pab Hills
Toba Kakar
Srinagar
Islamabad
Rawalpindi
Peshawar
Lahore
Faisalabad
Amritsar
Multan
Kabul
Herat
Qandahar
Quetta
Sukkur
Nawabshah
Jacobabad
Bahawalpur
Bikaner
Jodhpur
Jaipur
Ajmer
DELHI
Meerut
Moradabad
Bareilly
Aligarh
Agra
Mathura
Gwalior
Kanpur
Dehra Dun
Chandigarh
Simla
Ludhiana
Jullundur
Gujranwala
Sialkot

1:10 000 000

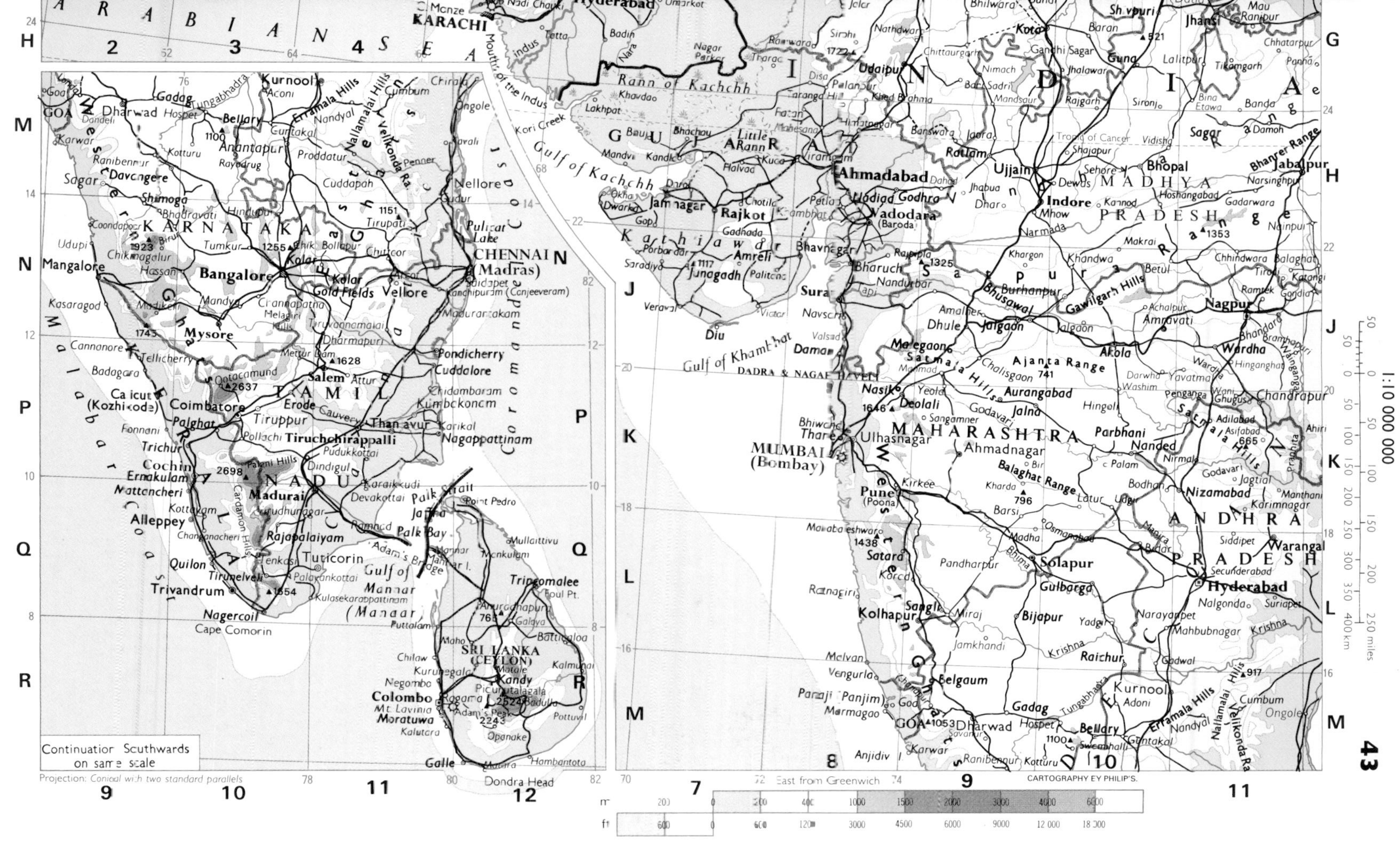

50 0 50 100 150 200 250 miles
50 0 50 100 150 200 250 300 350 400 km
ARABIAN SEA
KARACHI
Hyderabad
Rann of Kachchh
Gulf of Kachchh
GUJARAT
Ahmadabad
Vadodara (Baroda)
Rajkot
Jamnagar
Junagadh
Kathiawar
Diu
Gulf of Khambhat
Surat
Daman
DADRA & NAGAR HAVELI
MUMBAI (Bombay)
Thane
Ulhasnagar
Pune (Poona)
Nasik
MAHARASHTRA
Aurangabad
Ahmadnagar
Solapur
Kolhapur
Satara
GOA
Panaji (Panjim)
Belgaum
Dharwad
Bijapur
Gulbarga
Hyderabad
Secunderabad
ANDHRA PRADESH
Nagpur
Wardha
Akola
Amravati
Bhopal
Indore
Ujjain
Jabalpur
Jhansi
Sagar
MADHYA PRADESH
INDIA
Tropic of Cancer
Kurnool
Bellary
CHENNAI (Madras)
Bangalore
Mysore
Mangalore
KARNATAKA
TAMIL NADU
KERALA
Madurai
Coimbatore
Tiruchchirappalli
Pondicherry
Cochin
Trivandrum
Cape Comorin
Calicut (Kozhikode)
Coromandel Coast
Malabar Coast
Palk Strait
Palk Bay
Gulf of Mannar
Adam's Bridge
Jaffna
Trincomalee
SRI LANKA (CEYLON)
Kandy
Colombo
Galle
Dondra Head
Adam's Peak
East from Greenwich
m
ft
CARTOGRAPHY BY PHILIP'S
Continuation Southwards on same scale
Projection: Conical with two standard parallels

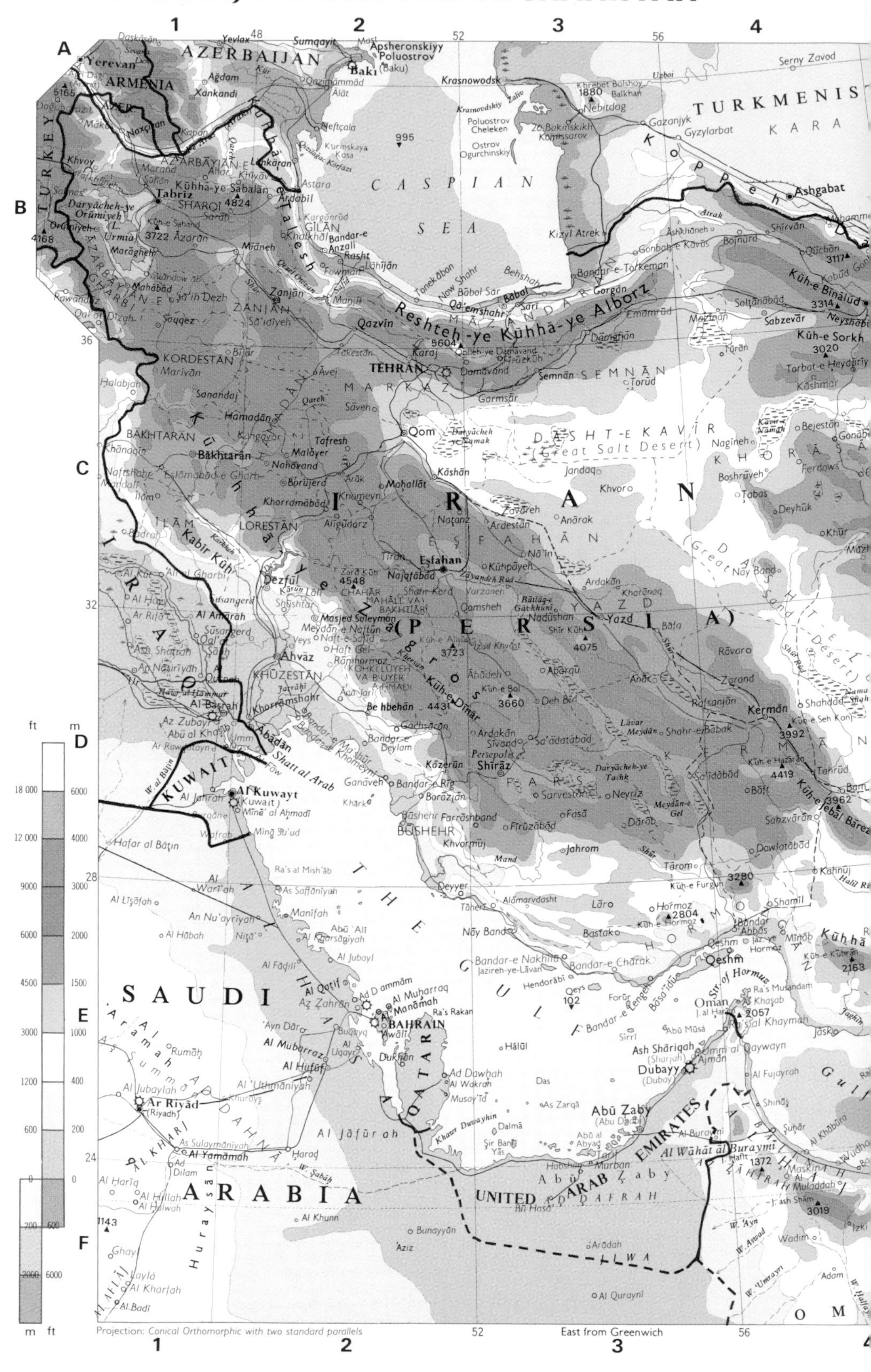

AZERBAIJAN
ARMENIA
Yerevan
Baki
(Baku)
Apsheronskiy
Poluostrov
Sumqayit
Yevlax
Ağdam
Xankandi
Qazimämmäd
Älät
Naxçivan
Kapan
Neftçala
Länkäran
Krasnovodsk
TURKMENIS
KARA
Serny Zavod
Nebitdag
Gazanjyk
Gyzylarbat
Ashgabat
CASPIAN
SEA
995
Poluostrov
Cheleken
Ostrov
Ogurchinskiy
Kizyl Atrek
TURKEY
Khvoy
Tabrīz
Kūhha-ye Sabalān
4824
Ardabīl
Astara
Daryācheh-ye
Orūmīyeh
Orūmīyeh
(Urmia)
3722
Marāgheh
Mīāneh
GĪLĀN
Bandar-e
Anzalī
Rasht
Lāhījān
4168
Mahābād
Zanjān
ZANJĀN
Saqqez
Qazvīn
Karaj
TEHRĀN
5604
Damāvand
Bābol Sar
Bābol
Sārī
Gorgān
Qā'emshahr
Bandar-e Torkeman
Gonbad-e Kāvūs
Bojnūrd
Shīrvān
Qūchān
3117
Kūh-e Bīnālūd
3314
Neyshābū
Sabzevār
Kūh-e Sorkh
3020
Torbat-e Heydarīyeh
Kāshmar
Reshteh-ye Kūhhā-ye Alborz
Kopet
MĀZANDARĀN
Dāmghān
Semnān
SEMNĀN
Torūd
Garmsār
MARKAZĪ
KORDESTĀN
Marīvān
Sanandaj
Hamadān
Sāveh
Qom
BĀKHTARĀN
Bākhtarān
Tafresh
Malāyer
Nahāvand
Borūjerd
Arāk
Kāshān
Mahallāt
Khomeyn
Khorramābād
Alīgūdarz
LORESTĀN
ĪLĀM
Īlām
Kabīr Kūh
DASHT-E KAVĪR
(Great Salt Desert)
Jandaq
Khvoro
Anārak
Naţanz
Ardestān
IRAN
(PERSIA)
EŞFAHĀN
Eşfahān
Najafābād
Nā'īn
Kūhpāyeh
Zard Kūh
4548
CHAHĀR MAHĀLL VA BAKHTĪĀRĪ
Shahr Kord
Dezfūl
Shūshtar
Masjed Soleymān
YAZD
Yazd
Ardakān
Kharānaq
Shīr Kūh
4075
Bāfq
Kūh-e Alījūq
3723
Ahvāz
KHŪZESTĀN
KOHKĪLŪYEH VA BŪYER AHMADĪ
Behbehān
4431
Kūh-e Bol
3660
Abarqū
Deh Bīd
Rāvar
Zarand
Kermān
Rafsanjān
3992
Shahr-e Bābak
Kūh-e Hazārān
4419
Bam
Kūh-e Jebāl Bārez
3962
Khorramshahr
Ābādān
Al Başrah
Shatt al Arab
Shīrāz
Persepolis
Kāzerūn
FĀRS
Neyrīz
Fasā
Dārāb
Fīrūzābād
Jahrom
BŪSHEHR
Būshehr
Bandar-e Rīg
Ganāveh
Khārk
Khvormūj
IRAQ
Al 'Amārah
An Nāşirīyah
Az Zubayr
KUWAIT
Al Kuwayt
(Kuwait)
Mīnā' al Aḩmadī
Al Jahrah
Hafar al Bāţin
Ra's al Mish'āb
As Saffānīyah
Manīfah
An Nu'ayrīyah
Al Wari'ah
THE GULF
Deyyer
Tāheri
Nāy Band
Lāro
Bastak
Hormoz
2804
HORMOZGĀN
Bandar-e Chārak
Bandar-e Lengeh
Bandar 'Abbās
Qeshm
Str. of Hormuz
Ra's Musandam
Oman
2057
Ra's al Khaymah
3280
Kūhhā
2163
SAUDI
ARABIA
Al Jubayl
Al Qaţīf
Ad Dammām
Az Zahrān
Al Muharraq
Al Manāmah
BAHRAIN
Dukhān
Al Mubarraz
Al Hufūf
QATAR
Ad Dawhah
Al Wakrah
Ra's Rakan
Hālūl
Das
Dalmā
Şīr Banī Yās
Abū Mūsā
Ash Shāriqah
(Sharjah)
Dubayy
(Dubai)
'Ajmān
Umm al Qaywayn
Al Fujayrah
Abū Zaby
(Abu Dhabi)
UNITED ARAB EMIRATES
Al Burāymī
Al Wāhāt al Buraymī
1372
Liwa
3019
OM
Ar Riyāḑ
(Riyadh)
Rumāh
Al Kharj
As Sulaymānīyah
Al Yamāmah
Haraḑ
Al Jāfūrah
Ad Dahnā'
1143
Al Kharfah
Layla
Al Badī
Bunayyān
Al Qurayni
Arādah
Projection: Conical Orthomorphic with two standard parallels
East from Greenwich
ft
m
18 000
12 000
9000
6000
4500
3000
1200
600
6000
4000
3000
2000
1500
1000
400
200
0

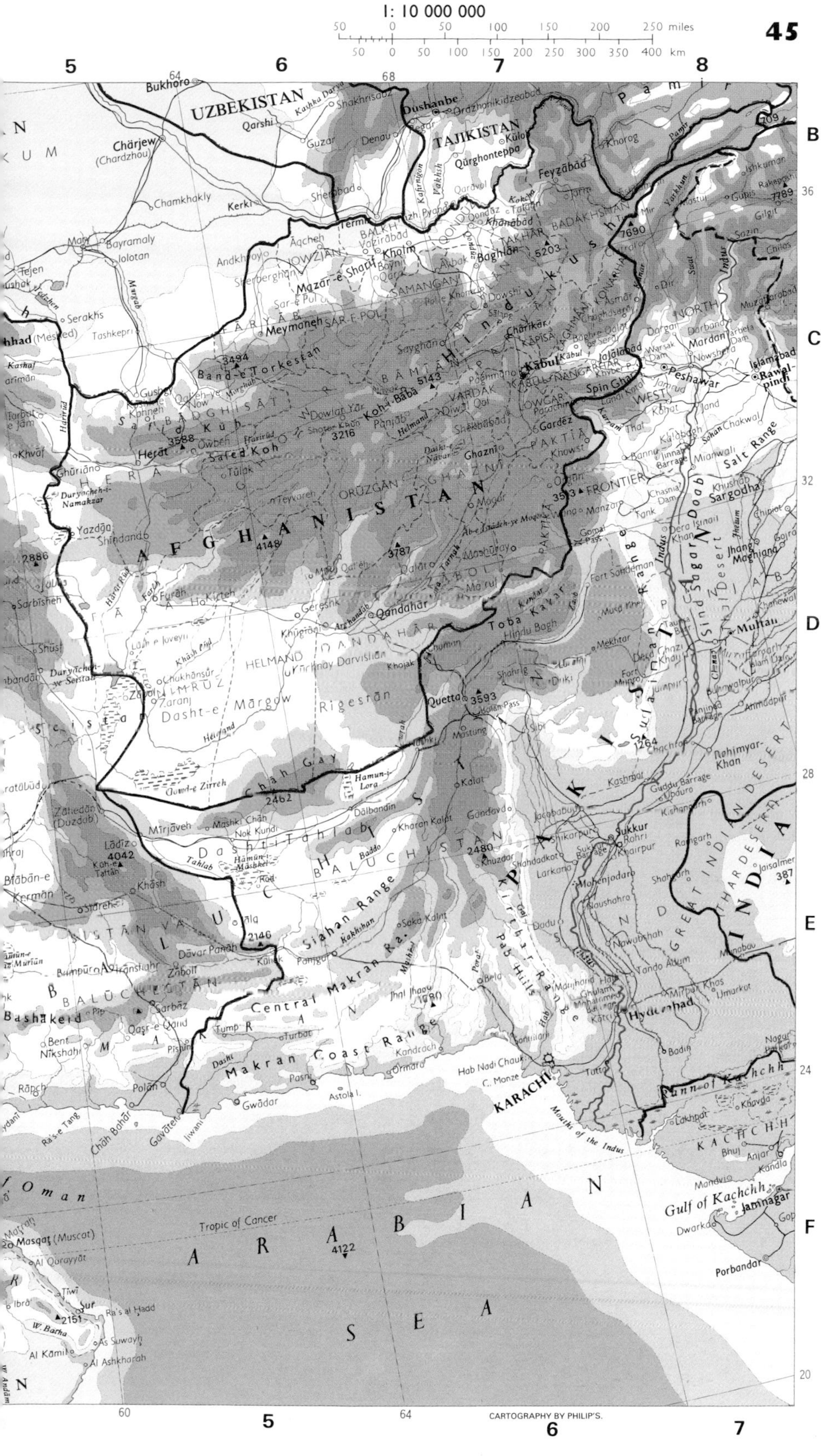
1: 10 000 000
50 0 50 100 150 200 250 miles
50 0 50 100 150 200 250 300 350 400 km
UZBEKISTAN
TAJIKISTAN
AFGHANISTAN
PAKISTAN
INDIA
Bukhoro
Qarshi
Chärjew
(Chardzhou)
Dushanbe
Qürghonteppa
Kerki
Termiz
Mary
Bayramaly
Chamkhakly
Serakhs
Tashkepri
Feyzābād
Khorog
Kondūz
Kholm
Mazār-e Sharīf
Baghlān
Tāloqān
Meymaneh
Band-e Torkestan
Chārīkār
Kābul
Jalālābād
Peshawar
Islāmābad
Rawalpindi
Mardan
Gilgit
Koh-i-Baba
Herāt
Safed Koh
Hindu Kush
Ghaznī
Gardēz
Khowst
Spin Ghar
Salt Range
Sargodha
Jhang Maghiana
Multan
Thal Desert
Sind Sagar Doab
Shindand
Farāh
Gereshk
Qandahār
Toba Kakar
Hindu Bagh
Quetta
3593
Rigestān
Dasht-e Mārgow
Zaranj
Zābol
Chah Gay
Hamun-i-Lora
Dālbandin
Kalat
Zāhedān
(Duzdab)
Mīrjāveh
Khāsh
BALUCHISTAN
Siahan Range
Central Makran Ra.
Makran Coast Range
Kirthar Range
Sukkur
Rohri
Shikarpur
Jacobabad
Larkana
Mohenjodaro
Hyderabad
Badin
KARACHI
C. Monze
Hab Nadi Chauk
Mouths of the Indus
Rann of Kachchh
KACHCHH
Bhuj
Anjar
Kandla
Gulf of Kachchh
Jamnagar
Dwarka
Porbandar
GREAT INDIAN (THAR) DESERT
Jaisalmer
Gwādar
Pasni
Ormara
Astola I.
Jiwani
Gavāter
Chāh Bahār
Tropic of Cancer
Masqat (Muscat)
Al Qurayyāt
Sur
Ra's al Hadd
As Suwayh
Al Ashkharah
Al Kāmil
ARABIAN SEA
4122
CARTOGRAPHY BY PHILIP'S.

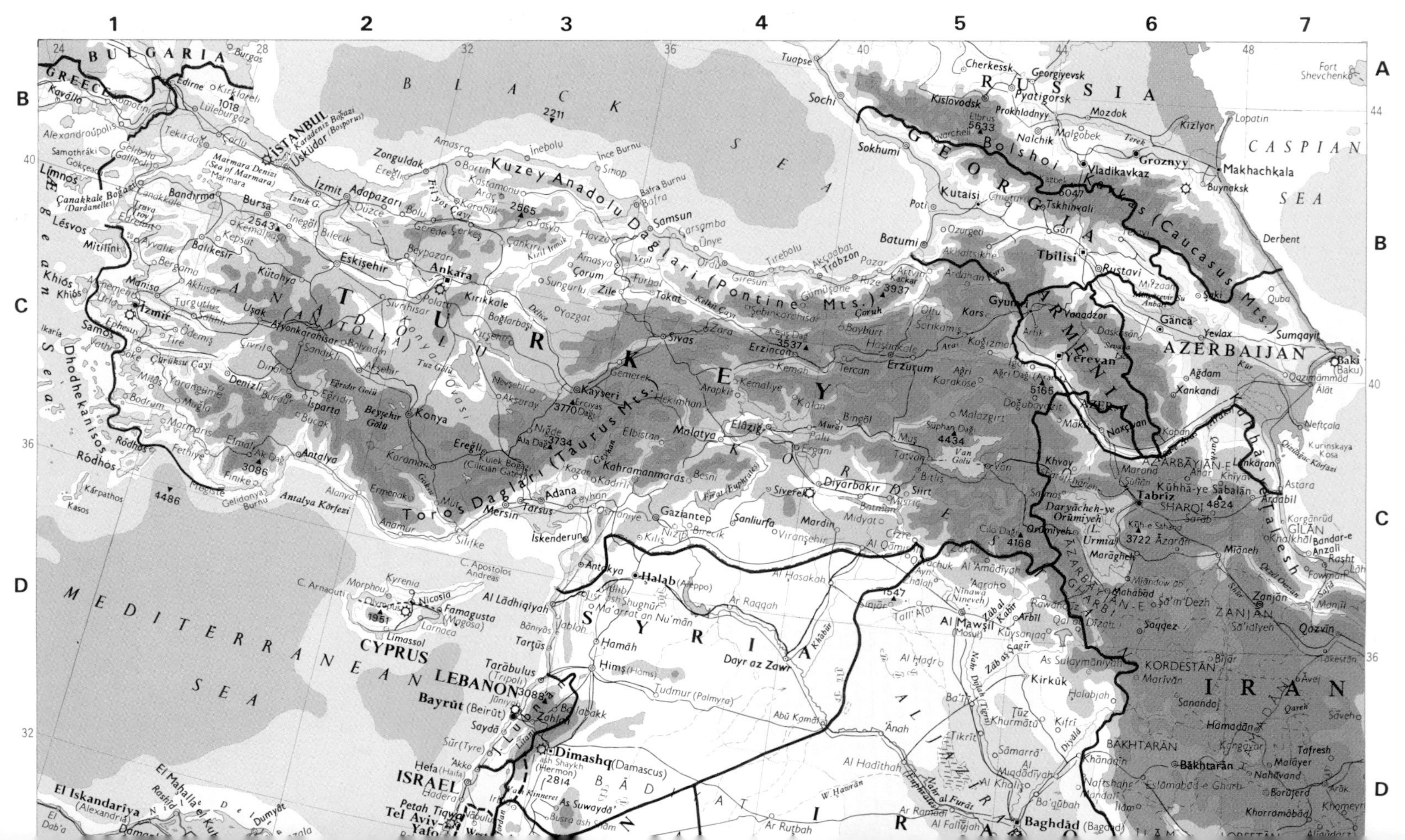
RUSSIA
GEORGIA
ARMENIA
AZERBAIJAN
IRAN
TURKEY
SYRIA
CYPRUS
LEBANON
ISRAEL
BULGARIA
GREECE
BLACK SEA
CASPIAN SEA
MEDITERRANEAN SEA
ANATOLIA
Bolshoi Kavkas (Caucasus Mts.)
Kuzey Anadolu Dağlari (Pontine Mts.)
Toros Dağlari (Taurus Mts.)
İSTANBUL
Ankara
Tbilisi
Yerevan
Baki (Baku)
Tabriz
Halab (Aleppo)
Dimashq (Damascus)
Bayrūt (Beirūt)
Baghdād (Bagdad)
Al Mawşil (Mosul)
Konya
İzmir
Adana
Kayseri
Erzurum
Trabzon
Samsun
Nicosia
Tel Aviv-Yafo
El Iskandarîya (Alexandria)

1:10 000 000

50 0 50 100 150 200 250 miles

50 0 50 100 150 200 250 300 350 400 km

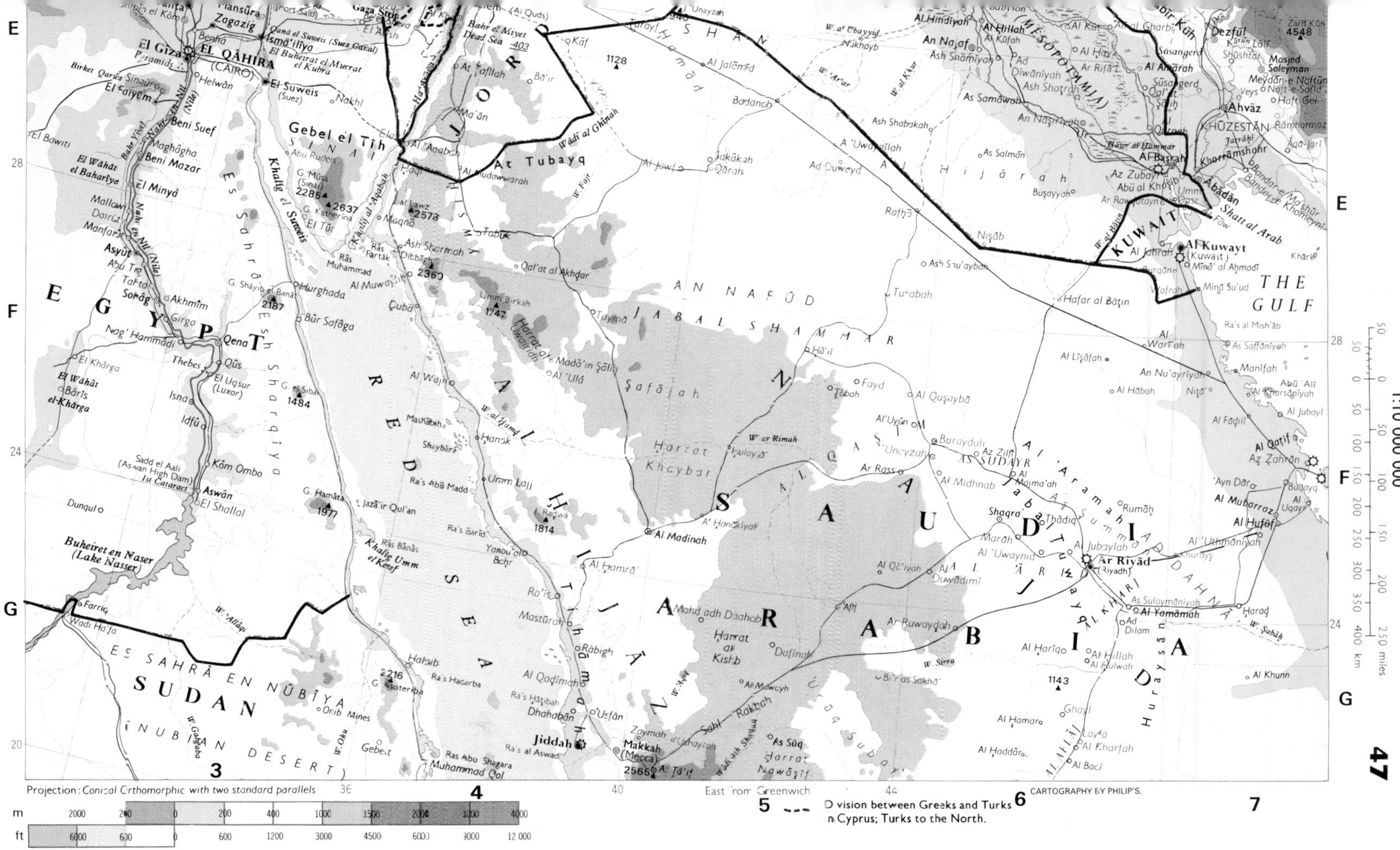

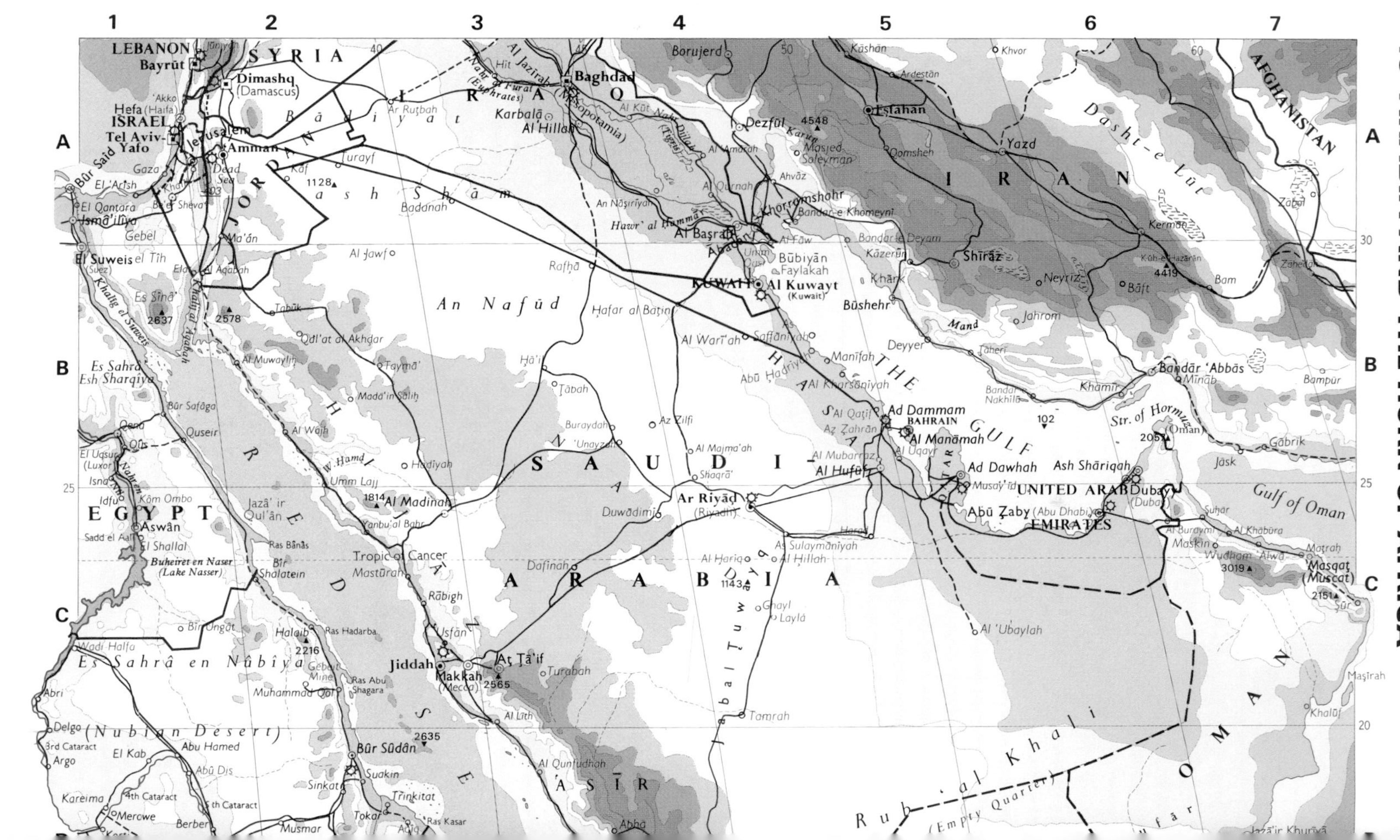
LEBANON
Bayrūt
SYRIA
Dimashq (Damascus)
ISRAEL
Hefa (Haifa)
Tel Aviv-Yafo
Jerusalem
'Ammān
Dead Sea
Gaza
JORDAN
Bûr Sa'îd
El Suweis (Suez)
Khalîg el Suweis
Khalīj al 'Aqabah
IRAQ
Baghdād
Karbalā'
Al Ḩillah
Al Jazīrah
Nahr al Furāt (Euphrates)
Nahr Dijlah (Tigris)
Mesopotamia
Al Başrah
KUWAIT
Al Kuwayt (Kuwait)
Būbiyān
Faylakah
Bādiyat ash Shām
An Nafūd
Ḩafar al Bāţin
SAUDI ARABIA
Ar Riyāḑ (Riyadh)
Al Madīnah
Makkah (Mecca)
Jiddah
Aţ Ţā'if
Tropic of Cancer
Ad Dammam
Al Hufūf
BAHRAIN
Al Manāmah
QATAR
Ad Dawhah
THE GULF
UNITED ARAB EMIRATES
Abū Ẓaby (Abu Dhabi)
Dubayy (Dubai)
Ash Shāriqah
Str. of Hormuz
Gulf of Oman
Masqaţ (Muscat)
OMAN
Rub' al Khālī (Empty Quarter)
'Asīr
RED SEA
IRAN
Borujerd
Dezfūl
Eşfahān
Kāshān
Yazd
Dasht-e Lūt
Kermān
Bam
Shīrāz
Būshehr
Bandar 'Abbās
Khorramshahr
AFGHANISTAN
EGYPT
Aswân
Buheiret en Naser (Lake Nasser)
Es Sahrâ en Nûbîya (Nubian Desert)
Bûr Sûdân
Suakin
1
2
3
4
5
6
7
A
B
C

1: 15 000 000

100 0 100 200 300 400 miles

100 0 100 200 300 400 500 600 km

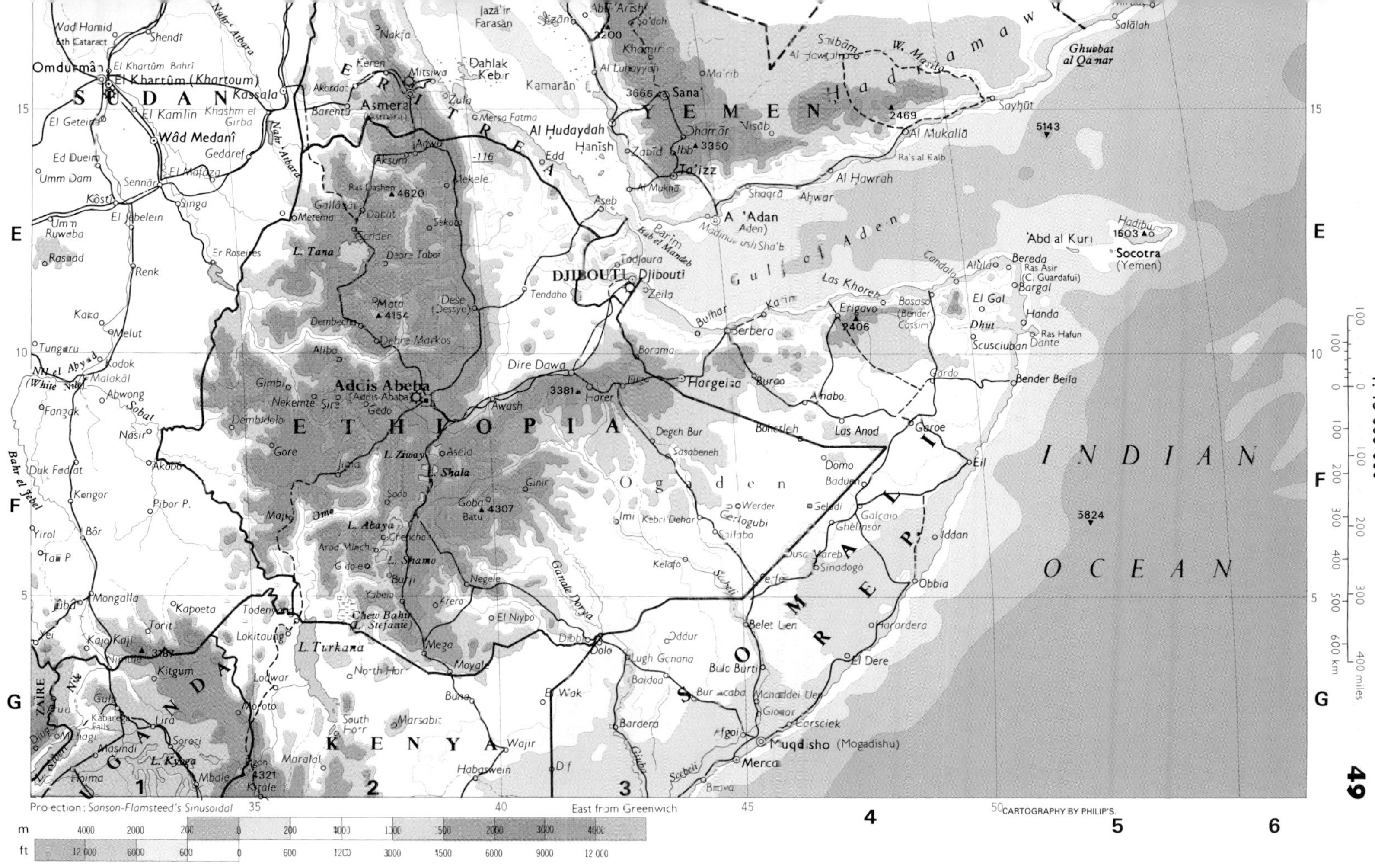

NORTH ATLANTIC OCEAN
Azores (Port.)
Madeira (Port.)
Canary Is. (Sp.)
CAPE VERDE IS.
Praia
B. of Biscay
UNITED KINGDOM
LONDON
FRANCE
PARIS
NETH.
BELG.
GERMANY
SWITZ.
SPAIN
Madrid
PORTUGAL
Lisbon
ITALY
Rome
Corsica
Sardinia
Sicily
MALTA
POLAND
Warsaw
CZECH REP.
Prague
SLOVAK REP.
AUSTRIA
Vienna
HUNGARY
CROATIA
BOS.-HERZ.
YUG.
ALB.
MAC.
GREECE
Athens
Crete
BULGARIA
ROMANIA
UKRAINE
Kiev
Odessa
RUSSIA
Volgograd
KAZAKSTAN
Aral Sea
TURKMEN.
Caspian Sea
GEORGIA
ARM.
AZER.
Baku
Black Sea
TURKEY
Ankara
CYPRUS
SYRIA
Aleppo
Damascus
LEB.
ISRAEL
Tel Aviv-Jaffa
Jerusalem
JORDAN
IRAQ
Mosul
Baghdād
Basra
Tigris
Euphrates
Syrian Desert
IRAN
TEHRĀN
Eşfahān
KUWAIT
BAHRAIN
QATAR
The Gulf
SAUDI ARABIA
Riyadh
Medina
Mecca
Jedda
YEMEN
G. of Aden
Socotra (Yemen)
Ras Asir
DJIBOUTI
Djibouti
Berbera
ERITREA
Asmera
Mesewa
Harer
Addis Ababa
L. Tana
Red Sea
Mediterranean Sea
Adriatic Sea
MOROCCO
Rabat
Casablanca
Marrakesh
Fès
Tetouan
ALGERIA
Algiers
Annaba
Constantine
Chott Djerid
In Salah
TUNISIA
Tunis
Sfax
LIBYA
Tripoli
Misrātah
Benghazi
Marzūq
Al Jawf
EGYPT
CAIRO
Alexandria
Port Said
Suez
El Faiyûm
Asyût
Aswân
Nile
Wadi Halfa
Port Sudan
SUDAN
Khartoum
Omdurmân
Atbara
'Atbara
Wad Medani
Blue Nile
White Nile
Malakâl
El Obeid
El Fâsher
CHAD
Abéché
Ndjamena
L. Chad
Chari
NIGER
Agadès
Niamey
NIGERIA
Kano
Maiduguri
Abuja
BENIN
BURKINA FASO
Ouagadougou
Bobo-Dioulasso
GHANA
IVORY COAST
MALI
Tombouctou
Bamako
Niger
MAURITANIA
Nouakchott
Fdérik
WESTERN SAHARA
El Aaiún
Dakhla
Ras Nouâdhibou
SENEGAL
Dakar
St-Louis
C. Vert
Senegal
GAMBIA
Banjul
GUINEA-BISSAU
Bissau
GUINEA
Conakry
SIERRA
Freetown
Sahara
Tropic of Cancer

1:56 000 000
200 0 200 400 600 800 1000 1200 miles
200 0 200 400 600 800 1000 1200 1400 1600 1800 km
INDIAN OCEAN
SOUTH ATLANTIC OCEAN
Gulf of Guinea
Bight of Benin
Mozambique Channel
Equator
Tropic of Capricorn
CAMEROON
CENTRAL AFRICAN REP.
CONGO
CONGO (DEM. REP. OF THE)
GABON
EQUATORIAL GUINEA
SÃO TOMÉ & PRINCIPE
UGANDA
KENYA
SOMALIA
RWANDA
BURUNDI
TANZANIA
ANGOLA
CABINDA (Angola)
ZAMBIA
MALAWI
MOZAMBIQUE
ZIMBABWE
NAMIBIA
BOTSWANA
SOUTH AFRICA
LESOTHO
SWAZ.
MADAGASCAR
COMOROS
SEYCHELLES
MAURITIUS
Réunion (Fr.)
Mayotte (Fr.)
Aldabra Is.
Ascension I. (U.K.)
St. Helena (U.K.)
Tristan da Cunha (U.K.)
Annobón
Monrovia
Abidjan
Sekondi-Takoradi
Accra
Porto Novo
Lagos
Enugu
Port Harcourt
Douala
Yaoundé
Malabo
Libreville
C. Lopez
Bangui
Mbandaka
Kisangani
Pointe Noire
Brazzaville
Kinshasa
Matadi
Karanga
Luanda
Lobito
Huambo
Nambe
C. Fria
Kampala
Kisumu
Nairobi
Mombasa
Kismayu
Mogadishu
Kigali
Bujumbura
Dodoma
Zanzibar
Dar es Salaam
C. Delgado
Likasi
Lubumbashi
Ndola
Lusaka
Lilongwe
Blantyre
Livingstone
Harare
Bulawayo
Beira
Moçambique
Windhoek
Gaborone
Pretoria
Johannesburg
Mbabane
Maputo
Kimberley
Maseru
Durban
East London
Port Elizabeth
Cape Town
C. of Good Hope
C. Agulhas
Antsiranana
Mahajanga
Toamasina
Antananarivo
Fianarantsoa
L. Albert
L. Edward
L. Kivu
L. Victoria
L. Turkana
L. Tanganyika
L. Mweru
L. Malawi
Congo
Oubangi
Lualaba
Kasai
Cuango
Cubango
Cunene
Zambezi
Limpopo
Vaal
Orange
Jebel
Shaballe
Juba
Tana
Projection: Azimuthal Equidistant
West from Greenwich
East from Greenwich
CARTOGRAPHY BY PHILIP'S.
Dakar Capital Cities
F
G
H
J
K
1
2
3
4
5
7
8
9

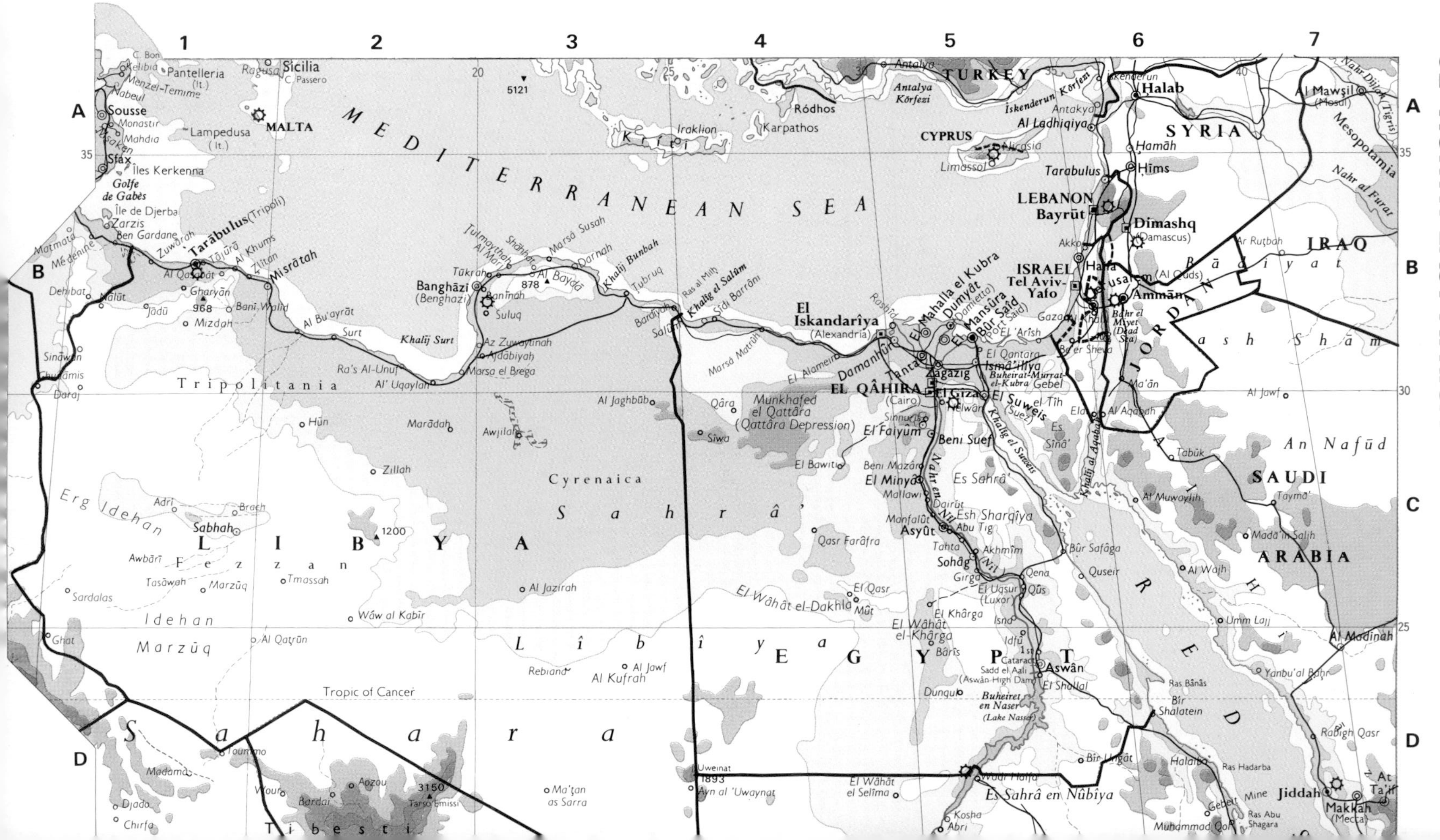
MEDITERRANEAN SEA
TURKEY
SYRIA
IRAQ
JORDAN
LEBANON
ISRAEL
CYPRUS
MALTA
SAUDI ARABIA
EGYPT
LIBYA
RED SEA
Sahrâ' Lîbîya
Sahara
Mesopotamia
Cyrenaica
Tripolitania
Fezzan
Tropic of Cancer
Tibesti
Halab
Dimashq (Damascus)
Hims
Hamāh
Bayrūt
Tarabulus
Tel Aviv-Yafo
Jerusalem (Al Quds)
'Ammān
Gaza
Bûr Sa'îd (Port Said)
El Iskandarîya (Alexandria)
EL QÂHIRA (Cairo)
El Gîza
El Suweis (Suez)
Asyût
Aswân
Sohâg
Qena
El Uqsur (Luxor)
Munkhafed el Qattâra (Qattâra Depression)
Siwa
Wadi Halfa
Es Sahrâ en Nûbîya
Makkah (Mecca)
Jiddah
Al Madīnah
Tabūk
Banghāzī (Benghazi)
Tarābulus (Tripoli)
Misrātah
Sabhah
Al Kufrah
Khalīj Surt
Golfe de Gabès
Sousse
Sfax
Lampedusa
Sicilia
Kríti
Ródhos
Karpathos
Limassol
Antalya
Iskenderun
An Nafūd
5121
878
1200
3150
1893

1: 15 000 000

100 0 100 200 300 400 miles

100 0 100 200 300 400 500 600 km

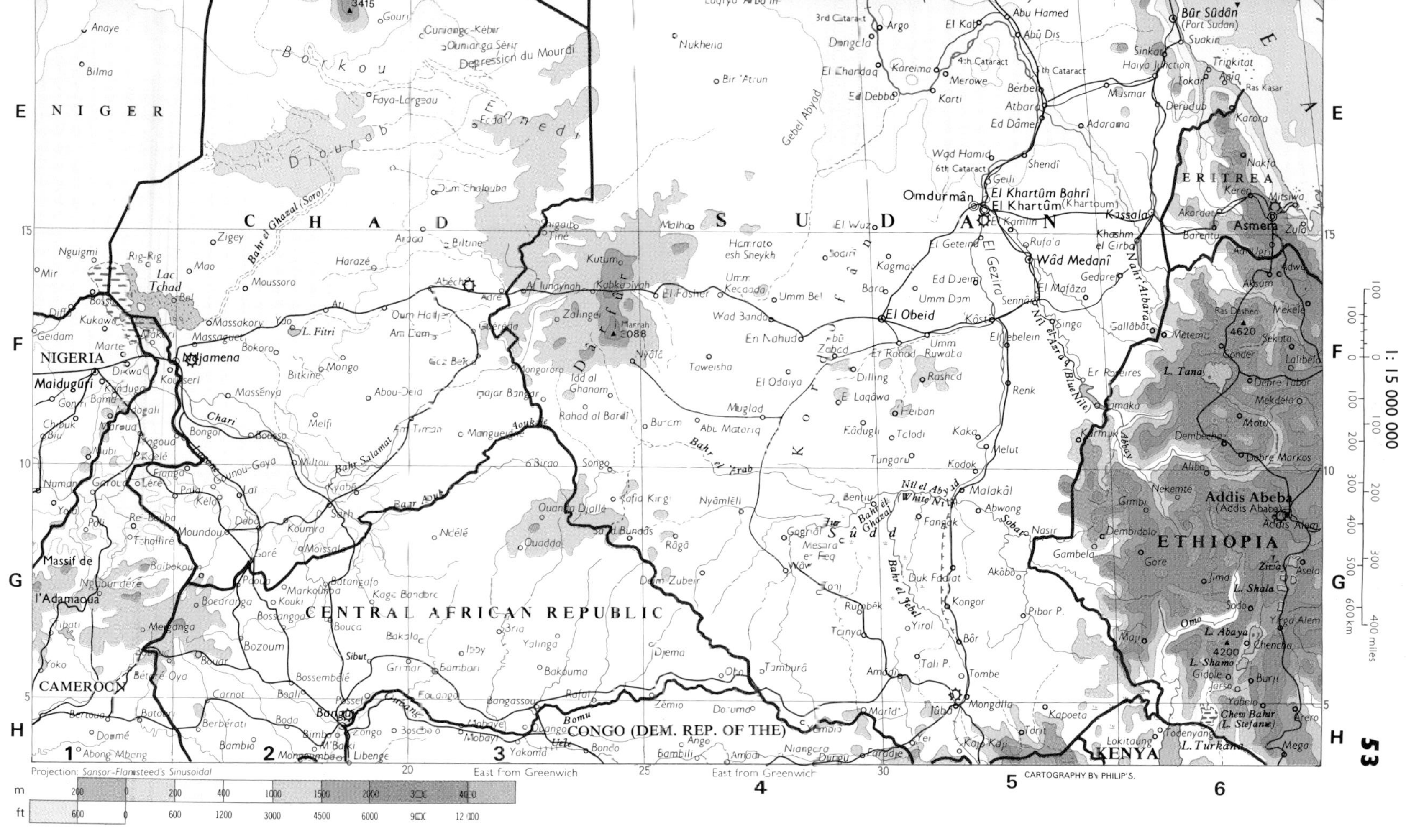

# 54 NORTH-WEST AFRICA

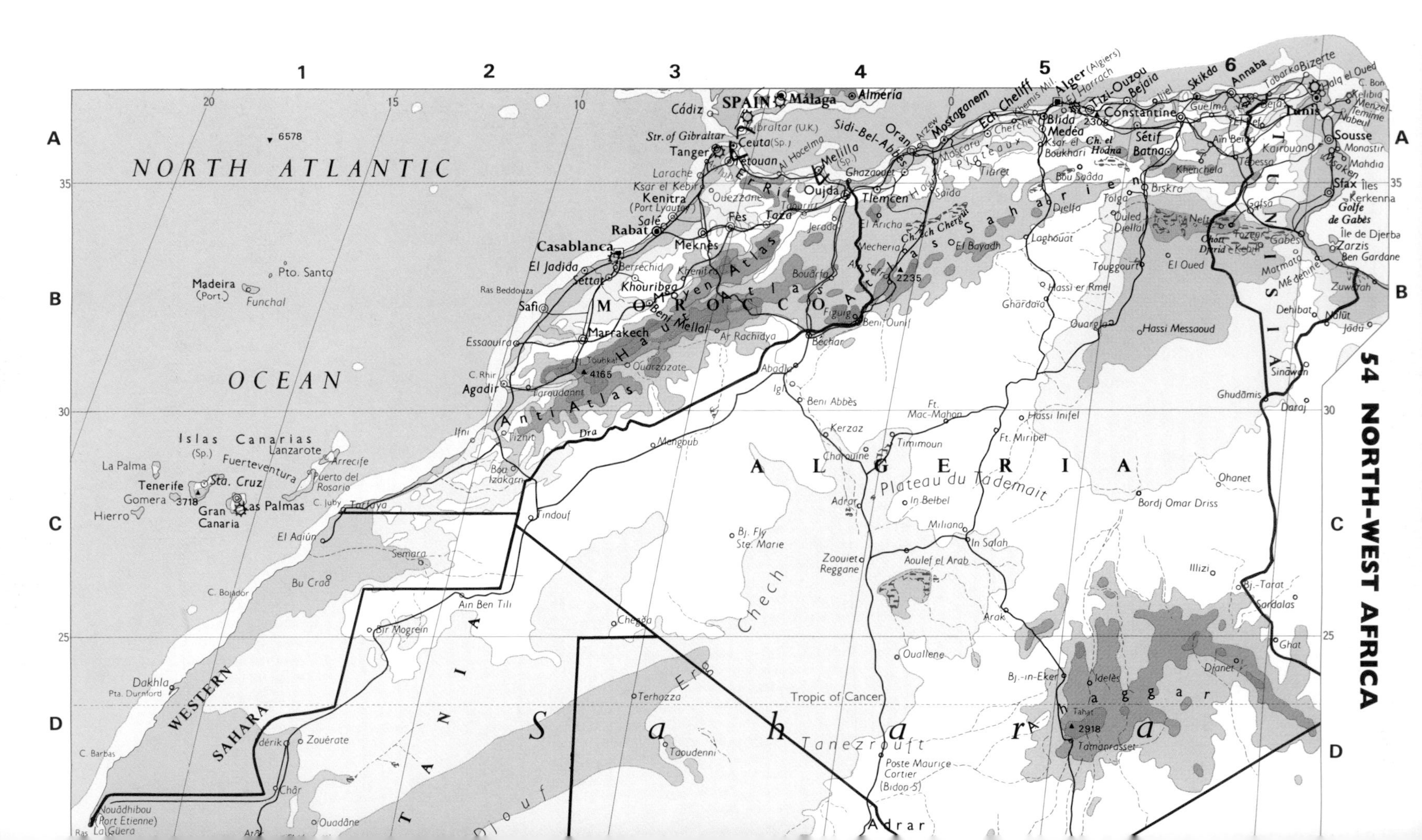

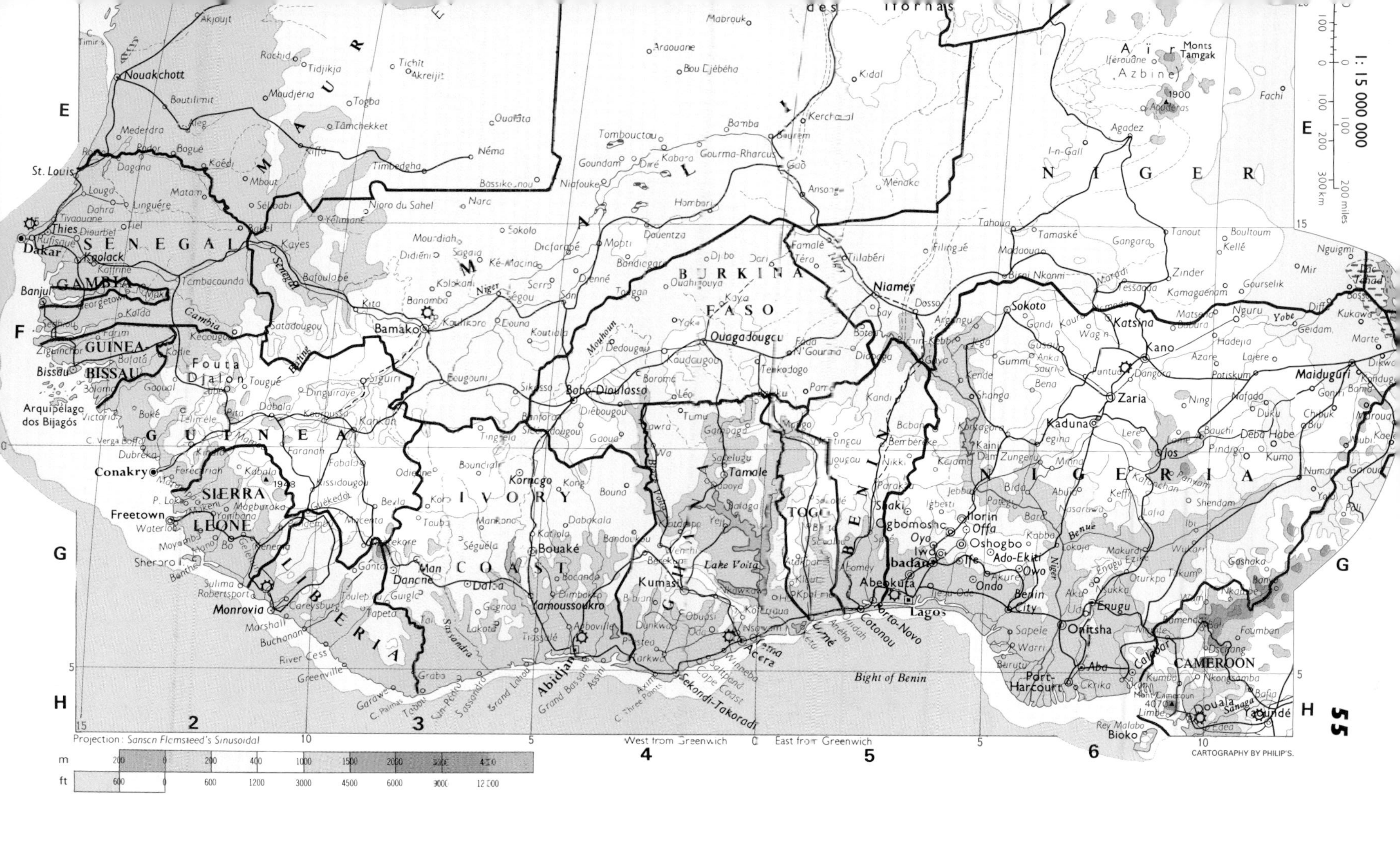
1: 15 000 000
200 miles
300 km
MAURITANIA
MALI
NIGER
BURKINA FASO
SENEGAL
GAMBIA
GUINEA-BISSAU
GUINEA
SIERRA LEONE
LIBERIA
IVORY COAST
GHANA
TOGO
BENIN
NIGERIA
CAMEROON
Nouakchott
St. Louis
Dakar
Thies
Kaolack
Banjul
Bissau
Arquipélago dos Bijagós
Conakry
Freetown
Monrovia
Bamako
Tombouctou
Gao
Mopti
Ségou
Kayes
Niamey
Ouagadougou
Bobo-Dioulasso
Agadez
Zinder
Maradi
Tahoua
Sokoto
Katsina
Kano
Zaria
Kaduna
Maiduguri
Jos
Ilorin
Ibadan
Oshogbo
Lagos
Porto-Novo
Cotonou
Lomé
Accra
Kumasi
Tamale
Lake Volta
Sekondi-Takoradi
Abidjan
Yamoussoukro
Bouaké
Korhogo
Man
Daloa
Benin City
Onitsha
Enugu
Port-Harcourt
Calabar
Douala
Yaoundé
Bioko
Bight of Benin
Fouta Djalon
Monts Tamgak
Aïr (Azbine)
Niger
Benue
Senegal
Gambia
West from Greenwich
East from Greenwich
Projection: Sanson Flamsteed's Sinusoidal
m
ft
CARTOGRAPHY BY PHILIP'S.

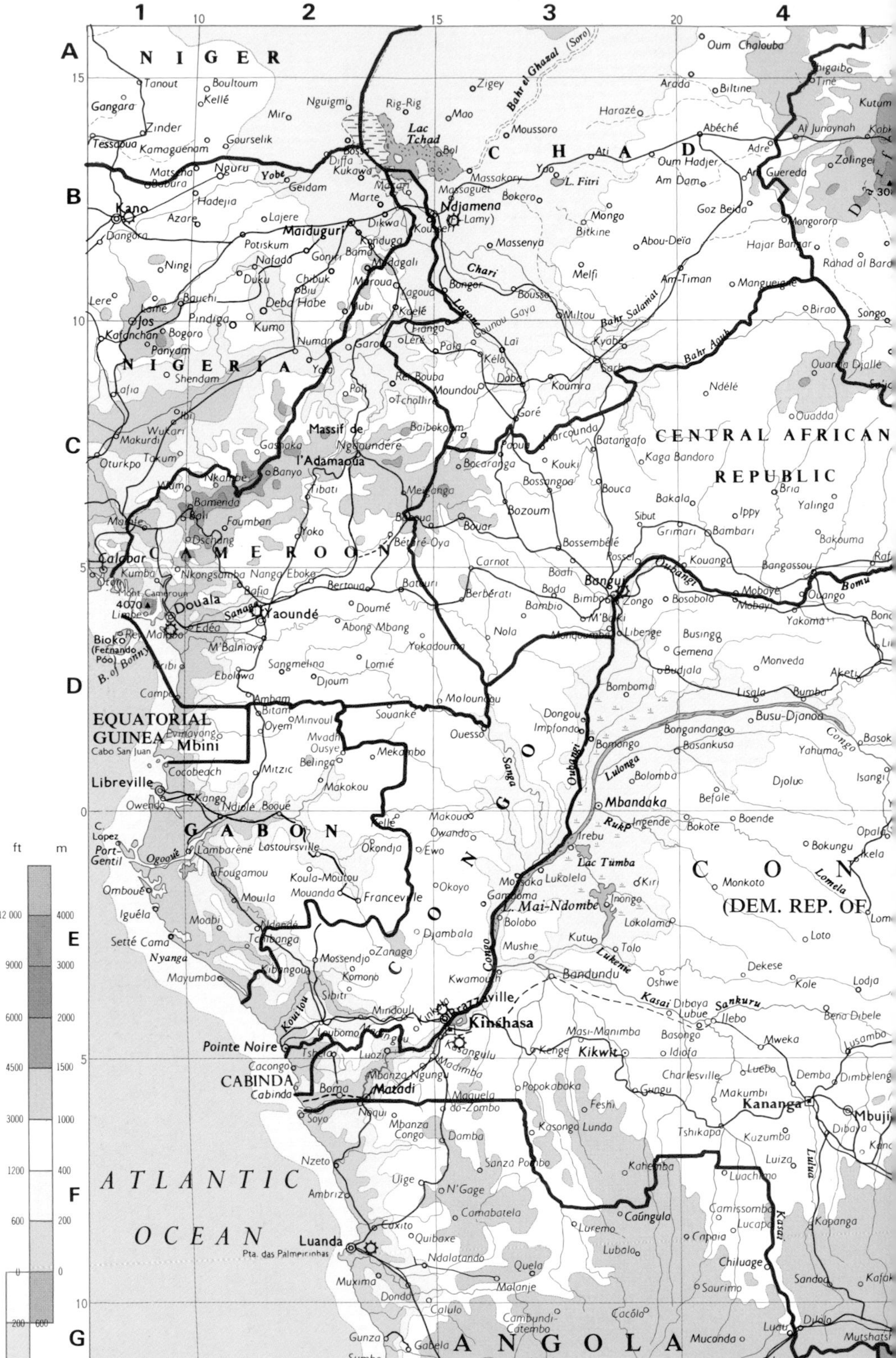

1 2 3 4

A B C D E F G

ft m

12 000 4000
9000 3000
6000 2000
4500 1500
3000 1000
1200 400
600 200
0 0
200 600

m ft

NIGER

CHAD

NIGERIA

CAMEROON

CENTRAL AFRICAN REPUBLIC

EQUATORIAL GUINEA

Mbini

GABON

CONGO

CONGO (DEM. REP. OF)

CABINDA

ANGOLA

ATLANTIC OCEAN

Lac Tchad

Massif de l'Adamaoua

Mont Cameroun 4070

Bioko (Fernando Póo)

B. of Bonny

L. Fitri

Lac Tumba

L. Mai-Ndombe

Kano

Maiduguri

Ndjamena (Lamy)

Yaoundé

Douala

Bangui

Libreville

Pointe Noire

Brazzaville

Kinshasa

Matadi

Luanda

Pta. das Palmeirinhas

Mbandaka

Kananga

Mbuji

Kikwit

Projection: Sanson Flamsteed's Sinusoidal

1: 15 000 000

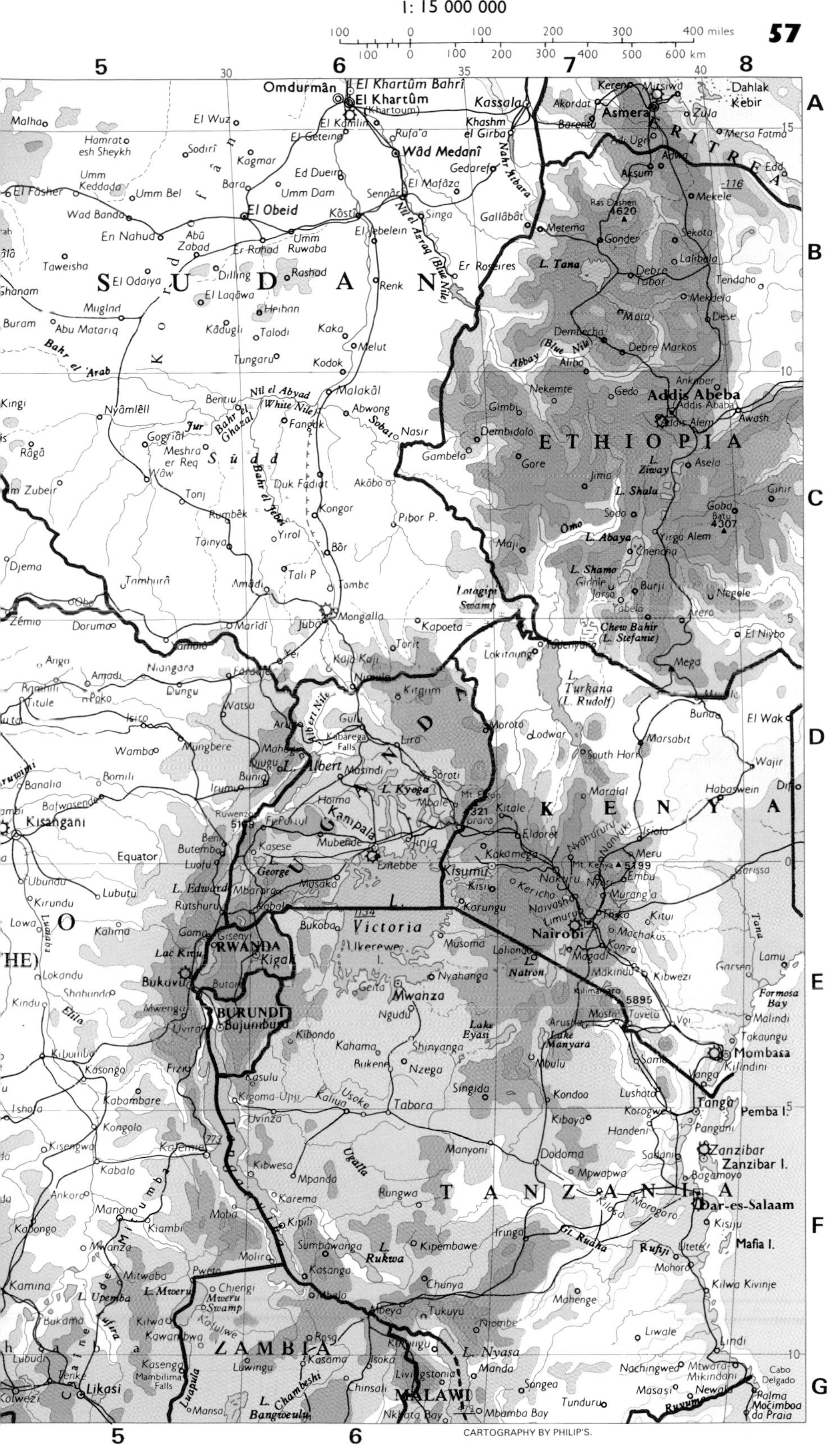


CARTOGRAPHY BY PHILIP'S.

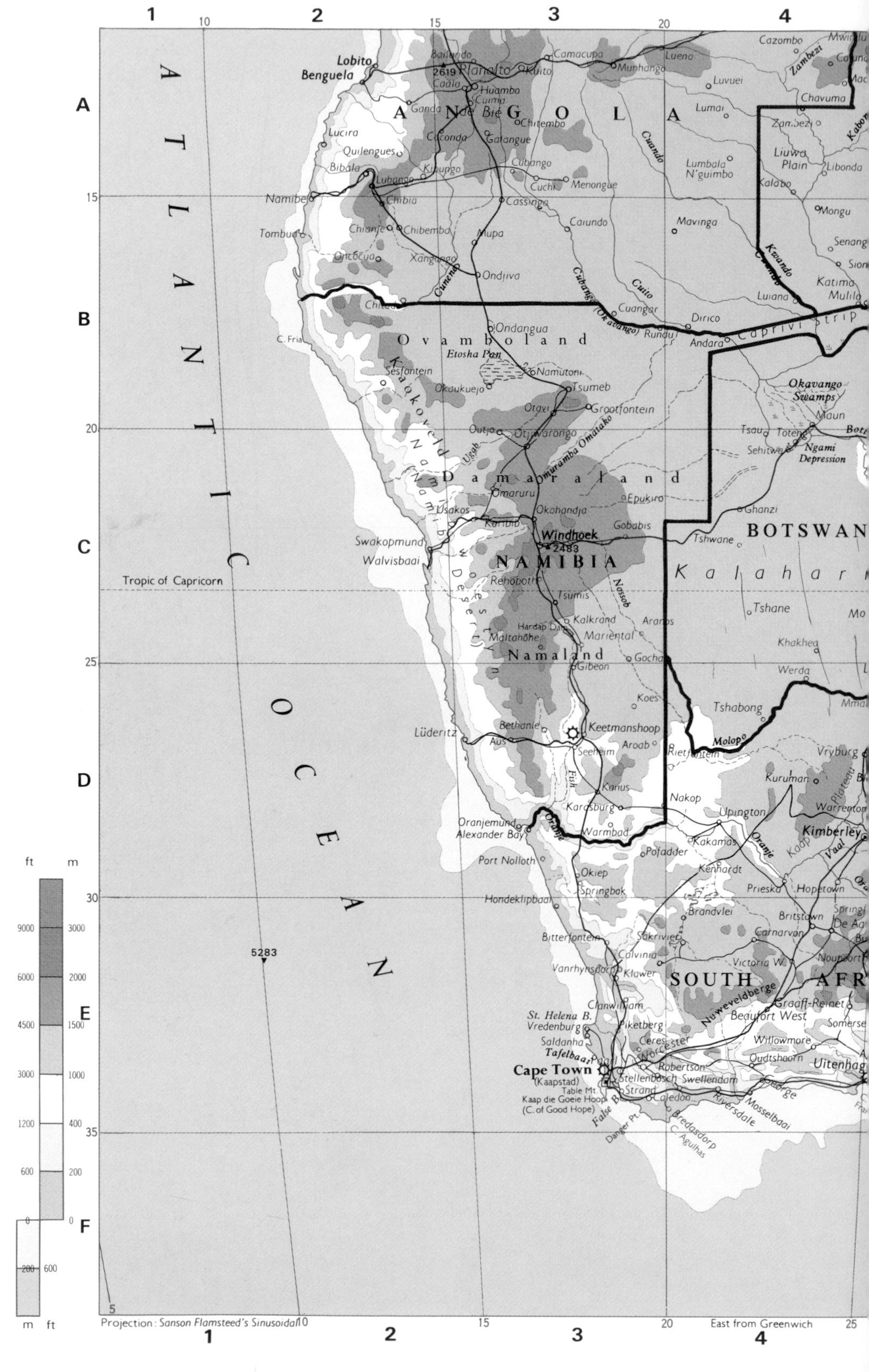

1
2
3
4
10
15
20
A
B
C
D
E
F
ATLANTIC OCEAN
ANGOLA
NAMIBIA
BOTSWAN
SOUTH AFR
Lobito
Benguela
Bailundo
2619
Planalto
Kuito
Camacupa
Munhango
Luena
Cazombo
Zambezi
Chavuma
Caála
Huambo
Cuima
Ganda
Nde Bié
Chitembo
Lucira
Caconda
Galangue
Quilengues
Bibala
Lubango
Kipungo
Cubango
Cuchi
Menongue
Cuando
Luvuei
Lumai
Lumbala N'guimbo
Liuwa Plain
Kalabo
Libonda
Mongu
Namibe
Chibia
Cassinga
Caiundo
Mavinga
Tombua
Chiange
Chibemba
Mupa
Xangongo
Cunene
Ondjiva
Cubango
Cuito
Kwando
Senanga
Katima Mulilo
Luiana
Cuangar
(Okavango)
Dirico
Rundu
Andara
Caprivi Strip
C. Fria
Ondangua
Ovamboland
Etosha Pan
Sesfontein
Kaokoveld
Namutoni
Okaukuejo
Tsumeb
Okavango Swamps
Maun
Otavi
Grootfontein
Omatako
Outjo
Otjiwarongo
Tsau
Toteng
Sehitwa
Ngami Depression
Ugab
Damaraland
Omaruru
Epukiro
Ghanzi
Usakos
Karibib
Okahandja
Gobabis
Swakopmund
Windhoek
2483
Tshwane
Walvisbaai
Namib Desert
Kalahari
Tropic of Capricorn
Rehoboth
Tsumis
Nossob
Tshane
Hardap Dam
Kalkrand
Maltahöhe
Mariental
Khakhea
Namaland
Gochas
Gibeon
Werda
Koes
Tshabong
Lüderitz
Bethanie
Keetmanshoop
Aus
Seeheim
Aroab
Rietfontein
Molopo
Vryburg
Fish
Kanus
Kuruman
Nakop
Karasburg
Upington
Oranjemund
Alexander Bay
Oranje
Warmbad
Kimberley
Kakamas
Pofadder
Vaal
Port Nolloth
Kenhardt
Okiep
Prieska
Hopetown
Springbok
Hondeklipbaai
Brandvlei
Britstown
Carnarvon
Bitterfontein
Sakrivier
Calvinia
Victoria W.
Vanrhynsdorp
Klawer
Nuweveldberge
Clanwilliam
Graaff-Reinet
Beaufort West
St. Helena B.
Vredenburg
Piketberg
Saldanha
Ceres
Worcester
Willowmore
Tafelbaai
Oudtshoorn
Cape Town
(Kaapstad)
Robertson
Stellenbosch
Swellendam
Table Mt.
Strand
Caledon
George
Kaap die Goeie Hoop
(C. of Good Hope)
False B.
Riversdale
Mosselbaai
Danger Pt.
Bredasdorp
C. Agulhas
5283
ft
m
9000
3000
6000
2000
4500
1500
1000
1200
400
600
200
0
5
Projection: Sanson Flamsteed's Sinusoidal
East from Greenwich
25

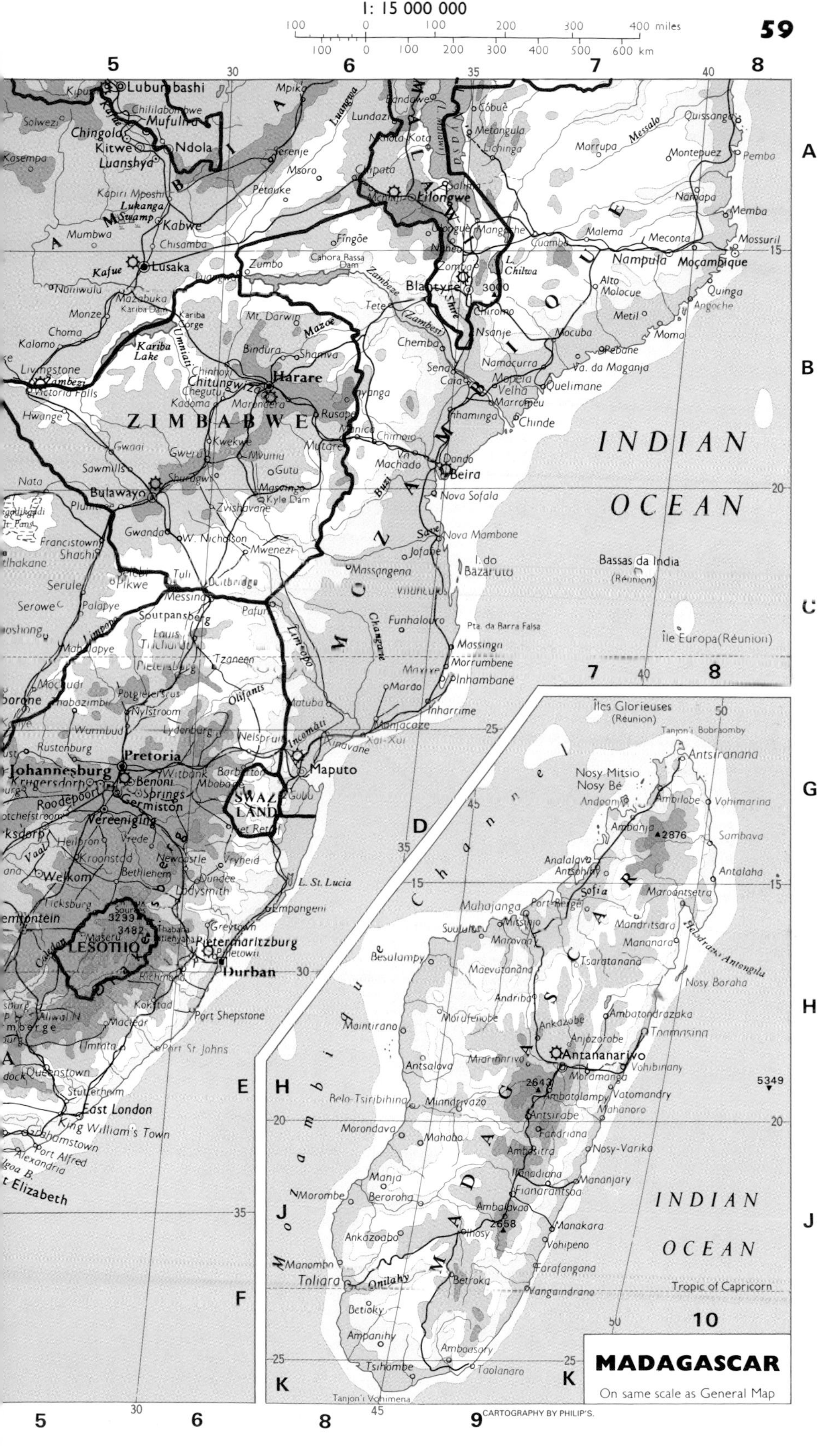
1: 15 000 000
100 0 100 200 300 400 miles
100 0 100 200 300 400 500 600 km
INDIAN OCEAN
ZIMBABWE
MOZAMBIQUE
ZAMBIA
MALAWI
SWAZILAND
LESOTHO
Lubumbashi
Chingola
Kitwe
Mufulira
Ndola
Luanshya
Kabwe
Lusaka
Livingstone
Victoria Falls
Kariba Lake
Harare
Chitungwiza
Bulawayo
Gweru
Mutare
Lilongwe
Blantyre
Zomba
Tete
Beira
Nampula
Moçambique
Quelimane
Chinde
Nova Sofala
Nova Mambone
I. do Bazaruto
Bassas da India (Réunion)
Île Europa (Réunion)
Inhambane
Maputo
Xai-Xai
Pretoria
Johannesburg
Germiston
Vereeniging
Welkom
Pietermaritzburg
Durban
Port Shepstone
Port St. Johns
Queenstown
East London
King William's Town
Grahamstown
Port Alfred
Port Elizabeth
L. St. Lucia
Îles Glorieuses (Réunion)
Mozambique Channel
Antsiranana
Nosy Bé
Mahajanga
Toamasina
Antananarivo
Antsirabe
Fianarantsoa
Toliara
Taolanaro
Tropic of Capricorn
MADAGASCAR
On same scale as General Map
CARTOGRAPHY BY PHILIP'S.

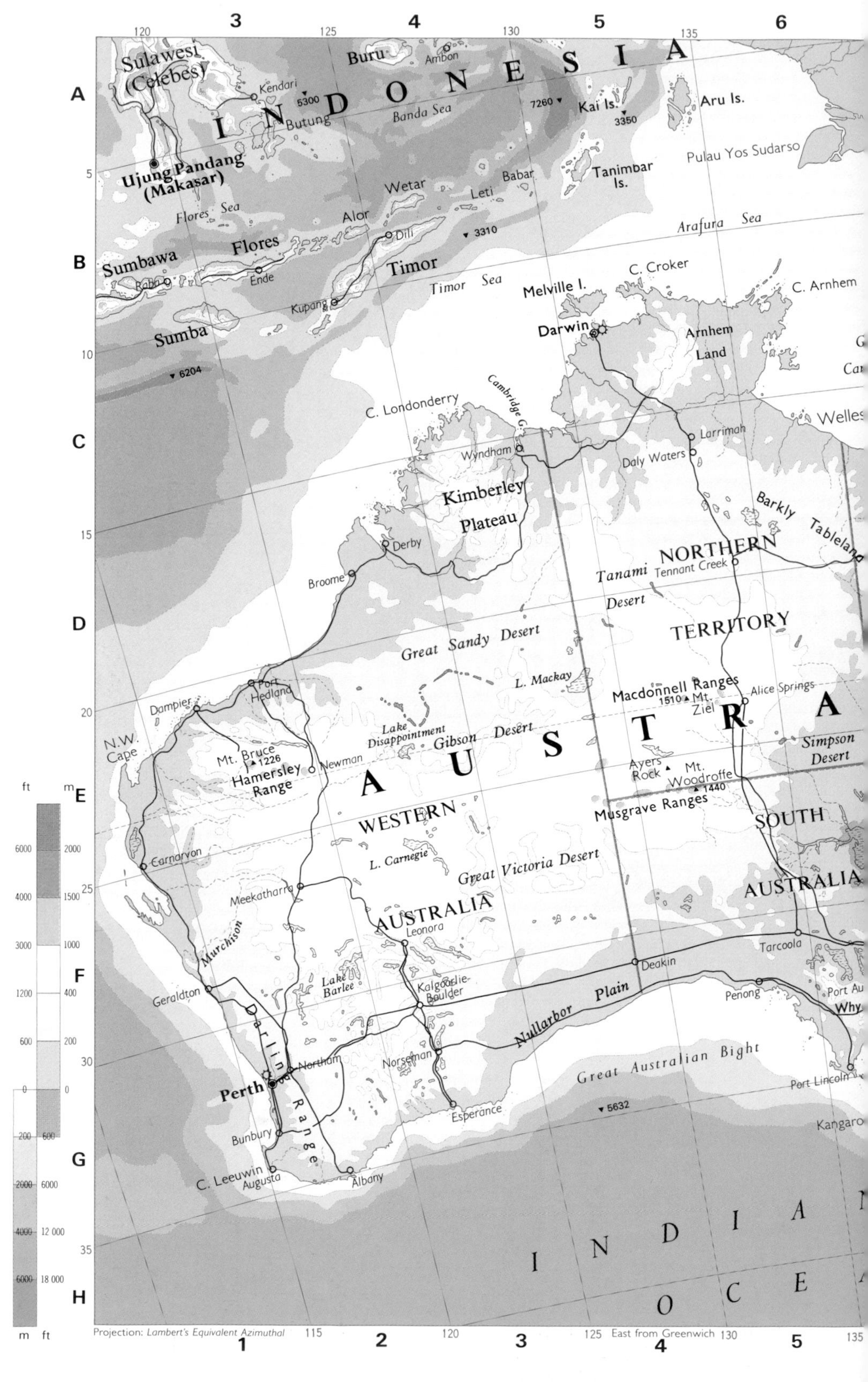
INDONESIA
Sulawesi (Celebes)
Ujung Pandang (Makasar)
Kendari
Buru
Ambon
Butung
Banda Sea
Kai Is.
Aru Is.
Pulau Yos Sudarso
Tanimbar Is.
Babar
Leti
Wetar
Alor
Flores Sea
Flores
Sumbawa
Ende
Dili
Timor
Kupang
Sumba
Arafura Sea
Timor Sea
Melville I.
C. Croker
C. Arnhem
Darwin
Arnhem Land
C. Londonderry
Cambridge G.
Wyndham
Larrimah
Daly Waters
Kimberley Plateau
Derby
Broome
Barkly Tableland
NORTHERN TERRITORY
Tennant Creek
Tanami Desert
Great Sandy Desert
L. Mackay
Port Hedland
Dampier
Macdonnell Ranges
Mt. Ziel
Alice Springs
Simpson Desert
N.W. Cape
Mt. Bruce
Hamersley Range
Newman
Lake Disappointment
Gibson Desert
AUSTRALIA
Ayers Rock
Mt. Woodroffe
Musgrave Ranges
WESTERN AUSTRALIA
SOUTH AUSTRALIA
L. Carnegie
Great Victoria Desert
Carnarvon
Meekatharra
Leonora
Tarcoola
Deakin
Murchison
Geraldton
Lake Barlee
Kalgoorlie-Boulder
Nullarbor Plain
Penong
Darling Range
Northam
Norseman
Perth
Great Australian Bight
Port Lincoln
Esperance
Bunbury
C. Leeuwin
Augusta
Albany
INDIAN OCEAN
Projection: Lambert's Equivalent Azimuthal
East from Greenwich

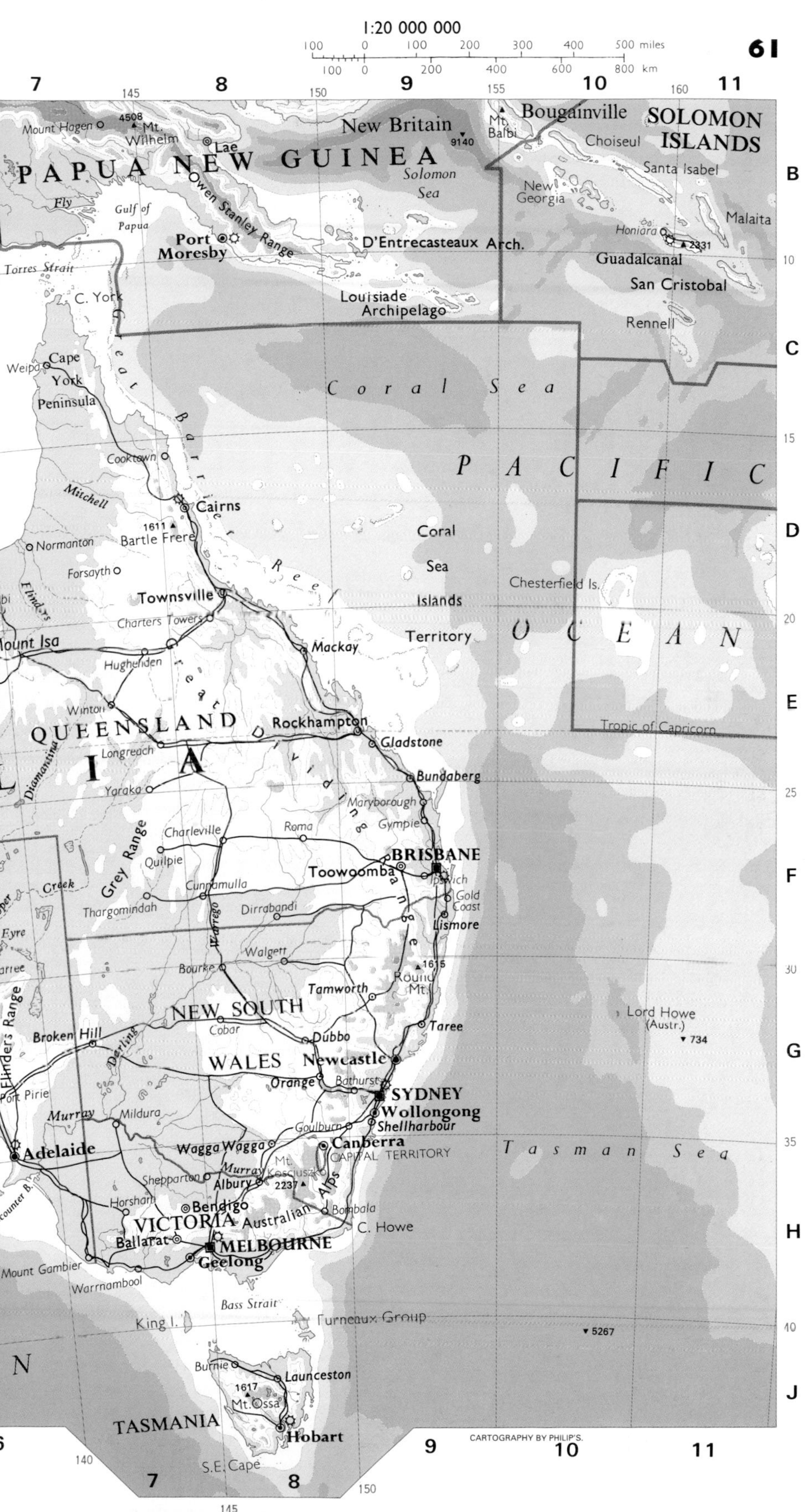
1:20 000 000
PAPUA NEW GUINEA
New Britain
Bougainville
SOLOMON ISLANDS
Solomon Sea
Coral Sea
PACIFIC OCEAN
Coral Sea Islands Territory
QUEENSLAND
NEW SOUTH WALES
VICTORIA
TASMANIA
Tasman Sea
BRISBANE
SYDNEY
MELBOURNE
Canberra
Hobart
Adelaide
Great Barrier Reef
Great Dividing Range
Tropic of Capricorn
CARTOGRAPHY BY PHILIP'S.

SOUTH AUSTRALIA
Lake Eyre (North)
L. Eyre (South)
Coober Pedy
Oodnadatta
Woomera
Port Augusta
Whyalla
Port Pirie
Port Lincoln
Eyre Peninsula
Spencer Gulf
ADELAIDE
Port Adelaide
Elizabeth
Glenelg
Brighton
Kangaroo I.
Victor Harbor
Murray Bridge
Mount Gambier
Broken Hill
Mildura
Lake Torrens
Lake Frome
Lake Gairdner
Flinders Ranges
Barrier Range
Kingston South East
Horsham
Ballarat
Warrnambool
Portland
King Island
TASMANIA
Flinders Island
Furneaux Group
Cape Barren I.
Wynyard
Burnie
Ulverstone
Devonport
George Town
Launceston
Queenstown
New Norfolk
Hobart
Glenorchy
Bruny I.
S.E. Cape
S.W. Cape
Projection: Bonne
East from Greenwich

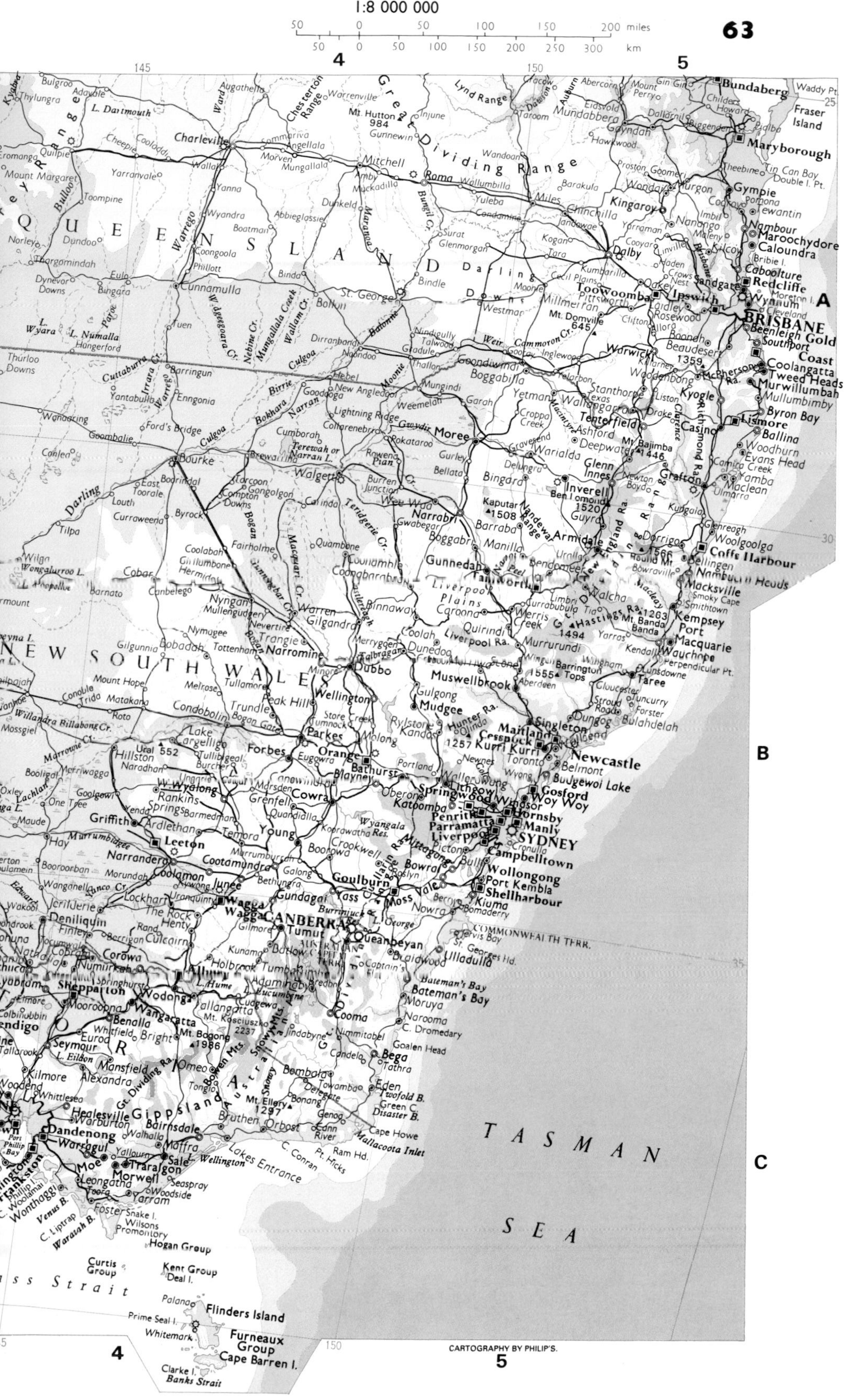
1:8 000 000
miles
km
QUEENSLAND
NEW SOUTH WALES
TASMAN SEA
Great Dividing Range
Darling Downs
Bundaberg
Fraser Island
Maryborough
Gympie
Nambour
Maroochydore
Caloundra
Caboolture
Redcliffe
Wynnum
BRISBANE
Ipswich
Toowoomba
Dalby
Kingaroy
Gold Coast
Southport
Coolangatta
Tweed Heads
Murwillumbah
Byron Bay
Lismore
Ballina
Casino
Grafton
Coffs Harbour
Armidale
Tamworth
Gunnedah
Narrabri
Moree
Inverell
Glenn Innes
Tenterfield
Warwick
Goondiwindi
St. George
Roma
Mitchell
Charleville
Cunnamulla
Bourke
Walgett
Dubbo
Orange
Bathurst
Parkes
Forbes
Wellington
Mudgee
Muswellbrook
Singleton
Maitland
Cessnock
Newcastle
Gosford
Woy Woy
Hornsby
Manly
SYDNEY
Parramatta
Penrith
Liverpool
Katoomba
Lithgow
Campbelltown
Wollongong
Port Kembla
Shellharbour
Kiama
Nowra
Goulburn
Yass
CANBERRA
Queanbeyan
Cooma
Bega
Eden
Batemans Bay
Ulladulla
Wagga Wagga
Griffith
Leeton
Narrandera
Cootamundra
Young
Cowra
Albury
Wodonga
Wangaratta
Shepparton
Benalla
Seymour
Dandenong
Frankston
Morwell
Traralgon
Sale
Bairnsdale
Lakes Entrance
Mt. Kosciusko 2237
Snowy Mts.
Gippsland
Port Macquarie
Kempsey
Taree
Bass Strait
Flinders Island
Furneaux Group
Cape Barren I.
Banks Strait
Kent Group
Hogan Group
Wilsons Promontory
COMMONWEALTH TERR.
Jervis Bay
Cape Howe
Mallacoota Inlet
CARTOGRAPHY BY PHILIP'S.

# NEW ZEALAND, CENTRAL AND SOUTH-WEST PACIFIC

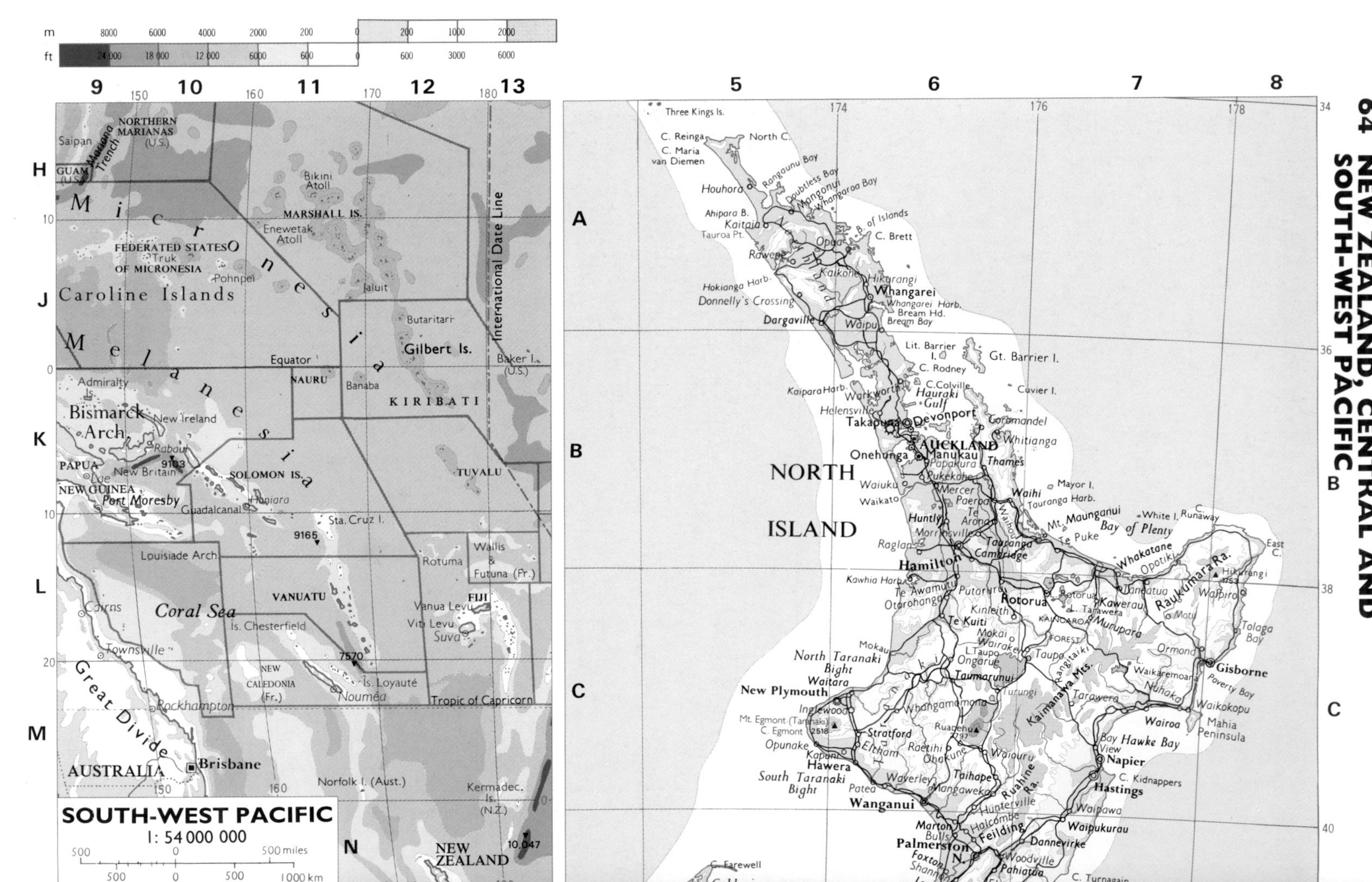

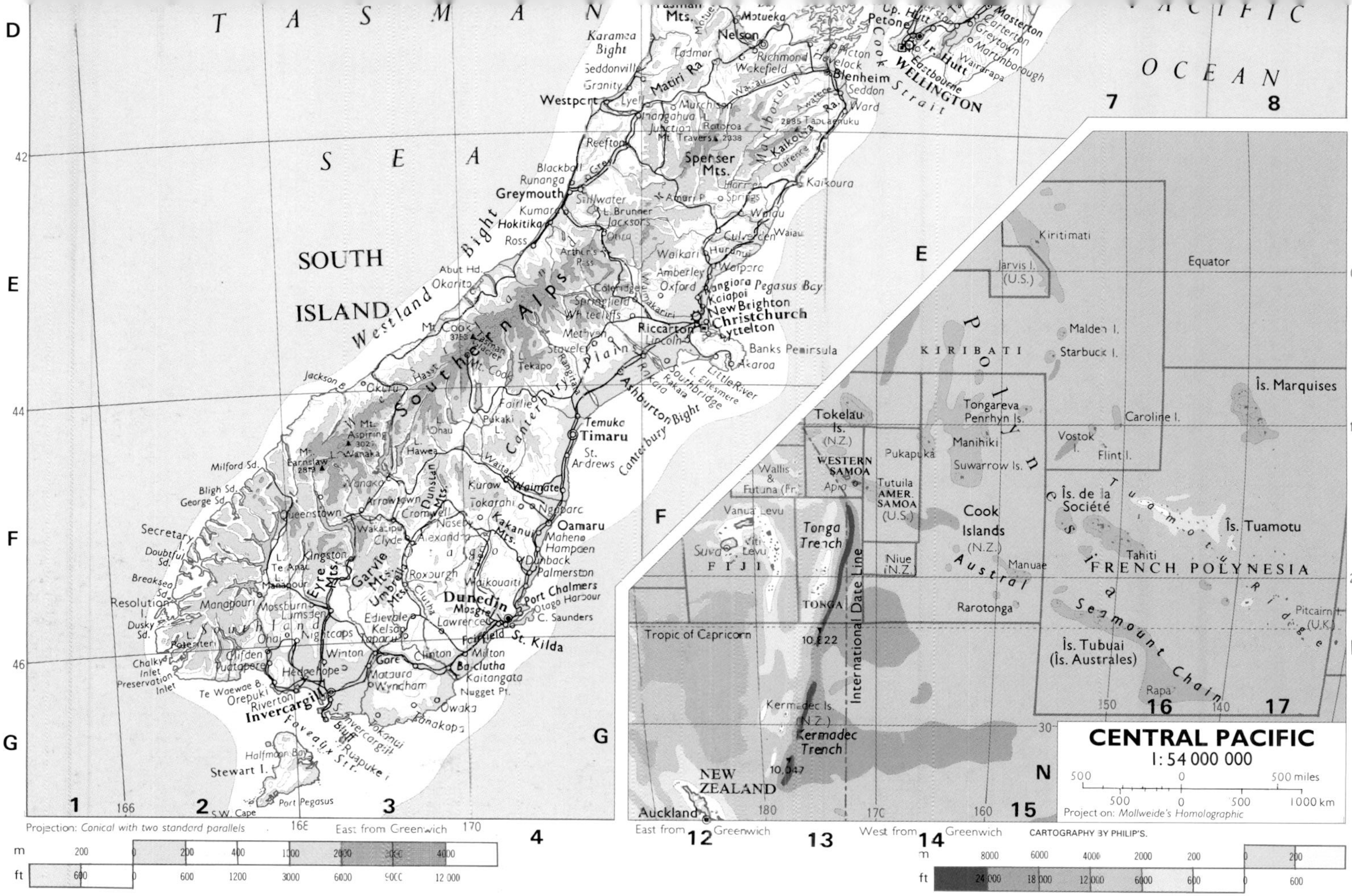

1: 6 000 000

50 0 50 100 miles

50 0 50 100 150 km

Projection: Conical with two standard parallels

East from Greenwich

| m | 200 | 0 | 200 | 400 | 1000 | 2000 | 3000 | 4000 |
|---|---|---|---|---|---|---|---|---|
| ft | 600 | 0 | 600 | 1200 | 3000 | 6000 | 9000 | 12 000 |

## CENTRAL PACIFIC

1: 54 000 000

500 0 500 miles

500 0 500 1000 km

Projection: *Mollweide's Homolographic*

East from Greenwich West from Greenwich

CARTOGRAPHY BY PHILIP'S.

| m | 8000 | 6000 | 4000 | 2000 | 200 | 0 | 200 |
|---|---|---|---|---|---|---|---|
| ft | 24 000 | 18 000 | 12 000 | 6000 | 600 | 0 | 600 |

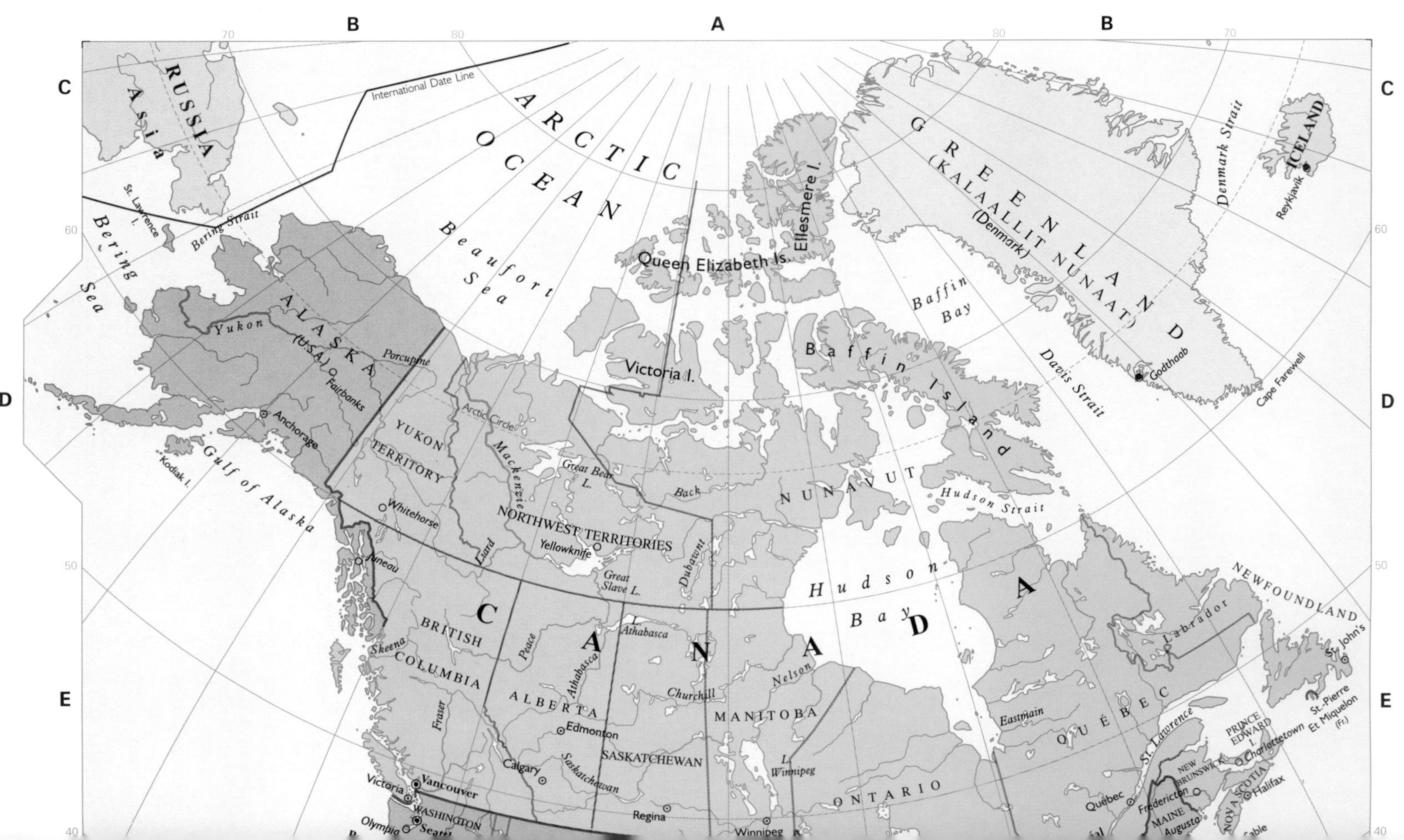
ARCTIC OCEAN
RUSSIA
Asia
International Date Line
St. Lawrence I.
Bering Strait
Bering Sea
ALASKA (U.S.A.)
Yukon
Porcupine
Fairbanks
Anchorage
Kodiak I.
Gulf of Alaska
Beaufort Sea
Queen Elizabeth Is.
Ellesmere I.
Victoria I.
GREENLAND (KALAALLIT NUNAAT) (Denmark)
Baffin Bay
Baffin Island
Davis Strait
Godthaab
Cape Farewell
Denmark Strait
ICELAND
Reykjavík
YUKON TERRITORY
Arctic Circle
Mackenzie
Whitehorse
Juneau
Great Bear L.
Back
NUNAVUT
Hudson Strait
NORTHWEST TERRITORIES
Yellowknife
Great Slave L.
Dubawnt
Liard
Hudson Bay
CANADA
BRITISH COLUMBIA
Skeena
Fraser
Peace
Athabasca
L. Athabasca
ALBERTA
Edmonton
Calgary
Saskatchewan
SASKATCHEWAN
Regina
Churchill
Nelson
MANITOBA
L. Winnipeg
Winnipeg
ONTARIO
Eastmain
QUÉBEC
Québec
St. Lawrence
Labrador
NEWFOUNDLAND
St. John's
St.-Pierre Et Miquelon (Fr.)
PRINCE EDWARD I.
Charlottetown
NEW BRUNSWICK
Fredericton
NOVA SCOTIA
Halifax
MAINE
Augusta
Vancouver
Victoria
WASHINGTON
Olympia
Seattle

1: 35 000 000
200 0 200 400 600 800 miles
400 0 400 800 1200 km
NORTH ATLANTIC OCEAN
PACIFIC OCEAN
UNITED STATES
MEXICO
Gulf of Mexico
Caribbean Sea
South America
Tropic of Cancer
OREGON
IDAHO
WYOMING
SOUTH DAKOTA
DAKOTA
NEBRASKA
IOWA
WISCONSIN
MICHIGAN
OHIO
ILLINOIS
INDIANA
KENTUCKY
VIRGINIA
W.V.
NORTH CAROLINA
SOUTH CAROLINA
TENNESSEE
GEORGIA
ALABAMA
MISSISSIPPI
LOUISIANA
ARKANSAS
MISSOURI
KANSAS
OKLAHOMA
TEXAS
NEW MEXICO
COLORADO
UTAH
NEVADA
ARIZONA
CALIFORNIA
FLORIDA
NEW YORK
PA.
MASS.
Helena
Boise
Snake
Bismarck
Minneapolis
Salt Lake City
Cheyenne
Denver
Carson City
Sacramento
SAN FRANCISCO
San Jose
Las Vegas
LOS ANGELES
San Diego
Colorado
Phoenix
Tucson
El Paso
Santa Fe
Albuquerque
Lincoln
Kansas City
Topeka
Oklahoma City
Dallas
Austin
Houston
Little Rock
Memphis
Mississippi
Jackson
Baton Rouge
New Orleans
Birmingham
Montgomery
Tallahassee
Jacksonville
Tampa
Miami
Atlanta
Columbia
Charleston
Charlotte
Raleigh
Richmond
Washington D.C.
Baltimore
PHILADELPHIA
NEW YORK CITY
Hartford
Providence
Boston
Buffalo
Toronto
L. Ontario
Huron
Detroit
Erie
Cleveland
Pittsburgh
Columbus
Toledo
Lansing
L. Michigan
Madison
Milwaukee
CHICAGO
Springfield
Indianapolis
Cincinnati
St. Louis
Nashville
Bermuda (U.K.)
Hermosillo
Culiacan
Rio Grande
Monterrey
Guadalajara
MÉXICO
Puebla
Acapulco
Mérida
Revilla Gigedo Is. (Mex.)
Guadalupe (Mex.)
Belmopan
BELIZE
GUATEMALA
Guatemala
HONDURAS
Tegucigalpa
San Salvador
EL SALVADOR
NICARAGUA
L. Nicaragua
Managua
COSTA RICA
San José
PANAMA
Panamá
COLOMBIA
Medellín
Barranquilla
Maracaibo
VENEZUELA
Florida Str.
Havana
CUBA
Cayman Is. (U.K.)
JAMAICA
Kingston
HAITI
Port-au-Prince
DOMINICAN REP.
Santo Domingo
PUERTO RICO (U.S.A.)
San Juan
BAHAMAS
Nassau
Turks & Caicos Is. (U.K.)
F
G
H
J
30
20
10
120
110
100
90
80
70
7
8
9
10
11
12
Projection: Bonne
West from Greenwich
■ MÉXICO Capital Cities
CARTOGRAPHY BY PHILIP'S.

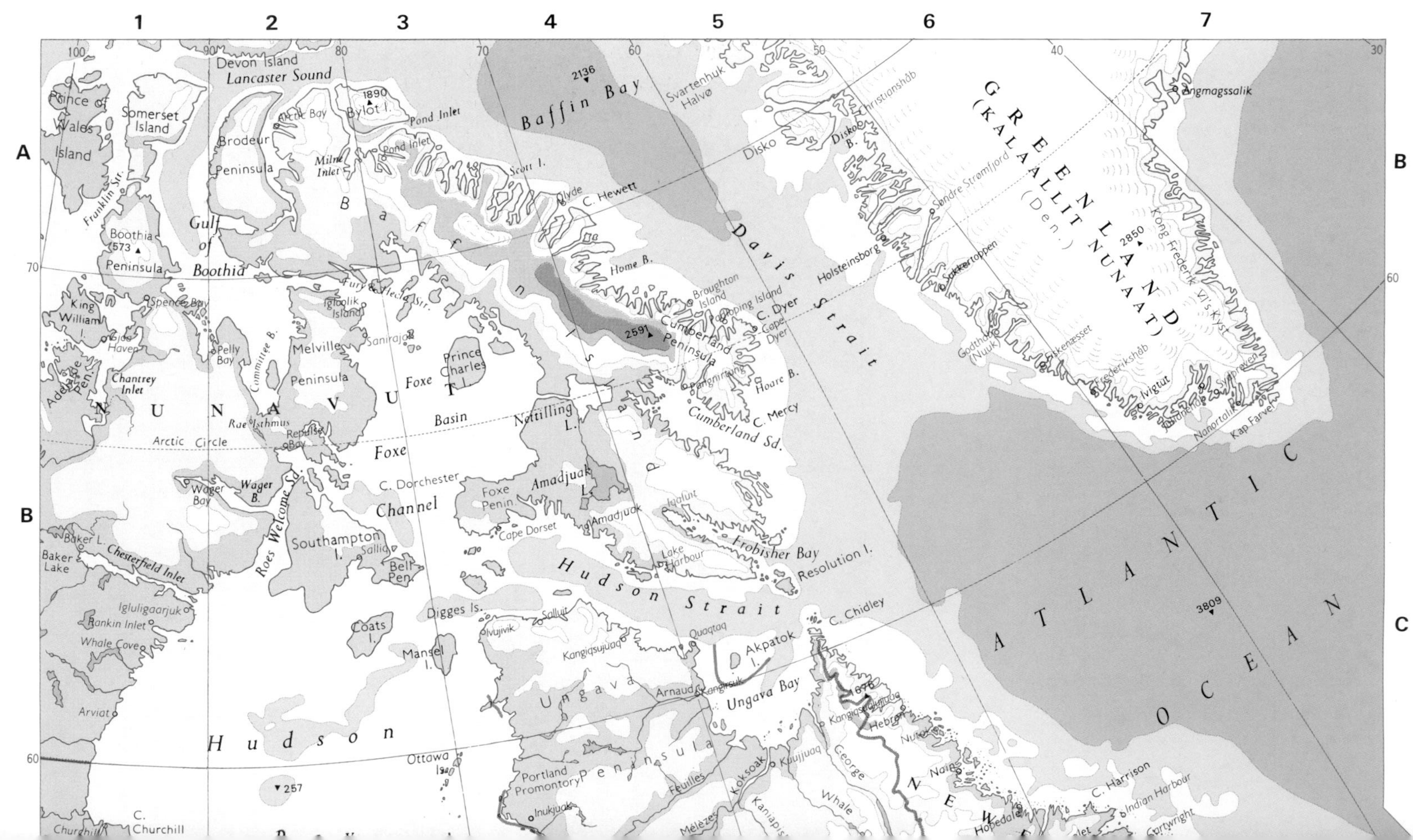
1
2
3
4
5
6
7
A
B
C
GREENLAND
(KALAALLIT NUNAAT)
(Den.)
Kong Frederik VI's Kyst
Kap Farvel
Angmagssalik
Christianshåb
Disko B.
Disko
Svartenhuk Halvø
Søndre Strømfjord
Holsteinsborg
Sukkertoppen
Godthåb (Nuuk)
Fiskenæsset
Frederikshåb
Ivigtut
Julianehåb
Nanortalik
2850
3809
ATLANTIC
OCEAN
Davis Strait
Baffin Bay
2136
Devon Island
Lancaster Sound
Prince of Wales Island
Somerset Island
Franklin Str.
Boothia Peninsula
573
Gulf of Boothia
Brodeur Peninsula
Arctic Bay
Bylot I.
1890
Pond Inlet
Milne Inlet
Scott I.
Clyde
C. Hewett
Home B.
Baffin Island
2591
Broughton Island
Qikiqtarjuaq
C. Dyer
Cape Dyer
Cumberland Peninsula
Pangnirtung
Hoare B.
C. Mercy
Cumberland Sd.
King William I.
Gjoa Haven
Spence Bay
Pelly Bay
Committee B.
Adelaide Pen.
Chantrey Inlet
NUNAVUT
Fury & Hecla Str.
Igloolik Island
Sanirajak
Melville Peninsula
Prince Charles I.
Foxe Basin
Nettilling L.
Rae Isthmus
Repulse Bay
Arctic Circle
Foxe Channel
C. Dorchester
Foxe Penin.
Amadjuak L.
Amadjuak
Cape Dorset
Iqaluit
Frobisher Bay
Lake Harbour
Resolution I.
Hudson Strait
Wager Bay
Wager B.
Roes Welcome Sd.
Southampton I.
Sallio
Bell Pen.
Baker L.
Baker Lake
Chesterfield Inlet
Igluligaarjuk
Rankin Inlet
Whale Cove
Arviat
Digges Is.
Salluit
Ivujivik
Coats I.
Mansel I.
Kangiqsujuaq
Quaqtaq
Akpatok I.
C. Chidley
Ungava
Arnaud
Kangirsuk
Ungava Bay
1676
Kangiqsualujjuaq
Hebron
Nutak
Nain
Hudson
Ottawa Is.
257
Peninsula
Portland Promontory
Inukjuak
Feuilles
Mélèzes
Koksoak
Kuujjuaq
Kaniapiscau
George
Whale
Hopedale
C. Harrison
Indian Harbour
Cartwright
C. Churchill
Churchill
100
90
80
70
60
50
40
30

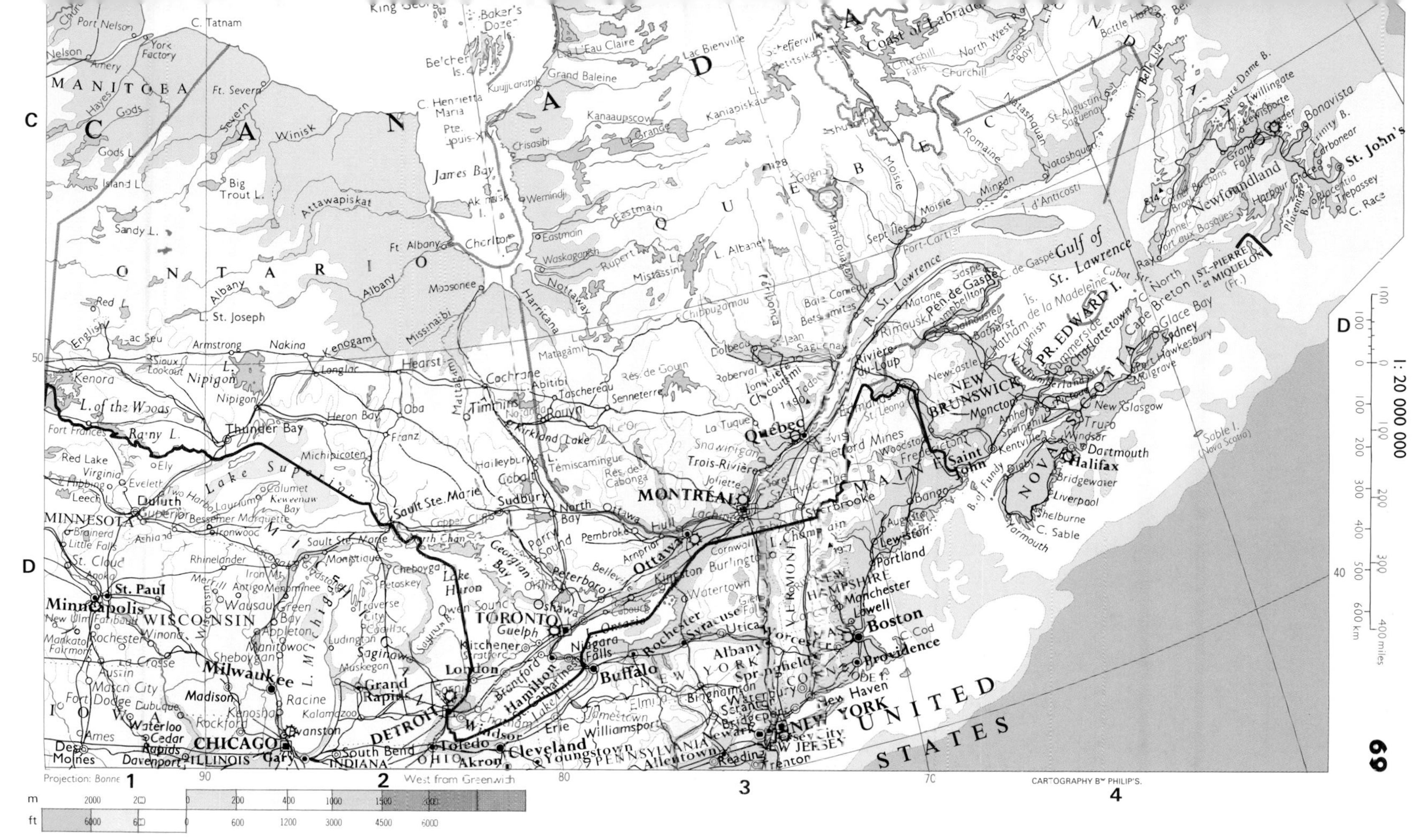
1: 20 000 000
100 0 100 200 300 400 miles
100 0 100 200 300 400 500 600 km
CANADA
UNITED STATES
ONTARIO
QUEBEC
MANITOBA
NEWFOUNDLAND
NEW BRUNSWICK
NOVA SCOTIA
PR. EDWARD I.
James Bay
Gulf of St. Lawrence
Lake Superior
Lake Huron
L. Michigan
MONTREAL
Québec
Ottawa
TORONTO
DETROIT
CHICAGO
Milwaukee
Minneapolis
St. Paul
Buffalo
Cleveland
Boston
NEW YORK
Halifax
St. John's
Projection: Bonne
West from Greenwich
CARTOGRAPHY BY PHILIP'S

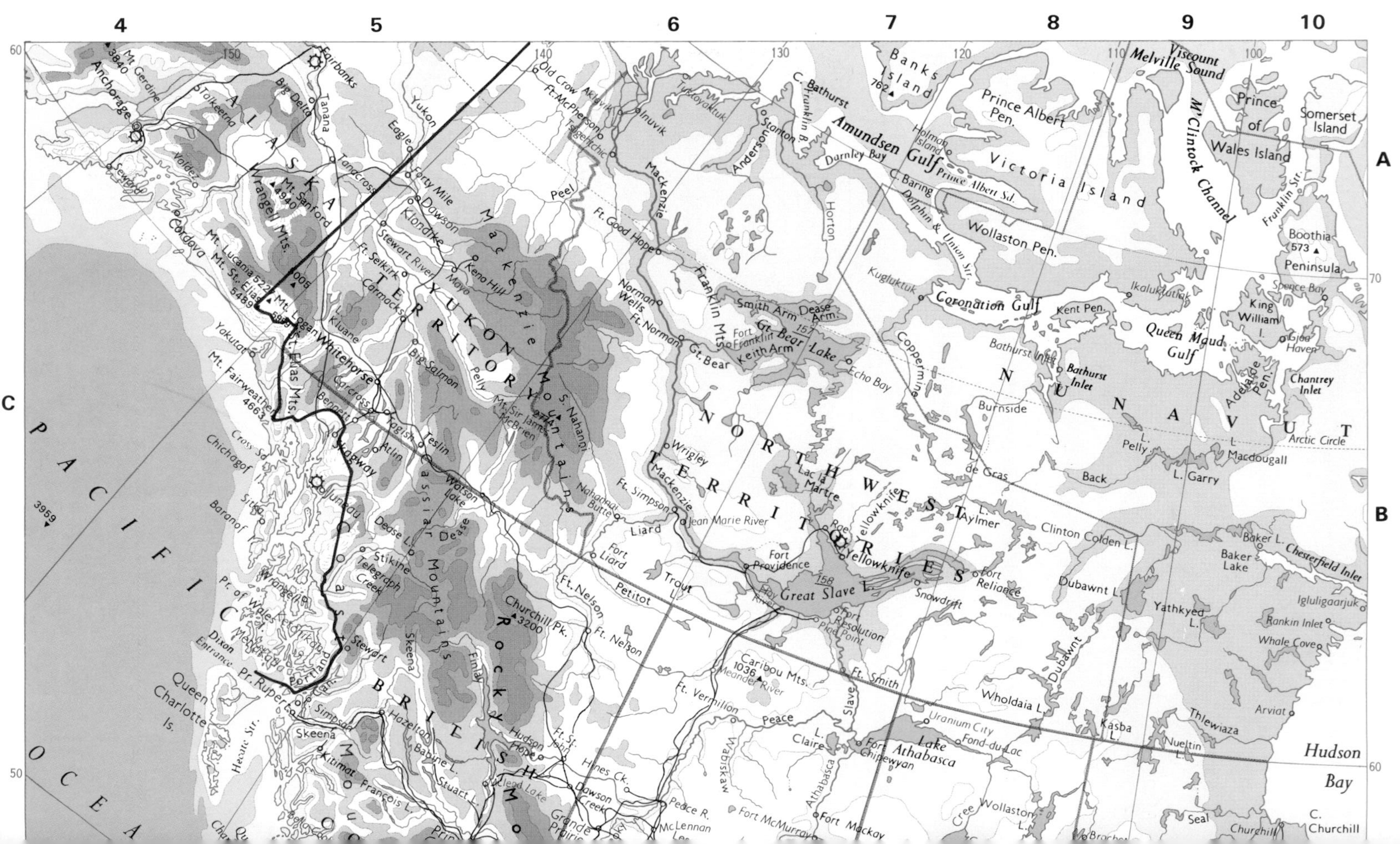
4
5
6
7
8
9
10
A
B
C
Mt Gerdine 3840
Anchorage
Seward
Talkeetna
Valdez
Cordova
ALASKA
Big Delta
Tanana
Fairbanks
Tanacross
Mt. Sanford 4940
Wrangell Mts.
Mt. Lucania 5226
Mt. St. Elias 5489
Mt. Logan
6050
St. Elias Mts.
Yakutat
Mt. Fairweather 4663
Cross Sd.
Chichagof I.
Sitka
Baranof
Juneau
Skagway
Wrangell
Pr. of Wales I.
Ketchikan
Metlakatla
Dixon Entrance
Pr. Rupert
Queen Charlotte Is.
Hecate Str.
Skeena
Kitimat
Simpson
Hazelton
Babine L.
Francois L.
Stuart L.
McLeod Lake
Portland Canal
Stewart
Stikine
Telegraph Creek
Dease L.
Atlin
Tagish
Carcross
Bennett
Whitehorse
Kluane
Carmacks
Ft. Selkirk
Stewart River
Klondike
Dawson
Forty Mile
Eagle
Yukon
Mayo
Keno Hill
Big Salmon
Pelly
Teslin
Watson Lake
Dease
Cassiar Mountains
YUKON TERRITORY
Mackenzie Mountains
Mt. Sir James McBrien
2762
S. Nahanni
Nahanni Butte
Old Crow
Aklavik
Ft. McPherson
Tsiigehtchic
Inuvik
Tuktoyaktuk
Peel
Mackenzie
Ft. Good Hope
Norman Wells
Ft. Norman
Gt. Bear
Franklin Mts.
Smith Arm
Dease Arm
Gt. Bear Lake
157
Fort Franklin
Keith Arm
Echo Bay
Wrigley
Ft. Simpson
Jean Marie River
Liard
Fort Liard
Ft. Nelson
Petitot
Trout L.
Fort Providence
Hay River
Great Slave L.
158
Yellowknife
Rae
Lac la Martre
Fort Resolution
Pine Point
Snowdrift
Fort Reliance
Ft. Smith
Caribou Mts.
1036
Meander River
Ft. Vermilion
Peace
Wabiskaw
L. Claire
Slave
Athabasca
Fort McMurray
Fort Mackay
Fort Chipewyan
Lake Athabasca
Uranium City
Fond-du-Lac
Cree
Wollaston L.
Peace R.
McLennan
Grande Prairie
Dawson Creek
Hines Ck.
Hudson Hope
Ft. St. John
Finlay
Churchill Pk.
3200
Rocky
BRITISH
NORTHWEST TERRITORIES
NUNAVUT
Horton
Anderson
Stanton
Franklin B.
C. Bathurst
Banks Island
762
Darnley Bay
Amundsen Gulf
Holman Island
Prince Albert Pen.
Prince Albert Sd.
Victoria Island
C. Baring
Dolphin & Union Str.
Wollaston Pen.
Kugluktuk
Coppermine
Coronation Gulf
Kent Pen.
Bathurst Inlet
Ikaluktutiak
Queen Maud Gulf
Burnside
de Gras
L. Pelly
Back
L. Garry
L. Macdougall
Arctic Circle
Adelaide Pen.
Chantrey Inlet
Gjoa Haven
King William I.
Spence Bay
Boothia Peninsula
573
Franklin Str.
M'Clintock Channel
Viscount Melville Sound
Prince of Wales Island
Somerset Island
L. Aylmer
Clinton Colden L.
Dubawnt L.
Dubawnt
Wholdaia L.
Kasba L.
Nueltin L.
Thlewiaza
Arviat
Yathkyed L.
Baker L.
Baker Lake
Chesterfield Inlet
Igluligaarjuk
Rankin Inlet
Whale Cove
Hudson Bay
Seal
Churchill
C. Churchill
PACIFIC OCEAN
3959
60
50
70
150
140
130
120
110
100

1: 15 000 000

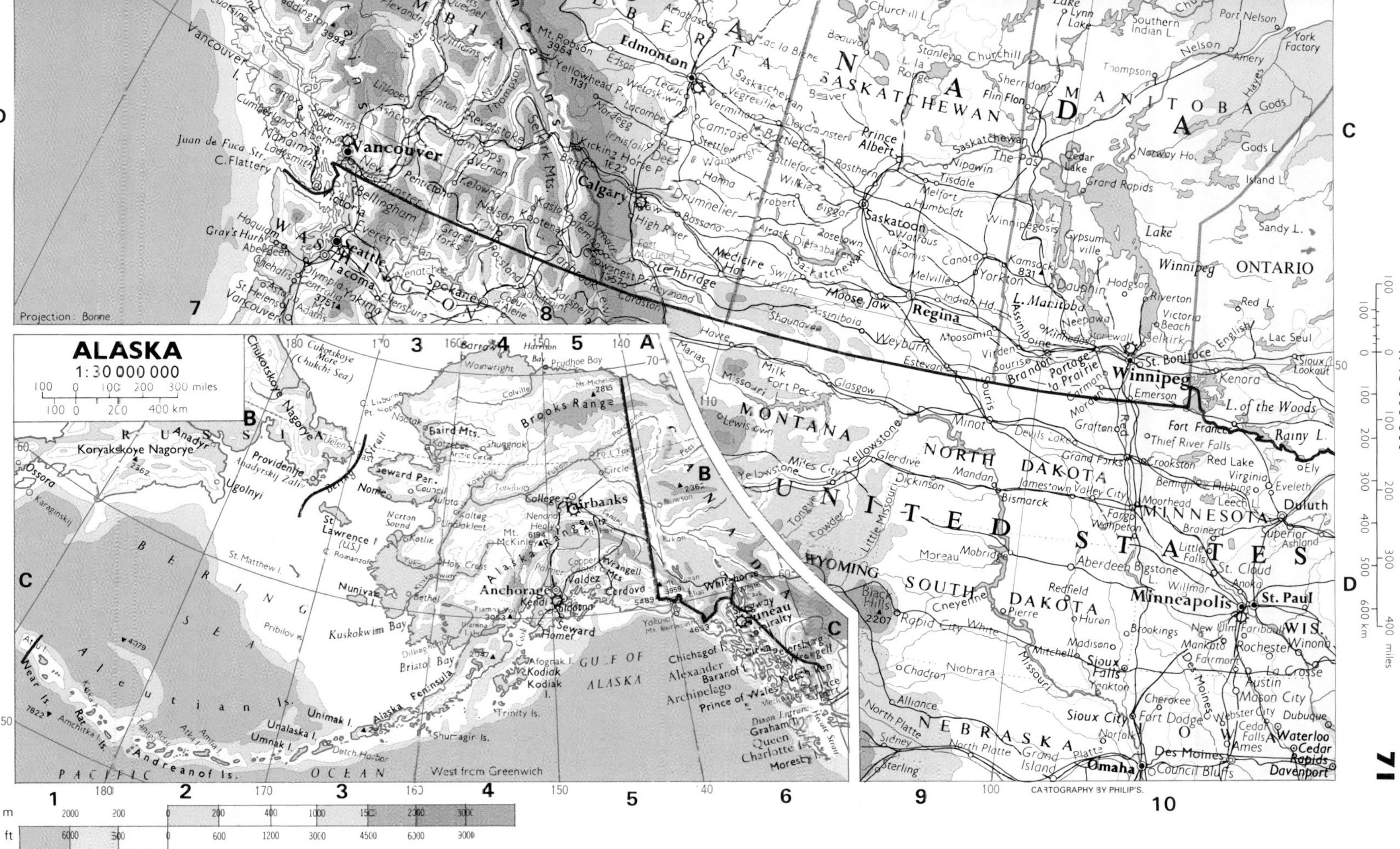
ALASKA
1:30 000 000
100 0 100 200 300 miles
100 0 200 400 km
ONTARIO
MANITOBA
SASKATCHEWAN
CANADA
MONTANA
NORTH DAKOTA
SOUTH DAKOTA
MINNESOTA
WYOMING
NEBRASKA
UNITED STATES
Winnipeg
Regina
Saskatoon
Edmonton
Calgary
Vancouver
Seattle
Minneapolis
St. Paul
Omaha
Fairbanks
Anchorage
Juneau
Brooks Range
BERING SEA
GULF OF ALASKA
PACIFIC OCEAN
Aleutian Is.
West from Greenwich
Projection: Bonne
CARTOGRAPHY BY PHILIP'S

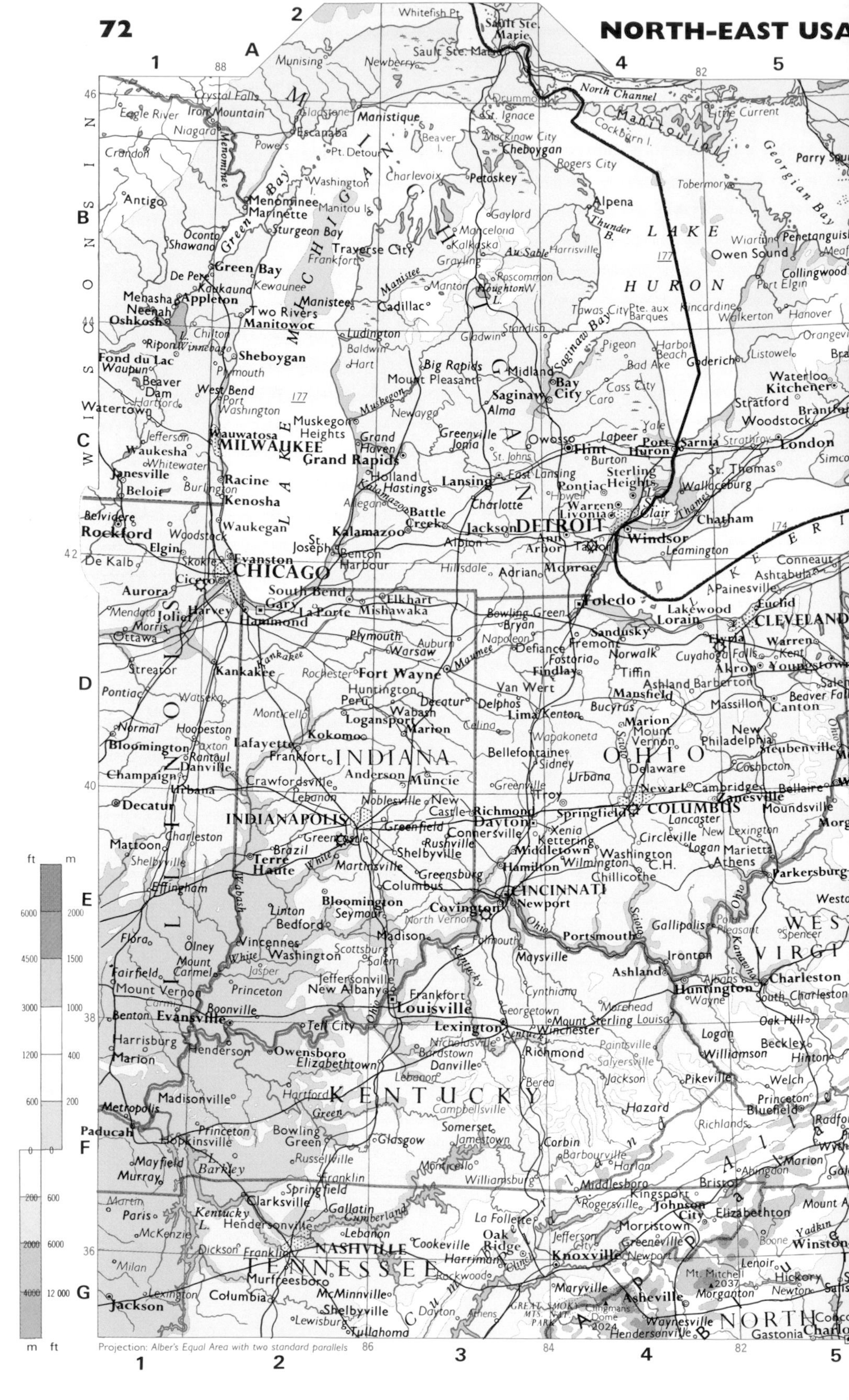


Projection: Alber's Equal Area with two standard parallels

1: 6 000 000

CARTOGRAPHY BY PHILIP'S.

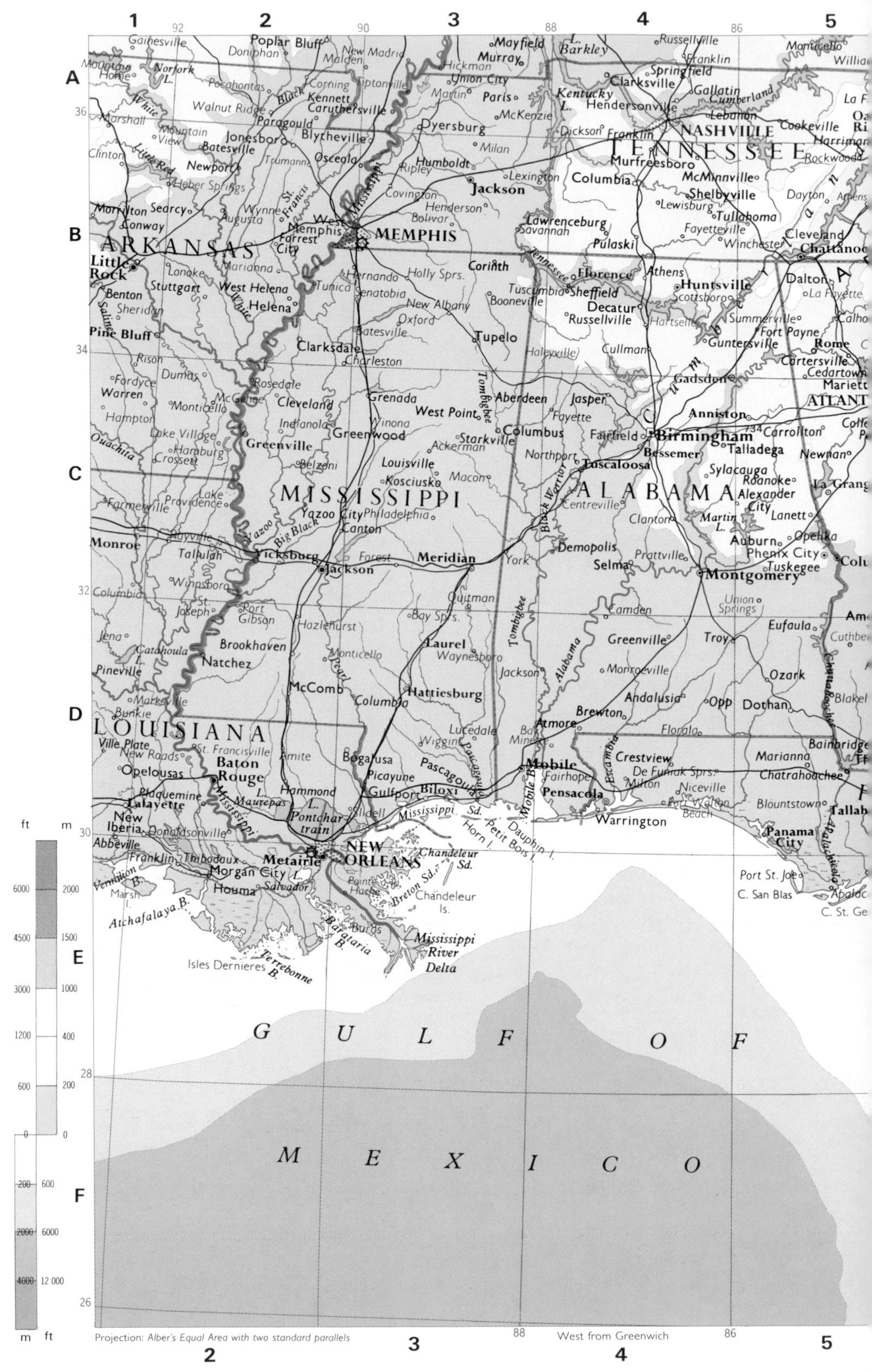

ARKANSAS
TENNESSEE
MISSISSIPPI
ALABAMA
LOUISIANA
MEMPHIS
NASHVILLE
NEW ORLEANS
Little Rock
Jackson
Birmingham
Montgomery
Mobile
Baton Rouge
Chattanooga
Huntsville
Meridian
Vicksburg
Tuscaloosa
Pensacola
Hattiesburg
Gulfport
Biloxi
G U L F O F
M E X I C O
Mississippi River Delta
Projection: Alber's Equal Area with two standard parallels
West from Greenwich

1: 6 000 000
50 0 50 100 miles
50 0 50 100 150 km
6
7
8
9
10
A
B
C
D
E
F
G
84
82
80
78
76
36
34
32
30
28
26
Harlan
Middlesboro
Kingsport
Bristol
Abingdon
Marion
Galax
Martinsville
Danville
Emporia
Currituck Sd.
Johnson City
Rogersville
Elizabethton
Mount Airy
Eden
Reidsville
Roxboro
Oxford
Roanoke Rapids
Henderson
Winton
Elizabeth City
Edenton
Albemarle Sd.
Manteo
Roanoke I.
Morristown
Jefferson City
Greeneville
Newport
Knoxville
Boone
Yadkin
Winston-Salem
Greensboro
High Point
Burlington
Graham
Durham
Chapel Hill
Raleigh
Rocky Mount
Wilson
Williamston
Greenville
Lenoir
Hickory
Statesville
Thomasville
Lexington
Mt. Mitchell 2037
Morganton
Newton
Salisbury
Asheboro
Kannapolis
Sanford
Smithfield
Washington
Pamlico
Pamlico Sound
Maryville
Asheville
Waynesville
Hendersonville
Brevard
NORTH CAROLINA
Concord
Gastonia
Shelby
Charlotte
Albemarle
Southern Pines
Dunn
Goldsboro
Neuse
Kinston
New Bern
C. Hatteras
GREAT SMOKY MTS. NAT. PARK
Clingmans Dome 2024
Murphy
Spartanburg
Gaffney
Rock Hill
Monroe
Fayetteville
Clinton
Jacksonville
Raleigh B.
Beaufort
C. Lookout
Onslow B.
Brasstown Bald 1458
Greenville
Easley
Union
Chester
Lancaster
Laurinburg
Cape Fear
Lumberton
Seneca
Toccoa
Belton
Anderson
Laurens
Broad
Bennettsville
Hartsville
Dillon
Darlington
Whiteville
Wilmington
Hartwell
Gainesville
Greenwood
Newberry
Camden
Florence
Mullins
Marion
Abbeville
Saluda
L. Murray
Columbia
Buford
Elberton
Athens
Lawrenceville
Clark Hill L.
Sumter
Lake City
Conway
Southport
C. Fear
Decatur
East Point
SOUTH CAROLINA
Manning
Kingstree
Myrtle Beach
Covington
Augusta
Aiken
Orangeburg
L. Marion
Georgetown
Griffin
Sparta
Savannah
Bamberg
L. Moultrie
GEORGIA
Milledgeville
Waynesboro
Summerville
Cooper
North Charleston
Walterboro
Charleston
Mt. Pleasant
Millen
Hampton
Thomaston
Macon
Warner Robins
Swainsboro
Ogeechee
Combahee
Dublin
Ridgeland
Beaufort
Parris I.
Perry
Cochran
Oconee
Statesboro
Vidalia
Eastman
Savannah
Ocmulgee
Cordele
Hazlehurst
Altamaha
Hinesville
Ossabaw I.
Fitzgerald
Buxley
Jesup
St. Catherines I.
Sylvester
Tifton
Douglas
Sapelo I.
Brunswick
Moultrie
Adel
Waycross
Satilla
Cairo
Valdosta
Okefenokee Swamp
Folkston
Cumberland I.
Quitman
Fernandina Beach
ATLANTIC
Monticello
Madison
Jasper
Live Oak
Suwannee
JACKSONVILLE
St. Johns
Jacksonville Beach
Lake City
Perry
Starke
Green Cove Springs
St. Augustine
Apalachee B.
High Springs
Palatka
Gainesville
Cross City
Bunnell
L. George
Ormond Beach
Ocala
Daytona Beach
New Smyrna Beach
OCEAN
De Land
Eustis
Sanford
Crystal River
Inverness
Leesburg
Titusville
Brooksville
Winter Park
Orlando
C. Canaveral
Cocoa
Merritt Island
Dade City
Kissimmee
Tarpon Springs
Lakeland
Haines City
Winter Haven
Melbourne
Indian
Clearwater
Largo
TAMPA
Bartow
St. Petersburg
Tampa Bay
Vero Beach
River
Sebring
L. Istokpoga
Fort Pierce
Kissimmee
Bradenton
Sarasota
Arcadia
Okeechobee
Stuart
Grand Cays
Little Abaco I.
Gt. Guana Cay
L. Okeechobee
Punta Gorda
Pahokee
Settlement Pt.
Hope Town
La Belle
Belle Glade
West Palm Beach
Grand Bahama I.
Charlotte Harb.
Fort Myers
Cape Coral
Immokalee
Delray Beach
Freeport
Great Abaco I.
Boca Raton
Pompano Beach
BAHAMAS
Naples
Big Cypress Swamp
Everglades
Fort Lauderdale
Hollywood
Carol City
Miami Beach
Hialeah
MIAMI
CARTOGRAPHY BY PHILIP'S.
EVERGLADES NAT. PARK
Biscayne B.
Homestead

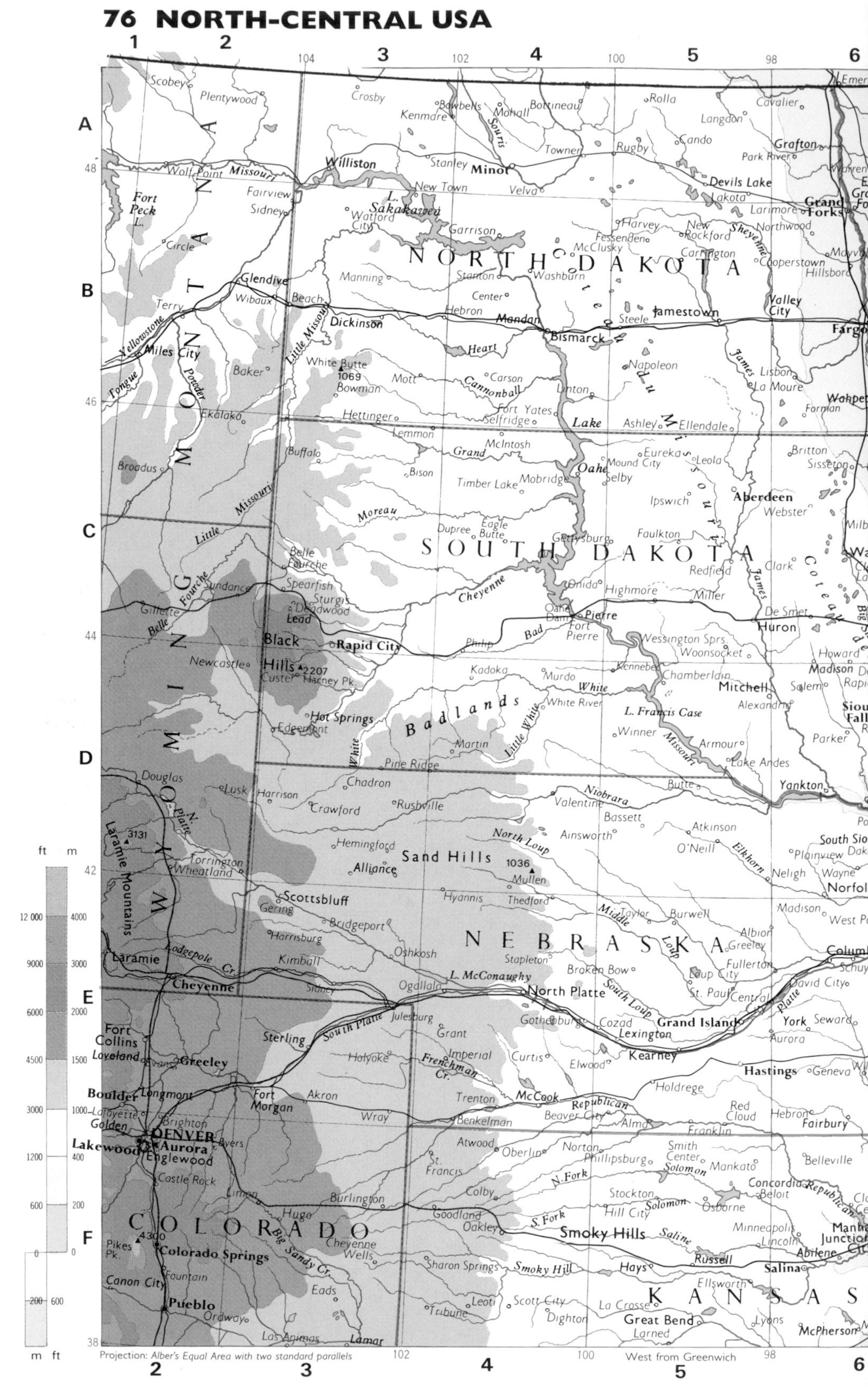

NORTH DAKOTA
SOUTH DAKOTA
NEBRASKA
KANSAS
COLORADO
WYOMING
MONTANA
Williston
Minot
Bismarck
Mandan
Jamestown
Fargo
Grand Forks
Devils Lake
Dickinson
Pierre
Rapid City
Black Hills
Aberdeen
Huron
Mitchell
Yankton
Sioux Falls
North Platte
Grand Island
Kearney
Lexington
Hastings
Scottsbluff
Cheyenne
Laramie
DENVER
Aurora
Lakewood
Englewood
Boulder
Greeley
Fort Collins
Colorado Springs
Pueblo
Salina
Hays
Great Bend
Sand Hills
Badlands
Smoky Hills
L. Sakakawea
L. Francis Case
L. McConaughy
Missouri
Platte
South Platte
Republican
Cheyenne
White
Niobrara
Projection: Alber's Equal Area with two standard parallels
West from Greenwich

CARTOGRAPHY BY PHILIP'S.

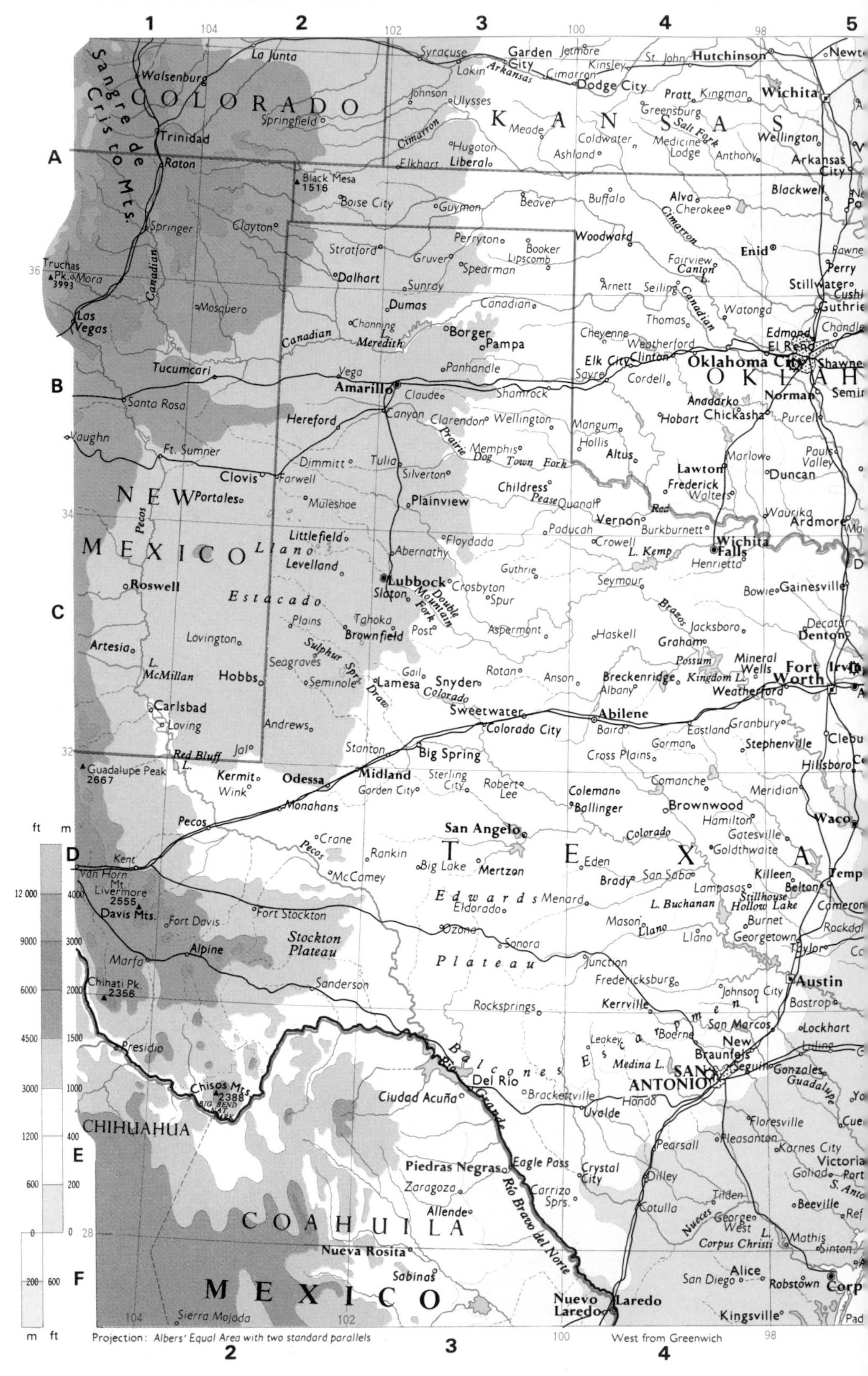
COLORADO
KANSAS
OKLAHOMA
NEW MEXICO
TEXAS
CHIHUAHUA
COAHUILA
MEXICO
Sangre de Cristo Mts.
Llano Estacado
Edwards Plateau
Stockton Plateau
Balcones Escarpment
Río Bravo del Norte
Rio Grande
La Junta
Walsenburg
Trinidad
Raton
Springer
Clayton
Truchas Pk. 3993
Mora
Las Vegas
Mosquero
Tucumcari
Santa Rosa
Vaughn
Ft. Sumner
Clovis
Portales
Roswell
Artesia
Carlsbad
Loving
Hobbs
Lovington
Amarillo
Lubbock
Dalhart
Dumas
Borger
Pampa
Midland
Odessa
Big Spring
San Angelo
Abilene
Wichita Falls
Fort Worth
Oklahoma City
Wichita
Dodge City
Hutchinson
Enid
Lawton
Austin
San Antonio
Waco
Laredo
Nuevo Laredo
Del Rio
Ciudad Acuña
Piedras Negras
Eagle Pass
Nueva Rosita
Sabinas
Sierra Mojada
Presidio
Marfa
Alpine
Fort Stockton
Pecos
Van Horn
Kent
Guadalupe Peak 2667
Mt. Livermore 2555
Davis Mts.
Chihati Pk. 2356
Chisos Mts. 2388
Black Mesa 1516
Projection: Albers' Equal Area with two standard parallels
West from Greenwich
ft
m
12 000
9000
6000
4500
3000
1200
600
0
200
4000
3000
2000
1500
1000
400
200
0
600
m
ft

1: 6 000 000
50 0 50 100 miles
50 0 50 100 150 km
6
7
8
9
96
94
92
90
A
B
C
D
E
F
MISSOURI
Ozark Plateau
ARKANSAS
TENNESSEE
MISSISSIPPI
LOUISIANA
GULF OF MEXICO
Nevada
Iola
Fort Scott
Yates Center
Chanute
Fredonia
Howard
Girard
Pittsburg
Parsons
Independence
Sedan
Coffeyville
Bartlesville
Camdenton
Rolla
Steelville
Lebanon
Buffalo
Bolivar
Stockton
Lamar
Greenfield
Marshfield
Springfield
Salem
Ironton
Perryville
Fredericktown
Murphysboro
Carbondale
Marion
Anna
Jackson
Cape Girardeau
Metropolis
Paducah
Cairo
Charleston
Sikeston
Mayfield
Houston
Cabool
Van Buren
Carthage
Joplin
Aurora
Ozark
Monett
Neosho
Miami
Cassville
Poplar Bluff
Dexter
New Madrid
Malden
Hickman
Union City
West Plains
Doniphan
Bull Shoals L.
Gainesville
Norfork L.
Vinita
Lake O' The Cherokees
Jay
Claremore
Pryor
Rogers
Springdale
Siloam Springs
Berryville
Mountain Home
Harrison
Pocahontas
Corning
Kennett
Caruthersville
Tiptonville
McKenzie
Dyersburg
Walnut Ridge
Paragould
Blytheville
Tulsa
Sapulpa
Wagoner
Haskell
Stilwell
Muskogee
Fayetteville
Boston Mts.
Marshall
Mountain View
Batesville
Jonesboro
Osceola
Trumann
Ripley
Humboldt
Jackson
Okmulgee
Henryetta
Clinton
Little Red
Newport
Heber Springs
Covington
Henderson
Bolivar
Ozark
Clarksville
Van Buren
Sallisaw
Ft. Smith
Arkansas
Russellville
Morrilton
Searcy
Augusta
Wynne
St. Francis
West Memphis
MEMPHIS
Forrest City
Eufaula
Stigler
Wewoka
Holdenville
McAlester
Eufaula L.
Poteau
Booneville
Conway
Ouachita Mts.
Waldron
Wilburton
Heavener
Ouachita L.
Little Rock
Benton
Lonoke
Stuttgart
Marianna
West Helena
Helena
Tunica
Hernando
Senatobia
Holly Sprs.
New Albany
Oxford
Tupelo
Batesville
Ada
Coalgate
Mena
Hot Springs
Malvern
Sheridan
Pine Bluff
Clarksdale
Charleston
Atoka
Antlers
Broken Bow Lake
Arkadelphia
Tishomingo
Lake Texoma
Durant
Red
Idabel
De Queen
Nashville
Millwood L.
Prescott
Hope
Rison
Fordyce
Warren
Dumas
Rosedale
McGehee
Cleveland
Grenada
Aberdeen
West Point
Columbus
Starkville
Winona
Greenwood
Indianola
Ackerman
Sherman
Paris
Bonham
Camden
Hampton
Monticello
Greenville
Clarksville
Texarkana
Magnolia
El Dorado
Ouachita
Lake Village
Hamburg
Crossett
Belzoni
Louisville
Kosciusko
Macon
McKinney
Greenville
Plano
Garland
DALLAS
Commerce
Sulphur Springs
Mount Pleasant
Pittsburg
Atlanta
Linden
Haynesville
Homer
Farmerville
Lake Providence
Yazoo
Big Black
Yazoo City
Philadelphia
Canton
Meridian
Forest
Quitman
Gilmer
Jefferson
Terrell
Marshall
Shreveport
Bossier City
Minden
Ruston
Monroe
Rayville
Tallulah
Vicksburg
Jackson
Longview
Kilgore
Tyler
Waxahachie
Ennis
Cedar Creek Res.
Athens
Henderson
Carthage
Jonesboro
Columbia
Winnsboro
St. Joseph
Port Gibson
Hazlehurst
Bay Sprs.
Laurel
Waynesboro
Trinity
Jacksonville
Tenaha
Mansfield
Coushatta
Winnfield
Natchitoches
Red
Brookhaven
Monticello
Pearl
Hattiesburg
Palestine
Nacogdoches
Center
Toledo Bend Reservoir
San Augustine
Many
Colfax
Jena
Catahoula L.
Pineville
Natchez
McComb
Columbia
Fairfield
Groesbeck
Crockett
Lufkin
Sam Rayburn Res.
Alexandria
Leesville
Marksville
Bunkie
Lucedale
Wiggins
Pascagoula
Centerville
Groveton
Jasper
Newton
Sabine
Oakdale
De Ridder
Ville Platte
New Roads
St. Francisville
Baton Rouge
Amite
Bogalusa
Picayune
Biloxi
Gulfport
Mississippi Sd.
Hearne
Madisonville
Livingston
Woodville
Huntsville
Opelousas
Eunice
Hammond
L. Maurepas
Slidell
L. Pontchartrain
Bryan
Brazos
L. Livingston
Trinity
L. Conroe
Kountze
Silsbee
Sulphur
Lake Charles
Crowley
Lafayette
Plaquemine
Mississippi
Navasota
Cleveland
Conroe
Beaumont
Orange
Calcasieu L.
New Iberia
Abbeville
Donaldsonville
Metairie
NEW ORLEANS
Chandeleur Sd.
Brenham
Hempstead
Liberty
Port Arthur
Sabine L.
Cameron
Grand L.
White L.
Franklin
Thibodaux
Morgan City
Salvador L.
Breton Sd.
Pointe-a-la-Hache
Chandeleur Is.
Bellville
Colorado
HOUSTON
Pasadena
Baytown
Vermilion B.
Marsh I.
Atchafalaya B.
Houma
Barataria B.
Burrs
Mississippi River Delta
Rosenberg
Richmond
Galveston B.
Texas City
Galveston
Wharton
Angleton
Isles Dernieres
Terrebonne B.
Campo
Edna
Bay City
Freeport
Matagorda B.
Matagorda I.
Kingsville
Hebbronville
Falfurrias
Sarita
Padre I.
Laguna Madre
Salado
Zapata
Falcon L.
MEXICO
Rio Grande City
Raymondville
Edinburg
McAllen
Harlingen
San Benito
Brownsville
28
26
Continuation Southwards on same scale
4
5
CARTOGRAPHY BY PHILIP'S.

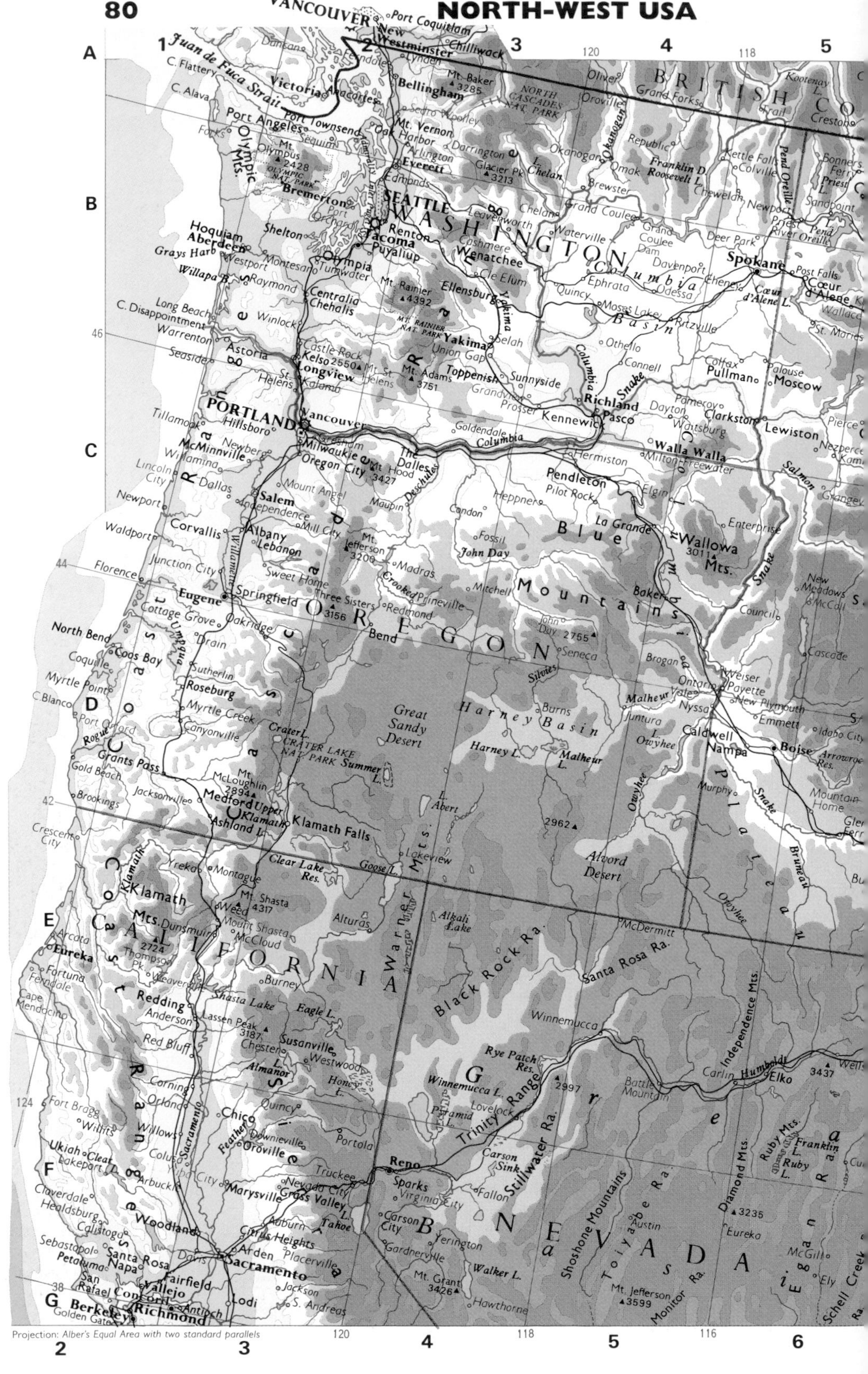


Projection: Alber's Equal Area with two standard parallels

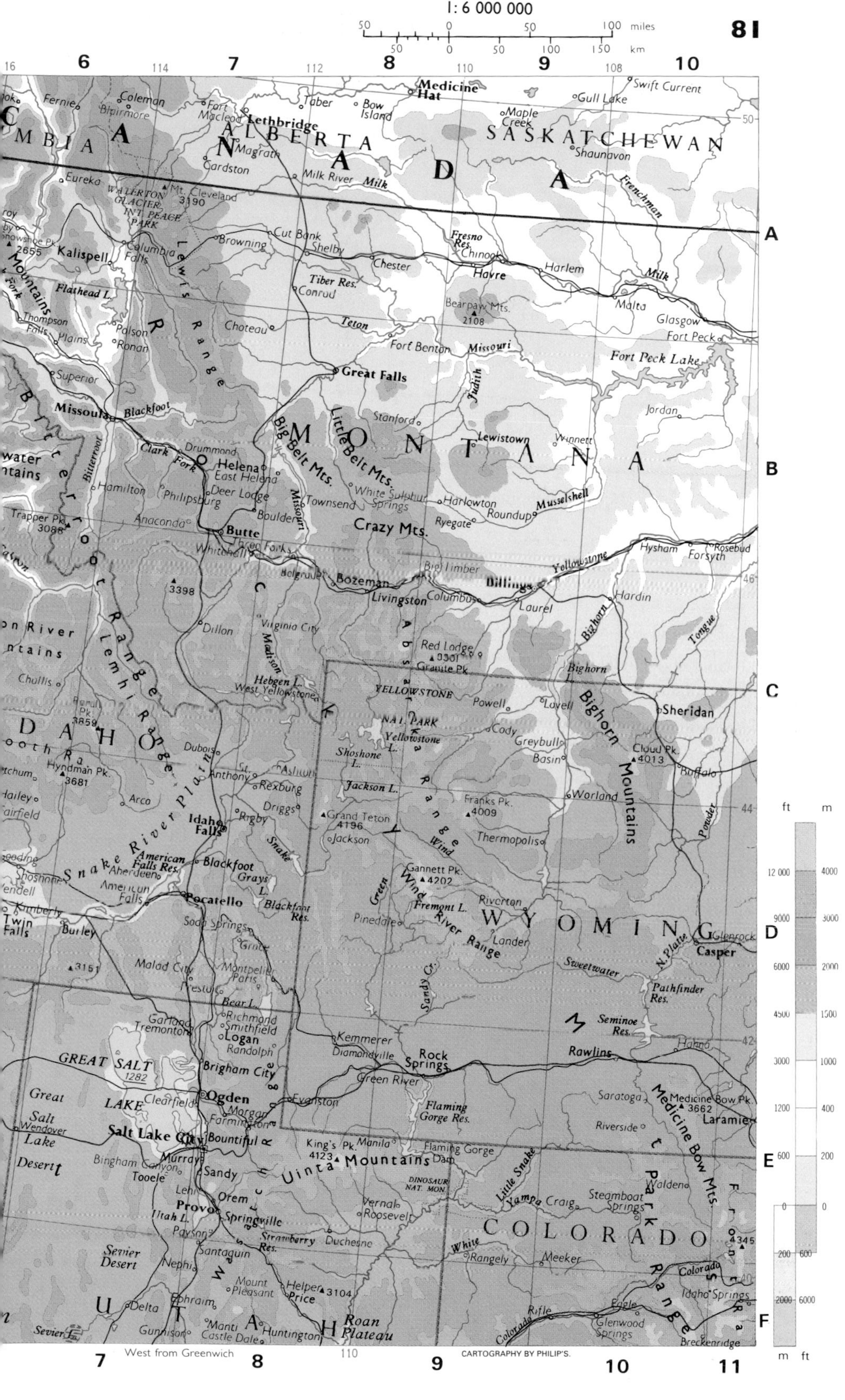
1: 6 000 000
miles
km
ALBERTA
SASKATCHEWAN
CANADA
MONTANA
WYOMING
IDAHO
UTAH
COLORADO
Medicine Hat
Lethbridge
Swift Current
Kalispell
Great Falls
Missoula
Helena
Butte
Bozeman
Billings
Sheridan
Casper
Idaho Falls
Pocatello
Ogden
Salt Lake City
Provo
Rock Springs
Rawlins
Laramie
GREAT SALT LAKE
Great Salt Lake Desert
Uinta Mountains
Bighorn Mountains
Wind River Range
Medicine Bow Mts.
Park Range
YELLOWSTONE NAT. PARK
ft
m
West from Greenwich
CARTOGRAPHY BY PHILIP'S.

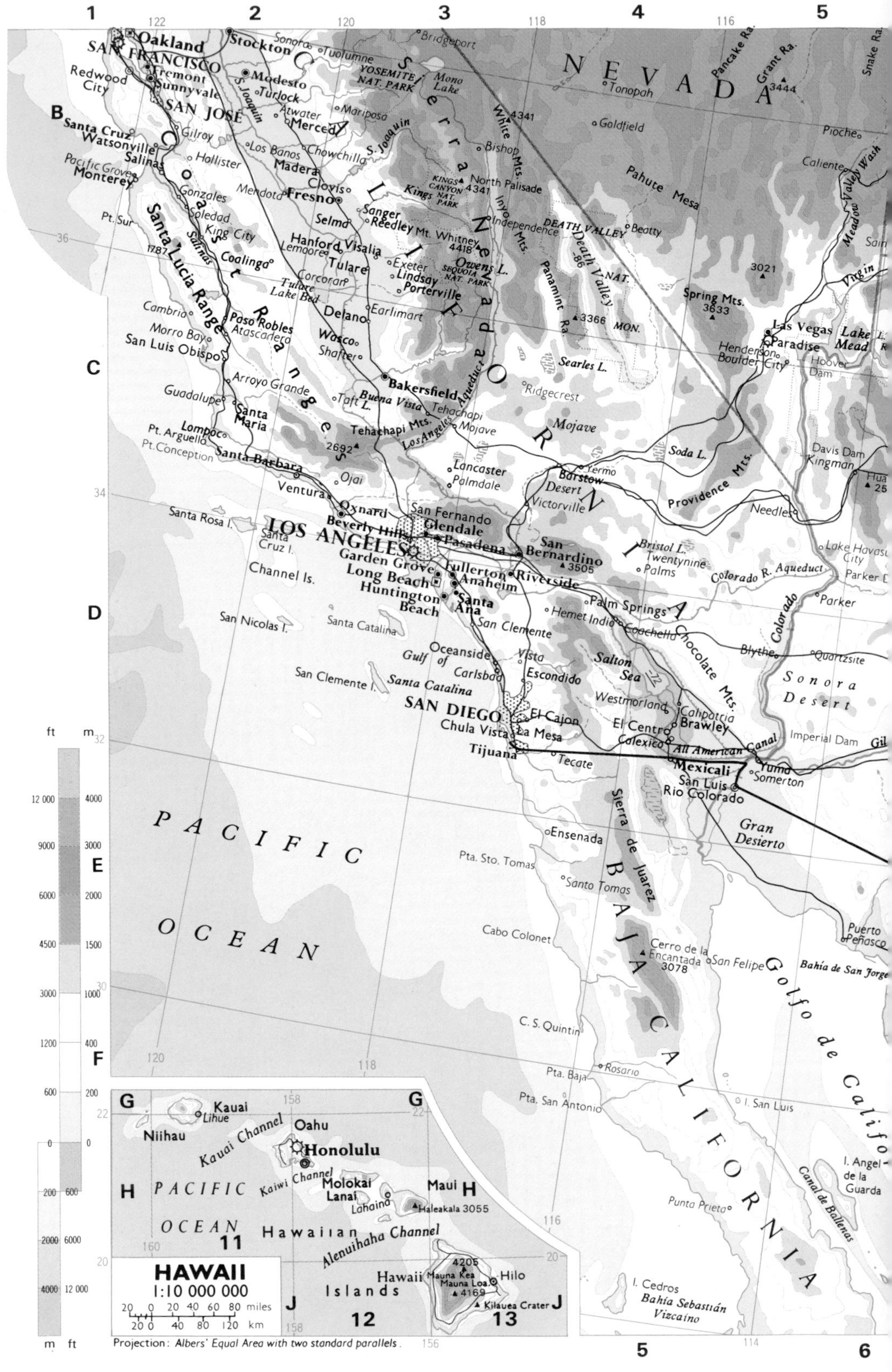
NEVADA
CALIFORNIA
PACIFIC OCEAN
BAJA CALIFORNIA
Golfo de California
San Francisco
Oakland
Stockton
Modesto
San Jose
Fresno
Bakersfield
Los Angeles
San Diego
Tijuana
Mexicali
Las Vegas
Sierra Nevada
Coast Ranges
Santa Lucia Range
Death Valley
Mojave
Salton Sea
Sonora Desert
Channel Is.
HAWAII
1:10 000 000
Kauai
Oahu
Honolulu
Niihau
Molokai
Lanai
Maui
Hawaii
Hawaiian Islands
Haleakala 3055
Mauna Kea 4205
Mauna Loa 4169
Hilo
Kilauea Crater
Projection: Albers' Equal Area with two standard parallels.

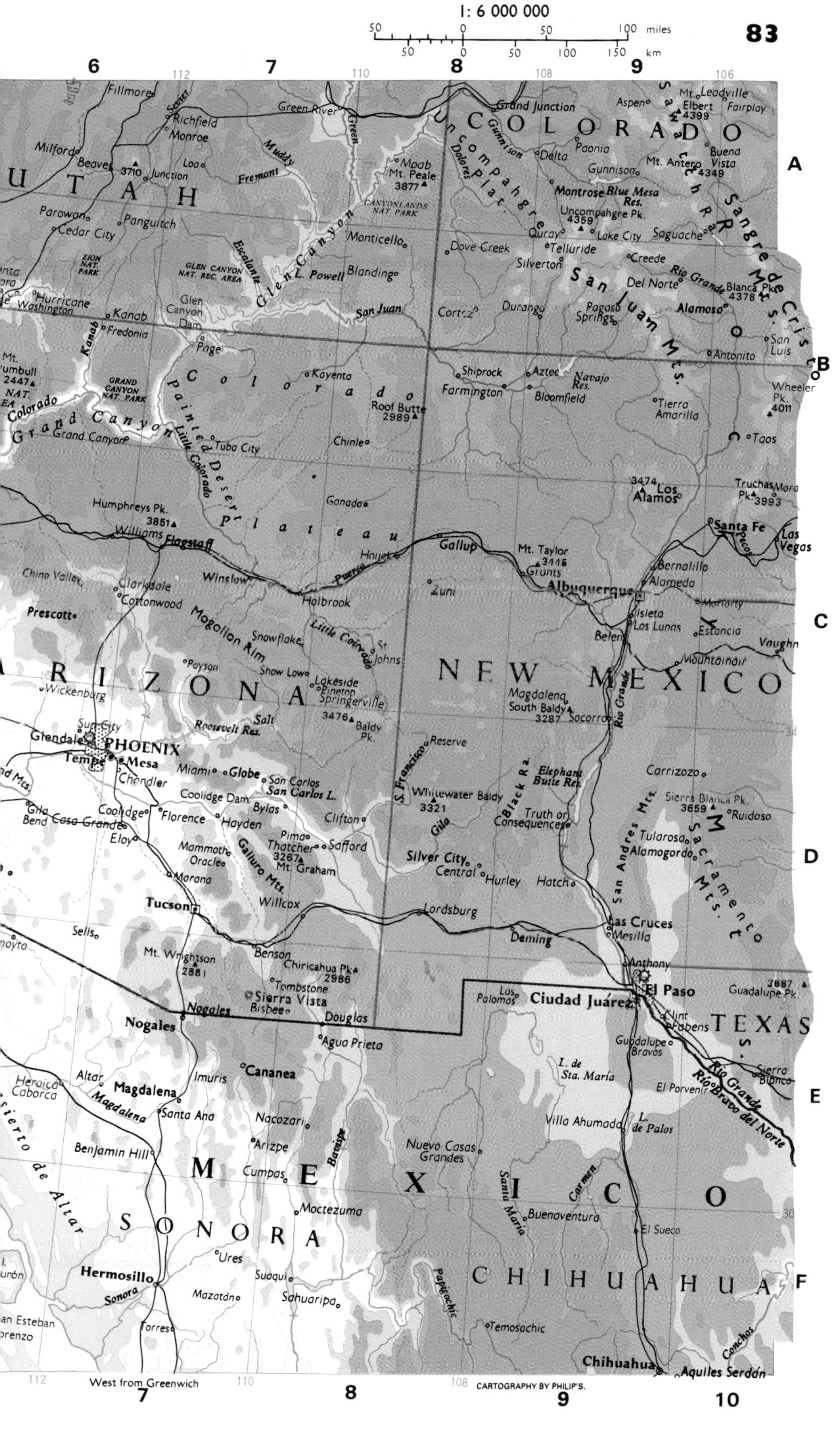
1: 6 000 000
UTAH
COLORADO
ARIZONA
NEW MEXICO
TEXAS
MEXICO
SONORA
CHIHUAHUA
Colorado Plateau
Painted Desert
Grand Canyon
Glen Canyon
San Juan Mts.
Sangre de Cristo Mts.
Sawatch R.
Uncompahgre Plat.
Mogollon Rim
Sacramento Mts.
San Andres Mts.
Desierto de Altar
Grand Junction
Aspen
Leadville
Fairplay
Mt. Elbert 4399
Buena Vista
Mt. Antero 4349
Delta
Paonia
Gunnison
Montrose
Blue Mesa Res.
Uncompahgre Pk. 4359
Ouray
Lake City
Saguache
Telluride
Silverton
Creede
Del Norte
Rio Grande
Blanca Pk. 4378
Alamosa
Pagosa Springs
Durango
Cortez
Dove Creek
Antonito
San Luis
Wheeler Pk. 4011
Taos
Tierra Amarilla
Shiprock
Aztec
Farmington
Bloomfield
Navajo Res.
Los Alamos 3474
Truchas Pk. 3993
Mora
Santa Fe
Pecos
Las Vegas
Bernalillo
Alameda
Albuquerque
Moriarty
Isleta
Los Lunas
Belen
Estancia
Vaughn
Mountainair
Mt. Taylor 3445
Grants
Gallup
Zuni
Magdalena
South Baldy 3287
Socorro
Carrizozo
Elephant Butte Res.
Truth or Consequences
Sierra Blanca Pk. 3659
Ruidoso
Tularosa
Alamogordo
Hatch
Las Cruces
Mesilla
Anthony
El Paso
Guadalupe Pk. 2667
Clint
Fabens
Guadalupe Bravos
Sierra Blanca
El Porvenir
Río Bravo del Norte
Ciudad Juárez
Los Palomas
Deming
Lordsburg
Hurley
Silver City
Central
Whitewater Baldy 3321
Gila
Black Ra.
Reserve
S. Francisco
Fillmore
Sevier
Richfield
Monroe
Green River
Green
Muddy
Fremont
Milford
Beaver
3710
Junction
Loa
Moab
Mt. Peale 3877
Canyonlands Nat. Park
Dolores
Gunnison
Parowan
Panguitch
Cedar City
Escalante
Monticello
Blanding
L. Powell
Zion Nat. Park
Glen Canyon Nat. Rec. Area
Hurricane
Washington
Kanab
Fredonia
Glen Canyon Dam
Page
San Juan
Kayenta
Roof Butte 2989
Mt. Trumbull 2447
Grand Canyon Nat. Park
Grand Canyon
Tuba City
Little Colorado
Chinle
Ganado
Humphreys Pk. 3851
Williams
Flagstaff
Houck
Puerco
Chino Valley
Clarkdale
Cottonwood
Winslow
Holbrook
Prescott
Snowflake
Little Colorado
St Johns
Payson
Show Low
Lakeside
Pinetop
Springerville
Wickenburg
3476 Baldy Pk.
Salt
Roosevelt Res.
Sun City
Glendale
PHOENIX
Tempe
Mesa
Chandler
Miami
Globe
San Carlos
San Carlos L.
Coolidge Dam
Bylas
Gila Bend
Casa Grande
Coolidge
Florence
Hayden
Clifton
Eloy
Pima
Thatcher
Safford
Mammoth
Oracle
3267 Mt. Graham
Galiuro Mts.
Marana
Tucson
Willcox
Sells
Benson
Mt. Wrightson 2881
Chiricahua Pk. 2986
Tombstone
Sierra Vista
Bisbee
Douglas
Nogales
Agua Prieta
Altar
Heroica Caborca
Magdalena
Imuris
Cananea
Santa Ana
Nacozari
Arizpe
Bavispe
Benjamin Hill
Cumpas
Moctezuma
Ures
Hermosillo
Sonora
Suaqui
Mazatán
Sahuaripa
Torres
San Esteban
Lorenzo
Nuevo Casas Grandes
Papigochic
Temosachic
L. de Sta. María
Villa Ahumada
L. de Palos
Santa Maria
Carmen
Buenaventura
El Sueco
Conchos
Chihuahua
Aquiles Serdán
West from Greenwich
CARTOGRAPHY BY PHILIP'S.

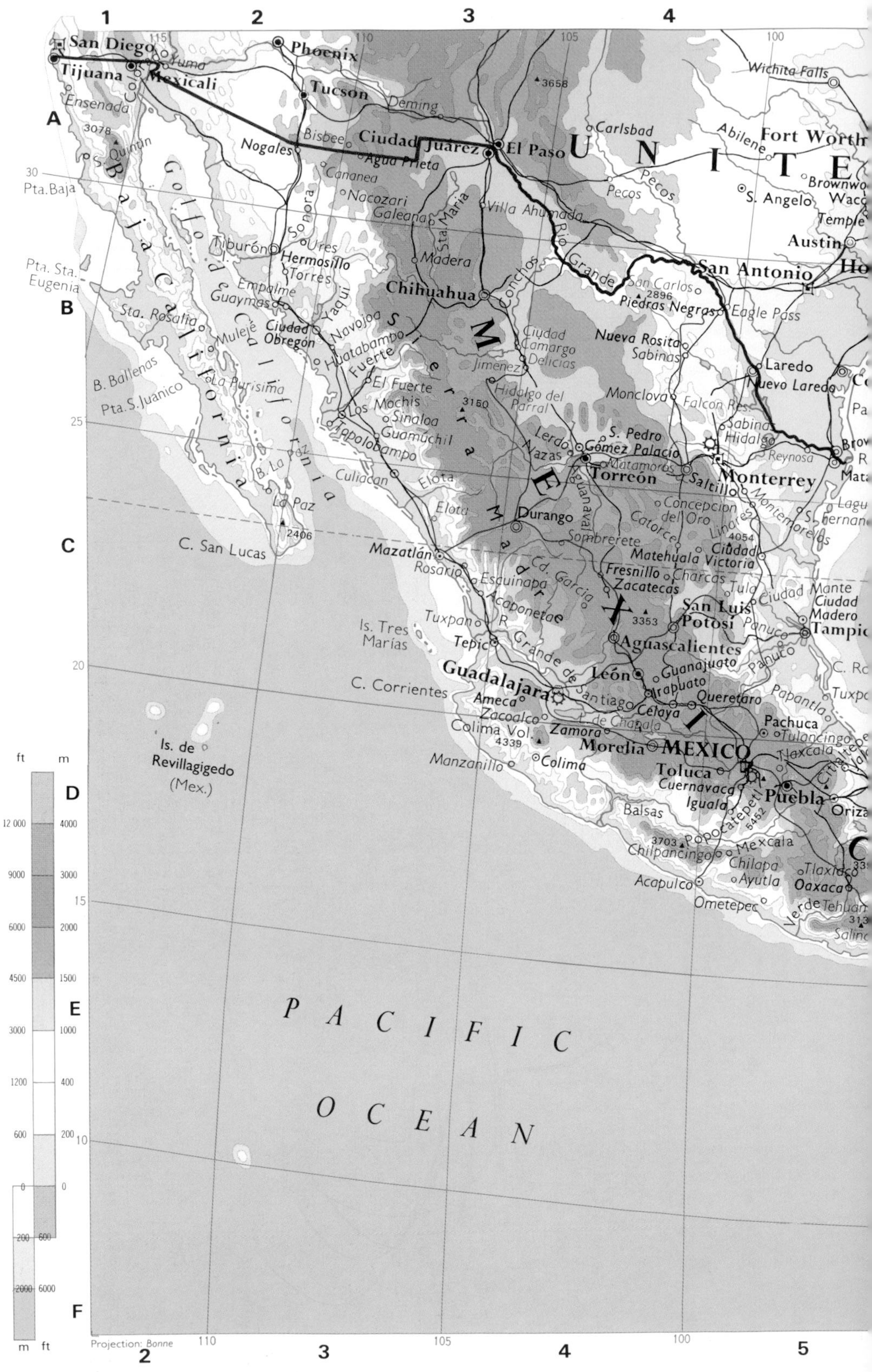
San Diego
Tijuana
Mexicali
Yuma
Phoenix
Tucson
Ensenada
Deming
Bisbee
Nogales
Ciudad Juárez
El Paso
Agua Prieta
Cananea
Nacozari
Galeana
Villa Ahumada
Carlsbad
Abilene
Fort Worth
Wichita Falls
Pecos
S. Angelo
Brownwood
Temple
Austin
San Antonio
UNITED
Golfo de California
Baja California
S. Quintín
Pta. Baja
Pta. Sta. Eugenia
Tiburón
Hermosillo
Ures
Torres
Empalme
Guaymas
Sonora
Yaqui
Sta. Maria
Madera
Chihuahua
Conchos
Río Grande
San Carlos
Piedras Negras
Eagle Pass
Sta. Rosalía
Mulegé
Ciudad Obregón
Navojoa
Huatabampo
Fuerte
El Fuerte
Los Mochis
Sinaloa
Guamúchil
Topolobampo
Culiacán
Elota
Sierra Madre
MEXICO
Ciudad Camargo
Delicias
Jiménez
Hidalgo del Parral
Nueva Rosita
Sabinas
Monclova
Falcon Res.
Laredo
Nuevo Laredo
Sabinas Hidalgo
Reynosa
B. Ballenas
Pta. S. Juanico
La Purísima
B. La Paz
La Paz
C. San Lucas
Lerdo
Nazas
S. Pedro
Gómez Palacio
Matamoros
Torreón
Saltillo
Monterrey
Montemorelos
Concepción del Oro
Catorce
Linares
Durango
Aguanaval
Sombrerete
Matehuala
Ciudad Victoria
Mazatlán
Rosario
Escuinapa
Acaponeta
Cd. García
Fresnillo
Zacatecas
Charcas
Tula
Ciudad Mante
Ciudad Madero
Tampico
San Luis Potosí
Pánuco
Is. Tres Marías
Tuxpan
Tepic
R. Grande de Santiago
Aguascalientes
Guadalajara
León
Guanajuato
Irapuato
Querétaro
C. Corrientes
Ameca
Zacoalco
L. de Chapala
Celaya
Colima Vol.
Zamora
Morelia
MEXICO
Pachuca
Tulancingo
Tlaxcala
Papantla
Tuxpan
Is. de Revillagigedo (Mex.)
Manzanillo
Colima
Toluca
Cuernavaca
Iguala
Puebla
Orizaba
Popocatépetl
Balsas
Chilpancingo
Mexcala
Chilapa
Ayutla
Tlaxiaco
Oaxaca
Acapulco
Ometepec
Verde
Tehuantepec
Salina
PACIFIC OCEAN
3078
3658
2896
3150
2406
4054
3353
4339
5452
3703
ft m
12 000 4000
9000 3000
6000 2000
4500 1500
3000 1000
1200 400
600 200
0 0
200 600
2000 6000
m ft
Projection: Bonne

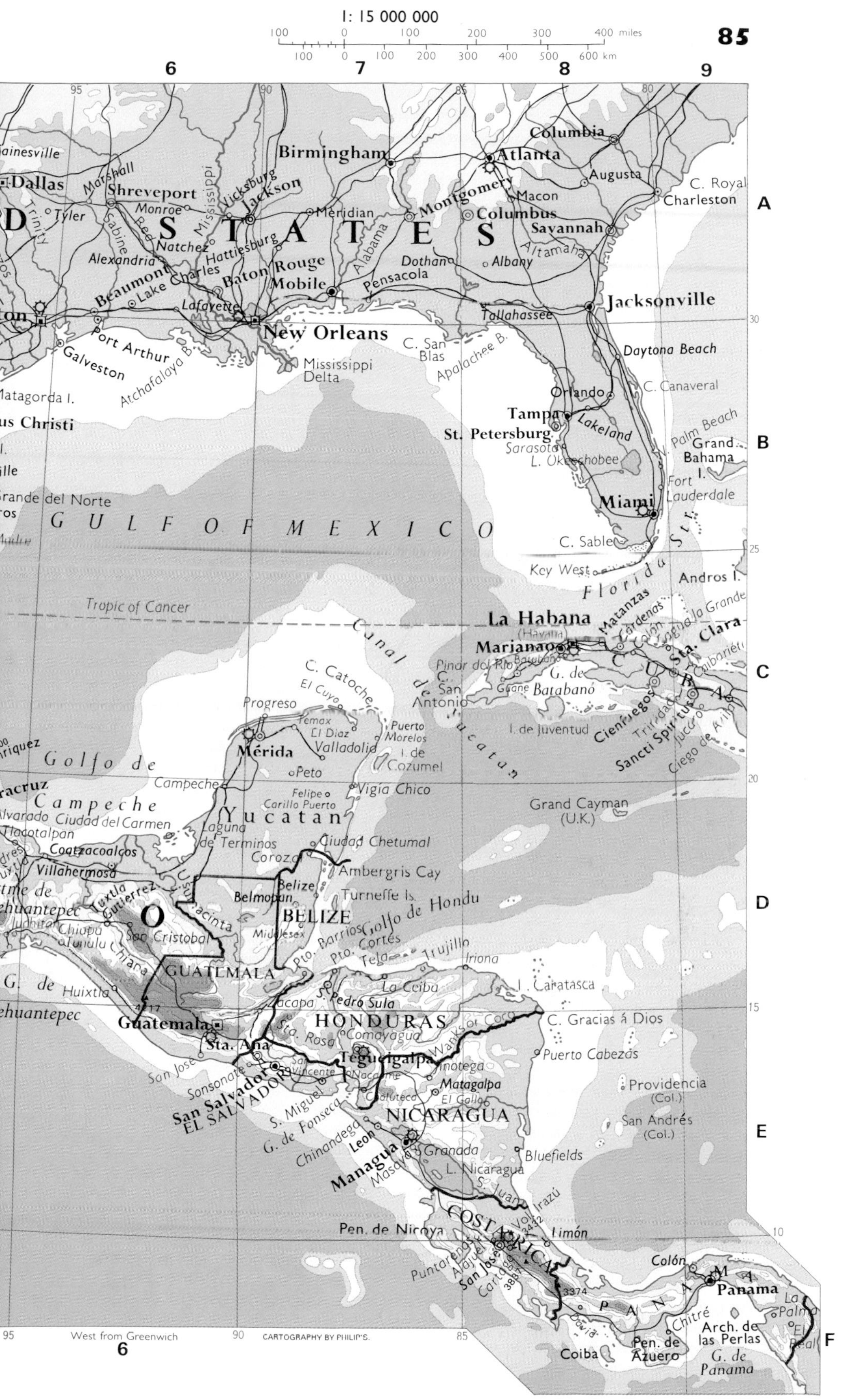

1: 15 000 000
miles
km
Birmingham
Atlanta
Columbia
Augusta
C. Royal
Charleston
Dallas
Marshall
Shreveport
Vicksburg
Jackson
Mississippi
Montgomery
Macon
Tyler
Monroe
Meridian
Columbus
Savannah
STATES
Natchez
Hattiesburg
Alabama
Altamaha
Alexandria
Baton Rouge
Dothan
Albany
Beaumont
Lake Charles
Mobile
Pensacola
Lafayette
Tallahassee
Jacksonville
New Orleans
Port Arthur
Galveston
C. San Blas
Apalachee B.
Mississippi Delta
Daytona Beach
Atchafalaya B.
Matagorda I.
C. Canaveral
Orlando
Tampa
Lakeland
St. Petersburg
Sarasota
L. Okeechobee
W. Palm Beach
Grand Bahama I.
Fort Lauderdale
Miami
GULF OF MEXICO
C. Sable
Key West
Florida Str.
Andros I.
Tropic of Cancer
La Habana
(Havana)
Matanzas
Cárdenas
Colón
Marianao
Sta. Clara
Canal de Yucatan
C. Catoche
El Cuyo
Pinar del Rio
Batabanó
G. de Batabanó
C. San Antonio
CUBA
Cienfuegos
Trinidad
Sancti Spiritus
Ciego de Avila
Progreso
Temax
El Diaz
Puerto Morelos
I. de Juventud
Mérida
Valladolid
I. de Cozumel
Golfo de Campeche
Peto
Campeche
Vigia Chico
Felipe Carillo Puerto
Grand Cayman (U.K.)
Yucatan
Alvarado
Ciudad del Carmen
Tlacotalpan
Laguna de Terminos
Ciudad Chetumal
Coatzacoalcos
Corozal
Villahermosa
Ambergris Cay
Belize
Belmopan
Turneffe Is.
Golfo de Hondu
BELIZE
Tuxtla Gutierrez
San Cristobal
Middlesex
Pto. Barrios
Pto. Cortés
Tela
Trujillo
Iriona
GUATEMALA
La Ceiba
I. Caratasca
G. de Tehuantepec
Huixtla
S. Pedro Sula
Guatemala
HONDURAS
C. Gracias á Dios
Sta. Ana
Comayagua
Sta. Rosa
Puerto Cabezas
San José
Tegucigalpa
Wanks or Coco
Sonsonate
San Vicente
Nacaome
Ocotal
Matagalpa
Providencia (Col.)
San Salvador
EL SALVADOR
S. Miguel
El Gallo
G. de Fonseca
Choluteca
NICARAGUA
San Andrés (Col.)
Chinandega
Leon
Managua
Masaya
Granada
Bluefields
L. Nicaragua
S. Juan
Irazú
COSTA RICA
Pen. de Nicoya
Limón
Colón
Puntarenas
Alajuela
San José
Cartago
PANAMA
Panama
David
Chitré
La Palma
Arch. de las Perlas
Pen. de Azuero
Coiba
G. de Panama
West from Greenwich
CARTOGRAPHY BY PHILIP'S

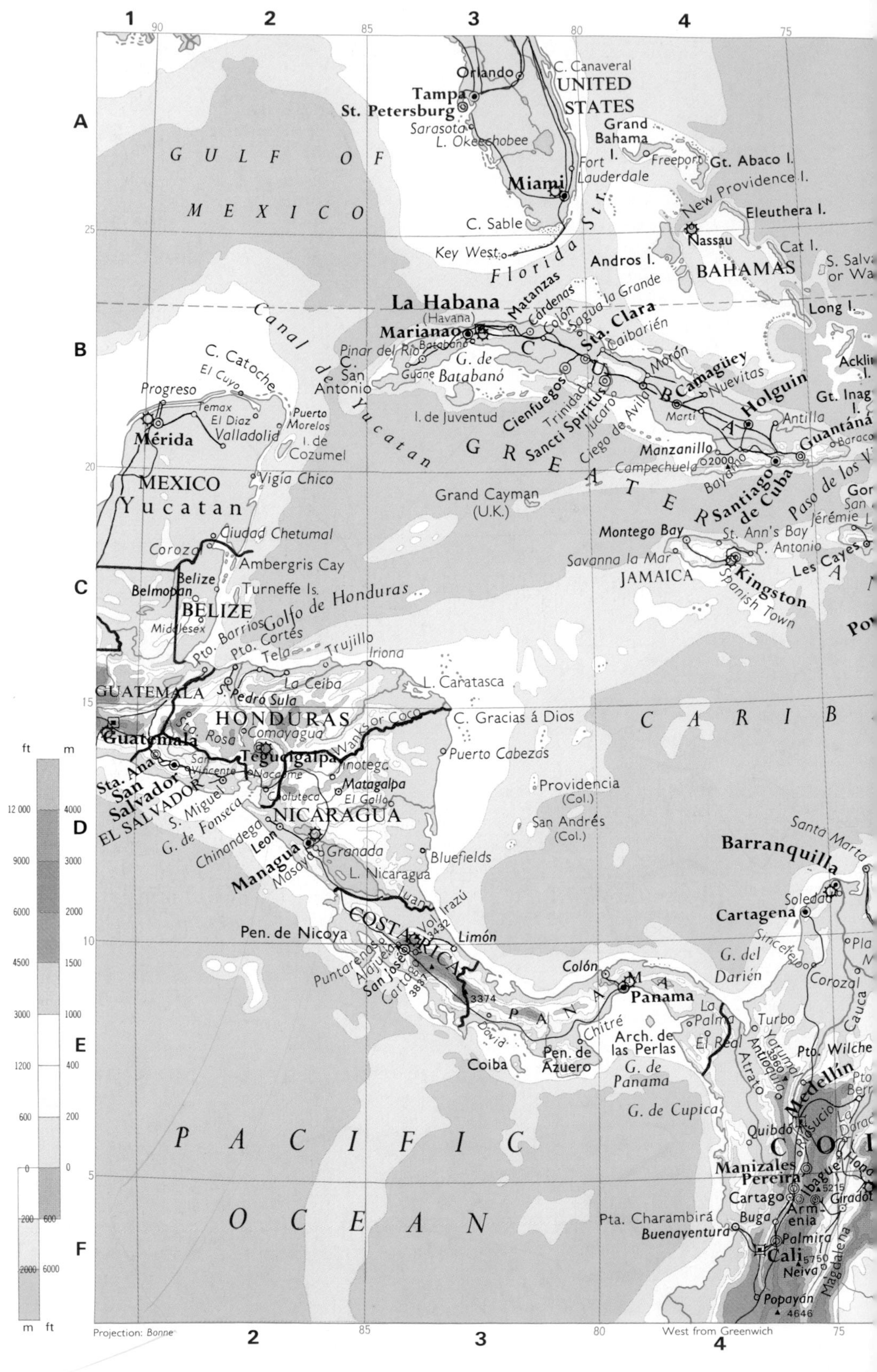
GULF OF MEXICO
UNITED STATES
Orlando
C. Canaveral
Tampa
St. Petersburg
Sarasota
L. Okeechobee
Grand Bahama I.
Freeport
Gt. Abaco I.
Fort Lauderdale
Miami
New Providence I.
Eleuthera I.
C. Sable
Nassau
Key West
Florida Str.
Andros I.
Cat I.
BAHAMAS
Long I.
La Habana
(Havana)
Marianao
Matanzas
Cárdenas
Colón
Sagua la Grande
Sta. Clara
Caibarién
Canal de Yucatan
C. Catoche
El Cuyo
Progreso
Temax
El Diaz
Mérida
Valladolid
Puerto Morelos
I. de Cozumel
Pinar del Rio
Batabanó
C. San Antonio
Guane
G. de Batabanó
I. de Juventud
Cienfuegos
Trinidad
Sancti Spiritus
Jucaro
Ciego de Avila
Morón
Camagüey
Nuevitas
Holguín
Marti
Antilla
Guantánamo
Baracoa
Manzanillo
Campechuela
2000
Bayamo
Santiago de Cuba
GREATER ANTILLES
CUBA
MEXICO
Yucatan
Vigía Chico
Grand Cayman
(U.K.)
Ciudad Chetumal
Corozal
Ambergris Cay
Belize
Belmopan
Turneffe Is.
BELIZE
Middlesex
Golfo de Honduras
Pto. Barrios
Pto. Cortés
Tela
Trujillo
Iriona
Montego Bay
St. Ann's Bay
P. Antonio
Savanna la Mar
JAMAICA
Kingston
Spanish Town
Les Cayes
Jérémie
Paso de los Vientos
La Ceiba
L. Caratasca
GUATEMALA
S. Pedro Sula
HONDURAS
Comayagua
Guatemala
Sta. Rosa
Wanks or Coco
C. Gracias á Dios
CARIBBEAN
Tegucigalpa
Puerto Cabezas
Sta. Ana
San Salvador
San Vicente
Nacaome
Jinotega
EL SALVADOR
S. Miguel
Choluteca
Matagalpa
El Gallo
Providencia
(Col.)
G. de Fonseca
NICARAGUA
San Andrés
(Col.)
Chinandega
Leon
Managua
Masaya
Granada
Bluefields
L. Nicaragua
San Juan
Santa Marta
Barranquilla
Soledad
Cartagena
COSTA RICA
Vol. Irazú
3432
Pen. de Nicoya
Limón
Puntarenas
Alajuela
San José
Cartago
3837
Colón
Panama
3374
PANAMA
David
Chitré
Pen. de Azuero
Arch. de las Perlas
La Palma
El Real
G. del Darién
Sinú
Corozal
Turbo
Coiba
G. de Panama
Atrato
Antioquia
Yarumal
3960
Medellín
Pto. Wilches
Cauca
G. de Cupica
Quibdó
Riosucio
PACIFIC OCEAN
Manizales
Pereira
Ibagué
5215
Girardot
Cartago
Armenia
Pta. Charambirá
Buga
Buenaventura
Palmira
Cali
5750
Neiva
Magdalena
Popayán
4646
ft
m
12 000
4000
9000
3000
6000
2000
4500
1500
3000
1000
1200
400
600
200
0
0
200
600
2000
6000
m
ft
Projection: Bonne
West from Greenwich

1: 15 000 000
100 0 100 200 300 400 miles
100 0 100 200 300 400 500 600 km
6
7
8
A
B
C
D
E
F
5
6
7
8
70
65
60
55
25
20
15
10
0
A T L A N T I C
O C E A N
Tropic of Cancer
gs I.
Mayaguana
Caicos I. (U.K.)
Turks Is. (U.K.)
Port de Paix
Cap Haitien
Monte Cristi
Velverde
Pto. Plata
Santiago
S. Francisco de Macoris
Sanchez
La Vega
3175
DOMINICAN REP.
La Romana
S. Pedro de Macoris
Santo Domingo
Barahona
Hispaniola
2680
Canal de la Mona
Aguadilla
Arecibo
PUERTO RICO (U.S.A.)
San Juan
1338
Caguas
Guayama
Mayagüez
Ponce
St. Thomas (U.S.A.)
Charlotte Amalie
Virgin Is. (U.K.)
St. Croix (U.S.A.)
Christiansted
Sombrero (U.K.)
Anguilla (U.K.)
St. Martin (Fr. & Neth.)
ST. KITTS-NEVIS
Basseterre
Charlestown
ANTIGUA & BARBUDA
St. John's
Plymouth
Montserrat (U.K.)
Guadeloupe (Fr.)
Pointe à Pitre
Leeward Islands
LESSER
DOMINICA
Roseau
Martinique (Fr.)
Fort de France
Castries
ST. LUCIA
BARBADOS
Bridgetown
ANTILLES
Windward
ST. VINCENT
& Kingstown
THE GRENADINES
Islands
GRENADA
St. George's
A N T I L L E S
E A N S E A
La Blanquilla (Ven.)
Tobago
Margarita
La Asunción
Carúpano
Port of Spain
TRINIDAD & TOBAGO
San Fernando
G. de Paria
Pta. Gallinas
Pen. de la Guajira
Golfo de Venezuela
Aruba (Neth.)
Curaçao
Willemstad
Bonaire
NETH. ANTILLES
Coro
Dabajuro
Pto. Cabello
Maiquetía
Caracas
La Tortuga (Ven.)
Cumaná
Maracaibo
Cabimas
L. de Maracaibo
Trujillo
Valera
Maracay
Valencia
San Felipe
Barquisimeto
Barcelona
Maturín
El Tigre
Las Mercedes
Tucupita
Calabozo
Ciudad Guayana
Orinoco
Ciudad Bolívar
Portuguesa
Cord. de Mérida
5007
Guanare
San Fernando de Apure
Apure
Tumeremo
El Callao
Caicara
San Cristóbal
Rubio
Pamplona
Bucaramanga
Arauca
Arauca
V E N E Z U E L A
Pto. Páez
Pto. Carreño
2285
Pto. Ayacucho
Meta
Caura
Caroni
2560
Roraima
2810
Cuyuni
Sierra Pacaraima
Georgetown
New Amsterdam
Bartica
Wismar
Essequibo
Corentyne
G U Y A N A
SURINAM
1280
O M B I A
Tunja
Bogotá
Guaviare
Casiquiare
Sa. Parima
B R A Z I L

NORTH ATLANTIC OCEAN
Caribbean Sea
Tropic of Cancer
Equator
BAHAMAS
Turks & Caicos Is. (U.K.)
CUBA
Havana
JAMAICA
Kingston
HAITI
Port-au-Prince
DOMINICAN REP.
PUERTO RICO (U.S.A.)
San Juan
Virgin Is. (U.K.)
ST. KITTS-NEVIS
ANTIGUA & BARBUDA
GUADELOUPE (Fr.)
Basse-Terre
DOMINICA
MARTINIQUE (Fr.)
Fort-de-France
ST. LUCIA
Castries
BARBADOS
Bridgetown
ST. VINCENT
Kingstown
GRENADA
St. George's
TRINIDAD & TOBAGO
Port of Spain
Aruba
Curaçao
MEXICO
BELIZE
GUATEMALA
Guatemala
HONDURAS
Tegucigalpa
EL SALVADOR
San Salvador
NICARAGUA
Managua
COSTA RICA
San José
PANAMA
Panamá
Gulf of Panamá
G. of Darién
Galapagos Is. (Ecuador)
VENEZUELA
Caracas
Valencia
Maracaibo
Barquisimeto
San Cristóbal
Ciudad Guayana
Orinoco
C. de la Aguja
Barranquilla
Cartagena
Cúcuta
Bucaramanga
COLOMBIA
Bogotá
Medellín
Cali
Magdalena
ECUADOR
Quito
Guayaquil
G. of Guayaquil
GUYANA
Georgetown
Essequibo
SURINAM
Paramaribo
FRENCH GUIANA
Cayenne
C. Orange
PERU
LIMA
Callao
Chiclayo
Trujillo
Chimbote
Iquitos
Cuzco
Napo
Marañón
Ucayali
Putumayo
Japurá
BRAZIL
AMAPÁ
RORAIMA
AMAZONAS
ACRE
RONDÔNIA
PARÁ
MATO GROSSO
TOCANTINS
MARANHÃO
PIAUÍ
CEARÁ
RIO G. DO NORTE
PARAÍBA
PERNAMBUCO
ALAGOAS
SERGIPE
BAHÍA
Amazon
Branco
Madeira
Purus
Juruá
Madre de Dios
Tapajós
Xingu
Tocantins
Araguaia
Parnaíba
Manaus
Santarém
Pôrto Velho
Belém
Marajó I.
São Luís
Teresina
Fortaleza
C. de São Roque
Natal
Campina Grande
Recife
Maceió
Aracaju
A
B
C
D
1
2
3
4
5
6
7

PACIFIC OCEAN
SOUTH ATLANTIC OCEAN
PARAGUAY
URUGUAY
CHILE
ARGENTINA
MATO GROSSO DO SUL
MINAS GERAIS
ESPIRITO SANTO
SÃO PAULO
PARANÁ
SANTA CATARINA
RIO GRANDE DO SUL
DIS. FED.
R. DE J.
Brasília
Goiânia
Belo Horizonte
Vitória
Campos
Juiz de Fora
Niterói
RIO DE JANEIRO
Ribeirão Prêto
Campinas
SÃO PAULO
Curitiba
Pôrto Alegre
Pelotas
Montevideo
Río de la Plata
Asunción
Corrientes
Córdoba
San Juan
Mendoza
Santa Fe
Rosario
BUENOS AIRES
Bahía Blanca
Mar del Plata
Arequipa
La Paz
Cochabamba
Santa Cruz
Iquique
Antofagasta
Tropic of Capricorn
San Ambrosio (Chile)
Viña del Mar
Valparaíso
SANTIAGO
Concepción
Valdivia
Puerto Montt
Gulf of Penas
Punta Arenas
Tierra del Fuego
C. Horn
West Falkland
East Falkland
South Georgia (U.K.)
Paraguay
Paraná
Uruguay
Colorado
Negro
Chubut
E
F
G
H
1
2
3
4
5
6
7
60 West from Greenwich
Projection: Lambert's Azimuthal Equal Area
Capital Cities
CARTOGRAPHY BY PHILIP'S.
1: 35 000 000
200 0 200 400 600 800 miles
400 0 400 800 1200 km

# SOUTH AMERICA-NORTH-WEST

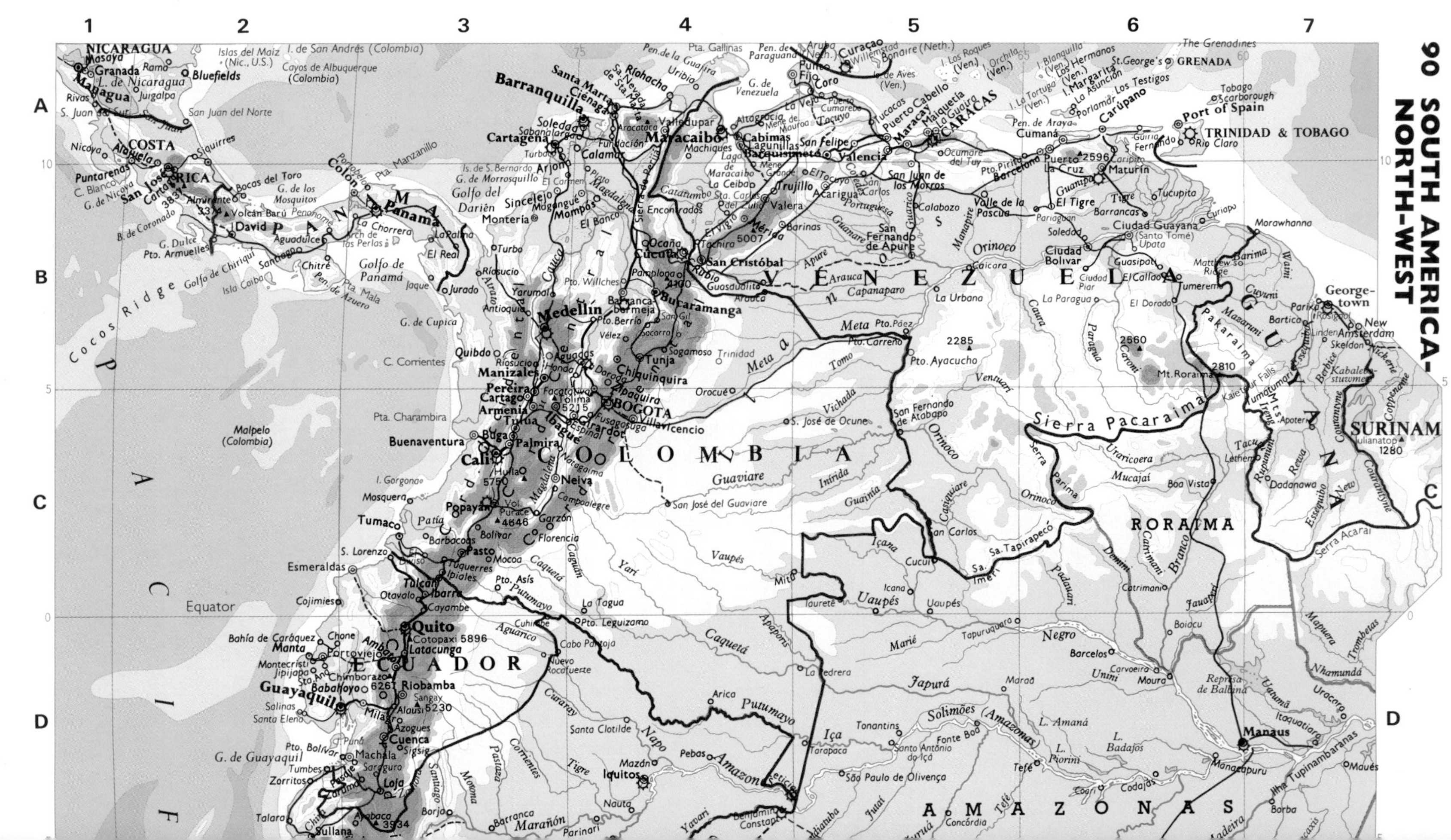

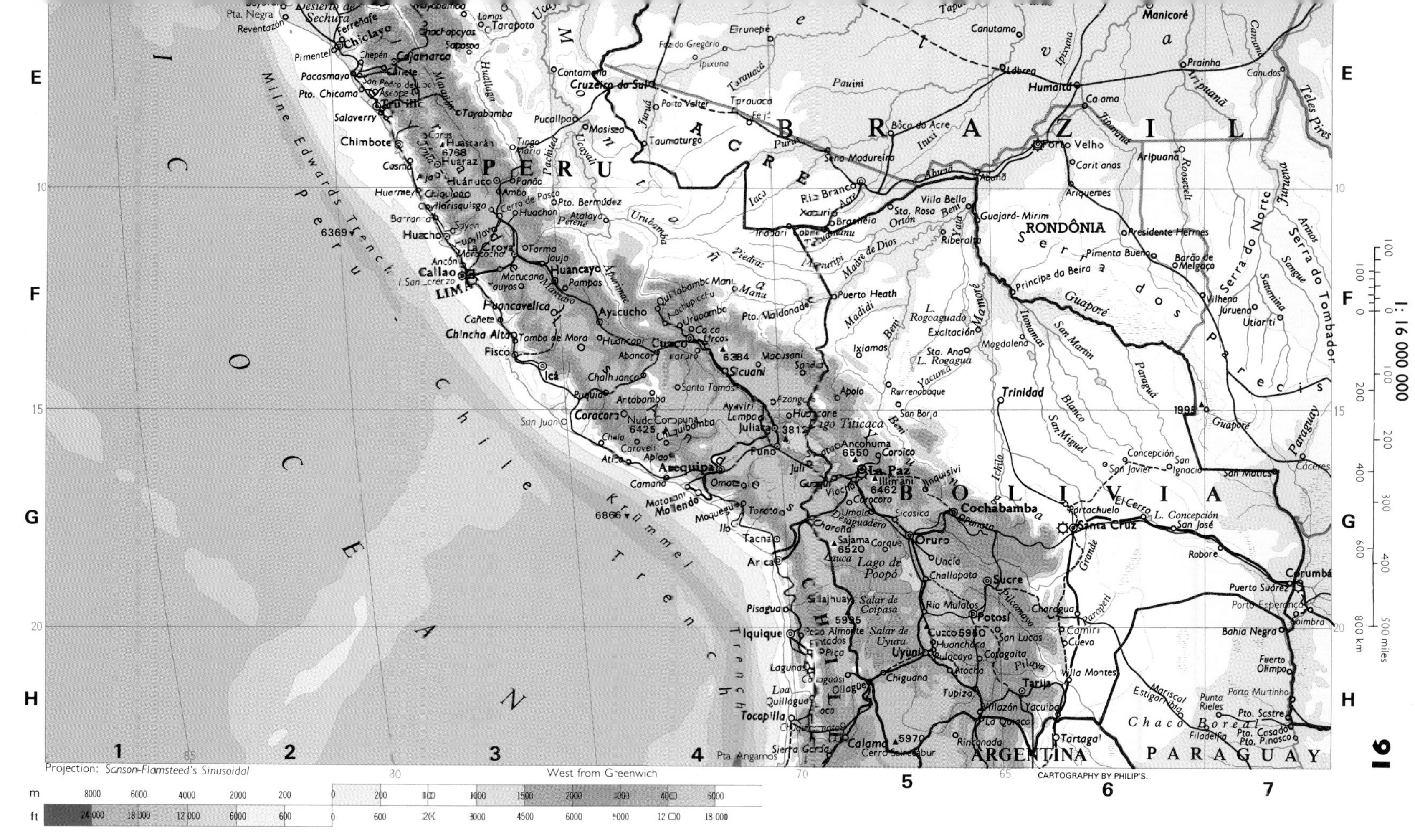
1: 16 000 000
100 0 100 200 300 400 500 miles
100 0 200 400 600 800 km
B R A Z I L
P E R U
B O L I V I A
C H I L E
ARGENTINA
P A R A G U A Y
A C R E
RONDÔNIA
Serra dos Parecis
Serra do Norte
Serra do Tombador
Chaco Boreal
P A C I F I C O C E A N
Peru Chile Trench
Milne Edwards Trench
Krümmel Trench
Lago Titicaca
Lago de Poopó
Salar de Coipasa
Salar de Uyuni
L. Rogoaguado
L. Rogagua
LIMA
Callao
Cuzco
Arequipa
Huancayo
Ayacucho
Chiclayo
Trujillo
Cajamarca
Chimbote
Iquitos
Tacna
Arica
Iquique
Tocopilla
Calama
La Paz
Cochabamba
Santa Cruz
Oruro
Sucre
Potosí
Tarija
Uyuni
Trinidad
Puerto Heath
Riberalta
Guajará-Mirim
Porto Velho
Humaitá
Rio Branco
Cruzeiro do Sul
Corumbá
Puerto Suárez
Bahia Negra
Illimani 6462
Ancohuma 6550
Sajama 6520
Huascarán 6768
Nudo Coropuna 6425
6384
5970
6369
6866
Pta. Negra
Reventazón
Pta. Angamos
Projection: Sanson-Flamsteed's Sinusoidal
West from Greenwich
CARTOGRAPHY BY PHILIP'S.
m 8000 6000 4000 2000 200 0 200 400 1000 1500 2000 3000 4000 6000
ft 24 000 18 000 12 000 6000 600 0 600 1200 3000 4500 6000 9000 12 000 18 000

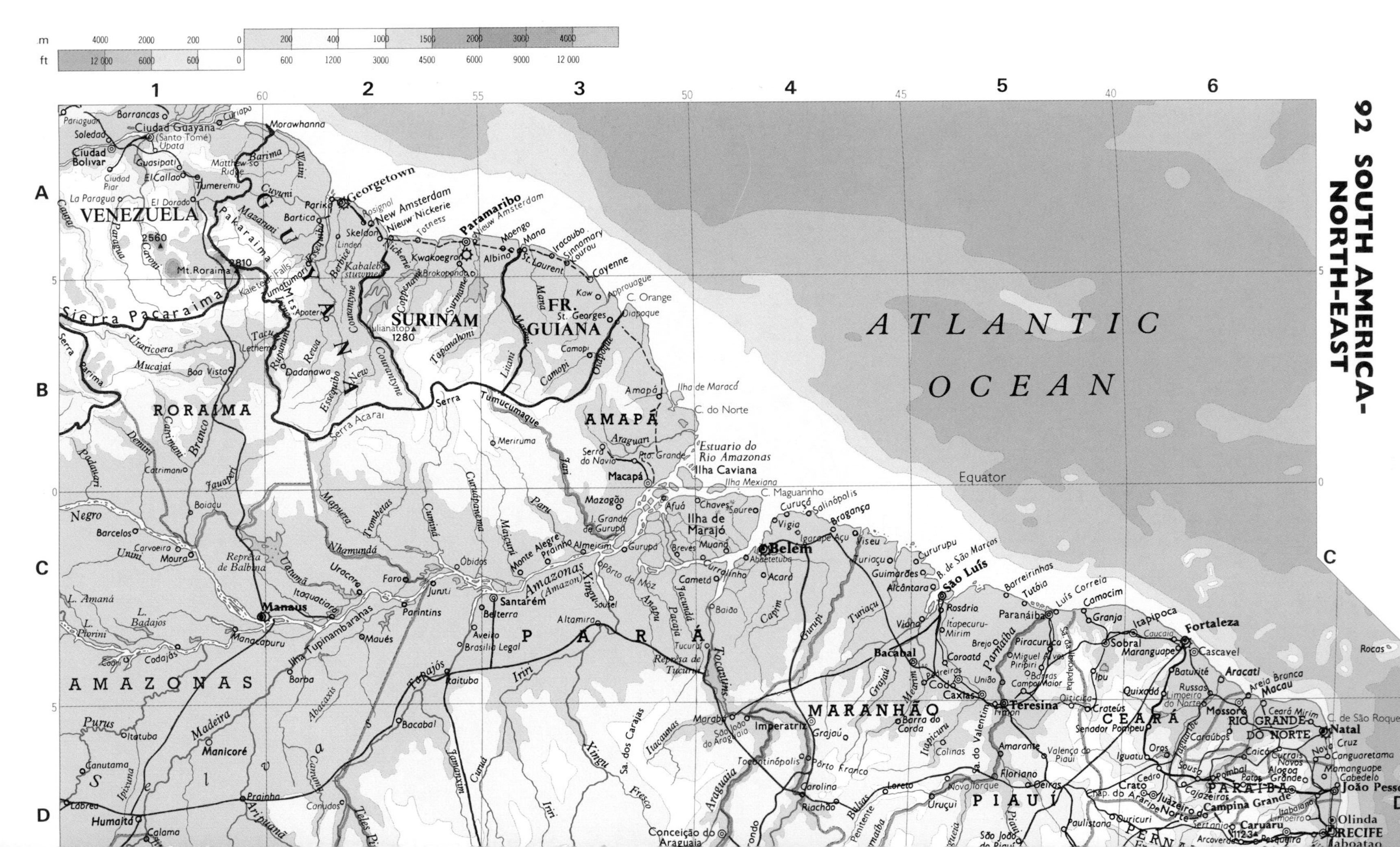
m
ft
4000
2000
200
0
400
1000
1500
3000
12 000
6000
600
1200
4500
9000
A T L A N T I C
O C E A N
Equator
VENEZUELA
G U Y A N A
SURINAM
FR. GUIANA
AMAPÁ
RORAIMA
A M A Z O N A S
P A R Á
MARANHÃO
CEARÁ
PIAUÍ
RIO GRANDE DO NORTE
PARAÍBA
Georgetown
Paramaribo
Cayenne
New Amsterdam
Macapá
Belém
São Luís
Teresina
Fortaleza
Natal
João Pessoa
RECIFE
Olinda
Manaus
Santarém
Mt. Roraima
2810
2560
Ciudad Guayana
Ciudad Bolívar
Sierra Pacaraima
Ilha de Marajó
Ilha Caviana
Estuario do Rio Amazonas
C. Orange
C. do Norte
C. de São Roque
Amazonas (Amazon)
Xingu
Tocantins
Madeira
Negro
Branco
Rocas
Imperatriz
Bacabal
Caxias
Campina Grande
Caruaru
Mossoró
Sobral
Humaitá
Manicoré
1
2
3
4
5
6
A
B
C
D

BRAZIL
BAHIA
MINAS GERAIS
GOIÁS
MATO GROSSO
MATO GROSSO DO SUL
SÃO PAULO
PARANÁ
RIO DE JANEIRO
ESPÍRITO SANTO
RONDÔNIA
TOCANTINS
DIST. FED.
BOLIVIA
PARAGUAY
ARGENTINA
ALAGOAS
SERGIPE
Maceió
Aracaju
Salvador
Feira de Santana
Vitória da Conquista
Ilhéus
Teófilo Otoni
Gov. Valadares
Montes Claros
Diamantina
Belo Horizonte
Juiz de Fora
Petrópolis
Niterói
Vitória
Campos
Brasília
Goiânia
Anápolis
Uberlândia
Ribeirão Prêto
Campinas
Curitiba
Ponta Grossa
Londrina
Maringá
Campo Grande
Cuiabá
Corumbá
Asunción
Concepción
Encarnación
Santa Cruz
Trinidad
Resistencia
Corrientes
Ilha do Bananal
Planalto do Mato Grosso
Serra do Roncador
Serra dos Parecis
Chaco Boreal
Chaco Central
Pilcomayo
Tropic of Capricorn
1 : 16 000 000
100 0 100 200 300 400 500 miles
100 0 200 400 600 800 km
West from Greenwich
Projection: Sanson-Flamsteed's Sinusoidal
CARTOGRAPHY BY PHILIP'S.

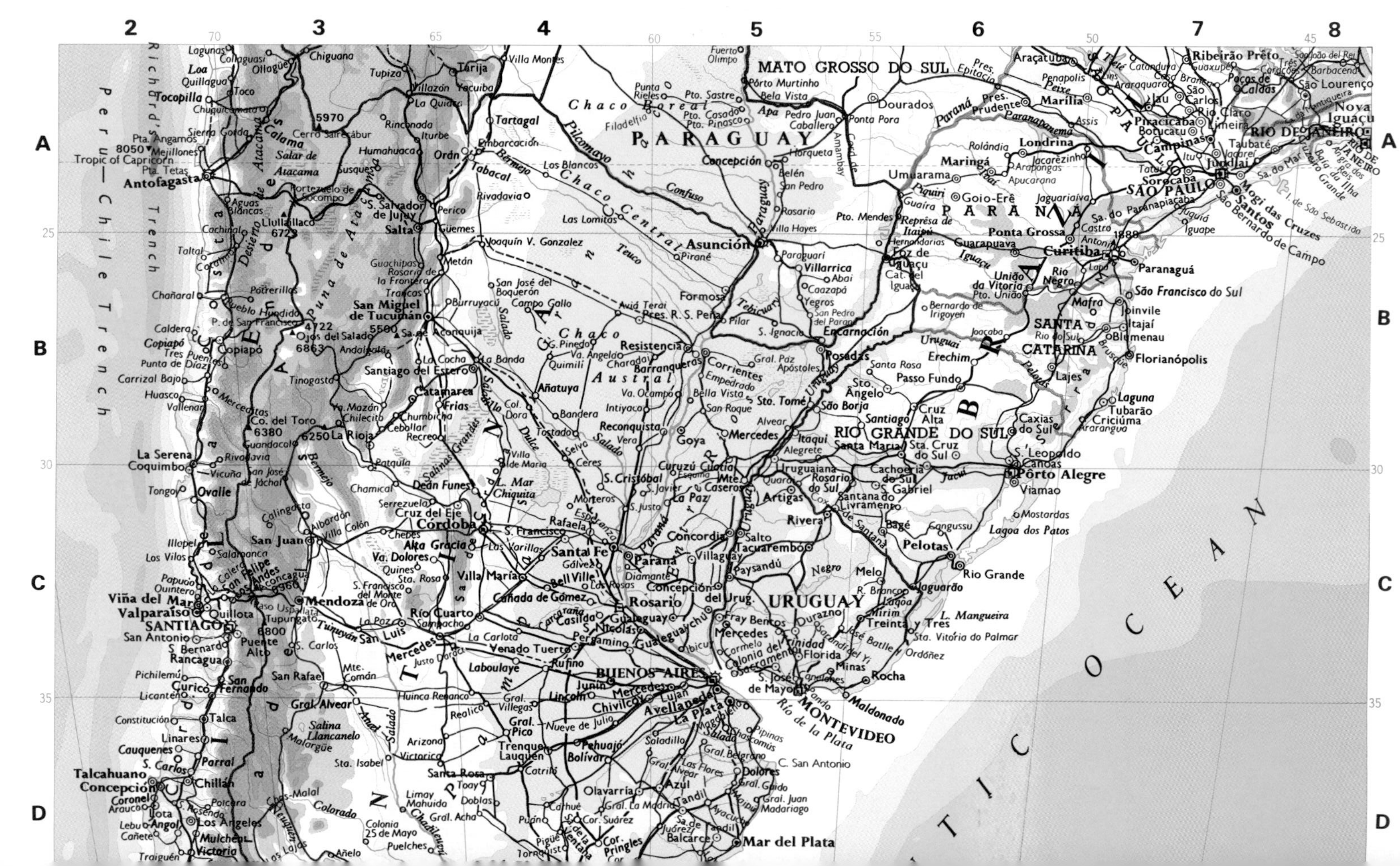

A
B
C
D
2
3
4
5
6
7
8
MATO GROSSO DO SUL
PARAGUAY
PARANÁ
SANTA CATARINA
RIO GRANDE DO SUL
URUGUAY
SÃO PAULO
RIO DE JANEIRO
MONTEVIDEO
BUENOS AIRES
SANTIAGO
Asunción
Pôrto Alegre
Florianópolis
Curitiba
Santos
Córdoba
Rosario
Mendoza
Valparaíso
Viña del Mar
Antofagasta
Salta
San Miguel de Tucumán
Mar del Plata
Río de la Plata
Peru — Chile Trench
Richard's Trench
Tropic of Capricorn
Chaco Boreal
Chaco Central
Chaco Austral
Puna de Atacama
Desierto de Atacama
A T L A N T I C   O C E A N

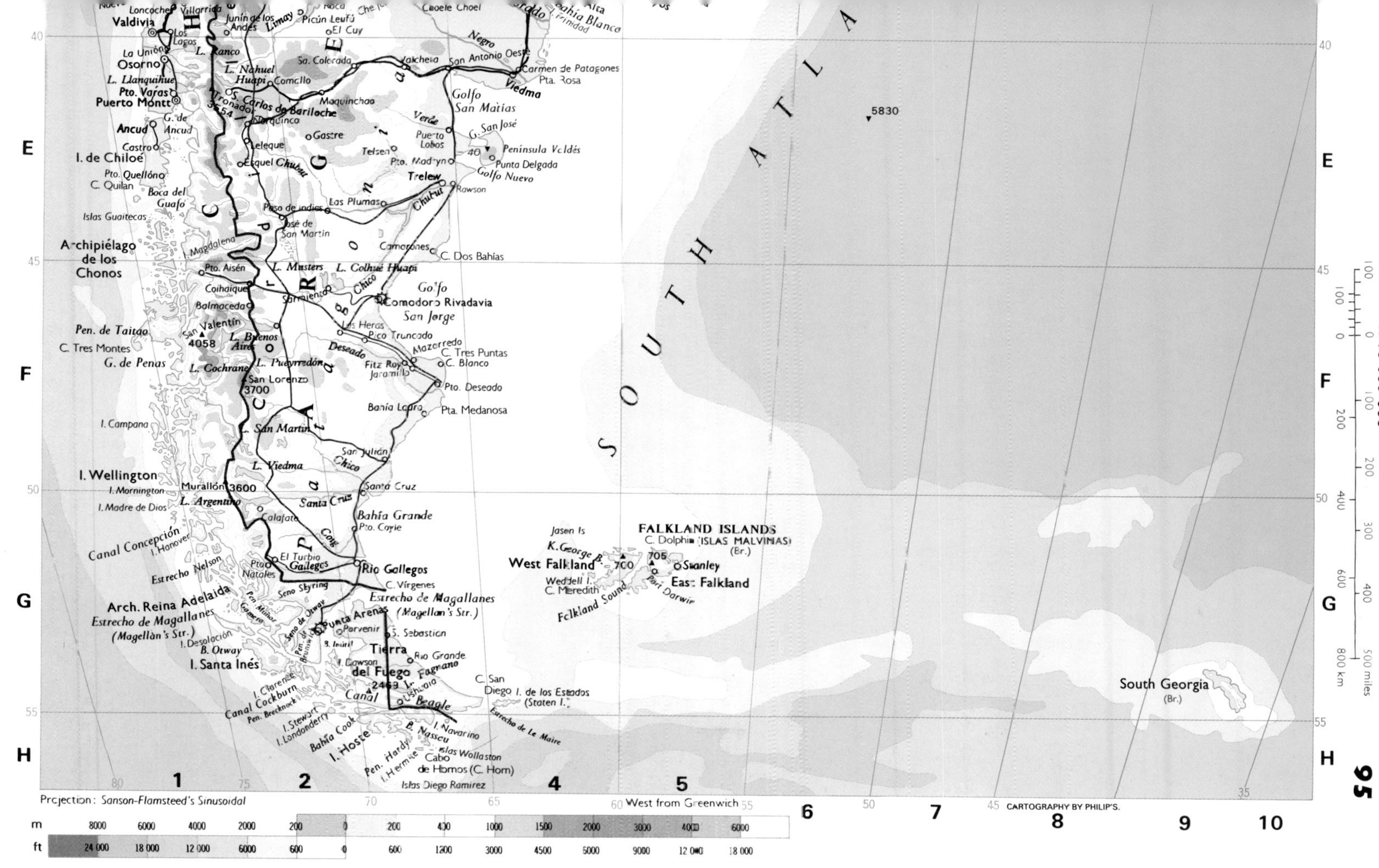
1: 16 000 000
100 0 100 200 300 400 500 miles
100 0 200 400 600 800 km
SOUTH ATLA
FALKLAND ISLANDS
(ISLAS MALVINAS)
(Br.)
West Falkland
East Falkland
Stanley
Falkland Sound
Port Darwin
Jasen Is
Weddell I.
C. Meredith
South Georgia
(Br.)
5830
Valdivia
Osorno
La Unión
L. Llanquihue
Pto. Varas
Puerto Montt
Ancud
G. de Ancud
I. de Chiloé
Castro
Pto. Quellón
C. Quilan
Boca del Guafo
Islas Guaitecas
Archipiélago de los Chonos
Pto. Aisén
Coihaique
Balmaceda
Pen. de Taitao
C. Tres Montes
G. de Penas
San Valentín 4058
L. Buenos Aires
L. Cochrane
San Lorenzo 3700
L. Pueyrredón
I. Campana
I. Wellington
I. Mornington
I. Madre de Dios
Murallón 3600
L. Argentino
L. Viedma
L. San Martín
Canal Concepción
I. Hanover
Estrecho Nelson
Arch. Reina Adelaida
Estrecho de Magallanes
(Magellan's Str.)
I. Desolación
B. Otway
I. Santa Inés
Punta Arenas
Porvenir
Tierra del Fuego
Rio Grande
Canal Beagle
Ushuaia
I. Hoste
I. Navarino
Cabo de Hornos (C. Horn)
Islas Wollaston
Islas Diego Ramirez
C. San Diego
I. de los Estados
(Staten I.)
Estrecho de Le Maire
Rio Gallegos
C. Vírgenes
Bahía Grande
Santa Cruz
San Julián
Pto. Deseado
Pta. Medanosa
C. Blanco
C. Tres Puntas
Golfo San Jorge
Comodoro Rivadavia
C. Dos Bahías
Camarones
Trelew
Rawson
Pto. Madryn
Golfo Nuevo
Punta Delgada
Península Valdés
G. San José
Golfo San Matías
Viedma
Carmen de Patagones
Pta. Rosa
San Antonio Oeste
Negro
Bahía Blanca
S. Carlos de Bariloche
L. Nahuel Huapi
Esquel
Chubut
Deseado
Projection: Sanson-Flamsteed's Sinusoidal
West from Greenwich
CARTOGRAPHY BY PHILIP'S.
m 8000 6000 4000 2000 200 0 200 400 1000 1500 2000 3000 4000 6000
ft 24 000 18 000 12 000 6000 600 0 600 1200 3000 4500 6000 9000 12 000 18 000
E F G H
1 2 4 5 6 7 8 9 10

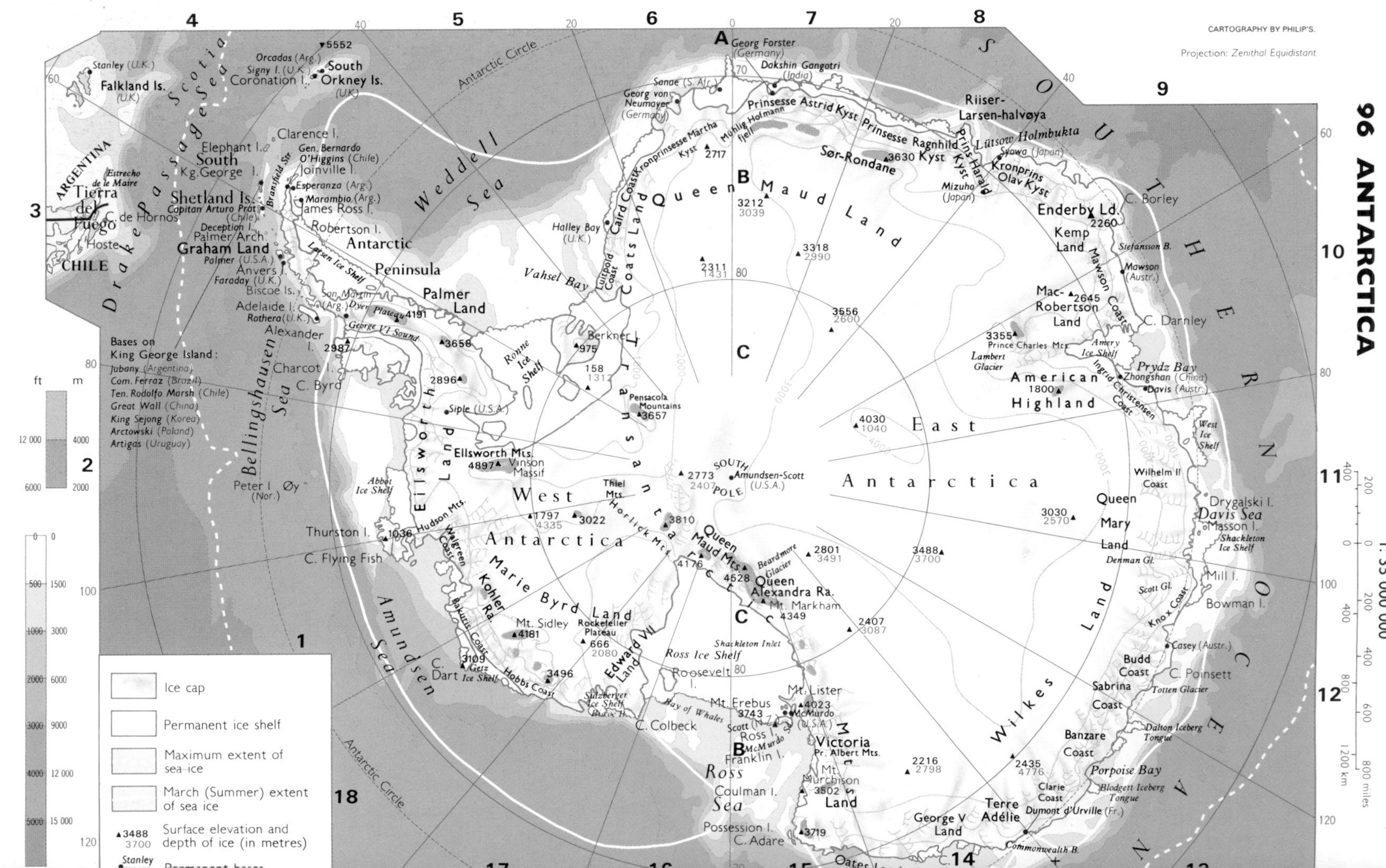
1: 35 000 000
200 0 200 400 600 800 miles
400 0 400 800 1200 km
CARTOGRAPHY BY PHILIP'S.
Projection: Zenithal Equidistant
SOUTHERN OCEAN
Weddell Sea
Amundsen Sea
Bellingshausen Sea
Ross Sea
Davis Sea
Drake Passage
Scotia Sea
Antarctic Circle
East Antarctica
West Antarctica
Transantarctic Mts.
Queen Maud Land
Enderby Ld.
Kemp Land
Mac-Robertson Land
American Highland
Queen Mary Land
Wilkes Land
Terre Adélie
George V Land
Victoria Land
Marie Byrd Land
Ellsworth Land
Palmer Land
Graham Land
Antarctic Peninsula
Coats Land
Ross Ice Shelf
Ronne Ice Shelf
Amery Ice Shelf
West Ice Shelf
Shackleton Ice Shelf
Vinson Massif 4897
Ellsworth Mts.
Queen Maud Mts.
Queen Alexandra Ra.
Mt. Markham 4349
Mt. Erebus
Amundsen-Scott (U.S.A.)
SOUTH POLE
McMurdo (U.S.A.)
Scott (N.Z.)
Mawson (Austr.)
Davis (Austr.)
Casey (Austr.)
Dumont d'Urville (Fr.)
Halley Bay (U.K.)
Georg von Neumayer (Germany)
Georg Forster (Germany)
Dakshin Gangotri (India)
Syowa (Japan)
Mizuho (Japan)
Zhongshan (China)
Siple (U.S.A.)
Rothera (U.K.)
Faraday (U.K.)
Palmer (U.S.A.)
Esperanza (Arg.)
Marambio (Arg.)
South Orkney Is.
South Shetland Is.
Falkland Is. (U.K.)
Stanley
Tierra del Fuego
C. de Hornos
ARGENTINA
CHILE
Peter I Øy (Nor.)
Thurston I.
Roosevelt I.
Ross I.
Coulman I.
C. Adare
Bases on King George Island:
Jubany (Argentina)
Com. Ferraz (Brazil)
Ten. Rodolfo Marsh (Chile)
Great Wall (China)
King Sejong (Korea)
Arctowski (Poland)
Artigas (Uruguay)
Ice cap
Permanent ice shelf
Maximum extent of sea-ice
March (Summer) extent of sea ice
Surface elevation and depth of ice (in metres)
3488 3700

# Index to Map Pages

The index contains the names of all principal places and features shown on the maps. Physical features composed of a proper name (Erie) and a description (Lake) are positioned alphabetically by the proper name. The description is positioned after the proper name and is usually abbreviated:

Erie, L. . . . . . . **72** **C5**

Where a description forms part of a settlement or administrative name however, it is always written in full and put in its true alphabetical position:

Lake Charles **79** **D7**

Names beginning St. are alphabetized under Saint, but Sankt, Sint, Sant, Santa and San are all spelt in full and are alphabetized accordingly.

The number in bold type which follows each name in the index refers to the number of the map page where that feature or place will be found. This is usually the largest scale at which the place or feature appears.

The letter and figure which are in bold type immediately after the page number give the grid square on the map page, within which the feature is situated.

Rivers carry the symbol → after their names. A solid square ■ follows the name of a country while an open square □ refers to a first order administrative area.

## A

A Coruña = La Coruña ..... **18 A1**
Aachen ....... **14 C4**
Aalborg = Ålborg ..... **9 G9**
Aalen ........ **14 D6**
Aarau ........ **13 C8**
Aare → ...... **13 C8**
Aarhus = Århus **9 G10**
Aba .......... **55 G6**
Abādān ...... **47 E7**
Ābādeh ...... **44 D3**
Abadla ....... **54 B4**
Abaetetuba ... **92 C4**
Abakan ....... **30 D7**
Abancay ...... **91 F4**
Abarqū ....... **44 D3**
Abashiri ...... **32 F12**
Abay ......... **29 E8**
Abaya, L. ..... **53 G6**
Abbay = Nîl el Azraq → ... **53 E5**
Abbeville ..... **12 A4**
Abbieglassie .. **63 A4**
Abbot Ice Shelf **96 B2**
Abbottabad ... **42 B8**
Abd al Kūrī ... **49 E5**
Abéché ....... **53 F3**
Abeokuta ..... **55 G5**
Abercorn = Mbala ...... **57 F6**
Abercorn ..... **63 A5**
Aberdeen, *Australia* .... **63 B5**
Aberdeen, *U.K.* **10 C5**
Aberdeen, *S. Dak., U.S.A.* **76 C5**
Aberdeen, *Wash., U.S.A.* **80 B2**
Aberystwyth .. **11 E4**
Abidjan ...... **55 G4**
Abilene ....... **78 C4**
Abitibi L. ..... **69 D3**
Abkhaz Republic □ = Abkhazia □ . **25 E5**
Abkhazia □ ... **25 E5**
Abminga ..... **62 A1**
Åbo = Turku .. **9 F12**
Abohar ....... **42 D9**
Aboméy ...... **55 G5**
Abong-Mbang . **56 D2**
Abou-Deïa .... **53 F2**
Abri ......... **52 D5**
Abrolhos, Banka **93 F6**
Abrud ........ **17 E6**
Absaroka Range **81 C9**
Abū al Khaşīb . **47 E6**
Abū 'Alī ...... **47 F7**
Abu 'Arīsh .... **49 D3**
Abu Dhabi = Abū Z̧āby ... **44 E3**
Abû Dis ...... **53 E5**
Abu Hamed ... **53 E5**
Abū Kamāl .... **46 D5**
Abū Madd, Ra's **47 F4**
Abu Matariq .. **53 F4**
Abu Rudeis ... **47 E3**
Abu Tig ...... **52 C5**
Abû Zabad .... **53 F4**
Abū Z̧āby ..... **44 E3**
Abuja ........ **55 G6**
Abukuma-Gawa → ... **33 G12**
Abunã ....... **91 E5**
Abunã → .... **91 E5**
Abut Hd. ..... **65 E4**
Abwong ...... **53 G5**
Acaponeta .... **84 C3**
Acapulco ..... **84 D5**
Acarigua ..... **90 B5**
Accra ........ **55 G4**
Aceh □ ....... **36 D1**
Achalpur ..... **43 J10**
Achill I. ....... **11 E1**
Achinsk ...... **30 D7**
Acireale ...... **21 F5**
Acklins I. ..... **86 B5**
Aconcagua, Cerro ....... **94 C3**
Aconquija, Mt. . **94 B3**
Açores, Is. dos = Azores ... **50 C1**
Acraman, L. ... **62 B2**
Acre = 'Akko .. **46 D3**
Acre □ ....... **91 E4**
Acre → ...... **91 E5**
Ad Dahnā ..... **47 F7**
Ad Dammām .. **47 F7**
Ad Dawhah ... **44 E2**
Ad Dilam ..... **47 G6**
Ad Dīwānīyah . **47 E6**
Ada .......... **79 B5**
Adaja → ..... **18 B3**
Adam ........ **44 F4**
Adamaoua, Massif de l' . **53 G1**
Adamawa Highlands = Adamaoua, Massif de l' . **53 G1**
Adamello, Mte. **20 A3**
Adaminaby ... **63 C4**
Adam's Bridge **43 Q11**
Adams Mt. .... **80 B3**
Adana ........ **46 C3**
Adapazarı ..... **46 B2**
Adarama ..... **53 E5**
Adare, C. ..... **96 B15**
Adaut ........ **39 F4**
Adavale ...... **63 A3**
Adda → ..... **20 B2**
Addis Ababa = Addis Abeba **53 G6**
Addis Abeba .. **53 G6**
Addis Alem ... **53 G6**
Adelaide ...... **62 B2**
Adelaide I. .... **96 A3**
Adelaide Pen. . **70 B10**
Adélie, Terre .. **96 A14**
Adélie Land = Adélie, Terre **96 A14**
Aden = Al 'Adan ...... **49 E4**
Aden, G. of ... **49 E4**
Adi .......... **39 E4**
Adi Ugri ...... **53 F6**
Adige → ..... **20 B4**
Adilabad ..... **43 K11**
Adirondack Mts. **73 C8**
Admer ....... **54 D6**
Admiralty I. ... **71 C6**
Admiralty Is. .. **64 K9**
Ado-Ekiti ..... **55 G6**
Adonara ...... **39 F2**
Adoni ........ **43 M10**
Adour → ..... **12 E3**
Adra ......... **18 D4**
Adrano ....... **21 F5**
Adrar ........ **54 C4**
Adré ......... **53 F3**
Adrī ......... **52 C1**
Adriatic Sea ... **20 C5**
Adua ......... **39 E3**

Adwa 53 F6
Adzhar Republic □ = Ajaria □ 25 E5
Ægean Sea 23 E5
Aerhtai Shan 34 B4
Afghanistan ■ 45 C6
Afgoi 49 G3
'Afif 47 G5
Afognak I. 71 C4
Afuá 92 C3
Afyonkarahisar 46 C2
Agadès = Agadez 55 E6
Agadez 55 E6
Agadir 54 B3
Agapa 30 B6
Agartala 41 F8
Agats 39 F5
Agboville 55 G4
Agde 13 E5
Agen 12 D4
Agra 42 F10
Agri → 21 D6
Ağrı Dağı 46 C6
Ağrı Karakose 46 C5
Agrigento 21 F4
Agrinion 23 E3
Água Clara 93 G3
Agua Prieta 84 A3
Aguadas 90 B3
Aguadilla 87 C6
Aguarico → 90 D3
Aguas Blancas 94 A3
Aguascalientes 84 C4
Aguilas 19 D5
Agulhas, C. 58 E4
Agung 37 F5
Agusan → 38 C3
Ahaggar 54 D6
Ahar 46 C6
Ahipara B. 64 A5
Ahiri 43 K12
Ahmadabad 43 H8
Ahmadnagar 43 K9
Ahmadpur 42 E7
Ahmedabad = Ahmadabad 43 H8
Ahmednagar = Ahmadnagar 43 K9
Ahvāz 47 E7
Ahvenanmaa = Åland 9 F11
Aḩwar 49 E4
Aigues-Mortes 13 E6
Aihui 35 A7
Aija 91 E3
Aiken 75 C7
Aimere 39 F2
Aimorés 93 F5
Ain Banaiyan 44 F2
Aïn Beïda 54 A6
Aïn Ben Tili 54 C3
Aïn-Sefra 54 B4
Ainabo 49 F4
Aïr 55 E6
Aisne → 13 B5
Aiud 17 E6
Aix-en-Provence 13 E6
Aix-la-Chapelle = Aachen 14 C4
Aix-les-Bains 13 D6
Aiyion 23 E4
Aizawl 41 F9
Ajaccio 13 F8
Ajanta Ra. 43 J9
Ajari Rep. = Ajaria □ 25 E5
Ajaria □ 25 E5
Ajdâbiyah 52 B3
Ajka 16 E3
'Ajmān 44 E3
Ajmer 42 F9
Ajo, C. de 18 A4
Akaroa 65 E5
Akashi 32 B4
Akelamo 39 D3
Aketi 56 D4
Akharnaí 23 E4
Akhelóös → 23 E3
Akhisar 23 E6
Akhmîm 52 C5
Akimiski I. 69 C2
Akita 33 G12
Akjoujt 55 E2
'Akko 46 D3
Akkol 29 E8
Aklavik 70 B6
Akmolinsk = Astana 29 D8
Akobo → 53 G5
Akola 43 J10
Akordat 53 E6
Akpatok I. 68 B4
Akreïjit 55 E3
Akron 72 D5
Aksai Chin 42 B11
Aksaray 46 C3
Aksarka 28 C7
Akşehir 46 C2
Aksu 34 B3
Aksum 53 F6
Aktogay 29 E8
Aktsyabrski 17 B9
Aktyubinsk = Aqtöbe 29 D6
Aku 55 G6
Akure 55 G6
Akyab = Sittwe 41 G9
Al 'Adan 49 E4
Al Aḩsā 47 F7
Al Amādīyah 46 C5
Al Amārah 47 E6
Al 'Aqabah 47 E3
Al 'Aramah 47 F6
Al Ashkhara 45 F4
Al Badī' 47 G6
Al Başrah 47 E6
Al Bayḑā 52 B3
Al Bu'ayrāt al Ḩasūn 52 B2
Al Fallūjah 46 D5
Al Fāw 47 E7
Al Fujayrah 44 E4
Al Hābah 47 F6
Al Haddār 47 G6
Al Hāmad 47 E4
Al Ḩamar 47 G6
Al Ḩamrā' 47 F4
Al Ḩarīq 47 G6
Al Ḩasakah 46 C5
Al Ḩawrah 49 E4
Al Ḩayy 47 D6
Al Ḩijāz 47 F4
Al Ḩillah, *Iraq* 47 D6
Al Ḩillah, *Si. Arabia* 47 G6
Al Hindīyah 47 D6
Al Hoceïma 54 A4
Al Ḩudaydah 49 E3
Al Hufūf 47 F7
Al Ḩulwah 47 G6
Al Ittihad = Madīnat ash Sha'b 49 E3
Al Jāfūrah 47 F7
Al Jaghbūb 52 C3
Al Jahrah 47 E6
Al Jalāmīd 47 E4
Al Jawf, *Libya* 52 D3
Al Jawf, *Si. Arabia* 47 E4
Al Jazirah, *Iraq* 46 D5
Al Jazirah, *Libya* 52 C3
Al Jubayl 47 F7
Al Jubaylah 47 F6
Al Junaynah 53 F3
Al Khābūra 44 F4
Al Khalīl 47 E3
Al Kharfah 47 G6
Al Kharj 47 F6
Al Khasab 44 E4
Al Kufrah 52 D3
Al Kūt 47 D6
Al Kuwayt 47 E7
Al Lādhiqīyah 46 D3
Al Luḩayyah 49 D3
Al Madīnah 47 F4
Al Majma'ah 47 F6
Al Manāmah 44 E2
Al Marj 52 B3
Al Mawşil 46 C5
Al Midhnab 47 F6
Al Mish'āb 47 E7
Al Mubarraz 47 F7
Al Muḩarraq 44 E2
Al Mukallā 49 E4
Al Mukhā 49 E3
Al Musayyib 47 D6
Al Muwayliḩ 47 F3
Al Qaḑīmah 47 G4
Al Qā'iyah 47 F5
Al Qāmishli 46 C5
Al Qaşabát 52 B1
Al Qaşīm 47 F5
Al Qaţīf 47 F7
Al Qaţrūn 52 D2
Al Qayşūmah 47 E6
Al Quaisūmah 47 E6
Al Quds = Jerusalem 47 E3
Al Qurayyāt 45 F4
Al Qurnah 47 E6
Al 'Ulā 47 F4
Al Uqaylah ash Sharqīgah 52 B2
Al Uqayr 47 F7
Al 'Uthmānīyah 47 F7
Al 'Uwaynid 47 F6
Al 'Uwayqīlah 47 E5
Al 'Uyūn 47 F5
Al Wakrah 44 E2
Al Wari'āh 47 F6
Al Yamāmah 47 F6
Alabama □ 74 C4
Alabama → 74 D4
Alaçam Dağları 23 E7
Alagoa Grande 92 D6
Alagoas □ 93 D6
Alagoinhas 93 E6
Alajuela 86 D3
Alamosa 83 B10
Åland 9 F11
Alania = North Ossetia □ 25 E5
Alanya 46 C2
Alapayevsk 29 D7
Alaşehir 23 E7
Alaska □ 71 B4
Alaska, G. of 71 C5
Alaska Peninsula 71 C4
Alaska Range 71 B4
Alataw Shankou 34 B3
Alatyr 24 C6
Alausi 90 D3
Alawoona 62 B3
Alba 20 B2
Alba-Iulia 17 E6
Albacete 19 C5
Albacutya, L. 62 C3
Albania ■ 23 D3
Albany, *Australia* 60 H2
Albany, *Ga., U.S.A.* 75 D5
Albany, *N.Y., U.S.A.* 73 C9
Albany, *Oreg., U.S.A.* 80 C2
Albany → 69 C2
Albardón 94 C3
Albemarle 75 B7
Alberche → 18 C3
Albert, L. 62 C2
Albert L. 57 D6
Albert Nile → 57 D6
Albertville 13 D7
Albi 12 E5
Albina 92 A3
Alborán 18 E4
Ålborg 9 G9
Alborz, Reshteh-ye Kūhhā-ye 44 B3
Albuquerque 83 C9
Albury 63 C4
Alcalá de Henares 18 B4
Alcalá la Real 18 D4
Alcamo 21 F4
Alcaníz 19 B5
Alcântara 92 C5
Alcántara, Embalse de 18 C2
Alcantarilla 19 D5
Alcaraz, Sierra de 19 C4
Alcaudete 18 D3
Alcázar de San Juan 18 C4
Alchevsk 25 D4
Alcira 19 C5
Alcoy 19 C5
Aldabra Is. 51 G8
Aldan → 31 C10
Alderney 11 G5
Aleg 55 E2
Alegrete 94 B5
Aleisk 29 D9
Aleksandriya = Oleksandriya 17 C8
Aleksandrovskoye 29 C8
Alemania 94 B3
Alençon 12 B4
Aleppo = Ḩalab 46 C4
Alès 13 D6
Alessándria 20 B2
Ålesund 8 F9
Aleutian Is. 71 C2
Alexander Arch. 71 C6
Alexander I. 96 A3
Alexandra, *Australia* 63 C4
Alexandra, *N.Z.* 65 F3
Alexandria = El Iskandarîya 52 B4
Alexandria, *Canada* 71 C7
Alexandria, *Romania* 22 C5
Alexandria, *S. Africa* 59 E5
Alexandria, *La., U.S.A.* 79 D7
Alexandria, *Va., U.S.A.* 73 E7

Alexandrina, L. 62 C2
Alexandroúpolis 22 D5
Alga 29 E6
Algarve 18 D1
Algeciras 18 D3
Algemesí 19 C5
Alger 54 A5
Algeria ■ 54 C5
Alghero 21 D2
Algiers = Alger 54 A5
Algoa B. 59 E5
Alhucemas = Al Hoceïma 54 A4
'Alī al Gharbī 47 D6
'Alī Khēl 42 C6
Aliağa 23 E6
Alibo 53 G6
Alicante 19 C5
Alice Springs 60 E5
Aligarh 42 F11
Alīgūdarz 46 D7
Alipur 42 E7
Alipur Duar 41 D7
Aliwal North 59 E5
Aljustrel 18 D1
Alkmaar 14 B3
All American Canal 82 D5
Allahabad 40 E3
Allanmyo 41 H10
Alleghony → 73 D5
Allegheny Plateau 73 F5
Allentown 73 D8
Alleppey 43 Q10
Aller → 14 B5
Allier → 13 C5
Allora 63 A5
Alma Ata = Almaty 29 E8
Almada 18 C1
Almadén 18 C3
Almansa 19 C5
Almanzor, Pico del Moro 18 B3
Almanzora → 19 D5
Almaty 29 E8
Almazán 19 B4
Almeirim 92 C3
Almelo 14 B4
Almendralejo 18 C2
Almería 19 D4
Almora 42 E11
Alnwick 10 D6
Alon 41 F10
Alor 39 F2
Alor Setar 36 C2
Alps 14 E5
Alsace 13 B7
Alsask 71 C9
Alsásua 19 A4
Alta Gracia 94 C4
Altagracia 90 A4
Altai = Aerhtai Shan 34 B4
Altamira 92 C3
Altamura 21 D6
Altanbulag 35 A5
Altay 34 B3
Altea 19 C5
Alto Araguaia 93 F3
Alto Molocue 59 B7
Alton 77 F9
Alton Downs 62 A2
Altoona 73 D6
Altun Shan 34 C3
Alùla 49 E5
Alusi 39 F4
Alvarado 85 D5
Alvear 94 B5
Alvie 62 C3
Alwar 42 F10
Alxa Zuoqi 35 C5
Am Dam 53 F3
Am-Timan 53 F3
Amâdi, *Sudan* 53 G5
Amadi, *Dem. Rep. of the Congo* 57 D5
Amadjuak 68 B3
Amadjuak L. 68 B3
Amagasaki 32 B4
Amakusa-Shoto 32 C2
Amaliás 23 F3
Amalner 43 J9
Amambay, Cordillera de 94 A5
Amangeldy 29 D7
Amapá 92 B3
Amapá □ 92 B3
Amarante 92 D5
Amargosa 93 E6
Amarillo 78 B3
Amaro, Mte. 20 C5
Amasra 46 B3
Amasya 46 B3
Amazon = Amazonas → 92 C3
Amazonas □ 90 D6
Amazonas → 92 C3
Ambala 42 D10
Ambalavao 59 J9
Ambam 56 D2
Ambanja 59 G9
Ambartsevo 29 D9
Ambato 90 D3
Ambatolampy 59 H9
Ambatondrazaka 59 H9
Amberg 16 D6
Ambergris Cay 85 D7
Amberley 65 E5
Ambikapur 40 F4
Ambilobé 59 G9
Ambo 91 F3
Amboise 12 C4
Ambon 39 E3
Ambositra 59 J9
Amboyna I. 36 C4
Ambriz 56 F2
Amby 63 A4
Amchitka I. 71 C1
Amderma 28 C7
Ameca 84 C4
Ameland 14 B3
American Highland 96 B10
American Samoa ■ 65 L13
Americus 75 C5
Amery 71 C10
Amery Ice Shelf 96 A10
Ames 77 D8
Amherst, *Burma* 41 J11
Amherst, *Canada* 69 D4
Amiata, Mte. 20 C3
Amiens 12 B5
Amirante Is. 26 K9
'Ammān 47 E3
Amorgós 23 F5
Amoy = Xiamen 35 D6
Ampanihy 59 J8
Ampenan 37 F5
Amper → 15 D6
Amravati 43 J10
Amreli 43 J7
Amritsar 42 D9
Amroha 42 E11
Amsterdam 14 B3
Amstetten 15 D8
Amudarya → 29 E6
Amundsen Gulf 70 A7
Amundsen Sea 96 B1
Amuntai 37 E5
Amur → 31 D12
Amurang 39 D2
Amuri Pass 65 E5
Amyderya = Amudarya → 29 E6
An Nafūd 47 E5
An Najaf 47 D6
An Nhon 36 B3
An Nu'ayrīyah 47 F7
Anabar → 30 B9
Anaconda 81 B7
Anadolu 46 C2
'Ānah 46 D5
Anaheim 82 D4
Anakapalle 40 J4
Analalava 59 G9
Anambas, Kepulauan 37 D3
Anambas Is. = Anambas, Kepulauan 37 D3
Anamur 46 C3
Anan 32 C4
Anantnag 42 C9
Ananyiv 17 E9
Anápolis 93 F4
Anār 44 D3
Anārak 44 C3
Anatolia = Anadolu 46 C2
Añatuya 94 B4
Anaye 53 E1
Anchorage 71 B5
Ancohuma, Nevada 91 G5
Ancón 91 F3
Ancona 20 C4
Ancud 95 F2
Ancud, G. de 95 E2
Andalgalá 94 B3
Andalucía □ 18 D3
Andalusia 74 D4
Andalusia □ = Andalucía □ 18 D3
Andaman Is. 27 H13
Andaman Sea 36 B1
Andara 58 B4
Anderson 72 D3
Anderson → 70 B7
Andes = Andes, Cord. de los 91 G4
Andes, Cord. de los 91 G4
Andhra Pradesh □ 43 L11
Andijon 29 E8
Andikíthira 23 G4
Andizhan = Andijon 29 E8
Andkhvoy 45 B6
Andoany 59 G9
Andorra ■ 19 A6
Andorra La Vella 19 A6
Andreanof Is. 71 C2
Andrewilla 62 A2
Ándria 20 D6
Andriba 59 H9
Andropov = Rybinsk 24 B4
Ándros 23 F5
Andros I. 86 B4
Andújar 18 C3
Andulo 56 G3
Aného 55 G5
Aneto, Pico de 19 A6
Angamos, Punta 94 A2
Ang'angxi 35 B7
Angara → 30 D7
Angarsk 30 D8
Angaston 62 B2
Ånge 8 F11
Angeles 38 A2
Angellala 63 A4
Ångermanälven → 8 F11
Angers 12 C3
Anglesey 11 E4
Ango 57 D5
Angola ■ 58 A3
Angoulême 12 D4
Angoumois 12 D4
Angra dos Reis 94 A8
Angren 29 E8
Anguilla ■ 87 C7
Anhui □ 35 C6
Anhwei □ = Anhui □ 35 C6
Anjidiv I. 43 M9
Anjou 12 C3
Anjozorobe 59 H9
Anju 35 C7
Anka 55 F6
Ankang 35 C5
Ankara 46 C3
Ankazoabo 59 J8
Ankazobe 59 H9
Ankoro 57 F5
Ann Arbor 72 C4
Annaba 54 A6
Annan 11 D5
Annapolis 73 E7
Annecy 13 D7
Anning 34 D5
Anniston 74 C5
Annobón 51 G4
Annuello 62 B3
Anqing 35 C6
Ansbach 14 D6
Anshan 35 B7
Anshun 35 D5
Ansirabe 59 H9
Ansongo 55 E5
Ansudu 39 E5
Antabamba 91 F4
Antakya 46 C4
Antalaha 59 G10
Antalya 46 C2
Antalya Körfezi 46 C2
Antananarivo 59 H9
Antarctic Pen. 96 A4
Antarctica 96 C
Antequera 18 D3
Anti Atlas 54 C3
Antibes 13 E7
Anticosti, I. d' 69 D4
Antigua & Barbuda ■ 87 C7
Antilla 86 B4
Antioquia 90 B3
Antofagasta 94 A2
Antofagasta de la Sierra 94 B3
Antongila, Helodrano 59 H9
Antonina 94 B7
Antrim 11 D3
Antsalova 59 H8
Antsiranana 59 G9
Antsohihy 59 G9
Antwerp = Antwerpen 14 C3
Antwerpen 14 C3

Anupgarh 42 E8
Anvers = Antwerpen 14 C3
Anvers I. 96 A3
Anxi 34 B4
Anxious B. 62 B1
Anyang 35 C6
Anzhero-Sudzhensk 29 D9
Ánzio 20 D4
Aomori 33 F12
Aosta 20 B1
Aoudéras 55 E6
Aoulef el Arab 54 C5
Apalachicola → 74 E5
Apaporis → 90 D5
Aparri 38 A2
Apeldoorn 14 B3
Apennines = Appennini 20 B3
Apia 65 L13
Apiacás, Serra dos 91 E7
Aplao 91 G4
Apo, Mt. 38 C3
Apollonia = Marsá Susah 52 B3
Apolo 91 F5
Apoteri 90 C7
Appalachian Mts. 73 F5
Appennini 20 B3
Appleton 72 B1
Approuague 92 B3
Aprília 20 D4
Apucarana 94 A6
Apure → 90 B5
Apurimac → 91 F4
Aqabah = Al 'Aqabah 47 E3
'Aqabah, Khalīj al 47 E3
Āqcheh 45 B6
Aqîq 53 E6
Aqmola = Astana 29 D8
Aqrah 46 C5
Aqtöbe 29 D6
Aquidauana 93 G2
Aquitain, Bassin 12 D3
Ar Rachidiya 54 B4
Ar Ramādī 46 D5
Ar Raqqah 46 D4
Ar Rass 47 F5
Ar Rifā'ī 47 E6
Ar Riyāḍ 47 F6
Ar Ruṭbah 46 D5
Ar Ruwayḍah 47 G6
Ara 40 E5
'Arab, Bahr el → 53 G4
Arab, Shatt al → 47 E7
Arabian Desert = Es Sahrâ' Esh Sharqîya 52 C5
Arabian Gulf = Gulf, The 44 E2
Arabian Sea 26 H10
Araç 46 B3
Aracaju 93 E6
Aracataca 90 A4
Aracati 92 C6
Araçatuba 93 G3
Aracena 18 D2
Araçuaí 93 F5
Arad 16 E5
Arada 53 F3
Arafura Sea 39 F4
Aragón □ 19 B5
Aragón → 19 A5
Araguacema 92 D4
Araguaia → 92 D4
Araguari 93 F4
Araguari → 92 B4
Arak 54 C5
Arakan Coast 41 H9
Arakan Yoma 41 H10
Araks = Aras, Rūd-e → 46 B7
Aral 29 E7
Aral Sea 29 E6
Aral Tengizi = Aral Sea 29 E6
Aralsk = Aral 29 E7
Aralskoye More = Aral Sea 29 E6
Aran I. 10 D2
Aran Is. 11 E2
Aranda de Duero 18 B4
Aranjuez 18 B4
Aranos 58 C3
Araouane 55 E4
Arapgir 46 C4
Arapiraca 93 D6
Arapongas 94 A6
Araranguá 94 B7
Araraquara 93 G4
Ararat 62 C3
Ararat, Mt. = Ağrı Dağı 46 C6
Araripe, Chapada do 92 D6
Aras, Rūd-e → 46 B7
Arauca 90 B4
Arauca → 90 B5
Arauco 94 D2
Araxá 93 F4
Araya, Pen. de 90 A6
Arbatax 21 E2
Arbīl 46 C6
Arbroath 10 C5
Arcachon 12 D3
Archangel = Arkhangelsk 28 C5
Arcila = Asilah 54 A3
Arckaringa 62 A1
Arckaringa Cr. → 62 A2
Arcos de la Frontera 18 D3
Arcot 43 N11
Arcoverde 92 D6
Arctic Bay 68 A2
Arctic Red River 70 B6
Arda → 22 D6
Ardabīl 46 C7
Ardahan 46 B5
Ardakān = Sepīdān 44 D3
Ardenne 14 D3
Ardennes = Ardenne 14 D3
Ardestān 44 C3
Ardlethan 63 B4
Ardmore 78 B5
Ardrossan 62 B2
Arecibo 87 C6
Areia Branca 92 C6
Arendal 9 G9
Arequipa 91 G4
Arero 53 H6
Arévalo 18 B3
Arezzo 20 C3
Argamakmur 37 E2
Arganda 18 B4
Argentan 12 B3
Argentário, Mte. 20 C3
Argentina ■ 94 D3
Argentina Is. 96 A3
Argentino, L. 95 G2
Argeş → 22 B6
Arghandab → 42 D4
Argo 53 E5
Argolikós Kólpos 23 F4
Árgos 23 F4
Argostólion 23 E3
Argungu 55 F5
Århus 9 G10
Arica, *Chile* 91 G4
Arica, *Colombia* 90 D4
Aridh 47 F6
Arinos → 91 F7
Aripuanã 91 E6
Aripuanã → 90 E6
Ariquemes 91 E6
Arizona 94 D3
Arizona □ 83 C7
Arjona 90 A3
Arkalyk = Arqalyk 29 D7
Arkansas □ 79 B7
Arkansas → 79 C8
Arkansas City 78 A5
Arkhangelsk 28 C5
Arklow 11 E3
Arkticheskiy, Mys 30 A7
Arlanzón → 18 A3
Arlberg P. 14 E6
Arles 13 E6
Arlington, *Va., U.S.A.* 73 E7
Arlington, *Wash., U.S.A.* 80 A2
Arlon 14 D3
Armagh 11 D3
Armavir 25 D5
Armenia 90 C3
Armenia ■ 25 E5
Armidale 63 B5
Armstrong 69 C2
Arnaud → 68 B3
Arnauti, C. 46 D3
Arnhem 14 C3
Arnhem, C. 60 C6
Arnhem Land 60 C5
Arno → 20 C3
Arno Bay 62 B2
Arnsberg 14 C5
Aroab 58 D3
Arqalyk 29 D7
Arrabury 62 A3
Arrah = Ara 40 E5
Arran 10 D4
Arras 13 A5
Arrecife 54 C2
Arrée, Mts. d' 12 B2
Arrowtown 65 F3
Árta 23 E3
Arthur → 62 D3
Arthur's Pass 65 E4
Artigas 94 C5
Artois 12 A5
Artsyz 17 E9
Artvin 46 B5
Aru, Kepulauan 39 F4
Aru Is. = Aru, Kepulauan 39 F4
Arua 57 D6
Aruanã 93 E3
Aruba ■ 87 D6
Arumpo 62 B3
Arunachal Pradesh □ 41 C10
Arusha 57 E7
Aruwimi → 56 D4
Arviat 70 B10
Arxan 35 B6
Arys 29 E7
Arzamas 24 B5
Arzew 54 A4
'As Saffānīyah 47 E7
As Samāwah 47 E6
As Sulaymānīyah, *Iraq* 46 D6
As Sulaymānīyah, *Si. Arabia* 47 F6
As Summān 47 F6
As Sūq 47 G5
As Suwaydā' 46 D4
As Suwayh 45 F4
As Ṣuwayrah 47 D6
Asahigawa 32 F12
Asansol 40 F6
Ascension I. 51 G2
Aschaffenburg 14 D5
Aschersleben 15 C6
Áscoli Piceno 20 C4
Ascope 91 E3
Aseb 49 E3
Asela 53 G6
Asenovgrad 22 C5
Ash Shām, Bādiyat 47 D4
Ash Shāmīyah 47 E6
Ash Shāriqah 44 E3
Ash Shaṭrah 47 E6
Ash Shaykh, J. 46 D3
Ash Shu'aybah 47 F6
Ash Shu'bah 47 E6
Ashburton 65 E4
Ashcroft 71 C7
Asheville 75 B6
Ashford, *Australia* 63 A5
Ashford, *U.K.* 11 F7
Ashgabat 29 F6
Ashikaga 32 A6
Ashizuri-Zaki 32 C3
Ashkhabad = Ashgabat 29 F6
Ashmyany 17 A7
Ashqelon 47 E3
Ashtabula 72 D5
Ashuanipi, L. 69 C4
Asia, Kepulauan 39 D4
Asifabad 43 K11
Asike 39 F6
Asilah 54 A3
Asinara 20 D2
Asinara, G. dell' 20 D2
Asino 29 D9
Asipovichy 17 B9
'Asīr □ 48 D3
Asir, Ras 49 E5
Asmara = Asmera 53 E6
Asmera 53 E6
Aspiring, Mt. 65 F3
Assam □ 41 D9
Assen 14 B4
Assini 55 G4
Assiniboia 71 D9
Assiniboine → 71 D10
Assis 94 A6
Assisi 20 C4
Astana 29 D8
Asti 20 B2
Astipálaia 23 F6
Astorga 18 A2
Astoria 80 B2
Astrakhan 25 D6
Astrakhan-Bazàr 25 F6

Asturias □ 18 A3
Asunción 94 B5
Aswân 52 D5
Aswân High Dam = Sadd el Aali 52 D5
Asyût 52 C5
At Ţafilah 47 E3
At Tā'if 48 C3
Atacama, Desierto de 94 A3
Atacama, Salar de 94 A3
Atakpamé 55 G5
Atalaya 91 F4
Atami 32 B6
Atapupu 39 F2
Atâr 54 D2
Atasu 29 E8
Atauro 39 F3
Atbara 53 E5
'Atbara → 53 E5
Atbasar 29 D7
Athabasca 71 C8
Athabasca → 70 C8
Athabasca, L. 70 C8
Athens = Athínai 23 F4
Athens, *Ala., U.S.A.* 74 B4
Athens, *Ga., U.S.A.* 75 C6
Athínai 23 F4
Athlone 11 E3
Athos 23 D5
Athy 11 E3
Ati 53 F2
Atico 91 G4
Atlanta 75 C5
Atlantic City 73 E8
Atlas Mts. = Haut Atlas 54 B3
Atrak = Atrek → 44 B3
Atrek → 44 B3
Attawapiskat → 69 C2
Attock 42 C8
Attopeu 36 B3
Attur 43 P11
Atuel → 94 D3
Atyraū 29 E6
Aubagne 13 E6
Aube → 13 B5
Auburn 74 C5
Auburn Ra. 63 A5
Aubusson 12 D5
Auch 12 E4
Auckland 64 B6
Aude → 13 E5
Augathella 63 A4
Augsburg 14 D6
Augusta, *Italy* 21 F5
Augusta, *Ga., U.S.A.* 75 C7
Augusta, *Maine, U.S.A.* 73 B11
Aunis 12 C3
Auponhia 39 E3
Aurangabad, *Bihar, India* 40 E5
Aurangabad, *Maharashtra, India* 43 K9
Aurich 14 B4
Aurillac 12 D5
Aurora, *Colo., U.S.A.* 76 F2
Aurora, *Ill., U.S.A.* 72 D1
Aus 58 D3
Auschwitz = Oświęcim 16 C4
Austin, *Minn., U.S.A.* 77 D8
Austin, *Tex., U.S.A.* 78 D5
Austral Is. = Tubuai Is. 65 M16
Austral Seamount Chain 65 M16
Australia ■ 60 E6
Australian Alps 63 C4
Australian Capital Territory □ 63 C4
Austria ■ 15 E8
Autun 13 C6
Auvergne 13 D5
Auvergne, Mts. d' 13 D5
Auxerre 13 C5
Avallon 13 C5
Aveiro, *Brazil* 92 C2
Aveiro, *Portugal* 18 B1
Āvej 46 D7
Avellaneda 94 C5
Avellino 21 D5
Aversa 21 D5
Avezzano 20 C4
Aviá Terai 94 B4
Aviemore 10 C5
Avignon 13 E6
Ávila 18 B3
Avilés 18 A3
Avoca → 62 C3
Avola 21 F5
Avranches 12 B3
'Awālī 44 E2
Awash 49 F3
Awatere → 65 D6
Awbārī 52 C1
Awjilah 52 C3
Axim 55 H4
Axiós → 23 D4
Ayabaca 90 D3
Ayabe 32 B4
Ayacucho, *Argentina* 94 D5
Ayacucho, *Peru* 91 F4
Ayaguz 29 E9
Ayamonte 18 D2
Ayaviri 91 F4
Āybak 45 B7
Aydın 23 F6
Ayers Rock 60 F5
Áyios Evstrátios 23 E5
Aylmer, L. 70 B8
Ayn Dār 47 F7
Ayn Zālah 46 C5
Ayr 10 D4
Aytos 22 C6
Ayu, Kepulauan 39 D4
Ayutla 84 D5
Ayvacık 23 E6
Ayvalık 23 E6
Az Ẓahrān 47 F7
Az Zarqā 46 D4
Az-Zilfī 47 F6
Az Zubayr 47 E6
Az Zuwaytīnah 52 B3
Azamgarh 40 D4
Azärbayjan = Azerbaijan ■ 25 E6
Āzarbāyjān-e Gharbī □ 46 C6
Āzarbāyjān-e Sharqī □ 46 C6
Azare 55 F7
Azbine = Aïr 55 E6
Azerbaijan ■ 25 E6
Azerbaijchan = Azerbaijan ■ 25 E6
Azogues 90 D3
Azores 50 C1
Azov 25 D4
Azov, Sea of 25 D4
Azovskoye More = Azov, Sea of 25 D4
Azovy 28 C7
Azúa 87 C5
Azuaga 18 C3
Azuero, Pen. de 86 E3
Azul 94 D5

## B

Ba Don 36 A3
Ba Ria 36 B3
Bab el Mandeb 49 E3
Baba Burnu 23 E6
Babadag 22 B7
Babadayhan 29 F7
Babaeski 22 D6
Babahoyo 90 D3
Babana 55 F5
Babar 39 F3
Babo 39 E4
Bābol 44 B3
Bābol Sar 44 B3
Baboua 56 C2
Babruysk 17 B9
Babura 55 F6
Babuyan Chan. 38 A2
Babylon 47 D6
Bacabal 92 C5
Bacan, Kepulauan 39 E3
Bacan, Pulau 39 E3
Bacarra 38 A2
Bacău 17 E8
Bachelina 29 D7
Back → 70 B9
Backstairs Passage 62 C2
Bacolod 38 B2
Bad Ischl 15 E7
Bad Kissingen 14 C6
Bad Lands 76 D3
Badagara 43 P9
Badajoz 18 C2
Badalona 19 B7
Badalzai 42 E4
Badampahar 40 F6
Badanah 47 E5
Badarinath 42 D11
Badas 36 D4
Badas, Kepulauan 37 D3
Baddo → 42 E4
Bade 39 F5
Baden 15 D9
Baden-Baden 14 D5
Baden-Württemberg □ 14 D5
Badgastein 15 E7
Bādghīsāt □ 42 B3
Badin 43 G6
Baduen 49 F4
Baena 18 D3
Baeza 18 D4
Bafatá 55 F2
Baffin B. 68 A4
Baffin I. 68 B3
Bafia 56 D2
Bafing → 55 F2
Bafoulabé 55 F2
Bāfq 44 D3
Bafra 46 B3
Bāft 44 D4
Bafwasende 57 D5
Bagamoyo 57 F7
Baganga 38 C3
Bagansiapiapi 37 D2
Bagdarin 30 D9
Bagé 94 C6
Baghdād 46 D6
Bagheria 21 E4
Baghlān 42 A6
Baghlān □ 45 C7
Baguio 38 A2
Bahamas ■ 86 A4
Baharampur 40 E7
Bahawalpur 42 E7
Bahía = Salvador 93 E6
Bahía □ 93 E5
Bahía Blanca 94 D4
Bahía de Caráquez 90 D2
Bahía Laura 95 F3
Bahía Negra 91 H7
Bahr Aouk → 56 C3
Bahr Salamat → 53 G2
Bahraich 40 D3
Bahrain ■ 44 E2
Baia Mare 17 E6
Baïbokoum 53 G2
Baidoa 49 G3
Baie Comeau 69 D4
Ba'ījī 46 D5
Baikal, L. = Baykal, Oz. 30 D8
Baile Atha Cliath = Dublin 11 E3
Băileşti 22 B4
Bailundo 58 A3
Bā'ir 47 E4
Baird Mts. 71 B3
Bairnsdale 63 C4
Baitadi 40 C3
Baiyin 35 C5
Baja 16 E4
Baja, Pta. 84 B1
Baja California 84 A1
Bajimba, Mt. 63 A5
Bakala 56 C4
Bakchar 29 D9
Bakel 55 F2
Baker, L. 70 B10
Baker I. 64 J13
Baker Lake 70 B10
Baker Mt. 80 A3
Baker's Dozen Is. 69 C3
Bakersfield 82 C3
Bākhtarān 46 D6
Bakı 25 E6
Bakony Forest = Bakony Hegyseg 16 E3
Bakony Hegyseg 16 E3
Bakouma 56 C4
Baku = Bakı 25 E6
Bakutis Coast 96 D1
Baky = Bakı 25 E6
Balabac I. 36 C5
Balabac Str. 36 C5
Balabalangan, Kepulauan 37 E5

Balaghat Ra. .. 43 K10
Balaguer ..... 19 B6
Balaklava, *Australia* .... 62 B2
Balaklava, *Ukraine* ..... 25 E3
Balakovo ..... 24 C6
Balashov ..... 24 C5
Balasore = Baleshwar .. 40 G6
Balaton ....... 16 E3
Balbina, Reprêsa de ......... 90 D7
Balchik ....... 22 C7
Balclutha ..... 65 G3
Baleares, Is. .... 19 C7
Balearic Is. = Baleares, Is. . 19 C7
Baler ......... 38 A2
Baleshwar .... 40 G6
Bali, *Cameroon* 55 G7
Bali, *Indonesia* 37 F5
Bali □ ........ 37 F5
Balikeşir ...... 23 E6
Balikpapan .... 37 E5
Balimbing .... 38 C1
Balipara ...... 41 D9
Baliza ........ 93 F3
Balkan Mts. = Stara Planina 22 C4
Balkh ........ 45 B6
Balkhash = Balqash .... 29 E8
Balkhash, Ozero = Balqash Köl 29 E8
Balla ......... 41 E8
Ballarat ....... 62 C3
Ballater ....... 10 C5
Ballina, *Australia* 63 A5
Ballina, *Ireland* 11 D2
Ballinasloe .... 11 E2
Ballymena .... 11 D3
Balmaceda .... 95 F2
Balmoral ..... 62 C3
Balonne → ... 63 A4
Balqash ...... 29 E8
Balqash Köl ... 29 E8
Balrampur .... 40 D4
Balranald ..... 62 B3
Balsas → .... 84 D4
Balta ......... 17 D9
Bălţi ......... 17 E8
Baltic Sea ..... 9 G11
Baltimore ..... 73 E7
Baluchistan □ . 42 F4
Balya ........ 23 E6
Bam ......... 44 D4
Bama ........ 53 F1
Bamako ...... 55 F3
Bamba ....... 55 E4
Bambari ...... 56 C4
Bamberg ..... 14 D6
Bambili ....... 57 D5
Bamenda ..... 55 G7
Bāmīān □ .... 42 B5
Bampūr ...... 45 E5
Ban Don = Surat Thani . 36 C1
Ban Mê Thuôt = Buon Me Thuot ...... 36 B3
Banaba ....... 64 K11
Banalia ....... 57 D5
Banam ....... 36 B3
Banamba ..... 55 F3
Bananal, I. do . 93 E3
Banaras = Varanasi .... 40 E4
Band-e Torkestān ... 45 C6
Banda, Kepulauan .. 39 E3
Banda Aceh ... 36 C1
Banda Banda, Mt. ........ 63 B5
Banda Elat .... 39 F4
Banda Is. = Banda, Kepulauan .. 39 E3
Banda Sea .... 39 F3
Bandanaira ... 39 E3
Bandar = Machilipatnam 40 J3
Bandār 'Abbās 44 E4
Bandar-e Anzalī 46 C7
Bandar-e Bushehr = Būshehr .... 44 D2
Bandar-e Chārak 44 E3
Bandar-e Deylam ..... 47 E7
Bandar-e Khomeynı ... 47 E7
Bandar-e Lengeh ..... 44 E3
Bandar-e Ma'shur .... 47 E7
Bandar-e Nakhīlū ..... 44 E3
Bandar-e Rīg .. 44 D2
Bandar-e Torkeman ... 44 B3
Bandar Maharani = Muar ....... 37 D2
Bandar Penggaram = Batu Pahat .. 37 D2
Bandar Seri Begawan ... 36 D5
Bandawe ..... 59 A6
Bandeira, Pico da ......... 93 G5
Bandera ...... 94 B4
Bandiagara ... 55 F4
Bandırma ..... 23 D7
Bandon ...... 11 F2
Bandundu .... 56 E3
Bandung ..... 37 F3
Banff, *Canada* . 71 C8
Banff, *U.K.* .... 10 C5
Banfora ...... 55 F4
Bang Saphan .. 36 B1
Bangalore .... 43 N10
Bangassou .... 56 D4
Banggai, Kepulauan .. 39 E2
Banggi, P. .... 36 C5
Banghāzī ..... 52 B3
Bangka, P., *Sulawesi, Indonesia* ... 39 D3
Bangka, P., *Sumatera, Indonesia* ... 37 E3
Bangka, Selat . 37 E3
Bangkinang ... 37 D2
Bangko ....... 37 E2
Bangkok ...... 36 B2
Bangladesh ■ . 41 E7
Bangong Co .. 42 B11
Bangor, *Down, U.K.* ........ 11 D4
Bangor, *Gwynedd, U.K.* ........ 11 E4
Bangor, *U.S.A.* 73 B11
Bangued ..... 38 A2
Bangui ....... 56 D3
Bangweulu, L. . 57 G6
Bani ......... 87 C5
Banī Walīd .... 52 B1
Banīnah ...... 52 B3
Bāniyās ...... 46 D3
Banja Luka .... 20 B6
Banjarmasin .. 37 E4
Banjul ........ 55 F1
Bankipore .... 40 E5
Banks I. ...... 70 A7
Banks Pen. .... 65 E5
Banks Str. .... 62 D4
Bankura ...... 40 F6
Banningville = Bandundu .. 56 E3
Bannu ........ 42 C7
Banská Bystrica 16 D4
Banswara ..... 43 H9
Bantry ....... 11 F2
Banu ......... 42 B6
Banyak, Kepulauan .. 37 D1
Banyo ........ 55 G7
Banzare Coast . 96 A13
Banzyville = Mobayi ..... 56 D4
Baoding ...... 35 C6
Baoji ......... 35 C5
Baoshan ...... 34 D4
Baotou ....... 35 B6
Bapatla ....... 40 K3
Ba'qūbah ..... 46 D6
Bar, *Montenegro, Yug.* ........... 22 C2
Bar, *Ukraine* .. 17 D8
Bar-le-Duc .... 13 B6
Barabai ....... 37 E5
Barabinsk ..... 29 D8
Baracaldo ..... 19 A4
Baracoa ...... 86 B5
Barahona ..... 87 C5
Barail Range .. 41 E9
Barakhola ..... 41 E9
Barakpur ..... 41 F7
Barakula ...... 63 A5
Baramula ..... 42 B9
Baran ........ 43 G10
Baranavichy ... 17 B8
Baranof I. ..... 71 C6
Barão de Melgaço .... 91 F6
Barapasi ...... 39 E5
Barat Daya, Kepulauan .. 39 F3
Barbacena .... 93 G5
Barbacoas .... 90 C3
Barbados ■ ... 87 D8
Barbastro ..... 19 A6
Barberton ..... 59 D6
Barcellona Pozzo di Gotto .... 21 E5
Barcelona, *Spain* 19 B7
Barcelona, *Venezuela* ... 90 A6
Barcelos ...... 90 D6
Bardai ........ 52 D2
Barddhaman .. 40 F6
Bardejov ..... 16 D5
Bardera ...... 49 G3
Bardi, Ra's .... 47 F4
Bardīyah ..... 52 B4
Bareilly ....... 42 E11
Barentu ...... 53 E6
Barfleur, Pte. de 12 B3
Barga ........ 34 C3
Bargal ........ 49 E5
Barhi ......... 40 E5
Bari .......... 20 D6
Bari Doab ..... 42 D8
Barīm ........ 49 E3
Barinas ....... 90 B4
Baring, C. ..... 70 B8
Bârîs ......... 52 D5
Barisal ....... 41 F8
Barisan, Bukit . 37 E2
Barito → ..... 37 E4
Barkly Tableland 60 D6
Barlee, L. ..... 60 F2
Barletta ...... 20 D6
Barmedman ... 63 B4
Barmer ....... 42 G7
Barmera ...... 62 B3
Barnato ...... 63 B4
Barnaul ...... 29 D9
Barnsley ...... 11 E6
Barnstaple .... 11 F4
Baro ......... 55 G6
Baroda = Vadodara ... 43 H8
Barpeta ...... 41 D8
Barquísimeto .. 90 A5
Barra, *Brazil* ... 93 E5
Barra, *U.K.* .... 10 C3
Barra do Corda 92 D4
Barra do Piraí . 93 G5
Barra Falsa, Pta. da ......... 59 C7
Barraba ...... 63 B5
Barrackpur = Barakpur .... 41 F7
Barraigh = Barra ....... 10 C3
Barranca, *Lima, Peru* ....... 91 F3
Barranca, *Loreto, Peru* . 90 D3
Barrancabermeja .......... 90 B4
Barrancas ..... 90 B6
Barrancos .... 18 C2
Barranqueras .. 94 B5
Barranquilla ... 90 A4
Barras ....... 92 C5
Barreiras ..... 93 E5
Barreirinhas ... 92 C5
Barreiro ...... 18 C1
Barreiros ..... 92 D6
Barretos ...... 93 G4
Barrier Ra. .... 62 B3
Barrington Tops 63 B5
Barringun ..... 63 A4
Barrow ....... 71 A4
Barrow-in-Furness ..... 11 D5
Barry ........ 11 F5
Barsi ......... 43 K9
Barsoi ........ 40 E6
Barstow ...... 82 C4
Bartica ....... 90 B7
Bartin ........ 46 B3
Bartle Frere ... 61 D8
Bartlesville .... 79 A6
Barysaw ...... 17 A9
Bāsa'idū ...... 44 E3
Basankusa .... 56 D3
Basarabeasca . 17 E9
Basel ........ 13 C7
Bashi Channel . 35 D7
Bashkir Republic = Bashkortostan □ .......... 29 D6
Bashkortostan □ 29 D6
Basilan ....... 38 C2
Basilan Str. ... 38 C2
Basildon ...... 11 F7
Basim = Washim .... 43 J10

Basingstoke 11 F6
Basle = Basel 13 C7
Basoka 56 D4
Basongo 56 E4
Basque Provinces = País Vasco □ 19 A4
Basra = Al Başrah 47 E6
Bass Str. 61 H8
Bassano 71 C8
Bassano del Grappa 20 B3
Bassas da India 59 C7
Bassein 41 J10
Basseterre 87 C7
Bassikounou 55 E3
Bastak 44 E3
Bastar 40 H3
Basti 40 D4
Bastia 13 E8
Bastogne 14 C3
Bata 56 D1
Bataan 38 B2
Batabanó 86 B3
Batabanó, G. de 86 B3
Batac 38 A2
Batagoy 31 C11
Batamay 31 C10
Batang 34 C4
Batangafo 56 C3
Batangas 38 B2
Batanta 39 E4
Bateman's B. 63 C5
Batemans Bay 63 C5
Bath 11 F5
Bathurst, *Australia* 63 B4
Bathurst, *Canada* 69 D4
Bathurst, C. 70 A7
Bathurst Harb. 62 D4
Bathurst Inlet 70 B9
Batinah 44 F4
Batlow 63 C4
Batman 46 C5
Batna 54 A6
Baton Rouge 79 D8
Batouri 56 D2
Battambang 36 B2
Battipáglia 21 D5
Battle Creek 72 C3
Battle Harbour 69 C5
Battleford 71 C9
Batu 49 F2
Batu, Kepulauan 37 E1
Batu Is. = Batu, Kepulauan 37 E1
Batu Pahat 37 D2
Batuata 39 F2
Batumi 25 E5
Baturaja 37 E2
Baturité 92 C6
Bau 37 D4
Baubau 39 F2
Bauchi 55 F6
Bauer, C. 62 B1
Baukau 39 F3
Bauru 93 G4
Baús 93 F3
Bautzen 15 C8
Bavaria = Bayern □ 15 D6
Bawdwin 41 F11
Bawean 37 F4
Bawku 55 F4
Bawlake 41 H11
Bay, L. de 38 B2
Bay City 72 C4
Bay View 64 C7
Bayamo 86 B4
Bayan Har Shan 34 C4
Bayan Hot = Alxa Zuoqi 35 C5
Bayanaūyl 29 D8
Bayanhongor 35 B5
Bayázeh 44 C3
Baybay 38 B2
Bayburt 46 B5
Bayern □ 15 D6
Bayeux 12 B3
Bayındır 23 E6
Baykal, Oz. 30 D8
Baykit 30 C7
Baykonur = Bayqongyr 29 E7
Bayombong 38 A2
Bayonne 12 E3
Bayovar 91 E2
Bayqongyr 29 E7
Bayram-Ali = Bayramaly 29 F7
Bayramaly 29 F7
Bayramiç 23 E6
Bayreuth 15 D6
Bayrūt 46 D3
Baytown 79 E6
Baza 19 D4
Bazaruto, I. do 59 C7
Beachport 62 C2
Beagle, Canal 96 G3
Beardmore Glacier 96 C14
Béarn 12 E3
Beauce, Plaine de la 12 B4
Beaudesert 63 A5
Beaufort 36 C5
Beaufort Sea 66 B6
Beaufort West 58 E4
Beaumont 79 D6
Beaune 13 C6
Beauvais 12 B5
Beauval 71 C9
Beaver 71 B5
Beaver → 71 C9
Beawar 42 F9
Bečej 22 B3
Béchar 54 B4
Bedford 11 E6
Beenleigh 63 A5
Be'er Sheva 47 E3
Beersheba = Be'er Sheva 47 E3
Befale 56 D4
Bega 63 C4
Behbehān 47 E7
Behshahr 44 B3
Bei Jiang → 35 D6
Bei'an 35 B7
Beibei 35 D5
Beihai 35 D5
Beijing 35 C6
Beilpajah 63 B3
Beinn na Faoghla = Benbecula 10 C3
Beira 59 B6
Beirut = Bayrūt 46 D3
Beitbridge 59 C6
Beja, *Portugal* 18 C2
Béja, *Tunisia* 54 A6
Bejaia 54 A6
Béjar 18 B3
Bejestān 44 C4
Békéscsaba 16 E5
Bela, *India* 40 E4
Bela, *Pakistan* 42 F5
Bela Crkva 22 B3
Bela Vista 94 A5
Belarus ■ 24 C2
Belau = Palau ■ 38 C4
Belawan 37 D1
Belaya Tserkov = Bila Tserkva 17 D10
Belcher Is. 69 C3
Belém 92 C4
Belén 94 A5
Belet Uen 49 G4
Belev 24 C4
Belfast 11 D4
Belfort 13 C7
Belgaum 43 M9
Belgium ■ 14 C3
Belgorod 24 C4
Belgorod-Dnestrovskiy = Bilhorod-Dnistrovskyy 25 D3
Belgrade = Beograd 22 B3
Beli Drim → 22 C3
Belinga 56 D2
Belinyu 37 E3
Beliton Is. = Belitung 37 E3
Belitung 37 E3
Belize ■ 85 D7
Belize City 85 D7
Belkovskiy, Ostrov 30 B11
Bell Bay 62 D4
Bell Peninsula 68 B2
Bell Ville 94 C4
Bella Unión 94 C5
Bella Vista 94 B5
Bellary 43 M10
Bellata 63 A4
Belle-Ile 12 C2
Belle Isle 69 C5
Belle Isle, Str. of 69 C5
Belleville, *Canada* 69 D3
Belleville, *U.S.A.* 77 F10
Bellin = Kangirsuk 68 C4
Bellingen 63 B5
Bellingham 80 A2
Bellingshausen Sea 96 A2
Bellinzona 13 C8
Belluno 20 A4
Belmont 63 B5
Belmonte 93 F6
Belmopan 85 D7
Belo Horizonte 93 F5
Belo-Tsiribihina 59 H8
Beloit 77 D10
Belokorovichi 17 C9
Belomorsk 28 C4
Belonia 41 F8
Belorussia ■ = Belarus ■ 24 C2
Belovo 29 D9
Beloye, Ozero 24 A4
Beloye More 28 C4
Belozersk 24 A4
Beltana 62 B2
Belterra 92 C3
Beltsy = Bălţi 17 E8
Belukha 29 E9
Beluran 36 C5
Belyy, Ostrov 28 B8
Belyy Yar 29 D9
Bembéréke 55 F5
Bemidji 77 B7
Ben Gardane 52 B1
Ben Lomond, *N.S.W., Australia* 63 B5
Ben Lomond, *Tas., Australia* 62 D4
Ben Nevis 10 C4
Bena 55 F6
Bena Dibele 56 E4
Benagerie 62 B3
Benalla 63 C4
Benambra, Mt. 63 C4
Benares = Varanasi 40 E4
Benavente 18 A3
Benbecula 10 C3
Benbonyathe 62 B2
Bend 80 C3
Bender Beila 49 F5
Bendery = Tighina 17 E9
Bendigo 63 C3
Benevento 20 D5
Bengal, Bay of 41 J7
Bengbu 35 C6
Benghazi = Banghāzī 52 B3
Bengkalis 37 D2
Bengkulu 37 E2
Bengkulu □ 37 E2
Benguela 58 A2
Beni 57 D5
Beni → 91 F5
Beni Abbès 54 B4
Beni Mazâr 52 C5
Beni Mellal 54 B3
Beni Ounif 54 B4
Beni Suef 52 C5
Benidorm 19 C5
Benin ■ 55 G5
Benin, Bight of 55 H5
Benin City 55 G6
Benjamin Constant 90 D4
Benoni 59 D5
Bent 44 E4
Benteng 39 F2
Benton Harbor 72 C2
Benue → 55 G6
Benxi 35 B7
Beo 38 D3
Beograd 22 B3
Beppu 32 C2
Berati 23 D2
Berau, Teluk 39 E4
Berber 53 E5
Berbera 49 E4
Berbérati 56 D3
Berbice → 90 B7
Berdichev = Berdychiv 17 D9
Berdsk 29 D9
Berdyansk 25 D4
Berdychiv 17 D9
Berebere 39 D3
Bereda 49 E5
Berehove 17 D6
Berekum 55 G4
Berestechko 17 C7
Bereza 17 B7
Berezhany 17 D7
Berezina = Byarezina → 17 B10
Berezniki 28 D6
Berezovo 28 C7
Berga 19 A6
Bergama 23 E6
Bérgamo 20 B2
Bergen 8 F9
Bergerac 12 D4

Berhala, Selat . 37 E2
Berhampore = Baharampur . 40 E7
Berhampur = Brahamapur . 40 H5
Bering Sea .... 71 C1
Bering Strait .. 71 B3
Berja ......... 19 D4
Berkeley ...... 80 G2
Berkner I. ..... 96 B4
Berlin ........ 15 B7
Bermejo →, *Formosa, Argentina* ... 94 B5
Bermejo →, *San Juan, Argentina* ... 94 C3
Bermuda ■ ... 67 F13
Bern ......... 13 C7
Bernardo de Irigoyen .... 94 B6
Bernburg ..... 15 C6
Berne = Bern . 13 C7
Bernina, Piz ... 13 C8
Beroroha ..... 59 J9
Beroun ....... 16 D2
Berrechid ..... 54 B3
Berri ......... 62 B3
Berry, *Australia* 63 B5
Berry, *France* .. 12 C5
Bershad ...... 17 D9
Bertoua ...... 56 D2
Berwick-upon-Tweed ...... 10 D6
Besalampy .... 59 H8
Besançon ..... 13 C7
Besar ........ 37 E5
Besni ........ 46 C4
Bessarabiya ... 17 E9
Bessarabka = Basarabeasca 17 E9
Bessemer ..... 74 C4
Betanzos ..... 18 A1
Bétaré Oya .... 56 C2
Bethanien .... 58 D3
Bethel ........ 71 B3
Bethlehem, *S. Africa* .... 59 D5
Bethlehem, *U.S.A.* ...... 73 D8
Béthune ...... 13 A5
Bethungra .... 63 B4
Betioky ....... 59 J8
Betroka ....... 59 J9
Betsiamites ... 69 D4
Bettiah ....... 40 D5
Betul ......... 43 J10
Betung ....... 37 D4
Beverley ...... 11 E6
Beverly Hills .. 82 C3
Beyla ........ 55 G3
Beyneu ....... 29 E6
Beypazarı ..... 46 B2
Beyşehir Gölü . 46 C2
Bezhitsa ...... 24 C3
Béziers ....... 13 E5
Bezwada = Vijayawada . 40 J3
Bhachau ...... 43 H7
Bhadrakh ..... 40 G6
Bhadravati .... 43 N9
Bhagalpur .... 40 E6
Bhakra Dam ... 42 D10
Bhamo ....... 41 E11
Bhandara ..... 43 J11
Bhanrer Ra. ... 43 H11
Bharat = India ■ ..... 43 J10
Bharatpur ..... 42 F10
Bhatpara ..... 41 F7
Bhaunagar = Bhavnagar .. 43 J8
Bhavnagar .... 43 J8
Bhawanipatna . 40 H3
Bhilsa = Vidisha 43 H10
Bhilwara ...... 43 G9
Bhima → .... 43 L10
Bhimavaram .. 40 J3
Bhind ........ 42 F11
Bhiwandi ..... 43 K8
Bhiwani ...... 42 E10
Bhola ........ 41 F8
Bhopal ....... 43 H10
Bhubaneshwar 40 G5
Bhuj ......... 43 H6
Bhumiphol Dam = Phumiphon, Khuan ...... 36 A1
Bhusaval ..... 43 J9
Bhutan ■ ..... 41 D8
Biafra, B. of = Bonny, Bight of .......... 56 D1
Biak ......... 39 E5
Biała Podlaska . 17 B6
Białogard ..... 16 A2
Białystok ..... 17 B6
Biaro ......... 39 D3
Biarritz ....... 12 E3
Bibala ........ 58 A2
Biberach ...... 14 D5
Bibiani ....... 55 G4
Bida ......... 55 G6
Bidar ......... 43 L10
Biddeford ..... 73 C10
Bidon 5 = Poste Maurice Cortier ..... 54 D5
Bié, Planalto de 58 A3
Biel .......... 13 C7
Bielefeld ...... 14 B5
Biella ........ 20 B2
Bielsk Podlaski 17 B6
Bielsko-Biała .. 16 D4
Bien Hoa ..... 36 B3
Bienne = Biel . 13 C7
Bienville, L. ... 69 C3
Big Horn Mts. = Bighorn Mts. 81 C10
Big Spring .... 78 C3
Big Trout L. ... 69 C2
Biğa ......... 23 D6
Bigadiç ....... 23 E7
Biggar ....... 71 C9
Biggenden .... 63 A5
Bighorn → ... 81 B10
Bighorn Mts. .. 81 C10
Bihać ........ 20 B5
Bihar ......... 40 E5
Bihar □ ...... 40 E5
Bihor, Munţii .. 17 E6
Bijagós, Arquipélago dos ........ 55 F1
Bijapur, *Karnataka, India* ....... 43 L9
Bijapur, *Mad. P., India* ....... 40 H3
Bījār ......... 46 D6
Bijeljina ...... 20 B7
Bijnor ........ 42 E11
Bikaner ....... 42 E8
Bikini Atoll .... 64 H11
Bila Tserkva ... 17 D10
Bilara ........ 42 F8
Bilaspur ...... 40 F4
Bilauk Taungdan 36 B1
Bilbao ........ 19 A4
Bilbo = Bilbao . 19 A4
Bilecik ........ 46 B2
Bilhorod-Dnistrovskyy 25 D3
Bilir .......... 31 C11
Billings ....... 81 C9
Billiton Is. = Belitung .... 37 E3
Bilma ........ 53 E1
Biloxi ........ 79 D9
Biltine ........ 53 F3
Bima ......... 39 F1
Bimbo ....... 56 D3
Bina-Etawah .. 43 G11
Binalbagan ... 38 B2
Binalong ..... 63 B4
Bīnālūd, Kūh-e 44 B4
Binatang ..... 37 D4
Binda ........ 63 A4
Bindle ........ 63 A4
Bindura ...... 59 B6
Bingara, *N.S.W., Australia* .... 63 A5
Bingara, *Queens., Australia* .... 63 A3
Bingham Canyon ..... 81 E7
Binghamton ... 73 C8
Bingöl ........ 46 C5
Binh Dinh = An Nhon ....... 36 B3
Binh Son ..... 36 A3
Binjai ........ 37 D1
Binnaway ..... 63 B4
Binongko ..... 39 F2
Bintan ........ 37 D2
Bintulu ....... 37 D4
Bintuni ....... 39 E4
Binzert = Bizerte 54 A6
Bioko ........ 56 D1
Bir ........... 43 K9
Bir Autrun .... 53 E4
Bir Mogrein ... 54 C2
Bîr Ungât ..... 52 D5
Bira .......... 39 E4
Birao ......... 53 F3
Birchip ....... 62 C3
Birecik ....... 46 C4
Bireuen ...... 36 C1
Bîrlad ........ 17 E8
Bîrlad → ..... 17 F8
Birmingham, *U.K.* ........ 11 E6
Birmingham, *U.S.A.* ...... 74 C4
Birmitrapur ... 40 F5
Birni Nkonni .. 55 F6
Birnin Kebbi .. 55 F5
Birr .......... 11 E3
Birrie → ..... 63 A4
Birsk ......... 29 D6
Birur ......... 43 N9
Bisa ......... 39 E3
Biscay, B. of .. 12 D2
Biscoe Bay .... 96 B17
Biscoe Is. ..... 96 A3
Bishkek ....... 29 E8
Biskra ........ 54 B6
Bislig ........ 38 C3
Bismarck ..... 76 B4
Bismarck Arch. 64 K9
Bissagos = Bijagós, Arquipélago dos ........ 55 F1
Bissau ....... 55 F1
Bistriţa ....... 17 E7
Bistriţa → .... 17 E8
Bitam ........ 56 D2
Bitkine ....... 53 F2
Bitlis ......... 46 C5
Bitola ........ 22 D3
Bitolj = Bitola . 22 D3
Bitter L. = Buheirat-Murrat-el-Kubra ...... 52 B5
Bitterfontein .. 58 E3
Bitterroot Range 81 B6
Biu .......... 53 F1
Biwa-Ko ...... 32 B5
Biysk ......... 29 D9
Bizerte ....... 54 A6
Bjelovar ...... 20 B6
Black Forest = Schwarzwald 14 D5
Black Hills .... 76 D3
Black Sea ..... 25 E3
Black Volta → 55 G4
Blackball ..... 65 E4
Blackburn ..... 11 E5
Blackpool ..... 11 E5
Blackwater → . 11 E2
Blagodarnoye = Blagodarnyy 25 D5
Blagodarnyy .. 25 D5
Blagoevgrad .. 22 C4
Blagoveshchensk .......... 31 D10
Blairmore ..... 71 D8
Blanc, Mont ... 13 D7
Blanca, B. ..... 95 D4
Blanca Peak ... 83 B10
Blanche, C. ... 62 B1
Blanche, L. .... 62 A2
Blanes ....... 19 B7
Blantyre ...... 59 B6
Blayney ...... 63 B4
Blednaya, Gora 28 B7
Blenheim ..... 65 D5
Blida ......... 54 A5
Bligh Sound .. 65 F2
Blitta ......... 55 G5
Blodgett Iceberg Tongue ..... 96 A13
Bloemfontein .. 59 D5
Bloemhof ..... 59 D5
Blois ......... 12 C4
Bloomington, *Ill., U.S.A.* ... 77 E10
Bloomington, *Ind., U.S.A.* .. 72 E2
Blue Mts., *Oreg., U.S.A.* ...... 80 C4
Blue Mts., *Pa., U.S.A.* ...... 73 D7
Blue Nile = Nîl el Azraq → . 53 E5
Blue Ridge Mts. 75 A7
Bluefields ..... 86 D3
Bluff ......... 65 G3
Blumenau .... 94 B7
Bo ........... 55 G2
Bo Duc ....... 36 B3
Bo Hai ....... 35 C6
Boa Vista ..... 90 C6
Boatman ..... 63 A4
Bobadah ..... 63 B4
Bobbili ....... 40 H4
Bobo-Dioulasso 55 F4
Bóbr → ...... 16 B2
Bobraomby, Tanjon' i .... 59 G9
Bobruysk = Babruysk ... 17 B9
Bôca do Acre .. 91 E5

Boca Raton 75 F7
Bocaiúva 93 F5
Bocanda 55 G4
Bocaranga 56 C3
Bochnia 16 D5
Bochum 14 C4
Boda 56 D3
Bodaybo 30 D9
Boden 8 E12
Bodensee 13 C8
Bodhan 43 K10
Bodø 8 E10
Bodrog → 16 D5
Bodrum 23 F6
Boende 56 E4
Boffa 55 F2
Bogalusa 79 D9
Bogan Gate 63 B4
Boggabilla 63 A5
Boggabri 63 B5
Bogo 38 B2
Bogong, Mt. 63 C4
Bogotá 90 C4
Bogotol 29 D9
Bogra 41 E7
Bogué 55 E2
Bohemian Forest = Böhmerwald 15 D7
Bohena Cr. → 63 B4
Böhmerwald 15 D7
Bohol 38 C2
Bohol Sea 38 C2
Bohotleh 49 F4
Boise 80 D5
Boise City 78 A2
Bojador C. 54 C2
Bojana → 22 D2
Bojnūrd 44 B4
Boké 55 F2
Bokhara → 63 A4
Bokoro 53 F2
Bokote 56 E4
Bokungu 56 E4
Bol 53 F1
Bolama 55 F1
Bolan Pass 42 E5
Bolbec 12 B4
Bole 34 B3
Bolekhiv 17 D6
Bolekhov = Bolekhiv 17 D6
Bolesławiec 16 C2
Bolgrad = Bolhrad 17 F9
Bolhrad 17 F9
Bolinao C. 38 A1
Bolívar, *Argentina* 94 D4
Bolívar, *Colombia* 90 C3
Bolivia ■ 91 G6
Bollon 63 A4
Bolobo 56 E3
Bologna 20 B3
Bologoye 24 B3
Bolomba 56 D3
Bolong 38 C2
Bolsena, L. di 20 C3
Bolshereche 29 D8
Bolshevik, Ostrov 30 B8
Bolshoi Kavkas = Caucasus Mountains 25 E5
Bolshoy Atlym 28 C7
Bolshoy Begichev, Ostrov 30 B9
Bolshoy Lyakhovskiy, Ostrov 31 B12
Bolton 11 E5
Bolu 46 B2
Bolvadin 46 C2
Bolzano 20 A3
Bom Despacho 93 F4
Bom Jesus da Lapa 93 E5
Boma 56 F2
Bomaderry 63 B5
Bombala 63 C4
Bombay 43 K8
Bomboma 56 D3
Bomili 57 D5
Bomongo 56 D3
Bomu → 56 D4
Bon, C. 52 A1
Bonaire 87 D6
Bonang 63 C4
Bonavista 69 D5
Bondo 56 D4
Bondoukou 55 G4
Bone, Teluk 39 E2
Bonerate 39 F2
Bonerate, Kepulauan 39 F2
Bong Son = Hoai Nhon 36 B3
Bongandanga 56 D4
Bongor 53 F2
Bonifacio 13 F8
Bonn 14 C4
Bonney, L. 62 C3
Bonny, Bight of 56 D1
Bonoi 39 E5
Bontang 37 D5
Bonthain 39 F1
Bonthe 55 G2
Bontoc 38 A2
Boolaboolka L. 62 B3
Booligal 63 B3
Boonah 63 A5
Boorindal 63 B4
Boorowa 63 B4
Boothia, Gulf of 68 A2
Boothia Pen. 70 A10
Booué 56 E2
Bor, *Serbia, Yug.* 22 B4
Bôr, *Sudan* 53 G5
Borama 49 F3
Borås 9 G10
Borāzjān 44 D2
Borba 90 D7
Borda, C. 62 C2
Bordeaux 12 D3
Bordertown 62 C3
Bordj Fly Ste. Marie 54 C4
Bordj-in-Eker 54 D6
Bordj Omar Driss 54 C6
Bordj-Tarat 54 C6
Borger 78 B3
Borisoglebsk 24 C5
Borisov = Barysaw 17 A9
Borja 90 D3
Borkou 53 E2
Borkum 14 B4
Borley, C. 96 A9
Borneo 37 D4
Bornholm 9 G11
Boromo 55 F4
Borongan 38 B3
Borovichi 24 B3
Borşa 17 E7
Borūjerd 46 D7
Boryslav 17 D6
Bosa 21 D2
Bosanska Gradiška 20 B6
Bosaso 49 E4
Boshan 35 C6
Boshrūyeh 44 C4
Bosna → 20 B7
Bosna i Hercegovina = Bosnia-Herzegovina ■ 20 B6
Bosnia-Herzegovina ■ 20 B6
Bosnik 39 E5
Bosobolo 56 D3
Bosporus = Karadeniz Boğazı 22 D7
Bossangoa 56 C3
Bossembélé 53 G2
Bosso 53 F1
Boston Hu 34 B3
Boston, *U.K.* 11 E6
Boston, *U.S.A.* 73 C10
Botany B. 63 B5
Bothnia, G. of 8 F12
Bothwell 62 D4
Botletle → 58 C4
Botoşani 17 E8
Botswana ■ 58 C4
Botucatu 94 A7
Bou Djébéha 55 E4
Bou Izakarn 54 C3
Bouaké 55 G3
Bouar 56 C3
Bouârfa 54 B4
Bouca 56 C3
Bougie = Bejaia 54 A6
Bougouni 55 F3
Boulder 76 E2
Boulder Dam = Hoover Dam 82 B5
Boulogne-sur-Mer 12 A4
Boultoum 55 F7
Bouna 55 G4
Boundiali 55 G3
Bourbonnais 13 C5
Bourem 55 E4
Bourg-en-Bresse 13 C6
Bourg-St.-Maurice 13 D7
Bourges 12 C5
Bourgogne 13 C6
Bourke 63 B4
Bournemouth 11 F6
Bousso 53 F2
Boutilimit 55 E2
Bowen Mts. 63 C4
Bowman I. 96 A12
Bowmans 62 B2
Bowral 63 B5
Bowraville 63 B5
Boyne → 11 E3
Boyni Qara 45 B6
Boz Dağları 23 E7
Bozburun 23 F7
Bozcaada 23 E6
Bozdoğan 23 F7
Bozeman 81 C8
Bozen = Bolzano 20 A3
Bozoum 56 C3
Bra 20 B1
Brač 20 C6
Bracciano, L. di 20 C4
Brach 52 C1
Bräcke 8 F11
Brad 17 E6
Bradenton 75 F6
Bradford 11 E6
Braemar 62 B2
Braga 18 B1
Bragança, *Brazil* 92 C4
Bragança, *Portugal* 18 B2
Brahamapur 40 H5
Brahmanbaria 41 F8
Brahmani → 40 G6
Brahmaputra → 41 F7
Braidwood 63 C4
Brăila 17 F8
Branco → 90 D6
Brandenburg = Neubrandenburg 15 B7
Brandenburg 15 B7
Brandenburg □ 15 B7
Brandon 71 D10
Brandvlei 58 E4
Braniewo 16 A4
Bransfield Str. 96 A4
Brantford 69 D2
Branxholme 62 C3
Brasiléia 91 F5
Brasília 93 F4
Braşov 17 F7
Brassey, Banjaran 36 D5
Bratislava 16 D3
Bratsk 30 D8
Braunau 15 D7
Braunschweig 14 B6
Brava 49 G3
Bravo del Norte, R. → = Grande, Rio → 79 F5
Brawley 82 D5
Bray 11 E3
Bray, Pays de 12 B4
Brazil ■ 93 E4
Brazos → 79 E6
Brazzaville 56 E3
Brčko 20 B7
Breaksea Sd. 65 F2
Bream B. 64 A6
Bream Hd. 64 A6
Brecon 11 F5
Breda 14 C3
Bredasdorp 58 E4
Bredbo 63 C4
Bregenz 14 E5
Brejo 92 C5
Bremen 14 B5
Bremerhaven 14 B5
Bremerton 80 B2
Brenner P. 15 E6
Bréscia 20 B3
Breslau = Wrocław 16 C3
Bressanone 20 A3
Brest, *Belarus* 17 B6
Brest, *France* 12 B1
Brest-Litovsk = Brest 17 B6
Bretagne 12 B2
Brett, C. 64 A6
Brewarrina 63 A4
Brezhnev = Naberezhnyye Chelny 29 D6
Bria 56 C4
Briançon 13 D7
Bribie I. 63 A5
Bridgeport 73 D9

Bridgetown 87 D8
Bridgewater 69 D4
Bridgewater, C. 62 C3
Bridlington 11 D6
Bridport 62 D4
Brig 13 C7
Brigham City 81 E7
Bright 63 C4
Brighton, *Australia* 62 C2
Brighton, *U.K.* 11 F6
Bríndisi 21 D6
Brinkworth 62 B2
Brisbane 63 A5
Brisbane → 63 A5
Bristol, *U.K.* 11 F5
Bristol, *U.S.A.* 75 A6
Bristol B. 71 C3
Bristol Channel 11 F4
Britstown 58 E4
Brittany = Bretagne 12 B2
Brive-la-Gaillarde 12 D4
Brixen = Bressanone 20 A3
Brlik 29 E8
Brno 16 D3
Brocken 14 C6
Brodeur Pen. 68 A2
Brodnica 16 B4
Brody 17 C7
Broken Hill = Kabwe 59 A5
Broken Hill 62 B3
Bronte Park 62 D4
Brooks Ra. 71 B5
Brooloo 63 A5
Broome 60 D3
Broughton Island 68 B4
Brown, Pt. 62 B1
Brownsville 78
Brownwood 78 D4
Bruay-en-Artois 13 A5
Bruce, Mt. 60 E2
Bruck an der Mur 15 E8
Bruges = Brugge 14 C2
Brugge 14 C2
Brumado 93 E5
Brunei = Bandar Seri Begawan 36 D5
Brunei ■ 36 D4
Brunner, L. 65 E4
Brunswick = Braunschweig 14 B6
Brunswick 75 D7
Brunswick, Pen. de 95 G2
Brusque 94 B7
Brussel 14 C3
Brussels = Brussel 14 C3
Bruthen 63 C4
Bruxelles = Brussel 14 C3
Bryan 79 D5
Bryan, Mt. 62 B2
Bryansk 24 C3
Bu Craa 54 C2
Buapinang 39 E2
Buayan 38 C3
Bucak 46 C2
Bucaramanga 90 B4
Buchach 17 D7
Buchanan 55 G2
Buchans 69 D5
Bucharest = Bucureşti 22 B6
Buckie 10 C5
Buckleboo 62 B2
Bucureşti 22 B6
Budalin 41 F10
Budapest 16 E4
Budd Coast 96 A12
Bude 11 F4
Budennovsk 25 E5
Budgewoi 63 B5
Budjala 56 D3
Buenaventura 90 C3
Buenos Aires 94 C5
Buenos Aires, L. 95 F2
Buffalo 73 C6
Bug → = Buh → 25 D3
Bug → 16 B5
Buga 90 C3
Bugel, Tanjung 37 F4
Bugsuk 36 C5
Bugun Shara 35 B5
Buguruslan 29 D6
Buh → 25 D3
Buheirat-Murrat-el-Kubra 52 B5
Buir Nur 35 B6
Bujumbura 57 E5
Bukama 57 F5
Bukavu 57 E5
Bukene 57 E6
Bukhara = Bukhoro 29 F7
Bukhoro 29 F7
Bukittinggi 37 E2
Bukoba 57 E6
Bula 39 E4
Bulahdelah 63 B5
Bulan 38 B2
Bulandshahr 42 E10
Bulawayo 59 C5
Buldan 23 E7
Bulgan 35 B5
Bulgaria ■ 22 C5
Bulgroo 63 A3
Bulgunnia 62 B1
Bulhar 49 E3
Buli, Teluk 39 D3
Buliluyan, C. 36 C5
Bulli 63 B5
Bulloo → 63 A3
Bulloo Downs 62 A3
Bulloo L. 62 A3
Bulls 64 D6
Bulo Burti 49 G4
Bulsar = Valsad 43 J8
Bulukumba 39 F2
Bulun 30 B10
Bumba 56 D4
Bumhpa Bum 41 D11
Buna 57 D7
Bunbah, Khalīj 52 B3
Bunbury 60 G2
Buncrana 11 D3
Bundaberg 63
Bundi 43 G9
Bundoran 11 D2
Bungo-Suidō 32 C3
Bunia 57 D6
Bunji 42 B9
Buntok 37 E4
Bunyu 37 D5
Buol 39 D2
Buon Me Thuot 36 B3
Buorkhaya, Mys 31 B11
Buqayq 47 F7
Bur Acaba 49 G3
Bûr Safâga 52 C5
Bûr Sa'îd 52 B5
Bûr Sûdân 53 E6
Burao 49 F4
Buraydah 47 F6
Buraymī, Al Wāhāt al 44 E3
Burcher 63 B4
Burdur 46 C2
Burdwan = Barddhaman 40 F6
Burgas 22 C6
Burgersdorp 59 E5
Burgos 18 A4
Burgundy = Bourgogne 13 C6
Burhaniye 23 E6
Burhanpur 43 J10
Burias 38 B2
Buriram 36 A2
Burji 53 G6
Burkina Faso ■ 55 F4
Burlington, *Iowa, U.S.A.* 77 E9
Burlington, *N.C., U.S.A.* 75 A8
Burlington, *Vt., U.S.A.* 73 B9
Burlyu-Tyube 29 E8
Burma ■ 41 G11
Burnie 62 D4
Burnley 11 E5
Burnside → 70 B9
Burqān 47 E6
Burqin 34 B3
Burra 62 B2
Burren Junction 63 B4
Burrendong Dam 63 B4
Burrinjuck Res. 63 C4
Burruyacú 94 B4
Bursa 23 D7
Burtundy 62 B3
Buru 39 E3
Burundi ■ 57 E6
Burutu 55 G6
Bury St. Edmunds 11 E7
Buşayyah 47 E6
Būshehr 44 D2
Būshehr □ 44 D2
Bushire = Būshehr 44 D2
Businga 56 D4
Busra ash Shām 46 D4
Busto Arsízio 20 B2
Busu-Djanoa 56 D4
Busuanga 38 B1
Buta 57 D4
Butare 57 E5
Butaritari 64 J12
Butembo 57 D5
Butha Qi 35 B7
Buton 39 E2
Butte 81 B7
Butterworth 36 C2
Butuan 38 C3
Butung = Buton 39 E2
Buturlinovka 24 C5
Buxtehude 14 B5
Buy 24 B5
Büyük Menderes → 23 F6
Büyükçekmece 22 D7
Buzău 17 F8
Buzău → 17 F8
Buzen 32 C2
Buzi → 59 B6
Buzuluk 29 D6
Byarezina → 17 B10
Bydgoszcz 16 B3
Byelarus = Belarus ■ 24 C2
Byelorussia = Belarus ■ 24 C2
Bykhaw 17 B10
Bykhov = Bykhaw 17 B10
Bylot I. 68 A3
Byrd, C. 96 A3
Byrock 63 B4
Byron Bay 63 A5
Byrranga, Gory 30 B8
Byrranga Mts. = Byrranga, Gory 30 B8
Bytom 16 C4
Bytów 16 A3

## C

Ca Mau = Quan Long 36 C3
Caála 58 A3
Cabanatuan 38 A2
Cabedelo 92 D7
Cabimas 90 A4
Cabinda 56 F2
Cabinda □ 56 F2
Cabinet Mts. 81 B6
Cabo Blanco 95 F3
Cabo Frio 93 G5
Cabo Pantoja 90 D3
Cabonga, Réservoir 69 D3
Caboolture 63 A5
Cabora Bassa Dam = Cahora Bassa Dam 59 B6
Cabot Str. 69 D5
Cabra 18 D3
Cabrera 19 C7
Cabriel → 19 C5
Čačak 22 C3
Cáceres, *Brazil* 91 G7
Cáceres, *Spain* 18 C2
Cachimbo, Serra do 93 D2
Cachoeira 93 E6
Cachoeira de Itapemirim 93 G5
Cachoeira do Sul 94 C6
Cacólo 56 G3
Caconda 58 A3
Cacongo 56 F2
Cadibarrawirracanna, L. 62 A2
Cadiz, *Phil.* 38 B2
Cádiz, *Spain* 18 D2
Cádiz, G. de 18 D2
Cadney Park 62 A1
Caen 12 B3
Caeté 93 F5
Caetité 93 E5
Cagayan → 38 A2
Cagayan de Oro 38 C2
Cágliari 21 E2
Cágliari, G. di 21 E2
Caguas 87 C6
Cahora Bassa Dam 59 B6
Cahors 12 D4
Cahuapanas 91 E3
Cahul 17 F9

Caia . . . . . . . . . 59 B7
Caibarién . . . . . 86 B4
Caicara . . . . . . . 90 B5
Caicó . . . . . . . . 92 D6
Caicos Is. . . . . . 87 B5
Caird Coast . . . 96 B5
Cairns . . . . . . . . 61 D8
Cairo = El Qâhira . . . . . . 52 B5
Cairo . . . . . . . . . 79 A9
Caiundo . . . . . . 58 B3
Caiza . . . . . . . . . 91 H5
Cajamarca . . . . 91 E3
Cajàzeiras . . . . 92 D6
Calabar . . . . . . . 55 H6
Calábria □ . . . . 21 E6
Calafate . . . . . . 95 G2
Calahorra . . . . . 19 A5
Calais . . . . . . . . 12 A4
Calama, *Brazil* . 91 E6
Calama, *Chile* . 94 A3
Calamar, *Bolívar, Colombia* . . . 90 A4
Calamar, *Vaupés, Colombia* . . . 90 C4
Calamian Group 38 B1
Calamocha . . . . 19 B5
Calang . . . . . . . 36 D1
Calapan . . . . . . 38 B2
Călăraşi . . . . . . 22 B6
Calatayud . . . . . 19 B5
Calauag . . . . . . 38 B2
Calavite, C. . . . 38 B2
Calbayog . . . . . 38 B2
Calca . . . . . . . . 91 F4
Calcutta . . . . . . 41 F7
Caldas da Rainha . . . . . 18 C1
Caldera . . . . . . . 94 B2
Caldwell . . . . . . 80 D5
Caledon . . . . . . 58 E3
Caledon → . . . 59 E5
Calgary . . . . . . . 71 C8
Cali . . . . . . . . . . 90 C3
Calicut . . . . . . . 43 P9
California □ . . . 82 B3
California, G. de 84 B2
Calingasta . . . . 94 C3
Callabonna, L. . 62 A3
Callao . . . . . . . . 91 F3
Caloundra . . . . 63 A5
Caltagirone . . . 21 F5
Caltanissetta . . 21 F5
Calulo . . . . . . . . 56 G2
Calunda . . . . . . 58 A4
Calvi . . . . . . . . . 13 E8
Calviá . . . . . . . . 19 C7
Calvinia . . . . . . 58 E3
Camabatela . . . 56 F3
Camacupa . . . . 58 A3
Camagüey . . . . 86 B4
Camaná . . . . . . 91 G4
Camargo . . . . . 91 H5
Camargue . . . . 13 E6
Camarones . . . 95 E3
Cambay = Khambhat . . 43 H8
Cambay, G. of = Khambat, G. of . . . . . . . . . 43 J8
Cambodia ■ . . 36 B3
Cambrai . . . . . . 13 A5
Cambrian Mts. 11 E5
Cambridge, *N.Z.* 64 B6
Cambridge, *U.K.* 11 E7
Cambridge, *U.S.A.* . . . . . . 73 C10
Cambridge Bay = Ikaluktutiak 70 B9
Cambridge G. . 60 C4
Cambundi-Catembo . . . . 56 G3
Camden, *Ark., U.S.A.* . . . . . . 79 C7
Camden, *N.J., U.S.A.* . . . . . . 73 E8
Cameroon ■ . . 56 C2
Cameroun, Mt. 56 D1
Cametá . . . . . . . 92 C4
Caminha . . . . . 18 B1
Camira Creek . . 63 A5
Camissombo . . 56 F4
Camocim . . . . . 92 C5
Camopi → . . . 92 B3
Campana, I. . . . 95 F1
Campánia □ . . 21 D5
Campbell Town 62 D4
Campbellton . . 69 D4
Campbelltown . 63 B5
Campbeltown . 10 D4
Campeche . . . . 85 D6
Campeche, B. de 85 D6
Camperdown . . 62 C3
Campina Grande 92 D6
Campinas . . . . . 94 A7
Campo . . . . . . . 56 D1
Campo Belo . . . 93 G4
Campo Formoso 93 E5
Campo Grande 93 G3
Campo Maíor . 92 C5
Campo Mourão 93 G3
Campoalegre . . 90 C3
Campobasso . . 20 D5
Campos . . . . . . 93 G5
Campos Belos . 93 E4
Campuya → . . 90 D4
Camrose . . . . . 71 C8
Çan . . . . . . . . . . 23 D6
Can Tho . . . . . . 36 B3
Canada ■ . . . . . 70 C8
Cañada de Gómez . . . . . 94 C4
Çanakkale . . . . 23 D6
Çanakkale Boğazı . . . . . . 23 D6
Cananea . . . . . . 84 A2
Canarias, Is. . . . 54 C1
Canary Is. = Canarias, Is. . 54 C1
Canavieiras . . . 93 F6
Canbelego . . . . 63 B4
Canberra . . . . . . 63 C4
Candala . . . . . . 49 E4
Candelo . . . . . . 63 C4
Candia = Iráklion . . . . . 23 G5
Canea = Khaniá 23 G5
Canelones . . . . 94 C5
Cañete, *Chile* . . 94 D2
Cañete, *Peru* . . 91 F3
Cangas de Narcea . . . . . 18 A2
Canguaretama . 92 D6
Canguçu . . . . . . 94 C6
Canicattì . . . . . . 21 F4
Canigou, Mt. . . 12 E5
Canipaan . . . . . 36 C5
Çankırı . . . . . . . 46 B3
Cann River . . . . 63 C4
Cannanore . . . . 43 P9
Cannes . . . . . . . 13 E7
Canoas . . . . . . . 94 B6
Canora . . . . . . . 71 C9
Canowindra . . . 63 B4
Cantabria □ . . . 18 A4
Cantabrian Mts. = Cantábrica, Cordillera . . . 18 A3
Cantábrica, Cordillera . . . 18 A3
Cantal, Plomb du . . . . . . . . . 13 D5
Canterbury . . . . 11 F7
Canterbury □ . 65 E4
Canterbury Bight . . . . . . . 65 F4
Canterbury Plains . . . . . . 65 E4
Canton = Guangzhou . 35 D6
Canton . . . . . . . 72 D5
Canudos . . . . . . 91 E7
Canutama . . . . 91 E6
Cap-Haïtien . . . 87 C5
Cap St.-Jacques = Vung Tau . 36 B3
Capaia . . . . . . . 56 F4
Capanaparo → 90 B5
Cape Barren I. . 62 D4
Cape Breton I. . 69 D4
Cape Coast . . . 55 G4
Cape Dorset . . . 68 B3
Cape Dyer . . . . 68 B4
Cape Girardeau 79 A9
Cape Jervis . . . 62 C2
Cape Town . . . 58 E3
Cape Verde Is. ■ 50 E1
Cape York Peninsula . . . 61 C7
Capela . . . . . . . 93 E6
Capim → . . . . 92 C4
Capraia . . . . . . . 20 C2
Capri . . . . . . . . . 21 D5
Caprivi Strip . . 58 B4
Captain's Flat . 63 C4
Caquetá → . . . 90 D5
Caracal . . . . . . . 22 B5
Caracas . . . . . . 90 A5
Caracol . . . . . . . 93 D5
Caradoc . . . . . . 62 B3
Carajás, Serra dos . . . . . . . . 92 D3
Carangola . . . . 93 G5
Caransebeş . . . 17 F6
Caratasca, L. . . 86 C3
Caratinga . . . . . 93 F5
Caraúbas . . . . . 92 D6
Caravaca . . . . . 19 C5
Caravelas . . . . . 93 F6
Caraveli . . . . . . 91 G4
Carballo . . . . . . 18 A1
Carbonara, C. . 21 E2
Carbondale . . . 79 A9
Carbonear . . . . 69 D5
Carbonia . . . . . 21 E2
Carcassonne . . 12 E5
Carcross . . . . . . 70 B6
Cardamon Hills 43 Q10
Cárdenas . . . . . 86 B3
Cardiff . . . . . . . 11 F5
Cardigan B. . . . 11 E4
Cardston . . . . . 71 D8
Carei . . . . . . . . . 17 E6
Careysburg . . . 55 G2
Carhué . . . . . . . 94 D4
Caria . . . . . . . . . 23 F7
Cariacica . . . . . 93 G5
Caribbean Sea . 86 D5
Cariboo Mts. . . 71 C7
Carinda . . . . . . 63 B4
Carinhanha . . . 93 E5
Carinthia □ = Kärnten □ . . 15 E7
Caripito . . . . . . 90 A6
Caritianas . . . . . 91 E6
Carlisle . . . . . . . 11 D5
Carlow . . . . . . . 11 E3
Carlsbad . . . . . . 78 C1
Carmacks . . . . . 70 B6
Carman . . . . . . 71 D10
Carmarthen . . . 11 F4
Carmaux . . . . . 12 D5
Carmelo . . . . . . 94 C5
Carmen . . . . . . 90 B3
Carmen de Patagones . . 95 E4
Carmona . . . . . 18 D3
Carnac . . . . . . . 12 C2
Carnarvon, *Australia* . . . . 60 E1
Carnarvon, *S. Africa* . . . . 58 E4
Carnegie, L. . . . 60 F3
Carnic Alps = Karnische Alpen . . . . . . 20 A4
Carniche Alpi = Karnische Alpen . . . . . . 20 A4
Carnot . . . . . . . 56 D3
Carnot, C. . . . . 62 B2
Carolina . . . . . . 92 D4
Caroline I. . . . . 65 K15
Caroline Is. . . . 64 J10
Caroni → . . . . 90 B6
Caronie = Nébrodi, Monti . . . . . . 21 F5
Caroona . . . . . . 63 B5
Carpathians . . . 16 D5
Carpaţii Meridionali . . 17 F7
Carpentaria, G. of . . . . . . . . . . 60 C6
Carpentras . . . . 13 D6
Carpi . . . . . . . . . 20 B3
Carpolac = Morea . . . . . . 62 C3
Carrara . . . . . . . 20 B3
Carrauntoohill . 11 E2
Carrick-on-Suir 11 E3
Carrieton . . . . . 62 B2
Carrizal Bajo . . 94 B2
Çarşamba . . . . 46 B4
Carson City . . . 80 F4
Cartagena, *Colombia* . . . 90 A3
Cartagena, *Spain* . . . . . . 19 D5
Cartago, *Colombia* . . . 90 C3
Cartago, *Costa Rica* . . 86 E3
Carterton . . . . . 65 D6
Carthage . . . . . 79 A6
Cartwright . . . . 68 C5
Caruaru . . . . . . 92 D6
Carúpano . . . . . 90 A6
Carvoeiro . . . . . 90 D6
Carvoeiro, C. . . . 18 C1
Casablanca . . . 54 B3
Cascade Ra. . . . 80 B3
Cascais . . . . . . . 18 C1
Cascavel . . . . . . 94 A6
Cáscina . . . . . . 20 C3
Caserta . . . . . . . 20 D5
Casiguran . . . . 38 A2
Casilda . . . . . . . 94 C4
Casino . . . . . . . 63 A5
Casiquiare → . 90 C5
Casma . . . . . . . . 91 E3
Caspe . . . . . . . . 19 B5
Casper . . . . . . . 81 D10

Caspian Sea **29 E6**
Cassinga **58 B3**
Castellammare di Stábia **21 D5**
Castellón de la Plana **19 C5**
Castelo Branco **18 C2**
Castelsarrasin **12 D4**
Castelvetrano **21 F4**
Casterton **62 C3**
Castilla La Mancha □ **18 C4**
Castilla y Leon □ **18 A3**
Castlebar **11 E2**
Castleblaney **11 D3**
Castlemaine **63 C3**
Castlereagh → **63 B4**
Castres **12 E5**
Castries **87 D7**
Castro **95 E2**
Castro Alves **93 E6**
Castuera **18 C3**
Cat I. **86 B4**
Catacáos **91 E2**
Catalão **93 F4**
Çatalca **22 D7**
Catalonia = Cataluña □ **19 B6**
Cataluña □ **19 B6**
Catamarca **94 B3**
Catanduanes **38 B2**
Catanduva **93 G4**
Catánia **21 F5**
Catanzaro **21 E6**
Catarman **38 B2**
Cateel **38 C3**
Catoche, C. **85 C7**
Catrimani **90 C6**
Catskill Mts. **73 C8**
Cauca → **90 B4**
Caucaia **92 C6**
Caucasus Mountains **25 E5**
Caúngula **56 F3**
Cauquenes **94 D2**
Caura → **90 B6**
Cauvery → **43 P11**
Caux, Pays de **12 B4**
Cavan **11 D3**
Cavendish **62 C3**
Caviana, I. **92 B3**
Cavite **38 B2**
Cawndilla L. **62 B3**
Cawnpore = Kanpur **40 D3**
Caxias **92 C5**
Caxias do Sul **94 B6**
Caxito **56 F2**
Cayambe **90 C3**
Cayenne **92 A3**
Cayman Is. ■ **67 H11**
Cazombo **58 A4**
Ceadâr-Lunga **17 E9**
Ceanannus Mor **11 E3**
Ceará = Fortaleza **92 C6**
Ceará □ **92 D6**
Ceará Mirim **92 D6**
Cebollar **94 B3**
Cebu **38 B2**
Cecil Plains **63 A5**
Cedar L. **71 C10**
Cedar Rapids **77 E9**
Cedro **92 D6**
Ceduna **62 B1**
Cefalù **21 E5**
Cegléd **16 E4**
Celaya **84 C4**
Celebes = Sulawesi □ **39 E2**
Celebes Sea **39 D2**
Celje **20 A5**
Celle **14 B6**
Celtic Sea **11 F2**
Central, Cordillera **90 C3**
Central African Rep. ■ **56 C4**
Central Makran Range **42 F4**
Cephalonia = Kefallinía **23 E3**
Ceram = Seram **39 E3**
Ceram Sea = Seram Sea **39 E3**
Ceres, *Argentina* **94 B4**
Ceres, *S. Africa* **58 E3**
Cerignola **20 D5**
Cerigo = Kíthira **23 F4**
Çerkeş **46 B3**
Çerkeşköy **22 D6**
Cervera **19 B6**
Cesena **20 B4**
Česka Republika = Czech Rep. ■ **16 D2**
České Budějovice **16 D2**
Ceskomoravská Vrchovina **16 D2**
Çeşme **23 E6**
Cessnock **63 B5**
Cetinje **22 C2**
Cetraro **21 E5**
Ceuta **18 E3**
Cévennes **13 D5**
Ceyhan **46 C3**
Ceylon = Sri Lanka ■ **43 R12**
Chachapoyas **91 E3**
Chachran **42 E7**
Chad ■ **53 E2**
Chad, L. = Tchad, L. **53 F1**
Chadileuvú → **94 D3**
Chadyr-Lunga = Ceadâr-Lunga **17 E9**
Chagai Hills **42 E3**
Chagos Arch. **27 K11**
Chāh Bahār **45 E5**
Chāh Gay Hills **45 D6**
Chahar Burjak **42 D3**
Chaibasa **40 F5**
Chakhānsūr **42 D3**
Chakradharpur **40 F5**
Chakwal **42 C8**
Chala **91 G4**
Chalcis = Khalkís **23 E4**
Chalhuanca **91 F4**
Chalisgaon **43 J9**
Chalky Inlet **65 G2**
Challapata **91 G5**
Chalon-sur-Saône **13 C6**
Châlons-en-Champagne **13 B6**
Chaman **42 D5**
Chamba, *India* **42 C10**
Chamba, *Tanzania* **59 A7**
Chambal → **42 F11**
Chambéry **13 D6**
Chamical **94 C3**
Chamonix-Mont Blanc **13 D7**
Champagne **13 B6**
Champaign **72 D1**
Champlain, L. **73 B9**
Chañaral **94 B2**
Chandigarh **42 D10**
Chandler **62 A1**
Chandmani **34 B4**
Chandpur **41 F8**
Chandrapur **43 K11**
Chang Jiang → **35 C7**
Changanacheri **43 Q10**
Changane → **59 C6**
Changchiak'ou = Zhangjiakou **35 B6**
Ch'angchou = Changzhou **35 C6**
Changchun **35 B7**
Changde **35 D6**
Changhai = Shanghai **35 C7**
Changjiang **35 E5**
Changsha **35 D6**
Changting **35 D6**
Changzhi **35 C6**
Changzhou **35 C6**
Channapatna **43 N10**
Channel Is. **11 G5**
Chantada **18 A2**
Chanthaburi **36 B2**
Chantrey Inlet **70 B10**
Chanute **79 A6**
Chao Phraya → **36 B2**
Chao'an **35 D6**
Chaoyang **35 D6**
Chapala, L. de **84 C4**
Chapayevsk **24 C6**
Chapra = Chhapra **40 E5**
Châr **54 D2**
Chara **31 D9**
Charadai **94 B5**
Charagua **91 G6**
Charaña **91 G5**
Chardara **29 E7**
Chardzhou = Chärjew **29 F7**
Charente → **12 D3**
Chari → **53 F1**
Chārīkār **42 B6**
Chärjew **29 F7**
Charleroi **14 C3**
Charles, C. **73 F8**
Charleston, *S.C., U.S.A.* **75 C8**
Charleston, *W. Va., U.S.A.* **72 E5**
Charlesville **56 F4**
Charleville **63 A4**
Charleville-Mézières **13 B6**
Charlotte **75 B7**
Charlotte Amalie **87 C7**
Charlottesville **73 E6**
Charlottetown **69 D4**
Charlton **62 C3**
Charolles **13 C6**
Charouine **54 C4**
Charters Towers **61 E8**
Chartres **12 B4**
Chascomús **94 D5**
Châteaubriant **12 C3**
Châteaulin **12 B1**
Châteauroux **12 C4**
Châtellerault **12 C4**
Chatham, *N.B., Canada* **69 D4**
Chatham, *Ont., Canada* **69 D2**
Chatham, *U.K.* **11 F7**
Chatrapur **40 H5**
Chattahoochee → **74 D5**
Chattanooga **74 B5**
Chauk **41 G10**
Chaukan La **41 D11**
Chaumont **13 B6**
Chaves, *Brazil* **92 C4**
Chaves, *Portugal* **18 B2**
Chavuma **58 A4**
Cheb **16 C1**
Cheboksary **24 B6**
Chech, Erg **54 D4**
Chechenia □ **25 E6**
Checheno-Ingush Republic = Chechenia □ **25 E6**
Chechnya = Chechenia □ **25 E6**
Cheduba I. **41 H9**
Cheepie **63 A4**
Chegga **54 C3**
Chegutu **59 B6**
Chehalis **80 B2**
Cheju Do **35 C7**
Chekiang = Zhejiang □ **35 D7**
Cheleken **29 F6**
Chelforó **95 D3**
Chelkar = Shalqar **29 E6**
Chelkar Tengiz, Solonchak **29 E7**
Chełm **17 C6**
Chełmno **16 B4**
Chelmsford **11 F7**
Cheltenham **11 F5**
Chelyabinsk **29 D7**
Chemnitz **15 C7**
Chen Xian **35 D6**
Chenab → **42 D7**
Chencha **53 G6**
Chenchiang = Zhenjiang **35 C6**
Chengde **35 B6**
Chengdu **35 C5**
Chengjiang **34 D5**
Ch'engtu = Chengdu **35 C5**
Chennai = Madras **43 N12**
Cheo Reo **36 B3**
Cheom Ksan **36 B2**
Chepén **91 E3**
Chepes **94 C3**
Cher → **12 C4**
Cherbourg **12 B3**
Cherchell **54 A5**
Cherdyn **28 C6**
Cherepanovo **29 D9**
Cherepovets **24 B4**
Chergui, Chott ech **54 B5**
Cherikov = Cherykaw **17 B10**
Cherkasy **24 D3**
Cherlak **29 D8**
Chernaya **30 B6**
Chernigov = Chernihiv **24 C3**
Chernihiv **24 C3**
Chernivtsi **17 D7**
Chernobyl = Chornobyl **17 C10**
Chernovtsy = Chernivtsi **17 D7**
Chernyakhovsk **28 D3**
Cherquenco **94 D2**
Cherrapunji **41 E8**

Cherven ...... 17 B9
Chervonohrad . 17 C7
Cherykaw ..... 17 B10
Chesapeake ... 73 F7
Chesapeake B. . 73 E7
Cheshskaya Guba ....... 28 C5
Chester, *U.K.* .. 11 E5
Chester, *U.S.A.* 73 E8
Chesterfield ... 11 E6
Chesterfield, Is. 64 L10
Chesterfield Inlet 70 B10
Chesterton Ra. 63 A4
Cheviot Hills .. 10 D5
Chew Bahir ... 53 H6
Cheyenne ..... 76 E2
Cheyenne → . 76 C4
Chhapra ...... 40 E5
Chhatarpur ... 43 G11
Chhindwara ... 43 H11
Chhlong ...... 36 B3
Chi → ....... 36 A2
Chiamussu = Jiamusi ..... 35 B8
Chiange ...... 58 B2
Chiapa → .... 85 D6
Chiávari ...... 20 B2
Chiavenna .... 20 A2
Chiba ........ 32 B7
Chibemba ..... 58 B2
Chibia ........ 58 B2
Chibougamau . 69 D3
Chibuk ....... 53 F1
Chicacole = Srikakulam .. 40 H4
Chicago ...... 72 D2
Chichagof I. ... 71 C6
Chichibu ...... 32 A6
Ch'ich'ihaerh = Qiqihar ..... 35 B7
Chickasha .... 78 B5
Chiclana de la Frontera .... 18 D2
Chiclayo ...... 91 E3
Chico ........ 80 F3
Chico →, *Chubut, Argentina* ... 95 E3
Chico →, *Santa Cruz, Argentina* ... 95 F3
Chicoutimi .... 69 D3
Chidambaram . 43 P11
Chidley, C. .... 68 B4
Chiemsee ..... 15 E7
Chiengi ....... 57 F5
Chiese → .... 20 B3
Chieti ........ 20 C5
Chiguana ..... 91 H5
Chihli, G. of = Bo Hai ...... 35 C6
Chihuahua .... 84 B3
Chiili ........ 29 E7
Chik Bollapur .. 43 N10
Chikmagalur .. 43 N9
Chilapa ....... 84 D5
Chilas ........ 42 B9
Chilaw ....... 43 R11
Childers ...... 63 A5
Chile ■ ....... 94 D2
Chilete ....... 91 E3
Chililabombwe 59 A5
Chilin = Jilin .. 35 B7
Chilka L. ...... 40 H5
Chillán ....... 94 D2
Chiloé, I. de ... 95 E2
Chilpancingo .. 84 D5
Chiluage ...... 56 F4
Chilwa, L. ..... 59 B7
Chimbay ..... 29 E6
Chimborazo ... 90 D3
Chimbote ..... 91 E3
Chimkent = Shymkent ... 29 E7
Chimoio ...... 59 B6
Chin ☐ ....... 41 F9
China ■ ...... 35 C5
Chinan = Jinan 35 C6
Chinandega ... 85 E7
Chincha Alta .. 91 F3
Chinchilla ..... 63 A5
Chinchou = Jinzhou ..... 35 B7
Chinde ....... 59 B7
Chindwin → .. 41 G10
Chingola ..... 59 A5
Ch'ingtao = Qingdao .... 35 C7
Chinguetti .... 54 D2
Chinhoyi ..... 59 B6
Chiniot ....... 42 D8
Chinju ........ 35 C7
Chinnampo ... 35 C7
Chinon ....... 12 C4
Chinsali ...... 57 G6
Chióggia ..... 20 B4
Chíos = Khíos . 23 E6
Chipata ....... 59 A6
Chiquián ..... 91 F3
Chiquinquira .. 90 B4
Chirchiq ...... 29 E7
Chirmiri ...... 40 F4
Chiromo ...... 59 B7
Chisamba ..... 59 A5
Chisapani Garhi 40 D5
Chişinău ...... 17 E9
Chistopol ..... 24 B7
Chita ......... 30 D9
Chitado ...... 58 B2
Chitembo ..... 58 A3
Chitral ....... 42 B7
Chitré ........ 86 E3
Chittagong .... 41 F8
Chittagong ☐ .. 41 E8
Chittaurgarh .. 43 G9
Chittoor ...... 43 N11
Chiusi ........ 20 C3
Chivasso ..... 20 B1
Chivilcoy ..... 94 B4
Chkalov = Orenburg ... 29 D6
Choele Choel .. 95 D3
Chojnice ...... 16 B3
Cholet ........ 12 C3
Choluteca ..... 85 E7
Choma ....... 59 B5
Chomutov .... 16 C1
Chon Buri .... 36 B2
Chone ........ 90 D3
Chŏngjin ..... 35 B7
Chŏngju ...... 35 C7
Chongqing .... 35 D5
Chŏnju ....... 35 C7
Chonos, Arch. de los ...... 95 F2
Chop ......... 17 D6
Chornobyl .... 17 C10
Chortkiv ...... 17 D7
Chorzów ...... 16 C4
Chos-Malal ... 94 D2
Chōshi ....... 32 B7
Choszczno .... 16 B2
Chotila ....... 43 H7
Choybalsan ... 35 B6
Christchurch .. 65 E5
Christiana .... 59 D5
Christmas I. = Kiritimati ... 65 J15
Chu = Shu .... 29 E8
Ch'uanchou = Quanzhou ... 35 D6
Chubut → .... 95 E3
Chudskoye, Oz. 24 B2
Chūgoku-Sanchi 32 B3
Chula Vista ... 82 D4
Chulucanas ... 90 E2
Chulym → ... 29 D9
Chumbicha ... 94 B3
Chumphon .... 36 B1
Chuna → .... 30 D7
Chunchŏn .... 35 C7
Chungking = Chongqing .. 35 D5
Chunya ....... 57 F6
Chuquibamba . 91 G4
Chuquicamata . 94 A3
Chur ......... 13 C8
Churachandpur 41 E9
Churchill ..... 70 C10
Churchill →, *Man., Canada* 70 C10
Churchill →, *Nfld., Canada* 69 C4
Churchill, C. ... 70 C10
Churchill Falls . 69 C4
Churchill L. ... 71 C9
Churu ........ 42 E9
Chushal ...... 42 C11
Chusovoy ..... 28 D6
Chuvash Republic ☐ = Chuvashia ☐ 24 B6
Chuvashia ☐ .. 24 B6
Cicero ........ 72 D2
Ciechanów .... 16 B5
Ciego de Avila . 86 B4
Ciénaga ...... 90 A4
Cienfuegos ... 86 B3
Cieszyn ....... 16 D4
Cieza ........ 19 C5
Cijara, Pantano de ........ 18 C3
Cilician Gates P. 46 C3
Cill Chainnigh = Kilkenny .... 11 E3
Cimişlia ...... 17 E9
Cimone, Mte. .. 20 B3
Cîmpina ...... 17 F7
Cîmpulung .... 17 F7
Cinca → ..... 19 B6
Cincar ........ 20 C6
Cincinnati ..... 72 E3
Çine ......... 23 F7
Cinto, Mte. .... 13 E8
Circle ........ 71 B5
Cirebon ...... 37 F3
Citlaltépetl .... 84 D5
Città di Castello 20 C4
Ciudad Bolívar 90 B6
Ciudad Chetumal ... 85 D7
Ciudad del Carmen ..... 85 D6
Ciudad Delicias = Delicias ... 84 B3
Ciudad Guayana 90 B6
Ciudad Juárez . 84 A3
Ciudad Madero 84 C5
Ciudad Mante . 84 C5
Ciudad Obregón 84 B3
Ciudad Real ... 18 C4
Ciudad Rodrigo 18 B2
Ciudad Trujillo = Santo Domingo ... 87 C6
Ciudad Victoria 84 C5
Civitanova Marche ..... 20 C4
Civitavécchia .. 20 C3
Cizre ......... 46 C5
Clanwilliam ... 58 E3
Clare ......... 62 B2
Clarence →, *Australia* .... 63 A5
Clarence →, *N.Z.* ........ 65 E5
Clarence, I. .... 95 G2
Clarence I. .... 96 A4
Clarie Coast ... 96 A13
Clarke I. ...... 62 D4
Clarksdale .... 79 B8
Clarksville .... 74 A4
Claveria ...... 38 A2
Clear, C. ...... 11 F2
Clearwater .... 75 F6
Clearwater Mts. 81 B6
Clermont-Ferrand ..... 13 D5
Cleveland, *Australia* .... 63 A5
Cleveland, *U.S.A.* ...... 72 D5
Clifden ....... 65 G2
Clifton ....... 63 A5
Clifton Hills ... 62 A2
Clinton, *Canada* 71 C7
Clinton, *N.Z.* .. 65 G3
Clinton, *U.S.A.* 77 E9
Clinton Colden L. .......... 70 B9
Clones ....... 11 D3
Clonmel ...... 11 E3
Clovis ........ 78 B2
Cluj-Napoca .. 17 E6
Clunes ....... 62 C3
Clutha → .... 65 G3
Clyde ........ 65 F3
Clyde → ..... 10 D4
Clyde, Firth of . 10 D4
Clyde River ... 68 A4
Coari ......... 90 D6
Coast Mts. .... 70 C7
Coast Ranges . 80 F2
Coats I. ....... 68 B2
Coats Land ... 96 B5
Coatzacoalcos . 85 D6
Cobalt ........ 69 D3
Cobar ........ 63 B4
Cóbh ........ 11 F2
Cobham ...... 62 B3
Cobija ........ 91 F5
Cobourg ...... 69 D3
Cobram ...... 63 C4
Cóbué ........ 59 A6
Coburg ....... 15 C6
Cocanada = Kakinada ... 40 J4
Cochabamba .. 91 G5
Cochin ....... 43 Q10
Cochin China = Nam-Phan .. 36 B3
Cochrane ..... 69 D2
Cochrane, L. .. 95 F2
Cockburn ..... 62 B3
Cockburn, Canal 95 G2
Coco → ...... 86 D3
Cocobeach .... 56 D1
Cod, C. ....... 73 C10
Codajás ...... 90 D6
Codó ......... 92 C5
Cœur d'Alene . 80 B5
Coffeyville .... 79 A6
Coffin B. ...... 62 B2
Coffin Bay Peninsula ... 62 B2
Coffs Harbour . 63 B5
Cognac ....... 12 D3

Cohuna 63 C3
Coiba, I. 86 E3
Coig → 95 G3
Coihaique 95 F2
Coimbatore 43 P10
Coimbra, *Brazil* 91 G7
Coimbra, *Portugal* 18 B1
Coín 18 D3
Cojimies 90 C3
Colac 62 C3
Colatina 93 F5
Colbeck, C. 96 B17
Colbinabbin 63 C3
Colchester 11 F7
Colebrook 62 D4
Coleman 71 D8
Coleraine, *Australia* 62 C3
Coleraine, *U.K.* 11 D3
Coleridge, L. 65 E4
Colesberg 59 E5
Colhué Huapi, L. 95 F3
Colima 84 D4
Colinas 92 D5
Coll 10 C3
Collaguasi 91 H5
Collarenebri 63 A4
Collingwood 64 D5
Colmar 13 B7
Colo → 63 B5
Cologne = Köln 14 C4
Colomb-Béchar = Béchar 54 B4
Colômbia 93 G4
Colombia ■ 90 C4
Colombo 43 R11
Colón, *Cuba* 86 B3
Colón, *Panama* 85 F9
Colonia 94 C5
Colonia Dora 94 B4
Colonsay 10 C3
Colorado □ 83 A10
Colorado →, *Argentina* 95 D4
Colorado →, *N. Amer.* 82 E5
Colorado Plateau 83 B7
Colorado Springs 76 F2
Columbia, *Mo., U.S.A.* 77 F8
Columbia, *S.C., U.S.A.* 75 B7
Columbia, *Tenn., U.S.A.* 74 B4
Columbia → 80 B1
Columbia, District of □ 73 E7
Columbia Basin 80 B4
Columbretes, Is. 19 C6
Columbus, *Ga., U.S.A.* 74 C5
Columbus, *Miss., U.S.A.* 74 C3
Columbus, *Ohio, U.S.A.* 72 E4
Colville → 71 A4
Colville, C. 64 B6
Colwyn Bay 11 E5
Comácchio 20 B4
Comallo 95 E2
Comilla 41 F8
Comino, C. 21 D2
Committee B. 68 B2
Commonwealth B. 96 A14
Commoron Cr. → 63 A5
Communism Pk. = Kommunizma, Pik 29 F8
Como 20 B2
Como, L. di 20 B2
Comodoro Rivadavia 95 F3
Comorin, C. 43 Q10
Comoro Is. = Comoros ■ 51 H8
Comoros ■ 51 H8
Comox 71 D7
Compiègne 13 B5
Compton Downs 63 B4
Comrat 17 E9
Conakry 55 G2
Conara Junction 62 D4
Concarneau 12 C2
Conceição da Barra 93 F6
Concepción, *Bolivia* 91 G6
Concepción, *Chile* 94 D2
Concepción, *Paraguay* 94 A5
Concepción, L. 91 G6
Concepción del Oro 84 C4
Concepción del Uruguay 94 C5
Conchos → 84 B3
Concord, *N.C., U.S.A.* 75 B7
Concord, *N.H., U.S.A.* 73 C10
Concordia, *Argentina* 94 C5
Concórdia, *Brazil* 90 D5
Condamine 63 A5
Condeúba 93 E5
Condobolin 63 B4
Conegliano 20 B4
Confuso → 94 B5
Congo ■ 56 E3
Congo → 56 F2
Congo, Dem. Rep. of the ■ 56 E4
Conjeeveram = Kanchipuram 43 N11
Conlea 63 B3
Conn, L. 11 D2
Connacht □ 11 E2
Connecticut □ 73 D9
Connecticut → 73 D9
Connemara 11 E2
Conoble 63 B3
Cononaco → 90 D3
Conran, C. 63 C4
Conselheiro Lafaiete 93 G5
Constance = Konstanz 14 E5
Constance, L. = Bodensee 13 C8
Constanţa 22 B7
Constantine 54 A6
Constitución 94 D2
Contai 40 G6
Contamana 91 E4
Contas → 93 E6
Conway, L. 62 A2
Coober Pedy 62 A1
Cooch Behar = Koch Bihar 41 D7
Cook, B. 95 H2
Cook, Mt. 65 E4
Cook Inlet 71 C4
Cook Is. 65 L14
Cook Strait 65 D6
Cooktown 61 D8
Coolabah 63 B4
Cooladdi 63 A4
Coolah 63 B4
Coolamon 63 B4
Coolangatta 63 A5
Cooma 63 C4
Coonabarabran 63 B4
Coonamble 63 B4
Coondapoor 43 N9
Coongie 62 A3
Coongoola 63 A4
Cooninie, L. 62 A2
Cooper Cr. →, *N. Terr., Australia* 60 C5
Cooper Cr. →, *S. Austral., Australia* 62 A2
Cooroy 63 A5
Cootamundra 63 B4
Cooyar 63 A5
Copenhagen = København 9 G10
Copiapó 94 B2
Copiapó → 94 B2
Copley 62 B2
Copper Center 71 B5
Copper Cliff 69 D2
Coppermine = Kugluktuk 70 B8
Coppermine → 70 B8
Coquimbo 94 C2
Corabia 22 C5
Coracora 91 G4
Coral Harbour = Salliq 68 B2
Coral Sea 64 L10
Corato 21 D6
Corby 11 E6
Corcaigh = Cork 11 F2
Corcubión 18 A1
Córdoba, *Argentina* 94 C4
Córdoba, *Spain* 18 D3
Córdoba, Sierra de 94 C4
Cordon 38 A2
Cordova 71 B5
Corfu = Kérkira 23 E2
Coria 18 C2
Corigliano Cálabro 21 E6
Corinna 62 D4
Corinth = Kórinthos 23 F4
Corinth, G. of = Korinthiakós Kólpos 23 E4
Corinto 93 F5
Cork 11 F2
Çorlu 22 D6
Corner Brook 69 D5
Corneşti 17 E9
Cornwall 69 D3
Corny Pt. 62 B2
Coro 90 A5
Coroatá 92 C5
Corocoro 91 G5
Coroico 91 G5
Coromandel 64 B6
Corona 62 B3
Coronation Gulf 70 B8
Coronation I. 96 A4
Coronel 94 D2
Coronel Dorrego 94 D4
Coronel Suárez 94 D4
Corowa 63 C4
Corpus Christi 78 F5
Corque 91 G5
Corrib, L. 11 E2
Corrientes 94 B5
Corrientes → 90 D4
Corrientes, C., *Colombia* 90 B3
Corrientes, C., *Mexico* 84 C3
Corse 13 E8
Corse, C. 13 E8
Corsica = Corse 13 E8
Corsicana 79 C5
Corte 13 E8
Çorum 46 B3
Corumbá 91 G7
Corumbá de Goiás 93 F4
Corunna = La Coruña 18 A1
Corvallis 80 C2
Cosenza 21 E6
Costa Blanca 19 C5
Costa Brava 19 B7
Costa del Sol 18 D3
Costa Dorada 19 B6
Costa Rica ■ 86 E3
Cotabato 38 C2
Cotagaita 91 H5
Côte d'Azur 13 E7
Côte-d'Ivoire ■ = Ivory Coast ■ 55 G3
Cotentin 12 B3
Cotonou 55 G5
Cotopaxi 90 D3
Cotswold Hills 11 F5
Cottbus 15 C8
Couedic, C. du 62 C2
Coulman I. 96 B15
Council 71 B3
Council Bluffs 77 E7
Courantyne → 90 B7
Courtrai = Kortrijk 14 C2
Coventry 11 E6
Covilhã 18 B2
Covington 72 E3
Cowal, L. 63 B4
Cowangie 62 C3
Cowarie 62 A2
Cowell 62 B2
Cowra 63 B4
Coxim 93 F3
Cox's Bazar 41 G8
Cozumel, I. de 85 C7
Craboon 63 B4
Cracow = Kraków 16 C4
Cracow 63 A5
Cradock 59 E5
Craigavon 11 D3
Crailsheim 14 D6
Craiova 22 B4
Cranbrook, *Australia* 62 D4
Cranbrook, *Canada* 71 D8
Crateús 92 D5
Crato 92 D6
Crawley 11 F6
Crazy Mts. 81 B8
Crema 20 B2
Cremona 20 B3
Cres 20 B5
Cressy 62 C3
Crete = Kríti 23 G5
Créteil 12 B5

Creus, C. de . . . 19 A7
Creuse → . . . . 12 C4
Crewe . . . . . . . . 11 E5
Criciúma . . . . . 94 B7
Crimean Pen. = Krymskyy Pivostriv . . . . 25 D3
Crişul Alb → . 16 E5
Crişul Negru → 16 E5
Crna Gora = Montenegro □ 22 C2
Crna Gora . . . . 22 C3
Crna Reka → . 22 D3
Croatia ■ . . . . . 20 B6
Crocker, Banjaran . . . . 36 C5
Croker, C. . . . . . 60 C5
Cromer . . . . . . . 11 E7
Cromwell . . . . . 65 F3
Cronulla . . . . . . 63 B5
Crookwell . . . . . 63 B4
Cross Sound . . 71 C6
Crotone . . . . . . 21 E6
Crows Nest . . . 63 A5
Crowsnest Pass 71 D8
Cruz Alta . . . . . 94 B6
Cruz del Eje . . . 94 C4
Cruzeiro . . . . . . 93 G5
Cruzeiro do Sul 91 E4
Crystal Brook . . 62 B2
Csongrád . . . . . 16 E5
Cuamba . . . . . . 59 A7
Cuando → . . . 58 D4
Cuarto → . . . . 94 C4
Cuba ■ . . . . . . . 86 B4
Cubango → . . 58 B4
Cuchi . . . . . . . . 58 A3
Cúcuta . . . . . . . 90 B4
Cuddalore . . . . 43 P11
Cuddapah . . . . 43 M11
Cudgewa . . . . . 63 C4
Cuenca, *Ecuador* 90 D3
Cuenca, *Spain* . 19 B4
Cuenca, Serranía de . 19 C5
Cuernavaca . . . 84 D5
Cuevas del Almanzora . . 19 D5
Cuevo . . . . . . . . 91 H6
Cuiabá . . . . . . . 93 F2
Cuiabá → . . . . 93 F2
Cuima . . . . . . . . 58 A3
Cuito → . . . . . 58 B4
Cukai . . . . . . . . 36 D2
Culcairn . . . . . . 63 C4
Culgoa → . . . . 63 A4
Culiacán . . . . . . 84 C3
Culion . . . . . . . . 38 B2
Cullarin Ra. . . . 63 B4
Cullera . . . . . . . 19 C5
Culuene → . . . 93 E3
Culverden . . . . 65 E5
Cumaná . . . . . . 90 A6
Cumberland, *Canada* . . . . . 71 D7
Cumberland, *U.S.A.* . . . . . . 73 E6
Cumberland Pen. . . . . . . . . 68 B4
Cumberland Plateau . . . . . 72 F3
Cumberland Sd. 68 B4
Cumborah . . . . 63 A4
Cumbum . . . . . 43 M11
Cummins . . . . . 62 B2
Cumnock . . . . . 63 B4
Cunene → . . . 58 B2
Cúneo . . . . . . . . 20 B1
Cunnamulla . . . 63 A4
Cupica, G. de . . 90 B3
Curaçao . . . . . . 87 D6
Curaray → . . . 90 D4
Curiapo . . . . . . 90 B6
Curicó . . . . . . . . 94 C2
Curitiba . . . . . . 94 B7
Currabubula . . 63 B5
Currais Novos . 92 D6
Curralinho . . . . 92 C4
Curraweena . . . 63 B4
Currie . . . . . . . . 62 C3
Curtea de Argeş 17 F7
Curtis Group . . 62 C4
Curuápanema → . . . . . . . . . . . 92 C2
Curuçá . . . . . . . 92 C4
Curup . . . . . . . . 37 E2
Cururupu . . . . . 92 C5
Curuzú Cuatiá . 94 B5
Cuttaburra → . 63 A3
Cuttack . . . . . . . 40 G5
Cuvier I. . . . . . . 64 B6
Cuxhaven . . . . . 14 B5
Cuyo . . . . . . . . . 38 B2
Cuzco, *Bolivia* . 91 H5
Cuzco, *Peru* . . . 91 F4
Cwmbran . . . . . 11 F5
Cyclades = Kikládhes . . . 23 F5
Cygnet . . . . . . . 62 D4
Cyprus ■ . . . . . 46 D3
Cyrenaica . . . . . 52 C3
Cyrene = Shaḥḥāt . . . . 52 B3
Czech Rep. ■ . . 16 D2
Częstochowa . . 16 C4

## D

Da Hinggan Ling 35 B7
Da Lat . . . . . . . . 36 B3
Da Nang . . . . . . 36 A3
Da Qaidam . . . . 34 C4
Da Yunhe → . . 35 C7
Daba Shan . . . . 35 C5
Dabakala . . . . . 55 G4
Dabo . . . . . . . . . 37 E2
Dabola . . . . . . . 55 F2
Daboya . . . . . . . 55 G4
Dacca = Dhaka 41 F8
Dacca = Dhaka □ . . . . 41 E8
Dachau . . . . . . . 15 D6
Dadanawa . . . . 90 C7
Dadra and Nagar Haveli □ . . . . 43 J8
Dadu . . . . . . . . . 42 F5
Daet . . . . . . . . . 38 B2
Dagana . . . . . . . 55 E1
Dagestan □ . . . 25 E6
Daghestan Republic = Dagestan □ . 25 E6
Dagö = Hiiumaa 24 B1
Dagupan . . . . . 38 A2
Dahlak Kebir . . 49 D3
Dahod . . . . . . . 43 H9
Dahomey = Benin ■ . . . . 55 G5
Dahra . . . . . . . . 55 E1
Daiō-Misaki . . . 32 B5
Dairût . . . . . . . . 52 C5
Dakar . . . . . . . . 55 F1
Dakhla . . . . . . . 54 D1
Dakhla, El Wâhât el- . . . 52 C4
Dakhovskaya . . 25 E5
Đakovica . . . . . 22 C3
Dalaman → . . 23 F7
Dalandzadgad . 35 B5
Dālbandīn . . . . 42 E4
Dalby . . . . . . . . 63 A5
Dalhousie . . . . . 69 D4
Dali . . . . . . . . . . 34 D5
Dalian . . . . . . . . 35 C7
Daliang Shan . . 34 D5
Dallarnil . . . . . . 63 A5
Dallas . . . . . . . . 79 C5
Dalmacija . . . . . 20 C6
Dalmatia = Dalmacija . . . 20 C6
Daloa . . . . . . . . 55 G3
Dalton . . . . . . . 74 B5
Dalton Iceberg Tongue . . . . . 96 A13
Daly Waters . . . 60 D5
Daman . . . . . . . 43 J8
Damanhûr . . . . 52 B5
Damar . . . . . . . 39 F3
Damaraland . . . 58 C3
Damascus = Dimashq . . . . 46 D4
Damāvand . . . . 44 C3
Damāvand, Qolleh-ye . . . 44 C3
Damba . . . . . . . 56 F3
Dāmghān . . . . . 44 B3
Damiel . . . . . . . 18 C4
Damietta = Dumyât . . . . . 52 B5
Dammam = Ad Dammām . . . 47 F7
Damoh . . . . . . . 43 H11
Dampier . . . . . . 60 E2
Dampier, Selat 39 E4
Danbury . . . . . . 73 D9
Dandeldhura . . 40 C3
Dandeli . . . . . . . 43 M9
Dandenong . . . 63 C4
Dandong . . . . . . 35 B7
Danger Is. = Pukapuka . . . 65 L14
Danger Pt. . . . . 58 E3
Dangora . . . . . . 55 F6
Danilov . . . . . . . 24 B5
Dankhar Gompa 42 C11
Dannemora . . . 9 F11
Dannevirke . . . 64 D7
Dante . . . . . . . . 49 E5
Danube = Dunărea → . 17 F9
Danville . . . . . . 75 A8
Danzig = Gdańsk . . . . . 16 A4
Dao . . . . . . . . . . 38 B2
Daoud = Aïn Beïda . . . . . . 54 A6
Dar el Beida = Casablanca . . 54 B3
Dar es Salaam . 57 F7
Dārāb . . . . . . . . 44 D3
Daraj . . . . . . . . . 54 B7
Darband . . . . . . 42 B8
Darbhanga . . . . 40 D5
Dardanelles = Çanakkale Boğazı . . . . . . 23 D6
Dârfûr . . . . . . . . 53 F3
Dargai . . . . . . . . 42 B7
Dargan Ata . . . 29 E7
Dargaville . . . . 64 A5
Darica . . . . . . . . 22 D7
Darién, G. del . 90 B3
Darjeeling = Darjiling . . . . 40 D7
Darjiling . . . . . . 40 D7
Darling → . . . . 62 B3
Darling Downs 63 A5
Darling Ra. . . . . 60 G2
Darlington . . . . 11 D6
Darłowo . . . . . . 16 A3
Darmstadt . . . . 14 D5
Darnah . . . . . . . 52 B3
Darnley, C. . . . . 96 A10
Darnley B. . . . . 70 B7
Dart, C. . . . . . . . 96 B18
Dartmoor . . . . . 11 F5
Dartmouth . . . . 69 D4
Dartmouth, L. . 63 A4
Darvaza . . . . . . 29 E6
Darvel, Teluk . . 38 D1
Darwha . . . . . . . 43 J10
Darwin . . . . . . . 60 C5
Daryoi Amu = Amudarya → 29 E6
Dās . . . . . . . . . . 44 E3
Dashhowuz . . . 29 E6
Dasht → . . . . . 42 G2
Dasht-e Kavīr . . 44 C3
Dasht-e Mārgow 42 D3
Datça . . . . . . . . 23 F6
Datia . . . . . . . . . 43 G11
Datong . . . . . . . 35 B6
Datu, Tanjung . 37 D3
Datu Piang . . . . 38 C2
Daugava → . . 24 B1
Daugavpils . . . . 24 B2
Daulpur . . . . . . 42 F10
Dauphin . . . . . . 71 C9
Dauphiné . . . . . 13 D6
Davangere . . . . 43 M9
Davao . . . . . . . . 38 C3
Davao, G. of . . 38 C3
Dāvar Panāh . . 45 E5
Davenport . . . . 77 E9
David . . . . . . . . 86 E3
David Gorodok = Davyd Haradok . . . . 17 B8
Davis Sea . . . . . 96 A11
Davis Str. . . . . . 68 B5
Davos . . . . . . . . 13 C8
Davyd Haradok 17 B8
Dawson . . . . . . 70 B6
Dawson, I. . . . . 95 G2
Dax . . . . . . . . . . 12 E3
Daxian . . . . . . . 35 C5
Daxue Shan . . . 34 C5
Daylesford . . . . 62 C3
Dayr az Zawr . . 46 D5
Dayton . . . . . . . 72 E3
Daytona Beach 75 E7
Dead Sea . . . . . 47 E3
Deakin . . . . . . . 60 G4
Deal I. . . . . . . . . 62 C4
Deán Funes . . . 94 C4
Death Valley . . 82 B4
Deba Habe . . . . 55 F7
Debar . . . . . . . . 22 D3
Dębica . . . . . . . 16 C5
Debre Markos . 53 F6
Debre Tabor . . 53 F6
Debrecen . . . . . 16 E5
Decatur, *Ala., U.S.A.* . . . . . . 74 B4
Decatur, *Ill., U.S.A.* . . . . . . 77 F10
Deccan . . . . . . . 43 L11
Děčín . . . . . . . . 16 C2
Dedéagach = Alexandroúpolis . . . . . . . . . . . 22 D5

Dédougou 55 F4
Dee → 10 C5
Deepwater 63 A5
Degeh Bur 49 F3
Deggendorf 15 D7
Deh Bīd 44 D3
Dehi Titan 42 C3
Dehibat 54 B7
Dehkareqan 46 C6
Dehra Dun 42 D11
Dej 17 E6
Dekese 56 E4
Delano 82 C3
Delaware □ 73 E8
Delaware → 73 E8
Delegate 63 C4
Delgado, C. 57 G8
Delgo 53 D5
Delhi 42 E10
Delice → 46 C3
Delicias 84 B3
Delmenhorst 14 B5
Delmiro Gouveia 93 D6
Deloraine 62 D4
Delungra 63 A5
Delvinë 23 E3
Demanda, Sierra de la 18 A4
Demavand = Damāvand 44 C3
Demba 56 F4
Dembecha 53 F6
Dembidolo 53 G5
Demini → 90 D6
Demirci 23 E7
Demirköy 22 D6
Dempo 37 E2
Den Haag = 's-Gravenhage 14 B3
Den Helder 14 B3
Denau 29 F7
Dendang 37 E3
Denia 19 C6
Denial B. 62 B1
Deniliquin 63 C3
Denman Glacier 96 A11
Denmark ■ 9 G9
Denmark Str. 66 C17
Denpasar 37 F5
Denton 78 C5
D'Entrecasteaux Is. 61 B9
Denver 76 F2
Deoghar 40 E6
Deolali 43 K8
Deoria 40 D4
Deosai Mts. 42 B9
Dêqên 34 D4
Dera Ghazi Khan 42 D7
Dera Ismail Khan 42 D7
Derbent 25 E6
Derby, *Australia* 60 D3
Derby, *U.K.* 11 E6
Derg, L. 11 E2
Dergaon 41 D9
Derry = Londonderry 11 D3
Derudub 53 E6
Des Moines 77 E8
Des Moines → 77 E9
Desaguadero → 91 G5
Dese 49 E2
Desna → 17 C10
Desolación, I. 95 G2
Despeñaperros, Paso 18 C4
Dessau 15 C7
Dessye = Dese 49 E2
D'Estrees B. 62 C2
Detmold 14 C5
Detroit 72 C4
Deutsche Bucht 14 A5
Deva 17 F6
Devakottai 43 Q11
Deventer 14 B4
Devonport, *Australia* 62 D4
Devonport, *N.Z.* 64 B6
Dewas 43 H10
Deyhūk 44 C4
Deyyer 44 E2
Dezfūl 47 D7
Dezhneva, Mys 31 C16
Dhafra 44 F3
Dhahira 44 F4
Dhahran = Az̧ Z̧ahrān 47 F7
Dhaka 41 F8
Dhaka □ 41 E8
Dhamar 49 E3
Dhamtari 40 G3
Dhanbad 40 F6
Dhangarhi 40 C3
Dhankuta 40 D6
Dhar 43 H9
Dharmapuri 43 N11
Dharwad 43 M9
Dhaulagiri 40 C4
Dhenkanal 40 G5
Dhíkti Óros 23 G5
Dhírfis 23 E4
Dhodhekánisos 23 F6
Dhrol 43 H7
Dhubaibah 44 F3
Dhuburi 41 D7
Dhule 43 J9
Dhut → 49 E5
Diafarabé 55 F4
Diamantina 93 F5
Diamantina → 62 A2
Diamantino 93 E2
Diamond Harbour 40 F7
Diapaga 55 F5
Dībā 44 E4
Dibaya 56 F4
Dibaya-Lubue 56 E3
Dibbi 49 G3
Dibrugarh 41 D10
Dickson 28 B9
Didiéni 55 F3
Diébougou 55 F4
Diefenbaker L. 71 C9
Dieppe 12 B4
Digby 69 D4
Digges Is. 68 B3
Dighinala 41 F9
Digne-les-Bains 13 D7
Digos 38 C3
Digul → 39 F5
Dihang → 41 D10
Dijlah, Nahr → 47 E6
Dijon 13 C6
Dikimdya 31 D10
Dikson = Dickson 28 B9
Dikwa 53 F1
Dili 39 F3
Dilling 53 F4
Dillingham 71 C4
Dilolo 56 G4
Dilston 62 D4
Dimashq 46 D4
Dimbokro 55 G4
Dimboola 62 C3
Dîmboviţa → 22 B6
Dimitrovgrad, *Bulgaria* 22 C5
Dimitrovgrad, *Russia* 24 C6
Dimitrovo = Pernik 22 C4
Dinagat 38 B3
Dinajpur 41 E7
Dinan 12 B2
Dinant 14 C3
Dinar 46 C2
Dīnār, Kūh-e 44 D2
Dinara Planina 20 B6
Dinard 12 B2
Dinaric Alps = Dinara Planina 20 B6
Dindigul 43 P11
Dingle 11 E1
Dinguiraye 55 F2
Dingwall 10 C4
Dinosaur National Monument 81 E9
Diourbel 55 F1
Dipolog 38 C2
Dir 42 B7
Diré 55 E4
Dire Dawa 49 F3
Dirico 58 B4
Dirranbandi 63 A4
Disa 43 G8
Disappointment, L. 60 E3
Disaster B. 63 C4
Discovery B. 62 C3
Disteghil Sar 42 A9
Distrito Federal □ 93 F4
Diu 43 J7
Divinópolis 93 G5
Divnoye 25 D5
Dīwāl Kol 42 B5
Diyarbakır 46 C5
Diz Chah 44 C3
Djado 52 D1
Djakarta = Jakarta 37 F3
Djambala 56 E2
Djanet 54 D6
Djawa = Jawa 37 F3
Djelfa 54 B5
Djema 57 C5
Djenné 55 F4
Djerba, I. de 52 B1
Djerid, Chott 54 B6
Djibo 55 F4
Djibouti 49 E3
Djibouti ■ 49 E3
Djolu 56 D4
Djougou 55 G5
Djoum 56 D2
Djourab 53 E2
Djugu 57 D6
Dmitriya Lapteva, Proliv 31 B12
Dnepr → = Dnipro → 25 D3
Dneprodzerzhinsk = Dniprodzerzhynsk 25 D3
Dnepropetrovsk = Dnipropetrovsk 25 D4
Dnestr → = Dnister → 17 E10
Dnestrovski = Belgorod 24 C4
Dnieper = Dnipro → 25 D3
Dniester = Dnister → 17 E10
Dnipro → 25 D3
Dniprodzerzhynsk 25 D3
Dnipropetrovsk 25 D4
Dnister → 17 E10
Dnistrovskyy Lyman 17 E10
Dnyapro = Dnipro → 25 D3
Doba 53 G2
Doberai, Jazirah 39 E4
Doblas 94 D4
Dobo 39 F4
Doboj 20 B7
Dobreta-Turnu-Severin 22 B4
Dobrich 22 C6
Dobruja 22 B7
Dobrush 17 B10
Dodecanese = Dhodhekánisos 23 F6
Dodge City 78 A3
Dodoma 57 F7
Dogi 42 C3
Doha = Ad Dawhah 44 E2
Dohazari 41 F9
Doi 39 D3
Dois Irmãos, Sa. 93 D5
Dolbeau 69 D3
Dole 13 C6
Dolomites = Dolomiti 20 A3
Dolomiti 20 A3
Dolores 94 D5
Dolphin, C. 95 G5
Dolphin and Union Str. 70 B8
Dombarovskiy 29 D6
Dominica ■ 87 C7
Dominican Rep. ■ 87 C5
Domo 49 F4
Domodóssola 20 A2
Domville, Mt. 63 A5
Don →, *Russia* 25 D4
Don →, *U.K.* 10 C5
Don Benito 18 C3
Donald 62 C3
Donau = Dunărea → 17 F9
Donauwörth 14 D6
Doncaster 11 E6
Dondo, *Angola* 56 F2
Dondo, *Mozam.* 59 B6
Dondo, Teluk 39 D2
Donegal 11 D2
Donets → 25 D5
Donetsk 25 D4
Donggala 39 E1
Dongola 53 E5
Dongou 56 D3
Dongting Hu 35 D6
Dongxing 35 D5
Donington, C. 62 B2
Donnelly's Crossing 64 A5
Donostia = San Sebastián 19 A5
Dora Báltea → 20 B2
Dorchester, C. 68 B3
Dordogne → 12 D3
Dordrecht 14 C3
Dori 55 F4
Dornbirn 14 E5
Dorohoi 17 E8

Döröö Nuur 34 B4
Dorrigo 63 B5
Dortmund 14 C4
Doruma 57 D5
Dos Bahías, C. 95 E3
Dos Hermanas 18 D3
Dosso 55 F5
Dothan 74 D5
Douai 13 A5
Douala 56 D1
Douarnenez 12 B1
Double Island Pt. 63 A5
Doubs → 13 C6
Doubtful Sd. 65 F2
Doubtless B. 64 A5
Douentza 55 F4
Douglas, *U.K.* 11 D4
Douglas, *U.S.A.* 83 E8
Doumé 56 D2
Dourados 94 A6
Douro → 18 B1
Dover, *Australia* 62 D4
Dover, *U.K.* 11 F7
Dover, Str. of 11 F7
Dovrefjell 8 F9
Dowlat Yār 45 C6
Dowlatābād 44 D4
Dowshī 45 C7
Draa, Oued → 54 C2
Drăgăşani 22 B5
Dragichyn 17 B7
Dragoman, Prokhod 22 C4
Draguignan 13 E7
Drake 63 A5
Drakensberg 59 E5
Dráma 22 D5
Drammen 9 G10
Drau = Drava → 20 B7
Drava → 20 B7
Dresden 15 C7
Dreux 12 B4
Drina → 20 B7
Drini → 22 C2
Drochia 17 D8
Drogheda 11 E3
Drogichin = Dragichyn 17 B7
Drogobych = Drohobych 17 D6
Drohobych 17 D6
Droichead Atha = Drogheda 11 E3
Dromedary, C. 63 C5
Drumheller 71 C8
Drummond Pt. 62 B2
Drut → 17 B10
Drygalski I. 96 A11
Dschang 55 G7
Ḑubā 47 F3
Dubai = Dubayy 44 E3
Dubăsari 17 E9
Dubăsari Vdkhr. 17 E9
Dubawnt → 70 B9
Dubawnt, L. 70 B9
Dubayy 44 E3
Dubbo 63 B4
Dublin, *Ireland* 11 E3
Dublin, *U.S.A.* 75 C6
Dubno 17 C7
Dubossary = Dubăsari 17 E9
Dubossary Vdkhr. = Dubăsari Vdkhr. 17 E9
Dubovka 24 D5
Dubréka 55 G2
Dubrovitsa = Dubrovytsya 17 C8
Dubrovnik 20 C7
Dubrovytsya 17 C8
Dudhi 40 E4
Dudinka 30 C6
Duero = Douro → 18 B1
Dugi Otok 20 B5
Duisburg 14 C4
Dukelský Průsmyk 16 D5
Dukhān 44 E2
Duki 42 D6
Duku 55 F7
Dulce → 94 C4
Dulit, Banjaran 37 D4
Duluth 77 B8
Dum Duma 41 D10
Dum Hadjer 53 F2
Dumaguete 38 C2
Dumai 37 D2
Dumaran 38 B1
Dumfries 11 D5
Dumyât 52 B5
Dún Dealgan = Dundalk 11 D3
Dun Laoghaire 11 E3
Duna = Dunărea → 17 F9
Dunaj = Dunărea → 17 F9
Dunakeszi 16 E4
Dunărea → 17 F9
Dunaújváros 16 E4
Dunav = Dunărea → 17 F9
Dunback 65 F4
Dunbar 10 D5
Duncan 78 B5
Dundalk 11 D3
Dundee, *S. Africa* 59 D6
Dundee, *U.K.* 10 C5
Dundoo 63 A3
Dunedin 65 F4
Dunfermline 10 C5
Dungarvan 11 E3
Dungog 63 B5
Dungu 57 D5
Dunhuang 34 B4
Dunkerque 12 A5
Dunkirk = Dunkerque 12 A5
Dunkwa 55 G4
Dúnleary = Dun Laoghaire 11 E3
Dunolly 62 C3
Dunqul 52 D5
Dunstan Mts. 65 F3
Durance → 13 E6
Durango, *Mexico* 84 C4
Durango, *Spain* 19 A4
Durazno 94 C5
Durazzo = Durrësi 22 D2
Durban 59 D6
Düren 14 C4
Durg 40 G3
Durgapur 40 F6
Durham, *U.K.* 11 D6
Durham, *U.S.A.* 75 B8
Durham Downs 63 A4
Durmitor 22 C2
Durrësi 22 D2
Dursunbey 23 E7
D'Urville, Tanjung 39 E5
D'Urville I. 65 D5
Dusa Mareb 49 F4
Dushak 29 F7
Dushanbe 29 F7
Dusky Sd. 65 F2
Düsseldorf 14 C4
Dutch Harbor 71 C3
Duwādimi 47 F6
Duyun 35 D5
Düzce 46 B2
Duzdab = Zāhedān 45 D5
Dvina, Severnaya → 28 C5
Dvinsk = Daugavpils 24 B2
Dwarka 43 H6
Dyatlovo = Dzyatlava 17 B7
Dyer, C. 68 B4
Dyer Plateau 96 B3
Dyersburg 79 A9
Dymer 17 C10
Dynevor Downs 63 A3
Dzamin Üüd 35 B6
Dzerzhinsk 24 B5
Dzhambul = Zhambyl 29 E8
Dzhankoy 25 D3
Dzhardzhan 30 C10
Dzhezkazgan = Zhezqazghan 29 E7
Dzhizak = Jizzakh 29 E7
Działdowa 16 B5
Dzierzoniów 16 C3
Dzungaria = Junggar Pendi 34 B3
Dzungarian Gate = Alataw Shankou 34 B3
Dzuumod 35 B5
Dzyarzhynsk 17 B8
Dzyatlava 17 B7

## E

Earnslaw, Mt. 65 F3
East Bengal 41 E7
East Beskids = Vychodné Beskydy 17 D5
East C. 64 B8
East China Sea 35 C7
East Falkland 95 G5
East Kilbride 10 D4
East London 59 E5
East Main = Eastmain 69 C3
East Orange 73 D8
East St. Louis 77 F9
East Toorale 63 B4
Eastbourne, *N.Z.* 65 D6
Eastbourne, *U.K.* 11 F7
Eastern Ghats 43 N11
Eastmain 69 C3
Eastmain → 69 C3
Eau Claire 77 C9
Eberswalde Finow 15 B7
Ebolowa 56 D2
Ebro → 19 B6
Eceabat 23 D6
Ech Cheliff 54 A5
Echo Bay 70 B8
Echuca 63 C3
Ecija 18 D3
Ecuador ■ 90 D3
Ed Dâmer 53 E5
Ed Debba 53 E5
Ed Dueim 53 F5
Edd 49 E3
Eddystone Pt. 62 D4
Édea 56 D2
Eden 63 C4
Eder → 14 C5
Édhessa 23 D4
Edievale 65 F3
Edinburg 78 F4
Edinburgh 10 D5
Ediniţa 17 D8
Edirne 22 D6
Edithburgh 62 C2
Edmonton 71 C8
Edmundston 69 D4
Edremit 23 E6
Edremit Körfezi 23 E6
Edson 71 C8
Edward → 62 C3
Edward, L. 57 E5
Edward VII Land 96 C17
Edwards Plateau 78 D3
Égadi, Ísole 21 F4
Eger = Cheb 16 C1
Eger 16 E5
Egersund 9 G9
Egmont, C. 64 C5
Egmont, Mt. 64 C6
Eğridir 46 C2
Eğridir Gölü 46 C2
Egypt ■ 52 C5
Eibar 19 A4
Eidsvold 63 A5
Eifel 14 C4
Eigg 10 C3
Eil 49 F4
Eildon, L. 63 C4
Eindhoven 14 C3
Eire = Ireland ■ 11 E3
Eirunepé 91 E5
Eisenach 14 C6
Eisenerz 15 E8
Eivissa = Ibiza 19 C6
Eketahuna 64 D6
Ekibastuz 29 D8
El Aaiún 54 C2
El Alamein 52 B4
El Aricha 54 B4
El 'Arîsh 52 B5
El Asnam = Ech Cheliff 54 A5
El Bawiti 52 C4
El Bayadh 54 B5
El Callao 90 B6
El Centro 82 D5
El Cerro 91 G6
El Cuy 95 D3
El Cuyo 85 C7
El Dere 49 G4
El Diviso 90 C3
El Djouf 55 D3
El Dorado, *Ark., U.S.A.* 79 C7
El Dorado, *Kans., U.S.A.* 78 A5
El Dorado, *Venezuela* 90 B6
El Escorial 18 B3
El Faiyûm 52 C5
El Fâsher 53 F4
El Ferrol 18 A1
El Fuerte 84 B3
El Gal 49 E5

| Name | Page | Grid |
|---|---|---|
| El Geneina = Al Junaynah | 53 | F3 |
| El Geteina | 53 | F5 |
| El Gîza | 52 | C5 |
| El Iskandarîya | 52 | B4 |
| El Jadida | 54 | B3 |
| El Jebelein | 53 | F5 |
| El Kab | 53 | E5 |
| El Kala | 54 | A6 |
| El Kamlin | 53 | E5 |
| El Kef | 54 | A6 |
| El Khandaq | 53 | E5 |
| El Khârga | 52 | C5 |
| El Khartûm | 53 | E5 |
| El Khartûm Bahrî | 53 | E5 |
| El Laqâwa | 53 | F4 |
| El Mafâza | 53 | F5 |
| El Mahalla el Kubra | 52 | B5 |
| El Mansûra | 52 | B5 |
| El Minyâ | 52 | C5 |
| El Obeid | 53 | F5 |
| El Odaiya | 53 | F4 |
| El Oued | 54 | B6 |
| El Paso | 83 | E9 |
| El Prat de Llobregat | 19 | B7 |
| El Puerto de Santa María | 18 | D2 |
| El Qâhira | 52 | B5 |
| El Qantara | 52 | B5 |
| El Qasr | 52 | C4 |
| El Reno | 78 | B5 |
| El Salvador ■ | 85 | E7 |
| El Shallal | 52 | D5 |
| El Suweis | 52 | C5 |
| El Tigre | 90 | B6 |
| El Tocuyo | 90 | B5 |
| El Turbio | 95 | G2 |
| El Uqsur | 52 | C5 |
| El Vigía | 90 | B4 |
| El Wak | 57 | D8 |
| El Wuz | 53 | E5 |
| Elat | 47 | E3 |
| Elâzığ | 46 | C4 |
| Elba | 20 | C3 |
| Elbasani | 22 | D3 |
| Elbe → | 14 | B5 |
| Elbert, Mt. | 83 | A9 |
| Elbeuf | 12 | B4 |
| Elbidtan | 46 | C4 |
| Elbing = Elbląg | 16 | A4 |
| Elbląg | 16 | A4 |
| Elbrus | 25 | E5 |
| Elburz Mts. = Alborz, Reshteh-ye Kūhhā-ye | 44 | B3 |
| Elche | 19 | C5 |
| Elda | 19 | C5 |
| Elde → | 15 | B6 |
| Eldoret | 57 | D7 |
| Elektrostal | 24 | B4 |
| Elephant I. | 96 | A4 |
| Eleuthera | 86 | A4 |
| Elgin, *U.K.* | 10 | C5 |
| Elgin, *U.S.A.* | 72 | C1 |
| Elgon, Mt. | 57 | D6 |
| Eliase | 39 | F4 |
| Elisabethville = Lubumbashi | 59 | A5 |
| Elista | 25 | D5 |
| Elizabeth, *Australia* | 62 | B2 |
| Elizabeth, *U.S.A.* | 73 | D8 |
| Elizabeth City | 75 | A9 |
| Elizabethton | 75 | A6 |
| Ełk | 16 | B6 |
| Elkhart | 72 | D3 |
| Elkhovo | 22 | C6 |
| Elko | 80 | E6 |
| Ellery, Mt. | 63 | C4 |
| Ellesmere, L. | 65 | G5 |
| Ellice Is. = Tuvalu ■ | 64 | K12 |
| Elliston | 62 | B1 |
| Ellore = Eluru | 40 | J3 |
| Ellsworth Land | 96 | B2 |
| Ellsworth Mts. | 96 | B2 |
| Elmore | 63 | C3 |
| Elmshorn | 14 | B5 |
| Eltham | 64 | C6 |
| Eluru | 40 | J3 |
| Elvas | 18 | C2 |
| Elx = Elche | 19 | C5 |
| Ely | 11 | E7 |
| Emāmrūd | 44 | B3 |
| Emba = Embi | 29 | E6 |
| Emba → = Embi → | 29 | E6 |
| Embarcación | 94 | A4 |
| Embi | 29 | E6 |
| Embi → | 29 | E6 |
| Embrun | 13 | D7 |
| Embu | 57 | E7 |
| Emden | 14 | B4 |
| Emerson | 71 | D10 |
| Emet | 23 | E7 |
| Emi Koussi | 53 | E2 |
| Emine, Nos | 22 | C6 |
| Emmen | 14 | B4 |
| Empalme | 84 | B2 |
| Empangeni | 59 | D6 |
| Empedrado | 94 | B5 |
| Empty Quarter = Rub' al Khali | 48 | D4 |
| Ems → | 14 | B4 |
| En Nahud | 53 | F4 |
| Enaratoli | 39 | E5 |
| Enare = Inarijärvi | 8 | E13 |
| Encanto, C. | 38 | A2 |
| Encarnación | 94 | B5 |
| Encounter B. | 62 | C2 |
| Ende | 39 | F2 |
| Enderby Land | 96 | A9 |
| Enewetak Atoll | 64 | H11 |
| Enez | 23 | D6 |
| Engadin | 13 | C9 |
| Engaño, C. | 38 | A2 |
| Engels | 24 | C6 |
| Enggano | 37 | F2 |
| Engkilili | 37 | D4 |
| England □ | 11 | E6 |
| Englewood | 76 | F2 |
| English Bazar = Ingraj Bazar | 40 | E7 |
| English Channel | 11 | F5 |
| Enid | 78 | A5 |
| Enna | 21 | F5 |
| Ennedi | 53 | E3 |
| Enngonia | 63 | A4 |
| Ennis | 11 | E2 |
| Enniskillen | 11 | D3 |
| Enns → | 15 | D8 |
| Enschede | 14 | B4 |
| Ensenada | 84 | A1 |
| Entebbe | 57 | D6 |
| Entroncamento | 18 | C1 |
| Enugu | 55 | G6 |
| Enugu Ezike | 55 | G6 |
| Eólie, Ís. | 21 | E5 |
| Épernay | 13 | B5 |
| Ephesus | 23 | F6 |
| Épinal | 13 | B7 |
| Epukiro | 58 | C3 |
| Equatorial Guinea ■ | 56 | D1 |
| Er Rahad | 53 | F5 |
| Er Rif | 54 | A4 |
| Er Roseires | 53 | F5 |
| Erāwadī Myit = Irrawaddy → | 41 | K10 |
| Erbil = Arbīl | 46 | C6 |
| Ercıyaş Dağı | 46 | C3 |
| Érd | 16 | E4 |
| Erdek | 23 | D6 |
| Erebus, Mt. | 96 | B15 |
| Erechim | 94 | B6 |
| Ereğli, *Konya, Turkey* | 46 | C3 |
| Ereğli, *Zonguldak, Turkey* | 46 | B2 |
| Eresma → | 18 | B3 |
| Erewadi Myitwanya | 41 | K10 |
| Erfurt | 15 | C6 |
| Ergani | 46 | C4 |
| Érice | 21 | E4 |
| Erie | 73 | C5 |
| Erie, L. | 72 | C5 |
| Erigavo | 49 | E4 |
| Erímanthos | 23 | F3 |
| Erimo-misaki | 32 | F12 |
| Eritrea ■ | 49 | E2 |
| Erlangen | 15 | D6 |
| Ermenak | 46 | C3 |
| Ermoúpolis = Síros | 23 | F5 |
| Ernakulam = Cochin | 43 | Q10 |
| Erne, Lower L. | 11 | D3 |
| Erode | 43 | P10 |
| Eromanga | 63 | A3 |
| Erramala Hills | 43 | M11 |
| Ertis → = Irtysh → | 28 | C7 |
| Erzgebirge | 15 | C7 |
| Erzincan | 46 | C4 |
| Erzurum | 46 | C5 |
| Es Sahrâ' Esh Sharqîya | 52 | C5 |
| Es Sînâ' | 52 | C5 |
| Esbjerg | 9 | G9 |
| Esch-sur-Alzette | 13 | B6 |
| Escuinapa | 84 | C3 |
| Eşfahān | 44 | C2 |
| Esh Sham = Dimashq | 46 | D4 |
| Esil → = Ishim → | 29 | D8 |
| Eskilstuna | 9 | G11 |
| Eskimo Pt. = Arviat | 70 | B10 |
| Eskişehir | 46 | C2 |
| Esla → | 18 | B2 |
| Eslāmābād-e Gharb | 46 | D6 |
| Eşme | 23 | E7 |
| Esmeraldas | 90 | C3 |
| Esperance | 60 | G3 |
| Esperanza | 94 | C4 |
| Espichel, C. | 18 | C1 |
| Espinal | 90 | C4 |
| Espinazo, Sierra del = Espinhaço, Serra do | 93 | F5 |
| Espinhaço, Serra do | 93 | F5 |
| Espírito Santo □ | 93 | G5 |
| Esquel | 95 | E2 |
| Esquina | 94 | C5 |
| Essaouira | 54 | B3 |
| Essen | 14 | C4 |
| Essequibo → | 90 | B7 |
| Esslingen | 14 | D5 |
| Estados, I. de Los | 95 | G4 |
| Estância | 93 | E6 |
| Estevan | 71 | D9 |
| Estonia ■ | 24 | B2 |
| Estrêla, Serra da | 18 | B2 |
| Estremoz | 18 | C2 |
| Estrondo, Serra do | 92 | D4 |
| Esztergom | 16 | E4 |
| Etadunna | 62 | A2 |
| Étampes | 12 | B5 |
| Etawah | 42 | F11 |
| Ethiopia ■ | 49 | F2 |
| Etna | 21 | F5 |
| Etosha Pan | 58 | B3 |
| Euboea = Évvoia | 23 | E5 |
| Eucumbene, L. | 63 | C4 |
| Eufaula | 74 | D5 |
| Eugene | 80 | C2 |
| Eugowra | 63 | B4 |
| Eulo | 63 | A4 |
| Euphrates = Furāt, Nahr al → | 47 | E6 |
| Eureka | 80 | E1 |
| Euroa | 63 | C4 |
| Europa, I. | 59 | J8 |
| Europa, Picos de | 18 | A3 |
| Europa, Pta. de | 18 | D3 |
| Europa Pt. = Europa, Pta. de | 18 | D3 |
| Evans Head | 63 | A5 |
| Evanston | 72 | C2 |
| Evansville | 72 | F2 |
| Everard, L. | 62 | B1 |
| Everest, Mt. | 40 | C6 |
| Everett | 80 | B2 |
| Everglades National Park | 75 | G7 |
| Evinayong | 56 | D2 |
| Évora | 18 | C2 |
| Évreux | 12 | B4 |
| Évros → | 22 | D6 |
| Evry | 12 | B5 |
| Évvoia | 23 | E5 |
| Ewo | 56 | E2 |
| Exaltación | 91 | F5 |
| Exeter | 11 | F5 |
| Exmoor | 11 | F5 |
| Exmouth | 11 | F5 |
| Extremadura □ | 18 | C2 |
| Eyasi, L. | 57 | E6 |
| Eyre (North), L. | 62 | A2 |
| Eyre (South), L. | 62 | A2 |
| Eyre, L. | 60 | F6 |
| Eyre Cr. → | 62 | A2 |
| Eyre Mts. | 65 | F3 |
| Eyre Pen. | 62 | B2 |
| Ezine | 23 | E6 |

## F

| Name | Page | Grid |
|---|---|---|
| F.Y.R.O.M. = Macedonia ■ | 22 | D3 |
| Fabriano | 20 | C4 |
| Facatativá | 90 | C4 |
| Fachi | 55 | E7 |
| Fada | 53 | E3 |
| Fada-n-Gourma | 55 | F5 |
| Faddeyevskiy, Ostrov | 31 | B12 |

Fāḍilī ........ 47 F7
Faenza ....... 20 B3
Færoe Is. = Føroyar ..... 6 C4
Făgăras ...... 17 F7
Fagnano, L. ... 95 G3
Fahraj ........ 45 D4
Fahūd ........ 44 F4
Fair Isle ...... 10 B6
Fairbanks ..... 71 B5
Fairfield, *Ala., U.S.A.* ...... 74 C4
Fairfield, *Calif., U.S.A.* ...... 80 F2
Fairlie ........ 65 F4
Fairweather, Mt. 71 C6
Faisalabad .... 42 D8
Faizabad ...... 40 D4
Fakfak ........ 39 E4
Falaise ....... 12 B3
Falam ........ 41 F9
Falconara Maríttima ... 20 C4
Falcone, C. .... 20 D2
Faleshty = Făleşti ...... 17 E8
Făleşti ........ 17 E8
Falkland Is. □ . 95 G5
Falkland Sd. ... 95 G5
Fall River ..... 73 D10
Falmouth ..... 11 F4
False B. ...... 58 E3
Fălticeni ...... 17 E8
Falun ........ 9 F11
Famagusta .... 46 D3
Fandriana ..... 59 J9
Fano ......... 20 C4
Fao = Al Fāw . 47 E7
Faradje ....... 57 D5
Farafangana .. 59 J9
Farāh ........ 42 C3
Farāh □ ...... 42 C3
Faranah ...... 55 F2
Farasān, Jazā'ir 49 D3
Farasan Is. = Farasān, Jazā'ir ...... 49 D3
Fareham ...... 11 F6
Farewell, C. ... 64 D5
Farewell C. = Farvel, Kap .. 68 C6
Farghona ..... 29 E8
Fargo ........ 76 B6
Farim ........ 55 F1
Farīmān ...... 45 C4
Farina ........ 62 B2
Faro, *Brazil* ... 92 C2
Faro, *Portugal* . 18 D2
Farrāshband .. 44 D3
Farrell Flat .... 62 B2
Farrukhabad-cum-Fatehgarh ... 42 F11
Fārs □ ....... 44 D3
Fársala ....... 23 E4
Fartak, Râs .... 47 E3
Farvel, Kap ... 68 C6
Fāryāb □ ..... 45 B6
Fasā ......... 44 D3
Fasano ....... 21 D6
Fastiv ........ 17 C9
Fastov = Fastiv 17 C9
Fatagar, Tanjung 39 E4
Fatehgarh .... 42 F11
Fatehpur, *Raj., India* ....... 42 F9
Fatehpur, *Ut. P., India* ....... 40 E3
Favara ....... 21 F4
Favignana .... 21 F4
Faya-Largeau .. 53 E2
Fayd ......... 47 F5
Fayetteville, *Ark., U.S.A.* . 79 A6
Fayetteville, *N.C., U.S.A.* . 75 B8
Fazilka ....... 42 D9
Fdérik ........ 54 D2
Feather → ... 80 F3
Featherston ... 65 D6
Fécamp ...... 12 B4
Fehmarn ..... 15 A6
Feilding ...... 64 D6
Feira de Santana 93 E6
Feldkirch ..... 14 E5
Felipe Carrillo Puerto ...... 85 D7
Felixstowe .... 11 F7
Fengjie ....... 35 C5
Fenyang ...... 35 C6
Feodosiya .... 25 D4
Ferdows ...... 44 C4
Ferfer ........ 49 F4
Fergana = Farghona ... 29 E8
Fermo ........ 20 C4
Fernando de Noronha .... 92 C7
Fernando Póo = Bioko ...... 56 D1
Ferozepore = Firozpur .... 42 D9
Ferrara ....... 20 B3
Ferreñafe ..... 91 E3
Ferret, C. ..... 12 D3
Ferrol = El Ferrol ...... 18 A1
Fès .......... 54 B4
Feshi ........ 56 F3
Feteşti ....... 22 B6
Fetlar ........ 10 A6
Feuilles → ... 68 C3
Fezzan ....... 52 C2
Fianarantsoa .. 59 J9
Fianga ....... 53 G2
Ficksburg ..... 59 D5
Fieri ......... 23 D2
Figeac ........ 12 D5
Figueira da Foz 18 B1
Figueras ...... 19 A7
Figuig ........ 54 B4
Fiji ■ ........ 64 L12
Filiatrá ....... 23 F3
Filyos → ..... 46 B3
Fingōe ....... 59 A6
Finike ........ 46 C2
Finisterre, C. .. 18 A1
Finke → ..... 62 A2
Finland ■ ..... 8 F13
Finland, G. of . 9 G13
Finlay → ..... 70 C7
Finley ........ 63 C4
Finniss, C. .... 62 B1
Fiora → ...... 20 C3
Firat = Furāt, Nahr al → .. 47 E6
Firenze ....... 20 C3
Firozabad ..... 42 F11
Firozpur ...... 42 D9
Fīrūzābād ..... 44 D3
Fīrūzkūh ...... 44 C3
Fish → ...... 58 D3
Fishguard ..... 11 E4
Fitri, L. ....... 53 F2
Fitz Roy ...... 95 F3
Fiume = Rijeka 20 B5
Fizi .......... 57 E5
Flagstaff ...... 83 C7
Flaming Gorge Reservoir ... 81 E9
Flamingo, Teluk 39 F5
Flandre ....... 14 C2
Flathead L. .... 81 B6
Flattery, C. .... 80 A1
Flensburg ..... 14 A5
Flers ......... 12 B3
Flesko, Tanjung 39 D2
Flin Flon ...... 71 C9
Flinders → ... 61 D7
Flinders I. ..... 62 C4
Flinders Ras. .. 62 B2
Flint ......... 72 C4
Flint I. ........ 65 L15
Flinton ....... 63 A4
Florence = Firenze ..... 20 C3
Florence, *Ala., U.S.A.* ...... 74 B4
Florence, *S.C., U.S.A.* ...... 75 B8
Florence, L. ... 62 A2
Flores ........ 39 F2
Flores Sea .... 39 F2
Floreşti ....... 17 E9
Floriano ...... 92 D5
Florianópolis .. 94 B7
Florida ....... 94 C5
Florida □ ..... 75 F6
Florida, Straits of .......... 86 B3
Flórina ....... 23 D3
Florø ......... 8 F9
Fluk ......... 39 E3
Flushing = Vlissingen .. 14 C2
Fly → ....... 61 B7
Flying Fish, C. . 96 B1
Foça ......... 23 E6
Focşani ....... 17 F8
Fóggia ....... 20 D5
Föhr ......... 14 A5
Foix ......... 12 F4
Foligno ....... 20 C4
Folkestone .... 11 F7
Fond du Lac .. 77 D10
Fondi ........ 20 D4
Fonsagrada ... 18 A2
Fonseca, G. de 85 E7
Fontainebleau . 13 B5
Fonte Boa .... 90 D5
Fontenay-le-Comte ...... 12 C3
Foochow = Fuzhou ..... 35 D6
Forbes ....... 63 B4
Ford's Bridge .. 63 A4
Forécariah .... 55 G2
Forestier Pen. . 62 D4
Forfar ........ 10 C5
Forlì ......... 20 B4
Formentera ... 19 C6
Formentor, C. de 19 C7
Former Yugoslav Republic of Macedonia = Macedonia ■ 22 D3
Fórmia ....... 20 D4
Formosa = Taiwan ■ ... 35 D7
Formosa ...... 94 B5
Formosa, Serra 93 E3
Formosa Bay .. 57 E8
Føroyar = Føroyar ..... 6 C4
Føroyar ...... 6 C4
Forrest ....... 62 C3
Forsayth ...... 61 D7
Forst ......... 15 C8
Forster ....... 63 B5
Fort Albany ... 69 C2
Fort Collins ... 76 E2
Fort-de-France . 87 D7
Fort de Possel = Possel ...... 56 C3
Fort Dodge ... 77 D7
Fort Franklin .. 70 B7
Fort Good-Hope 70 B7
Fort Hertz = Putao ...... 41 D11
Fort Lauderdale 75 F7
Fort Liard ..... 70 B7
Fort Macleod .. 71 D8
Fort MacMahon 54 C5
Fort McPherson 70 B6
Fort Miribel ... 54 C5
Fort Myers .... 75 F7
Fort Norman .. 70 B7
Fort Peck L. ... 81 B10
Fort Pierce .... 75 F7
Fort Portal .... 57 D6
Fort Providence 70 B8
Fort Resolution 70 B8
Fort Rosebery = Mansa ...... 57 G5
Fort Rupert = Waskaganish 69 C3
Fort Sandeman 42 D6
Fort Scott ..... 79 A6
Fort Severn ... 69 C2
Fort Shevchenko 29 E6
Fort Simpson . 70 B7
Fort Smith, *Canada* ..... 70 B8
Fort Smith, *U.S.A.* ...... 79 B6
Fort Trinquet = Bir Mogrein . 54 C2
Fort Walton Beach ...... 74 D4
Fort Wayne ... 72 D3
Fort William ... 10 C4
Fort Worth .... 78 C5
Fort Yukon .... 71 B5
Fortaleza ..... 92 C6
Forūr ........ 44 E3
Foshan ....... 35 D6
Fossano ...... 20 B1
Fougamou .... 56 E2
Fougères ..... 12 B3
Foula ........ 10 A5
Foumban ..... 55 G7
Foúrnoi ...... 23 F6
Fouta Djalon .. 55 F2
Foveaux Str. .. 65 G3
Foxe Basin .... 68 B3
Foxe Chan. ... 68 B2
Foxe Pen. ..... 68 B3
Foxton ....... 64 D6
Foz do Gregório 91 E4
Foz do Iguaçu . 94 B6
Franca ....... 93 G4
Francavilla Fontana .... 21 D6
France ■ ..... 13 C5
Frances ...... 62 C3
Franceville .... 56 E2
Franche-Comté 13 C6
Francistown ... 59 C5
Frankfurt, *Brandenburg, Germany* ... 15 B8
Frankfurt, *Hessen, Germany* ... 14 C5
Fränkische Alb 15 D6

Franklin B. 70 B7
Franklin I. 96 B15
Franklin Mts. 70 B7
Franklin Str. 70 A10
Frankston 63 C4
Frantsa Iosifa, Zemlya 28 A6
Franz 69 D2
Franz Josef Land = Frantsa Iosifa, Zemlya 28 A6
Fraser → 71 D7
Fraser I. 63 A5
Fraserburgh 10 C5
Fray Bentos 94 C5
Fredericksburg 73 E7
Fredericton 69 D4
Fredrikstad 9 G10
Freeport, *Bahamas* 86 A4
Freeport, *U.S.A.* 77 D10
Freetown 55 G2
Fregenal de la Sierra 18 C2
Freibourg = Fribourg 13 C7
Freiburg 14 E4
Freire 95 D2
Freising 15 D6
Freistadt 15 D8
Fréjus 13 E7
Fremont 82 B2
French Guiana ■ 92 B3
French Polynesia ■ 65 M16
Fresco → 92 D3
Freshfield, C. 96 A14
Fresnillo 84 C4
Fresno 82 B3
Freycinet Pen. 62 D4
Fria, C. 58 B2
Frías 94 B3
Fribourg 13 C7
Friedrichshafen 14 E5
Friendly Is. = Tonga ■ 65 L13
Frobisher B. 68 B4
Frobisher Bay = Iqaluit 68 B4
Frome, L. 62 B2
Frome Downs 62 B2
Front Range 81 E11
Frosinone 20 D4
Frunze = Bishkek 29 E8
Frutal 93 F4
Frýdek-Místek 16 D4
Fuchou = Fuzhou 35 D6
Fuengirola 18 D3
Fuentes de Oñoro 18 B2
Fuerte → 84 B3
Fuerte Olimpo 91 H7
Fuerteventura 54 C2
Fuhai 34 B3
Fuji-San 32 B6
Fujian □ 35 D6
Fujinomiya 32 B6
Fujisawa 32 B6
Fukien = Fujian □ 35 D6
Fukuchiyama 32 B4
Fukui 32 A5
Fukuoka 32 C2
Fukushima 33 G12
Fukuyama 32 B3
Fulda 14 C5
Fulda → 14 C5
Fullerton 82 D4
Funabashi 32 B7
Funchal 54 B1
Fundación 90 A4
Fundão 18 B2
Fundy, B. of 69 D4
Funtua 55 F6
Furāt, Nahr al → 47 E6
Furneaux Group 62 D4
Fürstenwalde 15 B8
Fürth 14 D6
Fury and Hecla Str. 68 B2
Fusagasuga 90 C4
Fushun 35 B7
Futuna 64 L12
Fuxin 35 B7
Fuyuan 35 B8
Fuzhou 35 D6
Fyn 9 G10

## G

Gabela 56 G2
Gabès 54 B7
Gabès, G. de 52 B1
Gabon ■ 56 E2
Gaborone 59 C5
Gabrovo 22 C5
Gachsārān 44 D2
Gadag 43 M9
Gadarwara 43 H11
Gadhada 43 J7
Gadsden 74 B4
Gadwal 43 L10
Gafsa 54 B6
Gagnoa 55 G3
Gagnon 69 C4
Gaillimh = Galway 11 E2
Gainesville, *Fla., U.S.A.* 75 E6
Gainesville, *Ga., U.S.A.* 75 B6
Gainesville, *Tex., U.S.A.* 78 C5
Gairdner, L. 62 B2
Galangue 58 A3
Galashiels 10 D5
Galaţi 17 F9
Galatina 21 D7
Galcaio 49 F4
Galdhøpiggen 8 F9
Galela 39 D3
Galesburg 77 E9
Galich 24 B5
Galicia □ 18 A2
Galilee, Sea of = Yam Kinneret 46 D3
Gallabat 53 F6
Gállego → 19 B5
Gallegos → 95 G3
Gallinas, Pta. 90 A4
Gallipoli = Gelibolu 23 D6
Gallípoli 21 D6
Gällivare 8 E12
Galloway, Mull of 11 D4
Galong 63 B4
Galveston 79 E6
Gálvez 94 C4
Galway 11 E2
Galway B. 11 E2
Gambaga 55 F4
Gambela 53 G5
Gambia ■ 55 F1
Gambia → 55 F1
Gambier Is. 62 C2
Gamboma 56 E3
Gan Jiang → 35 D6
Ganāveh 44 D2
Gäncä 25 E6
Gand = Gent 14 C2
Ganda 58 A2
Gandak → 40 E5
Gandava 42 E5
Gander 69 D5
Gandhi Sagar 43 G9
Gandi 55 F6
Gandía 19 C5
Ganedidalem = Gani 39 E3
Ganga → 41 F8
Ganganagar 42 E8
Gangara 55 F6
Gangaw 41 F10
Gangdisê Shan 40 B3
Ganges = Ganga → 41 F8
Gangtok 41 D7
Gani 39 E3
Gansu □ 34 C5
Ganta 55 G3
Gantheaume, C. 62 C2
Gantsevichi = Hantsavichy 17 B8
Ganyem 39 E6
Ganzhou 35 D6
Gaoua 55 F4
Gaoual 55 F2
Gaoxiong 35 D7
Gap 13 D7
Gar 34 C2
Garabogazköl Aylagy 29 E6
Garanhuns 92 D6
Garawe 55 H3
Gard 49 F4
Garda, L. di 20 B3
Garden City 78 A3
Garden Grove 82 D4
Gardēz 42 C6
Gargano, Mte. 20 D5
Garigliano → 20 D4
Garland 81 E7
Garm 29 F8
Garmisch-Partenkirchen 14 E6
Garmsār 44 C3
Garoe 49 F4
Garonne → 12 D3
Garoua 53 G1
Garrison Res. = Sakakawea, L. 76 B4
Garry, L. 70 B9
Garsen 57 E8
Garvie Mts. 65 F3
Garwa = Garoua 53 G1
Gary 72 D2
Garzê 34 C5
Garzón 90 C3
Gasan Kuli = Hasan Kuli 29 F6
Gascogne 12 E4
Gascogne, G. de 12 D2
Gascony = Gascogne 12 E4
Gashaka 55 G7
Gaspé 69 D4
Gaspé, C. de 69 D4
Gaspé, Pén. de 69 D4
Gasteiz = Vitoria 19 A4
Gastonia 75 B7
Gastre 95 E3
Gata, C. de 19 D4
Gata, Sierra de 18 B2
Gateshead 11 D6
Gauhati 41 D8
Gavāter 45 E5
Gávdhos 23 G5
Gävle 8 F11
Gawilgarh Hills 43 J10
Gawler 62 B2
Gaxun Nur 34 B5
Gaya, *India* 40 E5
Gaya, *Niger* 55 F5
Gayndah 63 A5
Gaysin = Haysyn 17 D9
Gayvoron = Hayvoron 17 D9
Gaza 47 E3
Gaziantep 46 C4
Gazli 29 E7
Gdańsk 16 A4
Gdańska, Zatoka 16 A4
Gdov 24 B2
Gdynia 16 A4
Gebe 39 D3
Gebeit Mine 52 D6
Gebze 22 D7
Gedaref 53 F6
Gede, Tanjung 37 F3
Gediz → 23 E6
Gedser 9 H10
Geelong 63 C3
Geesthacht 14 B6
Geidam 53 F1
Geili 53 E5
Geita 57 E6
Gejiu 34 D5
Gela 21 F5
Geladi 49 F4
Gelehun 55 G2
Gelibolu 23 D6
Gelsenkirchen 14 C4
Gemas 37 D2
Gemena 56 D3
Gemerek 46 C4
Gemlik 23 D7
General Acha 94 D4
General Alvear, *Buenos Aires, Argentina* 94 D5
General Alvear, *Mendoza, Argentina* 94 D3
General Artigas 94 B5
General Belgrano 94 D5
General Guido 94 D5
General Juan Madariaga 94 D5
General La Madrid 94 D4
General MacArthur 38 B3
General Martin Miguel de Güemes 94 A4
General Paz 94 B5
General Pico 94 D4
General Pinedo 94 B4
General Santos 38 C3
General Villegas 94 D4
Geneva = Genève 13 C7

Geneva, L. = Léman, L. 13 C7
Genève 13 C7
Genil → 18 D3
Gennargentu, Mti. del 21 D2
Genoa = Génova 20 B2
Genoa 63 C4
Génova 20 B2
Génova, G. di 20 C2
Gent 14 C2
Georga, Zemlya 28 A5
George 58 E4
George → 68 C4
George, L., *N.S.W., Australia* 63 C4
George, L., *S. Austral., Australia* 62 C3
George, L., *Uganda* 57 D6
George River = Kangiqsualujjuaq 68 C4
George Sound 65 F2
George Town 36 C2
George V Land 96 A14
George VI Sound 96 B3
Georgetown, *Gambia* 55 F2
Georgetown, *Guyana* 90 B7
Georgia □ 75 C6
Georgia ■ 25 E5
Georgian B. 69 D2
Georgiu-Dezh = Liski 24 C4
Georgiyevsk 25 E5
Gera 15 C7
Geral de Goiás, Serra 93 E4
Geraldton 60 F1
Gerede 46 B3
Gereshk 42 D4
Gerlogubi 49 F4
Germany ■ 14 C6
Germiston 59 D5
Gerona 19 B7
Geser 39 E4
Getafe 18 B4
Gettysburg 73 E7
Getz Ice Shelf 96 B18
Ghaghara → 40 E5
Ghana ■ 55 G4
Ghanzi 58 C4
Ghardaïa 54 B5
Gharyān 52 B1
Ghat 54 D7
Ghawdex = Gozo 21 F5
Ghayl 47 G6
Ghazal, Bahr el →, *Chad* 53 F2
Ghazâl, Bahr el →, *Sudan* 57 C6
Ghazaouet 54 A4
Ghaziabad 42 E10
Ghazipur 40 E4
Ghaznı 42 C6
Ghaznī □ 42 C6
Ghèlinsor 49 F4
Ghent = Gent 14 C2
Ghizao 42 C4
Ghowr □ 42 C4
Ghugus 43 K11
Ghūrīān 42 B2
Gia Lai = Pleiku 36 B3
Gian 38 C3
Giarabub = Al Jaghbūb 52 C3
Giarre 21 F5
Gibraltar ■ 18 D3
Gibraltar, Str. of 18 E3
Gibson Desert 60 E4
Gidole 53 G6
Giessen 14 C5
Gifu 32 B5
Giglio 20 C3
Gijón 18 A3
Gila → 82 D5
Gīlān □ 46 C7
Gilbert Is. 64 J12
Gilgandra 63 B4
Gilgit 42 B9
Gilles, L. 62 B2
Gilmore 63 C4
Gimbi 53 G6
Gin Gin 63 A5
Ginir 49 F3
Giohar 49 G4
Gióna, Óros 23 E4
Girardot 90 C4
Giresun 46 B4
Girga 52 C5
Giridih 40 E6
Girilambone 63 B4
Girne = Kyrenia 46 D3
Girona = Gerona 19 B7
Gironde → 12 D3
Girvan 10 D4
Gisborne 64 C8
Gisenyi 57 E5
Gitega 57 E5
Giuba → 49 G3
Giurgiu 22 C5
Giza = El Gîza 52 C5
Giżycko 16 A5
Gjirokastra 23 D3
Gjoa Haven 70 B10
Glace Bay 69 D5
Gladstone, *Queens., Australia* 61 E9
Gladstone, *S. Austral., Australia* 62 B2
Glåma = Glomma → 9 G10
Glasgow 10 D4
Glazov 28 D6
Gleiwitz = Gliwice 16 C4
Glen Canyon National Recreation Area 83 B7
Glen Innes 63 A5
Glendale 82 C3
Glenelg 62 B2
Glenelg → 62 C3
Glenmorgan 63 A4
Glenorchy 62 D4
Glenreagh 63 B5
Glenrothes 10 C5
Glens Falls 73 C9
Gliwice 16 C4
Głogów 16 C3
Glomma → 9 G10
Glorieuses, Is. 59 G9
Gloucester, *Australia* 63 B5
Gloucester, *U.K.* 11 F5
Glusk 17 B9
Gmünd 15 D8
Gmunden 15 E7
Gniezno 16 B3
Go Cong 36 B3
Goa 43 M8
Goa □ 43 M8
Goalen Hd. 63 C5
Goalpara 41 D8
Goba, *Ethiopia* 49 F2
Goba, *Mozam.* 59 D6
Gobabis 58 C3
Gobi 35 B6
Gochas 58 C3
Godavari → 40 J4
Godavari Point 40 J4
Godhra 43 H8
Gods → 71 C10
Gods L. 71 C10
Godthåb 68 B5
Godwin Austen = K2 42 B10
Goeie Hoop, Kaap die = Good Hope, C. of 58 E3
Gogra = Ghaghara → 40 E5
Goiânia 93 F4
Goiás 93 F3
Goiás □ 93 E4
Goio-Ere 94 A6
Gojra 42 D8
Gökçeada 23 D5
Goktelk 41 F11
Gold Coast 63 A5
Golden Gate 80 G2
Goldsboro 75 B9
Goleniów 16 B2
Golfo Aranci 20 D2
Golspie 10 C5
Goma 57 E5
Gomel = Homyel 17 B10
Gomera 54 C1
Gómez Palacio 84 B4
Gomogomo 39 F4
Gomoh 40 F6
Gompa = Ganta 55 G3
Gonābād 44 C4
Gonaïves 87 C5
Gonbab-e Kāvūs 44 B3
Gonda 40 D3
Gonder 53 F6
Gönen 23 D6
Gonghe 34 C5
Gongolgon 63 B4
Goniri 53 F1
Good Hope, C. of 58 E3
Goodooga 63 A4
Goolgowi 63 B4
Goombalie 63 A4
Goondiwindi 63 A5
Gooray 63 A5
Gop 43 H6
Göppingen 14 D5
Gorakhpur 40 D4
Goražde 20 C7
Gordon → 62 D4
Gore, *Australia* 63 A5
Goré, *Chad* 53 G2
Gore, *Ethiopia* 53 G6
Gore, *N.Z.* 65 G3
Gorgān 44 B3
Gorgona, I. 90 C3
Gorizia 20 B4
Gorki = Nizhniy Novgorod 24 B5
Gorkiy = Nizhniy Novgorod 24 B5
Gorkovskoye Vdkhr. 24 B5
Görlitz 15 C8
Gorlovka = Horlivka 25 D4
Gorna Dzhumayo = Blagoevgrad 22 C4
Gorna Oryakhovitsa 22 C5
Gorno-Altay □ 29 D9
Gorno-Altaysk 29 D9
Gorno Slinkino = Gornopravdinsk 29 C8
Gornopravdinsk 29 C8
Gorodenka = Horodenka 17 D7
Gorodok = Horodok 17 D6
Gorokhov = Horokhiv 17 C7
Gorontalo 39 D2
Gorzów Wielkopolski 16 B2
Gosford 63 B5
Goslar 14 C6
Gospič 20 B5
Göta kanal 9 G11
Göteborg 9 G10
Gotha 14 C6
Gothenburg = Göteborg 9 G10
Gotland 9 G11
Göttingen 14 C5
Gottwaldov = Zlin 16 D3
Gouda 14 B3
Gouin, Rés. 69 D3
Goulburn 63 B4
Gounou-Gaya 53 G2
Gouri 53 E2
Gourma Rharous 55 E4
Gourock Ra. 63 C4
Governador Valadares 93 F5
Gowd-e Zirreh 42 E3
Goya 94 B5
Goyder Lagoon 62 A2
Goyllarisquisga 91 F3
Goz Beîda 53 F3
Gozo 21 F5
Graaff-Reinet 58 E4
Gračac 20 B5
Gracias a Dios, C. 86 D3
Grado 18 A2
Gradule 63 A4
Grafton 63 A5
Graham Bell, Os. 28 A7
Graham Land 96 A3
Grahamstown 59 E5
Grajaú 92 D4
Grajaú → 92 C5
Grampian Highlands = Grampian Mts. 10 C4
Grampian Mts. 10 C4
Gran Canaria 54 C1
Gran Chaco 94 B4
Gran Paradiso 20 B1
Gran Sasso d'Italia 20 C4
Granada, *Nic.* 85 E7
Granada, *Spain* 18 D4

Granby 69 D3
Grand Bahama 86 A4
Grand Bassam 55 G4
Grand Canyon 83 B6
Grand Cayman 86 C3
Grand Coulee Dam 80 B4
Grand Forks, *Canada* 71 D8
Grand Forks, *U.S.A.* 76 B6
Grand Island 76 E5
Grand Lahou 55 G3
Grand Rapids, *Canada* 71 C10
Grand Rapids, *U.S.A.* 72 C3
Grand St.-Bernard, Col du 13 D7
Grand Teton 81 D8
Grande →, *Argentina* 94 A3
Grande →, *Bolivia* 91 G6
Grande →, *Bahia, Brazil* 93 E5
Grande →, *Minas Gerais, Brazil* 93 G3
Grande, B. 95 G3
Grande, Rio → 79 F5
Grande Baleine, R. de la → 69 C3
Grande de Santiago → 84 C3
Granite City 77 F9
Granity 65 D4
Granja 92 C5
Granollers 19 B7
Grantham 11 E6
Granville 12 B3
Gras, L. de 70 B8
Grasse 13 E7
Grassmere 62 B3
Graulhet 12 E4
's-Gravenhage 14 B3
Gravesend 63 A5
Graz 15 E8
Great Abaco I. 86 A4
Great Australian Bight 60 G4
Great Barrier I. 64 B6
Great Barrier Reef 61 D8
Great Basin 80 F5
Great Bear → 70 B7
Great Bear L. 70 B7
Great Belt = Store Bælt 9 G10
Great Dividing Ra. 61 E8
Great Falls 81 B8
Great Inagua I. 86 B5
Great Indian Desert = Thar Desert 42 F7
Great Karoo 58 E4
Great Lake 62 D4
Great Ouse → 11 E7
Great Ruaha → 57 F7
Great Saint Bernard P. = Grand St.-Bernard, Col du 13 D7
Great Salt L. 81 E7
Great Salt Lake Desert 81 E7
Great Sandy Desert 60 E3
Great Sangi = Sangihe, P. 39 D3
Great Slave L. 70 B8
Great Smoky Mts. Nat. Pk. 75 B6
Great Victoria Desert 60 F4
Great Wall 35 C5
Great Yarmouth 11 E7
Greater Antilles 86 C5
Greater Sunda Is. 37 F4
Gredos, Sierra de 18 B3
Greece ■ 23 E4
Greeley 76 E2
Green → 83 A8
Green Bay 72 B2
Green C. 63 C5
Greenland ■ 66 C9
Greenock 10 D4
Greensboro 75 A8
Greenville, *Liberia* 55 G3
Greenville, *Ala., U.S.A.* 74 D4
Greenville, *Miss., U.S.A.* 79 C8
Greenville, *N.C., U.S.A.* 75 B9
Greenville, *S.C., U.S.A.* 75 B6
Greenwood, *Miss., U.S.A.* 79 C8
Greenwood, *S.C., U.S.A.* 75 B6
Gregory, L. 62 A2
Greifswald 15 A7
Greiz 15 C7
Gremikha 28 C4
Grenada ■ 87 D7
Grenfell 63 B4
Grenoble 13 D6
Grey → 65 E4
Grey Ra. 63 A3
Greymouth 65 E4
Greytown, *N.Z.* 65 D6
Greytown, *S. Africa* 59 D6
Griffin 75 C5
Griffith 63 B4
Grimari 56 C4
Grimaylov = Hrymayliv 17 D8
Grimsby 11 E6
Gris-Nez, C. 12 A4
Grodno = Hrodna 17 B6
Grodzyanka = Hrodzyanka 17 B9
Grójec 16 C5
Groningen 14 B4
Grootfontein 58 B3
Gross Glockner 15 E7
Grosser Arber 15 D7
Grosseto 20 C3
Groznyy 25 E6
Grudziądz 16 B4
Gryazi 24 C4
Gryazovets 28 D5
Gua 40 F5
Guadalajara, *Mexico* 84 C4
Guadalajara, *Spain* 18 B4
Guadalcanal 64 K11
Guadalete → 18 D2
Guadalquivir → 18 D2
Guadalupe = Guadeloupe ■ 87 C7
Guadalupe, Sierra de 18 C3
Guadarrama, Sierra de 18 B4
Guadeloupe ■ 87 C7
Guadiana → 18 D2
Guadix 18 D4
Guafo, Boca del 95 E2
Guaíra 94 A6
Guaitecas, Is. 95 E2
Guajará-Mirim 91 F5
Guajira, Pen. de la 90 A4
Gualeguay 94 C5
Gualeguaychú 94 C5
Guam ■ 64 H9
Guamúchil 84 B3
Guan Xian 34 C5
Guanahani = San Salvador 86 B5
Guanajuato 84 C4
Guandacol 94 B3
Guane 86 B3
Guangdong □ 35 D6
Guanghua 35 C6
Guangxi Zhuangzu Zizhiqu □ 35 D5
Guangzhou 35 D6
Guanipa → 90 B6
Guantánamo 86 B4
Guaporé → 91 F5
Guaqui 91 G5
Guarapuava 94 B6
Guarda 18 B2
Guardafui, C. = Asir, Ras 49 E5
Guasdualito 90 B4
Guasipati 90 B6
Guatemala 85 E6
Guatemala ■ 85 D6
Guatire 90 A5
Guaviare □ 90 C4
Guaviare → 90 C5
Guaxupé 93 G4
Guayama 87 C6
Guayaquil 90 D3
Guayaquil, G. de 90 D2
Guaymas 84 B2
Guddu Barrage 42 E6
Gudivada 40 J3
Gudur 43 M11
Guecho 19 A4
Guékédou 55 G2
Guelma 54 A6
Guelph 69 D2
Guéréda 53 F3
Guéret 12 C4
Guernica 19 A4
Guernsey 11 G5
Guidónia-Montecélio 20 C4
Guiglo 55 G3
Guildford 11 F6
Guilin 35 D6
Guimarães, *Brazil* 92 C5
Guimarães, *Portugal* 18 B1
Guimaras 38 B2
Guinea ■ 55 F2
Guinea, Gulf of 51 F3
Guinea-Bissau ■ 55 F1
Guingamp 12 B2
Guiping 35 D6
Güiria 90 A6
Guiuan 38 B3
Guiyang 35 D5
Guizhou □ 35 D5
Gujarat □ 43 H7
Gujranwala 42 C9
Gujrat 42 C9
Gulbarga 43 L10
Gulf, The 44 E2
Gulgong 63 B4
Güllük 23 F6
Gulshad 29 E8
Gulu 57 D6
Gum Lake 62 B3
Gummi 55 F6
Gümüşhane 46 B4
Gumzai 39 F4
Guna 43 G10
Gundagai 63 C4
Gungu 56 F3
Gunnedah 63 B5
Gunningbar Cr. → 63 B4
Guntakal 43 M10
Guntur 40 J3
Gunungapi 39 F3
Gunungsitoli 37 D1
Gunza 56 G2
Gupis 42 A8
Gūrchān 46 D7
Gurdaspur 42 C9
Gurgaon 42 E10
Gurkha 40 C5
Gurley 63 A4
Gurupá 92 C3
Gurupá, I. Grande de 92 C3
Gurupi → 92 C4
Guryev = Atyraū 29 E6
Gusau 55 F6
Güstrow 15 B7
Gütersloh 14 C5
Guthrie 78 B5
Guyana ■ 90 B7
Guyane française ■ = French Guiana ■ 92 B3
Guyenne 12 D4
Guyra 63 B5
Gwa 41 J10
Gwaai 59 B5
Gwabegar 63 B4
Gwādar 42 G3
Gwalior 42 F11
Gwanda 59 C5
Gweru 59 B5
Gwydir → 63 A4
Gyandzha = Gäncä 25 E6
Gyaring Hu 34 C4
Gydanskiy P-ov. 28 B8
Gympie 63 A5
Gyöngyös 16 E4
Györ 16 E3
Gypsumville 71 C10
Gyula 16 E5
Gyumri 25 E5
Gyzylarbat 29 F6

## H

Ha 'Arava → 47 E3
Haarlem 14 B3
Haast → 65 E3
Habaswein 57 D7
Hachinohe 33 F12
Hadarba, Ras 52 D6

Hadd, R'as al 45 F4
Hadejia 55 F7
Haden 63 A5
H̱adera 46 D3
Hadhramaut = Haḍramawt 49 D4
Haḍramawt 49 D4
Haeju 35 C7
Haerhpin = Harbin 35 B7
Hafar al Bāţin 47 E6
Hafizabad 42 C8
Haflong 41 E9
Haft Gel 47 E7
Hafun, Ras 49 E5
Hagen 14 C4
Hagerstown 73 E7
Hagi 32 B2
Hagondange-Briey 13 B7
Hague, C. de la 12 B3
Hague, The = 's-Gravenhage 14 B3
Haguenau 13 B7
Hai'an 35 C7
Haifa = H̱efa 46 D3
Haikou 35 D6
Ḥā'il 47 F5
Hailar 35 B6
Haileybury 69 D3
Hailun 35 D7
Hainan □ 35 E5
Haiphong 35 D5
Haiti ■ 87 C5
Haiya Junction 53 E6
Hajar Bangar 53 F3
Hajdúböszörmény 16 E5
Hajnówka 17 B6
Hakken-Zan 32 B4
Hakodate 32 F12
Hala 42 G6
Ḥalab 46 C4
Ḥalabjah 46 D6
Halaib 52 D6
Halberstadt 15 C6
Halcombe 64 D6
Halcon, Mt. 38 B2
Halden 9 G10
Haldia 40 F7
Haldwani 42 E11
Halifax, *Canada* 69 D4
Halifax, *U.K.* 11 E6
Halīl → 44 E4
Hall Beach = Sanirajak 68 B2
Halle 15 C6
Hallett 62 B2
Halmahera 39 D3
Halmstad 9 G10
Halq el Oued 52 A1
Hälsingborg = Helsingborg 9 G10
Halul 44 E3
Hamada 32 B3
Hamadān 46 D7
Hamadān □ 46 D7
Hamāh 46 D4
Hamamatsu 32 B5
Hamar 8 F10
Hamburg 14 B5
Hameln 14 B5
Hamersley Ra. 60 E2
Hamhung 35 C7
Hami 34 B4
Hamilton, *Australia* 62 C3
Hamilton, *Canada* 69 D3
Hamilton, *N.Z.* 64 B6
Hamilton, *U.K.* 10 D4
Hamley Bridge 62 B2
Hamlin = Hameln 14 B5
Hamm 14 C4
Hammerfest 8 D12
Hammond 72 D2
Hampden 65 F4
Hampton 73 F7
Hamrat esh Sheykh 53 F4
Han Pijesak 20 B7
Hanamaki 33 G12
Hanau 14 C5
Hancock 77 C7
Handa 49 E5
Handan 35 C6
Handeni 57 F7
Hangayn Nuruu 34 B4
Hangchou = Hangzhou 35 C7
Hangu 35 C6
Hangzhou 35 C7
Hangzhou Wan 35 C7
Ḥanīsh 49 E3
Hanle 42 C11
Hanmer Springs 65 E5
Hanna 71 C8
Hannibal 77 F9
Hannover 14 B5
Hanoi 35 D5
Hanover = Hannover 14 B5
Hanover, I. 95 G2
Hanson, L. 62 B2
Hantsavichy 17 B8
Hanzhong 35 C5
Haora 40 F7
Haparanda 8 E12
Happy Valley-Goose Bay 69 C4
Hapur 42 E10
Ḥaql 47 E3
Har 39 F4
Har Hu 34 C4
Har Us Nuur 34 B4
Ḥaraḍ 47 F7
Haraisan Plateau = Huraysan 47 G6
Harardera 49 G4
Harare 59 B6
Harazé 53 F2
Harbin 35 B7
Harbour Grace 69 D5
Hardangerfjorden 8 F9
Hardap Dam 58 C3
Hardwar = Haridwar 42 E11
Hardy, Pen. 95 H3
Harer 49 F3
Hargeisa 49 F3
Hari → 37 E2
Haridwar 42 E11
Haringhata → 41 G7
Harīrūd 45 C5
Harīrūd → 42 A2
Harlingen 78 F5
Harlow 11 F7
Harney Basin 80 D4
Härnösand 8 F11
Ḥarrat al Kishb 47 G5
Harrat al 'Uwairidh 47 F4
Harris 10 C3
Harris L. 62 B2
Harrisburg 73 D7
Harrison, C. 68 C5
Harrison Bay 71 A4
Harrogate 11 D6
Hart, L. 62 B2
Hartford 73 D9
Hartlepool 11 D6
Harvey 72 D2
Harwich 11 F7
Haryana □ 42 E10
Haryn → 17 B8
Harz 14 C6
Hasa 47 F7
Hasan Kuli 29 F6
Hassi Inifel 54 C5
Hassi Messaoud 54 B6
Hastings, *N.Z.* 64 C7
Hastings, *U.K.* 11 F7
Hastings, *U.S.A.* 76 E5
Hastings Ra. 63 B5
Hatay = Antalya 46 C2
Hatfield P.O. 62 B3
Hatgal 34 A5
Hathras 42 F11
Hatia 41 F8
Hattah 62 B3
Hatteras, C. 75 B10
Hattiesburg 79 D9
Hatvan 16 E4
Hau Bon = Cheo Reo 36 B3
Haugesund 9 G9
Hauraki G. 64 B6
Haut Atlas 54 B3
Hautah, Wahāt al 47 G6
Hauts Plateaux 54 B4
Havana = La Habana 86 B3
Havant 11 F6
Havel → 15 B7
Havelock 65 D5
Haverfordwest 11 F4
Havlíčkův Brod 16 D2
Havre 81 A9
Havza 46 B3
Hawaii □ 82 J12
Hawaiian Is. 82 H12
Hawea, L. 65 F3
Hawera 64 C6
Hawick 10 D5
Hawke B. 64 C7
Hawker 62 B2
Hawkwood 63 A5
Hay 63 B3
Hay River 70 B8
Haya 39 E3
Hayes → 71 C10
Hayrabolu 22 D6
Haysyn 17 D9
Hayvoron 17 D9
Hazaribag 40 F5
Healesville 63 C4
Hearst 69 D2
Hebei □ 35 C6
Hebel 63 A4
Hebron = Al Khalīl 47 E3
Hebron 68 C4
Hechi 35 D5
Hechuan 35 C5
Heerlen 13 A6
H̱efa 46 D3
Hefei 35 C6
Hegang 35 B8
Heidelberg 14 D5
Heilbron 59 D5
Heilbronn 14 D5
Heilongjiang □ 35 B7
Heilunkiang = Heilongjiang □ 35 B7
Heinze Is. 41 K11
Hejaz = Al Ḥijāz 47 F4
Hekımhan 46 C4
Hekou 34 D5
Helena, *Ark., U.S.A.* 79 B8
Helena, *Mont., U.S.A.* 81 B7
Helensville 64 B6
Helgoland 14 A4
Heligoland = Helgoland 14 A4
Heligoland B. = Deutsche Bucht 14 A5
Hellín 19 C5
Helmand □ 42 D3
Helmand → 42 D2
Helmand, Hamun 45 D5
Helmsdale 10 B5
Helsingborg 9 G10
Helsingfors = Helsinki 9 F13
Helsinki 9 F13
Helwân 52 C5
Hemel Hempstead 11 F6
Henan □ 35 C6
Henares → 18 B4
Henderson 75 A8
Hendon 63 A5
Hengyang 35 D6
Henrietta Maria, C. 69 C2
Hentiyn Nuruu 35 B5
Henty 63 C4
Henzada 41 J10
Herāt 42 B3
Herāt □ 42 B3
Hercegnovi 22 C2
Hereford 11 E5
Herford 14 B5
Hermidale 63 B4
Hermitage 65 E4
Hermite, I. 95 H3
Hermon, Mt. = Ash Shaykh, J. 46 D3
Hermosillo 84 B2
Hernád → 16 E5
Hernandarias 94 B6
Heroica Nogales = Nogales 84 A2
Heron Bay 69 D2
Herrick 62 D4
's-Hertogenbosch 14 C3
Hesse = Hessen □ 14 C5
Hessen □ 14 C5
Hewett, C. 68 A4
Hexham 11 D5
Heyfield 63 C4
Heywood 62 C3
Hibbing 77 B8
Hibbs B. 62 D4
Hickory 75 B7
Hicks, Pt. 63 C4
Hida-Sammyaku 32 A5
Hidalgo del Parral 84 B3
Higashiōsaka 32 B4
High Atlas = Haut Atlas 54 B3

High Point 75 B8
High River 71 C8
High Tatra = Tatry 16 D4
High Wycombe 11 F6
Hiiumaa 24 B1
Ḩijārah, Şaḩrā' al 47 E6
Ḩijāz □ 48 C2
Hijo = Tagum 38 C3
Hikone 32 B5
Hikurangi 64 A6
Hikurangi, Mt. 64 C7
Hildesheim 14 B5
Hillston 63 B4
Hilo 82 J13
Hilversum 14 B3
Himachal Pradesh □ 42 D10
Himalaya 40 C5
Himatnagar 43 H8
Himeji 32 B4
Himi 32 A5
Ḩimş 46 D4
Hindmarsh, L. 62 C3
Hindu Kush 42 B7
Hindubagh 42 D5
Hindupur 43 N10
Hinganghat 43 J11
Hingoli 43 K10
Hinna = Imi 49 F3
Hinojosa del Duque 18 C3
Hirakud Dam 40 G4
Hiratsuka 32 B6
Hirosaki 33 F12
Hiroshima 32 B3
Hisar 42 E9
Hispaniola 87 C5
Hita 32 C2
Hitachi 32 A7
Hjälmaren 9 G11
Hlyboka 17 D7
Ho 55 G5
Ho Chi Minh City = Phanh Bho Ho Chi Minh 36 B3
Hoai Nhon 36 B3
Hoare B. 68 B4
Hobart 62 D4
Hobbs Coast 96 B18
Hodgson 71 C10
Hódmezövásárhely 16 E5
Hodna, Chott el 54 A5
Hodonín 16 D3
Hoek van Holland 14 B3
Hof 15 C6
Hōfu 32 B2
Hogan Group 62 C4
Hoggar = Ahaggar 54 D6
Hoh Xil Shan 34 C3
Hohe Rhön 14 C5
Hohhot 35 B6
Hoi An 36 A3
Hokianga Harbour 64 A5
Hokitika 65 E4
Hokkaidō □ 32 F12
Holbrook 63 C4
Holguín 86 B4
Hollandia = Jayapura 39 E6
Holman Island 70 A8
Holy Cross 71 B4
Holyhead 11 E4
Homalin 41 E10
Hombori 55 E4
Home B. 68 B4
Homer 71 C4
Homs = Ḩimş 46 D4
Homyel 17 B10
Hon Chong 36 B2
Honan = Henan □ 35 C6
Honda 90 B4
Hondeklipbaai 58 E3
Honduras ■ 85 E7
Honduras, G. de 85 D7
Honfleur 12 B4
Hong Kong 35 D6
Hongjiang 35 D5
Hongshui He → 35 D5
Hongze Hu 35 C6
Honiara 64 K10
Honolulu 82 H12
Honshū 32 G11
Hood, Mt. 80 C3
Hooghly → = Hughli → 40 G7
Hook of Holland = Hoek van Holland 14 B3
Hoorn 14 B3
Hoover Dam 82 B5
Hope, L. 62 A2
Hope, Pt. 71 B3
Hopedale 68 C4
Hopei = Hebei □ 35 C6
Hopetoun 62 C3
Hopetown 58 D4
Hoquiam 80 B2
Horlick Mts. 96 C1
Horlivka 25 D4
Hormoz 44 E3
Hormoz, Jaz. ye 44 E4
Hormozgān □ 44 E3
Hormuz, Str. of 44 E4
Horn 15 D8
Horn, Cape = Hornos, C. de 95 H3
Hornavan 8 E11
Hornos, C. de 95 H3
Hornsby 63 B5
Horodenka 17 D7
Horodok, *Khmelnytskyy, Ukraine* 17 D8
Horodok, *Lviv, Ukraine* 17 D6
Horokhiv 17 C7
Horqin Youyi Qianqi 35 B7
Horqueta 94 A5
Horsham 62 C3
Horton → 70 B7
Hose, Gunung-Gunung 37 D4
Hoshangabad 43 H10
Hoshiarpur 42 D9
Hospet 43 M10
Hospitalet de Llobregat 19 B7
Hoste, I. 95 H3
Hot Springs 79 B7
Hotan 34 C2
Houhora Heads 64 A5
Houlton 73 A12
Houma 79 E8
Houston 79 E6
Hovd 34 B4
Hövsgöl Nuur 34 A5
Howard 63 A5
Howe, C. 63 C5
Howitt, L. 62 A2
Howrah = Haora 40 F7
Höxter 14 C5
Hoy 10 B5
Høyanger 8 F9
Hoyerswerda 15 C8
Hpungan Pass 41 D11
Hradec Králové 16 C2
Hrodna 17 B6
Hrodzyanka 17 B9
Hron → 16 E4
Hrvatska = Croatia ■ 20 B6
Hrymayliv 17 D8
Hsenwi 41 F11
Hsiamen = Xiamen 35 D6
Hsian = Xi'an 35 C5
Hsinhailien = Lianyungang 35 C6
Hsisha Chuntao 36 A4
Hsüchou = Xuzhou 35 C6
Hua Hin 36 B1
Huacho 91 F3
Huachón 91 F3
Huai He → 35 C6
Huainan 35 C6
Huallaga → 90 E3
Huambo 58 A3
Huancabamba 91 E3
Huancane 91 G5
Huancapi 91 F4
Huancavelica 91 F3
Huancayo 91 F3
Huang Hai = Yellow Sea 35 C7
Huang He → 35 C6
Huangliu 35 E5
Huangshi 35 C6
Huánuco 91 E3
Huaraz 91 E3
Huarmey 91 F3
Huascarán 91 E3
Huasco 94 B2
Huatabampo 84 B3
Huayllay 91 F3
Hubei □ 35 C6
Hubli-Dharwad = Dharwad 43 M9
Huddersfield 11 E6
Hudiksvall 8 F11
Hudson → 73 D8
Hudson Bay 68 B2
Hudson Mts. 96 B2
Hudson Str. 68 B4
Hue 36 A3
Huelva 18 D2
Huesca 19 A5
Hughenden 61 E7
Hughli → 40 G7
Huila, Nevado del 90 C3
Huinca Renancó 94 C4
Huize 34 D5
Hukawng Valley 41 D11
Hulan 35 B7
Ḩulayfā' 47 F5
Huld 35 B5
Hull = Kingston upon Hull 11 E6
Hull 69 D3
Hulun Nur 35 B6
Humahuaca 94 A3
Humaitá, *Brazil* 91 E6
Humaitá, *Paraguay* 94 B5
Humber → 11 E6
Humboldt 71 C9
Humboldt → 80 F4
Hume, L. 63 C4
Humenné 16 D5
Hūn 52 C2
Hunan □ 35 D6
Hunedoara 17 F6
Hungary ■ 16 E4
Hungerford 63 A3
Hŭngnam 35 C7
Hunsrück 14 D4
Hunter I. 62 D3
Hunter Ra. 63 B5
Hunterville 64 C6
Huntington 72 E4
Huntington Beach 82 D3
Huntly, *N.Z.* 64 B6
Huntly, *U.K.* 10 C5
Huntsville 74 B4
Huonville 62 D4
Hupeh = Hubei □ 35 C6
Huraysān 47 G6
Huron, L. 72 B4
Hurunui → 65 E5
Huşi 17 E9
Hutchinson 78
Hutton, Mt. 63 A4
Hvar 20 C6
Hwang Ho = Huang He → 35 C6
Hwange 59 B5
Hyargas Nuur 34 B4
Hyderabad, *India* 43 L11
Hyderabad, *Pakistan* 42 G6
Hyères 13 E7
Hyères, Is. d' 13 E7

## I

I-n-Gall 55 E6
Iaco → 91 E5
Ialomiţa → 22 B6
Iaşi 17 E8
Iba 38 A2
Ibadan 55 G5
Ibagué 90 C3
Ibar → 22 C3
Ibarra 90 C3
Ibi 55 G6
Ibiá 93 F4
Ibicuy 94 C5
Ibioapaba, Sa. da 92 C5
Ibiza 19 C6
Ibonma 39 E4
Ibotirama 93 E5
Ibu 39 D3
Icá 91 F3
Iça → 90 D5
Içana 90 C5
Içel = Mersin 46 C3
Iceland ■ 8 B4
Ich'ang = Yichang 35 C6
Ichchapuram 40 H5
Ichihara 32 B7
Ichikawa 32 B6
Ichilo → 91 G6
Ichinomiya 32 B5
Idaho □ 81 C6
Idaho Falls 81 D7
Idar-Oberstein 14 D4
Idd el Ghanam 53 F3

Iddan . . . . . . . . 49 F4
Idehan . . . . . . . 52 C1
Idehan Marzūq 52 D1
Idelès . . . . . . . . 54 D6
Idfû . . . . . . . . . 52 D5
Ídhi Óros . . . . . 23 G5
Ídhra . . . . . . . . . 23 F4
Idi . . . . . . . . . . 36 C1
Idiofa . . . . . . . . 56 E3
Idlip . . . . . . . . . 46 D4
Ierápetra . . . . . 23 G5
Iesi . . . . . . . . . . 20 C4
Ifanadiana . . . . 59 J9
Ife . . . . . . . . . . . 55 G5
Ifni . . . . . . . . . . 54 C2
Iforas, Adrar des 54
Igarapava . . . . . 93 G4
Igarapé Açu . . . 92 C4
Igarka . . . . . . . . 28 C9
Igbetti . . . . . . . . 55 G5
Iglésias . . . . . . . 21 E2
Igli . . . . . . . . . . 54 B4
Igloolik . . . . . . . 68 B2
Igluligaarjuk . . . 68 B1
İğneada Burnu 22 D7
Igoumenítsa . . 23 E3
Iguaçu → . . . . 94 B6
Iguaçu, Cat. del 94 B6
Iguaçu Falls = Iguaçu, Cat. del . . . . . . . . 94 B6
Iguala . . . . . . . . 84 D5
Igualada . . . . . . 19 B6
Iguassu = Iguaçu → . . 94 B6
Iguatu . . . . . . . . 92 D6
Iguéla . . . . . . . . 56 E1
Ihosy . . . . . . . . 59 J9
Iida . . . . . . . . . . 32 B5
Iisalmi . . . . . 8 F13
Iizuka . . . . . . . . 32 C2
Ijebu-Ode . . . . . 55 G5
IJsselmeer . . . . 14 B3
Ikaluktutiak . . . 70 B9
Ikaría . . . . . . . . 23 F6
Ikela . . . . . . . . . 56 E4
Iki . . . . . . . . . . . 32 C1
Ilagan . . . . . . . . 38 A2
Īlām . . . . . . . . . 46 D6
Iława . . . . . . . . . 16 B4
Île-de-France . . 12 B5
Ilebo . . . . . . . . . 56 E4
Ilhéus . . . . . . . . 93 E6
Ili → . . . . . . . . 29 E8
Ilich . . . . . . . . . . 29 E7
Iligan . . . . . . . . 38 C2
Illampu = Ancohuma, Nevada . . . . . 91 G5
Illana B. . . . . . . 38 C2
Illapel . . . . . . . . 94 C2
Iller → . . . . . . . 14 D5
Illimani . . . . . . . 91 G5
Illium = Troy . . 23 E6
Ilmen, Ozero . . 24 B3
Ilo . . . . . . . . . . . 91 G4
Iloilo . . . . . . . . . 38 B2
Ilorin . . . . . . . . . 55 G5
Ilwaki . . . . . . . . 39 F3
Imabari . . . . . . . 32 B3
Imandra, Ozero 28 C4
Imari . . . . . . . . . 32 C1
imeni 26 Bakinskikh Komissarov = Neftçala . . . . 46 C7
Imeri, Serra . . . 90 C5
Imi . . . . . . . . . . 49 F3
Imola . . . . . . . . 20 B3
Imperatriz . . . . 92 D4
Impéria . . . . . . . 20 C2
Imperial Dam . 82 D5
Impfondo . . . . . 56 D3
Imphal . . . . . . . 41 E9
İmroz = Gökçeada . . . 23 D5
Imuruan B. . . . . 38 B1
In Belbel . . . . . . 54 C5
In Salah . . . . . . 54 C5
Ina . . . . . . . . . . 32 B5
Inangahua Junction . . . . 65 D4
Inanwatan . . . . 39 E4
Iñapari . . . . . . . 91 F5
Inarijärvi . . . . . . 8 E13
Inca . . . . . . . . . . 19 C7
İnce-Burnu . . . . 46 B3
Inchon . . . . . . . 35 C7
İncirliova . . . . . 23 F6
Incomáti → . . 59 D6
Indalsälven → 8 F11
Indaw . . . . . . . . 41 E11
Independence, *Kans., U.S.A.* 79 A6
Independence, *Mo., U.S.A.* . 77 F7
India ■ . . . . . . . 43 J10
Indian → . . . . . 75 F7
Indian Harbour 68 C5
Indian Head . . . 71 C9
Indiana □ . . . . . 72 D3
Indianapolis . . . 72 E2
Indiga . . . . . . . . 28 C5
Indigirka → . . 31 B12
Indonesia ■ . . . 37 E4
Indore . . . . . . . . 43 H9
Indravati → . . 40 H3
Indre → . . . . . 12 C4
Indus → . . . . . 43 G5
Inebolu . . . . . . . 46 B3
Ingende . . . . . . 56 E3
Inglewood, *Queens., Australia* . . . . 63 A5
Inglewood, *Vic., Australia* . . . . 62 C3
Inglewood, *N.Z.* 64 C6
Ingolstadt . . . . . 15 D6
Ingraj Bazar . . . 40 E7
Ingrid Christensen Coast . . . . . . 96 A10
Ingulec = Inhulec . . . . . 25 D3
Inhambane . . . 59 C7
Inhaminga . . . . 59 B7
Inharrime . . . . . 59 C7
Inhulec . . . . . . . 25 D3
Ining = Yining . 34 B3
Inírida → . . . . 90 C5
Injune . . . . . . . . 63 A4
Inle L. . . . . . . . . 41 G11
Inn → . . . . . . . 15 D7
Innamincka . . . 62 A3
Inner Hebrides 10 C3
Inner Mongolia = Nei Monggol Zizhiqu □ . . . 35 B6
Innisfail . . . . . . 71 C8
Innsbruck . . . . . 15 E6
Inongo . . . . . . . 56 E3
Inoucdjouac = Inukjuak . . . . 68 C3
Inowrocław . . . 16 B4
Inquisivi . . . . . . 91 G5
Insein . . . . . . . . 41 J11
Interlaken . . . . . 13 C7
International Falls . . . . . . . 77 A8
Intiyaco . . . . . . 94 B4
Inukjuak . . . . . . 68 C3
Inútil, B. . . . . . . 95 G2
Inuvik . . . . . . . . 70 B6
Invercargill . . . . 65 G3
Inverell . . . . . . . 63 A5
Invergordon . . . 10 C4
Inverness . . . . . 10 C4
Inverurie . . . . . 10 C5
Investigator Group . . . . . . 62 B1
Investigator Str. 62 C2
Inya . . . . . . . . . 29 D9
Inza . . . . . . . . . . 24 C6
Ioánnina . . . . . . 23 E3
Ionian Is. = Iónioi Nísoi . 23 E3
Ionian Sea . . . . 21 F6
Iónioi Nísoi . . . 23 E3
Íos . . . . . . . . . . . 23 F5
Iowa □ . . . . . . . 77 D8
Iowa City . . . . . 77 E9
Ipameri . . . . . . . 93 F4
Ipatinga . . . . . . 93 F5
Ipiales . . . . . . . . 90 C3
Ipin = Yibin . . . 35 D5
Ipixuna . . . . . . . 91 E4
Ipoh . . . . . . . . . 36 D2
Ippy . . . . . . . . . 56 C4
İpsala . . . . . . . . 22 D6
Ipswich, *Australia* . . . . 63 A5
Ipswich, *U.K.* . . 11 E7
Ipu . . . . . . . . . . 92 C5
Iqaluit . . . . . . . . 68 B4
Iquique . . . . . . . 91 H4
Iquitos . . . . . . . 90 D4
Iracoubo . . . . . . 92 A3
Iráklion . . . . . . . 23 G5
Iran ■ . . . . . . . . 44 C3
Iran, Gunung-Gunung . . . . 37 D4
Iran Ra. = Iran, Gunung-Gunung . . . . 37 D4
Īrānshahr . . . . . 45 E5
Irapuato . . . . . . 84 C4
Iraq ■ . . . . . . . . 46 D5
Irbid . . . . . . . . . 46 D3
Irebu . . . . . . . . . 56 E3
Ireland ■ . . . . . 11 E3
Irian Jaya □ . . . 39 E5
Iringa . . . . . . . . 57 F7
Iriri → . . . . . . . 92 C3
Irish Sea . . . . . . 11 E4
Irkineyeva . . . . 30 D7
Irkutsk . . . . . . . 30 D8
Iron Baron . . . . 62 B2
Iron Gate = Portile de Fier 22 B4
Iron Knob . . . . . 62 B2
Ironwood . . . . . 77 B9
Irpin . . . . . . . . . 17 C10
Irrara Cr. → . . 63 A4
Irrawaddy □ . . 41 J10
Irrawaddy → . 41 K10
Irtysh → . . . . . 28 C7
Irumu . . . . . . . . 57 D5
Irún . . . . . . . . . . 19 A5
Irunea = Pamplona . . . 19 A5
Irvine . . . . . . . . 10 D4
Irymple . . . . . . . 62 B3
Isabella . . . . . . . 38 C2
Isangi . . . . . . . . 56 D4
Isar → . . . . . . . 15 D7
Íschia . . . . . . . . 21 D4
Ise . . . . . . . . . . . 32 B5
Ise-Wan . . . . . . 32 B5
Isère → . . . . . . 13 D6
Isérnia . . . . . . . 20 D5
Ishikari-Wan . . 32 F12
Ishim → . . . . . 29 D8
Ishinomaki . . . . 33 G12
Ishkuman . . . . . 42 A8
Isil Kul . . . . . . . 29 D8
Isiolo . . . . . . . . 57 D7
Isiro . . . . . . . . . 57 D5
İskenderun . . . . 46 C4
Iskŭr → . . . . . . 22 C5
Islamabad . . . . 42 C8
Island L. . . . . . . 71 C10
Island Lagoon . 62 B2
Islay . . . . . . . . . 10 D3
Isle → . . . . . . . 12 D3
Isle of Wight □ 11 F6
Ismail = Izmayil 17 F9
Ismâ'ilîya . . . . . 47 E3
Isna . . . . . . . . . . 52 C5
İsparta . . . . . . . 46 C2
Íspica . . . . . . . . 21 F5
Israel ■ . . . . . . 46 E3
Issoire . . . . . . . 13 D5
Issyk-Kul, Ozero = Ysyk-Köl, Ozero . . . . . . 29 E8
İstanbul . . . . . . 22 D7
Istiaía . . . . . . . . 23 F4
Istra . . . . . . . . . 20 B4
İstranca Dağlari 22 D6
Istres . . . . . . . . 13 E6
Istria = Istra . . 20 B4
Itabaiana . . . . . 92 D6
Itaberaba . . . . . 93 E5
Itabira . . . . . . . . 93 F5
Itabuna . . . . . . . 93 E6
Itaipú, Reprêsa de . . . . . . . . 94 B6
Itaituba . . . . . . . 92 C2
Itajaí . . . . . . . . . 94 B7
Italy ■ . . . . . . . 20 C4
Itapecuru-Mirim 92 C5
Itaperuna . . . . . 93 G5
Itapicuru →, *Bahia, Brazil* . 93 E6
Itapicuru →, *Maranhão, Brazil* . . . . . . . 92 C5
Itapipoca . . . . . 92 C6
Itaquatiara . . . . 90 D7
Itaqui . . . . . . . . 94 B5
Itatuba . . . . . . . 91 E6
Ithaca = Itháki . 23 E3
Itháki . . . . . . . . 23 E3
Ito . . . . . . . . . . . 32 B6
Itonamas → . . 91 F6
Ituaçu . . . . . . . . 93 E5
Ituiutaba . . . . . . 93 F4
Itumbiara . . . . . 93 F4
Iturbe . . . . . . . . 94 A3
Itzehoe . . . . . . . 14 B5
Ivanava . . . . . . . 17 B7
Ivanhoe . . . . . . 63 B3
Ivano-Frankivsk 17 D7
Ivano-Frankovsk = Ivano-Frankivsk . . . 17 D7
Ivanovo = Ivanava . . . . . 17 B7
Ivanovo . . . . . . 24 B5
Ivatsevichy . . . . 17 B7
Ivory Coast ■ . 55 G3
Ivrea . . . . . . . . . 20 B1
Ivujivik . . . . . . . 68 B3
Iwahig . . . . . . . 36 C5
Iwaki . . . . . . . . . 33 G12

Iwakuni 32 B3
Iwata 33 H11
Iwate-San 33 G12
Iwo 55 G5
Ixiamas 91 F5
Izhevsk 28 D6
Izmayil 17 F9
İzmir 23 E6
İzmit 25 E2
İznik Gölü 23 D7
Izumi-sano 32 B4
Izumo 32 B3
Izyaslav 17 C8

## J

Jabalpur 43 H11
Jablah 46 D4
Jablanica 22 D3
Jablonec 16 C2
Jaboatão 92 D6
Jaca 19 A5
Jacareí 94 A7
Jacarèzinho 94 A7
Jackson, *Australia* 63 A4
Jackson, *Mich., U.S.A.* 72 C3
Jackson, *Miss., U.S.A.* 79 C8
Jackson, *Tenn., U.S.A.* 74 B3
Jackson B. 65 E3
Jacksons 65 E4
Jacksonville, *Fla., U.S.A.* 75 D7
Jacksonville, *Ill., U.S.A.* 77 F9
Jacksonville, *N.C., U.S.A.* 75 B9
Jacmel 87 C5
Jacobabad 42 E6
Jacobina 93 E5
Jacundá → 92 C3
Jadotville = Likasi 57 G5
Jādū 52 B1
Jaén, *Peru* 91 E3
Jaén, *Spain* 18 D4
Jaffa = Tel Aviv-Yafo 46 D3
Jaffa, C. 62 C2
Jaffna 43 Q12
Jagadhri 42 D10
Jagdalpur 40 H3
Jagraon 42 D9
Jagtial 43 K11
Jaguariaíva 94 A7
Jaguaribe → 92 C6
Jahrom 44 D3
Jailolo 39 D3
Jailolo, Selat 39 D3
Jaipur 42 F9
Jakarta 37 F3
Jalalabad 42 B7
Jalapa Enríquez 84 D5
Jalas, Jabal al 47 F4
Jalgaon, *Maharashtra, India* 43 J10
Jalgaon, *Maharashtra, India* 43 J9
Jalna 43 K9
Jalón → 19 B5
Jalpaiguri 41 D7
Jalq 45 E5
Jaluit I. 64 J11
Jamaica ■ 86 C4
Jamalpur, *Bangla.* 41 E7
Jamalpur, *India* 40 E6
Jamanxim → 92 C2
Jambe 39 E4
Jambi 37 E2
Jambi □ 37 E2
James → 76 D6
James B. 69 C2
James Ross I. 96 A4
Jamestown, *Australia* 62 B2
Jamestown, *N. Dak., U.S.A.* 76 B5
Jamestown, *N.Y., U.S.A.* 73 C6
Jamkhandi 43 L9
Jammu 42 C9
Jammu & Kashmir □ 42 B10
Jamnagar 43 H7
Jamrud 42 C7
Jamshedpur 40 F6
Jand 42 C8
Jandaq 44 C3
Jandowae 63 A5
Janesville 77 D10
Januária 93 F5
Jaora 43 H9
Japan ■ 33 G11
Japan, Sea of 33 G11
Japen = Yapen 39 E5
Japurá → 90 D5
Jaque 90 B3
Jarama → 18 B4
Jargalant = Hovd 34 B4
Jarosław 17 C6
Jarso 53 G6
Jarvis I. 65 K15
Jarwa 40 D4
Jāsk 44 E4
Jasło 16 D5
Jasper 74 C4
Jászberény 16 E4
Jataí 93 F3
Játiva 19 C5
Jaú 93 G4
Jauja 91 F3
Jaunpur 40 E4
Java = Jawa 37 F3
Java Sea 37 E3
Javhlant = Ulyasutay 34 B4
Jawa 37 F3
Jaya, Puncak 39 E5
Jayanti 41 D7
Jayapura 39 E6
Jayawijaya, Pegunungan 39 E5
Jaynagar 40 D6
Jean Marie River 70 B7
Jebba 55 G5
Jebel, Bahr el → 53 G5
Jedburgh 10 D5
Jedda = Jiddah 47 G4
Jędrzejów 16 C5
Jefferson City 77 F8
Jega 55 F5
Jelenia Góra 16 C2
Jelgava 24 B1
Jemaja 37 D3
Jembongan 36 C5
Jena 15 C6
Jeparit 62 C3
Jequié 93 E5
Jequitinhonha 93 F5
Jequitinhonha → 93 F6
Jerada 54 B4
Jerantut 37 D2
Jérémie 86 C5
Jerez de la Frontera 18 D2
Jerez de los Caballeros 18 C2
Jerilderie 63 C4
Jersey 11 G5
Jersey City 73 D8
Jerusalem 47 E3
Jervis B. 63 C5
Jesselton = Kota Kinabalu 36 C5
Jessore 41 F7
Jeypore 40 H4
Jhal Jhao 42 F4
Jhalawar 43 G10
Jhang Maghiana 42 D8
Jhansi 43 G11
Jharsaguda 40 G5
Jhelum 42 C8
Jhelum → 42 D8
Jhunjhunu 42 E9
Jiamusi 35 B8
Ji'an 35 D6
Jianchuan 34 D4
Jiangling 35 C6
Jiangmen 35 D6
Jiangsu □ 35 C6
Jiangxi □ 35 D6
Jian'ou 35 D6
Jianshui 34 D5
Jiao Xian 35 C7
Jiaozuo 35 C6
Jiaxing 35 C7
Jiayi 35 D7
Jibuti = Djibouti ■ 49 E3
Jiddah 47 G4
Jido 41 C10
Jihlava 16 D2
Jihlava → 16 D3
Jijel 54 A6
Jijiga 49 F3
Jilin 35 B7
Jilong 35 D7
Jima 53 G6
Jiménez 84 B4
Jinan 35 C6
Jindabyne 63 C4
Jindrichuv Hradeç 16 D2
Jingdezhen 35 D6
Jinggu 34 D5
Jingxi 35 D5
Jinhua 35 D6
Jining, *Nei Mongol Zizhiqu, China* 35 B6
Jining, *Shandong, China* 35 C6
Jinja 57 D6
Jinnah Barrage 42 C7
Jinotega 85 E7
Jinshi 35 D6
Jinzhou 35 B7
Jiparaná → 91 E6
Jipijapa 90 D2
Jisr ash Shughūr 46 D4
Jiu → 22 C4
Jiujiang 35 D6
Jiuquan 34 C4
Jixi 35 B8
Jizzakh 29 E7
Joaçaba 94 B6
João Pessoa 92 D7
Joaquín V. González 94 B4
Jodhpur 42 F8
Jofane 59 C6
Jogjakarta = Yogyakarta 37 F4
Johannesburg 59 D5
Johnson City 75 A6
Johnston Falls = Mambilima Falls 57 G5
Johnstown 73 D6
Johor Baharu 37 D2
Joinvile 94 B7
Joinville I. 96 A4
Joliet 72 D1
Joliette 69 D3
Jolo 38 C2
Jome 39 E3
Jonesboro 79 B8
Jönköping 9 G10
Jonquière 69 D3
Joplin 79 A6
Jordan ■ 47 E4
Jorhat 41 D10
Jorong 37 E4
Jos 55 G6
Jowzjān □ 45 B6
Juan de Fuca Str. 80 A1
Juan de Nova 59 H8
Juan Fernández, Arch. de 89 G3
Juárez 94 D5
Juàzeiro 93 D5
Juàzeiro do Norte 92 D6
Jubbulpore = Jabalpur 43 H11
Juby, C. 54 C2
Júcar → 19 C5
Juchitán 85 D5
Jugoslavia = Yugoslavia ■ 22 B3
Juiz de Fora 93 G5
Juli 91 G5
Juliaca 91 G4
Jullundur 42 D9
Jumilla 19 C5
Jumla 40 C4
Jumna = Yamuna → 40 E3
Junagadh 43 J7
Jundiaí 94 A7
Juneau 71 C6
Junee 63 B4
Jungfrau 13 C7
Junggar Pendi 34 B3
Junín 94 C4
Junín de los Andes 95 D2
Jūniyah 46 D3
Jur, Nahr el → 53 G4
Jura = Jura, Mts. du 13 C7
Jura = Schwäbische Alb 14 D5
Jura 10 D4
Jura, Mts. du 13 C7
Jurado 90 B3
Juruá → 90 D5
Juruena → 91 E7
Juruti 92 C2

Justo Daract 94 C3
Jutland = Jylland 9 G9
Juventud, I. de la 86 B3
Juwain 42 D2
Jylland 9 G9
Jyväskylä 8 F13

## K

K2 42 B10
Kaapkruis 58 C2
Kaapstad = Cape Town 58 E3
Kabaena 39 F2
Kabala 55 G2
Kabale 57 E6
Kabalo 57 F5
Kabambare 57 E5
Kabanjahe 37 D1
Kabara 55 E4
Kabardino-Balkar Republic = Kabardino Balkaria □ 25 E5
Kabardino Balkaria □ 25 E5
Kabare 39 E4
Kabarega Falls 57 D6
Kabasalan 38 C2
Kabba 55 G6
Kabīr, Zab al → 46 C5
Kabīr Kūh 47 D6
Kabkabīyah 53 F3
Kabompo → 58 A4
Kabongo 57 F5
Kabūd Gonbad 44 B4
Kābul 42 B6
Kābul □ 42 B6
Kabul → 42 C8
Kaburuang 39 D3
Kabwe 59 A5
Kachchh, Gulf of 43 H6
Kachchh, Rann of 43 G6
Kachin □ 41 D11
Kachiry 29 D8
Kaçkar 46 B5
Kadan Kyun 36 B1
Kadina 62 B2
Kadirli 46 C4
Kadiyevka = Stakhanov 25 D4
Kadoma 59 B5
Kâdugli 53 F4
Kaduna 55 F6
Kaédi 55 E2
Kaelé 53 F1
Kaesŏng 35 C7
Kāf 47 E4
Kafakumba 56 F4
Kafan = Kapan 25 F6
Kafanchan 55 G6
Kaffrine 55 F1
Kafia Kingi 53 G3
Kafirévs, Ákra 23 E5
Kafue → 59 B5
Kafulwe 57 F5
Kaga Bandoro 56 C3
Kagan 29 F7
Kağizman 46 B5
Kagoshima 33 D2
Kagoshima-Wan 33 D2
Kagul = Cahul 17 F9
Kahama 57 E6
Kahayan → 37 E4
Kahemba 56 F3
Kahnūj 44 E4
Kahoolawe 82 H12
Kahramanmaraş 46 C4
Kai, Kepulauan 39 F4
Kai Besar 39 F4
Kai Is. = Kai, Kepulauan 39 F4
Kai Kecil 39 F4
Kaiama 55 G5
Kaiapoi 65 E5
Kaieteur Falls 90 B7
Kaifeng 35 C6
Kaikohe 64 A5
Kaikoura 65 E5
Kaikoura Ra. 65 D5
Kaimana 39 E4
Kaimanawa Mts. 64 C6
Kaingaroa Forest 64 C7
Kainji Res. 55 F5
Kaipara Harbour 64 B6
Kaironi 39 E4
Kairouan 54 A7
Kaiserslautern 14 D4
Kaitaia 64 A5
Kaitangata 65 G3
Kajaani 8 F13
Kajabbi 61 D6
Kajana = Kajaani 8 F13
Kajo Kaji 53 H5
Kaka 53 F5
Kakamas 58 D4
Kakamega 57 D6
Kakanui Mts. 65 F4
Kakhovka 25 D3
Kakhovske Vdskh. 25 D3
Kakinada 40 J4
Kalaallit Nunaat = Greenland ■ 66 C9
Kalabagh 42 C7
Kalabahi 39 F2
Kalabo 58 A4
Kalach 24 C5
Kaladan → 41 G9
Kalahari 58 C4
Kalakan 31 D9
Kalámai 23 F4
Kalamata = Kalámai 23 F4
Kalamazoo 72 C3
Kalan 46 C4
Kalao 39 F2
Kalaotoa 39 F2
Kalat 42 E5
Kalce 20 B5
Kale 23 F7
Kalegauk Kyun 41 K11
Kalemie 57 F5
Kalewa 41 F10
Kalgan = Zhangjiakou 35 B6
Kalgoorlie-Boulder 60 G3
Kaliakra, Nos 22 C7
Kalianda 37 F3
Kalibo 38 B2
Kalima 57 E5
Kalimantan 37 E4
Kalimantan Barat □ 37 D4
Kalimantan Selatan □ 37 E5
Kalimantan Tengah □ 37 E4
Kalimantan Timur □ 37 D5
Kálimnos 23 F6
Kalinin = Tver 24 B4
Kaliningrad, *Kaliningd., Russia* 24 C1
Kaliningrad, *Moskva, Russia* 24 B4
Kalinkavichy 17 B9
Kalinkovichi = Kalinkavichy 17 B9
Kalispell 81 A6
Kalisz 16 C4
Kaliua 57 F6
Kalkrand 58 C3
Kalmar 9 G11
Kalmyk Republic = Kalmykia □ 25 D6
Kalmykia □ 25 D6
Kalocsa 16 E4
Kalomo 59 B5
Kaluga 24 C4
Kalush 17 D7
Kalutara 43 R11
Kama → 29 D6
Kamaishi 33 G12
Kamaran 49 D3
Kamchatka, P-ov. 31 D13
Kamchatka Pen. = Kamchatka, P-ov. 31 D13
Kamchiya → 22 C6
Kamen 29 D9
Kamenjak, Rt. 20 B4
Kamenka Bugskaya = Kamyanka-Buzka 17 C7
Kamensk Uralskiy 29 D7
Kamin-Kashyrskyy 17 C7
Kamina 57 F5
Kamloops 71 C7
Kampala 57 D6
Kampar → 37 D2
Kampen 14 B3
Kampot 36 B2
Kampuchea = Cambodia ■ 36 B3
Kampung → 39 F5
Kampungbaru = Tolitoli 39 D2
Kamrau, Teluk 39 E4
Kamsack 71 C9
Kamyanets-Podilskyy 17 D8
Kamyanka-Buzka 17 C7
Kamyshin 24 C6
Kanaaupscow 69 C3
Kananga 56 F4
Kanash 24 B6
Kanastraíon, Ákra = Palioúrion, Ákra 23 E4
Kanazawa 32 A5
Kanchanaburi 36 B1
Kanchenjunga 40 D7
Kanchipuram 43 N11
Kanda Kanda 56 F4
Kandahar = Qandahār 42 D4
Kandalaksha 28 C4
Kandalu 42 E3
Kandangan 37 E5
Kandi 55 F5
Kandla 43 H7
Kandos 63 B4
Kandy 43 R12
Kangaroo I. 62 C2
Kangāvar 46 D7
Kangean, Kepulauan 37 F5
Kangean Is. = Kangean, Kepulauan 37 F5
Kangiqsualujjuaq 68 C4
Kangiqsujuaq 68 B3
Kangirsuk 68 C4
Kangnŭng 35 C7
Kango 56 D2
Kangto 41 D9
Kaniapiskau → 68 C4
Kaniapiskau L. 69 C4
Kanin, Poluostrov 28 C5
Kanin Nos, Mys 28 C5
Kanin Pen. = Kanin, Poluostrov 28 C5
Kaniva 62 C3
Kankakee 72 D2
Kankan 55 F3
Kankendy = Xankändi 25 F6
Kanker 40 G3
Kannapolis 75 B7
Kannauj 42 F11
Kannod 43 H10
Kano 55 F6
Kanowit 37 D4
Kanoya 33 D2
Kanpetlet 41 G9
Kanpur 40 D3
Kansas □ 76 F5
Kansas City, *Kans., U.S.A.* 77 F7
Kansas City, *Mo., U.S.A.* 77 F7
Kansk 30 D7
Kansu = Gansu □ 34 C5
Kantang 36 C1
Kanuma 32 A6
Kanye 59 C5
Kaohsiung = Gaoxiong 35 D7
Kaokoveld 58 B2
Kaolack 55 F1
Kapan 25 F6
Kapanga 56 F4
Kapchagai = Qapshaghay 29 E8
Kapfenberg 15 E8
Kapiri Mposhi 59 A5
Kāpīsā □ 45 C7
Kapit 37 D4
Kapoeta 53 H5
Kaposvár 16 E3
Kapuas → 37 E3
Kapuas Hulu, Pegunungan 37 D4
Kapuas Hulu Ra. = Kapuas Hulu, Pegunungan 37 D4
Kapunda 62 B2
Kapuni 64 C6
Kaputar 63 B5
Kara 28 C7

Kara Bogaz Gol, Zaliv = Garabogazköl Aylagy 29 E6
Kara Kalpak Republic □ = Karakalpakstan □ 29 E6
Kara Kum 29 F6
Kara Sea 28 B8
Karabiğa 23 D6
Karabük 46 B3
Karaburun 23 E6
Karabutak = Qarabutaq 29 E7
Karacabey 23 D7
Karacasu 23 F7
Karachi 43 G5
Karad 43 L9
Karadeniz Boğazı 22 D7
Karaganda = Qaraghandy 29 E8
Karagayly 29 E8
Karaikal 43 P11
Karaikkudi 43 P11
Karaj 44 C2
Karakalpakstan □ 29 E6
Karakas 29 E9
Karakelong 38 D3
Karakitang 39 D3
Karaklis = Vanadzor 25 E5
Karakoram Pass 42 B10
Karakoram Ra. 42 B10
Karalon 30 D9
Karaman 46 C3
Karamay 34 B3
Karambu 37 E5
Karamea Bight 65 D4
Karasburg 58 D3
Karasino 28 C9
Karasuk 29 D8
Karatau = Qaratau 29 E8
Karatau, Khrebet 29 E7
Karawanken 20 A5
Karazhal 29 E8
Karbalā 47 D6
Karcag 16 E5
Kardhítsa 23 E3
Karelia □ 28 C4
Karelian Republic □ = Karelia □ 28 C4
Kargānrūd 46 C7
Kargasok 29 D9
Kargat 29 D9
Kargil 42 B10
Kariba, L. 59 B5
Kariba Dam 59 B5
Kariba Gorge 59 B5
Karibib 58 C3
Karimata, Kepulauan 37 E3
Karimata, Selat 37 E3
Karimata Is. = Karimata, Kepulauan 37 E3
Karimnagar 43 K11
Karimunjawa, Kepulauan 37 F4
Karin 49 E4
Karkaralinsk = Qarqaraly 29 E8
Karkinitska Zatoka 25 D3
Karkinitskiy Zaliv = Karkinitska Zatoka 25 D3
Karl-Marx-Stadt = Chemnitz 15 C7
Karlovac 20 B5
Karlovo 22 C5
Karlovy Vary 16 C1
Karlsbad = Karlovy Vary 16 C1
Karlskrona 9 G11
Karlsruhe 14 D5
Karlstad 9 G10
Karnal 42 E10
Karnali → 40 C3
Karnaphuli Res. 41 F9
Karnataka □ 43 N10
Karnische Alpen 20 A4
Kärnten □ 15 E7
Karonga 57 F6
Karoonda 62 C2
Karora 53 E6
Kárpathos 23 G6
Kars 46 B5
Karsakpay 29 E7
Karshi = Qarshi 29 F7
Karsun 24 C6
Karufa 39 E4
Karungu 57 E6
Karviná 16 D4
Karwar 43 M9
Kasai → 56 E3
Kasama 57 G6
Kasanga 57 F6
Kasangulu 56 E3
Kasaragod 43 N9
Kasba L. 70 B9
Kasempa 59 A5
Kasenga 57 G5
Kāshān 44 C2
Kashi 34 C2
Kashk-e Kohneh 42 B3
Kāshmar 44 C4
Kashun Noerh = Gaxun Nur 34 B5
Kasimov 24 C5
Kasiruta 39 E3
Kasongo 57 E5
Kasongo Lunda 56 F3
Kásos 23 G6
Kassalâ 53 E6
Kassel 14 C5
Kassue 39 F5
Kastamonu 46 B3
Kasulu 57 E6
Kasur 42 D9
Katako Kombe 56 E4
Katamatite 63 C4
Katanga = Shaba □ 57 F4
Katangi 43 J11
Kateríni 23 D4
Katha 41 E11
Kathiawar 43 H7
Katihar 40 E6
Katima Mulilo 58 B4
Katingan = Mendawai → 37 E4
Katiola 55 G3
Katmandu 40 D5
Katoomba 63 B5
Katowice 16 C4
Katsina 55 F6
Kattegat 9 G10
Kauai 82 G11
Kaunas 24 C1
Kaura Namoda 55 F6
Kaválla 22 D5
Kaw 92 B3
Kawagoe 32 B6
Kawaguchi 32 B6
Kawambwa 57 F5
Kawardha 40 G3
Kawasaki 32 B6
Kawerau 64 C7
Kawhia Harbour 64 C6
Kawio, Kepulauan 38 D3
Kawnro 41 F12
Kawthoolei = Kawthule □ 41 H11
Kawthule □ 41 H11
Kaya 55 F4
Kayah □ 41 H11
Kayan → 37 D5
Kayeli 39 E3
Kayes 55 F2
Kayoa 39 D3
Kayrunnera 62 B3
Kayseri 46 C3
Kayuagung 37 E2
Kazachye 31 B11
Kazakstan ■ 29 E7
Kazan 24 B6
Kazanlŭk 22 C5
Kazatin = Kozyatyn 17 D9
Kāzerūn 44 D2
Kazumba 56 F4
Kazym → 28 C7
Ké-Macina 55 F3
Kéa 23 F5
Kebnekaise 8 E11
Kebri Dehar 49 F3
Kecskemét 16 E4
Kediri 37 F4
Kédougou 55 F2
Keetmanshoop 58 D3
Kefallinía 23 E3
Kefamenanu 39 F2
Keffi 55 G6
Keighley 11 E6
Keith 62 C3
Keith Arm 70 B7
Kekri 42 G9
Kël 30 C10
Kelang 37 D2
Kelibia 52 A1
Kellé 56 E2
Kells = Ceanannus Mor 11 E3
Kélo 53 G2
Kelowna 71 D8
Kelso 65 F3
Keluang 37 D2
Kem 28 C4
Kema 39 D3
Kemah 46 C4
Kemerovo 29 D9
Kemi 8 E12
Kemi älv = Kemijoki → 8 E12
Kemijoki → 8 E12
Kemp Land 96 A9
Kempsey 63 B5
Kempten 14 E6
Kendal 37 F4
Kendall 63 B5
Kendari 39 E2
Kendawangan 37 E4
Kende 55 F5
Kendrapara 40 G6
Kenema 55 G2
Keng Tawng 41 G12
Keng Tung 41 G12
Kenge 56 E3
Kenhardt 58 D4
Kenitra 54 B3
Kennedy Taungdeik 41 F9
Kennewick 80 B4
Kenogami → 69 C2
Kenosha 72 C2
Kent Group 62 C4
Kent Pen. 70 B9
Kentau 29 E7
Kentucky □ 72 F3
Kentville 69 D4
Kenya ■ 57 D7
Kenya, Mt. 57 E7
Kepi 39 F5
Kerala □ 43 P10
Kerang 62 C3
Kerch 25 D4
Kerchoual 55 E5
Keren 53 E6
Kericho 57 E7
Kerinci 37 E2
Kerki 29 F7
Kérkira 23 E2
Kermadec Is. 64 M13
Kermadec Trench 65 N13
Kermān 44 D4
Kermān □ 44 D4
Kermānshāh = Bākhtarān 46 D6
Kerme Körfezi 23 F6
Kerrobert 71 C9
Kerulen → 35 B6
Kerzaz 54 C4
Keşan 22 D6
Kestenga 28 C4
Ket → 29 D9
Keta 55 G5
Ketapang 37 E4
Ketchikan 71 C6
Kętrzyn 16 A5
Keweenaw B. 69 D2
Key West 86 B3
Khabarovo 28 C7
Khabarovsk 31 E11
Khābūr → 46 D5
Khairpur 42 F6
Khakassia □ 30 D6
Khakhea 58 C4
Khalkhāl 46 C7
Khalkís 23 E4
Khalmer-Sede = Tazovskiy 28 C8
Khalmer Yu 28 C7
Khalturin 24 B6
Khalūf 48 C6
Khambat, G. of 43 J8
Khambhat 43 H8
Khamir 49 D3
Khānābād 45 B7
Khānaqīn 46 D6
Khandwa 43 J10
Khanewal 42 D7
Khaniá 23 G5
Khaníon, Kólpos 23 G4
Khankendy = Xankändi 25 F6
Khanty-Mansiysk 29 C7
Khapcheranga 30 E9
Kharagpur 40 F6
Kharan Kalat 42 E4
Kharānaq 44 C3
Kharda 43 K9
Khârga, El Wâhât el 52 C5
Khargon 43 J9
Khārk, Jazireh 47 E7
Kharkiv 24 D4

Kharkov = Kharkiv 24 D4
Kharovsk 24 B5
Kharsānīya 47 F7
Kharta 22 D7
Khartoum = El Khartûm 53 E5
Khāsh 42 E2
Khashm el Girba 53 F6
Khaskovo 22 D5
Khatanga 30 B8
Khatanga ⟶ 30 B8
Khaybar, Harrat 47 F5
Khed Brahma 43 G8
Khemmarat 36 A3
Khenchela 54 A6
Khenifra 54 B3
Kherson 25 D3
Kheta ⟶ 30 B8
Khilok 30 D9
Khíos 23 E6
Khiuma = Hiiumaa 24 B1
Khiva 29 E7
Khīyāv 46 C6
Khmelnik 17 D8
Khmelnitskiy = Khmelnytskyy 17 D8
Khmelnytskyy 17 D8
Khmer Rep. – Cambodia ■ 36 B3
Khodoriv 17 D7
Khodzent = Khudzhand 29 E7
Khojak P. 42 D5
Kholm, *Afghan.* 45 B6
Kholm, *Russia* 24 B3
Khomeyn 44 C2
Khon Kaen 36 A2
Khoper ⟶ 29 E5
Khóra Sfakíon 23 G5
Khorat = Nakhon Ratchasima 36 B2
Khorramābād 46 D7
Khorrāmshahr 47 E7
Khotyn 17 D8
Khouribga 54 B3
Khowai 41 E8
Khoyniki 17 C9
Khu Khan 36 B2
Khudzhand 29 E7
Khūgīānī 42 D4
Khulna 41 F7
Khulna □ 41 F7
Khūr 44 C4
Khuraysṣ 47 F7
Khūrīyā Mūrīyā, Jazā 'ir 48 D6
Khush 42 C3
Khushab 42 C8
Khust 17 D6
Khuzdar 42 F5
Khvor 44 C3
Khvormūj 44 D2
Khvoy 46 C6
Khyber Pass 42 B7
Kiama 63 B5
Kiamba 38 C2
Kiangsi = Jiangxi □ 35 D6
Kiangsu = Jiangsu □ 35 C6
Kibangou 56 F2
Kibombo 57 E5
Kibondo 57 E6
Kibwesa 57 F5
Kibwezi 57 E7
Kicking Horse Pass 71 C8
Kidal 55 E5
Kidnappers, C. 64 C7
Kiel 14 A6
Kiel Canal = Nord-Ostsee-Kanal ⟶ 14 A5
Kielce 16 C5
Kieler Bucht 14 A6
Kiev = Kyyiv 17 C10
Kiffa 55 E2
Kifrī 46 D6
Kigali 57 E6
Kigoma-Ujiji 57 E5
Kihee 62 A3
Kii-Suidō 32 C4
Kikinda 22 B3
Kikládhes 23 F5
Kikwit 56 E3
Kilcoy 63 A5
Kilimanjaro 57 E7
Kilindini 57 E7
Kilis 46 C4
Kiliya 17 F9
Kilkenny 11 E3
Kilkís 23 D4
Killarney, *Australia* 63 A5
Killarney, *Ireland* 11 E2
Killeen 78 D5
Killíni 23 F4
Kilmarnock 10 D4
Kilmore 63 C3
Kilosa 57 F7
Kilrush 11 E2
Kilwa Kivinje 57 F7
Kimaam 39 F5
Kimba 62 B2
Kimberley 58 D4
Kimberley Plateau 60 D4
Kimry 24 B4
Kinabalu, Gunong 36 C5
Kindia 55 G2
Kindu 57 E5
Kineshma 24 B5
King George B. 95 G4
King George I. 96 A4
King George Is. 69 C2
King I. = Kadan Kyun 36 B1
King I. 62 C3
King William I. 70 B10
King William's Town 59 E5
Kingaroy 63 A5
Kingoonya 62 B2
Kings Canyon National Park 82 B3
King's Lynn 11 E7
Kingscote 62 C2
Kingsport 75 A6
Kingston, *Canada* 69 D3
Kingston, *Jamaica* 86 C4
Kingston, *N.Z.* 65 F3
Kingston South East 62 C2
Kingston upon Hull 11 E6
Kingstown 87 D7
Kingsville 78 F5
Kınık 23 E6
Kinkala 56 E2
Kinleith 64 C6
Kinsale 11 F2
Kinshasa 56 E3
Kinston 75 B9
Kintampo 55 G4
Kintap 37 E5
Kiparissía 23 F3
Kiparissiakós Kólpos 23 F3
Kipembawe 57 F6
Kipili 57 F6
Kipushi 59 A5
Kirghizia ■ = Kyrgyzstan ■ 29 E8
Kirghizstan = Kyrgyzstan ■ 29 E8
Kiri 56 E3
Kiribati ■ 64 K12
Kırıkkale 46 C3
Kirillov 24 B4
Kirin = Jilin 35 B7
Kiritimati 65 J15
Kirkcaldy 10 C5
Kirkcudbright 11 D4
Kirkee 43 K8
Kirkenes 8 E14
Kirkland Lake 69 D2
Kırklareli 22 D6
Kirkūk 46 D6
Kirkwall 10 B5
Kirov 28 D5
Kirovabad = Gäncä 25 E6
Kirovakan = Vanadzor 25 E5
Kirovograd = Kirovohrad 25 D3
Kirovohrad 25 D3
Kirovsk = Babadayhan 29 F7
Kirovsk 28 C4
Kirsanov 24 C5
Kırşehir 46 C3
Kīrteh 45 C5
Kirthar Range 42 F5
Kiruna 8 E12
Kirundu 57 E5
Kiryū 32 A6
Kisangani 57 D5
Kisar 39 F3
Kiselevsk 29 D9
Kishanganj 40 D7
Kishangarh 42 F7
Kishinev = Chişinău 17 E9
Kishiwada 32 B4
Kishtwar 42 C9
Kisii 57 E6
Kisiju 57 F7
Kiska I. 71 C1
Kiskőrös 16 E4
Kiskunfélegyháza 16 E4
Kiskunhalas 16 E4
Kislovodsk 25 E5
Kiso-Sammyaku 32 B5
Kissidougou 55 G2
Kisumu 57 E6
Kita 55 F3
Kitab 29 F7
Kitakami-Gawa ⟶ 33 G12
Kitakyūshū 32 C2
Kitale 57 D7
Kitchener 69 D2
Kitega = Gitega 57 E5
Kitgum 57 D6
Kíthira 23 F4
Kíthnos 23 F5
Kittakittaooloo, L. 62 A2
Kitui 57 E7
Kitwe 59 A5
Kivertsi 17 C7
Kivu, L. 57 E5
Kiyev = Kyyiv 17 C10
Kiyevskoye Vdkhr. = Kyyivske Vdskh. 17 C10
Kızıl Irmak ⟶ 25 E4
Kizlyar 25 E6
Kizyl-Arvat = Gyzylarbat 29 F6
Kladno 16 C2
Klagenfurt 15 E8
Klaìpeda 24 B1
Klamath Falls 80 D3
Klamath Mts. 80 E2
Klarälven ⟶ 9 G10
Klatovy 16 D1
Klawer 58 E3
Klerksdorp 59 D5
Kletsk = Klyetsk 17 B8
Klin 28 D4
Kłodzko 16 C3
Klondike 70 B6
Klouto 55 G5
Kluane L. 70 B6
Kluczbork 16 C4
Klyetsk 17 B8
Knossós 23 G5
Knox Coast 96 A12
Knoxville 75 B6
Koartac = Quaqtaq 68 B4
Koba, *Aru, Indonesia* 39 F4
Koba, *Bangka, Indonesia* 37 E3
Kobarid 20 A4
Kobdo = Hovd 34 B4
Kōbe 32 B4
København 9 G10
Koblenz 14 C4
Kobroor, Kepulauan 39 F4
Kobryn 17 B7
Kocaeli = İzmit 25 E2
Kočani 22 D4
Koch Bihar 41 D7
Kōchi 32 C3
Kochiu = Gejiu 34 D5
Kodiak 71 C4
Kodiak I. 71 C4
Koes 58 D3
Kofiau 39 E3
Koforidua 55 G4
Kōfu 32 B6
Kogan 63 A5
Koh-i-Bābā 42 B5
Kohat 42 C7
Kohima 41 E10
Kohkīlūyeh va Būyer Aḥmadi □ 44 D2
Kohler Ra. 96 B1
Kokand = Qūqon 29 E8
Kokas 39 E4
Kokchetav = Kökshetaū 29 D7
Koko Kyunzu 41 K9
Kokomo 72 D2
Kokonau 39 E5
Kökshetaū 29 D7
Koksoak ⟶ 68 C4
Kokstad 59 E5
Kola, *Indonesia* 39 F4
Kola, *Russia* 28 C4
Kola Pen. = Kolskiy Poluostrov 28 C4

Kolaka 39 E2
Kolar 43 N11
Kolar Gold Fields 43 N11
Kolayat 42 F8
Kolchugino = Leninsk-Kuznetskiy 29 D9
Kolda 55 F2
Kole 56 E4
Kolepom = Yos Sudarso, Pulau 39 F5
Kolguyev, Ostrov 28 C5
Kolhapur 43 L9
Kolín 16 C2
Köln 14 C4
Koło 16 B4
Kołobrzeg 16 A2
Kolokani 55 F3
Kolomna 24 B4
Kolomyya 17 D7
Kolonodale 39 E2
Kolosib 41 E9
Kolpashevo 29 D9
Kolpino 24 B3
Kolskiy Poluostrov 28 C4
Kolwezi 57 G5
Kolyma → 31 C13
Komárno 16 E4
Komatsu 32 A5
Komi □ 28 C6
Kommunarsk = Alchevsk 25 D4
Kommunizma, Pik 29 F8
Komodo 39 F1
Komono 56 E2
Komoran, Pulau 39 F5
Komotini 22 D5
Kompong Cham 36 B3
Kompong Chhnang 36 B2
Kompong Som 36 B2
Komrat = Comrat 17 E9
Komsomolets, Ostrov 30 A7
Konarhá □ 42 B7
Konch 42 G11
Kondoa 57 E7
Konduga 53 F1
Köneürgench 29 E6
Kong 55 G4
Kong, Koh 36 B2
Konglu 41 D11
Kongolo 57 F5
Kongor 53 G5
Königsberg = Kaliningrad 24 C1
Konin 16 B4
Konjic 20 C6
Konosha 28 C5
Konotop 24 C3
Konqi He → 34 B4
Końskie 16 C5
Konstanz 14 E5
Kontagora 55 F6
Kontum 36 B3
Konya 46 C3
Konya Ovası 46 C3
Konza 57 E7
Kooloonong 62 B3
Koondrook 63 C3
Koonibba 62 B1
Koorawatha 63 B4
Kootenay L. 71 D8
Kopaonik 22 C3
Koper 20 B4
Kopeysk 29 D7
Kopi 62 B2
Koprivnica 20 A6
Kopychyntsi 17 D7
Korab 22 D3
Korça 23 D3
Korce = Korça 23 D3
Korčula 20 C6
Kordestan 46 D5
Kordestān □ 46 D6
Kordofân 53 F4
Korea, North ■ 35 C7
Korea, South ■ 35 C7
Korea Bay 35 C7
Korea Strait 35 C7
Korets 17 C8
Korhogo 55 G3
Korim 39 E5
Korinthiakós Kólpos 23 E4
Kórinthos 23 F4
Kōriyama 33 G12
Korneshty = Corneşti 17 E9
Koro, *Ivory C.* 55 G3
Koro, *Mali* 55 F4
Korogwe 57 F7
Koroit 62 C3
Koror 38 C4
Körös → 16 E5
Korosten 17 C9
Korostyshev 17 C9
Korti 53 E5
Kortrijk 14 C2
Kos 23 F6
Kościan 16 B3
Kosciuszko, Mt. 63 C4
Kosha 52 D5
K'oshih = Kashi 34 C2
Košice 16 D5
Kosovo □ 22 C3
Kosovska-Mitrovica 22 C3
Kôstî 53 F5
Kostopil 17 C8
Kostroma 24 B5
Kostrzyn 16 B2
Koszalin 16 A3
Kota 43 G9
Kota Baharu 36 C2
Kota Belud 36 C5
Kota Kinabalu 36 C5
Kota Tinggi 37 D2
Kotaagung 37 F2
Kotabaru 37 E5
Kotabumi 37 E2
Kotamobagu 39 D2
Kotawaringin 37 E4
Kotelnich 24 B6
Kotelnyy, Ostrov 31 B11
Kotka 9 F13
Kotlas 28 C5
Kotli 42 C8
Kotor 22 C2
Kotovsk 17 E9
Kotri 42 G6
Kottayam 43 Q10
Kotturu 43 M10
Kotuy → 30 B8
Kotzebue 71 B3
Kouango 56 D4
Koudougou 55 F4
Kouilou → 56 E2
Kouki 56 C3
Koula Moutou 56 E2
Koulen 36 B2
Koulikoro 55 F3
Koumra 53 G2
Kounradskiy 29 E8
Kouroussa 55 F3
Kousseri 53 F1
Koutiala 55 F3
Kovel 17 C7
Kovrov 24 B5
Kowloon 35 D6
Köyceğiz 23 F7
Koyuk 71 B3
Koyukuk → 71 B4
Kozan 46 C3
Kozáni 23 D3
Kozhikode = Calicut 43 P9
Kozyatyn 17 D9
Kpalimé 55 G5
Kra, Isthmus of = Kra, Kho Khot 36 B1
Kra, Kho Khot 36 B1
Kragujevac 22 B3
Krajina 20 B6
Krakatau = Rakata, Pulau 37 F3
Kraków 16 C4
Kraljevo 22 C3
Kramatorsk 25 D4
Kranj 20 A5
Kraśnik 16 C6
Krasnoarmeysk 29 D5
Krasnodar 25 D4
Krasnoperekopsk 25 D3
Krasnoselkupsk 28 C9
Krasnoturinsk 28 D7
Krasnoufimsk 29 D6
Krasnouralsk 29 D7
Krasnovodsk = Krasnowodsk 29 E6
Krasnowodsk 29 E6
Krasnoyarsk 30 D7
Krasnyy Luch 25 D4
Krasnyy Yar 25 D6
Kratie 36 B3
Krau 39 E6
Krefeld 14 C4
Kremen 20 B5
Kremenchug = Kremenchuk 24 D3
Kremenchuk 24 D3
Kremenchuksk Vdskh. 24 D3
Kremenets 17 C7
Krems 15 D8
Kribi 56 D1
Krichev = Krychaw 17 B10
Krishna → 40 K3
Krishnanagar 41 F7
Kristiansand 9 G9
Kristiansund 8 F9
Kríti 23 G5
Krivoy Rog = Kryvyy Rih 25 D3
Krk 20 B5
Kronprins Olav Kyst 96 A9
Kronshtadt 24 B2
Kroonstad 59 D5
Kropotkin, *Irkutsk, Russia* 30 D9
Kropotkin, *Krasnodar, Russia* 25 D5
Krosno 16 D5
Krotoszyn 16 C3
Krugersdorp 59 D5
Krung Thep = Bangkok 36 B2
Krupki 17 A9
Kruševac 22 C3
Krychaw 17 B10
Krymskiy Poluostrov = Krymskyy Pivostriv 25 D3
Krymskyy Pivostriv 25 D3
Kryvyy Rih 25 D3
Ksar el Boukhari 54 A5
Ksar el Kebir 54 B3
Ksar es Souk = Ar Rachidiya 54 B4
Kuala 37 D3
Kuala Kubu Baharu 37 D2
Kuala Lipis 37 D2
Kuala Lumpur 37 D2
Kuala Terengganu 36 C2
Kualajelai 37 E4
Kualakapuas 37 E4
Kualakurun 37 E4
Kualapembuang 37 E4
Kualasimpang 37 D1
Kuandang 39 D2
Kuangchou = Guangzhou 35 D6
Kuantan 37 D2
Kuba = Quba 25 E6
Kuban → 25 D4
Kucing 37 D4
Kuda 43 H7
Kudat 36 C5
Kudymkar 28 D6
Kueiyang = Guiyang 35 D5
Kufra Oasis = Al Kufrah 52 D3
Kufstein 15 E7
Kugluktuk 70 B8
Kūh-e 'Alijūq 44 D2
Kūh-e-Hazārām 44 D4
Kūh-e Sorkh 44 C4
Kūh-e Taftān 45 D5
Kūhak 42 F3
Kūhhā-ye-Bashākerd 45 E4
Kūhpāyeh 44 C3
Kuito 58 A3
Kujū-San 32 C2
Kukawa 53 F1
Kukësi 22 C3
Kula 23 E7
Kulasekarappattinam 43 Q11
Kuldja = Yining 34 B3
Kŭlob 29 F7
Kulsary 29 E6
Kulunda 29 D8
Kulwin 62 C3
Kulyab = Kŭlob 29 F7
Kum Tekei 29 E8
Kuma → 25 E6
Kumagaya 32 A6
Kumai 37 E4
Kumamba, Kepulauan 39 E5
Kumamoto 32 C2
Kumanovo 22 C3
Kumara 65 E4
Kumasi 55 G4
Kumayri = Gyumri 25 E5
Kumba 56 D1
Kumbakonam 43 P11

Kumbarilla 63 A5
Kumo 55 F7
Kumon Bum 41 D11
Kunama 63 C4
Kungala 63 A5
Kungrad = Qŭnghirot 29 E6
Kungur 29 D6
Kunlong 41 F12
Kunlun Shan 34 C3
Kunming 34 D5
Kunsan 35 C7
Kunya-Urgench = Köneürgench 29 E6
Kuopio 8 F13
Kupa → 20 B6
Kupyansk 28 E4
Kuqa 34 B3
Kür → 25 E6
Kura = Kür → 25 E6
Kurashiki 32 B3
Kurayoshi 32 B3
Kŭrdzhali 22 D5
Kure 32 B3
Kurgaldzhinskiy 29 D8
Kurgan 29 D7
Kuria Maria Is. = Khūrīyā Mūrīyā, Jazā 'ir 48 D6
Kurigram 41 E7
Kuril Is. = Kurilskiye Ostrova 31 E12
Kurilskiye Ostrova 31 E12
Kurmuk 53 F5
Kurnool 43 L11
Kurow 65 F4
Kurrajong 63 B5
Kurri Kurri 63 B5
Kursk 24 C4
Kuruktag 34 B3
Kuruman 58 D4
Kurume 32 C2
Kus Gölü 23 D6
Kuşadası 23 F6
Kushiro 32 F12
Kushtia 41 F7
Kuskokwim → 71 B3
Kuskokwim B. 71 C3
Kustanay = Qostanay 29 D7
Kütahya 46 C2
Kutaisi 25 E5
Kutaraja = Banda Aceh 36 C1
Kutch, Gulf of = Kachchh, Gulf of 43 H6
Kutch, Rann of = Kachchh, Rann of 43 G6
Kutno 16 B4
Kutu 56 E3
Kutum 53 F3
Kuujjuaq 68 C4
Kuwait = Al Kuwayt 47 E7
Kuwait ■ 47 E6
Kuwana 32 B5
Kuybyshev = Samara 24 C7
Kuybyshev 29 D8
Kuybyshevskoye Vdkhr. 24 B6
Kūysanjaq 46 C6
Kuyumba 30 C7
Kuzey Anadolu Dağları 46 B3
Kuznetsk 24 C6
Kvarner 20 B5
Kvarnerič 20 B5
Kwakoegron 92 A2
Kwamouth 56 E3
Kwando → 58 B4
Kwangju 35 C7
Kwangsi-Chuang = Guangxi Zhuangzu Zizhiqu □ 35 D5
Kwangtung = Guangdong □ 35 D6
Kwatisore 39 E4
Kweichow = Guizhou □ 35 D5
Kwekwe 59 B5
Kwidzyn 16 B4
Kwoka 39 E4
Kyabé 53 G2
Kyabra Cr. → 63 A3
Kyabram 63 C4
Kyancutta 62 B2
Kyangin 41 H10
Kyaukpadaung 41 G10
Kyaukpyu 41 H9
Kyaukse 41 G11
Kyle Dam 59 C6
Kyneton 63 C3
Kyō-ga-Saki 32 B4
Kyoga, L. 57 D6
Kyogle 63 A5
Kyongpyaw 41 J10
Kyōto 32 B4
Kyrenia 46 D3
Kyrgyzstan ■ 29 E8
Kystatyam 30 C10
Kytal Ktakh 31 C10
Kyunhla 41 F10
Kyūshū 32 C2
Kyūshū-Sanchi 32 C2
Kyustendil 22 C4
Kyusyur 30 B10
Kywong 63 B4
Kyyiv 17 C10
Kyyivske Vdskh. 17 C10
Kyzyl Kum 29 E7
Kyzyl-Kyya 29 E8
Kzyl-Orda = Qyzylorda 29 E7

## L

La Albufera 19 C5
La Alcarria 19 B4
La Asunción 90 A6
La Banda 94 B4
La Calera 94 C2
La Carlota 94 C4
La Ceiba 85 D7
La Chaux de Fonds 13 C7
La Cocha 94 B3
La Coruña 18 A1
La Crosse 77 D9
La Dorada 90 B4
La Estrada 18 A1
La Grange 74 C5
La Guaira 90 A5
La Güera 54 D1
La Habana 86 B3
La Línea de la Concepción 18 D3
La Mancha 19 C4
La Palma, *Canary Is.* 54 C1
La Palma, *Panama* 86 E4
La Palma del Condado 18 D2
La Paragua 90 B6
La Paz, *Entre Ríos, Argentina* 94 C5
La Paz, *San Luis, Argentina* 94 C3
La Paz, *Bolivia* 91 G5
La Paz, *Mexico* 84 C2
La Pedrera 90 D5
La Plata 94 D5
La Quiaca 94 A3
La Rioja 94 B3
La Rioja □ 19 A4
La Robla 18 A3
La Roche-sur-Yon 12 C3
La Rochelle 12 C3
La Roda 19 C4
La Romana 87 C6
La Serena 94 B2
La Seyne-sur-Mer 13 E6
La Spézia 20 B2
La Tortuga 87 D6
La Tuque 69 D3
La Unión 95 E2
La Urbana 90 B5
La Vega 87 C5
Labe = Elbe → 14 B5
Labé 55 F2
Labis 37 D2
Laboulaye 94 C4
Labrador, Coast of □ 69 C4
Lábrea 91 E6
Labuan, Pulau 36 C5
Labuha 39 E3
Labuhanbajo 39 F2
Labuk, Telok 36 C5
Labyrinth, L. 62 B2
Labytnangi 28 C7
Lac La Biche 71 C8
Lac la Martre 70 B8
Lacanau 12 D3
Laccadive Is. = Lakshadweep Is. 26 H11
Lacepede B. 62 C2
Lachine 69 D3
Lachlan → 63 B3
Lackawanna 73 C6
Lacombe 71 C8
Ladakh Ra. 42 B10
Lādīz 45 D5
Ladoga, L. = Ladozhskoye Ozero 28 C4
Ladozhskoye Ozero 28 C4
Ladysmith, *Canada* 71 D7
Ladysmith, *S. Africa* 59 D5
Lae 61 B8
Lafayette 79 D7
Lafia 55 G6
Laghmān □ 45 C7
Laghouat 54 B5
Lagonoy Gulf 38 B2
Lagos, *Nigeria* 55 G5
Lagos, *Portugal* 18 D1
Laguna 94 B7
Lagunas, *Chile* 91 H5
Lagunas, *Peru* 90 E3
Lahad Datu 38 C1
Lahat 37 E2
Lahewa 37 D1
Lāhījān 46 C7
Lahn → 14 C4
Lahore 42 D9
Lahti 8 F13
Lahtis = Lahti 8 F13
Laï 53 G2
Laibin 35 D5
Laidley 63 A5
Laila = Laylá 47 G6
Lairg 10 B4
Lajere 55 F7
Lajes 94 B6
Lake Cargelligo 63 B4
Lake Charles 79 D7
Lake City 75 D6
Lake Harbour 68 B4
Lake Worth 75 F7
Lakeland 75 E7
Lakes Entrance 63 C4
Lakewood 72 D5
Lakonikós Kólpos 23 F4
Lakor 39 F3
Lakota 55 G3
Lakshadweep Is. 26 H11
Lala Ghat 41 E9
Lalibela 53 F6
Lalín 18 A1
Lalitapur = Patan 40 D5
Lamaing 41 K11
Lamas 91 E3
Lambaréné 56 E2
Lambert Glacier 96 B10
Lame 55 F6
Lamego 18 B2
Lameroo 62 C3
Lamía 23 E4
Lamon Bay 38 B2
Lampa 91 G4
Lampedusa 21 G4
Lampione 21 G4
Lampung □ 37 F2
Lamu 57 E8
Lanai I. 82 H12
Lanak La 42 B11
Lanak'o Shank'ou = Lanak La 42 B11
Lanao, L. 38 C2
Lancaster, *U.K.* 11 D5
Lancaster, *U.S.A.* 73 D7
Lancaster Sd. 68 A2
Lanchow = Lanzhou 35 C5
Lanciano 20 C5
Landeck 14 E6
Landes 12 D3
Landi Kotal 42 B7
Land's End 11 F4
Landshut 15 D7
La'nga Co 40 B3
Langkawi, P. 36 C1
Langkon 36 C5
Langres 13 C6
Langres, Plateau de 13 C6
Langsa 36 D1
Languedoc 13 E5
Langzhong 35 C5
Lannion 12 B2
Lansdowne 63 B5
Lansing 72 C3
Lanusei 21 E2

Lanzarote 54 C2
Lanzhou 35 C5
Laoag 38 A2
Laoang 38 B3
Laon 13 B5
Laos ■ 36 A3
Lapa 94 B7
Laparan 38 C1
Lapland = Lappland 8 E12
Lappland 8 E12
Lapseki 23 D6
Laptev Sea 30 B10
L'Áquila 20 C4
Lār 44 E3
Larache 54 A3
Laramie 76 E2
Larantuka 39 F2
Larap 38 B2
Larat 39 F4
Laredo 78 F4
Lariang 39 E1
Lárisa 23 E4
Larnaca 46 D3
Larne 11 D4
Larrimah 60 D5
Larsen Ice Shelf 96 A3
Larvik 9 G9
Laryak 29 C8
Las Anod 49 F4
Las Cruces 83 D9
Las Flores 94 D5
Las Khoreh 49 E4
Las Lajas 94 D2
Las Lomitas 94 A4
Las Palmas 54 C1
Las Pipinas 94 D5
Las Plumas 95 E3
Las Rosas 94 C4
Las Varillas 94 C4
Las Vegas 82 B5
Lashio 41 F11
Lassen Pk. 80 E3
Lastoursville 56 E2
Lastovo 20 C6
Latacunga 90 D3
Latakia = Al Lādhiqīyah 46 D3
Latina 20 D4
Latium = Lazio □ 20 C4
Latrobe 62 D4
Latvia ■ 24 B1
Lauchhammer 15 C7
Launceston 62 D4
Laurel 79 D9
Lauria 21 D5
Laurium 69 D2
Lausanne 13 C7
Laut 36 D3
Laut Kecil, Kepulauan 37 E5
Laval 12 B3
Lávrion 23 F5
Lawas 36 D5
Lawele 39 F2
Lawng Pit 41 E11
Lawrence, *N.Z.* 65 F3
Lawrence, *U.S.A.* 77 F7
Lawton 78 B4
Laylá 47 G6
Lazio □ 20 C4
Le Creusot 13 C6
Le Havre 12 B4
Le Mans 12 C4
Le Mont-St.-Michel 12 B3
Le Moule 87 C7
Le Puy-en-Velay 13 D5
Le Touquet-Paris-Plage 12 A4
Le Tréport 12 A4
Le Verdon-sur-Mer 12 D3
Leamington Spa = Royal Leamington Spa 11 E6
Leandro Norte Alem 94 B5
Leavenworth 77 F7
Lebak 38 C2
Lebanon ■ 46 D3
Lębork 16 A3
Lebrija 18 D2
Lebu 94 D2
Lecce 23 D2
Lecco 20 B2
Lech → 14 D6
Łęczyca 16 B4
Leduc 71 C8
Leeds 11 E6
Leer 14 B4
Leeton 63 B4
Leeuwarden 14 B3
Leeuwin, C. 60 G2
Leeward Is. 87 C7
Leganés 18 B4
Legazpi 38 B2
Leghorn = Livorno 20 C3
Legionowo 16 B5
Legnago 20 B3
Legnica 16 C3
Legume 63 A5
Leh 42 B10
Leicester 11 E6
Leiden 14 B3
Leie → 14 C2
Leine → 14 B5
Leinster □ 11 E3
Leipzig 15 C7
Leiria 18 C1
Leitrim 11 D2
Leizhou Bandao 35 D6
Leksula 39 E3
Lékva Ori 23 G5
Leleque 95 E2
Léman, L. 13 C7
Lemhi Ra. 81 C7
Lena → 30 B10
Leninabad = Khudzhand 29 E7
Leninakan = Gyumri 25 E5
Leningrad = Sankt-Peterburg 24 B3
Leninogorsk = Ridder 29 D9
Leninsk 25 D6
Leninsk-Kuznetskiy 29 D9
Lenmalu 39 E4
Lens 13 A5
Lentini 21 F5
Leoben 15 E8
Leodhas = Lewis 10 B3
León, *Mexico* 84 C4
León, *Nic.* 85 E7
León, *Spain* 18 A3
León, Montañas de 18 A2
Leongatha 63 C4
Léopold II, Lac = Mai-Ndombe, L. 56 E3
Léopoldville = Kinshasa 56 E3
Leova 17 E9
Lepel = Lyepyel 24 C2
Lepikha 31 C10
Léré 53 G1
Lérida 19 B6
Lerwick 10 A6
Les Cayes 86 C5
Les Sables-d'Olonne 12 C3
Lesbos = Lésvos 23 E6
Leskovac 22 C3
Lesotho ■ 59 D5
Lesser Antilles 87 D7
Lesser Sunda Is. 39 F2
Lésvos 23 E6
Leszno 16 C3
Lethbridge 71 D8
Leti, Kepulauan 39 F3
Leti Is. = Leti, Kepulauan 39 F3
Leticia 90 D4
Letpadan 41 J10
Letpan 41 H10
Letterkenny 11 D3
Leuser, G. 37 D1
Leuven 14 C3
Levádhia 23 E4
Levice 16 D4
Levin 64 D6
Lévis 69 D3
Levkás 23 E3
Levkôsia = Nicosia 46 D3
Levskigrad = Karlovo 22 C5
Lewis 10 B3
Lewisporte 69 D5
Lewiston, *Idaho, U.S.A.* 80 B5
Lewiston, *Maine, U.S.A.* 73 B10
Lexington, *Ky., U.S.A.* 72 E3
Lexington, *N.C., U.S.A.* 75 B7
Leyte 38 B2
Lezha 22 D2
Lhasa 34 D4
Lhazê 34 D3
Lhokkruet 36 D1
Lhokseumawe 36 C1
Lhuntsi Dzong 41 D8
Lianga 38 C3
Lianyungang 35 C6
Liaoning □ 35 B7
Liaoyuan 35 B7
Liard → 70 B7
Libau = Liepāja 24 B1
Libenge 56 D3
Liberal 78 A3
Liberec 16 C2
Liberia ■ 55 G3
Lîbîya, Sahrâ' 52 C4
Libobo, Tanjung 39 E3
Libonda 58 A4
Libourne 12 D3
Libreville 56 D1
Libya ■ 52 C2
Libyan Desert = Lîbîya, Sahrâ' 52 C4
Licantén 94 D2
Licata 21 F4
Lichinga 59 A7
Lichtenburg 59 D5
Lida 17 B7
Liechtenstein ■ 14 E5
Liège 14 C3
Liegnitz = Legnica 16 C3
Lienyünchiangshih = Lianyungang 35 C6
Lienz 15 E7
Liepāja 24 B1
Liffey → 11 E3
Lifford 11 D3
Lightning Ridge 63 A4
Liguria □ 20 B2
Ligurian Sea 20 C2
Lijiang 34 D5
Likasi 57 G5
Lille 13 A5
Lillehammer 8 F10
Lilongwe 59 A6
Liloy 38 C2
Lim → 20 C7
Lima, *Indonesia* 39 E3
Lima, *Peru* 91 F3
Lima, *U.S.A.* 72 D3
Lima → 18 B1
Limassol 46 D3
Limay Mahuida 94 D3
Limbang 36 D5
Limbe 56 D1
Limbri 63 B5
Limburg 14 C5
Limeira 94 A7
Limerick 11 E2
Limfjorden 9 G9
Limia = Lima → 18 B1
Límnos 23 E5
Limoeiro do Norte 92 D6
Limoges 12 D4
Limón 86 E3
Limousin 12 D4
Limoux 12 E5
Limpopo → 59 D6
Limuru 57 E7
Linares, *Chile* 94 D2
Linares, *Mexico* 84 C5
Linares, *Spain* 18 C4
Linchuan 35 D6
Lincoln, *Argentina* 94 C4
Lincoln, *N.Z.* 65 E5
Lincoln, *U.K.* 11 E6
Lincoln, *U.S.A.* 77 E6
Linden 90 B7
Líndhos 23 F7
Lindi 57 F7
Lingayen 38 A2
Lingayen G. 38 A2
Lingen 14 B4
Lingga 37 E2
Lingga, Kepulauan 37 E2
Lingga Arch. = Lingga, Kepulauan 37 E2
Linguéré 55 E1
Lingyun 35 D5
Linhai 35 D7
Linhares 93 F5
Linköping 9 G11
Linosa, I. 21 G4
Lins 94 A7
Linville 63 A5
Linxia 34 C5
Linz 15 D8
Lion, G. du 13 E6
Lions, G. of = Lion, G. du 13 E6
Lipa 38 B2

Lípari 21 E5
Lípari, Is. = Eólie, Ís. 21 E5
Lipcani 17 D8
Lipetsk 24 C4
Lipkany = Lipcani 17 D8
Lipovets 17 D9
Lippe → 14 C4
Liptrap C. 63 C4
Lira 57 D6
Liria 19 C5
Lisala 56 D4
Lisboa 18 C1
Lisbon = Lisboa 18 C1
Lisburn 11 D3
Lisburne, C. 71 B3
Lishui 35 D6
Lisichansk = Lysychansk 25 D4
Lisieux 12 B4
Liski 24 C4
Lismore 63 A5
Lister, Mt. 96 B15
Liston 63 A5
Listowel 11 E2
Litang 38 C1
Litani → 46 D3
Lithgow 63 B5
Líthinon, Ákra 23 G5
Lithuania ■ 24 B1
Litoměřice 16 C2
Little Barrier I. 64 B6
Little Laut Is. = Laut Kecil, Kepulauan 37 E5
Little Missouri → 76 B3
Little River 65 E5
Little Rock 79 B7
Liukang Tenggaja 39 F1
Liuwa Plain 58 A4
Liuzhou 35 D5
Liverpool, *Australia* 63 B5
Liverpool, *Canada* 69 D4
Liverpool, *U.K.* 11 E5
Liverpool Plains 63 B5
Liverpool Ra. 63 B5
Livingstone 59 B5
Livingstonia 57 G6
Livny 24 C4
Livorno 20 C3
Livramento 94 C5
Liwale 57 F7
Ljubljana 20 A5
Ljungan → 8 F11
Ljusnan → 8 F11
Llancanelo, Salina 94 D3
Llanelli 11 F4
Llanes 18 A3
Llano Estacado 78 C2
Llanos 90 C4
Lleida = Lérida 19 B6
Llobregat → 19 B7
Lloret de Mar 19 B7
Lluchmayor 19 C7
Llullaillaco, Volcán 94 A3
Loa → 94 A2
Lobatse 59 D5
Lobería 94 D5
Lobito 58 A2
Locarno 13 C8
Loch Garman = Wexford 11 E3
Loches 12 C4
Lock 62 B2
Lodhran 42 E7
Lodi, *Italy* 20 B2
Lodi, *U.S.A.* 80 F3
Lodja 56 E4
Lodwar 57 D7
Łódź 16 C4
Lofoten 8 E10
Logan 81 E8
Logan, Mt. 70 B5
Logone → 53 F2
Logroño 19 A4
Lohardaga 40 F5
Loi-kaw 41 H11
Loir → 12 C3
Loire → 12 C2
Loja, *Ecuador* 90 D3
Loja, *Spain* 18 D3
Loji 39 E3
Lokandu 57 E5
Lokitaung 57 D7
Lokoja 55 G6
Lokolama 56 E3
Loliondo 57 E7
Lom 22 C4
Lomami → 56 D4
Lombárdia □ 20 B2
Lombardy = Lombárdia □ 20 B2
Lomblen 39 F2
Lombok 37 F5
Lomé 55 G5
Lomela 56 E4
Lomela → 56 E4
Lomié 56 D2
Lomond, L. 10 C4
Lompobatang 39 F1
Łomża 16 B6
Loncoche 95 D2
Londa 43 M9
London 11 F6
Londonderry 11 D3
Londonderry, C. 60 C4
Londonderry, I. 95 H2
Londrina 94 A6
Long Beach 82 D3
Long I., *Bahamas* 86 B4
Long I., *U.S.A.* 73 D9
Long Xuyen 36 B3
Longford, *Australia* 62 D4
Longford, *Ireland* 11 E3
Longiram 37 E5
Longlac 69 D2
Longnawan 37 D4
Longreach 61 E7
Longview, *Tex., U.S.A.* 79 C6
Longview, *Wash., U.S.A.* 80 B2
Lons-le-Saunier 13 C6
Lop Nor = Lop Nur 34 B4
Lop Nur 34 B4
Lopez, C. 56 E1
Lora → 42 D4
Lora, Hamun-i- 42 E4
Lora Cr. → 62 A2
Lora del Río 18 D3
Lorain 72 D4
Loralai 42 D6
Lorca 19 D5
Lorestān □ 46 D6
Loreto 92 D4
Lorient 12 C2
Lorne 62 C3
Lorraine 13 B7
Los Alamos 83 C9
Los Andes 94 C2
Los Angeles, *Chile* 94 D2
Los Angeles, *U.S.A.* 82 C3
Los Blancos 94 A4
Los Hermanos 90 A6
Los Mochis 84 B3
Los Roques 90 A5
Los Testigos 90 A6
Los Vilos 94 C2
Lošinj 20 B5
Lot → 12 D4
Lota 94 D2
Loubomo 56 E2
Louga 55 E1
Louis Trichardt 59 C5
Louis XIV, Pte. 69 C3
Louisiade Arch. 61 C9
Louisiana □ 79 D8
Louisville 72 E3
Loulé 18 D1
Lourdes 12 E3
Louth, *Australia* 63 B4
Louth, *U.K.* 11 E6
Louvain = Leuven 14 C3
Lovech 22 C5
Low Tatra = Nízké Tatry 16 D4
Lowell 73 C10
Lower California = Baja California 84 A1
Lower Hutt 65 D6
Lower Saxony = Niedersachsen □ 14 B5
Lower Tunguska = Tunguska, Nizhnyaya → 30 C6
Lowestoft 11 E7
Łowicz 16 B4
Lowyar □ 45 C7
Loxton 62 B3
Loyalty Is. = Loyauté, Is. 64 M11
Loyang = Luoyang 35 C6
Loyauté, Is. 64 M11
Loyev = Loyew 17 C10
Loyew 17 C10
Luachimo 56 F4
Luacono 56 G4
Lualaba → 57 D5
Luanda 56 F2
Luangwa 59 B6
Luangwa → 59 A6
Luanshya 59 A5
Luapula → 57 F5
Luarca 18 A2
Luashi 56 G4
Luau 56 G4
Lubalo 56 F3
Lubang Is. 38 B2
Lubbock 78 C3
Lübeck 15 B6
Lubefu 56 E4
Lubero = Luofu 57 E5
Lubin 16 C3
Lublin 17 C6
Lubuagan 38 A2
Lubuk Antu 37 D4
Lubuklinggau 37 E2
Lubuksikaping 37 D2
Lubumbashi 59 A5
Lubutu 57 E5
Lucca 20 C3
Lucena, *Phil.* 38 B2
Lucena, *Spain* 18 D3
Lučenec 16 D4
Lucerne = Luzern 13 C8
Lucira 58 A2
Luckenwalde 15 B7
Lucknow 40 D3
Lüda = Dalian 35 C7
Lüderitz 58 D3
Ludhiana 42 D9
Ludwigsburg 14 D5
Ludwigshafen 14 D5
Luebo 56 F4
Lufira → 57 F5
Lufkin 79 D6
Luga 24 B2
Lugano 13 C8
Lugansk = Luhansk 25 D4
Lugh Ganana 49 G3
Lugo, *Italy* 20 B3
Lugo, *Spain* 18 A2
Lugoj 17 F5
Lugovoy 29 E8
Luhansk 25 D4
Luiana 58 B4
Luimneach = Limerick 11 E2
Luís Correia 92 C5
Luitpold Coast 96 B5
Luiza 56 F4
Luján 94 C5
Lukanga Swamp 59 A5
Lukenie → 56 E3
Lukolela 56 E3
Łuków 17 C6
Lule älv → 8 E12
Luleå 8 E12
Lüleburgaz 22 D6
Lulonga → 56 D3
Lulua → 56 E4
Luluabourg = Kananga 56 F4
Lumai 58 A4
Lumbala N'guimbo 58 A4
Lumsden 65 F3
Lumut, Tg. 37 E3
Lundazi 59 A6
Lundu 37 D3
Lüneburg 14 B6
Lüneburg Heath = Lüneburger Heide 14 B6
Lüneburger Heide 14 B6
Lunéville 13 B7
Lunglei 41 F9
Luni 42 G8
Luni → 43 G7
Luninets = Luninyets 17 B8
Luninyets 17 B8
Luofu 57 E5
Luoyang 35 C6
Luozi 56 E2
Luremo 56 F3
Lurgan 11 D3
Lusaka 59 B5
Lusambo 56 E4
Lushnja 23 D2
Lushoto 57 E7
Luta = Dalian 35 C7
Luton 11 F6
Lutong 36 D4
Lutsk 17 C7

Lützow Holmbukta 96 A8
Luwuk 39 E2
Luxembourg 13 B7
Luxembourg ■ 14 D4
Luxor = El Uqsur 52 C5
Luza 24 A6
Luzern 13 C8
Luzhou 35 D5
Luziânia 93 F4
Luzon 38 A2
Lviv 17 D7
Lvov = Lviv 17 D7
Lyakhavichy 17 B8
Lyakhovskiye, Ostrova 31 B12
Lyallpur = Faisalabad 42 D8
Lydenburg 59 D6
Lydia 23 E7
Lyell 65 D5
Lyepyel 24 C2
Łyna → 16 A5
Lynchburg 73 F6
Lynd Ra. 63 A4
Lyndhurst 62 B2
Lynn Lake 71 C9
Lyon 13 D6
Lyonnais 13 D6
Lyons = Lyon 13 D6
Lys = Leie → 14 C2
Lysychansk 25 D4
Lyttelton 65 E5
Lyubertsy 24 B4
Lyuboml 17 C7

## M

Ma'alah 47 F6
Ma'ān 47 E3
Ma'anshan 35 C6
Ma'arrat an Nu'mān 46 D4
Maas → 14 C3
Maastricht 13 A6
Mabrouk 55 E4
Macaé 93 G5
McAllen 78 F4
Macao = Macau ■ 35 D6
Macapá 92 B3
Macau 92 D6
Macau ■ 35 D6
M'Clintock Chan. 70 A9
McComb 79 D8
Macdonnell Ras. 60 E5
McDouall Peak 62 A1
Macdougall L. 70 B10
Macedonia = Makedhonía □ 23 D4
Macedonia ■ 22 D3
Maceió 93 D6
Macenta 55 G3
Maçerata 20 C4
Macfarlane, L. 62 B2
Macgillycuddy's Reeks 11 F2
McGregor Ra. 62 A3
Mach 42 E5
Machado = Jiparaná → 91 E6
Machakos 57 E7
Machala 90 D3
Machilipatnam 40 J3
Machiques 90 A4
Machupicchu 91 F4
Macintyre → 63 A5
Mackay 61 E8
Mackay, L. 60 E4
Mackenzie → 70 B6
Mackenzie City = Linden 90 B7
Mackenzie Mts. 70 B6
McKinley, Mt. 71 B4
McKinney 79 C5
Macksville 63 B5
Maclean 63 A5
Maclear 59 E5
Macleay → 63 B5
McMurdo Sd. 96 B15
Mâcon, *France* 13 C6
Macon, *U.S.A.* 75 C6
Macondo 58 A4
McPherson Ra. 63 A5
Macquarie Harbour 62 D4
MacRobertson Land 96 B10
Madagali 53 F1
Madagascar ■ 59 J9
Madā'in Sālih 47 F4
Madama 52 D1
Madang 61 B8
Madaoua 55 F6
Madaripur 41 F8
Madauk 41 J11
Madaya 41 F11
Maddalena 20 D2
Madeira 54 B1
Madeira → 90 D7
Madha 43 L9
Madhya Pradesh □ 43 H10
Madikeri 43 N9
Madimba 56 E3
Madīnat ash Sha'b 49 E3
Madingou 56 E2
Madison 77 D10
Madiun 37 F4
Madras = Tamil Nadu □ 43 P10
Madras 43 N12
Madre, Laguna 78 F5
Madre, Sierra 38 A2
Madre de Dios → 91 F5
Madre de Dios, I. 95 G1
Madre Occidental, Sierra 84 B3
Madrid 18 B4
Madurai 43 Q11
Madurantakam 43 N11
Mae Sot 36 A1
Maebashi 32 A6
Maestrazgo, Mts. del 19 B5
Maevatanana 59 H9
Mafeking = Mafikeng 59 D5
Maffra 63 C4
Mafia I. 57 F7
Mafikeng 59 D5
Mafra, *Brazil* 94 B7
Mafra, *Portugal* 18 C1
Magadan 31 D13
Magadi 57 E7
Magallanes, Estrecho de 95 G2
Magangué 90 B4
Magburaka 55 G2
Magdalena, *Argentina* 94 D5
Magdalena, *Bolivia* 91 F6
Magdalena, *Malaysia* 36 D5
Magdalena → 90 A4
Magdeburg 15 B6
Magelang 37 F4
Magellan's Str. = Magallanes, Estrecho de 95 G2
Maggiore, L. 20 B2
Magnetic Pole (South) = South Magnetic Pole 96 A13
Magnitogorsk 29 D6
Magosa = Famagusta 46 D3
Maguarinho, C. 92 C4
Mağusa = Famagusta 46 D3
Magwe 41 G10
Mahābād 46 C6
Mahabo 59 J8
Mahagi 57 D6
Mahajanga 59 H9
Mahakam → 37 E5
Mahalapye 59 C5
Maḩallāt 44 C2
Mahanadi → 40 G6
Mahanoro 59 H9
Maharashtra □ 43 J9
Mahbubnagar 43 L10
Mahdia 52 A1
Mahenge 57 F7
Maheno 65 F4
Mahesana 43 H8
Mahia Pen. 64 C7
Mahilyow 17 B10
Mahón 19 C8
Mai-Ndombe, L. 56 E3
Maicurú → 92 C3
Maidstone 11 F7
Maiduguri 53 F1
Maijdi 41 F8
Maikala Ra. 40 G3
Main → 14 D5
Maine 12 C3
Maingkwan 41 D11
Mainit, L. 38 C3
Mainland, *Orkney, U.K.* 10 B5
Mainland, *Shet., U.K.* 10 A6
Maintirano 59 H8
Mainz 14 C5
Maipú 94 D5
Maiquetía 90 A5
Mairabari 41 D9
Maitland, *N.S.W., Australia* 63 B5
Maitland, *S. Austral., Australia* 62 B2
Maizuru 32 B4
Majene 39 E1
Maji 53 G6
Majorca = Mallorca 19 C7
Maka 55 F2
Makale 39 E1
Makari 56 B2
Makarikari = Makgadikgadi Salt Pans 59 C5
Makasar = Ujung Pandang 39 F1
Makasar, Selat 39 E1
Makasar, Str. of = Makasar, Selat 39 E1
Makat 29 E6
Makedhonía □ 23 D4
Makedonija = Macedonia ■ 22 D3
Makeni 55 G2
Makeyevka = Makiyivka 25 D4
Makgadikgadi Salt Pans 59 C5
Makhachkala 25 E6
Makian 39 D3
Makindu 57 E7
Makinsk 29 D8
Makiyivka 25 D4
Makkah 47 G4
Makó 16 E5
Makokou 56 D2
Makoua 56 E3
Makrai 43 H10
Makran 45 E5
Makran Coast Range 42 G4
Maksimkin Yar 29 D9
Mākū 46 C6
Makumbi 56 F4
Makurazaki 33 D2
Makurdi 55 G6
Malabang 38 C2
Malabar Coast 43 P9
Malabo = Rey Malabo 56 D1
Malacca, Str. of 36 D1
Maladzyechna 17 A8
Málaga 18 D3
Malakâl 53 G5
Malakand 42 B7
Malang 37 F4
Malanje 56 F3
Mälaren 9 G11
Malargüe 94 D3
Malaryta 17 C7
Malatya 46 C4
Malawi ■ 59 A6
Malawi, L. 59 A6
Malaybalay 38 C3
Malāyer 46 D7
Malaysia ■ 36 D4
Malazgirt 46 C5
Malbooma 62 B1
Malbork 16 A4
Malden I. 65 K15
Maldives ■ 26 J11
Maldonado 94 C6
Malé Karpaty 16 D3
Maléa, Ákra 23 F4
Malegaon 43 J9
Malema 59 A7
Malha 53 E4
Mali ■ 55 E4
Mali → 41 E11
Malik 39 E2
Malili 39 E2
Malin Hd. 10 D3
Malindi 57 E8
Malines = Mechelen 14 C3
Malino 39 D2
Malita 38 C3
Malkara 22 D6
Mallacoota 63 C4
Mallacoota Inlet 63 C4
Mallaig 10 C4
Mallawi 52 C5
Mallorca 19 C7
Mallow 11 E2

Malmö 9 G10
Malolos 38 B2
Malpelo 90 C2
Malta ■ 21 G5
Maltahöhe 58 C3
Maluku 39 E3
Maluku □ 39 E3
Maluku Sea = Molucca Sea 39 E2
Malvan 43 L8
Malvinas, Is. = Falkland Is. □ 95 G5
Malyn 17 C9
Malyy Lyakhovskiy, Ostrov 31 B12
Mamahatun 46 C5
Mamanguape 92 D6
Mamasa 39 E1
Mamberamo → 39 E5
Mambilima Falls 57 G5
Mamburao 38 B2
Mamfe 55 G6
Mamoré → 91 F5
Mamou 55 F2
Mamuju 39 E1
Man 55 G3
Man, I. of 11 D4
Man Na 41 F11
Mana 92 A3
Manaar, G. of = Mannar, G. of 43 Q11
Manacapuru 90 D6
Manacor 19 C7
Manado 39 D2
Managua 85 E7
Manakara 59 J9
Manama = Al Manamah 44 E2
Mananara 59 H9
Mananjary 59 J9
Manaos = Manaus 90 D7
Manapouri 65 F2
Manapouri, L. 65 F2
Manas 34 B3
Manas → 41 D8
Manasir 44 E2
Manaung 41 H9
Manaus 90 D7
Manay 38 C3
Manchester, *U.K.* 11 E5
Manchester, *U.S.A.* 73 C10
Mand → 44 D3
Manda 57 G6
Mandal 9 G9
Mandalay 41 F11
Mandale = Mandalay 41 F11
Mandalī 46 D6
Mandar, Teluk 39 E1
Mandaue 38 B2
Mandi 42 D10
Mandimba 59 A7
Mandioli 39 E3
Mandla 40 F3
Mandritsara 59 H9
Mandsaur 43 G9
Mandvi 43 H6
Mandya 43 N10
Manfalût 52 C5
Manfred 63 D3
Manfredónia 20 D5
Mangalia 22 C7
Mangalore 43 N9
Mangaweka 64 C6
Manggar 37 E3
Manggawitu 39 E4
Mangkalihat, Tanjung 39 D1
Mangla Dam 42 C8
Mangnai 34 C4
Mango 55 F5
Mangoche 59 A7
Mangole 39 E3
Mangonui 64 A5
Mangueigne 53 F3
Mangueira, L. da 94 C6
Mangyshlak Poluostrov 29 E6
Manhuaçu 93 G5
Manica 59 B6
Manicoré 91 E6
Manicouagan → 69 D4
Manīfah 47 F7
Manihiki 65 L14
Manila 38 B2
Manila B. 38 B2
Manilla 63 B5
Manipur □ 41 E9
Manipur → 41 F10
Manisa 23 E6
Manitoba □ 71 C10
Manitoba, L. 71 C10
Manitowoc 72 B2
Manizales 90 B3
Manja 59 J8
Manjacaze 59 C6
Manjhand 42 G6
Manjil 46 C7
Manjra → 43 K10
Mankono 55 G3
Manly 63 B5
Manmad 43 J9
Manna 37 E2
Mannahill 62 B3
Mannar 43 Q11
Mannar, G. of 43 Q11
Mannar I. 43 Q11
Mannheim 14 D5
Mannum 62 B2
Mano 55 G2
Manokwari 39 E4
Manombo 59 J8
Manono 57 F5
Manosque 13 E6
Manresa 19 B6
Mansa 57 G5
Mansel I. 68 B2
Mansfield, *Australia* 63 C4
Mansfield, *U.K.* 11 F6
Mansfield, *U.S.A.* 72 D4
Manta 90 D2
Mantalingajan, Mt. 36 C5
Mantes-la-Jolie 12 B4
Manthani 43 K11
Mantiqueira, Serra da 93 G5
Mántova 20 B3
Mantua = Mántova 20 B3
Manu 91 F4
Manuae 65 L15
Manuel Alves → 93 E4
Manui 39 E2
Manyara, L. 57 E7
Manych-Gudilo, Ozero 25 D5
Manyoni 57 F6
Manzai 42 C7
Manzanares 18 C4
Manzanillo, *Cuba* 86 B4
Manzanillo, *Mexico* 84 D4
Manzhouli 35 B6
Mao 53 F2
Maoke, Pegunungan 39 E5
Maoming 35 D6
Mapam Yumco 40 B3
Mapia, Kepulauan 39 D4
Mapuera → 90 D7
Maputo 59 D6
Maqnā 47 E3
Maquela do Zombo 56 F3
Maquinchao 95 E3
Mar, Serra do 94 B7
Mar Chiquita, L. 94 C4
Mar del Plata 94 D5
Mar Menor 19 D5
Maraā 90 D5
Marabá 92 D4
Maracá, I. de 92 B3
Maracaibo 90 A4
Maracaibo, L. de 90 B4
Maracay 90 A5
Marādah 52 C2
Maradi 55 F6
Marāgheh 46 C6
Marāh 47 F6
Marajó, I. de 92 C4
Maralal 57 D7
Marama 62 C3
Marampa 55 G2
Marand 46 C6
Maranguape 92 C6
Maranhão = São Luís 92 C5
Maranhão □ 92 D4
Maranoa → 63 A4
Marañón → 90 D4
Marão 59 C6
Maraş = Kahramanmaraş 46 C4
Maratua 39 D1
Marbella 18 D3
Marburg 14 C5
Marche 12 C4
Marchena 18 D3
Mardan 42 B8
Mardin 46 C5
Marek = Stanke Dimitrov 22 C4
Marek 39 E2
Margarita, I. de 90 A6
Margate 11 F7
Margelan = Marghilon 29 E8
Marghilon 29 E8
Mari El □ 24 B6
Mari Republic □ = Mari El □ 24 B6
Maria I. 62 D4
Maria van Diemen, C. 64 A5
Mariana Trench 64 H9
Marianao 86 B3
Ma'rib 49 D4
Maribor 20 A5
Marîdî 53 H4
Marie Byrd Land 96 B18
Marie-Galante 87 C7
Mariecourt = Kangiqsujuaq 68 B3
Mariental 58 C3
Mariinsk 29 D9
Marília 93 G3
Marín 18 A1
Marinduque 38 B2
Maringá 94 A6
Marion 79 A9
Mariscal Estigarribia 91 H6
Maritime Alps = Maritimes, Alpes 13 D7
Maritimes, Alpes 13 D7
Maritsa = Évros → 22 D6
Mariupol 25 D4
Marīvān 46 D6
Markazī □ 44 C2
Markham, Mt. 96 C15
Marks 24 C6
Marla 62 A1
Marmagao 43 M8
Marmara 23 D6
Marmara, Sea of = Marmara Denizi 22 D7
Marmara Denizi 22 D7
Marmaris 23 F7
Marmolada, Mte. 20 A3
Marne → 12 B5
Maroantsetra 59 H9
Marondera 59 B6
Maroni → 92 A3
Maroochydore 63 A5
Maroona 62 C3
Maroua 53 F1
Marovoay 59 H9
Marquesas Is. = Marquises, Is. 65 K17
Marquette 69 D2
Marquises, Is. 65 K17
Marrakech 54 B3
Marrawah 62 D3
Marree 62 A2
Marromeu 59 B7
Marrowie Cr. → 63 B4
Marrupa 59 A7
Marsá Matrûh 52 B4
Marsá Susah 52 B3
Marsabit 57 D7
Marsala 21 F4
Marsden 63 B4
Marseille 13 E6
Marseilles = Marseille 13 E6
Marshall, *Liberia* 55 G2
Marshall, *U.S.A.* 79 C6
Marshall Is. ■ 64 J12
Marshalltown 77 D8
Martaban 41 J11
Martaban, G. of 41 J11
Martapura, *Kalimantan, Indonesia* 37 E4
Martapura, *Sumatera, Indonesia* 37 E2
Marte 53 F1
Martigny 13 C7
Martigues 13 E6
Martin 16 D4
Martina Franca 21 D6
Martinborough 65 D6
Martinique ■ 87 D7
Martinique Passage 87 C7
Martinsville 75 A8
Marton 64 D6
Martos 18 D4
Marudi 37 D4

Ma'ruf . . . . . . . 42 D5
Marugame . . . . 32 B3
Marulan . . . . . . 63 B5
Marwar . . . . . . 42 G8
Mary . . . . . . . . . 29 F7
Maryborough = Port Laoise . . 11 E3
Maryborough, *Queens., Australia* . . . . 63 A5
Maryborough, *Vic., Australia* 62 C3
Maryland □ . . . 73 E7
Maryvale . . . . . 63 A5
Marzūq . . . . . . . 52 C1
Masaka . . . . . . . 57 E6
Masalembo, Kepulauan . . 37 F4
Masalima, Kepulauan . . 37 F5
Masamba . . . . . 39 E2
Masan . . . . . . . 35 C7
Masandam, Ras 44 E4
Masasi . . . . . . . 57 G7
Masaya . . . . . . 85 E7
Masbate . . . . . . 38 B2
Mascara . . . . . . 54 A5
Masela . . . . . . . 39 F3
Maseru . . . . . . . 59 D5
Mashābih . . . . . 47 F4
Mashhad . . . . . 44 B4
Mashike . . . . . . 32 F12
Mashkel, Hamun-i- . . . 42 E3
Mashki Chāh . . 42 E3
Masi Manimba 56 E3
Masindi . . . . . . 57 D6
Masisea . . . . . . 91 E4
Masjed Soleyman . . . 47 E7
Mask, L. . . . . . . 11 E2
Masohi . . . . . . . 39 E3
Mason City . . . 77 D8
Masqat . . . . . . . 45 F4
Massa . . . . . . . . 20 B3
Massachusetts □ . . . . . . . . . . . 73 C9
Massaguet . . . . 53 F2
Massakory . . . . 53 F2
Massangena . . 59 C6
Massawa = Mitsiwa . . . . . 53 E6
Massena . . . . . 73 B8
Massénya . . . . 53 F2
Massif Central . 13 D5
Massinga . . . . . 59 C7
Masson I. . . . . . 96 A11
Mastanli = Momchilgrad 22 D5
Masterton . . . . 65 D6
Mastuj . . . . . . . 42 A8
Mastung . . . . . . 42 E5
Masty . . . . . . . . 17 B7
Masuda . . . . . . 32 B2
Masvingo . . . . . 59 C6
Mataboor . . . . . 39 E5
Matad . . . . . . . . 35 B6
Matadi . . . . . . . 56 F2
Matagalpa . . . . 85 E7
Matagami, L. . . 69 D3
Matak, P. . . . . . 37 D3
Matakana . . . . . 63 B4
Matam . . . . . . . 55 E2
Matamoros, *Coahuila, Mexico* . . . . . 84 B4
Matamoros, *Tamaulipas, Mexico* . . . . . 84 B5
Ma'ṭan as Sarra 52 D3
Matane . . . . . . . 69 D4
Matanzas . . . . . 86 B3
Matapan, C. = Taínaron, Ákra 23 F4
Mataram . . . . . 37 F5
Matarani . . . . . 91 G4
Mataró . . . . . . . 19 B7
Mataura . . . . . . 65 G3
Matehuala . . . . 84 C4
Matera . . . . . . . 21 D6
Mathura . . . . . . 42 F10
Mati . . . . . . . . . 38 C3
Matiri Ra. . . . . . 65 D5
Matmata . . . . . 54 B6
Mato Grosso □ 93 E3
Mato Grosso, Planalto do . . 93 F3
Mato Grosso do Sul □ . . . . . . 93 F3
Matochkin Shar 28 B6
Matosinhos . . . 18 B1
Matrah . . . . . . . 45 F4
Matsue . . . . . . . 32 B3
Matsumoto . . . 32 A6
Matsusaka . . . . 32 B5
Matsuyama . . . 32 C3
Mattagami ⟶ . 69 C2
Mattancheri . . . 43 Q10
Matterhorn . . . 13 D7
Matthew's Ridge 90 B6
Matucana . . . . . 91 F3
Matun . . . . . . . . 42 C6
Maturín . . . . . . 90 B6
Mau Ranipur . . 43 G11
Maubeuge . . . . 13 A5
Maude . . . . . . . 63 B3
Maudin Sun . . . 41 K10
Maués . . . . . . . 90 D7
Mauganj . . . . . . 40 E3
Maui . . . . . . . . . 82 H12
Maulamyaing = Moulmein . . . 41 J11
Maumere . . . . . 39 F2
Maun . . . . . . . . 58 B4
Maungmagan Kyunzu . . . . . 41 K11
Mauritania ■ . . 55 D2
Mauritius ■ . . . 51 H9
Mavinga . . . . . . 58 B4
Mawk Mai . . . . 41 G11
Mawlaik . . . . . . 41 F10
Mawson Coast 96 A10
Maxixe . . . . . . . 59 C7
Mayaguana . . . 87 B5
Mayagüez . . . . 87 C6
Maydena . . . . . 62 D4
Mayenne ⟶ . . 12 C3
Maykop . . . . . . 25 E5
Mayo . . . . . . . . 70 B6
Mayo L. . . . . . . 70 B6
Mayon Volcano 38 B2
Mayor I. . . . . . . 64 B7
Mayu . . . . . . . . 39 D3
Mazabuka . . . . 59 B5
Mazagán = El Jadida . . . . . . 54 B3
Mazagão . . . . . 92 C3
Mazán . . . . . . . 90 D4
Māzandarān □ 44 B3
Mazar-e Sharīf . 45 B6
Mazara del Vallo 21 F4
Mazarredo . . . . 95 F3
Mazarrón . . . . . 19 D5
Mazaruni ⟶ . . 90 B7
Mazatlán . . . . . 84 C3
Māzhān . . . . . . 44 C4
Mazīnān . . . . . . 44 B4
Mazoe ⟶ . . . . 59 B6
Mazurian Lakes = Mazurski, Pojezierze . . . 16 B5
Mazurski, Pojezierze . . . 16 B5
Mazyr . . . . . . . . 17 C9
Mbabane . . . . . 59 D6
Mbaïki . . . . . . . 56 D3
Mbala . . . . . . . . 57 F6
Mbale . . . . . . . . 57 D6
Mbalmayo . . . . 56 D2
Mbamba Bay . . 57 G6
Mbandaka . . . . 56 D3
Mbanza Congo 56 F2
Mbanza Ngungu 56 F2
Mbarara . . . . . . 57 E6
Mbeya . . . . . . . 57 F6
Mbini □ . . . . . . 56 D2
Mbour . . . . . . . 55 F1
Mbout . . . . . . . 55 E2
Mbuji-Mayi . . . 56 F4
Mbulu . . . . . . . . 57 E7
Mchinji . . . . . . . 59 A6
Mead, L. . . . . . . 82 B5
Mearim ⟶ . . . 92 C5
Meaux . . . . . . . 13 B5
Mecca = Makkah . . . . . 47 G4
Mechelen . . . . . 14 C3
Mecheria . . . . . 54 B4
Mecklenburg . . 15 B6
Mecklenburger Bucht . . . . . . 15 A6
Meconta . . . . . . 59 A7
Medan . . . . . . . 37 D1
Medanosa, Pta. 95 F3
Medéa . . . . . . . 54 A5
Medellín . . . . . . 90 B3
Mederdra . . . . . 55 E1
Medford . . . . . . 80 D2
Medgidia . . . . . 22 B7
Mediaş . . . . . . . 17 E7
Medicine Bow Ra. . . . . . . . . 81 E10
Medicine Hat . . 71 C8
Medina = Al Madīnah . . . . 47 F4
Medina del Campo . . . . . 18 B3
Medina-Sidonia 18 D3
Medinipur . . . . 40 F6
Mediterranean Sea . . . . . . . . 50 C5
Médoc . . . . . . . 12 D3
Medveditsa ⟶ 24 D5
Medvezhyegorsk 28 C4
Meekatharra . . 60 F2
Meerut . . . . . . . 42 E10
Mega . . . . . . . . 53 H6
Mégara . . . . . . . 23 F4
Meghalaya □ . . 41 E8
Mei Xian . . . . . 35 D6
Meiganga . . . . . 56 C2
Meiktila . . . . . . 41 G10
Meissen . . . . . . 15 C7
Mejillones . . . . 94 A2
Mékambo . . . . . 56 D2
Mekdela . . . . . . 53 F6
Mekhtar . . . . . . 42 D6
Meknès . . . . . . 54 B3
Mekong ⟶ . . . 36 C3
Mekongga . . . . 39 E2
Mekvari = Kür ⟶ . . . . . 25 E6
Melagiri Hills . . 43 N10
Melaka . . . . . . . 37 D2
Melalap . . . . . . 36 C5
Melanesia . . . . 64 K10
Melbourne, *Australia* . . . . 63 C3
Melbourne, *U.S.A.* . . . . . . 75 E7
Mélèzes ⟶ . . . 68 C3
Melfi . . . . . . . . . 53 F2
Melfort . . . . . . . 71 C9
Melilla . . . . . . . 19 E4
Melitopol . . . . . 25 D4
Melk . . . . . . . . . 15 D8
Melo . . . . . . . . . 94 C6
Melolo . . . . . . . 39 F2
Melrose . . . . . . 63 B4
Melun . . . . . . . . 13 B5
Melut . . . . . . . . 53 F5
Melville . . . . . . 71 C9
Melville I. . . . . . 60 C5
Melville Pen. . . 68 B2
Memba . . . . . . . 59 G8
Memboro . . . . . 39 F1
Memel = Klaìpeda . . . . 24 B1
Memmingen . . 14 E6
Mempawah . . . 37 D3
Memphis, *Tenn., U.S.A.* . . . . . . 74 B3
Memphis, *Tex., U.S.A.* . . . . . . 78 B3
Ménaka . . . . . . 55 E5
Menan = Chao Phraya ⟶ . . 36 B2
Menate . . . . . . . 37 E4
Mendawai ⟶ . 37 E4
Mende . . . . . . . 13 D5
Mendocino, C. . 80 E1
Mendoza . . . . . 94 C3
Mene Grande . 90 B4
Menemen . . . . 23 E6
Menggala . . . . . 37 E3
Mengzi . . . . . . . 34 D5
Menindee . . . . . 62 B3
Menindee L. . . 62 B3
Meningie . . . . . 62 C2
Menominee . . . 72 B2
Menongue . . . . 58 A3
Menorca . . . . . . 19 C7
Mentawai, Kepulauan . . 37 E1
Menton . . . . . . 13 E7
Meppel . . . . . . . 14 B4
Merabéllou, Kólpos . . . . . 23 G5
Meran = Merano . . . . . 20 A3
Merano . . . . . . 20 A3
Merauke . . . . . . 39 F6
Merbein . . . . . . 62 B3
Merca . . . . . . . . 49 G3
Merced . . . . . . . 82 B2
Mercedes, *Buenos Aires, Argentina* . . . 94 C5
Mercedes, *Corrientes, Argentina* . . . 94 B5
Mercedes, *San Luis, Argentina* . . . 94 C3
Mercedes, *Uruguay* . . . . 94 C5
Merceditas . . . . 94 B2
Mercer . . . . . . . 64 B6
Mercy C. . . . . . 68 B4
Meredith, C. . . . 95 G4
Merga = Nukheila . . . . 53 E4
Mergui Arch. = Myeik Kyunzu 36 B1
Mérida, *Mexico* 85 C7
Mérida, *Spain* . 18 C2

Mérida, *Venezuela* . . . 90 B4
Mérida, Cord. de 87 E5
Meridian . . . . . 74 C3
Meriruma . . . . . 92 B3
Merowe . . . . . . 53 E5
Merriwa . . . . . . 63 B5
Merriwagga . . . 63 B4
Merrygoen . . . . 63 B4
Mersa Fatma . . 49 E3
Merseburg . . . . 15 C6
Mersin . . . . . . . 46 C3
Mersing . . . . . . 37 D2
Merthyr Tydfil . 11 F5
Mértola . . . . . . 18 D2
Meru . . . . . . . . . 57 D7
Mesa . . . . . . . . 83 D7
Meshed = Mashhad . . . 44 B4
Meshra er Req 53 G4
Mesolóngion . . 23 E3
Mesopotamia = Al Jazirah . . . 46 D5
Messina, *Italy* . 21 E5
Messina, *S. Africa* . . . . 59 C6
Messina, Str. di 21 E5
Messíni . . . . . . 23 F4
Messiniakós Kólpos . . . . . 23 F4
Mesta → . . . . . 22 D5
Meta → . . . . . . 90 B5
Metairie . . . . . . 79 E8
Metán . . . . . . . . 94 B4
Metangula . . . . 59 A6
Metema . . . . . . 53 F6
Methven . . . . . . 65 E4
Metil . . . . . . . . . 59 B7
Metlakatla . . . . 71 C6
Mettur Dam . . . 43 P10
Metz . . . . . . . . . 13 B7
Meulaboh . . . . 37 D1
Meureudu . . . . 36 C1
Meuse → . . . . 13 A6
Mexiana, I. . . . . 92 C4
Mexicali . . . . . . 84 A1
México . . . . . . . 84 D5
México □ . . . . . 84 D5
Mexico ■ . . . . . 84 C4
Mexico, G. of . . 85 B7
Meymaneh . . . 42 B4
Mezen . . . . . . . 28 C5
Mezen → . . . . 28 C5
Mézene . . . . . . 13 D6
Mezökövesd . . 16 E5
Mezötúr . . . . . . 16 E5
Mhow . . . . . . . . 43 H9
Miami . . . . . . . . 75 G7
Miami Beach . . 75 G7
Mīāndowāb . . . 46 C6
Miandrivazo . . . 59 H9
Mīāneh . . . . . . . 46 C6
Mianwali . . . . . 42 C7
Miaoli . . . . . . . . 35 D7
Miarinarivo . . . 59 H9
Miass . . . . . . . . 29 D7
Michalovce . . . 17 D5
Michigan □ . . . 72 C3
Michigan, L. . . . 72 C2
Michipicoten . . 69 D2
Michurin . . . . . 22 C6
Michurinsk . . . . 24 C5
Micronesia, Federated States of ■ . . 64 J10
Middelburg . . . 58 E5
Middlesbrough 11 D6
Midi, Canal du → . . . . . . 12 E4
Midland . . . . . . 78 D3
Midyat . . . . . . . 46 C5
Midzŏr . . . . . . . 22 C4
Międzychód . . . 16 B2
Międzyrzec Podlaski . . . . 17 C6
Mielec . . . . . . . 16 C5
Miercurea Ciuc 17 E7
Mieres . . . . . . . 18 A3
Miguel Alves . . 92 C5
Mihara . . . . . . . 32 B3
Mikhaylovgrad 22 C4
Míkonos . . . . . . 23 F5
Mikura-Jima . . 32 C6
Milagro . . . . . . 90 D3
Milan = Milano 20 B2
Milang . . . . . . . 62 B2
Milano . . . . . . . 20 B2
Milâs . . . . . . . . 23 F6
Milazzo . . . . . . . 21 E5
Mildura . . . . . . 62 B3
Miles . . . . . . . . 63 A5
Miletus . . . . . . . 23 F6
Milford Haven . 11 F4
Milford Sd. . . . 65 F2
Milḩ, Baḩr al . . 47 D5
Miliana . . . . . . . 54 C5
Mill I. . . . . . . . . 96 A12
Millau . . . . . . . . 13 D5
Millicent . . . . . . 62 C3
Millinocket . . . . 73 B11
Millmerran . . . . 63 A5
Milne Inlet . . . . 68 A2
Mílos . . . . . . . . 23 F5
Milparinka P.O. 62 A3
Milton . . . . . . . . 65 G3
Milton Keynes . 11 E6
Miltou . . . . . . . . 53 F2
Milwaukee . . . . 72 C2
Min Chiang → . 35 D6
Min Jiang → . 35 D5
Mina Pirquitas . 94 A3
Mīnā Su'ud . . . 47 E7
Mīnā'al Aḩmadī 47 E7
Mīnāb . . . . . . . . 44 E4
Minamata . . . . 32 C2
Minas . . . . . . . . 94 C5
Minas Gerais □ 93 F4
Minbu . . . . . . . . 41 G10
Mindanao . . . . 38 C2
Mindanao Sea = Bohol Sea . . 38 C2
Mindanao Trench . . . . . 38 B3
Minden . . . . . . . 14 B5
Mindiptana . . . 39 F6
Mindoro . . . . . . 38 B2
Mindoro Str. . . 38 B2
Mindouli . . . . . 56 E2
Mingäçevir Su Anbarı . . . . . . 25 E6
Mingan . . . . . . . 69 C4
Mingechaurskoye Vdkhr. = Mingäçevir Su Anbarı . . . . . . 25 E6
Mingin . . . . . . . 41 F10
Mingt'iehkaitafan = Mintaka Pass . . . . . . . 42 A9
Minho = Miño → . . . . 18 B1
Minho . . . . . . . . 18 B1
Minna . . . . . . . . 55 G6
Minneapolis . . . 77 C8
Minnedosa . . . . 71 C10
Minnesota □ . . 77 B7
Minnipa . . . . . . 62 B2
Miño → . . . . . 18 B1
Minorca = Menorca . . . . 19 C7
Minore . . . . . . . 63 B4
Minot . . . . . . . . 76 A4
Minsk . . . . . . . . 24 C2
Mińsk Mazowiecki . 16 B5
Mintaka Pass . . 42 A9
Minto . . . . . . . . 71 B5
Minutang . . . . . 41 C11
Minvoul . . . . . . 56 D2
Mir . . . . . . . . . . 53 F1
Mira . . . . . . . . . 20 B4
Miraj . . . . . . . . . 43 L9
Miram Shah . . 42 C7
Miranda . . . . . . 93 G2
Miranda de Ebro 19 A4
Miranda do Douro . . . . . . 18 B2
Miri . . . . . . . . . . 36 D4
Mirim, L. . . . . . 94 C6
Mirpur Khas . . 42 G6
Mirzapur . . . . . 40 E4
Mirzapur-cum-Vindhyachal = Mirzapur . . . . 40 E4
Mish'āb, Ra'as al . . . . . . . . . 47 E7
Mishan . . . . . . . 35 B8
Miskīn . . . . . . . 44 F4
Miskolc . . . . . . . 16 D5
Misool . . . . . . . . 39 E4
Misrātah . . . . . . 52 B2
Misriç . . . . . . . . 46 C5
Missinaibi → . 69 C2
Mississippi □ . 79 C9
Mississippi → 79 E9
Mississippi River Delta . . . . . . . 79 E9
Missoula . . . . . 81 B6
Missouri □ . . . . 77 F8
Missouri → . . 77 F9
Mistassini L. . . 69 C3
Misurata = Misrātah . . . . 52 B2
Mitchell, *Australia* . . . . 63 A4
Mitchell, *U.S.A.* 76 D5
Mitchell → . . . 61 D7
Mitilíni . . . . . . . 23 E6
Mito . . . . . . . . . 32 A7
Mitrovica = Titova-Mitrovica . . . 22 C3
Mitsinjo . . . . . . 59 H9
Mitsiwa . . . . . . 53 E6
Mittagong . . . . 63 B5
Mitú . . . . . . . . . 90 C4
Mitumba, Chaîne des . . 57 F5
Mitumba Mts. = Mitumba, Chaîne des . . 57 F5
Mitwaba . . . . . . 57 F5
Mitzic . . . . . . . . 56 D2
Miyake-Jima . . 32 B6
Miyako . . . . . . . 33 G12
Miyakonojō . . . 32 D2
Miyazaki . . . . . . 32 D2
Miyet, Bahr el = Dead Sea . . . 47 E3
Mizal . . . . . . . . . 47 G6
Mizdah . . . . . . . 52 B1
Mizoram □ . . . 41 F9
Mjøsa . . . . . . . . 8 F10
Mladá Boleslav 16 C2
Mława . . . . . . . 16 B5
Mljet . . . . . . . . . 20 C6
Mmabatho . . . . 59 D5
Moa . . . . . . . . . 39 F3
Moabi . . . . . . . . 56 E2
Moalie Park . . . 62 A3
Moba . . . . . . . . 57 F5
Mobaye . . . . . . 56 D4
Mobayi . . . . . . . 56 D4
Mobile . . . . . . . 74 D3
Mobutu Sese Seko, L. = Albert L. . . . . 57 D6
Moçambique . . 59 H8
Moçâmedes = Namibe . . . . . 58 B2
Mochudi . . . . . . 59 C5
Mocimboa da Praia . . . . . . . 57 G8
Mocoa . . . . . . . 90 C3
Mocuba . . . . . . 59 B7
Modane . . . . . . 13 D7
Módena . . . . . . 20 B3
Modesto . . . . . . 82 B2
Módica . . . . . . . 21 F5
Moe . . . . . . . . . 63 C4
Moengo . . . . . . 92 A3
Mogadishu = Muqdisho . . . 49 G4
Mogador = Essaouira . . . 54 B3
Mogami → . . . 33 G12
Mogaung . . . . . 41 E11
Mogi das Cruzes 94 A7
Mogi Mirim . . . 94 A7
Mogilev = Mahilyow . . . 17 B10
Mogilev-Podolskiy = Mohyliv Podilskyy . . . 17 D8
Mogoi . . . . . . . . 39 E4
Mogok . . . . . . . 41 F11
Mohács . . . . . . 16 F4
Moḩammadābād . . . . . . . . . . . 44 B4
Mohoro . . . . . . . 57 F7
Mohyliv-Podilskyy . . . 17 D8
Mointy . . . . . . . 29 E8
Moisie . . . . . . . 69 C4
Moisie → . . . . 69 C4
Moïssala . . . . . 53 G2
Mojave Desert . 82 C4
Mokai . . . . . . . . 64 C6
Mokokchung . . 41 D10
Mokra Gora . . . 22 C3
Molchanovo . . 29 D9
Moldavia ■ = Moldova ■ . . 17 E9
Molde . . . . . . . . 8 F9
Moldova ■ . . . 17 E9
Moldoveana . . 17 F7
Molepolole . . . 59 C5
Molfetta . . . . . . 20 D6
Moline . . . . . . . 77 E9
Moliro . . . . . . . 57 F6
Mollendo . . . . . 91 G4
Molodechno = Maladzyechna 17 A8
Molokai . . . . . . 82 H12
Molong . . . . . . 63 B4
Molopo → . . . 58 D4
Molotov = Perm 29 D6
Moloundou . . . 56 D3
Molu . . . . . . . . . 39 F4
Molucca Sea . . 39 E2
Moluccas = Maluku . . . . . 39 E3
Moma . . . . . . . . 59 B7
Mombasa . . . . . 57 E7
Momchilgrad . . 22 D5

Mompós 90 B4
Mon → 41 G10
Mona, Canal de la 87 C6
Monaco ■ 13 E7
Monahans 78 D2
Monastir = Bitola 22 D3
Monastir 52 A1
Moncayo, Sierra del 19 B5
Mönchengladbach 14 C4
Monchique 18 D1
Monclova 84 B4
Mondego → 18 B1
Mondeodo 39 E2
Mondovì 20 B1
Monforte de Lemos 18 A2
Mong Hsu 41 G12
Mong Kung 41 G11
Mong Nai 41 G11
Mong Pawk 41 F12
Mong Ton 41 G12
Mong Wa 41 G13
Mong Yai 41 F12
Mongalla 53 G5
Monghyr = Munger 40 E6
Mongibello = Etna 21 F5
Mongo 53 F2
Mongolia ■ 35 B5
Mongororo 53 F3
Mongu 58 B4
Monkoto 56 E4
Monópoli 21 D6
Monqoumba 56 D3
Monroe, *La., U.S.A.* 79 C7
Monroe, *N.C., U.S.A.* 75 B7
Monrovia 55 G2
Mons 14 C2
Monse 39 E2
Mont-de-Marsan 12 E3
Mont-St.-Michel, Le = Le Mont-St.-Michel 12 B3
Montalbán 19 B5
Montana □ 81 B9
Montargis 13 C5
Montauban 12 D4
Montbéliard 13 C7
Montceau-les-Mines 13 C6
Monte Alegre 92 C3
Monte Azul 93 F5
Monte-Carlo 20 C1
Monte Caseros 94 C5
Monte Comán 94 C3
Monte Santu, C. di 21 D2
Montecristi 90 D2
Montecristo 20 C3
Montego Bay 86 C4
Montélimar 13 D6
Montemorelos 84 B5
Montenegro □ 22 C2
Montepuez 59 A7
Monterey 82 B2
Montería 90 B3
Monterrey 84 B4
Montes Claros 93 F5
Montesilvano Marina 20 C5
Montevideo 94 C5
Montgomery = Sahiwal 42 D8
Montgomery 74 C4
Montijo 18 C2
Montilla 18 D3
Montluçon 13 C5
Montmorillon 12 C4
Montoro 18 C3
Montpellier 13 E5
Montréal 69 D3
Montreux 13 C7
Montrose, *U.K.* 10 C5
Montrose, *U.S.A.* 83 A9
Montserrat ■ 87 C7
Monveda 56 D4
Monywa 41 F10
Monza 20 B2
Monze 59 B5
Monze, C. 43 G5
Monzón 19 B6
Moolawatana 62 A2
Moomin Cr. → 63 A4
Moonie 63 A5
Moonie → 63 A4
Moonta 62 B2
Mooroopna 63 C4
Moose Jaw 71 C9
Moosomin 71 C9
Moosonee 69 C2
Mopeia Velha 59 B7
Mopti 55 F4
Moquegua 91 G4
Mora 8 F10
Moradabad 42 E11
Morafenobe 59 H8
Moramanga 59 H9
Moratuwa 43 R11
Morava →, *Serbia, Yug.* 22 B3
Morava →, *Slovak Rep.* 16 D3
Moravian Hts. = Ceskomoravská Vrchovina 16 D2
Morawhanna 90 B7
Moray Firth 10 C5
Morden 71 D10
Mordovian Republic □ = Mordvinia □ 24 C5
Mordvinia □ 24 C5
Morea 62 C3
Moree 63 A4
Morelia 84 D4
Morella 19 B5
Morena, Sierra 18 C3
Moreton I. 63 A5
Morgan 62 B2
Morgan City 79 E8
Morioka 33 G12
Morlaix 12 B2
Mornington 63 C4
Mornington, I. 95 F1
Moro G. 38 C2
Morocco ■ 54 B3
Morococha 91 F3
Morogoro 57 F7
Morombe 59 J8
Morón 86 B4
Mörön → 35 B6
Morón de la Frontera 18 D3
Morondava 59 J8
Morotai 39 D3
Moroto 57 D6
Morphou 46 D3
Morrinhos 93 F4
Morrinsville 64 B6
Morristown 75 A6
Morrumbene 59 C7
Morshansk 24 C5
Morteros 94 C4
Mortes, R. das → 93 E3
Mortlake 62 C3
Morundah 63 B4
Moruya 63 C5
Morvan 13 C6
Morven 63 A4
Morwell 63 C4
Moscos Is. 41 L11
Moscow = Moskva 24 B4
Moscow 80 B5
Mosel → 13 A7
Moselle = Mosel → 13 A7
Mosgiel 65 F4
Moshi 57 E7
Moskva 24 B4
Moskva → 24 B4
Moson-magyaróvar 16 E3
Mosquera 90 C3
Moss Vale 63 B5
Mossaka 56 E3
Mossburn 65 F3
Mosselbaai 58 E4
Mossendjo 56 E2
Mossgiel 63 B3
Mossoró 92 D6
Mossuril 59 G8
Most 16 C1
Mostaganem 54 A5
Mostar 20 C6
Mostardas 94 C6
Mostiska = Mostyska 17 D6
Mosty = Masty 17 B7
Mostyska 17 D6
Mosul = Al Mawşil 46 C5
Motihari 40 D5
Motril 18 D4
Motueka 65 D5
Motueka → 65 D5
Mouanda 56 E2
Moúdhros 23 E5
Moudjeria 55 E2
Mouila 56 E2
Moulamein 63 C3
Moulins 13 C5
Moulmein 41 J11
Moundou 53 G2
Mount Barker 62 C2
Mount Darwin 59 B6
Mount Eba 62 B2
Mount Gambier 62 C3
Mount Hope, *N.S.W., Australia* 63 B4
Mount Hope, *S. Austral., Australia* 62 B2
Mount Howitt 62 A3
Mount Isa 61 E6
Mount Lofty Ra. 62 B2
Mount McKinley National Park 71 B4
Mount Margaret 63 A3
Mount Maunganui 64 B7
Mount Olympus = Uludağ 23 D7
Mount Perry 63 A5
Mount Vernon 73 D9
Mountain View 82 B1
Moura, *Brazil* 90 D6
Moura, *Portugal* 18 C2
Mourdi, Dépression du 53 E3
Mourdiah 55 F3
Moussoro 53 F2
Moutohara 64 C7
Moutong 39 D2
Moyale 57 D7
Moyamba 55 G2
Moyen Atlas 54 B3
Moyo 37 F5
Moyyero → 30 C8
Mozambique = Moçambique 59 H8
Mozambique ■ 59 B7
Mozambique Chan. 59 H8
Mozdok 25 E5
Mozyr = Mazyr 17 C9
Mpanda 57 F6
Mpika 59 A6
Mpwapwa 57 F7
Msaken 52 A1
Msoro 59 A6
Mu Us Shamo 35 C5
Muaná 92 C4
Muar 37 D2
Muarabungo 37 E2
Muaraenim 37 E2
Muarajuloi 37 E4
Muarakaman 37 E5
Muaratebo 37 E2
Muaratembesi 37 E2
Muaratewe 37 E4
Mubarraz = Al Mubarraz 47 F7
Mubende 57 D6
Mubi 53 F1
Muckadilla 63 A4
Muconda 56 G4
Mucuri 93 F6
Mudanjiang 35 B7
Mudanya 23 D7
Mudgee 63 B4
Mufulira 59 A5
Muğla 23 F7
Mugu 40 C4
Muhammad Qol 52 D6
Mühlhausen 14 C6
Mühlig Hofmann fjell 96 B7
Mukacheve 17 D6
Mukachevo = Mukacheve 17 D6
Mukah 37 D4
Mukden = Shenyang 35 B7
Mukomuko 37 E2
Muktsar 42 D9
Mukur 42 C5
Mula 19 C5
Mulchén 94 D2
Mulde → 15 C7
Mulgathing 62 B1
Mulgrave 69 D4
Mulhacén 18 D4
Mulhouse 13 C7
Mull 10 C4
Mullengudgery 63 B4
Muller, Pegunungan 37 D4
Mullingar 11 E3
Mullumbimby 63 A5
Multan 42 D7
Mulwala 63 C4
Mumbaī = Bombay 43 K8
Mumbwa 59 A5
Muna 39 F2
München 15 D6

Munchen-Gladbach = Mönchengladbach ........... 14 C4
Muncie ....... 72 D3
Mundala ...... 39 E6
Münden ...... 14 C5
Mundo Novo .. 93 E5
Mungallala .... 63 A4
Mungallala Cr. → ...... 63 A4
Mungbere .... 57 D5
Munger ...... 40 E6
Mungindi ..... 63 A4
Munhango .... 58 A3
Munich = München ... 15 D6
Muñoz Gamero, Pen. ........ 95 G2
Münster ...... 14 C4
Munster □ .... 11 E2
Muntok ....... 37 E3
Mupa ........ 58 B3
Muqdisho .... 49 G4
Murallón, Cuerro ..... 95 F2
Murang'a ..... 57 E7
Murashi ...... 24 B6
Muratlı ....... 22 D6
Murchison → . 60 F1
Murchison, Mt. 96 B15
Murchison Falls = Kabarega Falls ...... 57 D6
Murcia ....... 19 C5
Murcia □ ..... 19 D5
Mureş → .... 16 E5
Mureşul = Mureş → ... 16 E5
Murfreesboro . 74 B4
Murgab = Murghob ... 29 F8
Murghob ..... 29 F8
Murgon ...... 63 A5
Müritz-see .... 15 B7
Murmansk .... 28 C4
Murom ....... 24 B5
Muroran ...... 32 F12
Muroto-Misaki . 32 C4
Murray → .... 62 C2
Murray Bridge . 62 C2
Murree ....... 42 C8
Murrumbidgee → ........... 62 B3
Murrumburrah 63 B4
Murrurundi ... 63 B5
Murtoa ....... 62 C3
Murwara ..... 40 F3
Murwillumbah . 63 A5
Mürzzuschlag . 15 E8
Muş ........ 46 C5
Mûsa, G. ..... 47 E3
Musa Khel .... 42 D6
Mūsá Qal'eh .. 42 C4
Musaffargarh .. 42 D7
Musala, *Bulgaria* 22 C4
Musala, *Indonesia* ... 37 D1
Musay'īd ..... 44 E2
Muscat = Masqat ..... 45 F4
Muscat & Oman = Oman ■ .. 48 C6
Muscatine .... 77 E9
Musgrave Ras. 60 F5
Mushie ....... 56 E3
Musi → ...... 37 E2
Muskogee .... 79 B6
Musmar ...... 53 E6
Musoma ...... 57 E6
Mussoorie .... 42 D11
Mustafakemalpaşa ........... 23 D7
Mustang ...... 40 C4
Musters, L. .... 95 F3
Muswellbrook . 63 B5
Mût, *Egypt* .... 52 C4
Mut, *Turkey* ... 46 C3
Mutare ....... 59 B6
Muting ....... 39 F6
Mutoray ...... 30 C8
Muxima ...... 56 F2
Muynak ...... 29 E6
Muzaffarabad . 42 B8
Muzaffarnagar . 42 E10
Muzaffarpur ... 40 D5
Muzhi ........ 28 C7
Muztag ....... 34 C3
Mvuma ....... 59 B6
Mwanza, *Tanzania* .... 57 E6
Mwanza, *Dem. Rep. of the Congo* ........... 57 F5
Mweka ....... 56 E4
Mwenezi ..... 59 C6
Mwenga ...... 57 E5
Mweru, L. .... 57 F5
Mwinilunga ... 58 A4
My Tho ...... 36 B3
Myanaung .... 41 H10
Myanmar = Burma ■ ... 41 G11
Myaungmya .. 41 J10
Mycenæ ...... 23 F4
Myeik Kyunzu . 36 B1
Myingyan ..... 41 G10
Myitkyina ..... 41 E11
Mykolayiv .... 25 D3
Mymensingh .. 41 E8
Mysia ........ 23 E6
Mysore = Karnataka □ . 43 N10
Mysore ....... 43 N10
Myszków ..... 16 C4
Mytishchi ..... 24 B4

# N

Na Hearadh = Harris ...... 10 C3
Naab → ..... 15 D7
Naberezhnyye Chelny ..... 29 D6
Nabeul ....... 52 A1
Nabire ....... 39 E5
Nablus = Nābulus .... 46 D3
Nābulus ...... 46 D3
Nachingwea .. 57 G7
Nackara ...... 62 B2
Nacogdoches . 79 D6
Nacozari ...... 84 A3
Nadiad ....... 43 H8
Nadūshan .... 44 C3
Nadvirna ..... 17 D7
Nadvornaya = Nadvirna ... 17 D7
Nadym ....... 28 C8
Nadym → .... 28 C8
Nafada ....... 55 F7
Nafūd ad Dahy 47 G6
Nafud Desert = An Nafūd ... 47 E5
Naga ........ 38 B2
Nagaland □ ... 41 E10
Nagano ...... 32 A6
Nagaoka ...... 33 G11
Nagappattinam 43 P11
Nagar Parkar .. 43 G7
Nagasaki ..... 32 C1
Nagaur ....... 42 F8
Nagercoil ..... 43 Q10
Nagīneh ...... 44 C4
Nagoya ...... 32 B5
Nagpur ....... 43 J11
Nagykanizsa .. 16 E3
Nagykörös .... 16 E4
Nahanni Butte . 70 B7
Nahāvand .... 46 D7
Nā'ifah ....... 48 D5
Nain, *Canada* .. 68 C4
Nā'īn, *Iran* .... 44 C3
Nairn ........ 10 C5
Nairobi ....... 57 E7
Naivasha ..... 57 E7
Najafābād .... 44 C2
Najd ......... 47 F5
Najibabad .... 42 E11
Nakamura .... 32 C3
Nakfa ........ 53 E6
Nakhichevan = Naxçıvan ... 25 F6
Nakhichevan Republic □ = Naxçıvan □ . 25 F6
Nakhodka ..... 31 E11
Nakhon Phanom 36 A2
Nakhon Ratchasima . 36 B2
Nakhon Sawan 36 A2
Nakhon Si Thammarat . 36 C2
Nakina ....... 69 C2
Nakuru ....... 57 E7
Nal → ....... 42 G4
Nalchik ....... 25 E5
Nalgonda ..... 43 L11
Nallamalai Hills 43 M11
Nālūt ........ 52 D1
Nam Co ...... 34 C4
Nam-Phan .... 36 B3
Namacurra .... 59 B7
Namak, Daryācheh-ye 44 C3
Namak, Kavir-e 44 C4
Namaland .... 58 C3
Namangan .... 29 E8
Namapa ...... 59 A7
Namber ...... 39 E4
Nambour ..... 63 A5
Nambucca Heads ...... 63 B5
Nameh ....... 37 D5
Namib Desert = Namibwoestyn ........... 58 C2
Namibe ...... 58 B2
Namibia ■ .... 58 C3
Namibwoestyn 58 C2
Namlea ...... 39 E3
Namoi → .... 63 B4
Nampa ....... 80 D5
Nampula ..... 59 B7
Namrole ...... 39 E3
Namse Shankou 40 C4
Namtu ....... 41 F11
Namur ....... 14 C3
Namutoni ..... 58 B3
Namwala ..... 59 B5
Nanaimo ..... 71 D7
Nanango ..... 63 A5
Nanao ....... 32 A5
Nanchang .... 35 D6
Nanching = Nanjing ..... 35 C6
Nanchong .... 35 C5
Nancy ........ 13 B7
Nanda Devi ... 42 D11
Nanded ...... 43 K10
Nandewar Ra. . 63 B5
Nandurbar .... 43 J9
Nandyal ...... 43 M11
Nanga-Eboko .. 56 D2
Nanga Parbat . 42 B9
Nangapinoh ... 37 E4
Nangarhár □ .. 42 B7
Nangatayap ... 37 E4
Nanjing ...... 35 C6
Nanking = Nanjing ..... 35 C6
Nanning ...... 35 D5
Nanping ...... 35 D6
Nansei-Shotō = Ryūkyū-rettō 35 D7
Nantes ....... 12 C3
Nanuque ..... 93 F5
Nanusa, Kepulauan .. 38 D3
Nanyang ..... 35 C6
Nanyuki ...... 57 D7
Nao, C. de la .. 19 C6
Naoetsu ...... 32 A6
Napa ......... 80 F2
Napier ....... 64 C7
Naples = Nápoli 21 D5
Naples ....... 75 F7
Napo → ..... 90 D4
Nápoli ....... 21 D5
Nappa Merrie . 62 A3
Nara, *Japan* ... 32 B4
Nara, *Mali* .... 55 E3
Naracoorte .... 62 C3
Naradhan ..... 63 B4
Narasapur .... 40 J3
Narathiwat .... 36 C2
Narayanganj .. 41 F8
Narayanpet ... 43 L10
Narbonne ..... 13 E5
Nardò ........ 23 D2
Narew → .... 16 B5
Narin ........ 42 A6
Narmada → .. 43 J8
Narooma ..... 63 C5
Narrabri ...... 63 B4
Narran → .... 63 A4
Narrandera ... 63 B4
Narromine .... 63 B4
Narsimhapur .. 43 H11
Narva ........ 24 B2
Narvik ........ 8 E11
Naryan-Mar ... 28 C6
Naryilco ...... 62 A3
Narym ....... 29 D9
Narymskoye .. 29 E9
Naryn ....... 29 E8
Nasarawa ..... 55 G6
Naseby ....... 65 F4
Naser, Buheirat en ........ 52 D5
Nashville ..... 74 A4
Nasik ........ 43 K8
Nasirabad .... 42 F9
Nassau ....... 86 A4
Nassau, B. .... 95 H3
Nasser, L. = Naser, Buheirat en . 52 D5
Nat Kyizin .... 41 K11
Nata ......... 59 C5
Natagaima .... 90 C3
Natal, *Brazil* ... 92 D6
Natal, *Indonesia* 37 D1

Naţanz 44 C2
Natashquan 69 C4
Natashquan → 69 C4
Natchez 79 D8
Nathalia 63 C4
Nathdwara 43 G8
Natitingou 55 F5
Natron, L. 57 E7
Natuna Besar, Kepulauan 37 D3
Natuna Is. = Natuna Besar, Kepulauan 37 D3
Natuna Selatan, Kepulauan 37 D3
Naturaliste, C. 62 D4
Naumburg 15 C6
Nauru ■ 64 K11
Naushahra = Nowshera 42 B8
Nauta 90 D4
Nautanwa 40 D4
Navahrudak 17 B7
Navalmoral de la Mata 18 C3
Navarino, I. 95 H3
Navarra □ 19 A5
Năvodari 22 B7
Navoi = Nawoiy 29 E7
Navojoa 84 B3
Návpaktos 23 E3
Návplion 23 F4
Navsari 43 J8
Nawabshah 42 F6
Nawakot 40 D5
Nawalgarh 42 F9
Nawāsīf, Harrat 47 G5
Nawoiy 29 E7
Naxçıvan 25 F6
Naxçıvan □ 25 F6
Náxos 23 F5
Nāy Band 44 E3
Nazas → 84 B4
Nazilli 23 F7
Nazir Hat 41 F8
Ncheu 59 A6
Ndalatando 56 F2
Ndélé 56 C4
Ndendé 56 E2
Ndjamena 53 F1
Ndjolé 56 E2
Ndola 59 A5
Neagh, Lough 11 D3
Near Is. 71 C1
Neath 11 F5
Nebine Cr. → 63 A4
Nebitdag 29 F6
Nebraska □ 76 E5
Nébrodi, Monti 21 F5
Neckar → 14 D5
Necochea 94 D5
Neemuch = Nimach 43 G9
Neepawa 71 C10
Nefta 54 B6
Neftçala 46 C7
Negapatam = Nagappattinam 43 P11
Negele 49 F2
Negombo 43 R11
Negotin 22 B4
Negra Pt. 38 A2
Negrais, C. = Maudin Sun 41 K10
Negro →, *Argentina* 95 E4
Negro →, *Brazil* 90 D6
Negro →, *Uruguay* 94 C5
Negros 38 C2
Nehbandān 45 D5
Nei Monggol Zizhiqu □ 35 B6
Neijiang 35 D5
Neiva 90 C3
Nejd = Najd 47 F5
Nekemte 53 G6
Nellore 43 M11
Nelson, *Canada* 71 D8
Nelson, *N.Z.* 65 D5
Nelson → 71 C10
Nelson, C. 62 C3
Nelson, Estrecho 95 G2
Nelspruit 59 D6
Néma 55 E3
Neman → 24 B1
Nemunas = Neman → 24 B1
Nemuro 32 F13
Nemuro-Kaikyō 32 F13
Nenagh 11 E2
Nenana 71 B5
Nenjiang 35 B7
Nepal ■ 40 D5
Nepalganj 40 C3
Neretva → 20 C6
Ness, L. 10 C4
Nesterov 17 C6
Nesvizh = Nyasvizh 17 B8
Netherlands ■ 14 B3
Netherlands Antilles ■ 87 D6
Nettilling L. 68 B3
Neubrandenburg 15 B7
Neuchâtel 13 C7
Neuchâtel, Lac de 13 C7
Neumünster 14 A5
Neunkirchen 14 D4
Neuquén 94 D3
Neuruppin 15 B7
Neustrelitz 15 B7
Neva → 24 B3
Nevada □ 80 F5
Nevada, Sierra, *Spain* 18 D4
Nevada, Sierra, *U.S.A.* 80 F3
Nevers 13 C5
Nevertire 63 B4
Nevinnomyssk 25 E5
Nevis 87 C7
Nevşehir 46 C3
New Amsterdam 90 B7
New Angledool 63 A4
New Bedford 73 D10
New Bern 75 B9
New Brighton 65 E5
New Britain, *Papua N. G.* 64 K10
New Britain, *U.S.A.* 73 D9
New Brunswick □ 69 D4
New Caledonia ■ 64 M11
New Delhi 42 E10
New England Ra. 63 B5
New Glasgow 69 D4
New Guinea 64
New Hampshire □ 73 C10
New Haven 73 D9
New Hebrides = Vanuatu ■ 64 L11
New Ireland 64 K10
New Jersey □ 73 E9
New London 73 D9
New Mexico □ 83 C9
New Norfolk 62 D4
New Orleans 79 E8
New Plymouth 64 C6
New Providence 86 A4
New Siberian Is. = Novosibirskiye Ostrova 31 B12
New South Wales □ 63 B4
New Westminster 71 D7
New York □ 73 C8
New York City 73 D9
New Zealand ■ 64 D7
Newala 57 G7
Newark 73 D8
Newburgh 73 D8
Newbury 11 F6
Newcastle, *Australia* 63 B5
Newcastle, *S. Africa* 59 D5
Newcastle-upon-Tyne 11 D6
Newfoundland □ 69 C5
Newman 60 E2
Newport, *I. of W., U.K.* 11 F6
Newport, *Newp., U.K.* 11 F5
Newport, *U.S.A.* 73 D10
Newport News 73 F7
Newquay 11 F4
Newry 11 D3
Newton Boyd 63 A5
Neya 24 B5
Neyrīz 44 D3
Neyshābūr 44 B4
Nezhin = Nizhyn 24 C3
Ngabang 37 D3
Ngabordamlu, Tanjung 39 F4
Ngami Depression 58 C4
Nganglong Kangri 40 A3
Ngaoundéré 56 C2
Ngapara 65 F4
Ngoring Hu 34 C4
Ngudu 57 E6
Nguigmi 53 F1
Nguru 55 F7
Nha Trang 36 B3
Nhill 62 C3
Niafounké 55 E4
Niagara Falls, *Canada* 69 D3
Niagara Falls, *U.S.A.* 73 C6
Niah 37 D4
Niamey 55 F5
Niangara 57 D5
Nias 37 D1
Nicaragua ■ 85 E7
Nicaragua, L. de 85 E7
Nicastro 21 E6
Nice 13 E7
Nichinan 33 D2
Nicobar Is. 27 J13
Nicosia 46 D3
Nicoya, Pen. de 85 F7
Niedersachsen □ 14 B5
Niemen = Neman → 24 B1
Nienburg 14 B5
Nieuw Amsterdam 92 A2
Nieuw Nickerie 92 A2
Niğde 46 C3
Niger ■ 55 E6
Niger → 55 G6
Nigeria ■ 55 G6
Nightcaps 65 F3
Nii-Jima 32 B6
Niigata 33 G11
Niihama 32 C3
Niihau 82
Nijmegen 14 C3
Nikiniki 39 F2
Nikki 55 G5
Nikolayev = Mykolayiv 25 D3
Nikolayevsk 24 C6
Nikopol 25 D3
Nīkshahr 45 E5
Nikšić 22 C2
Nîl, Nahr en → 52 B5
Nîl el Abyad → 53 E5
Nîl el Azraq → 53 E5
Nile = Nîl, Nahr en → 52 B5
Nimach 43 G9
Nîmes 13 E6
Nimfaíon, Ákra = Pínnes, Ákra 23 D5
Nimmitabel 63 C4
Nīmrūz □ 45 D5
Nimule 57 D6
Nīnawá 46 C5
Nindigully 63 A4
Nineveh = Nīnawá 46 C5
Ningbo 35 D7
Ningde 35 D6
Ningpo = Ningbo 35 D7
Ningsia Hui A.R. = Ningxia Huizu Zizhiqu □ 35 C5
Ningxia Huizu Zizhiqu □ 35 C5
Niobrara → 76 D5
Nioro du Sahel 55 E3
Niort 12 C3
Nipawin 71 C9
Nipigon, L. 69 D2
Niquelândia 93 E4
Nirmal 43 K11
Nirmali 40 D6
Niš 22 C3
Nişāb, *Si. Arabia* 47 E6
Nişāb, *Yemen* 49 E4
Nishinomiya 32 B4
Nistru = Dnister → 17 E10
Niţā' 47 F7
Niterói 93 G5
Nitra 16 D4
Nitra → 16 E4
Niue 65 L14
Niut 37 D4
Nivernais 13 C5
Nizamabad 43 K11
Nizamghat 41 C10
Nizhne-Vartovsk 29 C8
Nizhneyansk 31 B11
Nizhniy Novgorod 24 B5

Nizhniy Tagil .. 29 D6
Nizhyn ....... 24 C3
Nizip ......... 46 C4
Nízké Tatry ... 16 D4
Njombe ...... 57 F6
Nkambe ...... 55 G7
Nkawkaw ..... 55 G4
Nkhata Bay ... 57 G6
Nkhota Kota .. 59 A6
Nkongsamba .. 56 D1
Nmai → ..... 41 E11
Noakhali = Maijdi ...... 41 F8
Noatak ....... 71 B3
Nobeoka ..... 32 C2
Nocera Inferiore 21 D5
Nockatunga ... 62 A3
Nogales, *Mexico* 84 A2
Nogales, *U.S.A.* 83 E7
Nōgata ....... 32 C2
Noginsk ...... 30 C7
Noire, Mts. .... 12 B2
Noirmoutier, I. de ......... 12 C2
Nok Kundi .... 42 E3
Nokhtuysk .... 30 C9
Nokomis ..... 71 C9
Nola ......... 56 D3
Nome ........ 71 B3
Nong Khai .... 36 A2
Noondoo ..... 63 A4
Nóqui ........ 56 F2
Noranda ..... 69 D3
Nord-Ostsee-Kanal → ... 14 A5
Nordegg ...... 71 C8
Norderney .... 14 B4
Norderstedt ... 14 B5
Nordfriesische Inseln ...... 14 A5
Nordhausen ... 14 C6
Nordkapp ..... 8 D13
Nordrhein-Westfalen ☐ . 14 C4
Nordvik ...... 30 B9
Norfolk ....... 73 F7
Norfolk I. ..... 64 M11
Norilsk ....... 30 C6
Norley ....... 63 A3
Norman ...... 78 B5
Norman Wells . 70 B7
Normandie ... 12 B4
Normandy = Normandie .. 12 B4
Normanton ... 61 D7
Norquinco .... 95 E2
Norrköping ... 9 G11
Norrland ..... 8 F11
Norseman .... 60 G3
North Battleford 71 C9
North Bay .... 69 D3
North Bend ... 80 D1
North C. ...... 64 A5
North Cape = Nordkapp ... 8 D13
North Carolina ☐ .. 75 B7
North Channel, *Canada* ..... 69 D2
North Channel, *U.K.* ........ 11 D4
North Dakota ☐ 76 B4
North Frisian Is. = Nordfriesische Inseln ...... 14 A5
North I. ....... 64 B5
North Korea ■ 35 C7
North Lakhimpur .. 41 D10
North Minch .. 10 B4
North Ossetia ☐ 25 E5
North Pagai, I. = Pagai Utara . 37 E2
North Platte ... 76 E4
North Platte → 76 E4
North Rhine Westphalia ☐ = Nordrhein-Westfalen ☐ . 14 C4
North Saskatchewan → ........... 71 C8
North Sea .... 10 D8
North Sporades = Voríai Sporádhes .. 23 E4
North Taranaki Bight ....... 64 C6
North Thompson → 71 C7
North Uist .... 10 C3
North West C. . 60 E1
North West Frontier ☐ .. 42 B8
North West Highlands ... 10 C4
North West River ....... 69 C4
North West Territories ☐ 70 B7
Northampton .. 11 E6
Northern Circars 40 J4
Northern Ireland ☐ ... 11 D3
Northern Marianas ■ . 64 H9
Northern Territory ☐ .. 60 D5
Northland ☐ .. 64 A5
Northumberland, C. .......... 62 C3
Northumberland Str. ........ 69 D4
Norton Sd. .... 71 B3
Norway ■ .... 8 F10
Norway House 71 C10
Norwegian Sea 6 B6
Norwich ...... 11 E7
Nosok ........ 28 B9
Noşratabād ... 45 D4
Nossob → ... 58 D4
Nosy Bé ...... 59 G9
Nosy Boraha .. 59 H9
Nosy Mitsio ... 59 G9
Nosy Varika ... 59 J9
Noteć → ..... 16 B2
Noto-Hanto ... 33 G11
Notre Dame B. 69 D5
Notre Dame de Koartac = Quaqtaq .... 68 B4
Notre Dame d'Ivugivic = Ivujivik ..... 68 B3
Nottaway → .. 69 C3
Nottingham ... 11 E6
Nouâdhibou .. 54 D1
Nouâdhibou, Ras ........ 54 D1
Nouakchott ... 55 E1
Nouméa ...... 64 M11
Noupoort ..... 58 E4
Nouveau Comptoir = Wemindji ... 69 C3
Nouvelle-Calédonie = New Caledonia ■ . 64 M11
Nova Casa Nova 93 D5
Nova Cruz .... 92 D6
Nova Friburgo . 93 G5
Nova Gaia = Cambundi-Catembo .... 56 G3
Nova Iguaçu .. 93 G5
Nova Iorque .. 92 D5
Nova Lima .... 93 F5
Nova Mambone 59 C7
Nova Scotia ☐ . 69 D4
Nova Sofala ... 59 C6
Nova Venécia . 93 F5
Nova Zagora .. 22 C5
Novara ....... 20 B2
Novaya Ladoga 24 A3
Novaya Lyalya 29 D7
Novaya Zemlya 28 B6
Nové Zámky .. 16 D4
Novgorod .... 24 B3
Novgorod-Severskiy = Novhorod-Siverskyy ... 24 C3
Novhorod-Siverskyy ... 24 C3
Novi Lígure ... 20 B2
Novi Pazar .... 22 C3
Novi Sad ... 22 B2
Novo Mesto ... 20 B5
Novo Remanso 93 D5
Novoataysk ... 29 D9
Novocherkassk 25 D5
Novogrudok = Navahrudak . 17 B7
Novohrad-Volynskyy ... 17 C8
Novokazalinsk = Zhangaqazaly 29 E7
Novokuybyshevsk ........... 24 C6
Novokuznetsk . 29 D9
Novomoskovsk 24 C4
Novorossiysk .. 25 E4
Novorybnoye . 30 B8
Novoselytsya .. 17 D8
Novoshakhtinsk 25 D4
Novosibirsk ... 29 D9
Novosibirskiye Ostrova ..... 31 B12
Novotroitsk ... 29 D6
Novouzensk ... 24 C6
Novovolynsk .. 17 C7
Novska ....... 20 B6
Novyy Port ... 28 C8
Now Shahr ... 44 B2
Nowa Sól ..... 16 C2
Nowgong ..... 41 D9
Nowra ....... 63 B5
Nowshera .... 42 B8
Nowy Sącz .... 16 D5
Nowy Targ .... 16 D5
Nowy Tomyśl . 16 B3
Noyon ....... 13 B5
Nsanje ....... 59 B7
Nsawam ...... 55 G4
Nsukka ....... 55 G6
Nubian Desert = Nûbîya, Es Sahrâ En ... 52 D5
Nûbîya, Es Sahrâ En ... 52 D5
Nuboai ....... 39 E5
Nueltin L. ..... 70 B10
Nueva Imperial 94 D2
Nueva Rosita .. 84 B4
Nuéve de Julio 94 D4
Nuevitas ...... 86 B4
Nuevo, G. ..... 95 E4
Nuevo Laredo . 84 B5
Nugget Pt. .... 65 G3
Nuhaka ....... 64 C7
Nukey Bluff ... 62 B2
Nukheila ...... 53 E4
Nukus ........ 29 E6
Nulato ....... 71 B4
Nullarbor Plain 60 G4
Numalla, L. ... 63 A3
Numan ....... 53 G1
Numazu ...... 32 B6
Numfoor ..... 39 E4
Numurkah .... 63 C4
Nunavut ☐ .... 66 C10
Nuneaton ..... 11 E6
Nunivak I. .... 71 B3
Nunkun ...... 42 C10
Núoro ........ 21 D2
Nuremberg = Nürnberg ... 15 D6
Nuriootpa .... 62 B2
Nürnberg ..... 15 D6
Nurran, L. = Terewah, L. . 63 A4
Nusa Tenggara Barat ☐ ..... 37 F5
Nusa Tenggara Timur ☐ .... 39 F2
Nushki ....... 42 E5
Nutak ........ 68 C4
Nuuk = Godthåb .... 68 B5
Nuwakot ..... 40 C4
Nuweveldberge 58 E4
Nuyts Arch. ... 62 B1
Nyah West .... 62 C3
Nyahanga .... 57 E6
Nyahururu .... 57 D7
Nyainqentanglha Shan ....... 34 C4
Nyâlâ ........ 53 F3
Nyasa, L. = Malawi, L. .. 59 A6
Nyasvizh ..... 17 B8
Nyda ......... 28 C8
Nyeri ........ 57 E7
Nyíregyháza .. 17 E5
Nylstroom .... 59 C5
Nymagee ..... 63 B4
Nyngan ...... 63 B4
Nyoman = Neman → .. 24 B1
Nysa ......... 16 C3
Nysa → ...... 16 B2
Nyurbe ....... 30 C9
Nzega ........ 57 E6
N'Zérékoré .... 55 G3
Nzeto ........ 56 F2

## O

Ō-Shima ...... 32 B6
Oahe, L. ...... 76 C4
Oahu ........ 82 H12
Oak Ridge .... 75 A5
Oakbank ...... 62 B3
Oakey ........ 63 A5
Oakland ...... 82 B1
Oamaru ...... 65 F4
Oates Land ... 96 A15
Oaxaca ....... 84 D5
Ob → ....... 28 C7

| Place | Page | Grid |
|---|---|---|
| Oba | 69 | D2 |
| Oban | 10 | C4 |
| Obbia | 49 | F4 |
| Oberhausen | 14 | C4 |
| Oberon | 63 | B4 |
| Obi, Kepulauan | 39 | E3 |
| Obi Is. = Obi, Kepulauan | 39 | E3 |
| Óbidos | 92 | C2 |
| Obihiro | 32 | F12 |
| Obilatu | 39 | E3 |
| Obo | 57 | C5 |
| Obozerskaya = Obozerskiy | 28 | C5 |
| Obozerskiy | 28 | C5 |
| Obskaya Guba | 28 | C8 |
| Obuasi | 55 | G4 |
| Ocala | 75 | E6 |
| Ocaña | 18 | C4 |
| Occidental, Cordillera | 90 | C3 |
| Ocean I. = Banaba | 64 | K11 |
| Oceanside | 82 | D4 |
| Ocniţa | 17 | D8 |
| Ocumare del Tuy | 90 | A5 |
| Odate | 33 | F12 |
| Odawara | 32 | B6 |
| Oddur | 49 | G3 |
| Ödemiş | 23 | E7 |
| Odense | 9 | G10 |
| Oder → | 15 | B8 |
| Odesa | 25 | D3 |
| Odessa = Odesa | 25 | D3 |
| Odessa | 78 | D2 |
| Odienné | 55 | G3 |
| Odintsovo | 24 | B4 |
| Odorheiu Secuiesc | 17 | E7 |
| Odra = Oder → | 15 | B8 |
| Odra → | 16 | B2 |
| Oeiras | 92 | D5 |
| Ofanto → | 20 | D6 |
| Offa | 55 | G5 |
| Offenbach | 14 | C5 |
| Offenburg | 14 | D4 |
| Oga-Hantō | 33 | G11 |
| Ōgaki | 32 | B5 |
| Ogbomosho | 55 | G5 |
| Ogden | 81 | E8 |
| Ogdensburg | 73 | B8 |
| Oglio → | 20 | B3 |
| Ogooué → | 56 | E1 |
| Ogowe = Ogooué → | 56 | E1 |
| Ohai | 65 | F2 |
| Ohakune | 64 | C6 |
| Ohanet | 54 | C6 |
| Ohau, L. | 65 | F3 |
| Ohio □ | 72 | D4 |
| Ohio → | 72 | F1 |
| Ohre → | 16 | C2 |
| Ohrid | 22 | D3 |
| Ohridsko Jezero | 23 | D3 |
| Oise → | 12 | B5 |
| Ōita | 32 | C2 |
| Oiticica | 92 | D5 |
| Ojos del Salado, Cerro | 94 | B3 |
| Oka → | 28 | D5 |
| Okaba | 39 | F5 |
| Okahandja | 58 | C3 |
| Okahukura | 64 | C6 |
| Okandja | 56 | E2 |
| Okanogan → | 80 | A4 |
| Okara | 42 | D8 |
| Okarito | 65 | E4 |
| Okaukuejo | 58 | B3 |
| Okavango Swamps | 58 | B4 |
| Okaya | 32 | A6 |
| Okayama | 32 | B3 |
| Okazaki | 32 | B5 |
| Okeechobee, L. | 75 | F7 |
| Okefenokee Swamp | 75 | D6 |
| Okhotsk, Sea of | 31 | D12 |
| Oki-Shotō | 32 | A3 |
| Okiep | 58 | D3 |
| Okinawa-Jima | 35 | D7 |
| Oklahoma □ | 78 | B5 |
| Oklahoma City | 78 | B5 |
| Okmulgee | 79 | B6 |
| Oknitsa = Ocniţa | 17 | D8 |
| Okrika | 55 | H6 |
| Oktabrsk = Oktyabrsk | 29 | E6 |
| Oktyabrsk | 29 | E6 |
| Oktyabrskiy = Aktsyabrski | 17 | B9 |
| Oktyabrskoy Revolyutsii, Os. | 30 | B7 |
| Oktyabrskoye | 28 | C7 |
| Okuru | 65 | E3 |
| Okushiri-Tō | 32 | F11 |
| Öland | 9 | G11 |
| Olary | 62 | B3 |
| Olavarría | 94 | D4 |
| Oława | 16 | C3 |
| Ólbia | 20 | D2 |
| Old Crow | 70 | B6 |
| Oldenburg | 14 | B5 |
| Oldham | 11 | E5 |
| Olekma → | 31 | C10 |
| Olekminsk | 31 | C10 |
| Oleksandriya | 17 | C8 |
| Olenek | 30 | C9 |
| Olenek → | 30 | B10 |
| Oléron, I. d' | 12 | D3 |
| Oleśnica | 16 | C3 |
| Olevsk | 17 | C8 |
| Olhão | 18 | D2 |
| Olifants → | 59 | C6 |
| Ólimbos, Óros | 23 | D4 |
| Olinda | 92 | D7 |
| Oliveira | 93 | G5 |
| Olivenza | 18 | C2 |
| Ollagüe | 91 | H5 |
| Olomouc | 16 | D3 |
| Olongapo | 38 | B2 |
| Olot | 19 | A7 |
| Olsztyn | 16 | B5 |
| Olt → | 22 | C5 |
| Olteniţa | 22 | B6 |
| Oltu | 46 | B5 |
| Olympia, *Greece* | 23 | F3 |
| Olympia, *U.S.A.* | 80 | B2 |
| Olympic Mts. | 80 | B2 |
| Olympus, Mt. = Ólimbos, Óros | 23 | D4 |
| Om → | 29 | D8 |
| Omagh | 11 | D3 |
| Omaha | 77 | E7 |
| Oman ■ | 48 | C6 |
| Oman, G. of | 45 | E4 |
| Omaruru | 58 | C3 |
| Omate | 91 | G4 |
| Ombai, Selat | 39 | F2 |
| Omboué | 56 | E1 |
| Ombrone → | 20 | C3 |
| Omdurmân | 53 | E5 |
| Ometepec | 84 | D5 |
| Ōmiya | 32 | B6 |
| Omo → | 53 | G6 |
| Omsk | 29 | D8 |
| Omul, Vf. | 17 | F7 |
| Ōmura | 32 | C1 |
| Omuramba Omatako → | 58 | B4 |
| Ōmuta | 32 | C2 |
| Onang | 39 | E1 |
| Oncócua | 58 | B2 |
| Onda | 19 | C5 |
| Ondangua | 58 | B3 |
| Ondo | 55 | G5 |
| Öndörhaan | 35 | B6 |
| Onega | 28 | C4 |
| Onega → | 8 | F15 |
| Onega, G. of = Onezhskaya Guba | 28 | C4 |
| Onega, L. = Onezhskoye Ozero | 28 | C4 |
| Onehunga | 64 | B6 |
| Oneşti | 17 | E8 |
| Onezhskaya Guba | 28 | C4 |
| Onezhskoye Ozero | 28 | C4 |
| Ongarue | 64 | C6 |
| Onilahy → | 59 | J8 |
| Onitsha | 55 | G6 |
| Onoda | 32 | B2 |
| Ontario □ | 69 | D2 |
| Ontario, L. | 73 | C7 |
| Oodnadatta | 62 | A2 |
| Oostende | 14 | C2 |
| Ootacamund | 43 | P10 |
| Opala | 56 | E4 |
| Opava | 16 | D3 |
| Opole | 16 | C3 |
| Oporto = Porto | 18 | B1 |
| Opotiki | 64 | C7 |
| Opua | 64 | A6 |
| Opunake | 64 | C5 |
| Oradea | 17 | E5 |
| Orai | 42 | G11 |
| Oral = Zhayyq → | 29 | E6 |
| Oral | 24 | C7 |
| Oran, *Algeria* | 54 | A4 |
| Oran, *Argentina* | 94 | A4 |
| Orange = Oranje → | 58 | D3 |
| Orange, *Australia* | 63 | B4 |
| Orange, *France* | 13 | D6 |
| Orange, *U.S.A.* | 79 | D7 |
| Orange, C. | 92 | B3 |
| Orangeburg | 75 | C7 |
| Oranienburg | 15 | B7 |
| Oranje → | 58 | D3 |
| Oranjemund | 58 | D3 |
| Oras | 38 | B3 |
| Oraşul Stalin = Braşov | 17 | F7 |
| Orbetello | 20 | C3 |
| Orbost | 63 | C4 |
| Orchila, I. | 90 | A5 |
| Ordos = Mu Us Shamo | 35 | C5 |
| Ordu | 46 | B4 |
| Ordzhonikidze = Vladikavkaz | 25 | E5 |
| Ore Mts. = Erzgebirge | 15 | C7 |
| Örebro | 9 | G11 |
| Oregon □ | 80 | C3 |
| Orekhovo-Zuyevo | 24 | B4 |
| Orel | 24 | C4 |
| Ören | 23 | F6 |
| Orenburg | 29 | D6 |
| Orense | 18 | A2 |
| Orepuki | 65 | G2 |
| Øresund | 9 | G10 |
| Orgaz | 18 | C4 |
| Orgeyev = Orhei | 17 | E9 |
| Orgūn | 45 | C7 |
| Orhaneli | 23 | E7 |
| Orhangazi | 23 | D7 |
| Orhei | 17 | E9 |
| Orhon Gol → | 35 | A5 |
| Orient | 62 | A3 |
| Oriental, Cordillera | 90 | B4 |
| Orihuela | 19 | C5 |
| Orinoco → | 90 | B6 |
| Orissa □ | 40 | G5 |
| Oristano | 21 | E2 |
| Oristano, G. di | 21 | E2 |
| Orizaba | 84 | D5 |
| Orkney Is. | 10 | B5 |
| Orlando | 75 | E7 |
| Orléanais | 12 | C5 |
| Orléans | 12 | C4 |
| Ormara | 42 | G4 |
| Ormoc | 38 | B2 |
| Ormond | 64 | C7 |
| Örnsköldsvik | 8 | F11 |
| Orocué | 90 | C4 |
| Orol Dengizi = Aral Sea | 29 | E6 |
| Oroquieta | 38 | C2 |
| Orós | 92 | D6 |
| Orosháza | 16 | E5 |
| Orroroo | 62 | B2 |
| Orsha | 24 | C3 |
| Orsk | 29 | D6 |
| Orşova | 22 | B4 |
| Ortaca | 23 | F7 |
| Ortegal, C. | 18 | A2 |
| Orthez | 12 | E3 |
| Ortigueira | 18 | A2 |
| Ortles | 20 | A3 |
| Ortón → | 91 | F5 |
| Orūmīyeh | 46 | C6 |
| Orūmīyeh, Daryācheh-ye | 46 | C6 |
| Oruro | 91 | G5 |
| Oruzgān □ | 42 | C5 |
| Orvieto | 20 | C4 |
| Oryakhovo | 22 | C4 |
| Ōsaka | 32 | B4 |
| Ösel = Saaremaa | 24 | B1 |
| Osh | 29 | E8 |
| Oshawa | 69 | D3 |
| Oshkosh | 76 | E3 |
| Oshmyany = Ashmyany | 17 | A7 |
| Oshogbo | 55 | G5 |
| Oshwe | 56 | E3 |
| Osijek | 20 | B7 |
| Osipenko = Berdyansk | 25 | D4 |
| Osipovichi = Asipovichy | 17 | B9 |
| Oskarshamn | 9 | G11 |
| Öskemen | 29 | E9 |
| Oslo | 9 | G10 |
| Oslob | 38 | C2 |
| Oslofjorden | 9 | G10 |
| Osmanabad | 43 | K10 |
| Osmaniye | 46 | C4 |
| Osnabrück | 14 | B5 |
| Osorio | 94 | B6 |
| Osorno | 95 | E2 |
| Ossa, Mt. | 62 | D4 |
| Óssa, Oros | 23 | E4 |
| Ostend = Oostende | 14 | C2 |

Oster 17 C10
Österdalälven 8 F10
Östersund 8 F10
Ostfriesische Inseln 14 B4
Ostrava 16 D4
Ostróda 16 B4
Ostroh 17 C8
Ostrołęka 16 B5
Ostrów Mazowiecka 16 B5
Ostrów Wielkopolski 16 C3
Ostrowiec-Świętokrzyski 16 C5
Ostuni 21 D6
Ōsumi-Kaikyō 33 D2
Osuna 18 D3
Oswego 73 C7
Oświęcim 16 C4
Otago □ 65 F3
Otago Harbour 65 F4
Ōtake 32 B3
Otaki 64 D6
Otaru 32 F12
Otaru-Wan = Ishikari-Wan 32 F12
Otavalo 90 C3
Otavi 58 B3
Otira Gorge 65 E4
Otjiwarongo 58 C3
Otorohanga 64 C6
Otranto 23 D2
Otranto, C. d' 23 D2
Otranto, Str. of 23 D2
Ōtsu 32 B4
Ottawa 69 D3
Ottawa Is. 68 C2
Ottumwa 77 E8
Oturkpo 55 G6
Otway, B. 95 G2
Otway, C. 62 C3
Otwock 16 B5
Ouachita Mts. 79 B6
Ouadâne 54 D2
Ouadda 56 C4
Ouagadougou 55 F4
Ouahran = Oran 54 A4
Ouallene 54 D5
Ouanda Djallé 56 C4
Ouango 56 D4
Ouargla 54 B6
Ouarzazate 54 B3
Oubangi → 56 E3
Oudtshoorn 58 E4
Ouessant, I. d' 12 B1
Ouesso 56 D3
Ouezzane 54 B3
Ouidah 55 G5
Oujda 54 B4
Oujeft 55 D2
Ouled Djellal 54 B6
Oulu 8 E13
Oulujärvi 8 F13
Oulujoki → 8 E13
Oum Chalouba 53 E3
Ounianga-Kébir 53 E3
Ounianga Sérir 53 E3
Ourense = Orense 18 A2
Ouricuri 92 D5
Ouro Prêto 93 G5
Ouse 62 D4
Outer Hebrides 10 C3
Outjo 58 C3
Ouyen 62 C3
Ovalle 94 C2
Ovamboland 58 B3
Oviedo 18 A3
Ovruch 17 C9
Owaka 65 G3
Owambo = Ovamboland 58 B3
Owase 32 B5
Owbeh 42 B3
Owen Sound 69 D2
Owen Stanley Ra. 61 B8
Owendo 56 D1
Owo 55 G6
Owyhee → 80 D5
Oxford, *N.Z.* 65 E5
Oxford, *U.K.* 11 F6
Oxley 63 B3
Oxnard 82 C3
Oxus = Amudarya → 29 E6
Oya 37 D4
Oyama 32 A6
Oyem 56 D2
Oyo 55 G5
Ozamiz 38 C2
Ozark Plateau 79 A8
Ózd 16 D5

## P

Pa-an 41 J11
Paarl 58 E3
Pab Hills 42 F5
Pabianice 16 C4
Pabna 41 E7
Pacaja → 92 C3
Pacaraima, Sierra 90 C6
Pacasmayo 91 E3
Pachpadra 42 G8
Pachuca 84 C5
Padaido, Kepulauan 39 E5
Padang 37 E2
Padangpanjang 37 E2
Padangsidempuan 37 D1
Paderborn 14 C5
Padloping Island 68 B4
Pádova 20 B3
Padua = Pádova 20 B3
Paducah 72 F1
Paeroa 64 B6
Pafúri 59 C6
Pag 20 B5
Pagadian 38 C2
Pagai Selatan, P. 37 E2
Pagai Utara 37 E2
Pagalu = Annobón 51 G4
Pagastikós Kólpos 23 E4
Pagatan 37 E5
Pahiatua 64 D6
Painan 37 E2
Paint Hills = Wemindji 69 C3
Painted Desert 83 C7
País Vasco □ 19 A4
Paisley 10 D4
Paita 90 E2
Pajares, Puerto de 18 A3
Pakaraima Mts. 90 B6
Pakistan ■ 42 E7
Pakokku 41 G10
Pakse 36 A3
Paktīā □ 42 C6
Pala 53 G2
Palagruža 20 C6
Palam 43 K10
Palampur 42 C10
Palana 62 C4
Palanan 38 A2
Palanan Pt. 38 A2
Palangkaraya 37 E4
Palani Hills 43 P10
Palanpur 43 G8
Palanro 39 E1
Palapye 59 C5
Palau ■ 38 C4
Palawan 36 C5
Palayankottai 43 Q10
Paleleh 39 D2
Palembang 37 E2
Palencia 18 A3
Palermo 21 E4
Palestine 79 D6
Paletwa 41 G9
Palghat 43 P10
Pali 42 G8
Palioúrion, Ákra 23 E4
Palitana 43 J7
Palk Bay 43 Q11
Palk Strait 43 Q11
Pallanza = Verbánia 20 B2
Palm Springs 82 D4
Palma 57 G8
Palma → 93 E4
Palma, B. de 19 C7
Palma de Mallorca 19 C7
Palmares 92 D6
Palmas, C. 55 H3
Pálmas, G. di 21 E2
Palmeira dos Índios 93 D6
Palmeirinhas, Pta. das 56 F2
Palmer 71 B5
Palmer Arch. 96 A3
Palmer Land 96 B3
Palmerston 65 F4
Palmerston North 64 D6
Palmi 21 E5
Palmira 90 C3
Palmyra = Tudmur 40 D4
Palopo 39 E2
Palos, C. de 19 D5
Palu, *Indonesia* 39 E1
Palu, *Turkey* 46 C5
Paluan 38 B2
Pama 55 F5
Pamiers 12 E4
Pamirs 29 F8
Pamlico Sd. 75 B10
Pampa 78 B3
Pampa de las Salinas 94 C3
Pampanua 39 E2
Pampas, *Argentina* 94 D4
Pampas, *Peru* 91 F4
Pamplona, *Colombia* 90 B4
Pamplona, *Spain* 19 A5
Panaji 43 M8
Panamá 85 F9
Panama ■ 86 E4
Panamá, G. de 86 E4
Panama City 74 D5
Panão 91 E3
Panay 38 B2
Panay, G. 38 B2
Pančevo 22 B3
Pandan 38 B2
Pandharpur 43 L9
Pando 94 C5
Pando, L. = Hope, L. 62 A2
Panevėžys 24 B1
Panfilov 29 E8
Pang-Long 41 F12
Pang-Yang 41 F12
Pangani 57 F7
Pangfou = Bengbu 35 C6
Pangkajene 39 E1
Pangkalanbrandan 37 D1
Pangkalanbuun 37 E4
Pangkalansusu 37 D1
Pangkalpinang 37 E3
Pangkoh 37 E4
Pangnirtung 68 B4
Pangutaran Group 38 C2
Panjgur 42 F4
Panjim = Panaji 43 M8
Panjinad Barrage 42 E7
Panorama 94 A6
Pantar 39 F2
Pante Macassar 39 F2
Pantelleria 21 F3
Pánuco 84 C5
Panyam 55 G6
Paoting = Baoding 35 C6
Paot'ou = Baotou 35 B6
Paoua 56 C3
Pápa 16 E3
Papakura 64 B6
Papantla 84 C5
Papar 36 C5
Papua New Guinea ■ 61 B8
Papudo 94 C2
Papun 41 H11
Pará = Belém 92 C4
Pará □ 92 C3
Paracatu 93 F4
Paracel Is. = Hsisha Chuntao 36 A4
Parachilna 62 B2
Parachinar 42 C7
Paradip 40 G6
Parado 39 F1
Paragua → 90 B6
Paraguaçu → 93 E6
Paraguaná, Pen. de 90 A4
Paraguarí 94 B5
Paraguay ■ 94 A5
Paraguay → 94 B5
Paraíba = João Pessoa 92 D7
Paraíba □ 92 D6
Paraíba do Sul → 93 G5
Parakou 55 G5
Paramaribo 92 A2
Paraná, *Argentina* 94 C4
Paranã, *Brazil* 93 E4
Paraná □ 94 A6
Paraná → 94 C5
Paranaguá 94 B7
Paranaíba → 93 G3

Paranapanema → 94 A6
Paranapiacaba, Serra do 94 A7
Parang, *Jolo, Phil.* 38 C2
Parang, *Mindanao, Phil.* 38 C2
Paratinga 93 E5
Paratoo 62 B2
Parattah 62 D4
Parbhani 43 K10
Parchim 15 B6
Pardo →, *Bahia, Brazil* 93 F6
Pardo →, *Mato Grosso, Brazil* 93 G3
Pardo →, *São Paulo, Brazil* 93 G4
Pardubice 16 C2
Parecis, Serra dos 91 F7
Parepare 39 E1
Párga 23 E3
Pariaguán 90 B6
Pariaman 37 E2
Parigi 39 E2
Parika 90 B7
Parima, Serra 90 C6
Parinari 90 D4
Parîngul Mare 17 F6
Parintins 92 C2
Pariparit Kyun 41 K9
Paris, *France* 12 B5
Paris, *U.S.A.* 79 C6
Park Range 81 F10
Parkersburg 72 E5
Parkes 63 B4
Parla 18 B4
Parma 20 B3
Parnaguá 93 E5
Parnaíba, *Piauí, Brazil* 92 C5
Parnaíba, *São Paulo, Brazil* 93 F3
Parnaíba → 92 C5
Parnassós 23 E4
Parnu 24 B1
Paroo → 63 B3
Páros 23 F5
Parral 94 D2
Parramatta 63 B5
Parry Sound 69 D3
Partinico 21 E4
Paru → 92 C3
Paruro 91 F4
Parvān □ 42 B6
Parvatipuram 40 H4
Pasadena, *Calif., U.S.A.* 82 C3
Pasadena, *Tex., U.S.A.* 79 E6
Pasaje 90 D3
Pascagoula 79 D9
Paşcani 17 E8
Pasco 80 B4
Pasco, Cerro de 91 F3
Pashmakli = Smolyan 22 D5
Pašman 20 C5
Pasni 42 G3
Paso de Indios 95 E3
Passau 15 D7
Passero, C. 21 F5
Passo Fundo 94 B6
Passos 93 G4
Pastaza → 90 D3
Pasto 90 C3
Patagonia 95 F3
Patan, *India* 43 H8
Patan, *Nepal* 40 D5
Patani 39 D3
Patchewollock 62 C3
Patea 64 C6
Pategi 55 G6
Paternò 21 F5
Paterson 73 D8
Pathankot 42 C9
Patiala 42 D10
Patkai Bum 41 D10
Pátmos 23 F6
Patna 40 E5
Patos, L. dos 94 C6
Patos de Minas 93 F4
Patquía 94 C3
Pátrai 23 E3
Pátraikós Kólpos 23 E3
Patras = Pátrai 23 E3
Patrocínio 93 F4
Pattani 36 C2
Patuakhali 41 F8
Pau 12 E3
Pauini → 90 D6
Pauk 41 G10
Paulis = Isiro 57 D5
Paulistana 92 D5
Paulo Afonso 93 D6
Pavia 20 B2
Pavlodar 29 D8
Pavlograd = Pavlohrad 25 D4
Pavlohrad 25 D4
Pavlovo 24 B5
Pavlovsk 24 C5
Pawtucket 73 D10
Paxoí 23 E3
Payakumbuh 37 E2
Payne Bay = Kangirsuk 68 C4
Paysandú 94 C5
Paz, B. la 84 C2
Pazar 46 B5
Pazardzhik 22 C5
Peace → 70 C8
Peak Hill 63 B4
Peake 62 C2
Peake Cr. → 62 A2
Pebane 59 B7
Pebas 90 D4
Peć 22 C3
Pechenga 28 C4
Pechenizhyn 17 D7
Pechora → 28 C6
Pechorskaya Guba 28 C6
Pecos → 78 E3
Pécs 16 E4
Pedder, L. 62 D4
Pedirka 62 A2
Pedra Azul 93 F5
Pedreiras 92 C5
Pedro Afonso 93 D4
Pedro Juan Caballero 94 A5
Peebinga 62 B3
Peel →, *Australia* 63 B5
Peel →, *Canada* 70 B6
Peera Peera Poolanna L. 62 A2
Pegasus Bay 65 E5
Pegu 41 J11
Pegu Yoma 41 H10
Pehuajó 94 D4
Peine 14 B6
Peip'ing = Beijing 35 C6
Peipus, L. = Chudskoye, Oz. 24 B2
Peixe 93 E4
Pekalongan 37 F3
Pekanbaru 37 D2
Pekin 77 E10
Peking = Beijing 35 C6
Pelagie, Is. 21 G4
Pelaihari 37 E4
Peleaga, Vf. 17 F6
Peleng 39 E2
Pelješac 20 C6
Pelly → 70 B6
Pelly Bay 68 B2
Pelly L. 70 B9
Peloponnese = Pelopónnisos □ 23 F4
Pelopónnisos □ 23 F4
Peloro, C. 21 E5
Pelorus Sd. 65 D5
Pelotas 94 C6
Pelvoux, Massif du 13 D7
Pematangsiantar 37 D1
Pemba I. 57 F7
Pembroke, *Canada* 69 D3
Pembroke, *U.K.* 11 F4
Penang = Pinang 36 C2
Penápolis 94 A6
Peñarroya-Pueblonuevo 18 C3
Peñas, C. de 18 A3
Penas, G. de 95 F2
Pench'i = Benxi 35 B7
Pend Oreille L. 80 A5
Pendembu 55 G2
Pendleton 80 C4
Penedo 93 E6
Penguin 62 D4
Peniche 18 C1
Penida 37 F5
Peninsular Malaysia □ 37 D2
Penmarch, Pte. de 12 C1
Pennines 11 D5
Pennsylvania □ 73 D7
Penola 62 C3
Penong 60 G5
Penrith 63 B5
Pensacola 74 D4
Pensacola Mts. 96 C4
Penshurst 62 C3
Penticton 71 D8
Pentland Firth 10 B5
Penza 24 C6
Penzance 11 F4
Peoria 77 E10
Perabumulih 37 E2
Perche, Collines du 12 B4
Perdido, Mte. 19 A6
Perdu, Mt. = Perdido, Mte. 19 A6
Pereira 90 C3
Perekerten 62 B3
Pereyaslav-Khmelnytskyy 24 C3
Pergamino 94 C4
Péribonca → 69 D3
Perico 94 A3
Périgueux 12 D4
Perijá, Sierra de 90 B4
Perlas, Arch. de las 86 E4
Perm 29 D6
Pernambuco = Recife 92 D7
Pernatty Lagoon 62 B2
Pernik 22 C4
Perpendicular Pt. 63 B5
Perpignan 13 E5
Persepolis 44 D3
Pershotravensk 17 C8
Persian Gulf = Gulf, The 44 E2
Perth, *Australia* 60 G2
Perth, *U.K.* 10 C5
Perth Amboy 73 D8
Peru ■ 90 C3
Perúgia 20 C4
Pervomaysk 25 D3
Pervouralsk 29 D6
Pésaro 20 C4
Pescara 20 C5
Peshawar 42 B7
Peshkopi 22 D3
Pesqueira 92 D6
Petah Tiqwa 46 D3
Petauke 59 A6
Peter I.s Øy 96 A2
Peterborough, *Australia* 62 B2
Peterborough, *Canada* 69 D3
Peterborough, *U.K.* 11 E6
Peterhead 10 C6
Petersburg, *Alaska, U.S.A.* 71 C6
Petersburg, *Va., U.S.A.* 73 F7
Petitsikapau, L. 69 C4
Petlad 43 H8
Peto 85 C7
Petone 65 D6
Petrich 22 D4
Petrikov = Pyetrikaw 17 B9
Petrograd = Sankt-Peterburg 24 B3
Petrolândia 93 D6
Petrolina 93 D5
Petropavl 29 D7
Petropavlovsk = Petropavl 29 D7
Petropavlovsk-Kamchatskiy 31 D13
Petrópolis 93 G5
Petroşani 17 F6
Petrovaradin 22 B2
Petrovsk 24 C6
Petrozavodsk 28 C4
Peureulak 36 D1
Pforzheim 14 D5
Phagwara 42 D9
Phalodi 42 F8
Phan Rang 36 B3
Phangan, Ko 36 C2
Phangnga 36 C1
Phanh Bho Ho Chi Minh 36 B3
Phatthalung 36 C2
Phetchabun 36 A2
Philadelphia 73 E8
Philippines ■ 38 B2
Philippopolis = Plovdiv 22 C5
Phillip I. 63 C4

Phillott . . . . . . . 63 A4
Phitsanulok . . . 36 A2
Phnom Dangrek 36 B2
Phnom Penh . . 36 B2
Phoenix . . . . . . 83 D6
Phra Nakhon Si Ayutthaya . . . 36 B2
Phuket . . . . . . . 36 C1
Phumiphon, Khuan . . . . . . 36 A1
Piacenza . . . . . . 20 B2
Pialba . . . . . . . . 63 A5
Pian Cr. → . . . 63 B4
Pianosa . . . . . . 20 C3
Piatra Neamţ . . 17 E8
Piauí □ . . . . . . . 92 D5
Piave → . . . . . 20 B4
Pibor Post . . . . 53 G5
Pica . . . . . . . . . . 91 H5
Picardie . . . . . . 13 B5
Picardy = Picardie . . . . 13 B5
Pichilemu . . . . . 94 C2
Pico Truncado . 95 F3
Picton, *Australia* 63 B5
Picton, *N.Z.* . . . 65 D6
Pictou . . . . . . . . 69 D4
Picún Leufú . . . 95 D3
Piedmont = Piemonte □ . 20 B1
Piedras, R. de las → . . . . . . 91 F5
Piedras Negras 84 D4
Piemonte □ . . . 20 B1
Piet Retief . . . . 59 D6
Pietermaritzburg 59 D6
Pietersburg . . . 59 C5
Pietrosul, *Romania* . . . . 17 E7
Pietrosul, *Romania* . . . . 17 E7
Pigüé . . . . . . . . 94 D4
Piketberg . . . . . 58 E3
Piła . . . . . . . . . . 16 B3
Pilar, *Brazil* . . . 93 D6
Pilar, *Paraguay* 94 B5
Pilas Group . . . 38 C2
Pilcomayo → . 94 B5
Pilibhit . . . . . . . 42 E11
Pilica → . . . . . 16 C5
Pílos . . . . . . . . . 23 F3
Pilsen = Plzeň . 16 D1
Pimba . . . . . . . . 62 B2
Pimenta Bueno 91 F6
Pimentel . . . . . . 91 E3
Pinang . . . . . . . 36 C2
Pinar del Río . . 86 B3
Pınarhisar . . . . . 22 D6
Pińczów . . . . . . 16 C5
Pindiga . . . . . . . 55 G7
Pindos Óros . . . 23 E3
Pindus Mts. = Pindos Óros . 23 E3
Pine Bluff . . . . . 79 B7
Pine Point . . . . 70 B8
Pinega → . . . . 28 C5
Pinerolo . . . . . . 20 B1
Pinetown . . . . . 59 D6
Ping → . . . . . . 36 A2
Pingdong . . . . . 35 D7
Pingliang . . . . . 35 C5
Pingwu . . . . . . . 35 C5
Pingxiang . . . . . 35 D5
Pinhel . . . . . . . . 18 B2
Pini . . . . . . . . . . 37 D1
Piniós → . . . . . 23 E4
Pinnaroo . . . . . 62 C3
Pínnes, Ákra . . 23 D5
Pinrang . . . . . . 39 E1
Pinsk . . . . . . . . . 17 B8
Pintados . . . . . . 91 H5
Pinyug . . . . . . . 24 A6
Piombino . . . . . 20 C3
Pioner, Os. . . . . 30 B7
Piorini, L. . . . . . 90 D6
Piotrków Trybunalski . 16 C4
Pīp . . . . . . . . . . 45 E5
Piquiri → . . . . 94 A6
Piracicaba . . . . 94 A7
Piracuruca . . . . 92 C5
Piræus = Piraiévs . . . . . 23 F4
Piraiévs . . . . . . 23 F4
Pirané . . . . . . . . 94 B5
Pirapora . . . . . . 93 F5
Pírgos . . . . . . . . 23 F3
Pirin Planina . . 22 D4
Piripiri . . . . . . . 92 C5
Pirmasens . . . . 14 D4
Pirot . . . . . . . . . 22 C4
Piru . . . . . . . . . . 39 E3
Pisa . . . . . . . . . . 20 C3
Pisagua . . . . . . 91 G4
Pisciotta . . . . . . 21 D5
Pisco . . . . . . . . . 91 F3
Písek . . . . . . . . . 16 D2
Pishan . . . . . . . 34 C2
Pising . . . . . . . . 39 F2
Pistóia . . . . . . . 20 C3
Pisuerga → . . 18 B3
Pitarpunga, L. . 62 B3
Pitcairn I. . . . . . 65 M17
Piteå . . . . . . . . . . 8 E12
Piteşti . . . . . . . . 22 B5
Pithapuram . . . 40 J4
Pittsburg . . . . . 79 A6
Pittsburgh . . . . 73 D5
Pittsworth . . . . 63 A5
Piura . . . . . . . . . 90 E2
Placentia . . . . . 69 D5
Placentia B. . . . 69 D5
Plainview . . . . . 78 B3
Pláka, Ákra . . . . 23 G6
Plakhino . . . . . . 28 C9
Plasencia . . . . . 18 B2
Plata, Río de la 94 C5
Platani → . . . . 21 F4
Plato . . . . . . . . . 90 B4
Platte → . . . . . 77 F7
Plauen . . . . . . . 15 C7
Pleiku . . . . . . . . 36 B3
Plenty, B. of . . . 64 B7
Pleven . . . . . . . 22 C5
Plevlja . . . . . . . 22 C2
Płock . . . . . . . . . 16 B4
Plöckenstein . . 15 D7
Ploieşti . . . . . . . 22 B6
Plovdiv . . . . . . . 22 C5
Plumtree . . . . . 59 C5
Plymouth . . . . . 11 F4
Plzeň . . . . . . . . . 16 D1
Po → . . . . . . . . 20 B4
Po Hai = Bo Hai 35 C6
Pobedy Pik . . . . 29 E8
Pocatello . . . . . 81 D7
Poços de Caldas 93 G4
Podgorica . . . . 22 C2
Podilska Vysochyna . . 17 D8
Podkamennaya Tunguska → 30 C7
Podolsk . . . . . . 24 B4
Podor . . . . . . . . 55 E1
Pofadder . . . . . 58 D3
Poh . . . . . . . . . . 39 E2
Pohnpei . . . . . . 64 J10
Poinsett, C. . . . 96 A12
Pointe-à-Pitre . . 87 C7
Pointe Noire . . 56 E2
Poitiers . . . . . . . 12 C4
Poitou . . . . . . . . 12 C3
Pokaran . . . . . . 42 F7
Pokataroo . . . . 63 A4
Pokrovsk = Engels . . . . . . 24 C6
Pola = Pula . . . 20 B4
Polan . . . . . . . . . 45 E5
Poland ■ . . . . . 16 B5
Polatsk . . . . . . . 24 B2
Polcura . . . . . . . 94 D2
Polesye = Pripet Marshes . . . . 17 B9
Poli . . . . . . . . . . 56 C2
Police . . . . . . . . 16 B2
Polillo Is. . . . . . 38 B2
Políyiros . . . . . . 23 D4
Pollachi . . . . . . 43 P10
Polnovat . . . . . . 28 C7
Polonne . . . . . . 17 C8
Polonnoye = Polonne . . . . 17 C8
Poltava . . . . . . . 24 D3
Polunochnoye . 28 C7
Polynesia . . . . . 65 L15
Polynésie française = French Polynesia ■ . 65 M16
Pombal, *Brazil* . 92 D6
Pombal, *Portugal* . . . . 18 C1
Pomézia . . . . . . 20 D4
Pomorski, Pojezierze . . . 16 B3
Ponape = Pohnpei . . . . 64 J10
Ponca City . . . . 78 A5
Ponce . . . . . . . . 87 C6
Pond Inlet . . . . 68 A3
Pondicherry . . . 43 P11
Ponferrada . . . . 10 A2
Ponnani . . . . . . 43 P9
Ponnyadaung . 41 F10
Ponoy → . . . . 28 C5
Ponta Grossa . . 94 B6
Ponta Pora . . . . 94 A5
Pontarlier . . . . . 13 C7
Pontchartrain L. 79 D8
Ponte Nova . . . 93 G5
Pontevedra . . . 18 A1
Pontiac . . . . . . . 72 C4
Pontianak . . . . . 37 E3
Pontine Is. = Ponziane, Ísole . . . . . . . 21 D4
Pontine Mts. = Kuzey Anadolu Dağları . . . . . 46 B3
Pontivy . . . . . . . 12 B2
Pontoise . . . . . . 12 B5
Ponziane, Ísole 21 D4
Poochera . . . . . 62 B1
Poole . . . . . . . . 11 F6
Poona = Pune . 43 K8
Pooncarie . . . . . 62 B3
Poopelloe L. . . 63 B3
Poopó, L. de . . 91 G5
Popayán . . . . . . 90 C3
Popigay . . . . . . 30 B9
Popilta, L. . . . . . 62 B3
Popio L. . . . . . . 62 B3
Poplar Bluff . . . 79 A8
Popocatépetl, Volcán . . . . . 84 D5
Popokabaka . . . 56 F3
Poprád . . . . . . . 16 D5
Porbandar . . . . 43 J6
Porcupine → . 71 B5
Pordenone . . . . 20 B4
Pori . . . . . . . . . . 8 F12
Porkkala . . . . . . 9 G12
Porlamar . . . . . 90 A6
Poroshiri-Dake . 32 F12
Porpoise B. . . . 96 A13
Porretta, Passo di . . . . . . . . . . 20 B3
Port Adelaide . 62 B2
Port Alberni . . . 71 D7
Port Alfred . . . . 59 E5
Port Angeles . . 80 A2
Port Antonio . . 86 C4
Port Arthur, *Australia* . . . . 62 D4
Port Arthur, *U.S.A.* . . . . . . 79 E7
Port-au-Prince . 87 C5
Port Augusta . . 62 B2
Port Augusta West . . . . . . . 62 B2
Port Bergé Vaovao . . . . . 59 H9
Port Bou . . . . . . 19 A7
Port Broughton 62 B2
Port-Cartier . . . 69 C4
Port Chalmers . 65 F4
Port Darwin . . . 95 G5
Port Davey . . . . 62 D4
Port Dickson . . 37 D2
Port Elizabeth . 59 E5
Port Fairy . . . . . 62 C3
Port-Gentil . . . . 56 E1
Port Harcourt . . 55 H6
Port Harrison = Inukjuak . . . . 68 C3
Port Hawkesbury . 69 D4
Port Hedland . . 60 E2
Port Huron . . . . 72 C4
Port Kembla . . 63 B5
Port Kenny . . . . 62 B1
Port Lairge = Waterford . . . 11 E3
Port Laoise . . . 11 E3
Port Lincoln . . . 62 B2
Port Loko . . . . . 55 G2
Port MacDonnell 62 C3
Port Macquarie 63 B5
Port Moresby . . 61 B8
Port Nelson . . . 71 C10
Port Nolloth . . . 58 D3
Port Nouveau-Québec = Kangiqsualujjuaq . . . . . . . . . . . 68 C4
Port of Spain . . 87 D7
Port Pegasus . . 65 G2
Port Phillip B. . 63 C3
Port Pirie . . . . . 62 B2
Port Safaga = Bûr Safâga . . 52 C5
Port Said = Bûr Sa'îd . . . . . . . 52 B5
Port Shepstone 59 E6
Port Stanley = Stanley . . . . . 95 G5
Port Sudan = Bûr Sûdân . . 53 E6
Port Talbot . . . . 11 F5
Port-Vendres . . 13 E5
Port Wakefield . 62 B2
Port Weld . . . . . 36 D2
Porta Orientalis 22 B4

Portachuelo ... 91 G6
Portadown .... 11 D3
Portage La Prairie ...... 71 D10
Portalegre .... 18 C2
Portile de Fier . 22 B4
Portimão ..... 18 D1
Portland, *N.S.W., Australia* .... 63 B4
Portland, *Vic., Australia* .... 62 C3
Portland, *Maine, U.S.A.* ...... 73 C10
Portland, *Oreg., U.S.A.* ...... 80 C2
Portland B. ..... 62 C3
Portland Prom. 68 C3
Porto ........ 18 B1
Pôrto Alegre .. 94 C6
Porto Amboim = Gunza .... 56 G2
Pôrto de Móz .. 92 C3
Porto Empédocle .. 21 F4
Pôrto Esperança 91 G7
Pôrto Franco .. 92 D4
Porto Mendes . 94 A6
Pôrto Murtinho 91 H7
Pôrto Nacional 93 E4
Porto Novo ... 55 G5
Porto Santo ... 54 B1
Pôrto Seguro .. 93 F6
Porto Tórres .. 20 D2
Pôrto Uniâo ... 94 B6
Pôrto Válter ... 91 E4
Porto-Vecchio . 13 F8
Pôrto Velho ... 91 E6
Portoferráio ... 20 C3
Portoscuso .... 21 E2
Portovíejo .... 90 D2
Portree ....... 10 C3
Portsmouth, *U.K.* ........ 11 F6
Portsmouth, *U.S.A.* ...... 73 F7
Porttipahtan tekojärvi .... 8 E13
Portugal ■ .... 18 C1
Porvenir ...... 95 G2
Posadas ...... 94 B5
Poshan = Boshan ..... 35 C6
Poso ......... 39 E2
Posse ........ 93 E4
Possel ........ 56 C3
Possession I. .. 96 B15
Poste Maurice Cortier ..... 54 D5
Postojna ...... 20 B5
Potchefstroom . 59 D5
Potenza ...... 21 D5
Poteriteri, L. ... 65 G2
Potgietersrus .. 59 C5
Poti .......... 25 E5
Potiskum ..... 55 F7
Potomac → .. 73 E7
Potosí ........ 91 G5
Pototan ...... 38 B2
Potrerillos .... 94 B3
Potsdam ...... 15 B7
Poughkeepsie . 73 D9
Pouso Alegre .. 93 E2
Považská Bystrica .... 16 D4
Povenets ..... 28 C4
Poverty B. .... 64 C8
Póvoa de Varzim 18 B1
Powder → ... 76 B2
Powell L. ..... 83 B7
Poyang Hu .... 35 D6
Požarevac .... 22 B3
Poznań ....... 16 B3
Pozo Almonte . 91 H5
Pozoblanco ... 18 C3
Pozzuoli ...... 21 D5
Prachuap Khiri Khan ....... 36 B1
Prado ........ 93 F6
Prague = Praha 16 C2
Praha ........ 16 C2
Prainha, *Amazonas, Brazil* ....... 91 E6
Prainha, *Pará, Brazil* ....... 92 C3
Prairies ....... 71 C9
Prapat ........ 37 D1
Prata ......... 93 F4
Prato ......... 20 C3
Pravia ........ 18 A2
Praya ........ 37 F5
Preparis North Channel .... 41 K9
Preparis South Channel .... 41 K9
Přerov ....... 16 D3
Preservation Inlet ........ 65 G2
Presidencia Roque Saenz Peña ....... 94 B4
Presidente Epitácio .... 93 G3
Presidente Hermes ..... 91 F6
Presidente Prudente .... 93 G3
Prešov ....... 16 D5
Prespa, L. = Prespansko Jezero ...... 23 D3
Prespansko Jezero ...... 23 D3
Presque Isle ... 73 A11
Preston ....... 11 E5
Pretoria ...... 59 D5
Préveza ...... 23 E3
Příbram ...... 16 D2
Prichard ...... 74 D3
Prieska ....... 58 D4
Prievidza ..... 16 D4
Prilep ........ 22 D3
Priluki = Pryluky 24 C3
Prime Seal I. .. 62 D4
Prince Albert .. 71 C9
Prince Albert Mts. ........ 96 B15
Prince Albert Pen. ........ 70 A8
Prince Albert Sd. 70 A8
Prince Charles I. 68 B3
Prince Charles Mts. ........ 96 B10
Prince Edward I. □ ........ 69 D4
Prince of Wales I., *Canada* ... 70 A10
Prince of Wales I., *U.S.A.* ..... 71 C6
Principe da Beira ....... 91 F6
Prins Harald Kyst ........ 96 B8
Prinsesse Astrid Kyst ........ 96 B7
Prinsesse Ragnhild Kyst 96 B8
Pripet → = Prypyat → .. 17 C10
Pripet Marshes 17 B9
Pripyat Marshes = Pripet Marshes .... 17 B9
Pripyats = Prypyat → .. 17 C10
Priština ....... 22 C3
Privas ........ 13 D6
Privolzhskaya Vozvyshennost ........... 24 C6
Prizren ....... 22 C3
Proddatur ..... 43 M11
Progreso ..... 85 C7
Prokopyevsk .. 29 D9
Prokuplje ..... 22 C3
Prome = Pyè .. 41 H10
Propriá ....... 93 E6
Prostějov ..... 16 D3
Proston ...... 63 A5
Provence ..... 13 E6
Providence .... 73 D10
Providencia, I. de ......... 86 D3
Provins ....... 13 B5
Provo ........ 81 E8
Prozna → .... 16 B3
Pruszków ..... 16 B5
Prut → ...... 17 F9
Pruzhany ..... 17 B7
Prydz B. ...... 96 A10
Pryluky ....... 24 C3
Prypyat → ... 17 C10
Przemyśl ..... 17 D6
Przhevalsk .... 29 E8
Psará ........ 23 E5
Pskov ........ 24 B2
Ptich = Ptsich → ... 17 B9
Ptsich → ..... 17 B9
Puán ......... 94 D4
Pucallpa ...... 91 E4
Pudukkottai ... 43 P11
Puebla ....... 84 D5
Pueblo ....... 76 F2
Pueblo Hundido 94 B2
Puelches ..... 94 D3
Puente Alto ... 94 C2
Puente-Genil .. 18 D3
Puerto Aisén .. 95 F2
Puerto Ayacucho ... 90 B5
Puerto Barrios . 85 D7
Puerto Bermejo 94 B5
Puerto Bermúdez ... 91 F4
Puerto Bolívar . 90 D3
Puerto Cabello 90 A5
Puerto Cabezas 86 D3
Puerto Carreño 90 B5
Puerto Chicama 91 E3
Puerto Coig ... 95 G3
Puerto Cortés . 85 D7
Puerto Cumarebo .. 90 A5
Puerto del Rosario ..... 54 C2
Puerto Deseado 95 F3
Puerto Heath .. 91 F5
Puerto La Cruz 90 A6
Puerto Leguízamo .. 90 D4
Puerto Lobos .. 95 E3
Puerto Madryn 95 E3
Puerto Maldonado .. 91 F5
Puerto Montt .. 95 E2
Puerto Morelos 85 C7
Puerto Natales 95 G2
Puerto Páez ... 90 B5
Puerto Pinasco 94 A5
Puerto Pirámides ... 95 E4
Puerto Plata ... 87 C5
Puerto Princesa 38 C1
Puerto Quellón 95 E2
Puerto Rico ■ . 87 C6
Puerto Sastre . 91 H7
Puerto Suárez . 91 G7
Puerto Wilches 90 B4
Puertollano ... 18 C3
Pueyrredón, L. . 95 F2
Pugachev ..... 24 C6
Puget Sound .. 80 B2
Puigcerdá ..... 19 A6
Pukaki L. ..... 65 F4
Pukapuka ..... 65 L14
Pukekohe ..... 64 B6
Pula ......... 20 B4
Puławy ....... 16 C5
Pullman ...... 80 B5
Pulog ........ 38 A2
Pułtusk ...... 16 B5
Puna ......... 91 G5
Puná, I. ....... 90 D2
Punakha ...... 41 D7
Punata ....... 91 G5
Punch ........ 42 C9
Pune ......... 43 K8
Punjab □, *India* 42 D9
Punjab □, *Pakistan* .... 42 D8
Puno ......... 91 G4
Punta Alta .... 94 D4
Punta Arenas .. 95 G2
Punta de Díaz . 94 B2
Puntabie ...... 62 B1
Puntarenas ... 86 E3
Punto Fijo .... 90 A4
Puquio ....... 91 F4
Pur → ....... 28 C8
Purace, Vol. ... 90 C3
Puralia = Puruliya .... 40 F6
Puri .......... 40 H5
Purnia ........ 40 E6
Purukcahu .... 37 E4
Puruliya ...... 40 F6
Purus → ..... 90 D6
Pusan ........ 35 C7
Pushkino ..... 24 C6
Putao ........ 41 D11
Putaruru ...... 64 C6
Puthein Myit → 41 K10
Putignano .... 21 D6
Puting, Tanjung 37 E4
Putorana, Gory 30 C7
Puttalam ..... 43 Q11
Puttgarden .... 15 A6
Putumayo → . 90 D5
Putussibau .... 37 D4
Puy-de-Dôme . 13 D5
Pweto ........ 57 F5
Pwllheli ...... 11 E4
Pyapon ....... 41 J10
Pyasina → ... 30 B6
Pyatigorsk .... 25 E5
Pyè .......... 41 H10
Pyetrikaw ..... 17 B9
Pyinmana ..... 41 H11
P'yŏngyang ... 35 C7
Pyrénées ..... 19 A6
Pyu .......... 41 H11

## Q

Qādib 49 E5
Qā'emshahr 44 B3
Qahremānshahr = Bākhtarān 46 D6
Qaidam Pendi 34 C4
Qalāt 45 C6
Qal'at al Akhḍar 47 E4
Qal'eh Shaharak 42 B4
Qal'eh-ye Now 45 C5
Qamar, Ghubbat al 49 D5
Qamruddin Karez 42 D6
Qandahār 42 D4
Qandahār □ 42 D4
Qapshaghay 29 E8
Qâra 52 C4
Qarabutaq 29 E7
Qarachuk 46 C5
Qaraghandy 29 E8
Qārah 47 E5
Qarataū 29 E8
Qarqan 34 C3
Qarqan He → 34 C3
Qarqaraly 29 E8
Qarshi 29 F7
Qaşr-e Qand 45 E5
Qasr Farâfra 52 C4
Qatar ■ 44 E2
Qattâra, Munkhafed el 52 C4
Qattâra Depression = Qattâra, Munkhafed el 52 C4
Qāyen 44 C4
Qazaqstan = Kazakstan ■ 29 E7
Qazvin 46 C7
Qena 52 C5
Qeshm 44 E4
Qila Safed 42 E2
Qila Saifullāh 42 D6
Qilian Shan 34 C4
Qingdao 35 C7
Qinghai □ 34 C4
Qinghai Hu 34 C5
Qinhuangdao 35 C6
Qinzhou 35 D5
Qiqihar 35 B7
Qitai 34 B3
Qom 44 C2
Qomsheh 44 C2
Qondūz 45 B7
Qondūz □ 45 B7
Qostanay 29 D7
Qu Xian, *Sichuan, China* 35 C5
Qu Xian, *Zhejiang, China* 35 D6
Quambatook 62 C3
Quambone 63 B4
Quan Long 36 C3
Quandialla 63 B4
Quang Ngai 36 A3
Quanzhou 35 D6
Quaqtaq 68 B4
Quaraí 94 C5
Quartu Sant'Elena 21 E2
Quatsino 71 C7
Quba 25 E6
Qūchān 44 B4
Queanbeyan 63 C4
Québec 69 D3
Québec □ 69 D3
Queen Alexandra Ra. 96 C15
Queen Charlotte Is. 70 C6
Queen Charlotte Str. 71 C7
Queen Elizabeth Is. 66 B9
Queen Mary Land 96 B11
Queen Maud G. 70 B9
Queen Maud Land 96 B7
Queen Maud Mts. 96 C16
Queenscliff 63 C3
Queensland □ 61 E7
Queenstown, *Australia* 62 D4
Queenstown, *N.Z.* 65 F3
Queenstown, *S. Africa* 59 E5
Queimadas 93 E6
Quela 56 F3
Quelimane 59 B7
Quelpart = Cheju Do 35 C7
Quequén 94 D5
Querétaro 84 C4
Quetta 42 D5
Quezon City 38 B2
Qui Nhon 36 B3
Quibaxe 56 F2
Quibdo 90 B3
Quiberon 12 C2
Quilán, C. 95 E2
Quilengues 58 A2
Quillabamba 91 F4
Quillagua 91 H5
Quillota 94 C2
Quilon 43 Q10
Quilpie 63 A3
Quimilí 94 B4
Quimper 12 B1
Quimperlé 12 C2
Quincy 77 F9
Quines 94 C3
Quinga 59 H8
Quintanar de la Orden 18 C4
Quintero 94 C2
Quinyambie 62 B3
Quipungo 58 A2
Quirindi 63 B5
Quissanga 59 G8
Quitilipi 94 B4
Quito 90 D3
Quixadá 92 C6
Qŭnghirot 29 E6
Quondong 62 B3
Quorn 62 B2
Qŭqon 29 E8
Qûs 52 C5
Quseir 52 C5
Qyzylorda 29 E7

## R

Raahe 8 F12
Raba 39 F1
Rába → 16 E3
Rabat, *Malta* 21 G5
Rabat, *Morocco* 54 B3
Rabaul 64 K10
Rābigh 47 G4
Race, C. 69 D5
Rach Gia 36 B3
Racibórz 16 C4
Racine 72 C2
Rădăuţi 17 E7
Radekhiv 17 C7
Radekhov = Radekhiv 17 C7
Radhwa, Jabal 47 F4
Radom 16 C5
Radomsko 16 C4
Radomyshl 17 C9
Radstock, C. 62 B1
Rae 70 B8
Rae Bareli 40 D3
Rae Isthmus 68 B2
Raetihi 64 C6
Rafaela 94 C4
Rafai 56 D4
Rafḥā 47 E5
Rafsanjān 44 D4
Ragachow 17 B10
Ragama 43 R11
Raglan 64 B6
Ragusa 21 F5
Raha 39 E2
Rahad al Bardī 53 F3
Rahaeng = Tak 36 A1
Rahimyar Khan 42 E7
Raichur 43 L10
Raigarh 40 G4
Railton 62 D4
Rainier, Mt. 80 B3
Raipur 40 G3
Ra'is 47 G4
Raj Nandgaon 40 G3
Raja, Ujung 37 D1
Raja Ampat, Kepulauan 39 E3
Rajahmundry 40 J3
Rajang → 37 D4
Rajapalaiyam 43 Q10
Rajasthan □ 42 F8
Rajasthan Canal 42 F8
Rajgarh 43 G10
Rajkot 43 H7
Rajpipla 43 J8
Rajshahi 41 E7
Rakaia 65 E5
Rakaia → 65 E5
Rakan, Ra's 44 E2
Rakaposhi 42 A9
Rakata, Pulau 37 F3
Rakhiv 17 D7
Raleigh 75 B8
Ram Hd. 63 C4
Ramanathapuram 43 Q11
Ramechhap 40 D6
Ramelau 39 F3
Ramgarh, *Bihar, India* 40 F5
Ramgarh, *Raj., India* 42 F7
Rāmhormoz 47 E7
Ramnad = Ramanathapuram 43 Q11
Rampur 42 E11
Rampur Hat 40 E6
Ramree I. = Ramree Kyun 41 H9
Ramree Kyun 41 H9
Ramtek 43 J11
Ranaghat 41 F7
Ranau 36 C5
Rancagua 94 C2
Ranchi 40 F5
Randers 9 G10
Rangaunu B. 64 A5
Rangia 41 D8
Rangiora 65 E5
Rangitaiki → 64 B7
Rangitata → 65 E4
Rangon → 41 J11
Rangoon 41 J11
Rangpur 41 E7
Ranibennur 43 M9
Raniganj 40 F6
Raniwara 43 G8
Rankin Inlet 70 B10
Rankins Springs 63 B4
Ranong 36 C1
Ransiki 39 E4
Rantau 37 E5
Rantauprapat 37 D1
Rantemario 39 E1
Rapa 65 M16
Rapallo 20 B2
Rāpch 45 E4
Rapid City 76 C3
Rarotonga 65 M14
Ra's al Khaymah 44 E4
Ra's al-Unuf 52 B2
Ras Bânâs 52 D6
Ras Dashen 57 B7
Râs Timirist 55 E1
Rasa, Punta 95 E4
Rashad 53 F5
Rashîd 52 B5
Rasht 46 C7
Rat Islands 71 C1
Ratangarh 42 E9
Rathenow 15 B7
Ratibor = Racibórz 16 C4
Ratlam 43 H9
Ratnagiri 43 L8
Raukumara Ra. 64 C7
Raurkela 40 F5
Rava-Ruska 17 C6
Rava Russkaya = Rava-Ruska 17 C6
Rāvar 44 D4
Ravenna 20 B4
Ravensburg 14 E5
Ravi → 42 D7
Rawalpindi 42 C8
Rawāndūz 46 C6
Rawene 64 A5
Rawlins 81 E10
Rawson 95 E3
Ray, C. 69 D5
Rayadurg 43 M10
Rayagada 40 H4
Raymond 71 D8
Raz, Pte. du 12 B1
Razdel'naya = Rozdilna 17 E10
Razelm, Lacul 22 B7
Razgrad 22 C6
Ré, I. de 12 C3
Reading, *U.K.* 11 F6
Reading, *U.S.A.* 73 D8
Realicó 94 D4
Rebi 39 F4
Rebiana 52 D3
Rebun-Tō 32 E12
Rechytsa 17 B10
Recife 92 D7
Reconquista 94 B5
Recreo 94 B3
Red →, *La., U.S.A.* 79 D8
Red →, *N. Dak., U.S.A.* 76 A6
Red Cliffs 62 B3

Red Deer 71 C8
Red Sea 48 C2
Red Tower Pass = Turnu Roşu, P. 17 F7
Redcar 11 D6
Redcliffe 63 A5
Redding 80 E2
Redditch 11 E6
Redon 12 C2
Redondela 18 A1
Redwood City 82 B1
Ree, L. 11 E3
Reefton 65 E4
Regensburg 15 D7
Réggio di Calábria 21 E5
Réggio nell'Emília 20 B3
Reghin 17 E7
Regina 71 C9
Rehoboth 58 C3
Rehovot 46 E3
Rei-Bouba 53 G1
Reichenbach 15 C7
Reidsville 75 A8
Reigate 11 F6
Reims 13 B6
Reina Adelaida, Arch. 95 G2
Reindeer L. 71 C9
Reinga, C. 64 A5
Reinosa 18 A3
Reliance 70 B9
Remarkable, Mt. 62 B2
Remeshk 45 E4
Rendsburg 14 A5
Rengat 37 E2
Reni 17 F9
Renk 53 F5
Renmark 62 B3
Rennes 12 B3
Reno 80 F4
Reno → 20 B4
Rentería 19 A5
Republican → 76 F6
Repulse Bay 68 B2
Requena, *Peru* 90 E4
Requena, *Spain* 19 C5
Resadiye = Datça 23 F6
Resht = Rasht 46 C7
Resistencia 94 B5
Reşiţa 17 F5
Resolution I., *Canada* 68 B4
Resolution I., *N.Z.* 65 F2
Réthímnon 23 G5
Réunion ■ 51 J9
Reus 19 B6
Reutlingen 14 D5
Reval = Tallinn 24 B1
Revelstoke 71 C8
Rewa 40 E3
Rewari 42 E10
Rey Malabo 56 D1
Reykjavík 8 B2
Reynosa 84 B5
Rhein → 14 C4
Rhein-Main-Donau-Kanal → 15 D6
Rheine 14 B4
Rheinland-Pfalz □ 14 C4
Rhin = Rhein → 14 C4
Rhine = Rhein → 14 C4
Rhineland-Palatinate □ = Rheinland-Pfalz □ 14 C4
Rhode Island □ 73 D10
Rhodes = Ródhos 23 F7
Rhodope Mts. = Rhodopi Planina 22 D5
Rhodopi Planina 22 D5
Rhön = Hohe Rhön 14 C5
Rhondda 11 F5
Rhône → 13 E6
Rhum 10 C3
Riachão 92 D4
Riasi 42 C9
Riau □ 37 E2
Riau, Kepulauan 37 D2
Riau Arch. = Riau, Kepulauan 37 D2
Ribadeo 18 A2
Ribeirão Prêto 93 G4
Riberalta 91 F5
Rîbniţa 17 E9
Riccarton 65 E5
Richland 80 B4
Richmond, *Australia* 63 B5
Richmond, *N.Z.* 65 D5
Richmond, *Calif., U.S.A.* 80 G2
Richmond, *Va., U.S.A.* 73 F7
Richmond Ra. 63 A5
Ridder 29 D9
Ried 15 D7
Riesa 15 C7
Rieti 20 C4
Rig Rig 53 F1
Rīga 24 B1
Riga, G. of 24 B1
Rīgas Jūras Līcis = Riga, G. of 24 B1
Rīgestān □ 42 D4
Rigolet 68 C5
Riiser-Larsen-halvøya 96 A8
Rijeka 20 B5
Rimah, Wadi ar → 47 F5
Rímini 20 B4
Rîmnicu Sărat 17 F8
Rîmnicu Vîlcea 17 F7
Rimouski 69 D4
Rinca 39 F1
Rinconada 94 A3
Rinjani 37 F5
Rio Branco, *Brazil* 91 E5
Río Branco, *Uruguay* 94 C6
Río Cuarto 94 C4
Rio de Janeiro 93 G5
Rio de Janeiro □ 93 G5
Rio do Sul 94 B7
Río Gallegos 95 G3
Río Grande, *Argentina* 95 G3
Rio Grande, *Brazil* 94 C6
Rio Grande → 78
Rio Grande do Norte □ 92 D6
Rio Grande do Sul □ 94 B6
Rio Largo 93 D6
Río Mulatos 91 G5
Río Muni = Mbini □ 56 D2
Rio Negro 94 B7
Rio Verde 93 F3
Ríobamba 90 D3
Ríohacha 90 A4
Ríosucio, *Caldas, Colombia* 90 B3
Ríosucio, *Choco, Colombia* 90 B3
Rishiri-Tō 32 E12
Riva del Garda 20 B3
Rivadavia 94 B2
Rivera 94 C5
Riversdale 58 E4
Riverside 82 D4
Riverton, *Australia* 62 B2
Riverton, *Canada* 71 C10
Riverton, *N.Z.* 65 G2
Riviera di Levante 20 B2
Riviera di Ponente 20 B2
Rivière-du-Loup 69 D4
Rivne 17 C8
Rívoli 20 B1
Rivoli B. 62 C3
Riyadh = Ar Riyāḑ 47 F6
Rize 46 B5
Rizzuto, C. 21 E6
Roanne 13 C6
Roanoke 73 F6
Robbins I. 62 D4
Robertson 58 E3
Robertson I. 96 A4
Robertsport 55 G2
Robertstown 62 B2
Robinvale 62 B3
Roboré 91 G7
Robson, Mt. 71 C8
Roca, C. da 18 C1
Rocas, I. 92 C7
Rocha 94 C6
Rochefort 12 D3
Rochester, *Minn., U.S.A.* 77 C8
Rochester, *N.Y., U.S.A.* 73 C7
Rock Hill 75 B7
Rock Island 77 E9
Rock Springs 81 E9
Rockefeller Plateau 96 C18
Rockford 77 D10
Rockhampton 61 E9
Rocky Mount 75 B9
Rocky Mts. 70 C7
Rod 42 E3
Rodez 13 D5
Ródhos 23 F7
Rodney, C. 64 B6
Roes Welcome Sd. 68 B2
Rogachev = Ragachow 17 B10
Rogagua, L. 91 F5
Rogatyn 17 D7
Rogoaguado, L. 91 F5
Rohri 42 F6
Rohtak 42 E10
Roi Et 36 A2
Rojas 94 C4
Rojo, C. 84 C5
Rokan → 37 D2
Rolândia 94 A6
Roma, *Australia* 63 A4
Roma, *Italy* 20 D4
Roman 17 E8
Romang 39 F3
Romania ■ 22 B5
Romanovka = Basarabeasca 17 E9
Romans-sur-Isère 13 D6
Romblon 38 B2
Rome = Roma 20 D4
Rome 74 B5
Romorantin-Lanthenay 12 C4
Roncador, Serra do 93 E3
Ronda 18 D3
Rondônia □ 91 F6
Rondonópolis 93 F3
Ronge, L. la 71 C9
Ronne Ice Shelf 96 B3
Roodepoort 59 D5
Roorkee 42 E10
Roosevelt → 91 E6
Roosevelt I. 96 B16
Roquetas de Mar 19 D4
Roraima □ 90 C6
Roraima, Mt. 90 B6
Rosa 57 F6
Rosa, Monte 13 D7
Rosario, *Argentina* 94 C4
Rosário, *Brazil* 92 C5
Rosario, *Mexico* 84 C3
Rosario, *Paraguay* 94 A5
Rosario de la Frontera 94 B3
Rosário do Sul 94 C6
Rosas, G. de 19 A7
Roscommon 11 E2
Roseau, *Domin.* 87 C7
Roseau, *U.S.A.* 77 A7
Rosebery 62 D4
Roseburg 80 D2
Rosenheim 15 E7
Rosetown 71 C9
Rosetta = Rashîd 52 B5
Roseville 80 F3
Rosewood 63 A5
Rosignano Maríttimo 20 C3
Rosignol 90 B7
Roşiori-de-Vede 22 B5
Roslavl 24 C3
Roslyn 63 B4
Ross, *Australia* 62 D4
Ross, *N.Z.* 65 E4
Ross I. 96 B15
Ross Ice Shelf 96 C16
Ross Sea 96 B15
Rossano Cálabro 21 E6
Rossland 71 D8
Rosslare 11 E3
Rosso 55 E1
Rossosh 24 C4
Rosthern 71 C9
Rostock 15 A7
Rostov, *Don, Russia* 25 D4
Rostov, *Yarosl., Russia* 24 B4
Roswell 78 C1
Rotherham 11 E6
Roto 63 B4

Rotondo Mte. 13 E8
Rotorua 64 C7
Rotorua, L. 64 C7
Rotterdam 14 C3
Rottweil 14 D5
Rotuma 64 L12
Roubaix 13 A5
Rouen 12 B4
Round Mt. 63 B5
Roussillon 13 E5
Rouyn 69 D3
Rovaniemi 8 E13
Rovereto 20 B3
Rovigo 20 B3
Rovinj 20 B4
Rovno = Rivne 17 C8
Rovuma → 57 G8
Rowena 63 A4
Roxas 38 B2
Roxburgh 65 F3
Royal Leamington Spa 11 E6
Royan 12 D3
Rozdilna 17 E10
Rozhyshche 17 C7
Rtishchevo 24 C5
Ruahine Ra. 64 C7
Ruapehu 64 C6
Ruapuke I. 65 G3
Rub' al Khali 48 D4
Rubio 90 B4
Rubtsovsk 29 D9
Rudall 62 B2
Rudolf, Ostrov 28 A6
Rufa'a 53 F5
Rufiji → 57 F7
Rufino 94 C4
Rufisque 55 F1
Rugby 11 E6
Rügen 15 A7
Ruhr → 14 C4
Rukwa L. 57 F6
Rum = Rhum 10 C3
Rumāḩ 47 F6
Rumania = Romania ■ 22 B5
Rumbêk 53 G4
Rumia 16 A4
Rumoi 32 F12
Runanga 65 E4
Runaway, C. 64 B7
Rungwa 57 F6
Ruoqiang 34 C3
Rupa 41 D9
Rupat 37 D2
Rupert → 69 C3
Rupert House = Waskaganish 69 C3
Rurrenabaque 91 F5
Rusape 59 B6
Ruschuk = Ruse 22 C5
Ruse 22 C5
Rushworth 63 C4
Russas 92 C6
Russellkonda 40 H5
Russkaya Polyana 29 D8
Rustavi 25 E6
Rustenburg 59 D5
Ruteng 39 F2
Rutshuru 57 E5
Ruwenzori 57 D5
Ružomberok 16 D4
Rwanda ■ 57 E6
Ryazan 24 C4
Ryazhsk 24 C5
Rybache = Rybachye 29 E9
Rybachye 29 E9
Rybinsk 24 B4
Rybinskoye Vdkhr. 24 B4
Rybnitsa = Rîbniţa 17 E9
Rylstone 63 B4
Rypin 16 B4
Ryūkyū Is. = Ryūkyū-rettō 35 D7
Ryūkyū-rettō 35 D7
Rzeszów 16 C5
Rzhev 24 B3

## S

Sa Dec 36 B3
Sa'ādatābād 44 D3
Saale → 15 C6
Saalfeld 15 C6
Saar → 13 B7
Saarbrücken 14 D4
Saaremaa 24 B1
Šabac 22 B2
Sabadell 19 B7
Sabah □ 36 C5
Şabāḩ, Wadi → 47 G7
Sabalān, Kūhhā-ye 46 C6
Sábanalarga 90 A4
Sabang 36 C1
Sabará 93 F5
Saberania 39 E5
Sabhah 52 C1
Sabinas 84 B4
Sabinas Hidalgo 84 B4
Sablayan 38 B2
Sable, C., *Canada* 69 D4
Sable, C., *U.S.A.* 86 A3
Sable I. 69 D5
Sabrina Coast 96 A12
Sabulubek 37 E1
Sabzevār 44 B4
Sabzvārān 44 D4
Săcele 17 F7
Sachsen □ 15 C7
Sachsen-Anhalt □ 15 C7
Sacramento 80 F3
Sacramento → 80 F3
Sacramento Mts. 83 D10
Sadani 57 F7
Sadd el Aali 52 D5
Sado 33 G11
Sadon 41 E11
Safi 54 B3
Safīd Kūh 42 B3
Saga, *Indonesia* 39 E4
Saga, *Japan* 32 C2
Sagala 55 F3
Sagar 43 M9
Sagil 34 A4
Saginaw 72 C4
Şagīr, Zāb aş → 46 D5
Saglouc = Salluit 68 B3
Sagua la Grande 86 B3
Saguenay → 69 D3
Sagunto 19 C5
Sahagún 18 A3
Sahand, Kuh-e 46 C6
Sahara 54 D6
Saharan Atlas = Saharien, Atlas 54 B5
Saharanpur 42 E10
Saharien, Atlas 54 B5
Sahiwal 42 D8
Sa'id Bundas 53 G3
Saïda 54 B5
Sa'īdābād 44 D3
Sa'īdīyeh 46 C7
Saidpur 41 E7
Saidu 42 B8
Saigon = Phanh Bho Ho Chi Minh 36 B3
Saijō 32 C3
Saikhoa Ghat 41 D10
Saiki 32 C2
Sailolof 39 E4
St. Andrews 10 C5
St. Arnaud 62 C3
St-Augustin-Saguenay 69 C5
St. Augustine 75 E7
St. Austell 11 F4
St. Boniface 71 D10
St.-Brieuc 12 B2
St. Catharines 69 D3
St.-Chamond 13 D6
St. Christopher-Nevis ■ = St. Kitts & Nevis 87 C7
St. Cloud 77 C7
St. Croix 87 C7
St.-Denis 12 B5
St.-Dizier 13 B6
St. Elias, Mt. 70 B5
St.-Étienne 13 D6
St.-Flour 13 D6
St. Francis, C. 58 E4
St. Gallen = Sankt Gallen 13 C8
St.-Gaudens 12 E4
St. George 63 A4
St.-Georges, *Fr. Guiana* 92 B3
St. George's, *Grenada* 87 D7
St. George's Channel 11 F3
St. Georges Hd. 63 C5
St. Gotthard P. = San Gottardo, P. del 13 C8
St. Helena ■ 51 H3
St. Helena B. 58 E3
St. Helens 62 D4
St. Helier 11 G5
St-Hyacinthe 69 D3
St. John 69 D4
St. John's, *Antigua* 87 C7
St. John's, *Canada* 69 D5
St. Johns → 75 D7
St. Joseph 77 F7
St. Joseph, L. 69 C1
St. Kilda, *N.Z.* 65 F4
St. Kilda, *U.K.* 10 C2
St. Kitts & Nevis 87 C7
St.-Laurent 92 A3
St. Lawrence → 69 D4
St. Lawrence, Gulf of 69 D4
St. Lawrence I. 71 B2
St. Leonard 69 D4
St.-Lô 12 B3
St-Louis 55 E1
St. Louis 77 F9
St. Lucia ■ 87 D7
St. Lucia, L. 59 D6
St. Maarten 87 C7
St.-Malo 12 B2
St-Marc 87 C5
St. Mary Pk. 62 B2
St. Marys 62 D4
St.-Mathieu, Pte. 12 B1
St. Matthews, I. = Zadetkyi Kyun 36 C1
St.-Nazaire 12 C2
St.-Omer 12 A5
St. Paul 77 C8
St. Peter Port 11 G5
St. Petersburg = Sankt-Peterburg 24 B3
St. Petersburg 75 F6
St.-Pierre et Miquelon □ 69 D5
St.-Quentin 13 B5
St. Thomas I. 87 C7
St.-Tropez 13 E7
St. Vincent, G. 62 C2
St. Vincent & the Grenadines ■ 87 D7
Saintes 12 D3
Saintonge 12 D3
Saipan 64 H9
Sairang 41 F9
Sairecábur, Cerro 94 A3
Sajama 91 G5
Sajó 16 D5
Sakai 32 B4
Sakākah 47 E5
Sakakawea, L. 76 B4
Sakarya = Adapazarı 46 B2
Sakarya → 25 F3
Sakata 33 G11
Sakhalin 31 D12
Sakon Nakhon 36 A2
Sala 9 G11
Sala Consilina 21 D5
Saladillo 94 D5
Salado →, *Buenos Aires, Argentina* 94 D5
Salado →, *La Pampa, Argentina* 94 D3
Salado →, *Santa Fe, Argentina* 94 C4
Salaga 55 G4
Salālah 49 D5
Salamanca, *Chile* 94 C2
Salamanca, *Spain* 18 B3
Salamís 23 F4
Salar de Atacama 94 A3
Salar de Uyuni 91 H5
Salaverry 91 E3
Salawati 39 E4
Salayar 39 F2
Saldanha 58 E3
Sale, *Australia* 63 C4
Salé, *Morocco* 54 B3
Salekhard 28 C7
Salem, *India* 43 P11
Salem, *U.S.A.* 80 C2
Salerno 21 D5
Salgótarján 16 D4
Salihli 23 E7
Salihorsk 17 B8
Salima 59 A6

Salina, *Italy* . . . 21 E5
Salina, *U.S.A.* . 76 F6
Salina Cruz . . . 85 D5
Salinas, *Brazil* . 93 F5
Salinas, *Ecuador* 90 D2
Salinas, *U.S.A.* 82 B2
Salinas Grandes 94 C3
Salinópolis . . . . 92 C4
Salisbury, *Australia* . . . . 62 B2
Salisbury, *U.K.* 11 F6
Salisbury, *U.S.A.* 75 B7
Salliq . . . . . . . . 68 B2
Salluit . . . . . . . . 68 B3
Salmās . . . . . . . 46 C6
Salmon → . . . 80 C5
Salmon River Mts. . . . . . . . . 81 C6
Salon-de-Provence . . . 13 E6
Salonica = Thessaloníki . 23 D4
Salonta . . . . . . . 16 E5
Salsk . . . . . . . . . 25 D5
Salso → . . . . . 21 F4
Salt Creek . . . . 62 C2
Salt Lake City . 81 E8
Salta . . . . . . . . . 94 A3
Saltillo . . . . . . . 84 B4
Salto . . . . . . . . . 94 C5
Salto → . . . . . 20 C4
Salton Sea . . . . 82 D5
Saltpond . . . . . 55 G4
Salûm . . . . . . . . 52 B4
Salûm, Khâlig el 52 B4
Salur . . . . . . . . . 40 H4
Salvador . . . . . 93 E6
Salwa . . . . . . . . 44 E2
Salween → . . . 41 J11
Salyan . . . . . . . 25 F6
Salzach → . . . 15 D7
Salzburg . . . . . . 15 E7
Salzgitter . . . . . 14 B6
Salzwedel . . . . 15 B6
Sama . . . . . . . . 28 C7
Sama de Langreo . . . . 18 A3
Samales Group 38 C2
Samangán □ . . 45 B7
Samar . . . . . . . 38 B3
Samara . . . . . . 24 C7
Samarinda . . . . 37 E5
Samarkand = Samarqand . 29 F7
Samarqand . . . 29 F7
Sāmarrā . . . . . . 46 D5
Sambalpur . . . . 40 G5
Sambar, Tanjung . . . . 37 E4
Sambas . . . . . . 37 D3
Sambava . . . . . 59 G10
Sambhal . . . . . 42 E11
Sambhar . . . . . 42 F9
Sambiase . . . . . 21 E6
Sambir . . . . . . . 17 D6
Same . . . . . . . . 57 E7
Samokov . . . . . 22 C4
Sámos . . . . . . . 23 F6
Samothráki, *Évros, Greece* 23 D5
Samothráki, *Kérkira, Greece* . . . . . 23 E2
Sampacho . . . . 94 C4
Sampit . . . . . . . 37 E4
Sampit, Teluk . 37 E4
Samra . . . . . . . 47 F5
Samsun . . . . . . 46 B4
Samui, Ko . . . . 36 C2
Samut Prakan . 36 B2
Samut Songkhram → . . . . . . . . . . . 36 B2
San . . . . . . . . . . 55 F4
San → . . . . . . . 16 C5
San Agustin, C. 38 C3
San Andrés, I. de . . . . . . . . . 86 D3
San Andrés Tuxtla . . . . . . 85 D5
San Angelo . . . 78 D3
San Antonio, *Chile* . . . . . . . 94 C2
San Antonio, *Spain* . . . . . . 19 C6
San Antonio, *U.S.A.* . . . . . . 78 E4
San Antonio, C., *Argentina* . . . 94 D5
San Antonio, C., *Cuba* . . . . . . . 85 C8
San Antonio Oeste . . . . . . 95 E4
San Benedetto del Tronto . . 20 C4
San Bernardino 82 C4
San Bernardino Str. . . . . . . . . 38 B2
San Bernardo . 94 C2
San Bernardo, I. de . . . . . . . . . 90 B3
San Borja . . . . . 91 F5
San Carlos, *Argentina* . . . 94 C3
San Carlos, *Chile* . . . . . . . 94 D2
San Carlos, *Phil.* 38 B2
San Carlos, *Amazonas, Venezuela* . . . 90 C5
San Carlos, *Cojedes, Venezuela* . . . 90 B5
San Carlos de Bariloche . . . 95 E2
San Carlos del Zulia . . . . . . . 90 B4
San Cristóbal, *Argentina* . . . 94 C4
San Cristóbal, *Mexico* . . . . . 85 D6
San Cristóbal, *Venezuela* . . . 90 B4
San Diego . . . . 82 D4
San Diego, C. . 95 G3
San Felipe, *Chile* 94 C2
San Felipe, *Venezuela* . . . 90 A5
San Felíu de Guíxols . . . . . 19 B7
San Fernando, *Chile* . . . . . . . 94 C2
San Fernando, *La Union, Phil.* 38 A2
San Fernando, *Pampanga, Phil.* . . . . . . . . 38 A2
San Fernando, *Spain* . . . . . . 18 D2
San Fernando, *Trin. & Tob.* . 87 D7
San Fernando, *U.S.A.* . . . . . . 82 C3
San Fernando de Apure . . . 90 B5
San Fernando de Atabapo . 90 C5
San Francisco, *Argentina* . . . 94 C4
San Francisco, *U.S.A.* . . . . . . 82 B1
San Francisco de Macorîs . . 87 C5
San Francisco del Monte de Oro . . . . . . . . 94 C3
San Gil . . . . . . . 90 B4
San Gottardo, P. del . . . . . . . . . 13 C8
San Ignacio, *Bolivia* . . . . . 91 G6
San Ignacio, *Paraguay* . . . 94 B5
San Ildefonso, C. . . . . . . . . . . 38 A2
San Javier, *Argentina* . . . 94 C5
San Javier, *Bolivia* . . . . . 91 G6
San Joaquin → 82 A2
San Jorge, B. de 84 A2
San Jorge, G. . 95 F3
San Jorge, G. de 19 B6
San José, *Bolivia* . . . . . 91 G6
San José, *Costa Rica* . . 86 E3
San José, *Guatemala* . . 85 E6
San Jose, *Phil.* 38 A2
San Jose, *U.S.A.* 82 B2
San Jose de Buenovista . . 38 B2
San José de Jáchal . . . . . . 94 C3
San José de Mayo . . . . . . 94 C5
San José de Ocune . . . . . . 90 C4
San José del Guaviare . . . . 90 C4
San Juan, *Argentina* . . . 94 C3
San Juan, *Phil.* 38 C3
San Juan, *Puerto Rico* . 87 C6
San Juan → . . 86 D3
San Juan, C. . . 56 D1
San Juan de los Morros . . . . . 90 B5
San Juan Mts. . 83 B9
San Julián . . . . 95 F3
San Justo . . . . 94 C4
San Leandro . . 82 B1
San Lorenzo . . 90 C3
San Lorenzo, I. 91 F3
San Lorenzo, Mt. . . . . . . . . 95 F2
San Lucas . . . . 91 H5
San Lucas, C. . 84 C2
San Luis . . . . . . 94 C3
San Luis Obispo 82 C2
San Luis Potosí 84 C4
San Marino . . . 20 C4
San Marino ■ . 20 C4
San Martín, L. . 95 F2
San Matías . . . 91 G7
San Matías, G. 95 E4
San Miguel . . . 85 E7
San Miguel → 91 F6
San Miguel de Tucumán . . . 94 B3
San Narciso . . . 38 A2
San Nicolás de los Arroyas . 94 C4
San-Pédro . . . . 55 H3
San Pedro de las Colonias . 84 B4
San Pedro de Lloc . . . . . . . . 91 E3
San Pedro de Macorís . . . . 87 C6
San Pedro del Paraná . . . . . 94 B5
San Pedro Sula 85 D7
San Pieto . . . . . 21 E2
San Rafael, *Argentina* . . . 94 C3
San Rafael, *U.S.A.* . . . . . . 80 G2
San Ramón de la Nueva Orán 94 A4
San Remo . . . . 20 C1
San Roque, *Argentina* . . . 94 B5
San Roque, *Spain* . . . . . . 18 D3
San Rosendo . . 94 D2
San Salvador, *Bahamas* . . . 86 B5
San Salvador, *El Salv.* . . . . . 85 E7
San Salvador de Jujuy . . . . . . . 94 A4
San Sebastián, *Argentina* . . . 95 G3
San Sebastián, *Spain* . . . . . . 19 A5
San Severo . . . 20 D5
San Valentin, Mte. . . . . . . . 95 F2
San Vicente de la Barquera . 18 A3
Sana' . . . . . . . . 49 D3
Sana → . . . . . . 20 B6
Sanaga → . . . 56 D1
Sanana . . . . . . . 39 E3
Sanandaj . . . . . 46 D6
Sanco Pt. . . . . . 38 C3
Sancti-Spíritus . 86 B4
Sancy, Puy de . 13 D5
Sandakan . . . . . 36 C5
Sandanski . . . . 22 D4
Sanday . . . . . . . 10 B5
Sandgate . . . . . 63 A5
Sandía . . . . . . . 91 F5
Sandıklı . . . . . . 46 C2
Sandoa . . . . . . . 56 F4
Sandomierz . . . 16 C5
Sandoway . . . . 41 H10
Sandusky . . . . . 72 D4
Sandwip Chan. 41 F8
Sandy C. . . . . . 62 D3
Sandy L. . . . . . . 71 C10
Sanford, *Fla., U.S.A.* . . . . . . 75 E7
Sanford, *N.C., U.S.A.* . . . . . . 75 B8
Sanford, Mt. . . 71 B5
Sanga → . . . . 56 E3
Sangamner . . . 43 K9
Sangar . . . . . . . 31 C10
Sangasangadalam . . . . . . . . . . . 37 E5
Sangeang . . . . 39 F1
Sangerhausen . 15 C6
Sanggau . . . . . 37 D4
Sangihe, P. . . . 39 D3
Sangkapura . . . 37 F4
Sangli . . . . . . . . 43 L9
Sangmélina . . . 56 D2
Sangre de Cristo Mts. . . . . . . . 78 A1
Sanirajak . . . . . 68 B2
Sankt Gallen . . 13 C8
Sankt Moritz . . 13 C8
Sankt-Peterburg 24 B3

Sankt Pölten 15 D8
Sankuru → 56 E4
Sanliurfa 46 C4
Sanlúcar de Barrameda 18 D2
Sannicandro Gargánico 20 D5
Sanok 17 D6
Sanshui 35 D6
Santa Ana, *Bolivia* 91 F5
Santa Ana, *Ecuador* 90 D2
Santa Ana, *El Salv.* 85 E7
Santa Ana, *U.S.A.* 82 D4
Santa Barbara 82 C3
Santa Catalina I. 82 D3
Santa Catarina □ 94 B7
Santa Clara 86 B4
Santa Clotilde 90 D4
Santa Coloma de Gramanet 19 B7
Santa Cruz, *Argentina* 95 G3
Santa Cruz, *Bolivia* 91 G6
Santa Cruz, *Phil.* 38 B2
Santa Cruz, *U.S.A.* 82 B1
Santa Cruz → 95 G3
Santa Cruz de Tenerife 54 C1
Santa Cruz do Sul 94 B6
Santa Cruz I. 64 L11
Santa Elena 90 D2
Santa Eugenia, Pta. 84 B1
Santa Fe, *Argentina* 94 C4
Santa Fe, *U.S.A.* 83 C10
Santa Filomena 93 D4
Santa Inés, I. 95 G2
Santa Isabel = Rey Malabo 56 D1
Santa Isabel, *Argentina* 94 D3
Santa Isabel, *Brazil* 93 E3
Santa Lucia Range 82 C2
Santa Maria, *Brazil* 94 B6
Santa Maria, *U.S.A.* 82 C2
Santa Maria → 84 A3
Santa Maria da Vitória 93 E5
Santa Maria di Leuca, C. 23 E2
Santa Marta 90 A4
Santa Marta, Sierra Nevada de 90 A4
Santa Maura = Levkás 23 E3
Santa Rosa, *La Pampa, Argentina* 94 D4
Santa Rosa, *San Luis, Argentina* 94 C3
Santa Rosa, *Bolivia* 91 F5
Santa Rosa, *Brazil* 94 B6
Santa Rosa, *U.S.A.* 80 F2
Santa Rosa de Copán 85 E7
Santa Vitória do Palmar 94 C6
Santai 35 C5
Santana, Coxilha de 94 C5
Santana do Livramento 94 C5
Santander 18 A4
Sant'Antíoco 21 E2
Santarém, *Brazil* 92 C3
Santarém, *Portugal* 18 C1
Santiago, *Brazil* 94 B6
Santiago, *Chile* 94 C2
Santiago → 90 D3
Santiago de Compostela 18 A1
Santiago de Cuba 86 C4
Santiago de los Cabelleros 87 C5
Santiago del Estero 94 B4
Santo Amaro 93 E6
Santo Ângelo 94 B6
Santo Antonio 93 F2
Santo Corazón 91 G7
Santo Domingo 87 C6
Santo Tomás 91 F4
Santo Tomé 94 B5
Santo Tomé de Guayana = Ciudad Guayana 90 B6
Santoña 18 A4
Santoríni = Thíra 23 F5
Santos 94 A7
Santos Dumont 94 A8
Sanza Pombo 56 F3
São Anastácio 94 A6
São Bernado de Campo 93 G4
São Borja 94 B5
São Carlos 94 A7
São Cristóvão 93 E6
São Domingos 93 E4
São Francisco 93 F5
São Francisco → 93 E6
São Francisco do Sul 94 B7
São Gabriel 94 C6
São João da Madeira 18 B1
São João del Rei 93 G5
São João do Araguaia 92 D4
São João do Piauí 92 D5
São José do Rio Prêto 94 A7
São Leopoldo 94 B6
São Lourenço 93 G4
São Lourenço → 93 F2
São Luís 92 C5
São Marcos → 93 F4
São Marcos, B. de 92 C5
São Mateus 93 F8
São Paulo 94 A7
São Paulo □ 94 A7
São Roque, C. de 92 D6
São Sebastião, I. de 94 A7
São Tomé & Principe ■ 51 F4
São Vicente, C. de 18 D1
Saône → 13 D6
Saonek 39 E4
Saparua 39 E3
Sapele 55 G6
Saposoa 91 E3
Sapporo 32 F12
Sapulpa 79 B5
Saqqez 46 C6
Sar-e Pol 45 B6
Sar-e Pol □ 45 B6
Sar Planina 22 C3
Sarāb 46 C6
Sarada → 40 D3
Saragossa = Zaragoza 19 B5
Saraguro 90 D3
Sarajevo 20 C7
Saran, G. 37 E4
Sarandí del Yi 94 C5
Sarangani B. 38 C3
Sarangani Is. 38 C3
Sarangarh 40 G4
Saransk 24 C6
Sarapul 29 D6
Sarasota 75 F6
Saratov 24 C6
Saravane 36 A3
Sarawak □ 37 D4
Saray 22 D6
Sarayköy 23 F7
Sarbāz 45 E5
Sarbīsheh 45 C4
Sarda → = Sarada → 40 D3
Sardalas 54 C7
Sardarshahr 42 E9
Sardegna □ 21 D2
Sardinia = Sardegna □ 21 D2
Sardis 23 E7
Sargodha 42 C8
Sarh 53 G2
Sārī 44 B3
Sarıgöl 23 E7
Sarikamiş 46 B5
Sarikei 37 D4
Sark 11 G5
Şarköy 23 D6
Sarlat-la-Canéda 12 D4
Sarmi 39 E5
Sarmiento 95 F3
Sarnia 69 D2
Sarny 24 C2
Sarolangun 37 E2
Saronikós Kólpos 23 F4
Sarre = Saar → 13 B7
Sarreguemines 13 B7
Sarro 55 F3
Sarthe → 12 C3
Sartynya 28 C7
Sarvestān 44 D3
Sary-Tash 29 F8
Saryshagan 29 E8
Sasabeneh 49 F3
Sasaram 40 E5
Sasebo 32 C1
Saser 42 B10
Saskatchewan □ 71 C9
Saskatchewan → 71 C9
Saskatoon 71 C9
Saskylakh 30 B9
Sasovo 24 C5
Sassandra 55 H3
Sassandra → 55 H3
Sássari 21 D2
Sassnitz 15 A7
Sassuolo 20 B3
Sasyk, Ozero 17 F9
Sata-Misaki 33 D2
Satadougou 55 F2
Satara 43 L8
Satmala Hills 43 J9
Satna 40 E3
Sátoraljaújhely 16 D5
Satpura Ra. 43 J10
Satu Mare 17 E6
Satui 37 E5
Saturnina → 91 F7
Saudi Arabia ■ 47 F6
Sauerland 14 C4
Sault Ste. Marie, *Canada* 69 D2
Sault Ste. Marie, *U.S.A.* 72 A3
Saumlaki 39 F4
Saumur 12 C3
Saunders C. 65 F4
Sauri 55 F6
Saurimo 56 F4
Sava → 22 B3
Savage I. = Niue 65 L14
Savalou 55 G5
Savanna la Mar 86 C4
Savannah 75 C7
Savannah → 75 C7
Savannakhet 36 A2
Savanur 43 M9
Savé 55 G5
Save → 59 C6
Sāveh 46 D7
Savelugu 55 G4
Savoie □ 13 D7
Savona 20 B2
Sawahlunto 37 E2
Sawai 39 E3
Sawai Madhopur 42 F10
Sawara 32 B7
Sawatch Mts. 83 A9
Sawmills 59 B5
Sawu 39 F2
Sawu Sea 39 F2
Saxony, Lower = Niedersachsen □ 14 B5
Say 55 F5
Sayán 91 F3
Sayan, Zapadnyy 30 D7
Saydā 46 D3
Sayghān 45 C6
Sayhut 49 D5
Saynshand 35 B6
Sazanit 23 D2
Sázava → 16 D2
Sazin 42 B8
Scandicci 20 C3
Scandinavia 8 F10
Scarborough 11 D6
Scebeli, Wabi → 49 G3
Schaffhausen 13 C8
Schefferville 69 C4
Schelde → 14 C3
Schenectady 73 C9
Schiermonnikoog 14 B4
Schio 20 B3

Schleswig 14 A5
Schleswig-Holstein □ 14 A5
Schouten I. 62 D4
Schouten Is. = Supiori 39 E5
Schwäbische Alb 14 D5
Schwaner, Pegunungan 37 E4
Schwarzwald 14 D5
Schwedt 15 B8
Schweinfurt 14 C6
Schwenningen = Villingen-Schwenningen 14 D5
Schwerin 15 B6
Schwyz 13 C8
Sciacca 21 F4
Scilla 21 E5
Scilly, Isles of 11 G3
Scone 63 B5
Scotland □ 10 C4
Scott Glacier 96 A12
Scott Inlet 68 A3
Scottsbluff 76 E3
Scottsdale 62 D4
Scranton 73 D8
Scunthorpe 11 E6
Scusciuban 49 E5
Scutari = Üsküdar 25 E2
Seaspray 63 C4
Seattle 80 B2
Sebastopol = Sevastopol 25 E3
Sebha = Sabhah 52 C1
Şebinkarahisar 46 B4
Sebta = Ceuta 18 E3
Sebuku 37 E5
Sebuku, Teluk 37 D5
Secretary I. 65 F2
Secunderabad 43 L11
Sedalia 77 F8
Sedan, *Australia* 62 B2
Sedan, *France* 13 B6
Seddon 65 D6
Seddonville 65 D5
Sedhiou 55 F1
Sedova, Pik 28 B6
Seeheim 58 D3
Seferihisar 23 E6
Segamat 37 D2
Segesta 21 F4
Seget 39 E4
Ségou 55 F3
Segovia = Coco → 86 D3
Segovia 18 B3
Segre → 19 B6
Séguéla 55 G3
Segura → 19 C5
Sehitwa 58 C4
Sehore 43 H10
Seine → 12 B4
Seistan 45 D5
Seistan, Daryācheh-ye 45 D5
Sekayu 37 E2
Sekondi-Takoradi 55 H4
Selaru 39 F4
Selçuk 23 F6
Sele → 21 D5
Selenga = Selenge Mörön → 35 A5
Selenge Mörön → 35 A5
Seletan, Tg. 37 E4
Sélibabi 55 E2
Selîma, El Wâhât el 52 D4
Selkirk 71 C10
Selkirk Mts. 71 C8
Selma 75 B8
Selpele 39 E4
Selu 39 F4
Selva 94 B4
Selvas 91 E5
Semani → 23 D2
Semarang 37 F4
Semey 29 D9
Semiozernoye 29 D7
Semipalatinsk = Semey 29 D9
Semirara Is. 38 B2
Semisopochnoi I. 71 C1
Semitau 37 D4
Semiyarka 29 D8
Semiyarskoye = Semiyarka 29 D8
Semmering P. 15 E8
Semnān 44 C3
Semnān □ 44 C3
Semporna 38 D1
Semuda 37 E4
Sena Madureira 91 E5
Senador Pompeu 92 D6
Senaja 36 C5
Senanga 58 B4
Sendai, *Kagoshima, Japan* 32 D2
Sendai, *Miyagi, Japan* 33 G12
Senegal ■ 55 F2
Senegal → 55 E1
Senge Khambab = Indus → 43 G5
Sengkang 39 E2
Senhor-do-Bonfim 93 E5
Senigállia 20 C4
Senj 20 B5
Senja 8 E11
Senlis 13 B5
Senmonorom 36 B3
Sennâr 53 F5
Senneterre 69 D3
Sens 13 B5
Senta 22 B3
Sentani 39 E6
Seo de Urgel 19 A6
Seoul = Sŏul 35 C7
Sepīdān 44 D3
Sept-Îles 69 C4
Sequoia National Park 82 B3
Seram 39 E3
Seram Laut, Kepulauan 39 E4
Seram Sea 39 E3
Serasan 37 D3
Serbia □ 22 C3
Serdobsk 24 C5
Seremban 37 D2
Serenje 59 A6
Sereth = Siret → 17 F9
Sergino 28 C7
Sergipe □ 93 E6
Sergiyev Posad 24 B4
Seria 36 D4
Serian 37 D4
Seribu, Kepulauan 37 F3
Sérifos 23 F5
Sermata 39 F3
Serny Zavod 29 F6
Serov 28 D7
Serowe 59 C5
Serpukhov 24 C4
Sérrai 22 D4
Serrezuela 94 C3
Serrinha 93 E6
Sertânia 92 D6
Serua 39 F4
Serui 39 E5
Serule 59 C5
Sesepe 39 E3
Sesfontein 58 B2
Sesheke 58 B4
Sète 13 E5
Sete Lagôas 93 F5
Sétif 54 A6
Seto 32 B5
Settat 54 B3
Setté-Cama 56 E1
Setúbal 18 C1
Setúbal, B. de 18 C1
Seulimeum 36 C1
Sevan, Ozero = Sevana Lich 25 E6
Sevana Lich 25 E6
Sevastopol 25 E3
Severn →, *Canada* 69 C2
Severn →, *U.K.* 11 F5
Severnaya Zemlya 30 B7
Severnyye Uvaly 24 B6
Severo-Yeniseyskiy 30 C7
Severodvinsk 28 C4
Sevilla 18 D2
Seville = Sevilla 18 D2
Sevlievo 22 C5
Seward 71 B5
Seward Pen. 71 B3
Sewer 39 F4
Seychelles ■ 26 K9
Seymour 63 C4
Sfax 52 B1
Sfîntu Gheorghe 17 F7
Shaanxi □ 35 C5
Shaba □ 57 F4
Shabunda 57 E5
Shache 34 C2
Shackleton Ice Shelf 96 A11
Shackleton Inlet 96 C15
Shadrinsk 29 D7
Shāhābād 44 B4
Shahdād 44 D4
Shahdād, Namakzār-e 44 D4
Shahdadkot 42 F5
Shahgarh 42 F6
Shaḥḥāt 52 B3
Shahjahanpur 42 F11
Shahr Kord 44 C2
Shahrig 42 D5
Shaikhabad 42 B6
Shajapur 43 H10
Shakhty 25 D5
Shakhunya 24 B6
Shaki 55 G5
Shala, L. 53 G6
Shalqar 29 E6
Sham, J. ash 44 F4
Shamīl 44 E4
Shammar, Jabal 47 F5
Shamo = Gobi 35 B6
Shamo, L. 53 G6
Shamva 59 B6
Shan □ 41 G12
Shandong □ 35 C6
Shanghai 35 C7
Shangqiu 35 C6
Shangrao 35 D6
Shangshui 35 C6
Shannon 64 D6
Shannon → 11 E2
Shansi = Shanxi □ 35 C6
Shantou 35 D6
Shantung = Shandong □ 35 C6
Shanxi □ 35 C6
Shaoguan 35 D6
Shaowu 35 D6
Shaoxing 35 C7
Shaoyang 35 D6
Shaqra', *Si. Arabia* 47 F6
Shaqrā', *Yemen* 49 E4
Sharjah = Ash Shāriqah 44 E3
Sharon 72 D5
Sharya 24 B6
Shashi, *Botswana* 59 C5
Shashi, *China* 35 C6
Shasta, Mt. 80 E2
Shatt al'Arab → 47 E7
Shaunavon 71 D9
Shawan 34 B3
Shawinigan 69 D3
Shcherbakov = Rybinsk 24 B4
Shchuchinsk 29 D8
Shebele = Scebeli, Wabi → 49 G3
Sheboygan 72 C2
Sheffield 11 E6
Shekhupura 42 D8
Shelburne 69 D4
Shelby 75 B7
Shelbyville 74 B4
Shellharbour 63 B5
Shenandoah → 73 E7
Shendam 55 G6
Shendî 53 E5
Shensi = Shaanxi □ 35 C5
Shenyang 35 B7
Sheopur Kalan 42 G10
Shepetivka 17 C8
Shepetovka = Shepetivka 17 C8
Shepparton 63 C4
Sherbro I. 55 G2
Sherbrooke 69 D3
Sheridan 81 C10
Sherman 79 C5
Sherridon 71 C9
Shetland Is. 10 A6
Shibām 49 D4
Shigaib 53 E3
Shihchiachuangi = Shijiazhuang 35 C6
Shijiazhuang 35 C6
Shikarpur 42 F6
Shikoku 32 C3
Shikoku □ 33 H10
Shikoku-Sanchi 32 C3
Shilabo 49 F3
Shiliguri 40 D7
Shillong 41 E8
Shilong 35 D6
Shimada 32 B6
Shimizu 32 B6

Shimoga ..... 43 N9
Shimonoseki .. 32 C2
Shinano → ... 32 A6
Shīndand ..... 42 C3
Shingū ....... 32 C4
Shinyanga .... 57 E6
Shipehenski Prokhod .... 22 C5
Shipki La ..... 42 D11
Shīr Kūh ...... 44 D3
Shirane-San ... 32 A6
Shīrāz ........ 44 D3
Shire → ..... 59 B7
Shiretoko-Misaki 32 F13
Shiriya-Zaki ... 32 F12
Shīrvān ...... 44 B4
Shirwa, L. = Chilwa, L. ... 59 B7
Shivpuri ...... 43 G10
Shizuoka ..... 32 B6
Shklov = Shklow ..... 17 A10
Shklow ....... 17 A10
Shkoder = Shkodra .... 22 C2
Shkodra ...... 22 C2
Shkumbini → . 23 D2
Shmidta, O. ... 30 A7
Sholapur = Solapur ..... 43 L9
Shoshone Mts. 80 F5
Shoshong .... 59 C5
Shreveport .... 79 C7
Shrewsbury ... 11 E5
Shrirampur ... 40 F7
Shu .......... 29 E8
Shuangyashan 35 B8
Shule ........ 34 C2
Shumagin Is. .. 71 C4
Shungnak .... 71 B4
Shūr → ...... 44 D3
Shurugwi ..... 59 B5
Shūsf ........ 45 D5
Shūshtar ..... 47 D7
Shwebo ...... 41 F10
Shwegu ...... 41 E11
Shweli → .... 41 F11
Shymkent .... 29 E7
Shyok ........ 42 B11
Shyok → ..... 42 B9
Si Kiang = Xi Jiang → ... 35 D6
Si-ngan = Xi'an 35 C5
Si Racha ...... 36 B2
Siah ......... 47 G6
Siahan Range . 42 F4
Siaksrilndrapura 37 D2
Sialkot ....... 42 C9
Siantan, P. .... 37 D3
Sīāreh ........ 45 D5
Siargao ...... 38 C3
Siasi ......... 38 C2
Siau ......... 39 D3
Šiauliai ....... 24 B1
Šibenik ....... 20 C5
Siberut ....... 37 E1
Sibi .......... 42 E5
Sibil ......... 39 E6
Sibiti ........ 56 E2
Sibiu ......... 17 F7
Sibolga ....... 37 D1
Sibsagar ...... 41 D10
Sibu ......... 37 D4
Sibuco ....... 38 C2
Sibuguey B. ... 38 C2
Sibut ......... 56 C3
Sibutu ....... 38 D1
Sibutu Passage 38 D1
Sibuyan ...... 38 B2
Sibuyan Sea .. 38 B2
Sichuan □ .... 34 C5
Sicilia ....... 21 F5
Sicily = Sicilia . 21 F5
Sicuani ....... 91 F4
Siddipet ...... 43 K11
Sidéradougou . 55 F4
Sîdi Barrâni ... 52 B4
Sidi-bel-Abbès . 54 A4
Sidley, Mt. .... 96 B18
Sidon = Saydā 46 D3
Sidra, G. of = Surt, Khalīj .. 52 B2
Siedlce ....... 17 B6
Sieg → ...... 14 C4
Siegen ....... 14 C5
Siem Reap .... 36 B2
Siena ........ 20 C3
Sieradz ....... 16 C4
Sierra Colorada 95 E3
Sierra Gorda .. 94 A3
Sierra Leone ■ 55 G2
Sífnos ........ 23 F5
Sighetu-Marmatiei ... 17 E6
Sighişoara .... 17 E7
Sigli ......... 36 C1
Sigsig ........ 90 D3
Sigüenza ..... 19 B4
Siguiri ....... 55 F3
Sihanoukville = Kompong Som ....... 36 B2
Siirt .......... 46 C5
Sikar ......... 42 F9
Sikasso ....... 55 F3
Sikhote Alin, Khrebet ..... 31 E11
Sikhote Alin Ra. = Sikhote Alin, Khrebet 31 E11
Síkinos ....... 23 F5
Sikkim □ ..... 40 D7
Sil → ........ 18 A2
Silchar ....... 41 E9
Silesia = Śląsk 16 C3
Silgarhi Doti .. 40 C3
Silghat ....... 41 D9
Silifke ....... 46 C3
Siliguri = Shiliguri .... 40 D7
Siling Co ..... 34 C3
Silistra ....... 22 B6
Silivri ........ 22 D7
Sillajhuay, Cordillera ... 91 G5
Silva Porto = Kuito ....... 58 A3
Simanggang .. 37 D4
Simav ........ 23 E7
Simbirsk ..... 24 C6
Simeria ...... 17 F6
Simeulue ..... 37 D1
Simferopol .... 25 E3
Sími ......... 23 F6
Simikot ....... 40 C3
Simla ........ 42 D10
Simplon P. .... 13 C8
Simpson Desert 60 F6
Simunjan ..... 37 D4
Sinabang ..... 37 D1
Sinadogo ..... 49 F4
Sinai = Es Sînâ' 52 C5
Sinai, Mt. = Mûsa, G. .... 47 E3
Sinaloa de Levya ...... 84 B3
Sīnāwan ...... 54 B7
Sincelejo ..... 90 B3
Sincorá, Serra do ......... 93 E5
Sind □ ....... 42 F6
Sind Sagar Doab ....... 42 D7
Sindangan .... 38 C2
Sines ........ 18 D1
Sines, C. de ... 18 D1
Singa ........ 53 F5
Singapore ■ .. 37 D2
Singaraja ..... 37 F5
Singida ....... 57 E6
Singitikós Kólpos ..... 23 D5
Singkaling Hkamti ..... 41 E10
Singkawang ... 37 D3
Singleton ..... 63 B5
Singora = Songkhla ... 36 C2
Sinjai ........ 39 F2
Sinjār ........ 46 C5
Sinkat ........ 53 E6
Sinkiang Uighur = Xinjiang Uygur Zizhiqu □ ... 34 B3
Sinni → ..... 21 D6
Sinnuris ...... 52 C5
Sinop ........ 46 B3
Sintang ...... 37 D4
Sintra ....... 18 C1
Sinŭiju ....... 35 B7
Siocon ....... 38 C2
Siófok ........ 16 E4
Sioma ........ 58 B4
Sion ......... 13 C7
Sioux City .... 77 D6
Sioux Falls .... 76 D6
Sioux Lookout . 71 C10
Siping ........ 35 B7
Sipura ....... 37 E1
Siquijor ...... 38 C2
Siracusa ...... 21 F5
Sirajganj ..... 41 E7
Sirdaryo = Syrdarya → 29 E7
Siret → ...... 17 F9
Sirohi ........ 43 G8
Sironj ........ 43 G10
Síros ......... 23 F5
Sirsa ......... 42 E9
Sisak ........ 20 B6
Sisaket ....... 36 A2
Sisophon ..... 36 B2
Sīstan va Balūchestān □ 45 E5
Sitapur ....... 40 D3
Sitges ........ 19 B6
Sitía ......... 23 G6
Sitka ......... 71 C6
Sittang Myit → 41 J11
Sittwe ........ 41 G9
Siuri ......... 40 F6
Sīvand ....... 44 D3
Sivas ........ 46 C4
Siverek ....... 46 C4
Sivrihisar ..... 46 C2
Sîwa ......... 52 C4
Siwalik Range . 40 D4
Siwan ........ 40 D5
Sjælland ...... 9 G10
Sjumen = Šumen ..... 22 C6
Skadarsko Jezero ...... 22 C2
Skagerrak ..... 9 G9
Skagway ..... 71 C6
Skala-Podilska . 17 D8
Skala Podolskaya = Skala-Podilska 17 D8
Skalat ........ 17 D7
Skardu ....... 42 B9
Skarzysko-Kamienna ... 16 C5
Skeena → .... 70 C6
Skegness ..... 11 E7
Skeldon ...... 90 B7
Skellefte älv → 8 F12
Skellefteå ..... 8 F12
Skíathos ...... 23 E4
Skien ........ 9 G9
Skierniewice .. 16 C5
Skikda ....... 54 A6
Skipton ....... 62 C3
Skíros ........ 23 E5
Skole ........ 17 D6
Skópelos ..... 23 E4
Skopje ....... 22 C3
Skvyra ....... 17 D9
Skye ......... 10 C3
Skyros = Skíros 23 E5
Slamet ....... 37 F3
Śląsk ......... 16 C3
Slatina ....... 22 B5
Slave → ..... 70 B8
Slavgorod .... 29 D8
Slavonski Brod 20 B7
Slavuta ....... 17 C8
Slavyansk = Slovyansk ... 25 D4
Slawharad .... 17 B10
Sleaford B. .... 62 B2
Sleeper Is. .... 68 C2
Sligeach = Sligo 11 D2
Sligo ......... 11 D2
Sliven ........ 22 C6
Slobodskoy ... 24 B7
Slobozia ...... 22 B6
Slonim ....... 17 B7
Slough ....... 11 F6
Slovak Rep. ■ . 16 D5
Slovakia = Slovak Rep. ■ 16 D5
Slovakian Ore Mts. = Slovenské Rudohorie .. 16 D4
Slovenia ■ .... 20 B5
Slovenija = Slovenia ■ .. 20 B5
Slovenská Republika = Slovak Rep. ■ 16 D5
Slovenské Rudohorie .. 16 D4
Slovyansk .... 25 D4
Sluch → ..... 17 C8
Słupsk ...... 16 A3
Slutsk ....... 17 B8
Smara ....... 54 B3
Smarhon ..... 17 A8
Smederevo ... 22 B3
Smith Arm .... 70 B7
Smithton ..... 62 D4
Smithtown .... 63 B5
Smoky Bay ... 62 B1
Smolensk .... 24 C3
Smolikas, Óros 23 D3
Smolyan ..... 22 D5
Smorgon = Smarhon ... 17 A8
Smyrna = İzmir 23 E6
Snake → ..... 80 B4
Snake I. ...... 63 C4
Snake River Plain ....... 81 D7

Sneek . . . . . . . . 14 B3
Sněžka . . . . . . . 16 C2
Snøhetta . . . . . 8 F9
Snowdon . . . . . 11 E4
Snowdrift . . . . . 70 B8
Snowtown . . . . 62 B2
Snowy → . . . . 63 C4
Snowy Mts. . . . 63 C4
Snyatyn . . . . . . 17 D7
Snyder . . . . . . . 78 C3
Soalala . . . . . . . 59 H9
Sobat, Nahr → 53 G5
Sobral . . . . . . . 92 C5
Soc Trang . . . . 36 C3
Soch'e = Shache . . . . . 34 C2
Sochi . . . . . . . . 25 E4
Société, Is. de la 65 L15
Society Is. = Société, Is. de la . . . . . . . . . . 65 L15
Socompa, Portezuelo de 94 A3
Socorro . . . . . . 90 B4
Socotra . . . . . . 49 E5
Soda Plains . . . 42 B11
Söderhamn . . . 8 F11
Sodiri . . . . . . . . 53 F4
Sodo . . . . . . . . . 53 G6
Sofia = Sofiya . 22 C4
Sofia → . . . . . 59 H9
Sofiya . . . . . . . . 22 C4
Sogamoso . . . . 90 B4
Sognefjorden . 8 F9
Sohâg . . . . . . . . 52 C5
Soissons . . . . . 13 B5
Sokal . . . . . . . . 17 C7
Söke . . . . . . . . . 23 F6
Sokhumi . . . . . 25 E5
Sokodé . . . . . . . 55 G5
Sokol . . . . . . . . 24 B5
Sokółka . . . . . . 17 B6
Sokolo . . . . . . . 55 F3
Sokołów Podlaski . . . . 17 B6
Sokoto . . . . . . . 55 F6
Solano . . . . . . . 38 A2
Solapur . . . . . . 43 L9
Soledad . . . . . . 90 B6
Soligalich . . . . . 24 B5
Soligorsk = Salihorsk . . . 17 B8
Solikamsk . . . . 28 D6
Solimões = Amazonas → 92 C3
Solingen . . . . . 14 C4
Sóller . . . . . . . . 19 C7
Sologne . . . . . . 12 C4
Solok . . . . . . . . 37 E2
Solomon Is. ■ . 64 K10
Solomon Sea . 61 B9
Solon . . . . . . . . 35 B7
Solor . . . . . . . . 39 F2
Solothurn . . . . . 13 C7
Šolta . . . . . . . . . 20 C6
Solţānābād . . . 44 B4
Solunska Glava 22 D3
Solwezi . . . . . . 59 A5
Soma . . . . . . . . 23 E6
Somali Rep. ■ . 49 F4
Somalia = Somali Rep. ■ 49 F4
Sombor . . . . . . 22 B2
Sombrerete . . . 84 C4
Sombrero . . . . 87 C7
Somerset East . 59 E5
Somerset I. . . . 70 A10
Someş → . . . . 17 E6
Sommariva . . . 63 A4
Somme → . . . 12 A4
Somosierra, Puerto de . . . 18 B4
Somport, Puerto de . . . . . . . . . 12 E3
Søndre Strømfjord . . 68 B5
Sóndrio . . . . . . 20 A2
Sonepur . . . . . . 40 G4
Song Cau . . . . . 36 B3
Songea . . . . . . . 57 G7
Songhua Jiang → . . . 35 B8
Songkhla . . . . . 36 C2
Songpan . . . . . 34 C5
Sonipat . . . . . . 42 E10
Sonmiani . . . . . 42 G5
Sono → . . . . . 93 D4
Sonora → . . . . 84 B2
Sonsonate . . . . 85 E7
Soochow = Suzhou . . . . . 35 C7
Sopi . . . . . . . . . 39 D3
Sopot . . . . . . . . 16 A4
Sopron . . . . . . . 16 E3
Sør-Rondane . . 96 B8
Sorata . . . . . . . 91 G5
Sorel . . . . . . . . . 69 D3
Sorgono . . . . . . 21 D2
Soria . . . . . . . . . 19 B4
Sorkh, Kuh-e . . 44 C4
Soroca . . . . . . . 17 D9
Sorocaba . . . . . 94 A7
Soroki = Soroca 17 D9
Sorong . . . . . . . 39 E4
Soroti . . . . . . . . 57 D6
Sørøya . . . . . . . 8 D12
Sorrento . . . . . . 63 C3
Sorsogon . . . . . 38 B2
Sosnowiec . . . . 16 C4
Souanké . . . . . . 56 D2
Soúdhas, Kólpos 23 G5
Sŏul . . . . . . . . . 35 C7
Sound, The = Øresund . . . . 9 G10
Sources, Mt. aux 59 D5
Soure . . . . . . . . 92 C4
Souris . . . . . . . . 71 D9
Souris → . . . . 71 D10
Sousa . . . . . . . . 92 D6
Sousel . . . . . . . 92 C3
Sousse . . . . . . . 52 A1
South Africa ■ 58 E4
South Australia □ . . 62 B2
South Bend . . . 72 D2
South Carolina □ . . 75 C7
South China Sea 36 C4
South Dakota □ 76 C4
South East C. . 62 D4
South Horr . . . . 57 D7
South I. . . . . . . 65 E3
South Invercargill . . 65 G3
South Korea ■ 35 C7
South Magnetic Pole . . . . . . . . 96 A13
South Nahanni → . 70 B7
South Natuna Is. = Natuna Selatan, Kepulauan . . 37 D3
South Orkney Is. 96 A4
South Pagai, I. = Pagai Selatan, P. . . 37 E2
South Platte → 76 E4
South Pole . . . . 96 C
South Ronaldsay . . 10 B5
South Saskatchewan → . . . . . . . . . . . 71 C9
South Shetland Is. . . . . . . . . 96 A4
South Shields . 11 D6
South Taranaki Bight . . . . . . . 64 C6
South Uist . . . . 10 C3
South West C. . 62 D4
Southampton . 11 F6
Southampton I. 68 B2
Southbridge . . 65 E5
Southend-on-Sea . . . . . . . . 11 F7
Southern Alps . 65 E4
Southern Indian L. . . . . . . . . . 71 C10
Southern Ocean 96 A9
Southern Uplands . . . . 10 D5
Southport . . . . 63 A5
Southwest C. . . 65 G2
Soutpansberg . 59 C5
Sovetsk, *Kaliningd., Russia* . . . . . . 24 B1
Sovetsk, *Kirov, Russia* . . . . . . 24 B6
Sōya-Misaki . . . 32 E12
Soyo . . . . . . . . . 56 F2
Sozh → . . . . . . 17 C10
Spain ■ . . . . . . 18 C4
Spalding . . . . . 62 B2
Spanish Town . 86 C4
Sparta = Spárti 23 F4
Spartanburg . . 75 B7
Spárti . . . . . . . . 23 F4
Spartivento, C., *Calabria, Italy* 21 F6
Spartivento, C., *Sard., Italy* . . 21 E2
Spátha, Ákra . . 23 G4
Spence Bay . . . 70 B10
Spencer, C. . . . 62 C2
Spencer G. . . . . 62 B2
Spenser Mts. . . 65 E5
Spey → . . . . . . 10 C5
Speyer . . . . . . . 14 D5
Split . . . . . . . . . 20 C6
Spokane . . . . . . 80 B5
Spoleto . . . . . . . 20 C4
Sporyy Navolok, Mys . . . . . . . . 28 B7
Spratly I. . . . . . 36 C4
Spree → . . . . . 15 B7
Springbok . . . . 58 D3
Springfield, *N.Z.* 65 E4
Springfield, *Ill., U.S.A.* . . . . . . 77 F10
Springfield, *Mass., U.S.A.* 73 C9
Springfield, *Mo., U.S.A.* . . . . . . 79 A7
Springfield, *Ohio, U.S.A.* . 72 E4
Springfield, *Oreg., U.S.A.* 80 C2
Springfontein . 59 E5
Springhill . . . . . 69 D4
Springhurst . . . 63 C4
Springs . . . . . . 59 D5
Squamish . . . . 71 D7
Srbija = Serbia □ . . . . 22 C3
Sre Umbell . . . 36 B2
Srebrnica . . . . . 20 B7
Sredinny Ra. = Sredinnyy Khrebet . . . . . 31 D14
Sredinnyy Khrebet . . . . . 31 D14
Srednevilyuysk 31 C10
Śrem . . . . . . . . 16 B3
Sremska Mitrovica . . . 22 B2
Sri Lanka ■ . . . 43 R12
Srikakulam . . . . 40 H4
Srinagar . . . . . . 42 B9
Stade . . . . . . . . 14 B5
Stadlandet . . . . 8 F9
Stafford . . . . . . 11 E5
Stakhanov . . . . 25 D4
Stalingrad = Volgograd . . 25 D5
Staliniri = Tskhinvali . . . 25 E5
Stalino = Donetsk . . . . 25 D4
Stalinogorsk = Novomoskovsk . . . . . . . . . . . 24 C4
Stalowa Wola . 17 C6
Stamford . . . . . 73 D9
Stanislav = Ivano-Frankivsk . . . 17 D7
Stanke Dimitrov 22 C4
Stanley, *Australia* . . . . 62 D4
Stanley, *Canada* 71 C9
Stanley, *Falk. Is.* 95 G5
Stanovoy Khrebet . . . . . 31 D10
Stanovoy Ra. = Stanovoy Khrebet . . . . . 31 D10
Stanthorpe . . . . 63 A5
Stara Planina . . 22 C4
Stara Zagora . . 22 C5
Starachowice . . 16 C5
Staraya Russa . 24 B3
Starbuck I. . . . . 65 K15
Stargard Szczeciński . . 16 B2
Staritsa . . . . . . . 24 B3
Starogard Gdański . . . . 16 B4
Starokonstantinov = Starokonstyantyniv . . . . . . . . . . . 17 D8
Starokonstyantyniv . . . . . . . . . . . 17 D8
Staryy Chartoriysk . . 17 C7
Staryy Oskol . . 24 C4
State College . . 73 D7
Staten, I. = Estados, I. de Los . . . . . . . . 95 G4
Statesville . . . . 75 B7
Stavanger . . . . 9 G9
Staveley . . . . . . 65 E4
Stavropol . . . . . 25 D5
Stawell . . . . . . . 62 C3
Steenkool = Bintuni . . . . . 39 E4
Stefanie L. = Chew Bahir . 53 H6
Stefansson Bay 96 A9
Steiermark □ . . 15 E8
Steinkjer . . . . . . 8 F10
Stellenbosch . . 58 E3
Stendal . . . . . . . 15 B6

Steornabhaigh = Stornoway 10 B3
Stepanakert = Xankändi 25 F6
Stephens Creek 62 B3
Stepnoi = Elista 25 D5
Stepnyak 29 D8
Sterlitamak 29 D6
Stettin = Szczecin 16 B2
Stettiner Haff 15 B8
Stettler 71 C8
Steubenville 72 D5
Stevenage 11 F6
Stewart 70 B6
Stewart, I. 95 G2
Stewart I. 65 G2
Steyr 15 D8
Stillwater, *N.Z.* 65 E4
Stillwater, *U.S.A.* 78 A5
Štip 22 D4
Stirling 10 C5
Stockerau 15 D9
Stockholm 9 G11
Stockport 11 E5
Stockton 82 B2
Stockton-on-Tees 11 D6
Stoke on Trent 11 E5
Stokes Pt. 62 D3
Stolac 20 C6
Stolbovoy, Ostrov 30 B11
Stolbtsy = Stowbtsy 17 B8
Stolin 17 C8
Stonehaven 10 C5
Stonewall 71 C10
Stony Tunguska = Podkamennaya Tunguska → 30 C7
Stora Lulevatten 8 E11
Storavan 8 E11
Store Bælt 9 G10
Store Creek 63 B4
Storm B. 62 D4
Stormberge 59 E5
Stornoway 10 B3
Storozhinets = Storozhynets 17 D7
Storozhynets 17 D7
Storsjön 8 F10
Storuman 8 E11
Stowbtsy 17 B8
Strahan 62 D4
Stralsund 15 A7
Strand 58 E3
Stranraer 11 D4
Strasbourg 13 B7
Stratford, *Canada* 69 D2
Stratford, *N.Z.* 64 C6
Strathalbyn 62 C2
Straubing 15 D7
Streaky B. 62 B1
Streaky Bay 62 B1
Strelka 30 D7
Strezhevoy 29 C8
Strimón → 23 D4
Strimonikós Kólpos 23 D5
Strómboli 21 E5
Stronsay 10 B5
Stroud Road 63 B5
Strumica 22 D4
Stryy 17 D6
Strzelecki Cr. → 62 A2
Stuart Ra. 62 A1
Stung Treng 36 B3
Stutterheim 59 E5
Stuttgart 14 D5
Styria = Steiermark □ 15 E8
Suakin 53 E6
Subansiri → 41 D9
Subi 37 D3
Subotica 16 E4
Suceava 17 E8
Suchou = Suzhou 35 C7
Süchow = Xuzhou 35 C6
Sucre 91 G5
Sudair 47 F6
Sudan ■ 53 E4
Sudbury 69 D2
Sûdd 53 G4
Sudeten Mts. = Sudety 16 C3
Sudety 16 C3
Sudirman, Pegunungan 39 E5
Sueca 19 C5
Suez = El Suweis 52 C5
Suez, G. of = Suweis, Khalîg el 52 C5
Sugluk = Salluit 68 B3
Suhār 44 E4
Suhbaatar 35 A5
Suhl 14 C6
Suihua 35 B7
Sukadana, *Kalimantan, Indonesia* 37 E3
Sukadana, *Sumatera, Indonesia* 37 F3
Sukaraja 37 E4
Sukarnapura = Jayapura 39 E6
Sukhona → 28 C5
Sukhumi = Sokhumi 25 E5
Sukkur 42 F6
Sukkur Barrage 42 F6
Sula, Kepulauan 39 E3
Sulaiman Range 42 D6
Sulawesi □ 39 E2
Sulawesi Sea = Celebes Sea 39 D2
Sulima 55 G2
Sulina 17 F9
Sulitjelma 8 E11
Sullana 90 D2
Sultanpur 40 D4
Sulu Arch. 38 C2
Sulu Sea 38 C2
Suluq 52 B3
Sulzberger Ice Shelf 96 B17
Sumalata 39 D2
Sumatera □ 37 D2
Sumatra = Sumatera □ 37 D2
Sumba 39 F1
Sumba, Selat 39 F1
Sumbawa 37 F5
Sumbawa Besar 37 F5
Sumbe 56 G2
Šumen 22 C6
Sumgait = Sumqayıt 25 E6
Summerside 69 D4
Sumperk 16 D3
Sumqayıt 25 E6
Sumter 75 C7
Sumy 24 C3
Sunbury 63 C3
Sunda, Selat 37 F3
Sunda Str. = Sunda, Selat 37 F3
Sundarbans, The 41 G7
Sundargarh 40 F5
Sunderland 11 D6
Sundsvall 8 F11
Sungaigerong 37 E2
Sungailiat 37 E3
Sungaipakning 37 D2
Sungaipenuh 37 E2
Sungaitiram 37 E5
Sungari = Songhua Jiang → 35 B8
Sungguminasa 39 F1
Sunghua Chiang = Songhua Jiang → 35 B8
Sungurlu 46 B3
Sunnyvale 82 B1
Suntar 30 C9
Supaul 40 D6
Superior 77 B8
Superior, L. 69 D2
Suphan Dağı 46 C5
Supiori 39 E5
Sur, *Lebanon* 46 D3
Sūr, *Oman* 45 F4
Sura → 24 B6
Surabaja = Surabaya 37 F4
Surabaya 37 F4
Surakarta 37 F4
Surat, *Australia* 63 A4
Surat, *India* 43 J8
Surat Thani 36 C1
Suratgarh 42 E8
Surgut 29 C8
Suriapet 43 L11
Surigao 38 C3
Surinam ■ 92 B2
Suriname ■ = Surinam ■ 92 B2
Suriname → 92 A2
Surt 52 B2
Surt, Khalīj 52 B2
Suruga-Wan 32 B6
Sūsangerd 47 E7
Susanville 80 E3
Susquehanna → 73 E7
Susques 94 A3
Susunu 39 E4
Susurluk 23 E7
Sutherland Falls 65 F2
Sutlej → 42 E7
Suva 64 L12
Suva Planina 22 C4
Suvorov Is. = Suwarrow Is. 65 L14
Suwałki 17 A6
Suwarrow Is. 65 L14
Suweis, Khalîg el 52 C5
Suzdal 24 B5
Suzhou 35 C7
Suzu-Misaki 32 A5
Svealand □ 9 G10
Sverdlovsk = Yekaterinburg 29 D7
Svetlogorsk = Svyetlahorsk 17 B9
Svetozarevo 22 B3
Svishtov 22 C5
Svislach 17 B7
Svyetlahorsk 17 B9
Swabian Alps = Schwäbische Alb 14 D5
Swakopmund 58 C2
Swan Hill 62 C3
Swansea, *Australia* 63 B5
Swansea, *U.K.* 11 F5
Swatow = Shantou 35 D6
Swaziland ■ 59 D6
Sweden ■ 9 G10
Sweetwater 78 C3
Swellendam 58 E4
Świdnica 16 C3
Świdnik 17 C6
Świebodzin 16 B2
Świecie 16 B4
Swift Current 71 C9
Swindon 11 F6
Swinemünde = Świnoujście 16 B2
Świnoujście 16 B2
Switzerland ■ 13 C8
Sydney, *Australia* 63 B5
Sydney, *Canada* 69 D4
Sydra, G. of = Surt, Khalīj 52 B2
Syktyvkar 28 C6
Sylhet 41 E8
Sylt 14 A5
Syrin 29 C9
Syracuse 73 C7
Syrdarya → 29 E7
Syria ■ 46 D4
Syrian Desert = Ash Shām, Bādiyat 47 D4
Syzran 24 C6
Szczecin 16 B2
Szczecinek 16 B3
Szczytno 16 B5
Szechwan = Sichuan □ 34 C5
Szeged 16 E5
Székesfehérvár 16 E4
Szekszárd 16 E4
Szentes 16 E5
Szolnok 16 E5
Szombathely 16 E3

## T

Tabacal 94 A4
Tabaco 38 B2
Ţābah 47 F5
Tabarka 54 A6
Ţabas, *Khorāsān, Iran* 44 C4
Ţabas, *Khorāsān, Iran* 45 C5
Tabatinga, Serra da 93 E5
Tablas 38 B2
Table B. = Tafelbaai 58 E3
Table Mt. 58 E3
Tábor 16 D2
Tabora 57 F6
Tabou 55 H3
Tabrīz 46 C6
Tabūk 47 E4

Tacheng 34 B3
Tacloban 38 B2
Tacna 91 G4
Tacoma 80 B2
Tacuarembó 94 C5
Tademaït, Plateau du 54 C5
Tadjoura 49 E3
Tadmor 65 D5
Tadoussac 69 D4
Tadzhikistan = Tajikistan ■ 29 F8
Taegu 35 C7
Taejŏn 35 C7
Tafalla 19 A5
Tafelbaai 58 E3
Tafermaar 39 F4
Taft 38 B3
Taga Dzong 41 D7
Taganrog 25 D4
Tagbilaran 38 C2
Tagish 70 B6
Tagish L. 70 B6
Tagliamento → 20 B4
Taguatinga 93 E5
Tagum 38 C3
Tagus = Tejo → 18 C1
Tahakopa 65 G3
Tahan, Gunong 36 D2
Tahat 54 D6
Tāherī 44 E3
Tahiti 65 L16
Tahoe, L. 80 F3
Tahoua 55 F6
Tahta 52 C5
Tahulandang 39 D3
Tahuna 39 D3
Taï 55 G3
Tai Hu 35 C7
Taibei 35 D7
T'aichung = Taizhong 35 D7
Taidong 35 D7
Taieri → 65 G4
Taihape 64 C6
Tailem Bend 62 C2
Taimyr Peninsula = Taymyr, Poluostrov 30 B7
Tain 10 C4
Tainan 35 D7
Taínaron, Ákra 23 F4
T'aipei = Taibei 35 D7
Taiping 36 D2
Taitao, Pen. de 95 F1
Taiwan ■ 35 D7
Taïyetos Óros 23 F4
Taiyuan 35 C6
Taizhong 35 D7
Ta'izz 49 E3
Tajikistan ■ 29 F8
Tajo = Tejo → 18 C1
Tājūrā 52 B1
Tak 36 A1
Takada 32 A6
Takaka 65 D5
Takamatsu 32 B4
Takaoka 32 A5
Takapuna 64 B6
Takasaki 32 A6
Takatsuki 32 B4
Takaungu 57 E7
Takayama 32 A5
Takefu 32 B5
Takengon 36 D1
Takeo 36 B2
Tākestān 46 D7
Takhār □ 45 B7
Takum 55 G6
Talara 90 D2
Talas 29 E8
Talaud, Kepulauan 38 D3
Talaud Is. = Talaud, Kepulauan 38 D3
Talavera de la Reina 18 C3
Talayan 38 C2
Talbragar → 63 B4
Talca 94 D2
Talcahuano 94 D2
Talcher 40 G5
Taldy Kurgan = Taldyqorghan 29 E8
Taldyqorghan 29 E8
Ţalesh, Kūhhā-ye 46 C7
Tali Post 53 G5
Talibon 38 B2
Taliwang 37 F5
Tall 'Afar 46 C5
Talladega 74 C4
Tallahassee 75 D5
Tallangatta 63 C4
Tallarook 63 C4
Tallinn 24 B1
Talodi 53 F5
Taltal 94 B2
Talwood 63 A4
Talyawalka Cr. → 62 B3
Tamale 55 G4
Tamanrasset 54 D6
Tamarang 63 B5
Tamaské 55 F6
Tambacounda 55 F2
Tambelan, Kepulauan 37 D3
Tambo de Mora 91 F3
Tambora 37 F5
Tambov 24 C5
Tamburâ 53 G4
Tâmchekket 55 E2
Tamega → 18 B1
Tamenglong 41 E9
Tamgak, Mts. 55 E6
Tamil Nadu □ 43 P10
Tammerfors = Tampere 8 F12
Tamo Abu, Pegunungan 37 D5
Tampa 75 F6
Tampere 8 F12
Tampico 84 C5
Tamrida = Qādib 49 E5
Tamsagbulag 35 B6
Tamu 41 E10
Tamworth 63 B5
Tana →, *Kenya* 57 E8
Tana →, *Norway* 8 D13
Tana, L. 53 F6
Tanahbala 37 E1
Tanahgrogot 37 E5
Tanahjampea 39 F2
Tanahmasa 37 E1
Tanahmerah 39 F6
Tanami Desert 60 D5
Tanana 71 B4
Tanana → 71 B4
Tananarive = Antananarivo 59 H9
Tánaro → 20 B2
Tandag 38 C3
Tandil 94 D5
Tandil, Sa. del 94 D5
Tando Adam 42 G6
Tandou L. 62 B3
Tane-ga-Shima 33 D2
Taneatua 64 C7
Tanen Tong Dan 41 J12
Tanezrouft 54 D5
Tanga 57 F7
Tanganyika, L. 57 F5
Tanger = Tangier 54 A3
Tanggula Shan 34 C4
Tangier 54 A3
Tangshan 35 C6
Tanimbar, Kepulauan 39 F4
Tanimbar Is. = Tanimbar, Kepulauan 39 F4
Tanjay 38 C2
Tanjore = Thanjavur 43 P11
Tanjung 37 E5
Tanjungbalai 37 D1
Tanjungbatu 37 D5
Tanjungkarang Telukbetung 37 F3
Tanjungpandan 37 E3
Tanjungpinang 37 D2
Tanjungredeb 37 D5
Tanjungselor 37 D5
Tanout 55 F6
Tanta 52 B5
Tantung = Dandong 35 B7
Tanunda 62 B2
Tanzania ■ 57 F6
Taolanaro 59 K9
Taoudenni 54 D4
Taourirt 54 B4
Tapa Shan = Daba Shan 35 C5
Tapah 37 D2
Tapajós → 92 C3
Tapaktuan 37 D1
Tapanui 65 F3
Tapauá → 91 E6
Tapeta 55 G3
Tapi → 43 J8
Tapirapecó, Serra 90 C6
Tapuaenuku, Mt. 65 D5
Tapul Group 38 C2
Taquari → 91 G7
Tara, *Australia* 63 A5
Tara, *Russia* 29 D8
Tara →, *Montenegro, Yug.* 22 C2
Tara →, *Russia* 29 D8
Tarabagatay, Khrebet 29 E9
Tarābulus, *Lebanon* 46 D3
Tarābulus, *Libya* 52 B1
Tarakan 37 D5
Taralga 63 B4
Taranaki □ 64 C6
Tarancón 19 B4
Taranga Hill 43 H8
Táranto 21 D6
Táranto, G. di 21 D6
Tarapacá 90 D5
Tararua Ra. 64 D6
Tarashcha 17 D10
Tarauacá 91 E4
Tarauacá → 91 E5
Tarawera 64 C7
Tarawera L. 64 C7
Tarazona 19 B5
Tarbela Dam 42 B8
Tarbes 12 E4
Tarcoola 62 B1
Tarcoon 63 B4
Taree 63 B5
Tarfaya 54 C2
Tarifa 18 D3
Tarija 94 A4
Tariku → 39 E5
Tarim Basin = Tarim Pendi 34 C3
Tarim He → 34 C3
Tarim Pendi 34 C3
Taritatu → 39 E5
Tarkhankut, Mys 25 D3
Tarko Sale 28 C8
Tarkwa 55 G4
Tarlac 38 A2
Tarma 91 F3
Tarn → 12 D4
Tarnobrzeg 16 C5
Tarnów 16 C5
Tarnowskie Góry 16 C4
Taroom 63 A4
Taroudannt 54 B3
Tarragona 19 B6
Tarrasa 19 B7
Tarso Emissi 52 D2
Tarsus 46 C3
Tartagal 94 A4
Tartu 24 B2
Ţarţūs 46 D3
Tarutung 37 D1
Tasāwah 52 C1
Taschereau 69 D3
Tash-Kömür 29 E8
Tash-Kumyr = Tash-Kömür 29 E8
Tashauz = Dashhowuz 29 E6
Tashi Chho Dzong = Thimphu 41 D7
Tashkent = Toshkent 29 E7
Tashtagol 29 D9
Tasman B. 65 D5
Tasman Mts. 65 D5
Tasman Pen. 62 D4
Tasmania □ 62 D4
Tatabánya 16 E4
Tatar Republic □ = Tatarstan □ 29 D6
Tatarbunary 17 F9
Tatarsk 29 D8
Tatarstan □ 29 D6
Tateyama 32 B6
Tathra 63 C4
Tatra = Tatry 16 D4
Tatry 16 D4
Tatta 43 G5
Tatuī 94 A7
Tat'ung = Datong 35 B6
Tatvan 46 C5
Taubaté 94 A7
Tauern 15 E7
Taumarunui 64 C6
Taumaturgo 91 E4
Taungdwingyi 41 G10
Taunggyi 41 G11
Taungup 41 H10
Taungup Pass 41 H10
Taungup Taunggya 41 H9
Taunton 11 F5

Taunus ....... 14 C5
Taupo ........ 64 C7
Taupo, L. ..... 64 C6
Tauranga ..... 64 B7
Tauranga Harb. 64 B7
Taurianova ... 21 E6
Taurus Mts. = Toros Dağları 46 C3
Tavda ........ 29 D7
Tavda → ..... 29 D7
Taveta ....... 57 E7
Tavira ........ 18 D2
Tavoy ........ 36 B1
Tawau ....... 36 D5
Tawitawi ..... 38 C2
Tay → ....... 10 C5
Tayabamba ... 91 E3
Taylakova .... 29 D8
Taylakovy = Taylakova ... 29 D8
Taymā ....... 47 F4
Taymyr, Oz. ... 30 B8
Taymyr, Poluostrov .. 30 B7
Taytay ....... 38 B1
Taz → ....... 28 C8
Taza ......... 54 B4
Tazovskiy ..... 28 C8
Tbilisi ........ 25 E5
Tchad = Chad ■ 53 E2
Tchad, L. ..... 53 F1
Tch'eng-tou = Chengdu .... 35 C5
Tchibanga .. 56 E2
Tch'ong-k'ing = Chongqing .. 35 D5
Tczew ........ 16 A4
Te Anau, L. ... 65 F2
Te Aroha ..... 64 B6
Te Awamutu .. 64 C6
Te Kuiti ...... 64 C6
Te Puke ...... 64 B7
Te Waewae B. . 65 G2
Tebakang ..... 37 D4
Tébessa ...... 54 A6
Tebicuary → . 94 B5
Tebingtinggi .. 37 D1
Tecuci ........ 22 B6
Tedzhen = Tejen ....... 29 F7
Tefé ......... 90 D6
Tegal ........ 37 F3
Tegina ....... 55 F6
Tegucigalpa ... 85 E7
Tehachapi .... 82 C3
Tehrān ....... 44 C2
Tehuantepec .. 85 D5
Tehuantepec, G. de ......... 85 D5
Tehuantepec, Istmo de .... 85 D6
Tejen ........ 29 F7
Tejo → ...... 18 C1
Tekapo, L. .... 65 E4
Tekeli ........ 29 E8
Tekirdağ ...... 22 D6
Tekkali ....... 40 H5
Tel Aviv-Yafo .. 46 D3
Tela ......... 85 D7
Telanaipura = Jambi ...... 37 E2
Telavi ........ 25 E6
Telekhany = Tsyelyakhany 17 B7
Teles Pires → . 91 E7
Telford ....... 11 E5
Télimélé ...... 55 F2
Tellicherry .... 43 P9
Telsen ....... 95 E3
Teluk Anson .. 37 D2
Teluk Betung = Tanjungkarang Telukbetung . 37 F3
Teluk Intan = Teluk Anson . 37 D2
Telukbutun ... 37 D3
Telukdalem ... 37 D1
Tema ........ 55 G4
Temax ....... 85 C7
Temerloh ..... 37 D2
Temir ........ 29 E6
Temirtau, *Kazakstan* ... 29 D8
Temirtau, *Russia* 29 D9
Temma ....... 62 D3
Temora ...... 63 B4
Tempe ....... 83 D7
Temple ....... 78 D5
Temuco ...... 94 D2
Temuka ...... 65 F4
Tenali ........ 40 J3
Tenasserim ... 36 B1
Tenda, Col di .. 20 B1
Tendaho ...... 49 E3
Tenerife ...... 54 C1
Teng Xian .... 35 C6
Tengah □ ..... 39 E2
Tengah Kepulauan .. 37 F5
Tengchong ... 34 D4
Tenggara □ ... 39 E2
Tenggarong ... 37 E5
Tengiz, Ozero . 29 D7
Tenkasi ....... 43 Q10
Tenke ........ 57 G5
Tenkodogo ... 55 F4
Tennessee □ .. 74 R4
Tennessee → . 72 F1
Tenom ....... 36 C5
Tenryū-Gawa → ... 32 B5
Tenterfield .... 63 A5
Teófilo Otoni .. 93 F5
Tepa ......... 39 F3
Tepic ........ 84 C4
Teplice ....... 16 C1
Ter → ....... 19 A7
Téra ......... 55 F5
Téramo ...... 20 C4
Terang ....... 62 C3
Terebovlya .... 17 D7
Terek → ..... 25 E6
Teresina ...... 92 D5
Terewah, L. ... 63 A4
Terhazza ...... 54 D3
Teridgerie Cr. → ...... 63 B4
Termez = Termiz ..... 29 F7
Términi Imerese 21 F4
Termiz ....... 29 F7
Térmoli ...... 20 C5
Ternate ....... 39 D3
Terni ......... 20 C4
Ternopil ...... 17 D7
Ternopol = Ternopil .... 17 D7
Terowie, *N.S.W., Australia* .... 63 B4
Terowie, *S. Austral., Australia* .... 62 B2
Terracina ..... 20 D4
Terralba ...... 21 E2
Terranova = Ólbia ....... 20 D2
Terrassa = Tarrasa ..... 19 B7
Terre Haute ... 72 E2
Terschelling ... 14 B3
Teruel ........ 19 B5
Teryaweyna L. . 62 B3
Teshio-Gawa → 32 F12
Tesiyn Gol → . 34 A4
Teslin ........ 70 B6
Tessalit ....... 54 D5
Tessaoua ..... 55 F6
Tetas, Pta. .... 94 A2
Tete ......... 59 B6
Teterev → ... 17 C10
Teteven ...... 22 C5
Tetiyev ....... 17 D9
Tétouan ...... 54 A3
Tetovo ....... 22 C3
Teuco → ..... 94 B4
Teun ......... 39 F3
Teutoburger Wald ....... 14 B5
Tévere → .... 20 D4
Tewantin ..... 63 A5
Texarkana .... 79 C6
Texas ........ 63 A5
Texas □ ...... 78 D4
Texas City .... 79 E6
Texel ........ 14 B3
Teyvareh ..... 45 C6
Tezpur ....... 41 D9
Thabana Ntlenyana ... 59 D5
Thabazimbi ... 59 C5
Thailand ■ .... 36 A2
Thailand, G. of 36 B2
Thakhek ...... 36 A2
Thal ......... 42 C7
Thala La ..... 41 C11
Thallon ....... 63 A4
Thames ...... 64 B6
Thames → ... 11 F7
Thane ........ 43 K8
Thanh Pho Ho Chi Minh = Phanh Bho Ho Chi Minh ... 36 B3
Thanjavur .... 43 P11
Thar Desert ... 42 F7
Tharad ....... 43 G7
Thargomindah 63 A3
Tharrawaddy .. 41 J10
Thásos ....... 23 D5
Thaton ....... 41 J11
Thaungdut .... 41 E10
Thayetmyo ... 41 H10
Thazi ......... 41 G11
The Alberga → 62 A2
The Coorong .. 62 C2
The Frome → . 62 A2
The Grampians 62 C3
The Great Divide = Great Dividing Ra. . 61 E8
The Hague = 's-Gravenhage . 14 B3
The Hamilton → 62 A2
The Macumba → 62 A2
The Neales → 62 A2
The Pas ...... 71 C9
The Rock ..... 63 C4
The Salt L. .... 62 B3
The Stevenson → 62 A2
The Warburton → 62 A2
Thebes = Thívai 23 E4
Theebine ..... 63 A5
Thermaïkós Kólpos ..... 23 D4
Thermopylae P. 23 E4
Thessaloníki .. 23 D4
Thessaloniki, Gulf of = Thermaïkós Kólpos ..... 23 D4
Thetford ...... 11 E7
Thetford Mines 69 D3
Thevenard .... 62 B1
Thiel Mts. ..... 96 C2
Thiers ........ 13 D5
Thies ........ 55 F1
Thika ........ 57 E7
Thimphu ..... 41 D7
Thionville ..... 13 B7
Thíra ......... 23 F5
Thistle I. ...... 62 C2
Thívai ........ 23 E4
Thomas, L. .... 62 A2
Thomasville, *Ga., U.S.A.* .. 75 D6
Thomasville, *N.C., U.S.A.* . 75 B7
Thompson .... 71 C10
Thomson's Falls = Nyahururu 57 D7
Thrace ....... 22 D6
Three Hummock I. .......... 62 D3
Three Points, C. 55 H4
Thun ......... 13 C7
Thunder Bay .. 69 D2
Thung Song .. 36 C1
Thunkar ...... 41 D8
Thüringer Wald 14 C6
Thurles ....... 11 E3
Thurloo Downs 63 A3
Thurso ....... 10 B5
Thurston I. .... 96 B2
Thylungra .... 63 A3
Tia .......... 63 B5
Tian Shan .... 34 B3
Tianjin ....... 35 C6
Tianshui ...... 35 C5
Tiaret ........ 54 A5
Tiassalé ...... 55 G4
Tibati ........ 53 G1
Tiber = Tévere → .. 20 D4
Tiberias, L. = Yam Kinneret 46 D3
Tibesti ....... 52 D2
Tibet = Xizang □ ... 34 C3
Tibooburra .... 62 A3
Tiburón ...... 84 B2
Tîchît ........ 55 E3
Ticino → ..... 20 B2
Tiddim ....... 41 F9
Tidjikja ....... 55 E2
Tidore ........ 39 D3
Tiel .......... 55 F1
Tierra de Campos .... 18 A3
Tierra del Fuego, I. Gr. de ........ 95 G3
Tiétar → ..... 18 C2
Tieyon ....... 62 A1
Tiflis = Tbilisi . 25 E5
Tifu .......... 39 E3
Tighina ....... 17 E9
Tignish ....... 69 D4
Tigre → ..... 90 D4
Tigris = Dijlah, Nahr → .... 47 E6
Tigyaing ...... 41 F11

Tîh, Gebel el 52 C5
Tijuana 84 A1
Tikamgarh 43 G11
Tikhoretsk 25 D5
Tikrīt 46 D5
Tiksi 30 B10
Tilamuta 39 D2
Tilburg 14 C3
Tillabéri 55 F5
Tílos 23 F6
Tilpa 63 B3
Tilsit = Sovetsk 24 B1
Timaru 65 F4
Timbedgha 55 E3
Timboon 62 C3
Timbuktu = Tombouctou 55 E4
Timimoun 54 C5
Timişoara 16 F5
Timmins 69 D2
Timok → 22 B4
Timon 92 D5
Timor 39 F2
Tinaca Pt. 38 C3
Tindouf 54 C3
Tingo Maria 91 E3
Tinjoub 54 C3
Tinnevelly = Tirunelveli 43 Q10
Tinogasta 94 B3
Tínos 23 F5
Tintinara 62 C3
Tioman, Pulau 37 D2
Tipongpani 41 D10
Tipperary 11 E2
Tīrān 44 C2
Tirana 22 D2
Tiranë = Tirana 22 D2
Tiraspol 17 E9
Tire 23 E6
Tirebolu 46 B4
Tiree 10 C3
Tîrgovişte 22 B5
Tîrgu-Jiu 17 F6
Tîrgu Mureş 17 E7
Tirich Mir 42 A7
Tîrnăveni 17 E7
Tírnavos 23 E4
Tirodi 43 J11
Tirol □ 14 E6
Tirso → 21 E2
Tiruchchirappalli 43 P11
Tirunelveli 43 Q10
Tirupati 43 N11
Tiruppur 43 P10
Tiruvannamalai 43 N11
Tisa → 22 B3
Tisdale 71 C9
Tisza = Tisa → 22 B3
Tit-Ary 30 B10
Titicaca, L. 91 G5
Titograd = Podgorica 22 C2
Titov Veles 22 D3
Titova-Mitrovica = Kosovska-Mitrovica 22 C3
Titovo Užice 22 C2
Titule 57 D5
Tivaouane 55 F1
Tívoli 20 D4
Tiwī 45 F4
Tizi-Ouzou 54 A5
Tiznit 54 C3
Tjirebon = Cirebon 37 F3
Tlaxcala 84 D5
Tlaxiaco 84 D5
Tlemcen 54 B4
Tmassah 52 C2
Toamasina 59 H9
Toay 94 D4
Toba 32 B5
Toba Kakar 42 D6
Tobago 87 D7
Tobelo 39 D3
Tobermory 10 C3
Toboali 37 E3
Tobol → 29 D7
Toboli 39 E2
Tobolsk 29 D7
Tobruk = Tubruq 52 B3
Tobyl = Tobol → 29 D7
Tocantinópolis 92 D4
Tocantins □ 93 E4
Tocantins → 92 C4
Tochigi 32 A6
Tocopilla 94 A2
Tocumwal 63 C4
Tocuyo → 90 A5
Todeli 39 E2
Todenyang 57 D7
Todos os Santos, B. de 93 E6
Togba 55 E2
Togian, Kepulauan 39 E2
Togliatti 24 C6
Togo ■ 55 G5
Toinya 53 G4
Tojikiston = Tajikistan ■ 29 F8
Tojo 39 E2
Tokala 39 E2
Tōkamachi 32 A6
Tokanui 65 G3
Tokar 53 E6
Tokarahi 65 F4
Tokat 46 B4
Tokelau Is. 65 K13
Tokmak 29 E8
Tokushima 32 B4
Tokuyama 32 B2
Tōkyō 32 B6
Tolaga Bay 64 C8
Tolbukhin = Dobrich 22 C6
Toledo, *Spain* 18 C3
Toledo, *U.S.A.* 72 D4
Toledo, Montes de 18 C3
Tolga 54 B6
Toliara 59 J8
Tolima 90 C3
Tolitoli 39 D2
Tolo 56 E3
Tolo, Teluk 39 E2
Toluca 84 D5
Tomakomai 32 F12
Tomar 18 C1
Tomaszów Mazowiecki 16 C4
Tombé 53 G5
Tombouctou 55 E4
Tombua 58 B2
Tomelloso 18 C4
Tomingley 63 B4
Tomini 39 D2
Tomini, Teluk 39 E2
Tomorit 23 D3
Tomsk 29 D9
Tonantins 90 D5
Tonawanda 73 C6
Tondano 39 D2
Tonekābon 44 B2
Tong Xian 35 C6
Tonga ■ 65 L13
Tonga Trench 65 L13
Tongareva 65 K15
Tongchuan 35 C5
Tonghua 35 B7
Tongjiang 35 B8
Tongking, G. of = Tonkin, G. of 35 D5
Tongoy 94 C2
Tongren 35 D5
Tongsa Dzong 41 D8
Tongue → 76 B2
Tonk 42 F9
Tonkin, G. of 35 D5
Tonlé Sap 36 B2
Toompine 63 A3
Toora 63 C4
Toowoomba 63 A5
Topeka 77 F7
Topki 29 D9
Topol'čany 16 D4
Topolobampo 84 B3
Torata 91 G4
Torbalı 23 E6
Torbat-e Heydārīyeh 44 C4
Torbat-e Jām 45 C5
Torbay 11 F5
Tordesillas 18 B3
Torgau 15 C7
Torino 20 B1
Torit 53 H5
Tormes → 18 B2
Torne älv → 8 E12
Torneå = Tornio 8 E12
Torneträsk 8 E11
Tornio 8 E12
Tornquist 94 D4
Toro, Cerro del 94 B3
Toroníios Kólpos 23 D4
Toronto, *Australia* 63 B5
Toronto, *Canada* 69 D3
Toropets 24 B3
Tororo 57 D6
Toros Dağları 46 C3
Tôrre de Moncorvo 18 B2
Torre del Greco 21 D5
Torrejón de Ardoz 18 B4
Torrelavega 18 A3
Torremolinos 18 D3
Torrens, L. 62 B2
Torrente 19 C5
Torreón 84 B4
Torres 84 B2
Torres Vedras 18 C1
Torrevieja 19 D5
Tortosa 19 B6
Tortosa, C. de 19 B6
Ţorūd 44 C3
Toruń 16 B4
Tosa-Wan 32 C3
Toscana □ 20 C3
Toshkent 29 E7
Tostado 94 B4
Tosya 46 B3
Toteng 58 C4
Totma 24 A5
Totten Glacier 96 A12
Tottenham 63 B4
Tottori 32 B4
Touba 55 G3
Toubkal, Djebel 54 B3
Tougan 55 F4
Touggourt 54 B6
Tougué 55 F2
Toul 13 B6
Toulepleu 55 G3
Toulon 13 E6
Toulouse 12 E4
Toummo 52 D1
Toungoo 41 H11
Touraine 12 C4
Tourane = Da Nang 36 A3
Tourcoing 13 A5
Touriñán, C. 18 A1
Tournai 14 C2
Tournon 13 D6
Tours 12 C4
Towamba 63 C4
Towang 41 D8
Townsville 61 D8
Toyama 32 A5
Toyohashi 32 B5
Toyonaka 32 B4
Toyooka 32 B4
Toyota 32 B5
Tozeur 54 B6
Trá Li = Tralee 11 E2
Trabzon 46 B4
Trafalgar, C. 18 D2
Trail 71 D8
Tralee 11 E2
Trancas 94 B3
Trang 36 C1
Trangan 39 F4
Trangie 63 B4
Trani 20 D6
Transantarctic Mts. 96 C3
Transilvania 17 F7
Transilvanian Alps = Carpaţii Meridionali 17 F7
Transylvania = Transilvania 17 F7
Trápani 21 E4
Traralgon 63 C4
Trasimeno, L. 20 C4
Traun 15 D8
Travemünde 15 B6
Travers, Mt. 65 E5
Travnik 20 B6
Trébbia → 20 B2
Třebíč 16 D2
Trebinje 20 C7
Treinta y Tres 94 C6
Trelew 95 E3
Tremp 19 A6
Trenčín 16 D4
Trenque Lauquen 94 D4
Trent → 11 E6
Trento 20 A3
Trenton 73 D8
Trepassey 69 D5
Tres Arroyos 94 D4
Três Corações 93 G4
Três Lagoas 93 G3
Tres Montes, C. 95 F1
Tres Puentes 94 B2
Tres Puntas, C. 95 F3
Três Rios 93 G5
Treviso 20 B4
Triabunna 62 D4
Trichinopoly = Tiruchchirappalli 43 P11
Trichur 43 P10
Trida 63 B4
Trier 14 D4
Trieste 20 B4

Triglav 20 A4
Tríkkala 23 E3
Trikora, Puncak 39 E5
Trinidad, *Bolivia* 91 F6
Trinidad, *Colombia* 90 B4
Trinidad, *Cuba* 86 B3
Trinidad, *Uruguay* 94 C5
Trinidad, *U.S.A.* 78 A1
Trinidad, I. 95 D4
Trinidad & Tobago ■ 87 D7
Trinity → 79 E6
Trinity B. 69 D5
Trinity Range 80 E4
Trinkitat 53 E6
Tripoli = Tarābulus, *Lebanon* 46 D3
Tripoli = Tarābulus, *Libya* 52 B1
Trípolis 23 F4
Tripura □ 41 F8
Trivandrum 43 Q10
Trnava 16 D3
Troglav 20 C6
Trois-Rivières 69 D3
Troitsko Pechorsk 28 C6
Trollhättan 9 G10
Tronador 95 E2
Trondheim 8 F10
Trondheimsfjorden 8 F10
Trout L. 70 B7
Trouville-sur-Mer 12 B4
Troy, *Turkey* 23 E6
Troy, *Ala., U.S.A.* 74 D5
Troy, *N.Y., U.S.A.* 73 C9
Troyes 13 B8
Trucial States = United Arab Emirates ■ 44 F3
Trujillo, *Honduras* 85 D7
Trujillo, *Peru* 91 E3
Trujillo, *Spain* 18 C3
Trujillo, *Venezuela* 90 B4
Truk 64 J10
Trundle 63 B4
Truro, *Canada* 69 D4
Truro, *U.K.* 11 F4
Truskavets 17 D6
Trutnov 16 C2
Tsaratanana 59 H9
Tsarevo = Michurin 22 C6
Tsau 58 C4
Tselinograd = Astana 29 D8
Tsetserleg 34 B5
Tshabong 58 D4
Tshane 58 C4
Tshela 56 E2
Tshikapa 56 F4
Tshofa 57 F5
Tshwane 58 C4
Tsihombe 59 K9
Tsimlyansk Res. = Tsimlyanskoye Vdkhr. 25 D5
Tsimlyanskoye Vdkhr. 25 D5
Tsinan = Jinan 35 C6
Tsinghai = Qinghai □ 34 C4
Tsingtao = Qingdao 35 C7
Tskhinvali 25 E5
Tsna → 24 C5
Tsu 32 B5
Tsuchiura 32 A7
Tsugaru-Kaikyō 32 F12
Tsumeb 58 B3
Tsumis 58 C3
Tsuruga 32 B5
Tsurugi-San 32 C4
Tsuruoka 33 G11
Tsyelyakhany 17 B7
Tual 39 F4
Tuamotu Arch. = Tuamotu Is. 65 L16
Tuamotu Is. 65 L16
Tuamotu Ridge 65 M17
Tuao 38 A2
Tuapse 25 E4
Tuatapere 65 G2
Tubarão 94 B7
Tubau 37 D4
Tübingen 14 D5
Tubruq 52 B3
Tubuai Is. 65 M16
Tucacas 90 A5
Tucson 83 D7
Tucumcari 78 B2
Tucupita 90 B6
Tucuruí 92 C4
Tucuruí, Represa de 92 C4
Tudela 19 A5
Tudmur 46 D4
Tuen 63 A4
Tuguegarao 38 A2
Tukangbesi, Kepulauan 39 F2
Tūkrah 52 D3
Tuktoyaktuk 70 B6
Tukuyu 57 F6
Tula, *Mexico* 84 C5
Tula, *Russia* 24 C4
Tulak 45 C5
Tulancingo 84 C5
Tulare 82 B3
Tulcán 90 C3
Tulcea 17 F9
Tulchyn 17 D9
Tuli, *Indonesia* 39 E2
Tuli, *Zimbabwe* 59 C5
Tullamore, *Australia* 63 B4
Tullamore, *Ireland* 11 E3
Tulle 12 D4
Tullibigeal 63 B4
Ţulmaythah 52 B3
Tulsa 79 A6
Tulua 90 C3
Tulungagung 37 F4
Tum 39 E4
Tumaco 90 C3
Tumatumari 90 B7
Tumba, L. 56 E3
Tumbarumba 63 C4
Túmbes 90 D2
Tumby Bay 62 B2
Tumeremo 90 B6
Tumkur 43 N10
Tump 42 F3
Tumpat 36 C2
Tumu 55 F4
Tumucumaque, Serra 92 B3
Tumut 63 C4
Tuncurry 63 B5
Tunduru 57 G7
Tundzha → 22 D6
Tunga Pass 41 C10
Tungabhadra → 43 M11
Tungaru 53 F5
Tunguska, Nizhnyaya → 30 C6
Tunis 54 A7
Tunisia ■ 54 B6
Tunja 90 B4
Tunuyán → 94 C3
Tunxi 35 D6
Tupelo 74 B3
Tupinambaranas 90 D7
Tupiza 94 A3
Tupungato, Cerro 94 C3
Túquerres 90 C3
Tura 30 C8
Turabah 47 E5
Tūrān 44 C4
Turayf 47 E4
Turda 17 E6
Turek 16 B4
Turfan = Turpan 34 B3
Turfan Depression = Turpan Hami 34 B3
Tŭrgovishte 22 C6
Turgutlu 23 E6
Turhal 46 B4
Turia → 19 C5
Turiaçu 92 C4
Turiaçu → 92 C4
Turin = Torino 20 B1
Turkana, L. 57 D7
Turkestan = Türkistan 29 E7
Turkey ■ 46 C3
Türkistan 29 E7
Turkmenistan ■ 29 F6
Turks & Caicos Is. ■ 87 B5
Turku 9 F12
Turnagain, C. 64 D7
Turneffe Is. 85 D7
Turnhout 14 C3
Tŭrnovo = Veliko Tŭrnovo 22 C5
Turnu Măgurele 22 C5
Turnu Roşu, P. 17 F7
Turpan 34 B3
Turpan Hami 34 B3
Turukhansk 30 C6
Tuscaloosa 74 C4
Tuscany = Toscana □ 20 C3
Tuticorin 43 Q11
Tutóia 92 C5
Tutong 36 D4
Tutrakan 22 B6
Tuttlingen 14 E5
Tutuala 39 F3
Tutuila 65 L13
Tuvalu ■ 64 K12
Tuxpan 84 C5
Tuxtla Gutiérrez 85 D6
Tuy 18 A1
Tuz Gölü 46 C3
Ţūz Khurmātū 46 D6
Tuzla 20 B7
Tver 24 B4
Tweed Heads 63 A5
Twillingate 69 D5
Twin Falls 81 D6
Twofold B. 63 C4
Tyachiv 17 D6
Tychy 16 C4
Tyler 79 C6
Tyre = Sūr 46 D3
Tyrol = Tirol □ 14 E6
Tyrrell → 62 C3
Tyrrell, L. 62 C3
Tyrrhenian Sea 21 E4
Tyumen 29 D7
Tzaneen 59 C6
Tzukong = Zigong 35 D5

## U

U.S.A. = United States of America ■ 67 F10
Uarsciek 49 G4
Uato-Udo 39 F3
Uatumã → 90 D7
Uaupés 90 D5
Uaupés → 90 C5
Ubá 93 G5
Ubaitaba 93 E6
Ubangi = Oubangi → 56 E3
Ubauro 42 E6
Ube 32 C2
Ubeda 18 C4
Uberaba 93 F4
Uberlândia 93 F4
Ubon Ratchathani 36 A2
Ubort → 17 B9
Ubundu 57 E5
Ucayali → 90 D4
Uchiura-Wan 32 F12
Udaipur 43 G8
Udaipur Garhi 40 D6
Udgir 43 K10
Udhampur 42 C9
Udi 55 G6
Údine 20 A4
Udmurtia □ 28 D6
Udon Thani 36 A2
Udupi 43 N9
Ueda 32 A6
Uele → 57 D4
Uelzen 14 B6
Ufa 29 D6
Ugab → 58 C2
Ugalla → 57 F6
Uganda ■ 57 D6
Ugljane 20 B5
Ugolyak 30 C10
Uibhist a Deas = South Uist 10 C3
Uibhist a Tuath = North Uist 10 C3
Uíge 56 F2
Uinta Mts. 81 E8
Uitenhage 59 E5
Ujjain 43 H9
Ujung Pandang 39 F1
Ukerewe I. 57 E6
Ukhrul 41 E10
Ukhta 28 C6
Ukraine ■ 25 D3
Ulaanbaatar 35 B5
Ulaangom 34 A4
Ulan Bator = Ulaanbaatar 35 B5
Ulan Ude 30 D8
Ulcinj 22 D2

Ulhasnagar 43 K8
Ulladulla 63 C5
Ullapool 10 C4
Ulm 14 D5
Ulmarra 63 A5
Ulonguè 59 A6
Ulster □ 11 D3
Ulubat Gölü 23 D7
Uludağ 23 D7
Ulungur He → 34 B3
Uluru = Ayers Rock 60 F5
Ulutau 29 E7
Ulverstone 62 D4
Ulyanovsk = Simbirsk 24 C6
Ulyasutay 34 B4
Umala 91 G5
Uman 17 D10
Umaria 40 F3
Umarkot 43 G6
Umba 28 C4
Umbrella Mts. 65 F3
Ume älv → 8 F12
Umeå 8 F12
Umera 39 E3
Umm al Qaywayn 44 E3
Umm Bel 53 F4
Umm Lajj 47 F4
Umm Ruwaba 53 F5
Umnak I. 71 C3
Umniati → 59 B5
Umtata 59 E5
Umuarama 93 G3
Una → 20 B6
Unalaska 71 C3
Uncía 91 G5
Underbool 62 C3
Ungarie 63 B4
Ungarra 62 B2
Ungava B. 68 C4
Ungava Pen. 68 B3
Ungeny = Ungheni 17 E8
Ungheni 17 E8
União da Vitória 94 B6
Unimak I. 71 C3
United Arab Emirates ■ 44 F3
United Kingdom ■ 11 E5
United States of America ■ 67 F10
Unnao 40 D3
Unst 10 A6
Ünye 46 B4
Upata 90 B6
Upemba, L. 57 F5
Upington 58 D4
Upper Hutt 65 D6
Upper Volta = Burkina Faso ■ 55 F4
Uppsala 9 G11
Ur 47 E6
Uracara 90 D7
Ural = Zhayyq → 29 E6
Ural 63 B4
Ural Mts. = Uralskie Gory 28 D6
Uralla 63 B5
Uralsk = Oral 24 C7
Uralskie Gory 28 D6
Uranquinty 63 C4
Urawa 32 B6
Uray 29 C7
Urbana 72 D1
Urbino 20 C4
Urbión, Picos de 19 A4
Urcos 91 F4
Urda 25 D6
Urdzhar 29 E9
Ures 84 B2
Urfa = Sanliurfa 46 C4
Urganch 29 E7
Urgench = Urganch 29 E7
Uribia 90 A4
Urla 23 E6
Urmia = Orūmīyeh 46 C6
Urmia, L. = Orūmīyeh, Daryācheh-ye 46 C6
Uroševac 22 C3
Uruana 93 F4
Urubamba 91 F4
Urubamba → 91 F4
Uruçuí 92 D5
Uruguai → 94 B6
Uruguaiana 94 B5
Uruguay ■ 94 C5
Uruguay → 94 C5
Urumchi = Ürümqi 34 B3
Ürümqi 34 B3
Usakos 58 C3
Usedom 15 B8
Ush-Tobe 29 E8
Ushant = Ouessant, I. d' 12 B1
Ushuaia 95 G3
Üsküdar 25 E2
Usman 24 C4
Usoke 57 F6
Uspallata, P. de 94 C3
Uspenskiy 29 E8
Ussuriysk 31 E11
Ust-Aldan = Batamay 31 C10
Ust Ilimpeya = Yukti 30 C8
Ust Ishim 29 D8
Ust-Kamenogorsk = Öskemen 29 E9
Ust-Karenga 31 D9
Ust Kuyga 31 B11
Ust Muya 30 D9
Ust Olenek 30 B10
Ust Port 28 C9
Ust Tsilma 28 C6
Ust Urt = Ustyurt, Plateau 29 E6
Ust Vorkuta 28 C7
Ústí nad Labem 16 C2
Ustica 21 E4
Ustinov = Izhevsk 28 D6
Ustye 30 D7
Ustyurt, Plateau 29 E6
Usu 34 B3
Usuki 32 C2
Usumacinta → 85 D6
Usumbura = Bujumbura 57 E5
Uta 39 E5
Utah □ 81 F8
Utete 57 F7
Utiariti 91 F7
Utica 73 C8
Utrecht 14 B3
Utrera 18 D3
Utsunomiya 32 A6
Uttar Pradesh □ 42 F11
Uttaradit 36 A2
Uummannarsuaq = Farvel, Kap 68 C6
Uusikaupunki 8 F12
Uvat 29 D7
Uvinza 57 F6
Uvira 57 E5
Uvs Nuur 34 A4
Uwajima 32 C3
Uyuni 91 H5
Uzbekistan ■ 29 E7
Uzerche 12 D4
Uzh → 17 C10
Uzhgorod = Uzhhorod 17 D6
Uzhhorod 17 D6
Uzunköprü 22 D6

## V

Vaal → 58 D4
Vaasa 8 F12
Vác 16 E4
Vach → = Vakh → 29 C8
Vadodara 43 H8
Vadsø 8 D13
Vaduz 13 C8
Váh → 16 E4
Vahsel B. 96 B5
Vaigach 28 B6
Vakh → 29 C8
Val d'Or 69 D3
Valahia 22 B5
Valandovo 22 D4
Valcheta 95 E3
Valdayskaya Vozvyshennost 24 B3
Valdepeñas 18 C4
Valdés, Pen. 95 E4
Valdez 71 B5
Valdivia 95 D2
Valdosta 75 D6
Valença 93 E6
Valença do Piauí 92 D5
Valence 13 D6
Valencia, *Spain* 19 C5
Valencia, *Venezuela* 90 A5
Valencia □ 19 C5
Valencia, G. de 19 C6
Valencia de Alcántara 18 C2
Valencia I. 11 F1
Valenciennes 13 A5
Valentim, Sa. do 92 D5
Valera 90 B4
Valjevo 22 B2
Vall de Uxó 19 C5
Valladolid, *Mexico* 85 C7
Valladolid, *Spain* 18 B3
Valle de la Pascua 90 B5
Valledupar 90 A4
Vallejo 80 F2
Vallenar 94 B2
Valletta 21 G5
Valls 19 B6
Valognes 12 B3
Valona = Vlóra 23 D2
Valozhyn 17 A8
Valparaíso 94 C2
Vals, Tanjung 39 F5
Valsad 43 J8
Valverde del Camino 18 D2
Van 46 C5
Van, L. = Van Gölü 46 C5
Van Gölü 46 C5
Van Rees, Pegunungan 39 E5
Vanadzor 25 E5
Vancouver, *Canada* 71 D7
Vancouver, *U.S.A.* 80 C2
Vancouver I. 71 D7
Vänern 9 G10
Vanga 57 E7
Vangaindrano 59 J9
Vännäs 8 F11
Vannes 12 C2
Vanrhynsdorp 58 E3
Vanua Levu 64 L12
Vanuatu ■ 64 L11
Vapnyarka 17 D9
Varanasi 40 E4
Varangerfjorden 8 D13
Varaždin 20 A6
Varberg 9 G10
Vardak □ 45 C7
Vardar = Axiós → 23 D4
Varese 20 B2
Varna 22 C6
Varzaneh 44 C3
Vasa Barris → 93 E6
Vascongadas = País Vasco □ 19 A4
Vasht = Khāsh 42 E2
Vasilevichi 17 B9
Vasilkov = Vasylkiv 17 C10
Vaslui 17 E8
Västerås 9 G11
Västervik 9 G11
Vasto 20 C5
Vasylkiv 17 C10
Vatican City ■ 20 D4
Vatomandry 59 H9
Vatra-Dornei 17 E7
Vättern 9 G10
Vaupés = Uaupés → 90 C5
Vawkavysk 17 B7
Vaygach, Ostrov 28 C6
Vedea → 22 C5
Vega 8 E10
Vegreville 71 C8
Vejer de la Frontera 18 D3
Velebit Planina 20 B5
Vélez 90 B4
Vélez Málaga 18 D3
Vélez Rubio 19 D4
Velhas → 93 F5
Velika Kapela 20 B5
Velikaya → 24 B2
Veliki Ustyug 24 A6
Velikiye Luki 24 B3
Veliko Tŭrnovo 22 C5
Velikonda Range 43 M11
Velletri 20 D4
Vellore 43 N11
Venado Tuerto 94 C4
Vendée □ 12 C3
Vendôme 12 C4
Venézia 20 B4
Venézia, G. di 20 B4

Venezuela ■ 90 B5
Venezuela, G. de 90 A4
Vengurla 43 M8
Venice = Venézia 20 B4
Venkatapuram 40 H3
Ventotene 21 D4
Ventoux, Mt. 13 D6
Ventspils 24 B1
Ventuarí → 90 C5
Ventura 82 C3
Venus B. 63 C4
Vera, *Argentina* 94 B4
Vera, *Spain* 19 D5
Veracruz 84 D5
Veraval 43 J7
Verbánia 20 B2
Vercelli 20 B2
Verde → 95 E3
Verden 14 B5
Verdun 13 B6
Vereeniging 59 D5
Verga, C. 55 F2
Verín 18 B2
Verkhnevilyuysk 30 C10
Verkhniy Baskunchak 25 D6
Verkhoyansk 31 C11
Verkhoyansk Ra. = Verkhoyanskiy Khrebet 31 C10
Verkhoyanskiy Khrebet 31 C10
Vermilion 71 C8
Vermont □ 73 C9
Vernon, *Canada* 71 C8
Vernon, *U.S.A.* 78 B4
Véroia 23 D4
Verona 20 B3
Versailles 12 B5
Vert, C. 55 F1
Verviers 14 C3
Veselovskoye Vdkhr. 25 D5
Vesoul 13 C7
Vesterålen 8 E11
Vestfjorden 8 E10
Vesuvio 21 D5
Vesuvius, Mt. = Vesuvio 21 D5
Veszprém 16 E3
Vetlugu → 28 D5
Vettore, Mte. 20 C4
Veys 47 E7
Vezhen 22 C5
Viacha 91 G5
Viamão 94 C6
Viana 92 C5
Viana do Alentejo 18 C2
Viana do Castelo 18 B1
Vianópolis 93 F4
Viaréggio 20 C3
Vibo Valéntia 21 E6
Vicenza 20 B3
Vich 19 B7
Vichy 13 C5
Vicksburg 79 C8
Viçosa 93 D6
Victor 43 J7
Victor Harbor 62 C2
Victoria, *Canada* 71 D7
Victoria, *Chile* 94 D2
Victoria, *Guinea* 55 F2
Victoria, *Malaysia* 36 C5
Victoria □ 62 C3
Victoria, L., *Africa* 57 E6
Victoria, L., *Australia* 62 B3
Victoria Beach 71 C10
Victoria de Durango = Durango 84 C4
Victoria Falls 59 B5
Victoria I. 70 A8
Victoria Ld. 96 B14
Victoria Taungdeik 41 G9
Victoria West 58 E4
Victorica 94 D3
Vicuña 94 C2
Vidin 22 C4
Vidisha 43 H10
Viedma 95 E4
Viedma, L. 95 F2
Vienna = Wien 15 D9
Vienne 13 D6
Vienne → 12 C4
Vientiane 36 A2
Vierzon 12 C5
Vietnam ■ 36 A3
Vigan 38 A2
Vigévano 20 B2
Vigia 92 C4
Vigo 18 A1
Vijayawada 40 J3
Vikeke 39 F3
Vikna 8 F10
Vila da Maganja 59 D7
Vila de João Belo = Xai-Xai 59 D6
Vila do Bispo 18 D1
Vila Franca de Xira 18 C1
Vila Machado 59 B6
Vila Nova de Gaia 18 B1
Vila Real 18 B2
Vila Real de Santo António 18 D2
Vila Velha 93 G5
Vilaine → 12 C2
Vilanculos 59 C7
Vileyka 17 A8
Vilhelmina 8 F11
Vilhena 91 F6
Vilkitskogo, Proliv 30 B8
Vilkovo = Vylkove 17 F9
Villa Ahumada 84 A3
Villa Ángela 94 B4
Villa Bella 91 F5
Villa Bens = Tarfaya 54 C2
Villa Colón 94 C3
Villa de María 94 B4
Villa Dolores 94 C3
Villa Hayes 94 B5
Villa María 94 C4
Villa Mazán 94 B3
Villa Montes 94 A4
Villa Ocampo 94 B5
Villacarrillo 18 C4
Villach 15 E7
Villagarcía de Arosa 18 A1
Villaguay 94 C5
Villahermosa 85 D6
Villajoyosa 19 C5
Villalba 18 A2
Villanueva de la Serena 18 C3
Villanueva y Geltrú 19 B6
Villarreal 19 C5
Villarrica, *Chile* 95 D2
Villarrica, *Paraguay* 94 B5
Villarrobledo 19 C4
Villavicencio 90 C4
Villaviciosa 18 A3
Villazón 94 A3
Villena 19 C5
Villeneuve-d'Ascq 13 A5
Villeneuve-sur-Lot 12 D4
Villingen-Schwenningen 14 D5
Vilnius 24 C2
Vilyuy → 31 C10
Vilyuysk 31 C10
Viña del Mar 94 C2
Vinaroz 19 B6
Vindhya Ra. 43 H10
Vineland 73 E8
Vinkovci 20 B7
Vinnitsa = Vinnytsya 17 D9
Vinnytsya 17 D9
Virac 38 B2
Viramgam 43 H8
Viranşehir 46 C4
Virden 71 D9
Vire 12 B3
Virgenes, C. 95 G3
Virgin Is. (British) ■ 87 C7
Virginia □ 73 F0
Virginia Beach 73 F8
Virovitica 20 B6
Virudunagar 43 Q10
Vis 20 C6
Visalia 82 B3
Visayan Sea 38 B2
Visby 9 G11
Višegrad 20 C7
Viseu, *Brazil* 92 C4
Viseu, *Portugal* 18 B2
Vishakhapatnam 40 J4
Viso, Mte. 20 B1
Vistula = Wisła → 16 A4
Vitebsk = Vitsyebsk 24 B3
Viterbo 20 C4
Viti Levu 64 L12
Vitigudino 18 B2
Vitória, *Brazil* 93 G5
Vitoria, *Spain* 19 A4
Vitória da Conquista 93 E5
Vitsyebsk 24 B3
Vittória 21 F5
Vittório Véneto 20 B4
Vivero 18 A2
Vize 22 D6
Vizianagaram 40 H4
Vjosa → 23 D2
Vladikavkaz 25 E5
Vladimir 24 B5
Vladimir Volynskiy = Volodymyr-Volynskyy 17 C7
Vladivostok 31 E11
Vlissingen 14 C2
Vlóra 23 D2
Vltava → 16 C2
Vogelsberg 14 C5
Voghera 20 B2
Vohibinany 59 H9
Vohimarina 59 G10
Vohimena, Tanjon' i 59 K9
Vohipeno 59 J9
Voi 57 E7
Voiron 13 D6
Vojvodina □ 22 B2
Volga → 25 D6
Volga Hts. = Privolzhskaya Vozvyshennost 24 C6
Volgodonsk 25 D5
Volgograd 25 D5
Volgogradskoye Vdkhr. 24 C6
Volkhov → 24 A3
Volkovysk = Vawkavysk 17 B7
Volochanka 30 B7
Volodymyr-Volynskyy 17 C7
Vologda 24 B4
Vólos 23 E4
Volovets 17 D6
Volozhin = Valozhyn 17 A8
Volsk 24 C6
Volta → 55 G5
Volta, L. 55 G5
Volta Redonda 93 G5
Volterra 20 C3
Volturno → 20 D4
Volzhskiy 25 D6
Voríai Sporádhes 23 E4
Vorkuta 28 C7
Voronezh 24 C4
Voroshilovgrad = Luhansk 25 D4
Voroshilovsk = Alchevsk 25 D4
Vosges 13 B7
Vostok I. 65 L15
Vouga → 18 B1
Voznesensk 25 D3
Voznesenye 28 C4
Vrangelya, Ostrov 31 B15
Vranje 22 C3
Vratsa 22 C4
Vrbas → 20 B6
Vrede 59 D5
Vredenburg 58 E3
Vršac 22 B3
Vryburg 58 D4
Vryheid 59 D6
Vukovar 20 B7
Vulcan 17 F6
Vulcaneşti 17 F9
Vulcano 21 E5
Vulkaneshty = Vulcaneşti 17 F9
Vung Tau 36 B3
Vyatka = Kirov 28 D5
Vyatskiye Polyany 24 B7
Vyazma 24 B3
Vyborg 28 C3
Vychegda → 28 C5
Vychodné Beskydy 17 D5
Vylkove 17 F9
Vynohradiv 17 D6
Vyshniy Volochek 24 B3
Vyškov 16 D3

# W

Wa . . . . . . . . . . 55 F4
Waal → . . . . . . 14 C3
Wabash → . . . 72 F1
Waco . . . . . . . . 78 D5
Wad Banda . . . 53 F4
Wad Hamid . . . 53 E5
Wâd Medanî . . 53 F5
Waddington, Mt. 71 C7
Waddy Pt. . . . . 63
Wadi Halfa . . . . 52 D5
Wafrah . . . . . . . 47 E6
Wager B. . . . . . 68 B2
Wager Bay . . . . 68 B1
Wagga Wagga 63 C4
Waghete . . . . . 39 E5
Wah . . . . . . . . . 42 C8
Wahai . . . . . . . . 39 E3
Waiau → . . . . 65 E5
Waibeem . . . . . 39 E4
Waigeo . . . . . . . 39 E4
Waihi . . . . . . . . 64 B6
Waihou → . . . 64 B6
Waikabubak . . . 39 F1
Waikari . . . . . . . 65 E5
Waikato → . . . 64 B6
Waikerie . . . . . . 62 B2
Waikokopu . . . . 64 C7
Waikouaiti . . . . 65 F4
Waimakariri → 65 E5
Waimate . . . . . 65 F4
Wainganga → 43 K11
Waingapu . . . . 39 F2
Wainwright, *Canada* . . . . . 71 C8
Wainwright, *U.S.A.* . . . . . . 71 A3
Waiouru . . . . . . 64 C6
Waipara . . . . . . 65 E5
Waipawa . . . . . 64 C7
Waipiro . . . . . . 64 C8
Waipu . . . . . . . . 64 A6
Waipukurau . . . 64 D7
Wairakei . . . . . . 64 C7
Wairarapa, L. . . 65 D6
Wairoa . . . . . . . 64 C7
Waitaki → . . . . 65 F4
Waitara . . . . . . 64 C6
Waiuku . . . . . . . 64 B6
Wajima . . . . . . . 32 A5
Wajir . . . . . . . . . 57 D8
Wakasa-Wan . . 32 B4
Wakatipu, L. . . 65 F3
Wakayama . . . . 32 B4
Wakefield . . . . . 65 D5
Wakema . . . . . . 41 J10
Wakkanai . . . . . 32 E12
Wakool . . . . . . . 63 C3
Wakool → . . . 62 C3
Wakre . . . . . . . . 39 E4
Wałbrzych . . . . 16 C3
Walcha . . . . . . . 63 B5
Wałcz . . . . . . . . 16 B3
Wales □ . . . . . . 11 E4
Walgett . . . . . . 63 A4
Walgreen Coast 96 B1
Walhalla . . . . . . 63 C4
Walla Walla . . . 80 B4
Wallachia = Valahia . . . . . 22 B5
Wallal . . . . . . . . 63 A4
Wallaroo . . . . . 62 B2
Wallerawang . . 63 B5
Wallis & Futuna, Is. . . . . . . . . . 64 L13
Wallowa Mts. . 80 C5
Wallsend . . . . . 63 B5
Wallumbilla . . . 63 A4
Walvisbaai . . . . 58 C2
Wamba . . . . . . 57 D5
Wamena . . . . . 39 E5
Wamulan . . . . . 39 E3
Wana . . . . . . . . 42 C6
Wanaaring . . . . 63 A3
Wanaka . . . . . . 65 F3
Wanaka L. . . . . 65 F3
Wanapiri . . . . . 39 E5
Wanbi . . . . . . . . 62 B3
Wandoan . . . . . 63 A4
Wangal . . . . . . . 39 F4
Wanganella . . . 63 C3
Wanganui . . . . 64 C6
Wangaratta . . . 63 C4
Wangary . . . . . 62 B2
Wangerooge . . 14 B4
Wangiwangi . . 39 F2
Wanxian . . . . . . 35 C5
Warangal . . . . . 43 L11
Waratah . . . . . . 62 D4
Waratah B. . . . . 63 C4
Warburton . . . . 63 C4
Ward . . . . . . . . 65 D6
Ward → . . . . . 63 A4
Wardha . . . . . . 43 J11
Wardha → . . . 43 K11
Warialda . . . . . 63 A5
Wariap . . . . . . . 39 E4
Warkopi . . . . . . 39 E4
Warmbad, *Namibia* . . . . 58 D3
Warmbad, *S. Africa* . . . . 59 C5
Warner Mts. . . 80 E3
Warracknabeal 62 C3
Warragul . . . . . 63 C4
Warrego → . . 63 B4
Warren . . . . . . . 63 B4
Warrenton . . . . 58 D4
Warrenville . . . 63 A4
Warri . . . . . . . . 55 G6
Warrina . . . . . . 62 A2
Warrington, *U.K.* 11 E5
Warrington, *U.S.A.* . . . . . . 74 D4
Warrnambool . 62 C3
Warsa . . . . . . . . 39 E5
Warsaw = Warszawa . . . 16 B5
Warszawa . . . . 16 B5
Warta → . . . . . 16 B2
Warthe = Warta → . . . 16 B2
Waru . . . . . . . . 39 E4
Warwick . . . . . . 63 A5
Wasatch Ra. . . 81 E8
Wash, The . . . . 11 E7
Washim . . . . . . 43 J10
Washington . . . 73 E7
Washington □ . 80 B3
Washington, Mt. 73 B10
Wasian . . . . . . . 39 E4
Wasior . . . . . . . 39 E4
Waskaganish . . 69 C3
Wasserkuppe . . 14 C5
Watangpone . . 39 E2
Waterbury . . . . 73 D9
Waterford . . . . 11 E3
Waterloo, *S. Leone* . . . . 55 G2
Waterloo, *U.S.A.* 77 D8
Waterton-Glacier International Peace Park . . 81 A6
Watertown . . . . 73 C8
Waterville . . . . 73 B11
Watford . . . . . . 11 F6
Watling I. = San Salvador . . . . 86 B5
Watrous . . . . . . 71 C9
Watsa . . . . . . . . 57 D5
Watson Lake . . 70 B7
Watsonville . . . 82 B2
Wattiwarriganna Cr. → . . . . . . 62 A2
Watuata = Batuata . . . . . 39 F2
Watubela, Kepulauan . . 39 E4
Watubela Is. = Watubela, Kepulauan . . 39 E4
Wauchope . . . . 63 B5
Waukegan . . . . 72 C2
Waukesha . . . . 72 C1
Wausau . . . . . . 77 C10
Wauwatosa . . . 72 C2
Waverley . . . . . 64 C6
Wâw . . . . . . . . . 53 G4
Wāw al Kabīr . . 52 C2
Waxahachie . . . 79 C5
Wayabula Rau . 39 D3
Wayatinah . . . . 62 D4
Waycross . . . . . 75 D6
Wazirabad . . . . 42 C9
We . . . . . . . . . . 36 C1
Weda . . . . . . . . 39 D3
Weda, Teluk . . 39 D3
Weddell I. . . . . 95 G4
Weddell Sea . . 96 A4
Wedderburn . . 62 C3
Wee Waa . . . . . 63 B4
Weemelah . . . . 63 A4
Weiden . . . . . . . 15 D7
Weifang . . . . . . 35 C6
Weimar . . . . . . 15 C6
Weipa . . . . . . . . 61 C7
Weir → . . . . . . 63 A4
Wejherowo . . . 16 A4
Welbourn Hill . 62 A1
Welkom . . . . . . 59 D5
Wellesley Is. . . 60 D6
Wellington, *Australia* . . . . 63 B4
Wellington, *N.Z.* 65 D6
Wellington, I. . . 95 F1
Wellington, L. . 63 C4
Wels . . . . . . . . . 15 D8
Welshpool . . . . 11 E5
Wemindji . . . . . 69 C3
Wenatchee . . . . 80 B3
Wenchi . . . . . . . 55 G4
Wenchow = Wenzhou . . . 35 D7
Wendesi . . . . . . 39 E4
Wensu . . . . . . . 34 B3
Wentworth . . . . 62 B3
Wenut . . . . . . . 39 E4
Wenzhou . . . . . 35 D7
Werda . . . . . . . 58 D4
Werder . . . . . . . 49 F4
Weri . . . . . . . . . 39 E4
Werra → . . . . . 14 C5
Werribee . . . . . 63 C3
Werrimull . . . . . 62 B3
Werris Creek . . 63 B5
Wersar . . . . . . . 39 E4
Weser → . . . . 14 B5
Wesiri . . . . . . . . 39 F3
West Bengal □ 40 F7
West Beskids = Západné Beskydy . . . . 16 D4
West Falkland . 95 G4
West Fjord = Vestfjorden . 8 E10
West Ice Shelf . 96 A11
West Nicholson 59 C5
West Palm Beach . . . . . . 75 F7
West Pt. . . . . . . 62 C2
West Virginia □ 72 E5
West Wyalong . 63 B4
Westall Pt. . . . . 62 B1
Westbury . . . . . 62 D4
Westerland . . . 14 A5
Western Australia □ . . 60 F3
Western Dvina = Daugava → . 24 B1
Western Ghats 43 N9
Western Sahara ■ . . . 54 D2
Western Samoa ■ . . . 65 L13
Westerwald . . . 14 C4
Westland Bight 65 E4
Weston . . . . . . . 36 C5
Weston-super-Mare . . . . . . . 11 F5
Westport, *Ireland* . . . . . 11 E2
Westport, *N.Z.* . 65 D4
Westray . . . . . . 10 B5
Wetar . . . . . . . . 39 F3
Wetaskiwin . . . 71 C8
Wetzlar . . . . . . . 14 C5
Wewak . . . . . . . 61
Wexford . . . . . . 11 E3
Weyburn . . . . . 71 D9
Weymouth . . . . 11 F5
Whakatane . . . . 64 B7
Whale → . . . . 68 C4
Whale Cove . . . 70 B10
Whales, B. of . . 96 B16
Whangamomona . . . . . . . . . . . 64 C6
Whangarei . . . . 64 A6
Whangarei Harb. 64 A6
Wheeling . . . . . 72 D5
White →, *Ark., U.S.A.* . . . . . . 79 C8
White →, *Ind., U.S.A.* . . . . . . 72 E2
White Cliffs . . . 62 B3
White I. . . . . . . 64 B7
White Nile = Nîl el Abyad → 53 E5
White Russia = Belarus ■ . . . 24 C2
White Sea = Beloye More 28 C4
Whitecliffs . . . . 65 E4
Whitehaven . . . 11 D5
Whitehorse . . . 70 B6
Whitemark . . . . 62 D4
Whitfield . . . . . 63 C4
Whitianga . . . . 64 B6
Whitney, Mt. . . 82 B3
Whittlesea . . . . 63 C4
Wholdaia L. . . . 70 B9
Whyalla . . . . . . 62 B2
Whyjonta . . . . . 62 A3
Wichita . . . . . . . 78 A5
Wichita Falls . . 78 C4
Wick . . . . . . . . . 10 B5
Wickham, C. . . 62 C3
Wicklow Mts. . . 11 E3
Wieluń . . . . . . . 16 C4
Wien . . . . . . . . . 15 D9
Wiener Neustadt 15 E9
Wiesbaden . . . . 14 C5
Wilcannia . . . . . 62 B3
Wildspitze . . . . 14 E6
Wilhelm, Mt. . . 61 B8
Wilhelm II Coast 96 A11

Wilhelmshaven 14 B5
Wilkes-Barre .. 73 D8
Wilkie ........ 71 C9
Willandra Billabong Creek → ... 63 B4
Willemstad ... 87 D6
William Creek . 62 A2
Williams Lake . 71 C7
Williamsburg .. 73 F7
Williamsport .. 73 D7
Williamstown . 63 C3
Williston ...... 76 A3
Willowmore ... 58 E4
Willunga ..... 62 C2
Wilmington, *Australia* .... 62 B2
Wilmington, *Del., U.S.A.* . 73 E8
Wilmington, *N.C., U.S.A.* . 75 B9
Wilpena Cr. → 62 B2
Wilson ....... 75 B9
Wilson → .... 62 A3
Wilsons Promontory . 63 C4
Wimmera → . 62 C3
Winchester ... 11 F6
Wind River Range ...... 81 D9
Windau = Ventspils ... 24 B1
Windhoek .... 58 C3
Windsor, *Australia* .... 63 B5
Windsor, *N.S., Canada* ..... 69 D4
Windsor, *Ont., Canada* ..... 69 D2
Windward Is. .. 87
Wingen ...... 63 B5
Wingham .. 63 D5
Winisk → .... 69 C2
Winneba ..... 55 G4
Winnipeg ..... 71 D10
Winnipeg, L. .. 71 C10
Winnipegosis L. 71 C9
Winona ...... 77 C9
Winston-Salem 75 A7
Winterthur .... 13 C8
Winton, *Australia* .... 61 E7
Winton, *N.Z.* .. 65 G3
Wirrulla ...... 62 B1
Wisconsin □ .. 77 C10
Wisła → ..... 16 A4
Wismar ...... 15 B6
Witbank ...... 59 D5
Wittenberg .... 15 C7
Wittenberge ... 15 B6
Wkra → ..... 16 B5
Włocławek .... 16 B4
Włodawa ..... 17 C6
Wodonga ..... 63 C4
Wokam ....... 39 F4
Wolfsberg .... 15 E8
Wolfsburg .... 15 B6
Wolin ........ 16 B2
Wollaston, Is. . 95 H3
Wollaston Pen. 70 B8
Wollongong ... 63 B5
Wolseley ..... 62 C3
Wolverhampton 11 E5
Wondai ...... 63 A5
Wongalarroo L. 63 B3
Wŏnsan ...... 35 C7
Wonthaggi .... 63 C4
Woocalla ..... 62 B2
Woodburn .... 63 A5
Woodenbong . 63 A5
Woodend ..... 63 C3
Woodland .... 80 F3
Woodroffe, Mt. 60 F5
Woods, L. of the 71 D10
Woodstock .... 69 D4
Woodville .... 64 D6
Woolamai, C. .. 63 C4
Woolgoolga ... 63 B5
Woombye .... 63 A5
Woomera ..... 62 B2
Worcester, *S. Africa* .... 58 E3
Worcester, *U.K.* 11 E5
Worcester, *U.S.A.* ...... 73 C10
Workington ... 11 D5
Worms ....... 14 D5
Worthing ..... 11 F6
Wosi ......... 39 E3
Wou-han = Wuhan ..... 35 C6
Wour ........ 52 D2
Wousi = Wuxi . 35 C7
Wowoni ...... 39 E2
Woy Woy ..... 63 B5
Wrangel I. = Vrangelya, Ostrov ...... 31 B15
Wrangell ..... 71 C6
Wrangell Mts. . 71 B5
Wrath, C. ..... 10 B4
Wrexham ..... 11 E5
Wright ....... 38 B3
Wrigley ...... 70 B7
Wrocław ...... 16 C3
Września ..... 16 B3
Wu Jiang → .. 35 D5
Wuhan ....... 35 C6
Wuhsi = Wuxi . 35 C7
Wuhu ........ 35 C6
Wukari ....... 55 G6
Wuliaru ..... 39 F4
Wulumuchi = Ürümqi ..... 34 B3
Wum ........ 55 G7
Wuntho ...... 41 F10
Wuppertal .... 14 C4
Würzburg ..... 14 D5
Wutongqiao ... 34 D5
Wuwei ....... 34 C5
Wuxi ........ 35 C7
Wuyi Shan .... 35 D6
Wuzhi Shan ... 35 E5
Wuzhong ..... 35 C5
Wuzhou ...... 35 D6
Wyandotte .... 72 C4
Wyandra ..... 63 A4
Wyangala Res. 63 B4
Wyara, L. ..... 63 A3
Wycheproof ... 62 C3
Wynbring ..... 62 B1
Wyndham, *Australia* .... 60 D4
Wyndham, *N.Z.* 65 G3
Wynnum ..... 63 A5
Wynyard ..... 62 D4
Wyoming □ ... 81 D10
Wyong ....... 63 B5

## X

Xai-Xai ....... 59 D6
Xainza ....... 34 C3
Xangongo .... 58 B3
Xankändi ..... 25 F6
Xánthi ....... 22 D5
Xapuri ....... 91 F5
Xi Jiang → ... 35 D6
Xiaguan ...... 34 D5
Xiamen ...... 35 D6
Xi'an ......... 35 C5
Xiang Jiang → 35 D6
Xiangfan ..... 35 C6
Xiangtan ..... 35 D6
Xiao Hinggan Ling ........ 35 B7
Xiapu ........ 35 D6
Xichang ...... 34 D5
Xigazê ....... 34 D3
Xinavane ..... 59 D6
Xing'an ...... 35 D6
Xingren ...... 35 D5
Xingtai ....... 35 C6
Xingu → ..... 92 C3
Xining ....... 34 C5
Xinjiang Uygur Zizhiqu □ ... 34 B3
Xinjin ........ 35 C7
Xinxiang ..... 35 C6
Xinyang ...... 35 C6
Xinzhu ....... 35 D7
Xique-Xique .. 93 E5
Xisha Qundao = Hsisha Chuntao .... 36 A4
Xixabangma Feng ....... 40 C5
Xizang □ ..... 34 C3
Xuanhua ..... 35 B6
Xuchang ..... 35 C6
Xuzhou ....... 35 C6

## Y

Ya'an ........ 34 D5
Yaapeet ...... 62 C3
Yabelo ....... 53 H6
Yablonovy Ra. = Yablonovyy Khrebet ..... 30 D9
Yablonovyy Khrebet ..... 30 D9
Yacuiba ...... 94 A4
Yadgir ....... 43 L10
Yagoua ....... 56 B3
Yahuma ...... 56 D4
Yakima ....... 80 B3
Yakutat ....... 71 C6
Yakutsk ...... 31 C10
Yala ......... 36 C2
Yalinga ....... 56 C4
Yalong Jiang → 34 D5
Yalova ....... 22 D7
Yalta ......... 25 E3
Yalutorovsk ... 29 D7
Yam Ha Melaḥ = Dead Sea . 47 E3
Yam Kinneret . 46 D3
Yamagata .... 33 G12
Yamaguchi ... 32 B2
Yamal, Poluostrov .. 28 B8
Yamal Pen. = Yamal, Poluostrov .. 28 B8
Yamantau, Gora 29 D6
Yamba, *N.S.W., Australia* .... 63 A5
Yamba, *S. Austral., Australia* .... 62 B3
Yâmbiô ...... 53 H4
Yambol ...... 22 C6
Yamdena ..... 39 F4
Yamethin ..... 41 G11
Yamma-Yamma, L. .......... 62 A3
Yamoussoukro 55 G3
Yampil ....... 17 D9
Yampol = Yampil ..... 17 D9
Yamuna → ... 40 E3
Yamzho Yumco 34 D4
Yana → ...... 31 B11
Yanac ........ 62 C3
Yanbu 'al Baḥr 47 F4
Yancannia .... 62 B3
Yanco Cr. → .. 63 C4
Yandoon ..... 41 J10
Yangambi .... 56 D4
Yangch'ü = Taiyuan .... 35 C6
Yangchun .... 35 D6
Yangjiang .... 35 D6
Yangon = Rangoon .... 41 J11
Yangquan .... 35 C6
Yanji ......... 35 B7
Yanna ........ 63 A4
Yanqi ........ 34 B3
Yantabulla .... 63 A4
Yantai ........ 35 C7
Yanykurgan ... 29 E7
Yao .......... 53 F2
Yaoundé ..... 56 D2
Yapen ........ 39 E5
Yapen, Selat .. 39 E5
Yaqui → .... 84 B2
Yar-Sale ...... 28 C8
Yaraka ....... 61 E7
Yaransk ...... 24 B6
Yardea P.O. ... 62 B2
Yaremcha .. 17 D7
Yarensk ...... 28 C5
Yarí → ...... 90 D4
Yarkand = Shacho ..... 34 C2
Yarkhun → ... 42 A8
Yaroslavl ..... 24 B4
Yarram ....... 63 C4
Yarraman ..... 63 A5
Yarranvale .... 63 A4
Yarras ........ 63 B5
Yartsevo ...... 30 C7
Yaselda ...... 17 B8
Yasinya ...... 17 D7
Yass ......... 63 B4
Yatağan ...... 23 F7
Yathkyed L. ... 70 B10
Yatsushiro .... 32 C2
Yauyos ....... 91 F3
Yavari → .... 90 D4
Yavatmal ..... 43 J11
Yavoriv ....... 17 D6
Yavorov = Yavoriv ..... 17 D6
Yawatahama .. 32 C3
Yazd ......... 44 D3
Yazd □ ....... 44 C3
Yazdān ....... 45 C5
Yazoo → ..... 79 C8
Ye Xian ...... 35 C6
Yebyu ........ 41 K12
Yecla ........ 19 C5
Yedintsy = Edinița ..... 17 D8
Yeelanna ..... 62 B2
Yegros ....... 94 B5
Yei .......... 53 H5
Yekaterinburg . 29 D7
Yekaterinodar = Krasnodar .. 25 D4

Yelarbon 63 A5
Yelets 24 C4
Yelizavetgrad = Kirovohrad 25 D3
Yell 10 A6
Yellow Sea 35 C7
Yellowhead Pass 71 C8
Yellowknife 70 B8
Yellowknife → 70 B8
Yellowstone → 76 B3
Yellowstone National Park 81 C8
Yelsk 17 C9
Yemen ■ 49 E3
Yenangyaung 41 G10
Yenbo = Yanbu 'al Baḩr 47 F4
Yenda 63 B4
Yenice 23 E6
Yenisey → 28 B9
Yeniseysk 30 D7
Yeniseyskiy Zaliv 28 B9
Yenyuka 31 D10
Yeola 43 J9
Yeovil 11 F5
Yerbent 29 F6
Yerevan 25 E5
Yermak 29 D8
Yershov 24 C6
Yerushalayim = Jerusalem 47 E3
Yessey 30 C8
Yeu, I. d' 12 C2
Yevpatoriya 25 D3
Yeysk 25 D4
Yezd = Yazd 44 D3
Yiannitsa 23 D4
Yibin 35 D5
Yichang 35 C6
Yichun 35 B7
Yilan 35 D7
Yinchuan 35 C5
Yingkou 35 B7
Yingtan 35 D6
Yining 34 B3
Yinmabin 41 F10
Yishan 35 D5
Yíthion 23 F4
Yiyang 35 D6
Yog Pt. 38 B2
Yogyakarta 37 F4
Yokadouma 56 D2
Yokkaichi 32 B5
Yoko 53 G1
Yokohama 32 B6
Yokosuka 32 B6
Yola 53 G1
Yonago 32 B3
Yongji 35 C6
Yonibana 55 G2
Yonkers 73 D9
Yonne → 13 B5
York, *U.K.* 11 E6
York, *U.S.A.* 73 E7
York, C. 61 C7
Yorke Pen. 62 B2
Yorkton 71 C9
Yos Sudarso, Pulau 39 F5
Yosemite National Park 82 B3
Yoshkar Ola 24 B6
Youghal 11 F3
Young 63 B4
Younghusband, L. 62 B2
Younghusband Pen. 62 C2
Youngstown 72 D5
Yozgat 46 C3
Ysyk-Köl, Ozero 29 E8
Yu Jiang → 35 D6
Yu Shan 35 D7
Yuan Jiang → 35 D6
Yuanling 35 D6
Yuanyang 34 D5
Yuba City 80 F3
Yūbari 32 F12
Yucatán □ 85 C7
Yucatán, Canal de 85 C7
Yucatán, Península de 85 D7
Yucatan Str. = Yucatán, Canal de 85 C7
Yuci 35 C6
Yugoslavia ■ 22 B3
Yukon → 71 B3
Yukon Territory □ 70 B6
Yukti 30 C8
Yuma 82 D5
Yumen 34 C4
Yun Xian 35 C6
Yungas 91 G5
Yunnan □ 34 D5
Yunta 62 B2
Yurgao 29 D9
Yuribei 28 B8
Yurimaguas 91 E3
Yuryung Kaya 30 B9
Yushu 34 C4
Yuzhno-Sakhalinsk 31 E12
Yvetot 12 B4

## Z

Zabid 49 E3
Zābol 45 D5
Zābol □ 45 D6
Zābolī 45 E5
Zabrze 16 C4
Zacapa 85 E7
Zacatecas 84 C4
Zacoalco 84 C4
Zadar 20 B5
Zadetkyi Kyun 36 C1
Zafra 18 C2
Żagań 16 C2
Zagazig 52 B5
Zagorsk = Sergiyev Posad 24 B4
Zagreb 20 B6
Zāgros, Kūhhā-ye 44 C2
Zagros Mts. = Zāgros, Kūhhā-ye 44 C2
Zāhedān 45 D5
Zahlah 46 D3
Zaïre = Congo → 56 F2
Zaïre = Congo, Dem. Rep. of the ■ 56 E4
Zaječar 22 C4
Zakhodnaya Dzvina = Daugava → 24 B1
Zākhū 46 C5
Zákinthos 23 F3
Zakopane 16 D4
Zalaegerszeg 16 E3
Zalău 17 E6
Zaleshchiki = Zalishchyky 17 D7
Zalew Wiślany 16 A4
Zalingei 53 F3
Zalishchyky 17 D7
Zambeze → 59 B7
Zambezi = Zambeze → 59 B7
Zambezi 58 A4
Zambia ■ 59 B5
Zamboanga 38 C2
Zamora, *Mexico* 84 D4
Zamora, *Spain* 18 B3
Zamość 17 C6
Zanaga 56 E2
Zanesville 72 E4
Zanjān 46 C7
Zanjān □ 46 C7
Zante = Zákinthos 23 F3
Zanzibar 57 F7
Zaouiet El-Kala = Bordj Omar Driss 54 C6
Zaouiet Reggane 54 C5
Zap Suyu = Kabīr, Zab al → 46 C5
Zapadnaya Dvina 28 D4
Zapadnaya Dvina → = Daugava → 24 B1
Západné Beskydy 16 D4
Zaporizhzhya 25 D4
Zaporozhye = Zaporizhzhya 25 D4
Zara 46 C4
Zaragoza 19 B5
Zarand 44 D4
Zaranj 42 D2
Zaria 55 F6
Zaruma 90 D3
Żary 16 C2
Zarzis 52 B1
Zaskar Mts. 42 C10
Zavāreh 44 C3
Zawiercie 16 C4
Zāyandeh → 44 C3
Zaysan 29 E9
Zaysan, Oz. 29 E9
Zbarazh 17 D7
Zdolbuniv 17 C8
Zduńska Wola 16 C4
Zeebrugge 14 C2
Zeehan 62 D4
Zeerust 59 D5
Zeila 49 E3
Zeitz 15 C7
Zelenograd 24 B4
Zémio 57 C5
Zemun 22 B3
Zenica 20 B6
Žepce 20 B7
Zêzere → 18 C1
Zgorzelec 16 C2
Zhabinka 17 B7
Zhailma 29 D7
Zhambyl 29 E8
Zhangaqazaly 29 E7
Zhanghua 35 D7
Zhangjiakou 35 B6
Zhangye 34 C5
Zhangzhou 35 D6
Zhanjiang 35 D6
Zhanyi 34 D5
Zhaotong 34 D5
Zhashkiv 17 D10
Zhayyq → 29 E6
Zhdanov = Mariupol 25 D4
Zhejiang □ 35 D7
Zhengzhou 35 C6
Zhenjiang 35 C6
Zhenyuan 35 D5
Zhezqazghan 29 E7
Zhigansk 30 C10
Zhijiang 35 D5
Zhilinda 30 B9
Zhitomir = Zhytomyr 17 C9
Zhlobin 17 B10
Zhmerinka = Zhmerynka 17 D9
Zhmerynka 17 D9
Zhodino = Zhodzina 17 A9
Zhodzina 17 A9
Zhongdian 34 D4
Zhumadian 35 C6
Zhuzhou 35 D6
Zhytomyr 17 C9
Zibo 35 C6
Zielona Góra 16 C2
Zigey 53 F2
Zigong 35 D5
Zigui 35 C6
Ziguinchor 55 F1
Zile 46 B3
Žilina 16 D4
Zillah 52 C2
Zimbabwe ■ 59 B5
Zimnicea 22 C5
Zinder 55 F6
Zion National Park 83 B6
Zipaquirá 90 C4
Ziway, L. 53 G6
Zlatograd 22 D5
Zlatoust 29 D6
Zlin 16 D3
Zlītan 52 B1
Zmeinogorsk 29 D9
Znojmo 16 D3
Zolochev = Zolochiv 17 D7
Zolochiv 17 D7
Zomba 59 B7
Zongo 56 D3
Zonguldak 46 B2
Zorritos 90 D2
Zouar 52 D2
Zouérate 54 D2
Zrenjanin 22 B3
Zuetina = Az Zuwaytīnah 52 B3
Zufar 48 D5
Zug 13 C8
Zugspitze 14 E6
Zula 53 E6
Zumbo 59 B6
Zungeru 55 G6
Zunyi 35 D5
Zürich 13 C8
Zuwārah 52 B1
Zvishavane 59 C6
Zvolen 16 D4
Zwettl 15 D8
Zwickau 15 C7
Zwolle 14 B4
Żyrardów 16 B5
Zyryan 29 E9
Zyryanovsk = Zyryan 29 E9
Żywiec 16 D4